FINANCIAL PLANNING 2000

The American College's Guide to the State of the Art for Financial Services Professionals

FINANCIAL PLANNING 2000

The American College's Guide to the State of the Art for Financial Services Professionals

Fourth Edition

Edited by
John J. McFadden

Jennifer J. Alby
George Alden
Burton T. Beam, Jr.
Roger C. Bird
Alan C. Bugbee, Jr.
David M. Cordell
Charles S. DiLullo
Ronald F. Duska
Thomas A. Dziadosz
Constance J. Fontaine
Edward E. Graves
James F. Ivers III
Ted Kurlowicz
Thomas P. Langdon
Stephan R. Leimberg
David A. Littell
Michael J. Roszkowski
William J. Ruckstuhl

The American College
Bryn Mawr, Pennsylvania

ACKNOWLEDGMENTS

Financial Planning 2000, The American College's Guide to the State of the Art for Financial Services Professionals, fourth edition, is a project of the faculty and staff of The American College.

The following staff members were particularly involved in the creation and production of this book:

Patricia G. Berenson
Nancy A. Cornman
Wendy Cox
Keith de Pinho
Susan Doherty
Elizabeth B. Fahrig
Eva T. Goldman
Lynn Hayes
Deborah A. Jenkins
Sally A. Kennedy
Barbara G. Keyser

Susan P. Lerman
Maria Marlowe
Charlene McNulty
Rosemary J. Pagano
Suzanne W. Rettew
Evelyn M. Rice
Margaret D. Reeves
Christina Ruckstuhl
Emily C. Sims
Barbara J. Wilson

Production Director: Jane R. Hassinger

Cover: Joseph L. Brennan

© 1997 The American College
All rights reserved

Library of Congress Catalog Card Number 97-70789
ISBN 0-943590-91-4

Printed in the United States of America

CONTENTS

FOREWORD   ix

PREFACE   xiii

1. PERSONAL INCOME TAX PLANNING   James F. Ivers III

   Income Tax Treatment of Long-Term Care Insurance   1.1
   Income Tax Exclusion for Accelerated Benefits Paid to
       Terminally Ill or Chronically Ill Individuals   1.5
   Income Tax Credit for Adoption Expenses   1.8
   Joint Life Policies and IRC Sec. 1035   1.11
   Entity Ownership of Nonqualified Deferred Annuities   1.15

2. ESTATE PLANNING   Jennifer J. Alby, Constance J. Fontaine,
   Ted Kurlowicz, and Stephan R. Leimberg

   IRS Continues "Crummey" Attack   2.1
   Estate Planning for Retirement Benefits   2.9
   Estate Planning for Non-U.S. Citizens and Their Spouses   2.19
   Character-Building Trust (Family Goals Trust)   2.33
   Keeping a Living Will Alive   2.36
   Organ Donation in Estate Planning   2.43

3. BUSINESS PLANNING   James F. Ivers III, Ted Kurlowicz,
   Thomas P. Langdon, and Stephan R. Leimberg

   New Rules Make S Corporations More Flexible
       Planning Tools   3.1
   Increase in the Number of Permissible S Corporation
       Shareholders   3.2
   Permissible Shareholders   3.3
   Affiliated Groups   3.6
   1995 Final Regulations and Qualified Subchapter S
       Trusts (QSSTs)   3.7
   Electing Small Business Trusts (ESBTs)   3.11
       Changes to Safe Harbor Debt Rules   3.12
   S Corporation Stock and Sec. 1014 Step Up in Basis   3.13

Limited Liability Companies (LLCs) and the New Entity
   Classification Scheme   3.14
A Comparison of Limited Liability Companies and S Corporations in
   Planning for Closely Held or Family-Owned Businesses   3.19
Interest Deduction Limitations for COLI   3.28

4. SPLIT-DOLLAR LIFE INSURANCE ARRANGEMENTS   Stephan R. Leimberg

The Importance of Documentation   4.1
Rules for Use of Insurer's One-Year Term Rates
   Have Tightened   4.5
Sec. 83 Has Been Applied to Equity Split-Dollar   4.10
The Impact of Sec. 83 on Reverse Split-Dollar   4.30
More Favorable Controlling and Sole Shareholder Estate Tax
Implications   4.35
More Guidance on the Tax Implications of Private (Family)
   Split-Dollar   4.40
S Corporations and Second Class of Stock Issues   4.43
Partnerships, LLCs, and Split-Dollar Arrangements   4.45
A Warning and a Conclusion   4.47

5. QUALIFIED PLANS   David A. Littell and John J. McFadden

SIMPLES: Will They Fly?   5.1
401(k) Plans after the Small Business Job Protection Act
   of 1996   5.11
The 15 Percent Excise Tax Moratorium—Should
   You Bite?   5.16
Qualified Plan Options for Nonprofits   5.18

6. LIFE INSURANCE PRODUCTS AND SERVICES   Edward E. Graves

Equity-Indexed Annuities   6.1
Criminalization of Donors   6.7
Life Insurance Policy Illustrations   6.9
Replacement Questionnaire   6.15
Introduction to the Life Insurance Illustration
   Questionnaire (IQ)   6.18
Replacement Questionnaire (RQ) (A Policy Replacement
   Evaluation Form)   6.22
Life Insurance Illustrations Model Regulation   6.28

7. GROUP BENEFITS   Burton T. Beam, Jr.

   Increased Availability of Medical Expense Coverage   7.1
   Portability of Group Medical Expense   7.5
   COBRA Changes   7.9
   ERISA Modification for Group Health Plans   7.10
   Favorable Tax Treatment for Medical Savings Accounts   7.11
   Expanded Coverage for Newborns and Mothers   7.17
   Some Minor Changes in Mental Health Benefits   7.19

8. INVESTMENTS   George Alden, Thomas A. Dziadosz, and
                                                           William J. Ruckstuhl

   Asset Allocation   8.1
   Revised Stock Market Circuit Breakers   8.25
   New Twists on Corporate Dividend Reinvestment
      Plans (DRIPs)   8.28
   Financial Planning 2000—What Will It Be Like?   8.30
   Mutual Fund Capital Gains—A Conduit Is Not Always
      a Conduit   8.34
   Emergency Cash—Investment Alternatives   8.35
   ATM Cards, Debit Cards, and Credit Cards   8.39
   Recent Changes in Credit Card Terms   8.41

9. FINANCIAL PLANNING   David M. Cordell

   Changes in Registration Requirements for Investment
      Advisers   9.1

10. ECONOMICS   Roger C. Bird

    Competition in Financial Services: Who Is Ahead?   10.1
    Everything You Need to Know about Price Indices   10.10
    Public and Private Economic Security Mechanisms   10.19

11. HUMAN BEHAVIOR PERSPECTIVES   Michael J. Roszkowski

    Psychological Characteristics of the Entrepreneur   11.2
    Successful Family-Owned Business Succession   11.10
    Decision-Making Styles and Succession   11.14

12. USING THE INTERNET FOR INSURANCE
    AND FINANCIAL SERVICES   Alan C. Bugbee, Jr.

    Selected Web Sites   12.17

13. ETHICS   Ronald F. Duska

14. CHARITABLE GIVING   Jennifer J. Alby

    Fair-Market-Value Deduction for Gifts of Publicly Traded
        Stock to Private Foundations   14.1
    Charitable Gift Annuity Rates Raised   14.2
    Charitable Planning with S Corporation Stock   14.5
    Charitable Planning with Qualified Plan Assets   14.6

15. GAAP VERSUS SAP: CRITICAL INFORMATION
    FOUND IN FINANCIAL STATEMENTS   Charles S. DiLullo

    Differences in Principles, Objectives, and Audiences   15.1
    The Beginnings and Its Evolution   15.2
    Underlying Concepts   15.3
    Critical Differences   15.5
    Basic Financial Statements   15.7
    The Why and What of Evaluation   15.10
    Risk Based Capital   15.11

APPENDIX   A.1

ABOUT THE AUTHORS   B.1

INDEX   I.1

FOREWORD

70TH ANNIVERSARY OF THE AMERICAN COLLEGE

Education for Performance in a Rapidly Changing World

The American College was founded in 1927. That was the year Babe Ruth hit 60 home runs, Charles Lindbergh flew solo across the Atlantic, Al Jolson starred in the first talking movie called the *Jazz Singer*, and the life expectancy of a male in the United States was 54.1 years. The Dow Jones Industrial Average was 175, and a new car cost $495.

The world was a much different place in those days. The life insurance industry was also much different than it is today. For life insurers those were more stable times: Mentalities were slow to change, promotion from within was the tradition, and continuity of the past was the strategy for the future. They were also simpler times: The life insurance agent sold a few basic types of policies, and the career agency system was the dominant channel of sales that continued to grow and prosper. The only barrier to a successful career as a life insurance agent was "call reluctance."

Today there are many more barriers to a successful career as a life insurance agent. Life insurance products are far more complicated than in the past, and there are more of them. Agents are now selling a wide variety of products, and most of these products pass much of the financial risk to the consumer. This is a fundamental difference from years gone by. As a result, agents must accept greater responsibility for the advice and recommendations they give to clients because the financial consequences of today's financial decisions can have a profound impact on the long-term financial security of the client, the family, and the business. In this environment clients expect more from their agents, and these higher expectations are justified.

Today's successful life insurance agent is also a financial consultant, and this requires knowledge—gained through continuing education—that is both up-to-date and applicable to the client's situation. In addition to being knowledgeable, the professional agent must be ethical. The code by which The American College alumni are expected to adhere is a version of the Golden Rule. It states that insurance professionals will endeavor to provide the same advice and service to the client as they would apply to themselves. The professional must have knowledge *and* ethics—one without the other is unacceptable.

While the early environment was vastly different from the fast-changing, uncertain world of today, the early leaders of The American College made decisions relative to the founding of this institution that were as prudent then as they are now. Those early leaders set the philosophy of education that still prevails at the College. It was they who insisted upon the highest level of educational standards—the same level of standards that exists today.

The American College reflected the life insurance industry during those early years. Its sole designation was the Chartered Life Underwriter with a five-course curriculum. The only other educational programs offered were management certificate courses that were designed for field managers. There was no full-time faculty specializing in the various disciplines of financial services to write the textbooks for the courses. In 1962 the College employees fit nicely into Huebner Hall—with space for the American Society of CLU & ChFC, the American Institute of CPCU, and its Society.

The decade of the 1970s was the beginning of a rapidly changing environment for life insurance. Perhaps 1978 was the pivotal year. It was the year that universal life insurance was introduced to the general public. It was the beginning of the best of times and the worst of times for The American College. Over the next 2 decades the College would experience its most rapid rate of growth but also the largest buildup of indebtedness in its history. The decisions to build a full-time faculty, to operate a full-service library, and to attain academic accreditation with the introduction of a masters degree program were made in the mid-seventies. In 1976 the College decided to change its name from The American College of Life Underwriters to simply The American College. This decision was highly controversial at the time. However, in retrospect it was a visionary decision of a vastly changing industry that would be greatly influenced by the public's primary concern shifting from the financial risks of dying too soon to the financial risks of living too long. A monumental decision in 1978 was to build a modern, full-service conference center that included residency rooms.

Beginning in the 1980s, competition accelerated, and new products proliferated. Annuities and mutual funds became important financial products. The College's courses and curriculae began to mirror these changes. In 1982 the College introduced its Chartered Financial Consultant designation and 13 years later added the Registered Health Underwriter and the Registered Employee Benefits Consultant designations. It also added a five-course track for those who want to take the Certified Financial Planner® certification examination. By the late 1980s, the College had more than 40 courses in its various curriculae, as well as a wide variety of short continuing education courses. No longer does the College see its constituency as a homogenous group of life insurance agents. Today its students represent a broad and diversified financial services industry. This is the new era of The American College.

This publication illustrates the breadth of subjects that the College faculty can discuss in depth and with accuracy, and it is an example of the diversity of knowledge the financial services professional must possess for the years ahead.

For 70 years The American College has provided professional education to life insurance agents, expanding its curriclae in recent years to include all financial services professionals. The College is well positioned to be the dominant professional education provider for an integrated financial services industry. Financial planning will continue to grow as the methodology for solving financial problems. The American College will continue to educate those who want the knowledge to meet the financial planning needs of their clients.

The need for The American College over the next 70 years will be even greater than it has been over the past 70 years. The year 2000 is just ahead, but a new era for the financial services professional has already begun.

Samuel H. Weese
President and CEO

PREFACE

Financial Planning 2000 is the fourth in The American College's series of books presenting our perspective on the state of the art for financial services professionals. As with earlier versions of the book, our faculty and other authors have worked to create the single best source of up-to-date ideas on the wide range of topics you need to know to effectively help your clients.

As the table of contents indicates, the scope of the book is wide, ranging from current tax planning issues to psychological perspectives. The articles are action oriented, designed to help you advise clients on these complex issues. You'll find many helpful charts, checklists, graphs, examples, and references.

Our goal is to provide you with timely, relevant information as you and your clients approach the ever-changing future. Please let us know how we have met this goal.

John J. McFadden
Editor

PERSONAL INCOME TAX PLANNING

James F. Ivers III

Income Tax Treatment of Long-Term Care Insurance

What Was the Situation Before?

Insurance companies and policyowners faced a dilemma regarding the income tax treatment of long-term care insurance. Although there was existing authority to indicate that such insurance should be treated as health insurance under the income tax laws, the IRS refused to rule on the issue and the answer was uncertain. Were premiums deductible? Were benefits taxable?

What Is the Nature of the Change?

Long-term care insurance contracts issued after 1996 will generally be treated as health insurance under the income tax laws. There are special rules limiting tax-favored benefits, deductibility of premiums, applications of coverage in employer plans, and various policy features. There is the usual myriad of definitions and qualifications. Many of the rules apply more to policy design than to placement in the field. The following planning tips may be helpful to the financial services professional who is involved with placing long-term care coverage.

Exclusion for Benefits. Perhaps the most welcome part of this area of the 1996 tax legislation is the income tax *exclusion* for benefits payable under qualified long-term care policies. "Pure" indemnity-type contracts are eligible for an unlimited exclusion for benefits. Contracts providing per diem benefits are eligible for an exclusion of up to $175 per day, or a *greater* amount if *actual* expenses exceed $175 per day.

The exclusion basically eliminates the dilemma previously facing insurance companies as to whether (or *how*) to issue a Form 1099 when benefits are paid from a long-term care policy. The law provides certainty for payers who are required to file information returns for long-term care benefits paid to individuals.

Deductibility of Premiums. Long-term care premiums are now treated as deductible medical expenses under IRC Sec. 213(d). However, the law imposes special dollar limits for deductibility of long-term care premiums, ranging from $200 to $2,500 per year per covered individual, based on age. Remember that clients still generally face the 7.5 percent of adjusted gross income "floor" with respect to the deductibility of these premiums. Unless income is low or total medical expenses are high, all or a part of the deduction for the premiums is likely to be lost "under the floor." If the client is self-employed, however, a different situation occurs (see below). The special limitations on deductibility of premiums are shown in the following table.

Dollar Limits for Deductibility of Long-Term Care Insurance Premiums	
Age of Covered Individual	Maximum Annual Deductible Amount
40 or under	$ 200
41–50	375
51–60	750
61–70	2,000
over 70	2,500

Notice that there is a substantial increase in deductible premium between age 60 and 61. Also, because the dollar limits apply per covered individual, a married couple filing a joint return could buy two policies (thus covering each spouse), and the limits would apply separately to each policy. Finally, long-term care expenses are added to other deductible medical expenses for purposes of applying the 7.5 percent "floor" for deductibility of medical expenses. Medical expenses paid for the care of the taxpayer, his or her spouse, or dependents (without regard to the gross income test under the dependency exemption rules) are eligible for deductibility under Sec. 213.

Exchanges Involving Long-Term Care Contracts. The law provides that until January 1, 1998, long-term care contracts may be exchanged without causing a taxable event. This is essentially the equivalent of a Sec. 1035 exchange. A special rule allows a 60-day grace period for reinvesting any proceeds received upon cancellation of an old contract. This provision has limited applicability since most long-term care policies have no cash value and therefore no untaxed gain.

Effective Date Provisions. Generally the new rules apply to contracts issued after December 31, 1996. However, any contract that met the long-term care requirements of the state in which the contract was "sitused" at the time of issuance will be eligible for treatment under the new law. What does "state in which the contract was sitused" mean? The most likely meaning is the state in which the contract was placed (sold). Most existing contracts should be grandfathered under this provision.

Cafeteria Plans. A disappointing aspect of the new law is that long-term care benefits cannot be used in a cafeteria plan arrangement. With respect to employer-provided insurance coverage, stand-alone coverage only will be possible. Employees will not be able to choose between long-term care insurance and other benefits. For income tax purposes, however, no nondiscrimination rules apply to insured long-term care plans, since they are treated the same way as health plans.

Flexible Spending Accounts (FSAs). Long-term care benefits cannot be provided through a flexible spending account. This means that any portion of long-term care insurance premiums paid by employees will be subject to the 7.5 percent floor for deductibility, rather than payable on a before-tax basis by means of an FSA.

How Does This Change Affect Your Clients?

Long-term care insurance will now be perceived as a "legitimate" product because of the governmental imprimatur of tax-favored treatment. It *always was,* of course, a legitimate product. But now more people will perceive it that way, and that is good. Long-term care insurance will also serve as a vehicle to introduce many new clients to the products and services offered by versatile financial planning professionals.

What Should Be Done?

The correlation of the tax treatment of long-term care insurance and the "above-the-line" deduction for health insurance premiums of self-employed taxpayers should also be considered.

Under 1996 legislation, the partial "above-the-line" deduction for health insurance premiums of a self-employed taxpayer will be increased. For 1996 that deduction is 30 percent of such premiums paid. The allowable percentage will be increased as shown in the following table:

Deduction for Health Insurance Premiums of Self-Employed Taxpayers

Year	Deductible Percentage
1997	40%
1998–2002	45%
2003	50%
2004	60%
2005	70%
2006 and thereafter	80%

An "above-the-line" deduction is one taken from gross income in determining adjusted gross income, rather than one taken as an itemized deduction. Most medical expenses are deducted as itemized or "below-the-line" deductions subject to the 7.5 percent floor.

Note that *long-term care insurance premiums are eligible* for the "above-the-line" deduction for self-employed taxpayers!

Implications for Taxpayers with Self-Employment Income. A self-employed taxpayer for purposes of the above-the-line deduction includes a sole proprietor, a partner in a partnership, and a more-than-2 percent shareholder in an S corporation. Unlike employer-provided *medical expense* insurance, long-term care insurance premiums are typically paid substantially or in full from the covered individual's own funds, even under an employer-sponsored plan. Since FSAs cannot be used to fund such premiums, "employees" are facing the 7.5 percent "floor" for any premiums they pay, inside or outside a group plan, because the deduction for premiums is taken as an itemized deduction on Schedule A of Form 1040. But self-employed taxpayers can use the above-the-line deduction, which places them in a significantly better position to pay for long-term care insurance. Presumably anyone who files a Schedule C with Form 1040 can claim the above-the-line deduction, including "statutory employees" and *part-time* sole proprietors (moonlighters).

> *Example:* Chuck Hughes, aged 62, is retired from full-time employment, and he has begun distributions from his retirement plan. He supplements his income with a small consulting practice currently earning $22,000 annually. Chuck purchases a long-term care policy with an annual premium of $1,950. In 1997 he can deduct 40 percent of the premium above the line, or $780. By 2006 he will be able to deduct 80 percent of the premium as long as he continues to earn income from self-employment.

Can individuals who are already covered by subsidized *medical* insurance plans and who also buy *long-term care* coverage with their own funds claim the above-the-line deduction? Consider the restriction on the use of the above-the-line deduction under IRC Sec. 162 (l)(2)(B):

Other coverage: Paragraph (1) shall not apply to any taxpayer for any calendar month for which the taxpayer is eligible to participate in any subsidized health plan maintained by any employer of the taxpayer or of the spouse of the taxpayer.

Does this provision disallow the above-the-line deduction for taxpayers who have *medical* insurance at their full-time job, but who file a Schedule C with Form 1040 and buy their own *long-term care* policy? This was *not* the original intent of the provision. It was meant to prevent self-employed taxpayers who had access to subsidized medical insurance from using the above-the-line deduction for their share of the premium payments. However, Sec. 162(l)(2)(B) could be interpreted to mean that taxpayers who are covered by subsidized medical insurance provided by their employers will not be able to claim the above-the-line deduction for personally paid long-term care policies, even though they have self-employment income.

Where Can I Find Out More?

- HS 321 Income Taxation. The American College.
- Stephan R. Leimberg, James F. Ivers III, Martin J. Satinsky, Eric Johnson, and John J. McFadden. *Federal Income Tax Law,* 1997 ed. RIA Group, New York.
- IRC Sec. 7702B.
- IRC Sec. 213(a), 213(d).
- IRC Sec. 162(e).

Income Tax Exclusion for Accelerated Insurance Benefits Paid to Terminally Ill or Chronically Ill Individuals

What Was the Situation Before?

In 1992 the IRS issued proposed regulations regarding the treatment of certain accelerated death benefits under a life insurance contract. In those regulations, accelerated death benefits paid under a life insurance contract were treated for income tax purposes as amounts paid by reason of the death of the insured, and therefore excludible from gross income under IRC Sec. 101(a)(1), if certain requirements were met. The most important requirement was that the insured be "terminally ill" in order for accelerated benefits to qualify for the income tax exclusion. An insured was considered to be "terminally ill" if he or she had an illness which was reasonably expected to result in death within 12 months of the payment of the benefit. No provision for payments made by viatical settlement providers was included in these proposed regulations. Prior to the issuance of these regulations, there was no income tax exclusion available for accelerated benefits paid under a life insurance policy.

What Is the Nature of the Change?

The Health Reform Act of 1996 added Sec. 101(g) to the Internal Revenue Code, codifying the exclusion for certain accelerated death benefits. This statutory change is effective beginning in 1997 and overrides the previous proposed regulations. The new exclusion follows the philosophy of the 1992 regulations but is different in certain important respects.

Amounts received under a life insurance contract covering the life of an insured who is either terminally or chronically ill will now be excludible if certain requirements are met. Amounts may qualify for the exclusion if paid by either the insurance company that issued the policy or by a licensed viatical settlement provider. However, the exclusion does not apply if the amounts are paid to a taxpayer other than the insured if the insured is a director, officer, or employee of the taxpayer or has a financial interest in a business conducted by the taxpayer.

A *viatical settlement provider* is defined as one regularly engaged in the business of purchasing life insurance contracts insuring terminally or chronically ill individuals. The provider must be licensed in the state in which the insured resides. If that state has no licensing requirement for viatical providers, certain requirements of the Model Regulations and/or the Viatical Settlement Model Act of the NAIC must be met by the provider.

A *terminally ill* individual is one who has been certified by a physician as having an illness or condition that can be expected to result in death within 24 months of the date the certification is given.

> *Example:* Alvin is seriously ill. His personal physician believes that he has less than 2 years to live and certifies in writing that his illness can be expected to result in death within 2 years. Alvin owns a life insurance policy on his life, which he assigns to a licensed viatical settlement provider in exchange for a discounted percentage of the death benefit under the policy. Alvin may exclude the full amount he receives for the policy, regardless of his basis in the policy.

A *chronically ill* individual is one who is unable to perform at least two activities of daily living for at least 90 days. Activities of daily living include eating, toileting, transferring, bathing, dressing, and continence. Individuals suffering from severe cognitive impairment, such as Alzheimer's and related disorders, are also considered to be chronically ill.

There are additional requirements for the exclusion if the insured is chronically ill rather than terminally ill. In such cases, the benefit must be paid under a rider or provision of the life insurance policy that qualifies as a long-term care insurance contract within the meaning of IRC Sec. 7702B (as discussed in "long-term care"). Therefore a life policy without such a provision or rider can pay excludible accelerated benefits only to a terminally ill insured. This rule prevents pure life insurance contracts from being used as long-term care policies with excludible benefits.

The term *chronically ill* has the same meaning as that term has for purposes of the new income tax rules applicable to long-term care insurance contracts (except that the term does not include a terminally ill individual). In addition, the rules and limitations applicable to excludible benefits paid from qualified long-term care contracts also *generally* apply for purposes of the accelerated benefits exclusion.

How Does This Change Affect Your Clients?

It's important to understand how the new provision covering accelerated benefits differs from the previous regulations. The statute provides an exclusion for benefits paid to chronically ill individuals, and the regulations did not. Therefore persons insured under a life policy with a long-term care rider are in essentially the same income tax position regarding benefits paid in the event of chronic illness as are covered individuals under a separate long-term care policy.

The statute also allows an exclusion for benefits paid by viatical settlement providers, which the regulations did not.

With regard to benefits payable to a terminally ill insured, the statute provides that a physician must certify that the insured can reasonably be expected to die within 24 months. Under the regulations the period of time was 12 months.

The requirement for a physician's certification raises a couple of questions regarding the exclusion. First, can the physician making the certification be *any* physician? Apparently the answer is yes. There is no requirement that the physician be independent or be representing any particular party to the transaction. Second, what happens if the physician makes the certification and then the insured lives beyond the 24-month period? The answer is that the law does not address this situation. Therefore it must be presumed that the actual death or survival of the insured after the required certification is immaterial for purposes of the income tax exclusion.

Another question involves the coordination of the exclusion for benefits paid to a chronically ill insured with the income tax rules for long-term care contracts under IRC Sec. 7702B. If benefits paid under a long-term care rider to a life contract are excludible as qualified long-term care payments under that code section, why is an exclusion for benefits paid to chronically ill insureds under IRC Sec. 101 (certain death benefits) also necessary? Do the two provisions taken together constitute statutory surplusage? The answer is no. There are a couple of situations where the Sec. 101 exclusion will apply to chronically ill individuals even though all the requirements of Sec. 7702B are not met. First, Sec. 7702(B) applies only to insurance benefits paid by the insurance company, while Sec. 101(g) also applies to payments made by viatical settlement providers. However, practically speaking, a chronically ill individual with a normal life expectancy will probably not be involved in a viatical settlement. Second, certain policies that combine long-term care and life coverage without a complete segregation of the premium may qualify for the accelerated benefits exclusion for payments to chronically ill individuals under Sec. 101(g) even though such policies may not meet all the requirements of a qualified long-term care policy under Sec. 7702B.

What Should Be Done?

Financial services professionals involved in the placement of life insurance policies that provide for the payment of accelerated benefits must inform their clients of the income tax rules that apply in the event of payment of such benefits. Contracts offering such benefits may be desirable for individuals who are concerned about the cost of a protracted terminal illness, as well as for clients who would like to combine life and long-term care coverage. Generally it will be the responsibility of the insurance company to design contracts that properly qualify for the desired income tax benefits.

Where Can I Find Out More?

- HS 321 Income Taxation. The American College.
- IRC Sec. 101(g).
- IRC Sec. 818(g).
- IRC Sec. 7702B.
- Aaron G. Chambers and Frederic J. Gelfond. "Provisions for the Journey: Accelerated Death Benefits and Viatical Settlements for the Terminally or Chronically Ill," *The Insurance Tax Review,* February 1997, vol. 12, no. 2.
- Prop. Regs. Secs. 1.101-8, 1.7702-0, 1.7702-2.

Income Tax Credit for Adoption Expenses

What Was the Situation Before?

There was no provision in the income tax law that provided a tax benefit specifically to adoptive parents.

What Is the Nature of the Change?

Beginning in 1997, a tax credit of up to $5,000 per eligible child for qualified adoption expenses will be available to taxpayers who pay such expenses (IRC Sec. 23). A credit of up to $6,000 is available for expenses paid with respect to a child with special needs. The limit on the credit applies to total overall expenses for each child. The credit is phased out for taxpayers with adjusted gross income in excess of specified levels. For tax years in which an adoption becomes final, the taxpayer is allowed to claim the credit for expenses paid during that year. For years in which qualified expenses are paid, but in which the adoption does not become final, the taxpayer must claim the credit for the tax year following the year in which the expenses are paid. Expenses for a foreign adoption qualify for the credit only if the adoption becomes final and may be claimed only in that year.

There is a 5-year carryover period available for taxpayers whose allowable adoption credit exceeds their tax liability for the year the credit is first allowable.

The credit is currently scheduled to be available only for expenses paid until December 31, 2001. After that date the credit will be available only for expenses paid for the adoption of a child with special needs.

How Does This Change Affect Your Clients?

It is important for clients considering adoption or in the process of adoption to understand what expenses qualify for the credit and how the income limitation is applied. *Qualified adoption expenses* include legal fees, court costs, and other related fees and costs that have the principal purpose of a legal adoption of an *eligible child* or a *child with special needs* by the taxpayer. However, costs associated with the adoption of a child of the taxpayer's spouse are not qualified expenses. Costs for surrogate parenting arrangements are also not qualified expenses. In the case of foreign adoptions only, the adoption must actually be completed in order for the expenses to be eligible for the credit.

An *eligible child* for purposes of the credit is a person under the age of 18 or one who is physically or mentally incapable of self-care. A *child with special needs* is defined as a citizen or resident of the United States who is determined by state authorities to be unable to be placed for adoption without adoption assistance. There must be a determination by the state that the child should not be returned to his or her biological parents, and that there is a specific factor or condition that makes the child unable to be placed without adoption assistance.

The allowable amount of the adoption credit is phased out for taxpayers whose adjusted gross income for the year exceeds $75,000. For such taxpayers, the allowable credit is fully phased out when adjusted gross income (AGI) reaches $115,000. Adjusted gross income for this purpose is determined by including the calculation of taxable social security benefits, deductible IRA contributions, and allowable passive activity losses. The foreign earned income exclusion is not taken into account. To determine the amount phased out, the fraction resulting from dividing the amount of the taxpayer's adjusted gross income in excess of $75,000 by $40,000 is multiplied by the allowable amount of the credit ($5,000 or $6,000).

> *Example*: Jim and Denise Oliver pay $16,000 in legal fees, court costs, and other fees in 1997 to adopt Michael, a 2-year-old U.S. citizen. The adoption is completed in 1997. Michael is not a special needs child. The Olivers' adjusted gross income for 1997 is $100,000. The maximum allowable credit for their expenses is $5,000. This $5,000 amount must be reduced by a fraction equal to $25,000 (the amount of AGI in excess of $75,000) divided by $40,000, or 5/8. Therefore, the amount of the allowable credit that is "phased out" is $3,125 ($5,000 x 5/8). The allowable credit is $1,875 ($5,000 – $3,125). The tax credit may be claimed in 1997 because the adoption is completed in that year.

In planning for the adoption credit, it is important to know that there is also an income tax *exclusion* available for amounts paid by a taxpayer's employer for qualified adoption expenses on behalf of the taxpayer/employee. Such amounts must be furnished under a nondiscriminatory adoption assistance program. The rules defining and limiting this exclusion for adoption assistance payments are very similar to the rules just described for application of the adoption credit. For example, the dollar amounts of the available exclusion are the same as the dollar amounts of the credit. Any amounts excluded from gross income under such a program are not eligible to be treated as qualified expenses for purposes of the adoption credit.

What Should Be Done?

The adoption credit is the largest of any allowable tax credit for an expense of a personal nature that this writer can recall in the history of the income tax law. For that reason alone, it is significant. In addition, the credit reflects a congressional awareness of family values in a context that has not been so strongly recognized in the past. Since the first $5,000 spent to adopt a child will, in essence, be free for the majority of families, many fortunate children and their adoptive parents should benefit.

Planners should make sure that clients remember two things about the adoption credit. First, it is a per child, not a per year, credit. This means that the credit can be claimed up to the maximum amount only *once* for *each* child. However, it *also* means that the credit can be claimed *again* for the adoption of *another* child. Second, families have only until the end of the year 2001 to pay expenses eligible for the credit (except in the case of special needs children). Whether that date will be extended is unknown at this time.

With regard to tax benefits associated with adopted children, it should also be mentioned that the IRS will now allow adoptive parents to claim a dependency exemption or child care credit with respect to an adopted child before the adoption becomes final. Parents cannot obtain a social security number (SSN) for the child until the adoption becomes final, and that number is normally required to claim these tax benefits. However, since many adoptive parents have custody of the child before the adoption becomes final, the IRS is relaxing the general rule. Parents should write "U.S. adoption pending" in the exemption section of Form 1040 in place of the child's SSN and attach documentation of custody. For foreign adoptions, the procedure is somewhat different. An individual taxpayer identification number (ITIN) should be obtained for the child by filing Form W-7. That number can be used until the SSN is obtained. Alternatively, parents can file amended returns when an SSN is obtained.

Where Can I Find Out More?

- HS 321 Income Taxation. The American College.
- IRC Sec. 23.
- IRC Sec. 137.
- IRS Press Release IR-97-6.

Joint Life Policies and IRC Sec. 1035

What Was the Situation Before?

Many life underwriters had been faced with the issue of whether the favorable income tax treatment of IRC Sec. 1035 could be applied to life insurance policy replacements involving joint life policies. Could a single life policy be exchanged under Sec. 1035 for a policy insuring more than one life? Could two single life policies be exchanged for a joint life policy insuring the same two lives? Could a joint life policy be exchanged for one or more single life policies? Such questions arose in many cases and for a substantial period of time were left unanswered by the IRS.

What Is the Nature of the Change?

Through the issuance of a series of private letter rulings, the IRS has addressed these issues in the context of second-to-die policies. Unfortunately, for the most part their answers are not favorable to life underwriters and their clients who are attempting to legitimately achieve the most appropriate life insurance configurations. Let's take a look at the answers given by the IRS to some of these questions.

Question 1: Can a second-to-die policy be exchanged for a single life policy under Sec. 1035 where one of the insureds under the joint life policy has died and the new single life policy covers the life of the surviving insured?

Answer: The IRS says yes. This is the one situation in this whole area where the IRS has taken a position favorable to taxpayers. (See PLR 9330040, PLR 9248013.)

> *Example 1:* Sam and Ginny, a married couple, owned a second-to-die life insurance policy. Sam passed away last year. This year Ginny exchanged the policy for a new single-life policy insuring her life. The IRS says that this exchange qualifies under Sec. 1035.

Question 2: Can a single life policy be exchanged under Sec. 1035 for a second-to-die policy covering the life of the insured under the old policy plus the life of a new, additional insured person?

Answer: The IRS says no. (See PLR 9542037.) Such an exchange would involve the addition of a new insured person to the insurance arrangement. The Service says that this violates the "same insured" requirement of the Treasury regulations under Sec. 1035. Rev. Rul. 90-109, 1990-2 C.B. 191, is cited to support this conclusion. That ruling involved a policy that offered an option of substituting the insured person with another insured. In other words, the policy feature addressed under Rev. Rul. 90-109 involved a change of the insured person (person A) to another newly insured person (person B). Such a substitution is a clear violation of the "same insured" requirement, so the exercise of such an option clearly would not qualify as a Sec. 1035 exchange but rather is treated as a taxable surrender of the policy under Rev. Rul. 90-109.

In PLR 9542037 this same rationale was applied to the addition of a new insured in a single life to second-to-die exchange, and the Service concluded that such an exchange does not qualify under Sec. 1035. Since such an exchange involves the addition of a newly insured person, that conclusion is sensible.

> *Example 2*: Louise owns a life insurance policy covering her life. She exchanges the policy for a new policy insuring both her life and the life of her husband, Don. The IRS says that this exchange does *not* qualify under Sec. 1035.

Question 3: Can two single life policies insuring the lives of A and B be exchanged under Sec. 1035 for a second-to-die policy insuring the lives of both A and B?

Answer: The IRS says no. This issue was also addressed in PLR 9542037. It doesn't matter whether the policies are owned jointly by the spouses, by one spouse individually, or by a trust. Such an exchange, according to the IRS, will be taxable under the authority of Rev. Rul. 90-109, discussed above.

> *Example 3:* Rose owns a life insurance policy covering her life. Her husband, Tony, also owns a policy on his life. Rose and Tony exchange these single life policies for one second-to-die policy insuring both their lives. The IRS says that this exchange does *not* qualify under Sec. 1035.

This question was the one most frequently considered and wondered about before PLR 9542037 was released. Where an exchange involves the addition or subtraction of one or more insureds, a fairly clear violation of the "same insured" requirement under Sec. 1035 occurs. However, the scenario under question 3 does *not* involve the addition or subtraction of any insured person. It simply combines two life policies into one that covers the same lives. By denying Sec. 1035 treatment to such exchanges, the IRS seems to be saying that *each* policy involved in a Sec. 1035 exchange must insure the same, and only the same, life or lives as every *other* policy involved in the exchange. In other words, the IRS sees the "same insured" requirement as applying *separately* to each policy involved in an exchange rather than to the *overall effect* of the exchange. Curiously, the IRS cited Rev. Rul. 90-109 to support this position, even though that ruling is not on point regarding this question at all. It is, in fact, largely irrelevant from an analytical standpoint.

Commentators have, for the most part, meekly accepted this result as "logical" or "correct." But, in this writer's opinion, it is neither. How does such an exchange violate either the letter or the spirit of Sec. 1035 or its accompanying regulations? The purpose for enactment of Sec. 1035 was to allow individuals to modify their insurance arrangements to better suit their needs without the imposition of a taxable event. Sec. 1035 treatment was intended to apply in situations where the life insurance investment is being continued without a change in the life or lives being insured.

The IRS has never denied Sec. 1035 treatment to an exchange merely because there was a different number of policies on one end of the exchange than on the other end. (See PLR 9708016, PLR 9644016, and PLR 6212194820A.) Furthermore, the Service has never denied Sec. 1035 treatment on the basis of differences in policy design or economic attributes among the contracts involved in the exchange.

In one ruling, the IRS approved the exchange of individual policies under Sec. 1035 for interests in a group life policy. (See PLR 9017062.) Naturally, the group policy covered the lives of many other individuals not involved in the approved exchange. The group policy also did not previously cover the life of the individual involved in the exchange. It could be argued that the interest in the group policy was simply viewed as a separate contract for Sec. 1035 purposes by the IRS. However, a group contract is a single contract for most legal and underwriting purposes.

What, then, was the Service's logical analysis in PLR 9542037 for disallowing 1035 treatment for an exchange of two single life policies for one policy covering the same two insureds? There was, in fact, no logic. There was no explanation. There was no indication that the author of the ruling even understood the issue.

Ah, well, that's enough venting. Thank you, kind reader, for your patience.

How Does This Change Affect Your Clients?

The effect of PLR 9542037 is, of course, a negative one, particularly with regard to question 3 just discussed. Exchanges disapproved by the ruling will not be processed by most insurance companies. Unfortunately (although understandably), insurance companies do not want to process varieties of policy exchanges that have been the subject of an unfavorable ruling from the IRS. Although the private letter ruling applies only to the taxpayer to whom it is issued and cannot be cited as authority, it does cast a pall over industry practices in this case. Many legal issues involving the income taxation of life insurance and annuities have no clear authority on point other than private letter rulings. In such cases, the industry follows the rulings. Such is the situation here.

What Should Be Done?

With regard to question 3 discussed above (exchange of policy insuring A and policy covering B for a second-to-die policy covering A and B), a judicial challenge of the IRS position might produce a favorable result. This would require the following steps: the processing of such an exchange under Sec. 1035 by an insurance company, then an IRS audit of an affected taxpayer, then a court action. Absent a willingness to go that route (making your client famous), taxpayers and insurers will simply have to "grin and bear it."

A related question that some life underwriters are still unsure about involves the application of PLR 9542037 to exchanges involving first-to-die, rather than second-to-die policies. There is a school of thought that holds that first-to-die policies should receive more favorable treatment than second-to-die policies in exchanges like the one in question 3. Since a first-to-die policy pays a death benefit on the first insured's death (which a second-to-die does not), and since a first-to-die policy generally allows the remaining insured to continue coverage in some way after the first death, therefore (the argument goes) there is no violation of the same insured requirement where two single life policies are exchanged for a first-to-die policy covering the same two lives. The second-to-die policy does not qualify in such exchanges, it is argued, because it is really only *one* life that is insured in a second-to-die policy, since only one death benefit will be paid. This approach suggests that it is the *subtraction,* not the addition, of an insured in exchanges for second-to-die policies that violates Sec. 1035 principles.

Well, what about that? As the saying goes, the argument "proves too much." There is absolutely no indication in PLR 9542037 that it makes any difference to the IRS whether a first-to-die or second-to-die policy is received in such exchanges. The difference in mortality assumptions or, for that matter, any comparison of economic differences in any of the policies being examined was never a factor in the ruling. As previously stated, the Service never even got that far. They simply cited Rev. Rul. 90-109, which involved a completely different type of situation, and let it go at that.

In conclusion, there is nothing to indicate that the Service would approve an exchange of two single life policies for a first-to-die policy any more than for a second-to-die policy. There is also no indication that the result would be different if the exchange was reversed; that is, if a first- or second-to-die policy were surrendered in exchange for two single life policies. In this writer's opinion, any of these transactions should qualify under Sec. 1035. However, the Service has thrown a wet blanket, it seems, over all these planning possibilities. The entire situation is uncalled for, unfortunate, and unsettling.

Where Can I Find Out More?

- PLR 9708016.

- PLR 9644016.
- PLR 9542037.
- PLR 9330040.
- PLR 9248013.
- Rev. Rul. 90-109, 1990-2 C.B. 191.
- PLR 9017062.
- PLR 6212194820A.

Entity Ownership of Nonqualified Deferred Annuities

What Was the Situation Before?

When a trust or other entity is considered for annuity ownership, the first income tax problem that must be confronted is the "non-natural person" rule of IRC Sec. 72(u). If this rule applies, the annuity will not be treated as an annuity for income tax purposes, and the income on the contract will be taxed as ordinary income to the contract owner each year. In most cases, this tax result will result in the loss of the appropriateness of the annuity as a wealth building vehicle.

The non-natural person rule does not apply to annuities acquired by the estate of a decedent by reason of the decedent's death, to annuities held by qualified plans, or to immediate annuities.

More importantly, however, if an entity holds the annuity as "an agent for a natural person," the non-natural person rule will not apply. In what kinds of situations will the "agent for a natural person" exception to the "non-natural person" rule apply? This question has often been asked since the enactment of IRC Sec. 72(u). Recently several private letter rulings have been issued that help bring the picture into focus.

What Is the Nature of the Change?

The IRS has recognized the "agent for a natural person" (agency) exception in two types of situations that are distinct but related: single beneficiary trusts and certain grantor trusts.

Single Beneficiary Trusts. The IRS has approved the application of the agency exception in rulings involving single beneficiary trusts. First, let's examine PLR 9204010 and PLR 9204014. These two rulings are companion pieces issued under essentially the same ruling request. Annuity contracts were to be issued to trustee owners. There were age restrictions in the trusts on the beneficiary's unfettered access to the trust property. The IRS observed that "although trustee is the contract owner of the annuity contract, its ownership interest is nominal . . . " The Service concluded in both rulings that since the sole beneficiary of the trust was the beneficial owner of the annuity, the tax-deferred status of the annuity was preserved.

In PLR 9639057, a financial institution proposed to maintain trusts to hold annuity contracts for the benefit of its customers. The trusts in question were single beneficiary trusts that were essentially under the customer's complete control. The IRS also approved this arrangement under the agency exception to the non-natural person rule.

The trusts in question in these rulings were *not* grantor trusts for income tax purposes. (See below.)

It follows that where a trust has only one beneficiary and that beneficiary is a natural person, the agency exception to the non-natural person rule should apply, and the placement of an annuity will not cause income tax problems.

Grantor Trusts. In PLR 9120024, trusts were funded with annuities under a funeral trust arrangement. The trust model in question was treated as a grantor trust for income tax purposes because the grantors maintained reversionary interests in portions of the trust property that exceeded 5 percent of their value under IRC Sec. 673(a). The IRS concluded that the trust was an agent for a natural person because the trust was taxed as a grantor trust under IRC Sec. 673(a).

PLR 9316018 involved a trust established by an employee for the purposes of receiving bonuses from an employer. The employee had the right to decide whether to receive the bonuses personally or have them deposited into the trust. Also, the employee had the unilateral right to withdraw the trust's current income and/or any bonuses paid into the trust within 30 days of their contribution. However, except for those specified withdrawal rights, the employer had the right to approve any withdrawals from the trust prior to the employee's termination of employment. The employer's creditors had no interest or rights in the trust. The trust was a grantor trust under IRC Sec. 677 because the trust property could be distributed to the grantor (the employee) without the approval of an adverse party under IRC Sec. 677. The IRS concluded that the trust was an agent for a natural person, because the trust was a grantor trust under IRC Sec. 677.

How Does This Change Affect Your Clients?

We have examined the rulings that apply the agency exception to the non-natural person rule to grantor trusts and single beneficiary trusts. Now let's examine a few other related questions regarding the agency exception.

Question 1: Would *any* trust that is treated as a grantor trust under IRC Sec. 671-678 qualify for the "agent for a natural person" exception to the non-natural person rule under the logic in the existing rulings?

Answer: Sorry, but we don't know. Although the IRS has *not denied* the exception to any grantor trust in any private ruling, it has *specifically approved* the exception using a grantor trust analysis *only* in the rulings just discussed. Trusts that are grantor trusts, for example, under the "power to control beneficial enjoyment" rules of IRC Sec. 674 or the "administrative powers" provisions of IRC Sec. 675 have not been the subject of rulings involving the ownership of annuities. It is very possible, however, that *not all* grantor trusts would be treated as involving the type of agency relationship with the grantor that was found in the rulings cited. Also, the grantor trust rulings involved grantor trusts that, for all practical purposes, were also *single beneficiary* trusts. If a grantor trust had more than one beneficiary whose beneficial interests were subject to discretionary powers, the required agency relationship between the trust and a natural person might not be present in the eyes of the IRS.

Question 2: Could an annuity be placed in a trust that would not violate the non-natural person rule, and at the same time also avoid federal estate tax inclusion of the annuity in the estate of the individual who pays the premium?

Answer: Probably, if the right type of trust were used. This technique has been referred to as the *irrevocable annuity trust,* or IRAT. Its practical suitability, however, is probably limited to certain specific situations.

For example, suppose a father and mother wanted to purchase a deferred annuity contract for the benefit of a son but did not want the annuity to be included in their own estates or the son to have control over the disposition of the contract. The contract could be placed in a single beneficiary trust with an independent trustee delaying the son's control over the property until age 40. If the parents wanted to pay the annuity premiums, they would either have to make a taxable gift to the trust or limit the premiums to $20,000 a year using a present-interest exclusion approach with a Crummey power. In this way, the parents could exclude the annuity from their estates and still avoid the application of the non-natural person rule because the trust is a single beneficiary trust. Such a trust should work as an IRAT.

Note also that the IRS has stated that when an annuity is distributed *to the trust beneficiary from a single beneficiary trust,* that transfer is *not* a taxable gift of the annuity under IRC Sec. 72(e)(4)(C) because the trust making the transfer is not an "individual" within the meaning of that subsection. (See PLR 9204010.)

Although an IRAT may be a suitable technique in certain situations, it seems to lack major potential for general application. The IRAT presents certain problems. First, when an existing annuity is transferred *to* a trust by an individual, both a transfer tax and an income tax event will likely occur. Transfers of life insurance policies result only in a transfer tax event. Second, only certain types of trusts qualify for the agency exception to the non-natural person rule, as we have just discussed. Third, annuities do not present the same estate planning opportunity for amplification of wealth at death that life insurance does.

Question 3: Can a deferred annuity be used to fund a credit shelter (bypass) trust for estate tax planning purposes?

Answer: No. Such a trust is not a single beneficiary trust or a grantor trust. Use of an annuity in such a trust would trigger recognition of all existing gain in the contract, the same as if the contract had been surrendered. (See IRC Sec. 72(u)(2)(A).)

Question 4: Can a partnership or limited liability company own an annuity as an "agent for a natural person"?

Answer: We don't know. The legislative history of IRC Sec. 72(u) indicates that a major reason for the enactment of the rule was to prevent the use of annuities for nonqualified deferred compensation plans. The timing of taxable compensation to an owner would not be an issue with a pass-through tax entity such as a partnership or LLC. However, as previously discussed, entities that exist for the benefit of more than one person have not been the subject of any rulings on the agency exception. There would be a significant downside tax risk, therefore, in placing a deferred annuity in a partnership without a favorable IRS ruling on the issue.

Entity Ownership of Nonqualified Deferred Annuities			
Can a deferred annuity be owned under the agency exception to the non-natural person rule by:	Yes	No	We don't know.
a single beneficiary trust?	X		
a grantor trust under IRC Sec. 673(a)?	X		
a grantor trust under IRC Sec. 677?	X		
any grantor trust?			X
a credit shelter trust?		X	
a partnership or LLC?			X
a corporation?		X	

What Should Be Done?

If you have a situation, such as annuity ownership by a trust, that could result in problems with the non-natural person rule, you must consider the downside risk. Violation of the rule has serious tax consequences.

Most people think of the rule, if it applies, as resulting in the immediate taxation of the income on the contract to the contract owner. That is true, and it's not good. However, there are other implications that you may not have considered.

Since an annuity contract that violates the non-natural person rule is not treated as an annuity for tax purposes, consequences other than the taxation of income on the contract may result. For example, the contract would no longer qualify for a Sec. 1035 exchange. How can this be significant? For one thing, it has been suggested that a possible exit strategy for life insurance policies that carry an economic loss (where basis is higher than cash value) would be to exchange the policy for an annuity, then perhaps sometime later (for valid economic reasons) to surrender the annuity at a deductible loss, using the carryover basis from the life policy. But what if the owner of the life policy is an entity, such as a bank or a corporation, and exchanges the policy for an annuity contract that violates the non-natural person rule? Simply paying tax on the annual annuity income might not be so bad if the loss upon surrender would still be deductible. *But this technique won't work.* There will be no valid Sec. 1035 exchange because the annuity received in the exchange is not an "annuity for income tax purposes." Therefore, there will be *no carryover basis* and the exchange will be treated as a taxable *surrender of the life policy,* which will *not* result in a deductible loss.

It should be noted that to the extent that income on the contract is taxed, the contract owner receives additional basis in the contract, which can later be recovered upon disposition or annuitization. This ameliorates somewhat the harsh effects of the rule. However, it *still* doesn't make it a *good* rule.

Where Can I Find Out More?

- IRC Sec. 72(u).
- PLR 9639057.
- PLR 9322011.
- PLR 9316018.
- PLR 9204014.
- PLR 9204010.
- PLR 9120024.
- Ann St. Laurent, Esq. "Estate Planning with Tax-Deferred Annuities—Special Problems under Sec. 72," *Tax Management Estates, Gifts & Trusts Journal,* vol. 211, no. 6.

- James F. Ivers III. "Current Income Tax Considerations for the Insurance Professional," 13th Annual Tax Conference, The American College, 1996. Video tape, audio tape, and outline.

ESTATE PLANNING

IRS Continues "Crummey" Attack
Ted Kurlowicz and Stephan R. Leimberg

What Was the Situation Before?

We often recommend and implement accumulation trusts for our clients. To ensure the $10,000 annual federal gift tax exclusion for gifts to accumulation trusts, we must provide a present interest for the trust beneficiaries in the form of immediate temporary withdrawal rights. These withdrawal rights are usually referred to as "Crummey" powers in deference to the court case that approved the annual exclusion for such transfers (*Crummey v. Commissioner*, 397 F.2d 82 (9th Cir. 1968)).

A Crummey trust is an irrevocable trust that provides for accumulated income to be added to corpus for later distribution according to dispositive provisions of the trust. The typical Crummey trust is an irrevocable life insurance trust (ILIT), but the Crummey trust will work well with many other investments with accumulation potential. The Crummey trust provides each beneficiary with a temporary noncumulative right to withdraw his or her share of each gift made to the trust. These rights typically lapse in 15 or 30 days. However, the ability to immediately withdraw the gifts ensures the annual gift tax exclusion.

The IRS eventually acquiesced in the *Crummey* decision (Rev. Rul. 73-405, 1973-2 C.B. 321), but has attempted on many occasions to limit the annual exclusions available for gifts to Crummey trusts. For example, the IRS challenged the use of Crummey powers to create annual exclusion gifts for contingent remainder beneficiaries of a trust (*Cristofani v. Commissioner*, 97 T.C. 74). The IRS took the position that a Crummey power will create annual exclusion gifts only for beneficiaries who have "substantial, future economic benefits" in the Crummey trust. These beneficiaries would normally include the income beneficiaries whose future benefits in the trust would be enhanced if they currently forego their Crummey withdrawal rights. The court in *Cristofani* disagreed with the IRS and concluded, "We do not believe . . . that *Crummey* requires that the beneficiaries of a trust must have a vested present interest or vested remainder interest in the trust corpus or income, in order to qualify for the Sec. 2503(b) exclusion."

The IRS released an Action on Decision (AOD, 1992-009, I.R.B. 4) and acquiesced in the result of *Cristofani* in the ninth circuit (the jurisdiction where *Cristofani* took place). The AOD indicated that the IRS reserved its right to litigate Crummey trusts that it viewed as more abusive, particularly outside of the ninth circuit. Following this decision, for some time nothing significant was issued by the IRS concerning the abuse of the annual exclusion. It seemed that the IRS had backed off in its attacks on the Crummey trust.

What Is the Nature of the Change?

The IRS has renewed its attack on the Crummey trust and what it views as abuses of such trusts in proliferating annual exclusion opportunities for wealthy clients. Again, the focus of these attacks is on situations where the Crummey power is used to create annual exclusions where there is some factual question as to the reality of the withdrawal rights. The IRS accepts the validity of the Crummey power (1) when actual notice of the withdrawal rights are given to adult beneficiaries, (2) when the beneficiaries have adequate time to exercise their rights, (3) where there is sufficient cash or cash equivalent in the trust to satisfy all withdrawal rights, (4) when the facts do not reveal a prearranged understanding that the withdrawal rights would not be exercised, and (5) where exercising the withdrawal right would result in adverse consequences to its holder (for example, losing future benefits under the trust instrument or other beneficial arrangement). The recent rulings by the IRS concerning Crummey trusts are discussed below. It is important to discuss the facts in some detail to understand the holding of the IRS.

TAM 9532001. In a technical advice memorandum issued to the estate of a decedent, the service evaluated lifetime gifts made to the decedent's Crummey trust. The facts of TAM 9532001 present two interesting but separate issues. First, the decedent created a Crummey trust stating that each beneficiary would be given an immediate right to withdraw gifts to the trust up to $20,000 annually (the trust was created when both the grantor and the grantor's spouse were alive and gift-splitting presumably would have been in effect). However, the trust provided that the grantor must first inform the trustee to make the withdrawal rights available when annual gifts were made or no rights would be granted to the beneficiaries. (This is an interesting provision and is worthy of our consideration. Presumably, the grantor could annually examine the beneficiaries and control the Crummey withdrawal powers as appropriate. For example, the grantor could avoid granting the Crummey power to a beneficiary who is facing bankruptcy or divorce, or has become spendthrift.)

However, in this instance the grantor *never* informed the trustee to make the withdrawal powers available. The IRS concluded, in our opinion, appropriately, that no annual exclusion was available since the grantor never met the trust's specific requirement to make the Crummey powers available. This is a good example of how our clients need continuous guidance in the administration of Crummey trusts, particularly when the grantor and trustee are nonprofessionals.

Interestingly enough, the IRS did not end its examination of the facts at this point. A second issue was raised by the IRS in TAM 9532001 concerning the notice requirement for the Crummey withdrawal rights. All beneficiaries in this case executed statements waiving their initial withdrawal rights and the right to receive notice of future withdrawal rights. (The beneficiaries also retained the right to revoke this waiver and receive future notices.) This waiver is often suggested to avoid future notices, particularly when a nonprofessional fiduciary is selected. As we know, the notice requirement can be annoying when life insurance premiums paid by the Crummey trust are on a semiannual or even monthly basis. (Amazingly, even some high-income, high-net-worth clients have cash-flow problems and choose to make small periodic gifts to their trusts). The IRS concluded that "... without the current notice that a gift is being transferred, it is not possible for a donee to have the real and immediate benefit of the gift . . ." and the annual exclusions were denied.

Based on the facts of TAM 9532001, it is our opinion that the IRS didn't need to examine the issue of the waiver of the Crummey notices by the beneficiaries. The annual exclusions were effectively precluded by the failure of the grantor to notify the trustee to make the Crummey powers available. By examining this second issue, the IRS is probably issuing a warning to other taxpayers. We're not certain that the holding with respect to the waivers is correct. Each adult beneficiary in his or her waiver stated that he or she (1) was aware that annual gifts were to be made and (2) would have the right to withdraw the gifts. In addition, the beneficiaries also retained the right to revoke the waiver and receive actual notice in the future. However, right or wrong, this holding offers us a warning that the IRS will insist that all adult beneficiaries must be given actual notice of their Crummey withdrawal rights.

TAM 9628004. The facts of this TAM are somewhat lengthy and convoluted. It appears that the donor clearly had attempted to make maximum annual exclusion gifts. Prior to his death, the donor created three irrevocable trusts. The first trust (Trust #1) provided Crummey withdrawal rights to the donor's three children (and their spouses) and seven grandchildren. The Crummey notices were mailed on December 27th of the year of the purported gifts. Although the donor instructed the bank to make the transfer to the trust on December 31st of the same year, the funds were not transferred due to bank administrative rules until January 2nd of the following year. On the donor's Form 709 (gift tax return), he reported $130,000 in gifts for the calendar year and claimed 13 annual exclusions totaling $130,000. He made the same gifts and filed returns for four ensuing years for Trust #1.

The beneficiaries of Trust #1 were the three children and seven grandchildren. The spouses of the children had no beneficial interest other than the Crummey power. In other words, they had "naked" Crummey powers. In addition, the current benefits from Trust #1 to the actual beneficiaries were limited to discretionary nonguaranteed distribution potential. At the death of the donor, the remainder would be payable to one child and to the donor's second trust (Trust #2) in equal shares. Thus several Crummey beneficiaries of Trust #1 had contingent speculative interests only.

The donor created Trust #2 with similar terms, primarily benefiting one child. The donor, having used all his annual exclusions already, did not provide additional Crummey rights to the beneficiaries of Trust #2.

Undaunted, the donor created Trust #3 with similar terms, again primarily benefiting one child. Other beneficiaries again could receive discretionary payments while the donor was alive, but Trust #3 was primarily distributable to one child at the donor's death. In this instance the donor and his advisers became creative. Crummey rights and notices were sent to the donor's two great-grandchildren and the spouses of four of the donor's grandchildren. The great-grandchildren could potentially be discretionary distributees of Trust #3 (although it is difficult to determine this from the facts). However, the spouses of the grandchildren held only naked Crummey powers and were added only to increase the annual exclusions.

The IRS focused its analysis on the following facts:

- Notices with respect to Trusts #1 and #3 were, in the first year, sent only a few days before they would lapse, and before the trusts had been funded (no cash was actually in either trust in year one).
- Neither trust required that notice be given to the Crummey beneficiaries when gifts were made to the trusts.
- Only three out of 13 Crummey beneficiaries of Trust #1 had an interest in the trust aside from their withdrawal right. Seven of the other 10 had only discretionary income interests in the trust during the donor's lifetime. The three spouses of the donor's children held only naked Crummey powers.
- None of the six Crummey powerholders of Trust #3 had any other interest whatsoever in either trust income or corpus, aside from his or her withdrawal right. (Interestingly enough, the donor's attorney produced only five notice letters; the IRS will clearly ask for these on audit.)

None of the rights were ever exercised, even by those beneficiaries who held only Crummey withdrawal powers and had no economic incentive to allow funds to accumulate in the trust.

The IRS reached several conclusions, all of which could justify the denial of all annual exclusions in this case. First, the service determined that the donor chose to fund each trust in a manner that "severely restricted the time during which the beneficiaries could exercise their rights." In the first year and some subsequent years, the gifts were not made until shortly before the end of the tax year. Second, the trust instruments never required that notice be provided to the Crummey beneficiaries. Third, the IRS reasoned that the donor could not have achieved the same beneficial results of Trusts #1 and #3 if separate trusts were designed for all Crummey beneficiaries. Finally, and most troubling, the IRS speculated as to the intent of the donor and the Crummey beneficiaries and denied the gift tax annual exclusion based on speculation of this intent. Be aware that there are no facts that indicate intent one way or the other, and that intent is not a requirement of the gift tax rules or the holding of the *Crummey* case. Here are the actual words of the ruling:

> ". . . that as part of a prearranged understanding, all of the beneficiaries knew that their rights were paper rights only, or that exercising them would result in unfavorable consequences. There is no other logical reason why these individuals would choose not to withdraw $10,000 a year as a gift which would not be includible in their income or subject the Donor to the gift tax. . . ."

The IRS position creates a presumption of guilt. The IRS will assume a pre-arranged understanding between donor and the holder of the Crummey power that rights are not meant to be exercised (or that exercise will result in adverse consequences) if

- a Crummey beneficiary has no other trust rights except the withdrawal power,

- a Crummey beneficiary has only discretionary income interests, and

- a Crummey beneficiary has an interest in the remainder that is either remote or contingent.

AOD 1996-010. The IRS again issued an action on decision concerning the *Cristofani* case. Although it chose not to appeal, the Service restated its disagreement with the holding of the case. Specifically, the IRS feels that no annual exclusion should be available for Crummey beneficiaries who have only contingent or remote remainder interests in the trust. What differs from the 1992 AOD, mentioned above, is that the Service states an intent to litigate cases where "no bona fide gift of a present interest was intended." You will recall that the previous AOD suggested litigation of cases more abusive than *Cristofani*. In addition, the new AOD adds the language of TAM 9628004 that the facts and circumstances of a Crummey trust could indicate a "prearranged understanding that the withdrawal right would not be exercised or that doing so would result in adverse consequences to the holder." In other words, the IRS feels that unless the Crummey beneficiary has future economic benefit for his or her lapse of the Crummey power, a "wink" will be implied between the donor and the Crummey beneficiary if the power is lapsed.

When Does This Change Affect Clients?

These changes affect all Crummey trusts, either those already in existence or those that will be created after the changes.

What Should Be Done?

One question that we are frequently asked is, "How will the IRS know about gifts made by our clients?" This is a good question and the answer indicates when these changes will really affect clients.

The IRS has no reason or resources to audit gifts made by clients unless a gift tax return is filed alerting the IRS to such gifts. Since gift tax returns are filed only when taxable gifts (gifts not sheltered by annual exclusions or the marital deduction) are made or gift-splitting is in effect, there will generally be no return requirement for the average Crummey trust. (In fact, we don't understand why gift tax returns were filed in TAM 9628004 since all gifts purportedly received annual exclusions. Perhaps the client and his advisers felt that they were being aggressive and didn't want to have failure-to-file penalties if the annual exclusions were denied.) In addition, the IRS takes the position that it does not have to audit a gift tax return and that the 3-year statute of limitations does not apply unless (1) a gift tax return is filed and (2) gift tax is payable with the return. (Perhaps the advisers for the client in TAM 9628004 were attempting to create a 3-year statute of limitations by filing unnecessary gift tax returns).

Thus the only time the IRS generally will find out about these issues is when the donor dies. **If no statute of limitations applied to such non-taxed lifetime gifts, gifts could be examined at the donor's death that occurred many years earlier.** At this time the IRS does have the incentive and the means to discover your deceased client's gifts. First, any trusts created by the decedent must be filed with the estate tax return. This will alert the IRS to Crummey trusts and the tax years that gifts were made. In addition, all life insurance on the decedent's life, whether or not included in the decedent-insured's gross estate, must be reported on the return. At this time, the estate tax examiner will routinely request the following information pertinent to a Crummey trust:

- a copy of all notice letters
- all tax returns for the trust
- the decedent's banking records for at least 3 years prior to death, including all accounts in which the decedent had individual or joint checking privileges
- all banking records for the trust

Thus, from the estate tax return, any required supporting documents, and the audit information, the IRS can certainly determine the terms of the Crummey trust and whether the Crummey beneficiaries had (1) actual notice, (2) adequate time to exercise this notice, (3) sufficient available cash in the trust to satisfy their withdrawal rights, and (4) any noncontingent beneficial interests in the trust besides the Crummey power.

Unfortunately, the IRS seems to be speculating as to the intent of the donor and creating a presumption of guilt when the facts of cases like those discussed above present themselves on the estate tax audit. What makes matters worse is that the expert witness, the person most competent to testify as to his or her intent, is now deceased. This puts the estate and the heirs in a difficult position. They can request a TAM from the IRS, but the two rulings discussed above suggest that little comfort may be forthcoming from this avenue. Or, the estate and the heirs can litigate. This path was successful in *Cristofani*, but this has its costs—legal fees, uncertainty, and delays in settling the estate. The other choice is for the estate to attempt a settlement with the IRS. This will probably result in the use of some of the decedent's unified credit to shelter gifts where the annual exclusion is disallowed. Remember, there may not be sufficient tax dollars at stake (simply some disallowed annual exclusions) for the estate to justify the costs of litigation.

A Conservative Approach. For many of our clients, the options are probably more limited. They prefer not to make their estates famous. They prefer that the estate settlement process be as smooth and expense-free as possible. For these individuals, their Crummey trusts should be kept "squeaky clean." Fortunately (or maybe unfortunately), the majority of our clients are not so wealthy that they will need to be overly aggressive with annual exclusion gifts. To "audit-proof" our Crummey trusts, we need to be certain of two things. First, the trust should be drafted and administered properly. Second, we need to limit the Crummey beneficiaries to the actual income and vested remainder beneficiaries of the trust.

The conservative approach will involve careful drafting and follow-up during the period of administration of the Crummey powers. This will place a greater burden on professional advisers when laypersons, such as family members, are performing the duties of trustees. The steps that we believe will keep a client "audit proof" with respect to the annual gift tax exclusion for Crummey trusts are as follows:

Step One — Execute an irrevocable trust requiring the steps below to be followed by all affected parties. The trust should be clear as to the necessity and timing of the Crummey notices. Crummey notices should be provided for in the document only for the income and vested remainder beneficiaries.

Step Two — Have the donor make a gift of cash by writing a check to the trustee. (If the corpus consists of a life insurance policy, the check should not be written directly to the insurer.)

Step Three — Have the trustee send notices to the beneficiaries clearly indicating their rights to withdraw for the requisite time period (we recommend *at least* 15 days). It may be prudent to send notices with "return-receipt requested."

Step Four   Have the trustee deposit the funds in a checking or other cash-equivalent account. (We often recommend a tax-free municipal bond fund with checking privileges to avoid receiving taxable income and subjecting the trust to quarterly tax compliance.)

Step Five   Have the trustee pay the life insurance premium or invest in other non-cash-equivalent investments only after the withdrawal period expires. (The trustee may be able to pay the premiums earlier if the life insurance policy has enough cash surrender value to satisfy the withdrawal rights.)

A More Aggressive Approach. In some cases our clients may be both (1) so wealthy that they can't give it away fast enough and (2) sufficiently risk tolerant to live with the chance that the IRS may find some issues to prompt an audit of their estate tax return. When the aggressive approach is taken, we still recommend all the steps listed above with respect to the set-up, funding, and administration of the trust. However, the aggressive approach involves the multiplier approach with respect to beneficiaries. First, the *Cristofani* case involved the use of contingent remainder beneficiaries as Crummey power holders. The tax court agreed with Mrs. Cristofani that all Crummey beneficiaries, including the nonvested contingent remainder beneficiaries, were eligible to receive annual exclusion gifts.

Example: Suppose your client is married and has three children, two of whom have two children each. Your client is contemplating a second-to-die policy with an annual premium of $100,000 and will place it in a Crummey trust. The Crummey trust language provides that, "at the death of the survivor of the grantor and the grantor's spouse, divide the trust fund into as many equal shares as grantor has children then living and children then deceased with issue then living." If the Crummey powers are limited to $20,000 (assume gift-splitting between the spouses) each to the three children (the actual vested beneficiaries), the grantor would have to use $40,000 of unified credit each year to fund the trust. However, adding the four grandchildren as beneficiaries (the nonvested remainder beneficiaries) under the *Cristofani* reasoning and using gift-splitting will increase the available annual exclusions to seven or $140,000 annually. What's more, as more grandchildren are born, it is possible to give them Crummey powers beginning with the year of birth. Thus the Crummey trust can be built to grow with the family.

It may well be that the IRS is wrong on its anti-*Cristofani* position. Hopefully, we will see additional favorable cases or the IRS will back off its position in the near future.

What about the use of naked Crummey power holders? Certainly, the reasoning of *Crummey* would provide some argument that the only requirement for an annual exclusion gift is to provide the beneficiary with something now (that is, the current temporary right to withdraw from the trust). Neither *Crummey* nor *Cristofani* expressly require the Crummey beneficiary to have other significant beneficial interests. However, a word of warning is prudent. It is our opinion that the use of naked Crummey beneficiaries will attract certain, and not favorable, attention from the IRS. The naked Crummey case will certainly be litigated and will be more difficult to win than one with the less-aggressive *Cristofani* fact pattern. What's worse, Congress may react unfavorably to an abusive use of Crummey powers and provide legislative restriction on our use of such trusts in the future.

Where Can I Find Out More?

- HS 334 Fundamentals of Estate Planning II. The American College.
- Ted Kurlowicz. "Crummey News From the IRS." *NAEPC Insider's Newsletter* (Spring 1996).
- Howard M. Zaritsky and Stephan R. Leimberg. *Tax Planning with Life Insurance: Financial Professional's Edition.* New York: RIA Group. Phone (800) 950-1210.
- Stephan Leimberg et al. *The Tools and Techniques of Estate Planning.* 10th ed. Cincinnati: The National Underwriter Company, 1995. Phone (513) 721-2140 or (800) 543-0874.

Estate Planning for Retirement Benefits
Ted Kurlowicz and Jennifer J. Alby

What Was the Situation Before?

Planning for larger estates generally focused on transferring closely held businesses and/or preserving family wealth. Retirement plan account balances were usually not a significant problem for taxable estates. In fact, most recent IRS data indicates that only 30 percent of estate tax returns (Form 706) contained qualified retirement plan assets.

What is the Nature of the Change?

With the passage of ERISA in 1974 and the generally favorable long-term growth in the equity markets in the '80s and '90s, the funds accumulating in the various qualified and quasi-qualified retirement plans have reached unprecedented levels. These funds will grow even more as the baby boomer generation continues its mission to fund a comfortable retirement. The American Council of Life Insurance recently reported that over 65 million Americans were covered by pension plans with life insurance companies in 1995; reserves for these plans totaled over $972 billion. Assets in qualified retirement plans not funded with life insurance companies totaled over $2.6

trillion in 1995. Individual or self-employed retirement plans, such as IRAs, SEPs, or Keogh plans, are also used extensively as tax-advantaged retirement savings vehicles. The 1996 tax changes generally created more opportunities to establish and fund private retirement plans (perhaps as a foreshadowing of the federal government's desire to slow the growth of public retirement funding through social security).

For many individuals who took, or are continuing to take, advantage of the tax incentives to defer income through such retirement arrangements, these plans have become a primary estate planning concern. It is not unusual for business owners or executives who are currently near or beyond retirement age to have retirement account balances over $1 million. What makes the estate planning problems for such individuals even more troubling is that the retirement plan often represents a large percentage of their estates. As we will discuss below, retirement plan account balances are not a comfortable fit in the normal estate planning techniques for wealthy individuals. Over the last couple of years, the most frequent comment we've heard from financial services professionals is that they need guidance with respect to estate planning for clients with large retirement plans.

When Does This Change Affect Clients?

Planning for the accumulation, distribution, and transfer of retirement plans is an ongoing dilemma that will become more significant in the future.

What Should Be Done?

The estate planning decisions for qualified retirement plans will generally be subordinate to the retirement distribution decisions for clients to appropriately fund their own and their spouses' retirement. These decisions will be based on their financial needs and, for wealthier individuals, will generally focus on income tax deferral. Unfortunately, while the tax rules applicable to retirement plans are extremely efficient for accumulating retirement assets, the rules are very complex for planning distributions for the retiree. The tax treatment for transferring retirement plan assets to heirs could be viewed as confiscatory.

Retirement Plans Make Inefficient Inheritances. The tax treatment of retirement plan assets left to heirs can be summarized as follows:

- These assets do not receive an income tax basis step-up to date-of-death values and are treated as income in respect of a decedent (IRD). Therefore the income taxes lurking in retirement plan funds will be paid by survivors (in some cases very soon after the plan owner's death).
- These assets are also subject to federal estate taxes, generation-skipping taxes, and state inheritance taxes in some cases. The federal estate taxes paid on the retirement assets will be deductible from federal income taxes under IRC Sec. 691(c).

- Overfunded retirement plans are subject to a 15 percent federal excess-accumulations tax at the death of the plan owner (or his or her spouse if an election to defer the excess tax until the second death is made).

This tax treatment is often referred to as a "triple tax" on retirement plan assets held by a decedent. The bottom line is that retirement plan assets are income tax efficient for funding retirement benefits, but overall, tax inefficient for funding inheritances.

Example: Suppose Mrs. Adams, aged 75, owned her own business for many years prior to her recent retirement. She named her husband as beneficiary of her IRA when she reached age 70 1/2 and they elected to take a joint and survivor payout from the IRA, recalculating life expectancy to determine the required minimum distribution. Her husband predeceased her 2 years ago. Mrs. Adams dies this year with an estate of $6 million, with $2 million remaining in her IRA payable to her two children, aged 51 and 46. Assume the remainder of her estate contains no other income in respect of decedent (IRD) items. The taxes for her estate and her IRA are as follows *(financial calculations courtesy of Pension and Excise Tax Calculator Software (610) 527-5216)*:

Federal estate tax	$2,173,203
State death tax (taxes equal to the maximum state death tax credit allowable)	492,940
Excess accumulations tax	148,831
Income tax on the IRA (assuming a 39.6% marginal rate and after the Sec. 691(c) deduction)	472,981
Estate remaining after taxes	$2,712,045
Percentage of estate passing to heirs	45.2

Let's take a closer look at what happens to the IRA account. The IRA was $2 million at the time of her death. This is reduced by the excess accumulations tax of $148,831. If we assume the federal estate and state death taxes are divided proportionately between the IRA and the remainder of her estate, the death taxes attributable to the IRA are $742,827 and $168,493. In addition, the IRA creates an excess accumulations tax of $148,831 (based on a Sec. 7520 rate of 7.8 percent) and income taxes of $472,981. The income tax is payable in the tax year following the year of the decedent's death (the result of the recalculation method for determining the IRA minimum distribution chosen by Mrs. Adams). The inefficiency of the IRA as an inheritance is demonstrated by the following table:

IRA balance at death		$2,000,000
Less		
Excess accumulations tax	($148,831)	
Federal estate tax	($742,827)	
State death tax	($168,493)	
Income tax on IRA		($472,981)
Total reduction		$1,533,132
Net value of IRA for heirs		$466,868
Percentage of IRA passing to heirs		23.3

Mrs. Adam's estate shrinks by just over 54 percent, but her IRA shrinks by more than 76 percent (with taxes fairly proportioned). What's more, her IRA account balance will be subject to income taxes (compressed into the highest marginal bracket) in the year following the year of her death since she elected to recalculate life expectancy when determining her minimum required distribution.

At first glance, this result looks horrible. However, we need to remember that Mrs. Adams probably accumulated far more in her qualified plan account than she would have been able to accumulate in a taxable investment alternative. She probably took advantage of years of before-tax contributions and tax-deferred buildup in her qualified plan. Her family is probably better off in spite of the "triple tax." However, her heirs may not view the final result as a "victory."

General Guidelines Concerning Retirement Distribution and Estate Planning Choices. Although the estate planning implications for qualified retirement plans create some complex choices, there are several general rules to follow. The good news is that the standard choice of naming the surviving spouse as designated beneficiary and choosing a joint life payout will probably be the optimal choice in more than 90 percent of the cases.

In most retirement plans, a participant will be given annuity options. An annuity is a form of payout guaranteed for life or, in the case of a qualified joint and survivor annuity (QJSA), for the joint lives of a husband and wife. In other plans, the participant may have the choice of a lump-sum option or have an account balance that can be rolled over to an IRA. If income tax deferral is the goal, the rollover option generally provides the best alternative.

Generally, an individual must begin drawing from a pension plan or IRA no later than April 15th of the year following the tax year in which he or she attains age 70 1/2. The beneficiary designation for the account balance must also be made at this time. In advising your clients on how to take retirement plan distributions and selecting a beneficiary for their retirement plan, keep in mind the following general rules:

- Check the retirement provisions of the specific plan. Not all options are available in every plan.
- The financial needs of the participant, his or her spouse, and other heirs should be the primary concern.
- The income tax issues regarding the type of distribution option selected are more immediate and usually outweigh the estate planning issues. Thus, when in doubt, defer as long as possible or practical.
- The best choice for income tax deferral (annual recalculation of life expectancy) while the participant and/or his or her spouse are alive will create the worst income tax result after their deaths, since the remaining life expectancy will be zero after the second death. Thus as in the earlier example of Mrs. Adams, the income tax problem is immediate.
- A designated beneficiary should be selected. This will usually provide the longest income tax deferral. The participant's spouse or other family members can be designated beneficiaries; the individual's estate or trust cannot unless some special planning (discussed later) has been performed.
- Decisions about the retirement plan are extraordinarily complex (even in the context of the tax laws) and should not be made without appropriate professional advice. If you don't stay on top of the subject, you may consider referring to a specialist.

Factors That Affect the Choice of Beneficiary. Most married individuals will designate their spouses as beneficiaries of their retirement plans. Many retirement plan participants will need to provide for the nonparticipant spouse from the retirement plan since the other family assets will be insufficient to provide a comfortable retirement. Furthermore, there may be no choice in many types of qualified retirement plans. The Retirement Equity Act (REA) stipulates in many instances that a married individual covered by a qualified pension plan must provide his or her spouse with a qualified joint and 50 percent survivor annuity. This survivor annuity can be avoided only with the nonparticipant spouse's consent. The REA rules do not apply to IRAs, SEPs, or Sec. 403(b) plans. For qualified plans that permit rollovers to an IRA, the participant's spouse must generally consent to a rollover. The IRS recently released Notice 97-10 providing much needed explanations of a plan participant's spouse rights in a qualified plan and sample language for the waiver of a QJSA.

A married individual's decision to consent to a distribution different from a QJSA will depend on several factors. First, the surviving spouse must have sufficient funds outside of the retirement plan to provide for the remainder of his or her retirement. Quite often, these funds could come from life insurance, a far superior vehicle for funding inheritances than the retirement plan account balance. "Pension maximization" employs the technique of choosing a larger single life payout from a retirement plan and using some of the extra cash to buy life insurance for the surviving spouse as a replacement fund.

Second, the participant could have another beneficiary who would be the appropriate choice from a personal and tax standpoint. For example, the plan participant may have children from a prior marriage that would be his or her first choice for designated beneficiary.

Third, the income and estate tax consequences of a retirement distribution choice must be carefully considered. The choice of the designated beneficiary has the following important tax consequences:

- The choice of designated beneficiary will affect the size of the minimum distribution if a joint and survivor option is selected.
- The income tax deferral available to the heirs depends on the selection of the designated beneficiary.
- The availability of the marital deduction and the ability to defer the excess accumulations tax until the second death depends on the selection of the spouse or the appropriate marital trust as the designated beneficiary.

Unique Tax-Deferral Options of Naming the Spouse as Designated Beneficiary

Income Tax Issues. Naming the spouse as designated beneficiary of the IRA offers income-tax-deferral options. First, the minimum distribution requirements at age 70 1/2 provide for a longer payout period if the joint life expectancy of the married couple is used. The required payout period is 16 years for one life at age 70 but much longer if two lives are used. For example, it is 26.2 years if the participant's spouse is 10 years younger and a joint life payout is selected. Thus the income taxes on the account balance are spread over a longer period. In addition, if the surviving spouse is the designated beneficiary, he or she can roll over the account balance to his or her own IRA and delay distributions until he or she attains age 70 1/2. This gives more flexibility for deferral, particularly if the beneficiary-spouse is significantly younger. Better yet, the surviving spouse can name a new designated beneficiary of the rollover IRA (such as the couple's child or children). This permits the family to further defer the income taxes since the minimum required distributions can be taken over a new joint-life payout.

> *Example:* Suppose Mr. Jones, aged 68, is married to Mrs. Jones, aged 55, and has a large account balance in his IRA rollover. They have one child, Mitch, aged 35. If Mr. Jones dies this year and has designated Mrs. Jones as the beneficiary of the IRA, she can create her own IRA and roll over his account balance to her IRA. She will not have to take distributions from this IRA until she is age 70 1/2, or in about 16 years. She could then designate her child as sole beneficiary of the IRA and choose a joint-life payout. Her minimum required distributions would then be based on the joint life expectancy of herself and her child. However, the minimum distribution rules permit only

a maximum 10-year differential between joint-life expectancies if the beneficiary is not the participant's spouse. Thus a 26.2 year payout can be chosen. If Mrs. Jones dies before the balance is withdrawn and has not recalculated life expectancy, Mitch can spread the remaining payments over his actual life expectancy. Of course, this wonderful flexibility to defer income on the IRA presumes that the Jones family will not need sooner or larger distributions.

Estate Tax Issues. For estate tax purposes, the estate tax marital deduction will defer estate taxes until the second death (on any plan assets remaining at that time) if the designated beneficiary of the retirement plan is the surviving spouse. In addition, the estate of the participant can elect to defer the excess accumulations tax until the second death under these circumstances.

Marital Trust As Potential Beneficiary

Generally, a marital trust should be designated as the beneficiary only when the participant has an asset-protection goal. That is, the participant either (1) desires a trustee of the marital trust to control the management of the retirement plan account or (2) wants to preserve as much as possible of the principal of the retirement plan account for the next generation. For example, the participant may have children from a prior marriage. Using a marital trust as the designated beneficiary of the retirement plan will provide retirement income for the new spouse, but guarantee that the remaining retirement account balance will be distributed to the children at the surviving spouse's death.

The use of the marital trust adds significant complexity and may remove flexibility. In a pure QTIP trust, the principal will be protected from unlimited invasion by the surviving spouse. Thus the participant will be able to name the remainder beneficiaries of the IRA and preserve as much principal as possible for these heirs. However, the surviving spouse will not be able to roll over the account to his or her IRA. The rollover potential is foreclosed unless the surviving spouse has sufficient control over the IRA to treat it as his or her IRA for rollover purposes. This type of control is not normally provided in a QTIP trust. In fact, such control is contrary to the asset-protection goal. For example, a recent private ruling (Ltr. 9608036) permitted rollover if the surviving spouse has a general power of appointment over the marital trust. Other private rulings (most recently, Ltrs. 9703036 and 9620038) have permitted rollover treatment when the IRA was payable to the estate, which could include testamentary trusts not qualifying for rollover, but the surviving spouse as executor had the power to allocate the IRA balance to an outright marital bequest. In either of these instances, the surviving spouse could invade the IRA at his or her discretion. Thus the participant had to forego the asset-protection goal to achieve the rollover potential.

A QTIP trust as beneficiary of the IRA will qualify for the marital deduction if the requirements of Rev. Rul. 89-89, 1989-2 C.B. 231 are met. The trustee must be able to compel distribution of all income from the IRA, and the marital trust should receive the greater of the actual income or the minimum required IRA distribution. The annual distribution to the QTIP must be paid to the surviving spouse. Of course, the actual income earned by an IRA with a large account balance may be greater than the minimum required distribution under the normal IRA rules. Thus the QTIP requirement to distribute actual income may cause a larger required annual distribution and some income tax deferral may be lost if the QTIP trust is used as a beneficiary. In addition, the income tax deferral potential of a rollover is unavailable.

To some degree, the investment policy for the IRA could control the amount of annual income. For example, dividends, interest, or rent is normally allocated to income, while capital gains are normally allocated to principal. The IRA forms should be adapted to provide for the determination of principal and income.

If the surviving spouse is not a citizen of the United States, the qualified domestic trust rules must be followed, and the amount of the IRA distribution treated as principal must be determined to calculate the deferred estate tax applicable (see the next section of this chapter for a discussion of the deferred estate tax for a qualified domestic trust). In any event, significant additional compliance complexity and costs are associated with the selection of the marital trust as beneficiary if the beneficiary is a noncitizen.

Estate or Unified Credit Shelter/Bypass Trust Generally Not Recommended as Beneficiary

Naming the participant's estate or unified credit shelter trust (UCST) as the designated beneficiary of the retirement plan account balance is generally not recommended because of adverse income tax treatment. The estate and any testamentary trust (including the UCST) created under the participant's will cannot be designated beneficiaries for retirement plan purposes. Therefore the minimum required distributions at age 70 1/2 must be based solely on the participant's life if his or her estate or testamentary trust is the named beneficiary. This causes the income tax to be incurred over a shorter period since payout cannot be made over the life expectancy of a surviving designated beneficiary. Depending on the age of the participant at his or her death or the type of distribution selected, the beneficiaries would take the remaining balance either (1) at least as fast as the participant was taking distributions, (2) in five installments beginning in the year following the year of the participant's death, or (3) all in the year following the year of the participant's death (if recalculation was chosen by the participant).

In addition, the UCST should generally be designed with a goal of maximum growth since it is a bypass trust and estate taxes are not imposed on this trust until the next generation. Funding the trust with retirement plan assets will shrink the growth by the income taxes that the UCST will incur on these retirement assets. Thus it is usually recommended that the UCST be funded with retirement plan assets only if there are no other estate assets available and only if the estate tax savings outweigh the adverse income tax consequences. One option may be to use the UCST as a disclaimer option if the surviving spouse and his or her advisers think this would be an appropriate postmortem choice.

Living Trust Can Be Designated Beneficiary

It is possible to designate a living trust, perhaps designed to use the marital deduction or unified credit, as beneficiary of the retirement plan assets. If the requirements of proposed Treas. Reg. Sec. 1.401(a)(9)-1 (Q&A D-5(a)) are met, a trust beneficiary can qualify as a designated beneficiary. Thus the beneficiary's life expectancy can be used to determine the payout after the death of the participant. Of course, if the trust is a marital trust, the greater of the minimum distribution or the actual income must be paid to the spouse.

The proposed regulations give the following requirements for the living trust:

- The beneficiaries of the trust who are beneficiaries of the participant's retirement benefits are identifiable from the trust document.
- The trust is a valid trust under state law.
- The trust is irrevocable at the later of the time it is designated as the beneficiary or the participant's attainment of age 70 1/2.
- A copy of the trust is given to the plan administrator or custodian of the IRA.

Several private rulings have approved variations of this living trust beneficiary designation. Thus a living marital or UCST can be named as the designated beneficiary and the age of one of the trust beneficiaries can be used to determine the minimum distribution under a joint life payout option. One interesting question is whether the plan participant can change the beneficiary designation from the trust after reaching age 70 1/2. The living trust must be irrevocable at that time, but maybe the flexibility to change the beneficiary is not forgone.

Charitable Giving and Retirement Plan Benefits

A charity can be the beneficiary of a retirement plan, even though the plan account or an IRA is generally nonassignable. The charity makes an appropriate beneficiary if two circumstances coincide: First, the participant has a desire to benefit a charity. Second, the income and estate tax benefits from the charitable gift are important to the client.

The designation of a charity or a charitable remainder trust (CRT) solves several of the tax problems discussed above, and for this reason, it will probably be better to fund a charitable gift with retirement plan assets than with other family assets. If these tax problems are mitigated, the family, the charity, or both will receive greater net inheritances than if non-IRD assets are used to fund the charitable bequest.

If a charity or CRT is the named beneficiary, the following tax consequences occur:

- The estate receives a charitable deduction for the amount passing to charity.
- The charity or CRT is tax exempt, and the IRD may be avoided (or deferred if a CRT is the beneficiary). The excess-accumulations tax is not avoided.

Example: Suppose Mrs. Adams, from our previous example, would like to leave $2,000,000 to The American College. You will recall that her $6 million estate consisted of a $2 million IRA account balance and $4 million of non-IRD items. If she designates The American College as the beneficiary of her IRA and apportions all taxes and expenses to her residuary estate, The American College gets $2 million and her heirs receive $2,285,026. If she left the IRA to her children and made a bequest of $2 million of non-IRD items to The American College, the College would still receive its $2 million; however, her children would only receive $1,814,903. This result is far worse since the income tax on the IRA is not avoided. See chapter 14 for more details of this computation.

The use of a CRT solves a problem created by the recalculation method of determining the minimum required distribution. Suppose a participant named his or her surviving spouse as the beneficiary and elected a QJSA with recalculation. At the second death, the entire remaining balance is subject to estate taxes within 9 months and income taxes on the IRD in the year following the survivor's death. By naming a testamentary CRT as the remainder beneficiary, the retirement assets will be payable to a tax-exempt trust. Thus the IRD is not immediately taxable.

If the married couple names their children as the CRT's noncharitable annuity or unitrust payment recipients, the IRD can be spread over the lifetime(s) of the noncharitable beneficiaries, an alternative not available without the charitable donation. What's more, an estate tax deduction is available for the remainder interest passing to charity.

Example: Suppose Mrs. Adams, from our previous example, did not want to deprive her children of the use of the IRA during their lifetimes, but still wanted to make a substantial gift to The American College. She could designate a testamentary charitable remainder trust (CRT) as the beneficiary of the IRA. Her children would receive an annual distribution equal to 6 percent of the annual value of the CRT's principal, (payable at the end of the year) for the remainder of their lives. The American College would receive the balance of the principal at the death of the survivor of her children. In this scenario, her estate would receive a charitable deduction of $291,140, saving her estate $160,127 in state and federal death taxes. What's more, the income taxes on the IRA would not have to be taken until her children received their annual payments form the CRT. The actuarial value of their payments would be $1,708,860, providing them with substantial funds for the remainder of their lives.

Where Can I Find Out More?

- HS 334 Fundamentals of Estate Planning II. The American College.
- "Estate Planning: The Cutting Edge," Workbook and tape. The American College. Phone (610) 526-1449.
- Kenneth A. Hansen. "Estate Planning for IRA and Qualified Plan Distributions," *Taxation for Accountants,* May 1996.
- Robert S. Schwartz. "Estate and Income Tax Planning for IRA and Qualified Plan Accounts," *The Practical Tax Lawyer,* summer 1995.

Estate Planning for Non-U.S. Citizens and Their Spouses
Ted Kurlowicz

What Was the Situation Before?

The federal estate tax is imposed on the entire taxable estate of a decedent who is a resident of the United States at the date of death. This is true even in a situation in which such individual was not a U.S. citizen at the date of death. Prior to the enactment of the Technical and Miscellaneous Revenue Act of 1988 (TAMRA) transfer to a resident-alien spouse would generally avoid estate tax because of the availability of the unlimited federal estate tax marital deduction and the unlimited federal gift tax marital deduction. The key point is that prior to the enactment of TAMRA, these deductions were equally available for transfers to spouses who were U.S. citizens and to resident aliens.

The legislative history of TAMRA makes clear that Congress was concerned about situations involving a non-U.S.-citizen surviving spouse returning to his or her homeland following the death of his or her spouse without ever paying federal estate tax on the marital property. Sec. 2056(d) was enacted as part of TAMRA to deny the federal estate tax marital deduction if the surviving spouse is not a U.S. citizen. The effective date of this provision was November 10, 1988. TAMRA also added Sec. 2056A that provided an estate tax deferral if assets transferred to a noncitizen surviving spouse were placed in a qualified domestic trust (QDOT). The Revenue

Reconciliation Act of 1989 (RRA 89) made technical corrections to TAMRA with respect to the changes brought about on the estate and gift tax treatment of transfers to noncitizen spouses. The Revenue Reconciliation Act of 1990 (RRA 90) made further modifications. Finally, some proposed regulations were issued by the Treasury on December 31, 1992, to further explain the statutory changes. However, many items were unexplained or unclear, particularly with respect to security rules required for the collection of deferred estate taxes by a QDOT's trustee.

What Is the Nature of the Change?

Final regulations were issued on August 21, 1995, on many of the issues formerly addressed in the proposed regulations mentioned above. Some new proposed and temporary regulations were issued at that time concerning some of the rules relating to the bond or security requirements for QDOTs. Final regulations on the security requirements were issued December 29, 1996.

The first rule to remember is that these new rules apply to transfers to the noncitizen spouse. Transfers from the noncitizen spouse to the citizen spouse are treated with the same exclusions, deductions, and credits available to transfers between spouses who are both citizens. The two sets of new regulations clarify and add compliance and drafting requirements for transfer to the noncitizen spouse, particularly with respect to transfers to a QDOT.

What Are the Gift Tax Changes?

The status of the donor is immaterial for this portion of the discussion. What is pertinent to the changes in the gift tax rules is that the donee is a noncitizen; the donor could be a citizen, a resident alien, or a nonresident alien.

No gift tax marital deduction is available for gifts to a noncitizen spouse. However, as the discussion below indicates, the new rules do borrow some of the traditional marital-deduction rules.

Super Annual-Exclusion Gifts. The gift tax annual exclusion is raised for transfers to a noncitizen spouse from $10,000 to $100,000. It gets complicated here since both the annual-exclusion and marital-deduction rules apply. The usual annual-exclusion rules requiring a present-interest gift apply to the transfer to the noncitizen spouse. The annual exclusion requires (1) an outright transfer in property, (2) a current income interest in a trust, or (3) that a "Crummey" withdrawal power over a transfer in a future interest trust be provided for the resident-alien spouse. Otherwise, no exclusion will apply to the gifts since neither the regular nor super gift tax annual exclusion is applicable and the donor spouse's unified credit will be wasted. It appears from the regulations that gifts made between August 14, 1988, and June 29, 1989, must meet only the annual-exclusion and not the marital-deduction rules to qualify for this special $100,000 exclusion.

For lifetime gifts to a resident-alien spouse after June 29, 1989, the normal marital-deduction rules have to be followed for a gift to qualify for a super annual exclusion. However, the new regulations diverge somewhat from, and are not as broad as, the marital-deduction rules for gifts to a citizen spouse. The following types of transfers will qualify for the super annual exclusion: (1) outright transfers to the noncitizen spouse and (2) a life income interest in a trust coupled with a testamentary power of appointment (a power of appointment trust). The latter will qualify for the super annual exclusion to the extent of the actuarial value of the income interest. However, the regulations indicate that a gift to an inter vivos QTIP or estate trust will not qualify.

Qualified Plan Implications. The transfer of the qualified survivor annuity (the required default election under the qualified plan rules) from a qualified retirement plan will qualify for an unlimited marital deduction despite the general prohibition of these rules. Presumably, it makes no difference for tax revenue whether or not the nonparticipant surviving spouse is a citizen to avoid gift taxes on the creation of a survivor annuity.

Creation of a Joint Tenancy in Real Estate. There are special rules for the creation of joint tenancies or tenancies by the entireties where one spouse is not a citizen. The rules mysteriously refer to a now-repealed Code section (Sec. 2515) and the regulations thereunder. (Presumably, tax history is more significant to the IRS than it is to the rest of us.) Note that the joint tenancy rules discussed here apply to the gift tax treatment of the creation and termination of the property interest.

The creation of a joint tenancy with rights of survivorship or a tenancy by the entireties will result in a gift when one tenant contributes more than one-half the consideration. Normally, this is not an issue between spouses because of the unlimited marital deduction. However, there is no gift tax marital deduction when the donee spouse is a noncitizen. The creation of a joint tenancy in real property after August 13, 1988, that would otherwise be a gift is not treated as a gift if the donee spouse is a noncitizen. However, the gift is merely deferred until the property interest is severed or the donee spouse dies. The termination of a joint tenancy in real property created after August 13, 1988, may result in a gift if the donee resident-alien spouse gets too much of the proceeds on termination. A gift is made at the termination to the extent the donor spouse receives less than his or her proportionate share of the proceeds based on the portions of the initial purchase price provided by each.

> *Example:* Suppose Dr. Dana, a citizen of the U.S., provided $150,000 to help purchase a $200,000 home in 1989. The home is a tenancy by the entireties with her husband, Mr. Dana, a resident alien, who provides the remainder of the purchase price. The home is sold in 1996 for $300,000, and the proceeds are divided equally. Dr. Dana makes a gift of $75,000 when the proceeds of the sale are divided equally since she should have received her proportionate share of $225,000

($150,000/$200,000 multiplied by $300,000) when the home was sold. The gift on the termination of the joint tenancy should be eligible for the super annual exclusion since the transfer is an outright present interest in property when the joint tenancy in the home is terminated.

What Are the Estate Tax Changes?

The normal marital-deduction rules provide that transfers at death to a surviving spouse who is a U.S. citizen qualify for the unlimited estate tax marital deduction. The major change brought about by TAMRA generally disallows the marital deduction for transfers to a noncitizen surviving spouse. Although the new regulations are voluminous, this discussion will try to focus on the most important implications. Basically, there are a couple of possibilities to salvage the marital deduction, or at least to defer estate taxes where the surviving spouse is not a U.S. citizen. The surviving spouse could choose to become a citizen on a timely basis following the death of the spouse who leaves assets to such spouse, or the assets transferred to the surviving spouse by the decedent could be transferred to a qualified domestic trust (QDOT).

The Surviving Spouse Becomes a U.S. Citizen. The normal unlimited marital deduction rules will apply if the surviving spouse becomes a U.S. citizen on a timely basis. The new regulations clarify this procedure. The surviving spouse must become a citizen before the estate tax return is made and must have been a resident of the U.S. at all times after the deceased spouse's date of death and before becoming a citizen. An early return is considered filed on the last date that the return is required to be filed (including extensions), and a late return filed at any time after the due date is considered filed on the date that it is actually filed.

It has been suggested that it may be practically impossible to attain citizenship within the 15 months (the normal due date of the estate tax return including extensions) following the decedent's death. There are a couple of potential solutions. One solution would be to file late and apply for "reasonable cause" relief from late filing and payment penalties for the purposes of Sec. 6651, if the survivor decides to begin naturalization proceedings but it appears unlikely that the process can be completed on time. Another possibility is to qualify the transfers to the surviving noncitizen spouse for the estate tax deferral under the QDOT rules and then begin (or continue) the naturalization proceedings.

Estate Tax Deferral through the Use of a QDOT. An estate tax deferral was made possible by TAMRA for transfers to a QDOT for the benefit of a surviving noncitizen spouse. This estate tax deferral is not the same as (it is generally worse than) the traditional unlimited marital deduction and provides rules for a deferred estate tax to be paid by the decedent-spouse's estate.

A QDOT can be established in one of two manners. First, it can be created by the transferor spouse as a testamentary marital trust contained in a will or funded at the death of the transferor spouse through the provisions of a living trust. Thus in this instance the QDOT is the traditional marital trust with the addition of the new QDOT drafting and administrative requirements. The other choice is for the QDOT to be created postmortem by the surviving noncitizen spouse or the executor of the deceased spouse's estate.

Some of the requirements for a QDOT created by the transferor spouse as a testamentary transfer device differ from the requirements for a QDOT created postmortem solely to avoid the prohibition of the marital deduction. The QDOT created by the deceased spouse's will must meet the usual rules for the marital-deduction trust contained in Sec. 2056. Thus a QTIP, power of appointment, or estate trust may be selected. Or, a charitable remainder trust, in which the surviving noncitizen spouse will be the only noncharitable beneficiary, will qualify as a QDOT. A QDOT created postmortem does not have to meet the normal marital-deduction rules. However, to be effective, the postmortem QDOT must be created prior to the time the return is due and the QDOT election must be made. All QDOTs must generally meet the following requirements:

- Initially, it was required to be a U.S. trust. The regulations now provide that the trust can be created in a foreign jurisdiction but must be maintained and governed by the laws of a U.S. state or the District of Columbia. (The QDOT is maintained in a state if the records, or copies thereof, are kept in the state). In the case of a foreign trust, the instrument must specify the U.S. state as the governing law of choice. This gives significant flexibility in choosing the most favorable state's trust law.
- The trust must qualify as an ordinary trust under the rules of the regulations for entity tax classification.
- The QDOT must satisfy the trustee security rules.

If the QDOT created by the decedent does not qualify, it can be salvaged by a judicial reformation. The regulations provide that the property interest is treated as passing to the surviving spouse in a QDOT if the trust is reformed, either in accordance with the terms of the decedent's will or trust agreement or pursuant to a judicial proceeding, to meet the requirements of a QDOT. A reformation made pursuant to the terms of the decedent's will or trust instrument must be completed by the time prescribed (including extensions) for filing the decedent's estate tax return. A reformation pursuant to a judicial proceeding is permitted under these rules if the reformation is commenced on or before the due date (determined with regard to extensions actually granted) for filing the estate tax return, regardless of the date that the return is actually filed.

Assignment of Property to a QDOT. The QDOT rules provide for the deferral of estate taxes for property left by the deceased spouse to the QDOT.

However, what about transfers made to the surviving spouse that are not transferred to a marital trust? The new rules permit the surviving spouse to achieve the estate tax deferral by assigning or transferring such assets to a QDOT prior to filing the decedent's estate tax return. If no other property, other than the property passing to the noncitizen, is transferred to the QDOT, the QDOT need not be in the form of a marital-deduction trust. However, it is important to note that the survivor will be considered the transferor of the property transferred or assigned to the QDOT for all tax purposes (other than qualifying for the QDOT). Thus care should be taken to avoid making completed gifts of the remainder interest in the QDOT or immediate gift taxes may result.

> *Example:* Dr. Richards left all of his $2 million estate outright to his wife, Mrs. Richards, who is not a citizen of the United States. Mrs. Richards would like to inherit the wealth, but would like to defer the estate taxes on this transfer. She creates a QDOT and makes the election on a timely filed estate tax return for her husband's estate. She transfers approximately $1.4 million of the inherited estate to the QDOT and leaves approximately $600,000 outside of the QDOT to be sheltered by her husband's unified credit. How should the QDOT be designed? If a traditional QTIP is selected, she will receive all income from the QDOT and the remainder will go to their children. However, if the QDOT is irrevocable, she will have completed a gift of the remainder interest to the children when the property is transferred to the QDOT. Thus the actuarial value of the remainder (determined by her age and the Sec. 7520 rate) will be a taxable gift from her to her children. (Note: The new regulations exempt this type of transfer from the rules of Sec. 2702.) To avoid a taxable gift, she could retain the right to revoke or invade the principal of the QDOT and make the transfer of the remainder incomplete, and thus not a gift, until the time of her death.

What assets can be assigned to a QDOT? Virtually anything that passes to the surviving noncitizen spouse can be transferred or assigned. Certainly, outright bequests to the surviving will qualify for transfer to a QDOT. Life insurance benefits payable to the survivor, or joint property received by operation of law can also be transferred to the QDOT by the executor or the surviving spouse. In addition, the assignment rules permit the flexibility to be creative. The surviving spouse can choose to assign assets to a QDOT based on a pecuniary or other formula to mirror a traditional marital-deduction unified-credit-shelter trust arrangement. The regulations provide the details for such a formula assignment.

> *Example:* Under the terms of Decedent's will, the entire probate estate passes outright to Survivor. Prior to the date Decedent's estate tax return is filed and before the date that the

QDOT election must be made, the surviving noncitizen spouse establishes a QDOT and such survivor executes an irrevocable assignment to the QDOT equal to "that portion of the gross estate necessary to reduce the estate tax to zero, taking into account all available credits and deductions."

Assignment of Retirement Plan Assets. What about the assignment of retirement accounts and annuities? Retirement plan assets require special consideration. The retirement plan cannot be overlooked for the purposes of planning the client's estate. The beneficiary designation should be formed in conjunction with, and with all the due care that goes into the preparation of, the wills and trusts. In many instances, it is even more important because the retirement plan assets may dwarf the size of the probate estate.

Individual retirement annuities are generally not assignable. However, the new regulations provide for the ability to defer taxes on retirement plan assets left to the noncitizen spouse irrespective of the nonassignability of such assets. In the case of a retirement plan, annuity, or other arrangement that is not assignable or transferable (or is treated as such), the property passing under the plan from the decedent is treated as meeting the requirements of the QDOT estate tax deferral rules if either of the following two requirements are met:

- First, the surviving noncitizen spouse could agree to pay the deferred estate tax on principal distributions from the IRA as they are received each year as part of the retirement plan or IRA distributions.
- Second, the principal portion of a distribution or an annuity payment could be rolled over to a QDOT to defer the estate tax.

These new rules for the assignment of the retirement plan assets or IRAs provide for significant complexity (in addition to the already complex minimum-distribution rules) and the regulations must be followed carefully. The regulations provide model forms for the assignment for both of the options discussed above.

In addition, the principal portion of retirement plan or IRA distributions must now be determined to meet either of these options. The principal portion of each nonassignable annuity or other payment is determined in accordance with the following formula:

$$\text{Corpus amount} = \frac{\text{Total present value of annuity or other payment}}{\text{Expected annuity term}}$$

The total present value of the annuity or other payment is the present value of the nonassignable annuity or other payment as of the date of the decedent's death, determined in accordance with the interest rates and mortality data prescribed by Sec. 7520 (which generally provides valuation discount rates and mortality tables).

Example: At the time of Decedent's death, Decedent is a participant in an employees' pension plan described in Sec. 401(a). On Decedent's death, Decedent's spouse, Survivor, a noncitizen, becomes entitled to receive a survivor's annuity of $72,000 per year, payable monthly, for life. At the time of Decedent's death, Survivor is aged 60. Assume that under Sec. 7520, the appropriate discount rate to be used for valuing annuities in the case of this decedent is 7.4 percent. The annuity factor at 7.4 percent for a person aged 60 is 9.3865. The adjustment factor for monthly payments at 7.4 percent is 1.0335. Accordingly, the right to receive $72,000 a year on a monthly basis is equal to the right to receive $74,412 ($72,000 x 1.0335) on an annual basis.

The principal portion of each annuity payment received by Survivor is determined as follows: The first step is to determine the annuity factor for the number of years that would be required to exhaust a hypothetical fund that has a present value and a payout corresponding to Survivor's interest in the payments under the plan:

> Present value of survivor's annuity:
> $74,412 x 9.3865 = $698,468
>
> Annuity factor for expected annuity term:
> $698,468/$74,412 = 9.3865

The second step is to determine the number of years that would be required for Survivor's annuity to exhaust a hypothetical fund of $698,468. The term-certain annuity factor of 9.3865 falls between the annuity factors for 16 and 17 years in the 7.4 percent term-certain annuity table. Accordingly, the expected annuity term is 17 years.

The third step is to determine the principal amount by dividing the expected term of 17 years into the present value of the hypothetical fund as follows:

> Principal amount of annual payment:
> $698,468/17 = $41,086

In the fourth step, the principal portion of each annuity payment is determined by dividing the principal amount of each annual payment by the annual annuity payment as follows:

> Principal portion of each annuity payment:
> $41,086/$74,412 = .55

Accordingly, 55 percent of each payment to Survivor is deemed to be a distribution of principal. A marital deduction is allowed for $698,468, the present value of the annuity as of Decedent's date of death, if either (1) Survivor agrees to roll over the principal portion of each payment to a QDOT or (2) Survivor agrees to pay the tax due on the principal portion of each payment.

When and How Is Tax Imposed on a QDOT? Unfortunately, the QDOT is unlike a true marital-deduction transfer in that the tax ultimately paid will be based on the decedent-spouse's estate tax bracket as if included in his or her estate at that time. A new system of deferred estate tax is applicable on various distributions from a QDOT. An estate tax is imposed on the occurrence of a taxable event. The following four events can trigger an estate tax on QDOT assets:

- Any distribution made prior to the surviving spouse's death—other than (1) income to the surviving spouse or (2) a distribution to the surviving spouse on account of hardship—will trigger an estate tax.

- At the surviving spouse's death the entire value of the property in the QDOT at that time will be subject to federal estate tax.

- An estate tax is imposed anytime the QDOT fails to meet any QDOT requirements.

- The payment of the deferred QDOT tax upon the first of the above triggering events (even if the U.S. trustee withholds such tax) is considered a taxable distribution that sets off yet another tax. In other words, the QDOT's payment of the deferred estate tax on a distribution is itself a distribution (equal to the amount of the tax) subject to a further estate tax.

The regulations provide normal definitions of principal and income. However, only nonhardship definitions of principal trigger a tax. A distribution is treated as being made on account of hardship if the distribution is made to the spouse from the QDOT in response to an immediate and substantial financial need relating to the spouse's health, maintenance, education, or support, or the health, maintenance, education, or support of any person that the surviving spouse is legally obligated to support. A distribution is not treated as a hardship if the amount distributed may be obtained from other sources that are reasonably available to the surviving spouse—for example, from the sale by the surviving spouse of personally owned, publicly traded stock or from the cashing in of a certificate of deposit owned by the surviving spouse. Fortunately, assets such as closely held business interests, real estate, and tangible personal property are not considered sources that are reasonably available to the surviving spouse.

Calculating the QDOT Tax. The tax payable on the occurrence of any of the four triggering taxable events discussed above is computed (in a cumulative manner similar to the tax on taxable gifts) as follows:

Step 1: State the amount of property involved in the taxable event.

Step 2: Add all previous taxable events.

Step 3: Compute the federal estate tax on the estate of first spouse to die if total of steps 1 and 2 above were included in decedent's gross estate.

Step 4: Compute the federal estate tax on the estate of first spouse to die if only amount of previous taxable events were included in decedent's gross estate.

Step 5: Subtract tax computed in step 4 from tax computed in step 3.

Result: Deferred estate tax imposed as result of current taxable event.

Example: Debra Decedent, a United States citizen, dies in 1996 as a resident of State X, with a gross estate of $2,000,000. Under Debra's will, a pecuniary bequest of $700,000 passes to a QDOT for the benefit of Debra's spouse, Donald, who is a resident but not a citizen of the United States. Debra's estate pays $70,000 in death taxes to State X. Debra's estate tax is computed as follows:

Gross estate		$2,000,000
Marital deduction		(700,000)
Taxable estate		$1,300,000
Gross tax		$469,800
Less unified credit	$192,800	
State death tax credit limitation (lesser of $51,600 or $70,000 tax paid)	$ 51,600	(244,400)
Estate tax		$225,400

Donald dies in 1997, at which time he is still a resident of the United States and the value of the QDOT's assets is $800,000. Donald's estate pays $40,000 in State X death taxes with respect to the inclusion of the QDOT in Donald's gross estate for state death tax purposes. Assuming there were no taxable events during Donald's lifetime with respect to the QDOT, the deferred estate tax is $ 304,800, computed as follows:

Debra's actual taxable estate	$1,300,000
QDOT property left at Donald's death	800,000
Total	$2,100,000
Gross tax	829,800
Less unified credit	(192,800)
Pre-state death tax estate tax	$ 637,000

(A) State death tax credit computation:
 (1) State death tax paid by Donald's estate with respect to the QDOT ($40,000) plus state death tax previously paid by Debra's estate ($70,000) = $110,000.

 (2) Limit for state death tax credit = $106,800.

(B) State death tax credit allowable (106,800)

Net tax	$530,200
Less tax that would have been imposed on Debra's taxable estate of $1,300,000	225,400
Deferred estate tax on Debra's estate	$304,800

New Security Requirements for QDOTs. Congress was concerned about the ability to collect the QDOT tax. The law generally requires that at least one trustee must be an individual who is a U.S. citizen or a domestic corporation. In addition, Congress directed the Treasury to make regulations to provide for the collection of the QDOT tax when a taxable event occurs. For the purposes of the security requirements, the new regulations create a distinction between large (over $2 million) QDOTs and small ($2 million or less) QDOTS.

A small QDOT simply needs to meet the requirement of a U.S. trustee. Thus the trustee could generally be any individual or entity residing in the U.S.

For a large QDOT, special security arrangements were deemed necessary since the potential deferred estate taxes would be larger. Alternative requirements for QDOTs with assets in excess of $2 million (determined without regard to indebtedness encumbering the assets) are as follows:

- The QDOT must require that at least one trustee be a U.S. bank or a U.S. branch of a foreign bank (provided a U.S. trustee with a tax home in the U.S. serves as cotrustee),

- The QDOT must require an individual U.S. trustee that will post a bond in favor of the IRS equal to 65 percent of value the trust assets, or
- The QDOT must require that the U.S. trustee furnish an irrevocable letter of credit issued by a U.S. bank, or a U. S. branch of a foreign bank, or by a foreign bank and confirmed by a U.S. bank in an amount equal to 65 percent of the fair market value of the trust assets.
- The IRS will consider alternative security arrangements to ensure the collection of tax if proposed by the trustee and a request for a private letter ruling is made (for example, a major law firm with substantial assets as trustee for the QDOT).

Of course, there are many special rules for computing the value of the QDOT assets to determine its status as a large or small QDOT. These rules provide additional annual compliance burdens and the regulations must be followed carefully. The following are key issues for determining the large or small status of a QDOT:

- Indebtedness can be ignored. The fair market value of the assets passing, treated, or deemed to have passed to the QDOT (or in the form of a QDOT) is determined without reduction for any indebtedness with respect to the assets in the QDOT.
- Principal residences can be excluded. The value of the surviving spouse's home and one additional residence that is personal (that is, not rented) can be excluded up to a combined value of $600,000, including related furnishings.
- Foreign property limitation: The trust instrument must require that no more than 35 percent of the fair market value of the trust assets, determined annually on the last day of the taxable year of the trust (or on the last day of the calendar year if the QDOT does not have a taxable year), may consist of real property located outside of the United States, or the trust must meet the bank trustee, bond, or security requirements required for large QDOTs.

Miscellaneous Compliance Issues. The complexity and compliance requirements for QDOTs added by the regulations is astonishing and cannot be given full treatment here. However, the following key issues should be examined by the client's advisers if a QDOT will be used:

- The QDOT election is irrevocable and must be made timely.
- Annual reporting statements may be required to determine the value of the QDOT and the foreign property limitation.
- A QDOT *must* be drafted to meet all of the new rules, including the security arrangements.
- Tax returns must be filed for events triggering a deferred estate tax. The due date for payment of the deferred estate tax imposed on distributions during the noncitizen spouse's lifetime is April 15th of the year following the distribution. An extension of not more than 6

months may be obtained for filing Form 706-QDT. Other filings are required for hardship distributions.
- Each trustee (and not solely the U.S. trustee(s)) of a QDOT is personally liable for the amount of the estate tax imposed in the case of any taxable event. In the case of multiple QDOTs with respect to the same decedent, each trustee of a QDOT is personally liable for the amount of the deferred estate tax imposed on any taxable event with respect to that trustee's QDOT, but is not personally liable for tax imposed with respect to taxable events involving QDOTs of which that person is not a trustee.
- For multiple QDOTs, a designated return filer can be named. The designated filer must be a U.S. trustee.
- Watch out for the retirement plan or IRA. Additional information statements must be filed with the return to select the alternate approach to receive QDOT deferral for these assets.

When Do These Changes Affect Clients?

The date for the new regulations governing the gift tax treatment of lifetime interspousal gifts to noncitizen spouses is effective for gifts made after August 22, 1995, although the denial of the marital deduction and the availability of the super annual-exclusion gift generally go back to the effective date of TAMRA.

The date for the new regulations (except for the new security requirements) governing the estate tax treatment of transfers to surviving noncitizen spouses is also effective for decedent's dying after August 22, 1995. The denial of the marital deduction and the availability of the QDOT also generally go back to the effective date of TAMRA.

The effective date for the new security requirements is for QDOT elections made after December 9, 1996.

What Should Be Done?

Perhaps the most obvious conclusion that can be formed from the discussion of the new rules discussed above is that the QDOT approach will add incredible complexity and compliance requirements for marital transfers to the noncitizen spouse. Understanding the implications should lead to the following conclusions:

- Avoid the QDOT approach whenever possible.
- If a QDOT must be used, attempt to qualify as a small QDOT to reduce the expense of the security requirements.

How Do You Avoid the Funding of a QDOT? First, the surviving spouse could avoid the QDOT approach entirely by obtaining citizenship, which of course would have to be obtained on a timely basis. Even if the citizenship is obtained later, the QDOT can be avoided afterward and all QDOT distributions made prior to becoming a citizen will be treated as gifts by the surviving spouse. Such gifts can be sheltered by the surviving spouse's unified credit and the deferred estate tax will no longer apply to withdrawal of principal from the marital trust.

Second, if obtaining citizenship is impractical or undesirable, all other estate reduction techniques should be examined. Maximum use should be made of $100,000 super annual-exclusion gifts to the noncitizen spouse. If the estate is not that large, a combination of the use of the unified credit and lifetime super annual-exclusion gifts to the noncitizen spouse could be effective.

> *Example:* Mrs. Remington is married to Mr. Remington, who is not a citizen of the United States. She has an estate of approximately $1.2 million and her husband has insignificant wealth. She creates a will to leave an optimal marital formula to take maximum advantage of her unified credit. Her will creates a unified credit shelter trust (UCST) and QDOT. The UCST provides her husband with all income and the power for a trustee to invade for his support if he survives. She begins a pattern of $100,000 super annual-exclusion gifts to her husband. If she lives 6 more years, she will have transferred enough to her husband to fund a full unified credit transfer in his estate. In addition, she will have removed much of the excess over her unified credit-equivalent from her estate. This will reduce the funding of the QDOT that might be created by her will. If Mr. Remington is well-advised, he will use some of the annual gifts to buy life insurance on his wife's life. The life insurance will provide additional flexibility. For example, it would provide the liquidity to pay taxes at the death of his wife. If Mr. Remington and his advisers decide that they should avoid the QDOT approach, they can choose not to make the QDOT election. If her estate exceeds $600,000, this will result in some first-death taxes. The life insurance proceeds provide ability to freeze her estate tax costs by avoiding the future deferred estate taxes on the QDOT.

Third, the hardship exemption from QDOT tax should be investigated. This could allow the surviving noncitizen spouse to consume principal without tax. Of course, it will require the survivor to have insufficient non-QDOT funds for support. However, business interests held by the family will not have to be liquidated to qualify for hardship treatment.

Finally, life insurance can be used to effectively mitigate or avoid the QDOT tax. An inter vivos irrevocable life insurance trust (ILIT) would prevent the proceeds from enhancing either spouse's gross estate. The noncitizen spouse could own the policy covering the life of the citizen spouse. Or, the couple's children could own the policy. If survivorship (second to die) coverage is used, the impact of the QDOT can be mitigated at the second death.

Where Can I Find Out More?

- HS 334 Fundamentals of Estate Planning II. The American College.
- Treas. Reg. Secs. 20.2056A-1 to 13.
- IAFP Success Forum, *Wealth Transfer Planning for Non-U.S. Citizens and Their Spouses.* Audio tape and workbook. Phone (800) 241-7785.

Character-Building Trust (Family Goals Trust)
Constance J. Fontaine

How Does This Affect Clients?

The wealthy have concerns that their self-earned wealth will be the ruination of their children's and grandchildren's characters.

Creative estate planning can be developed to provide incentives for lineal descendants through the use of carefully drafted trusts that are centered on the settlor's values. Such provisions are appropriate for irrevocable life insurance trusts as well as many other situations. (Also see chapter 11, "Human Behavior Perspectives.")

Common Scenario. You are "well off" financially, perhaps downright wealthy, and are respected within your community. The family values you embrace are founded on love, caring, recognition, and respect. Perpetuation of these qualities through generations to follow would be the greatest gift and finest legacy you could leave. Yet you recognize that respect has to be earned—it can't be gifted and it can't be bought. To get where you are today you worked tirelessly, struggled for years, sacrificed many things, and did without. From your perspective your efforts broadened your shoulders and made you appreciate what you have and what you have achieved. In essence you believe that taking the rough road made you learn to manage life and money. It gave you confidence, values, standards, self-esteem. You love your children and grandchildren and can afford to lavish them with all sorts of money and privileges that were unavailable to you at their ages.

However, you begin to notice that there might already be some telltale signs that the kids are "spoiled," lazy, and take the good life for granted. Your concerns: Will they squander the wealth? Will they "waste" their lives and live off their inheritances? Will your money undermine their personal growth and chances for success? Your wish is that they live up to their individual potentials. You don't want your achievements to be a cause of their inability to lead constructive, respected lives in their own right. The quandary is how to instill a work ethic, promote self-reliance, develop a sense of responsibility, reinforce love, and continue to provide assistance to your lineal descendants.

The answer may be found in a "character-building" or "personal philosophies" trust.

What Should Be Done?

A carefully and creatively drafted character-building trust can be fashioned to help develop the settlor's most treasured personal characteristics and family values in his or her lineal descendants. The underpinnings of this kind of trust are quite different from the typical garden variety trust that is premised on the avoidance of gift and estate taxes and that mandates distributions of income and corpus at predetermined beneficiary ages. The character-building trust will not necessarily pay out income at certain specified intervals, nor will it dole out corpus to lineal descendant beneficiaries upon the attainment of chronological ages. Rather, this trust will make distributions of income and corpus when the benefi-ciaries have "earned" them in accordance with the personal philosophies of the one who originally earned them.

For instance, if the settlor considers education to be a primary source for gainful employment and self-worth, distributions could be related to academic achievements—a college degree, a graduate degree, etc. Of course, if the prerequisites for distribution are too narrow, that is, the college degrees must be from certain educational institutions or within certain fields of study, the limitations may discourage the intended beneficiaries from trying to meet the goals the settlor originally wanted them to achieve. Therefore the trust terms could provide latitude. If a beneficiary is not academically inclined, the trust could provide for distributions for the completion of a vocational or trade-oriented program. Perhaps the beneficiary is not a good academic student but is artistically or musically accomplished. In that case, satisfactory progression or completion of art or music school could meet the desired incentives expectation.

Maybe the settlor has determined that employment or some form of money-earning endeavor is the foundation for success. The reasoning here is that the settlor had to work hard to get where he or she is and therefore so should the kids. The harder the beneficiaries work, the more likely it is they will make it on their own. In this case, the trust might provide that every dollar earned in a year is matched with trust money. Limitations could be placed in the trust instructions. For example, earned dollars aren't matched by trust dollars until the beneficiary has earned a certain level of income. Conversely, there could be a limit on the amount of matching to discourage greed. Inflation and the possibility of changes in the economy and personal lives should be kept in mind, however, at the time of drafting.

Trust directions can also anticipate beneficiaries who aspire to government careers or to lives of public service as well as those who wish to give time and effort to philanthropic causes. The possibilities are endless and thought provoking. Clearly the creation of a values-oriented trust can be time consuming and may require a fair amount of ingenuity—the guidance and caring of others usually does.

The character-building trust does not have to (and probably would not be intended to) preclude beneficiaries from receiving any trust benefits unless they have jumped through exacting hoops. The trust terms can make provisions for emergency situations, hardships, and extraordinary or changing circumstances. The trust (and the settlor) is likely to be viewed in a positive light when it allows for some flexibility and discretion. Since the wealthy settlor probably stumbled several times on the road to his or her own success and fortune, the trust directions can provide for flexibility so that the beneficiaries won't be denied distributions entirely because of a mistake or two. After all, one of the values of the trust that the settlor wishes to convey is kindness.

The thrust of a personal goals type of trust is to encourage the beneficiaries to develop qualities and values that will serve them well throughout their lives, years after the settlor is available to provide guidance. If a trust that strives for the development of values is too rigid, it may thwart the very purpose for which it was originally created. To avoid the appearance of being too much like a carrot on the end of a stick, the trust directions could grant distributions at specified age intervals when desired accomplishments (a college degree, full-time employment, etc.) have been achieved. Should trust conditions and desired qualities in the beneficiaries not be met, the trust instructions could call for corpus to pass to charity or to the next generation and so forth. Understanding the settlor's intentions, concepts, and reasoning may be enhanced by the settlor gathering the family together for a discussion of the trust contents.

The selection of a financial adviser and attorney must be done with care. This is clearly a more customized and people-focused trust document than a conventional trust that is mostly money oriented. Computer software doesn't contain provisions for this kind of finely tailored instrument. A good balance may be achieved if there is an independent, institutional trustee and also a family or close family friend cotrustee. The corporate trustee has the tax and investment expertise while the individual trustee provides the personal family insights. A trust that encourages children and grandchildren to reach their potentials and establish sound values is an excellent way of being remembered and a fine family tradition to pass on.

Estate and Gift Tax Implications. The character-building trust will have some estate and/or gift tax implications since it involves a transfer of property. However, the estate and/or gift tax implications cannot be discussed without addressing the specific circumstances of the transfer or terms of the trust. For example, an inter vivos trust may or may not be a completed gift when it is created, depending on the types of powers retained by the grantor. A completed gift to an inter vivos trust may be included back in the grantor's estate at the time of his or her death under Secs. 2036 or 2038 if the grantor retains the right to sprinkle benefits or change beneficiaries. A testamentary trust will invariably invoke the estate tax system. Due to this complexity, please do not attempt to create a character-building trust without appropriate legal and tax advice.

Where Can I Find Out More?

- See chapter 11, "Human Behavior Perspectives."
- GS 816 Advanced Estate Planning II. The American College.

Keeping a Living Will Alive
Constance J. Fontaine

Generally speaking, both law and custom accept a competent individual's right to refuse life-prolonging medical treatment. However, the area of health care decisions regarding incapacitated and incompetent patients is where the conflict, uncertainty, and difficult issues prevail. The importance of formally expressing medical treatment wishes while competent—before a possible future state of incompetence—cannot be overemphasized. Life-prolonging measures may be withdrawn or withheld if there is reliable evidence that, under the existing circumstances, the patient did not want treatment.

An advance health care directive (commonly but misleadingly called a living will) is a document establishing a declarant's instructions for medical treatment at such time he or she is terminally ill and is incapable of communicating medical choices. The long and short of it is that in the majority of cases the declarant is trying to avoid being sustained by artificial life support when there is no hope of recovery. An advance medical directive is in most situations a declarant's attempt to provide for a dignified death. It may be an attempt to alleviate the fear of being held hostage by medical technology. It may be an attempt to avoid becoming the cause of a financial drain on the family coffers. Perhaps, above all, it may be an attempt to spare the family the anguish, disagreements, confusion, and guilt that abound with decisions related to medical issues surrounding the terminally ill.

Ninety percent of Americans say they do not want heroic measures to prolong their lives when there's no real hope of recovery. Out of the 90 percent only 15 percent have executed a document saying so.[1] Why?

- Procrastination ("I'll do it soon." "I'll let the family handle it if it ever comes to that.")
- Denial ("The likelihood of this happening to me. . . ." "I'm too young to worry about this now.")

---

1. Alfred Lewis. "How Living Wills Could Save Billions," *Business and Health*, page 68, September 1994.

- Reluctance to discuss incompetence or terminal condition with family, friends, or doctor ("Bringing this up will just upset my family.")
- Expense concerns ("I'll have to get a lawyer." "It will be expensive.")
- Lack of knowledge ("I don't know how to go about creating one." "I don't know where to go or what to say.")
- Viewed as worthless effort ("Nobody pays any attention to these things anyway.")

One problem area with advance health care directives is the distinction between the discontinuation of life-sustaining medical treatment and the omission of treatment in the first place. Society, and therefore family members and medical providers, seems to find it more morally and psychologically troublesome to stop treatment already commenced than to simply not consider the treatment in the first place. Perhaps this is because the discontinuation of treatment involves affirmative action, whereas failing to begin treatment is passive. Maybe the distinction rests with the attitude that the withdrawal of life support is perceived as euthanasia or as "killing" someone. Legally, however, there is a clear distinction between the removal of life-support treatment and affirmative euthanasia where a health care provider, such as a physician, actively assists the patient, at the patient's behest, to die. Currently, no state legalizes active euthanasia. In the last few years, however, the cases involving Dr. Jack Kevorkian have made the issues surrounding the terminally ill and those who are chronically in pain the subject of heated debates in the news, courts, and legislative bodies.

The medical, ethical, legal, religious, financial, emotional, and moral questions swirling around the subject of a person's right to die appear to be infinite. It involves a balancing of a person's right to medical self-determination about life when death is imminent, the medical oath to preserve life, and public policy to protect citizenry, allowing what inherently has a sense of being humane and compassionate while simultaneously seeming inhumane and disturbing. Congress and Uniform Laws Commissioners are striving to achieve more uniformity, "clarity," and acceptance concerning medical treatment decisions for those unable to express their wishes. The Patient Self-Determination Act is a federal law requiring health care providers participating in medicare and medicaid programs to inform and educate patients about their right to refuse medical treatment. In other words, medical personnel must tell patients of the right to execute, in accordance with state law, an advance medical directive to provide guidance in case of incapacity.

Another problem is the fact that although all states recognize at least some type of advance medical directive—be it in the form of a health care proxy, living will, or durable medical power of attorney—there are many discrepancies among them. Living wills become operative if a person is suffering from a "terminal condition" or is in a "persistent vegetative state." The way one state defines terminal condition may be different from another state. What constitutes a persistent vegetative state may vary from jurisdiction to jurisdiction. Some state statutes provide suggested forms but allow flexibility while other states require the use of a particular form. States also differ in their standards in determining the validity of advance medical directives, such as the number of witnesses, notarization, and so forth. In an attempt to alleviate jurisdictional discrepancy problems, many states have reciprocity agreements. (See figures 2–1 and 2–2 at the end of this section: "Reciprocity Provisions in Living Will Statutes" and "Reciprocity Provisions in Statutes Authorizing Health Care Agents.")

There are several uniform acts that help to bring about a degree of consensus among the states. The Uniform Durable Power of Attorney Act contains a checklist of the types of transactions that are widely accepted and that may be authorized in a power of attorney. The Uniform Statutory Form Power of Attorney Act provides a simple, universally accepted durable power of attorney form. The Uniform Health Care Decisions Act was approved by the Uniform Law Commissioners in 1993. The drafters recognized a need to provide for advance health care directives that can be either a power of attorney for health care or an "individual instruction" (terminology the drafters considered to be more appropriate than "living will") since these issues are typically addressed by separate statutes in most states. The act includes a combined durable power of attorney for health care and individual instruction form that can be modified by the declarant. Another benefit of the Uniform Health Care Decisions Act is the minimization of requirements for executing advance directives.[2] While most states require witnesses or acknowledgment in addition to the declarant's signature, the act provides that an individual instruction may be oral or in writing and that a medical power of attorney merely be written and signed.

What Should Be Done?

Reliance on federal legislation and uniform acts in most cases isn't going to be enough. Presently, the best protection of an individual's right to health care self-determination is by executing an advance medical directive such as a living will type of document and a durable power of attorney for health care or health care proxy. There are several ways to achieve acceptance of and reliance on these documents as well as convince family members and relevant medical providers of the declarant's intentions.

The declarant's wishes should be documented in writing, and the instrument should be dated and witnessed. Notarization may be required by the particular state, but, even if not required, notarization serves to validate the declarant's intent.

Any and all health care documents must comply with applicable state law, and therefore state law must be consulted. This is not as onerous as it sounds. There are numerous sources for achieving compliance including the local or

---

2. David M. English. "The Health-Care Decisions Act Represents a Major Advance," *Trusts and Estates*, May 1994, pages 32–38.

state bar association, which may provide information, and also certain organizations, such as Choice In Dying, that will furnish information that is state specific for a nominal cost, if any. (Choice In Dying is a nonprofit patients' rights organization that is based in New York. It produces state-specific advance directives and other materials and services relating to end-of-life medical care. Call Choice In Dying for information. (212) 366-5540.) Of course, an attorney who is knowledgeable in this area of the law can be consulted. Additionally, if the declarant has more than one medical decision-making document, each instrument can acknowledge the existence of the other.

The individual should openly express his or her feelings with respect to health care decisions with loved ones, close friends, doctors, and a lawyer. Specifically, those individuals who may be consulted about the declarant's health care should know what the declarant wanted. Although the document may state the declarant's wishes, hearing the wishes gives added meaning (and comfort).

Documents should be as specific and as flexible as possible. Clearly all situations and medical treatments can't be anticipated and considered. The benefit of having both a durable power of attorney for health care and an advance medical directive regarding artificial life support and the prolongation of life is that the power of attorney can be drafted to grant broad powers to the agent or proxy for decision-making situations that are not specifically addressed. To the extent possible, however, the more medical conditions and treatments delineated in the document, the less uncertainty for all concerned. General, overly broad descriptions of mental and physical conditions should be avoided. For instance, phrases such as "no heroic measures" or "no life-prolonging procedures if there's no hope of recovery" don't provide any real decision-making guidance to medical personnel and family. These types of phrases with no elaboration are too vague to be helpful. In this case the declarant's wishes need to be verbally expanded: "Should it be determined that I am terminally ill with irreversible brain damage resulting in family and friends being unrecognizable to me, and/or the inability to breathe on my own, or swallow, I would (or would not) want the following measures to be taken— (1) a respirator, (2) gastric feeding tube," and so forth.

Keep the advance medical directive where it can be easily located. Studies have shown that in 40 percent of the instances in which declarants have executed advance medical directives, the documents can't be found when needed. To solve this problem, Choice In Dying has developed an automated advance directive registry to provide document availability at any time.[3] The legal staff at Choice In Dying reviews submitted documents for state law compliance. Once compliance is determined, a copy of the advance directive

---

3. Joan R. Rose and Debra Potter. "News Beat," *Medical Economics*, July 10, 1995, page 24.

is entered into the registry database. Thereafter, a copy can be obtained and faxed within minutes of a request.

Last, reviewing and updating the advance medical directive is important. Although a periodic review every 2 to 3 years is advisable, the interval between reviews should not exceed 5 years. Updating in most cases merely constitutes signing or initialing, dating, and notarizing the update.

Once a person has taken the steps to execute a living will type of document, efforts to ensure its viability are not burdensome. The declarant's objectives are usually twofold—peace of body and peace of mind—and by putting this document in place, both objectives may be achieved.

Where Can I Find Out More?

- GS 816 Advanced Estate Planning II. The American College.
- Choice In Dying, Inc., 200 Varick Street, New York, N.Y. 10014 (1-[212]-366-5540)
- Joseph E. Beltran. *The Living Will and Other Life-and-Death Medical Choices.* 1994.
- Carolyn Brown, et al. (Nancy R. Hull, ed.) *Decide for Yourself: Life Support, Living Will, Power of Attorney for Health Care.* 1993.
- Norman L. Cantor. *Advance Directives and the Pursuit of Death with Dignity.* 1993.
- David J. Doukas and William Reichel. *Planning for Uncertainty: A Guide to Living Wills and Other Advance Directives for Health Care.* 1993.
- *Living Wills and Powers of Attorney.* (E-Z Legal Guide Ser.) 1995.
- *Take Control of Your Own Health Care Decisions: A State-by-State Guide to Preparing Your Living Will and Appointing Your Health Care Agent, with Forms. Regional Edition:* Midwest & Great Lakes Edition. 1995.
- Francis Collin, Jr., Esq., et al. *Durable Powers of Attorney and Health Care Directives.* 3d ed. 1995.

FIGURE 2-1

June 1996

Reciprocity Provisions in Living Will Statutes

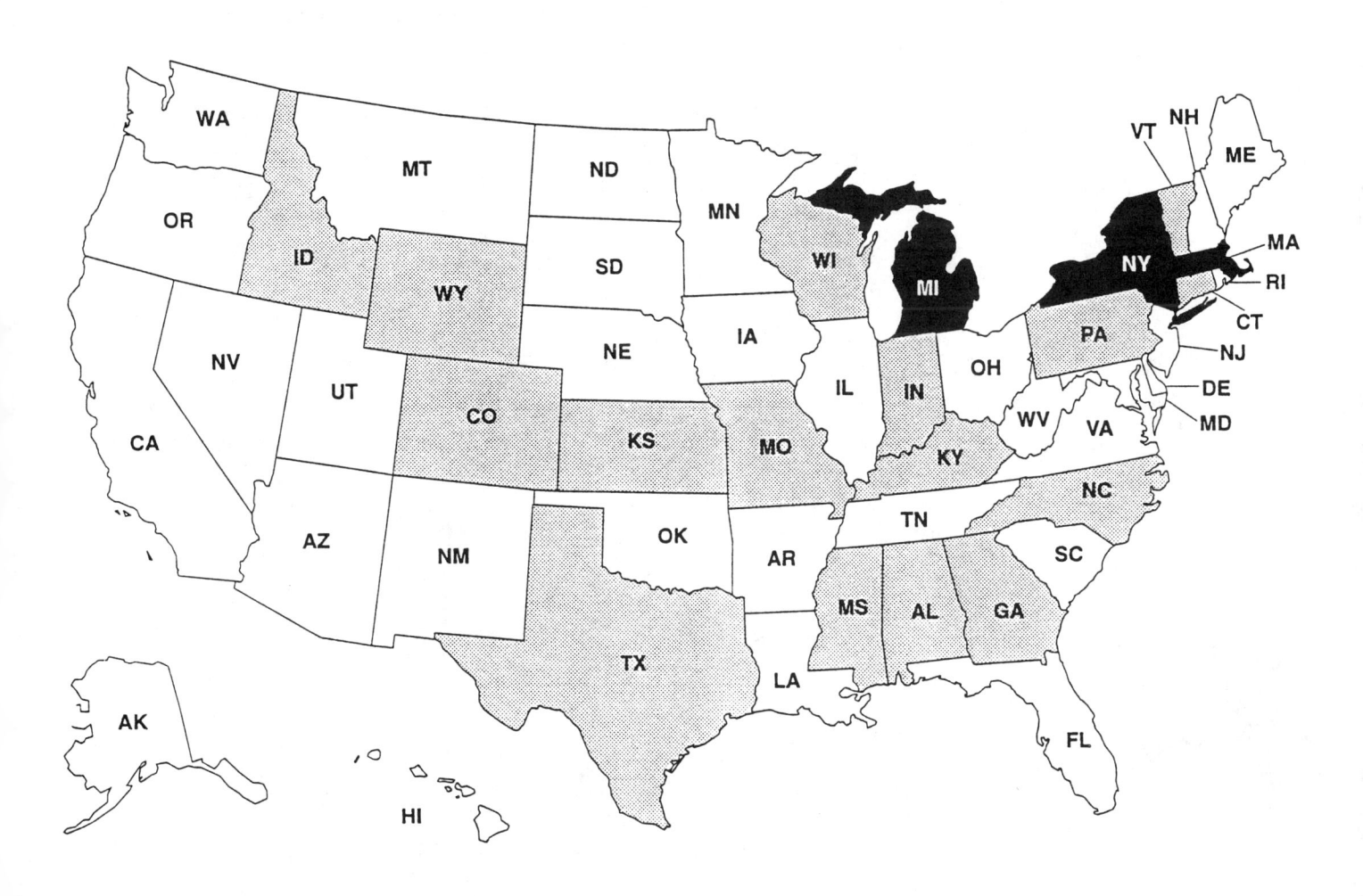

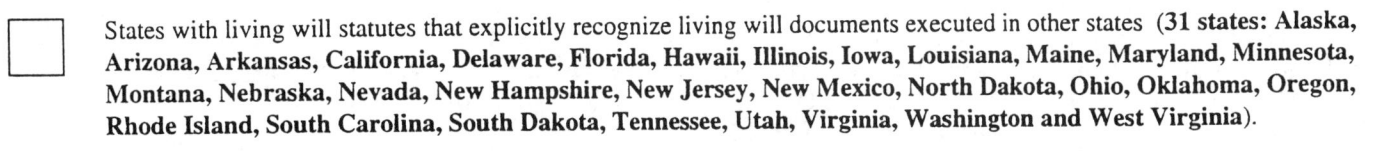

☐ States with living will statutes that explicitly recognize living will documents executed in other states (**31 states: Alaska, Arizona, Arkansas, California, Delaware, Florida, Hawaii, Illinois, Iowa, Louisiana, Maine, Maryland, Minnesota, Montana, Nebraska, Nevada, New Hampshire, New Jersey, New Mexico, North Dakota, Ohio, Oklahoma, Oregon, Rhode Island, South Carolina, South Dakota, Tennessee, Utah, Virginia, Washington and West Virginia**).

▒ Jurisdictions whose living will statutes do not explicitly address the issue of reciprocity (**the District of Columbia and 16 states: Alabama, Colorado, Connecticut, Georgia, Idaho, Indiana, Kansas, Kentucky, Mississippi, Missouri, North Carolina, Pennsylvania, Texas, Vermont, Wisconsin and Wyoming**).

■ States without living will statutes (**3 states: Massachusetts, Michigan and New York**).

© 1996 **Choice In Dying, Inc.**
200 Varick Street, 10th Floor   New York, NY 10014-4810   (212) 366-5540

---

*Figures 2-1 and 2-2 are reprinted with the permission of Choice In Dying, Inc.

FIGURE 2-2

June 1996

Reciprocity Provisions in Statutes Authorizing Health Care Agents

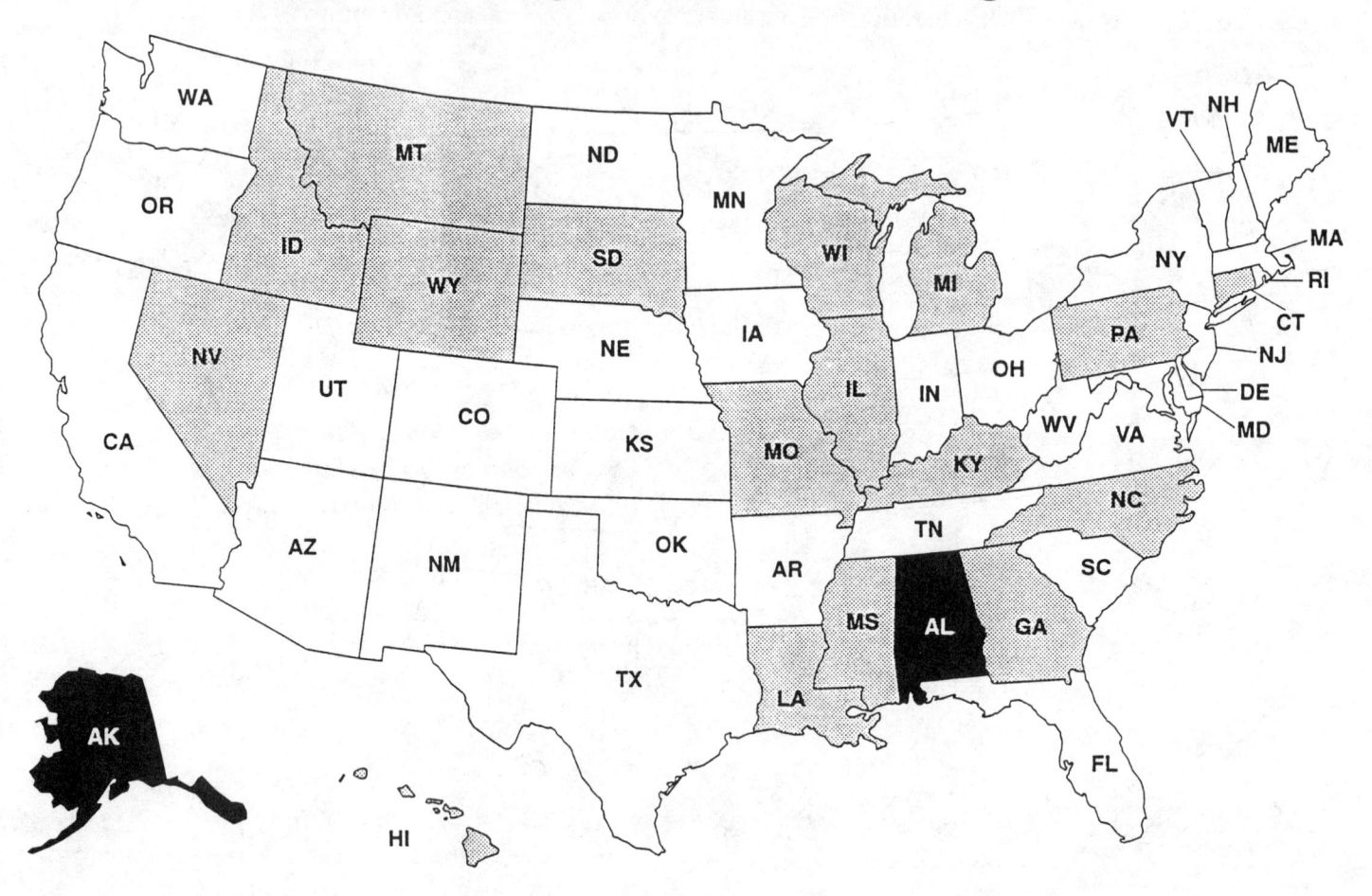

States with statutes that permit agents appointed in documents executed in other states to make health care decisions on behalf of incapacitated principals (**31 states: Arizona, Arkansas, California, Colorado, Delaware, Florida, Indiana, Iowa, Kansas, Maine, Maryland, Massachusetts, Minnesota, Nebraska, New Hampshire, New Jersey, New Mexico, New York, North Dakota, Ohio, Oklahoma, Oregon, Rhode Island, South Carolina, Tennessee, Texas, Utah, Vermont, Virginia, Washington and West Virginia**).

Jurisdictions whose statutes do not explicitly address reciprocity of health care agent appointments (**the District of Columbia and 17 states: Connecticut, Georgia, Hawaii, Idaho, Illinois, Kentucky, Louisiana, Michigan, Mississippi, Missouri, Montana, Nevada,* North Carolina, Pennsylvania, South Dakota, Wisconsin and Wyoming**).

States without statutes for appointing health care agents (**2 states: Alabama and Alaska**).

* While Nevada's medical power of attorney statute makes no mention of reciprocity, its living will statute explicitly recognizes living will documents executed in other states. The state's living will law permits individuals to appoint health care agents to make decisions regarding life-sustaining treatment.

© 1996 **Choice In Dying, Inc.**
200 Varick Street, 10th Floor   New York, NY 10014-4810   (212) 366-5540

Organ Donation in Estate Planning

Constance J. Fontaine

What Was the Situation Before?

A generation ago organ donation was unusual and uncommon. Medical technology and expertise weren't as sophisticated as they are today. The capabilities just weren't there to the extent that they are now.

What Is the Nature of the Change?

Organ donation is increasingly being brought to public attention partly through advertisements on television encouraging donation and also through the news media, which has brought the Nicholas Green story to the world. Nicholas was the California child gunned down while vacationing with his parents in Italy in 1994. His parents donated his organs and seven Italian citizens were the organ recipients. Organ donation in Italy has significantly increased as a result of the Green family's caring gesture. Nicholas's parents claim to find comfort in the fact that others continue to live because of their son. Other success stories having name recognition include actor Larry Hagman of television's "Dallas" J.R. Ewing fame. After being on a donation waiting list for six weeks, Mr. Hagman received a new liver and a new lease on life. Since his successful liver transplant, he has given a great deal of time and effort to furthering the organ donation cause. Several years ago Pennsylvania's then governor Robert Casey was the recipient of a "new" liver and heart in a successful double transplant operation.

Most individuals have a desire to make a contribution to society in some recognizable way—to "make a difference." Although many are in a better position than others to help mankind, organ and tissue donations are not limited to the wealthy, the people who have time, or even those who are medically healthy. Practically every person is capable of improving the lives of others—and society as a whole—through organ and tissue donations. No one may be in a better position than the estate planner to introduce the thought processes relating to organ donation.

What Could Be Done?

The most common topics that come to mind with estate planning are wills, trusts, various insurance needs, retirement plans, and durable powers of attorney. While many clients are reluctant to discuss their financial and personal family situations freely, getting them to address plans for incapacity, personal care, terminal illness, and organ donation is in most cases an even greater impasse. First, let's review the following documents used to address personal and physical care issues, including organ donations.

Medical Durable Power of Attorney. The durable power of attorney for health care is an instrument that appoints another individual, usually a close family member or friend, to make health-related decisions for the declarant when the declarant is no longer capable (as determined by the physician and/or spouse or children of the declarant) of making his or her own decisions. In most situations, the document spells out specific instructions concerning the decisions to be made under varying circumstances. In essence, the declarant is taking the precaution of making his or her own decisions in advance should a loss of decision-making capacity prevent him or her from doing so later. States often have example forms that can be used. A successor attorney-in-fact should also be named in the document in case the original agent is, for one reason or another, unable to act on behalf of the declarant. (For an example, see *Texas Durable Power of Attorney for Health Care* at the end of this chapter.)

Health Care Proxy. A health care proxy is a written document that appoints a named agent or surrogate to make decisions relating to the declarant's health care. This particular instrument typically is not specific regarding decisions to be made and instead merely names someone to act on the declarant's behalf. Some states, however, require that the declarant's wishes about certain issues be communicated to the proxy either orally or in writing. For example, under state law the proxy may need to know the declarant's wishes concerning artificial feeding and hydration by tube feeding. As with the medical durable power of attorney, a successor agent should be designated in the proxy instrument. Since both a durable power of attorney for health care and a health care proxy name an agent to act for the creator of the instrument and serve essentially the same basic purpose, an individual would need only one of these documents—having both would be redundant. (For an example, see *New York Health Care Proxy* at the end of this chapter.)

Individual Instruction/Advance Health Care Directive/Living Will. Although medical powers of attorney are sometimes referred to as advance medical directives, in most circumstances an advance medical directive is a more accurate reference to what is generically called a "living will." This instrument states more specifically the declarant's wishes regarding limitations on medical treatment upon the occurrence of a coma, persistent vegetative state, or terminal condition where there is no medical expectation of recovery. In most cases an advance medical directive is a declarant's statement that he or she does not want to be kept alive by machines or other artificial support when there's no hope of recovery. In most cases it's created as a "pull the plug" directive, but it may be used as a directive for medical providers to prolong life in spite of low medical expectations for recovery. For instance, under the Uniform Health Care Decisions Act there is a Choice Not to Prolong Life as well as a Choice to Prolong Life.[4] Additional credibility that this document represents the declarant's rational, clear-thinking views on the matters at hand is achieved with a video in which the declarant expresses his or her health care wishes about prolonging life. (For an example, see *Florida Living Will* at the end of this chapter.)

---

4. Uniform Health Care Decisions Act ("UHCDA") 1993 Sec. 4(a) and (b).

The Uniform Health Care Decisions Act was approved by the Uniform Law Commissioners in August 1993 for the purpose of facilitating the use of advance health care and surrogate decision-making directives, including powers of attorney for health care.[5] The act has provisions on executing and revoking advance medical directives as well as an optional statutory form. A space is provided on the form where a declarant can express a desire for anatomical gifting. The hope is that the use of a statutory form supported by statutory terms will reinforce the acceptance of a donor's intentions by third parties.

Although individuals may be willing to execute medical treatment documents while alive, they may not care about having control over their bodies, other than funeral and burial matters, after death, or they may simply be uncomfortable thinking about their remains at death. A 1993 Gallop survey found that one-third of survey respondents were somewhat uncomfortable thinking about their deaths.[6] Because of the estate planner's role in the client's life, he or she is in a good position to bring up and elicit the client's feelings about organ donation. The planner must, of course, remain conscious of the client's personal religious and cultural sensitivities. If the client doesn't want to think about it, or doesn't care one way or another, at least the planner can impart that much to family members if they are approached about donating the deceased client's organs and tissues. Although the planner may be rebuffed by the client with respect to this topic, bringing the subject up is sometimes all it takes to nudge the client into discussing his or her feelings about organ donation with family members.

Are documents necessary for organ and tissue donations? Clearly, an individual can express a desire for anatomical contributions in a medical power of attorney, to the agent of a health care proxy, and even in a living will type of medical directive. Generally a will should not contain organ donation provisions. Time is of the essence with organ and tissue transplantation. Gifts could become unusable and wasted when wills are not readily located by family members. (Specifically, hearts, livers, kidneys, pancreases, and lungs are considered to be organs; bone, bone marrow, skin, veins, corneas, and eyes are categorized as tissues.)

A model organ donation act called the Uniform Anatomical Gift Act (UAGA) 1987 (supersedes the Uniform Anatomical Gift Act as amended in 1980) is the force behind all 50 states and Washington D.C. partially or completely enacting some type of organ and tissue donation statute.[7] The UAGA requirements are that (1) the donor must be at least 18 years old, (2)

---

5. 9 U.L.A. (Pt. I (1994 Supp.)).
6. "The American Public's Attitudes Toward Organ Donation and Transplantation." Survey prepared by the Gallop Organization, Inc., for the Partnership for Organ Donation (Feb. 1993).
7. Fred H. Cate. "Human Organ Transplantation: The Role of Law." *Journal of Corporation Law*, Fall 1994, 71, 24.

donation may be made for the purposes of medical research, transplantation, and therapy, and (3) donation may be made to a hospital, physician, procurement organization, educational institution, or another specified person.

In addition to instructions in general medical directive document(s), a contributor should sign an organ donor card and/or complete a simple Organ Donor Declaration form. (For an example, see *Organ Donor Declaration*.) Copies of the donor card or form should be given to relevant family members and the donor's doctor. (For an example, see the *PA Department of Health Voluntary Uniform Anatomical Donor Card*.) The donor card does not have to be witnessed, and, like other health care instruments, it can be modified and revoked at any time either orally or in writing. Since these documents are recognized in every state as legal documents, relocations and vacations do not affect the intent of the gifts. Most jurisdictions include information about organ, tissue, and body donations with applications for drivers' licenses and renewals. (For an example, see the *Pennsylvania Voluntary Uniform Anatomical Donor Card* at the end of this chapter.) Many states also provide for the notation of anatomical gifts on drivers' licenses. In fact, most states require drivers to check off whether they do or do not want to be an organ donor at the time they register for their driver's license.

In spite of properly executed organ donation documents, however, hospitals and medical providers universally require the written permission of the deceased's available next-of-kin. Unfortunately, more than 50 percent of eligible family members refuse to make anatomical donations on behalf of their recently deceased relatives. This reluctance resulted in the deaths of approximately 3,100 Americans from a list of approximately 42,000 desperately waiting for organs.[8] There are estimates that for certain organs, one-third of those on waiting lists will die waiting.

Members of the National Coalition on Donation, based in Richmond, Virginia, have come to the conclusion that encouraging families to talk about organ donation prior to the death of a loved one will increase donations. The coalition's impression is that once families discuss their wishes about anatomical gifts, surviving family members will know what the deceased wanted and won't be in a quandary when the time arrives. Enter the estate planner . . . .

Is it fair for family members in their time of grief to have to make an emotional and perhaps wrenching decision when there are no earlier words of guidance from the deceased?

Does it cost to make donations? No, there is no expense to family or the deceased's estate for the donation of organs and tissue. Costs resulting from

---

8. Peter MacPherson. "A Pitch for Organ Donations." *Hospitals and Health Networks*, vol. 70, no. 4, page 76, February 20, 1996 (according to a study published in the *Annals of Internal Medicine*, July 1995).

donations are covered by the nearest regional Organ Procurement Organization (OPO). OPOs are organizations that procure and coordinate organ donations within their established regions. OPOs also maintain priority lists of recipients. More specifically, an OPO arranges for the surgery necessary to retrieve donated organs, oversees tissue typing, keeps lists for matching those in need of transplants with available donations, and makes arrangements for donation transport.[9] There are about 70 OPOs in the U.S.

Will organ donation interfere with funeral arrangements? No. Organ donation involves ordinary surgical procedure. Open casket services are not affected by anatomical gifts nor are funeral services delayed.

Do the benefits of transplantation outweigh the costs? There is no doubt that transplantation is expensive. However, as organ donation becomes more common and medical techniques become more advanced, the long-run benefits are certain to outweigh the initial expense. For example, kidney transplants are becoming increasingly successful and are more cost-efficient than long-term kidney dialysis. That's the objective value. Subjectively, there is no monetary amount that can be placed on the benefit to the recipient and his or her family.

What about religious considerations? If a potential donor has religious concerns about making anatomical gifts, he or she should discuss them with the appropriate members of the clergy. Today all major religions in the U.S. accept and endorse anatomical gifting.

Can donations be limited? Yes. A person can provide for the donation of any or all needed body organs and tissues or for only a certain, specific organ. An entire body may be gifted for medical research. Donations are not necessarily affected by the age of the donor.

If someone makes the decision to provide for anatomical donation before death, he or she is making an additional gift to family members—relief from having to make the decision at a time when they are already under stress when approached by the OPO and/or hospital staff members. The previously mentioned Gallop survey determined that 87 percent of Americans had a positive attitude about organ donation.[10] Although 69 percent stated a desired to actually become a donor at death, only half of them shared that desire with family members.

By bringing the subject of organ and tissue donation to the foreground with clients, the estate planner may be assisting clients in following through

---

9. Gloria S. Neuwirth. "Guidelines for Clients Contemplating Organ Donation." *Estate Planning*, vol. 23, no. 8, October 1996.
10. "The American Public's Attitudes Toward Organ Donation and Transplantation." Survey prepared by the Gallop Organization, Inc., for the Partnership for Organ Donation (Feb. 1993).

with an intention that heretofore had not been formally addressed. The result may provide emotional relief for surviving family members who can act one way or another according to a deceased family member's wishes. The discrepancy between the need for and the availability of organs may be narrowed. The quality of recipients' lives may be enhanced, and people's lives may be saved. Medical knowledge may be advanced and medical costs overall reduced. Society can make a difference and can benefit from it.

Where Can I Find Out More?

- HS 323 Individual Life Insurance. The American College.
- Coalition on Donation, 1100 Boulders Parkway, Suite 500, Richmond, VA 23225
- Uniform Anatomical Gift Act of 1987, 8A U.L.A.
- Uniform Determination of Death Act, 12 U.L.A. 414 (Supp. 1994)
- National Organ Transplant Act, Pub. L. No. 98-507, 98 Stat. 2339
- Brigid McMenamin. "Why People Die Waiting for Transplants." *Forbes,* vol. 157, no. 5, pages 140–148.
- United Network for Organ Sharing (UNOS)
- "The American Public's Attitudes Toward Organ Donation and Transplantation." Survey prepared by Gallup Organization, Inc., for the Partnership for Organ Donation (Feb. 1993).
- Bethany Spielman, ed. *Organ and Tissue Donation: Ethical, Legal, and Policy Issues*. 1996.

TEXAS DURABLE POWER OF ATTORNEY FOR HEALTH CARE*

Information Concerning the Durable Power of Attorney for Health Care

This is an important legal document. Before signing this document, you should know these important facts:

Except to the extent you state otherwise, this document gives the person you name as your agent the authority to make any and all health care decisions for you in accordance with your wishes, including your religious and moral beliefs, when you are no longer capable of making them yourself. Because "health care" means any treatment, service, or procedure to maintain, diagnose, or treat your physical or mental condition, your agent has the power to make a broad range of health care decisions for you. Your agent may consent, refuse to consent, or withdraw consent to medical treatment and may make decisions about withdrawing or withholding life-sustaining treatment. Your agent may not consent to voluntary inpatient mental health services, convulsive treatment, psychosurgery, or abortion. A physician must comply with your agent's instructions or allow you to be transferred to another physician.

Your agent's authority begins when your doctor certifies that you lack the capacity to make health care decisions.

Your agent is obligated to follow your instructions when making decisions on your behalf. Unless you state otherwise, your agent has the same authority to make decisions about your health care as you would have had.

It is important that you discuss this document with your physician or other health care provider before you sign it to make sure that you understand the nature and range of decisions that may be made on your behalf. If you do not have a physician, you should talk with someone else who is knowledgeable about these issues and can answer your questions. You do not need a lawyer's assistance to complete this document, but if there is anything in this document that you do not understand, you should ask a lawyer to explain it to you.

The person you appoint as agent should be someone you know and trust. The person must be 18 years of age or older or a person under 18 years of age who has had the disabilities of minority removed. If you appoint your health or residential care provider (e.g., your physician or an employee of a home health agency, hospital, nursing home, or residential care home, other than a relative), that person has to choose between acting as your agent or as your health or residential care provider; the law does not permit a person to do both at the same time.

---

*The Texas Durable Power of Attorney for Health Care, the New York Health Care Proxy, and the Florida Living Will are all reprinted by permission of Choice In Dying, 200 Varick Street, New York, NY 10014. Anyone who wishes further information about materials and services related to end-of-life medical care can contact the organization at the address noted or at (212) 366-5540.

You should inform the person you appoint that you want the person to be your health care agent. You should discuss this document with your agent and your physician and give each a signed copy. You should indicate on the document itself the people and institutions who have signed copies. Your agent is not liable for health care decisions made in good faith on your behalf.

Even after you have signed this document, you have the right to make health care decisions for yourself as long as you are able to do so and treatment cannot be given to you or stopped over your objection. You have the right to revoke the authority granted to your agent by informing your agent of your health or residential care provider orally or in writing, or by your execution of a subsequent durable power of attorney for health care. Unless you state otherwise, your appointment of a spouse dissolves on divorce.

This document may not be changed or modified. If you want to make changes in the document, you must make an entirely new one.

You may wish to designate an alternate agent in the event that your agent is unwilling, unable, or ineligible to act as your agent. Any alternate agent you designate has the same authority to make health care decisions for you.

This power of attorney is not valid unless it is signed in the presence of two or more qualified witnesses. The following persons may not act as witnesses:

(1) the person you have designated as your agent;
(2) your health or residential care provider or an employee of your health or residential care provider;
(3) your spouse;
(4) your lawful heirs or beneficiaries named in your will or a deed; or
(5) creditors or persons who have a claim against you.

TEXAS DURABLE POWER OF ATTORNEY FOR HEALTH CARE

INSTRUCTIONS

PRINT YOUR NAME

PRINT THE NAME, ADDRESS AND HOME AND WORK TELEPHONE NUMBERS OF YOUR AGENT

STATE LIMITATIONS ON YOUR AGENT'S POWER (IF ANY)

DESIGNATION OF HEALTH CARE AGENT.

I, _____ appoint:
　　　　　　　　　　(name)

_____
　　　　　　　　(name of agent)

_____
　　　　　　　　　(address)

_____
(work telephone number)　　(home telephone number)

as my agent to make any and all health care decisions for me, except to the extent I state otherwise in this document. This durable power of attorney for health care takes effect if I become unable to make my own health care decisions and this fact is certified in writing by my physician.

LIMITATIONS ON THE DECISION MAKING AUTHORITY OF MY AGENT ARE AS FOLLOWS.

TEXAS DURABLE POWER OF ATTORNEY FOR HEALTH CARE—PAGE 4 OF 6

PRINT THE NAME, ADDRESS AND HOME AND WORK TELEPHONE NUMBERS OF YOUR FIRST AND SECOND ALTERNATE AGENTS

FIRST ALTERNATE

SECOND ALTERNATE

LOCATION OF ORIGINAL

DESIGNATION OF ALTERNATE AGENT.
(You are not required to designate an alternate agent but you may do so. An alternate agent may make the same health care decisions as the designated agent if the designated agent is unable or unwilling to act as your agent. If the agent designated is your spouse, the designation is automatically revoked by law if your marriage is dissolved.)

If the person designated as my agent is unable or unwilling to make health care decisions for me, I designate the following persons to serve as my agent to make health care decisions for me as authorized by this document, who serve in the following order:

A. First Alternate Agent

_____
(name of first alternate agent)

_____
(home address)

_____
(work telephone number)   *(home telephone number)*

B. Second Alternate Agent

_____
(name of second alternate agent)

_____
(home address)

_____
(work telephone number)   *(home telephone number)*

The original of this document is kept at: _____

_____

LOCATION OF COPIES	The following individuals or institutions have signed copies: Name: _____ Address: _____ Name: _____ Address: _____ **DURATION.** I understand that this power of attorney exists indefinitely from the date I execute this document unless I establish a shorter time or revoke the power of attorney. If I am unable to make health care decisions for myself when this power of attorney expires, the authority I have granted my agent continues to exist until the time I become able to make health care decisions for myself. (IF APPLICABLE) This power of attorney ends on the following date:
EXPIRATION DATE (IF ANY)	_____ PRIOR DESIGNATIONS REVOKED. I revoke any prior power of attorney for health care. ACKNOWLEDGMENT OF DISCLOSURE STATEMENT. I have been provided with a disclosure statement explaining the effect of this document. I have read and understood that information contained in the disclosure statement. (YOU MUST DATE AND SIGN THIS POWER OF ATTORNEY)
PRINT THE DATE **PRINT YOUR LOCATION** **SIGN THE DOCUMENT** **PRINT YOUR NAME**	I sign my name to this durable power of attorney for health care on ____ *(date)* day of _____ 19 _____, at _____. *(month)* *(city and state)* _____ *(signature)* _____ *(print name)*

| TEXAS DURABLE POWER OF ATTORNEY FOR HEALTH CARE—PAGE 6 OF 6 |

WITNESSING PROCEDURE

YOUR TWO WITNESSES MUST SIGN AND DATE YOUR DOCUMENT BELOW

THEY MUST ALSO PRINT THEIR NAMES AND ADDRESSES

WITNESS #1

WITNESS #2

STATEMENT OF WITNESSES.

I declare under penalty of perjury that the principal has identified himself or herself to me, that the principal signed or acknowledged this durable power of attorney in my presence, that I believe the principal to be of sound mind, that the principal has affirmed that the principal is aware of the nature of the document and is signing it voluntarily and free from duress, that the principal requested that I serve as witness to the principal's execution of this document, that I am not the person appointed as agent by this document, and that I am not a provider of health or residential care, an employee of a provider of health or residential care, the operator of a community care facility, or an employee of an operator of a health care facility.

I declare that I am not related to the principal by blood, marriage, or adoption and that to the best of my knowledge I am not entitled to any part of the estate of the principal on the death of the principal under a will or by operation of law.

Witness Signature: _____

Print Name: _____ Date:_____

Address: _____

Witness Signature: _____

Print Name: _____ Date:_____

Address: _____

NEW YORK HEALTH CARE PROXY

INSTRUCTIONS	
PRINT YOUR NAME	(1) I, _____, hereby appoint:
PRINT NAME, HOME ADDRESS AND TELEPHONE NUMBER OF YOUR AGENT	_____ *(name, home address and telephone number of agent)* _____

as my health care agent to make any and all health care decisions for me, except to the extent that I state otherwise.

This Health Care Proxy shall take effect in the event I become unable to make my own health care decisions.

ADD PERSONAL INSTRUCTIONS (IF ANY)

(2) Optional instructions: I direct my agent to make health care decisions in accord with my wishes and limitations as stated below, or as he or she otherwise knows.

(Unless your agent knows your wishes about artificial nutrition and hydration [feeding tubes], your agent will not be allowed to make decisions about artificial nutrition and hydration.)

2.55

NEW YORK HEALTH CARE PROXY—PAGE 2 OF 2

PRINT NAME, HOME ADDRESS AND TELEPHONE NUMBER OF YOUR ALTERNATE AGENT

(3) Name of substitute or fill-in agent if the person I appoint above is unable, unwilling or unavailable to act as my health care agent.

_____
(name, home address and telephone number of alternate agent)
_____

ENTER A DURATION OR A CONDITION (IF ANY)

(4) Unless I revoke it, this proxy shall remain in effect indefinitely, or until the date or condition I have stated below. This proxy shall expire (specific date or conditions, if desired): _____

_____

SIGN AND DATE THE DOCUMENT AND PRINT YOUR ADDRESS

(5) Signature _____ Date _____

Address _____

WITNESSING PROCEDURE

Statement by Witnesses (must be 18 or older)

I declare that the person who signed this document appeared to execute the proxy willingly and free from duress. He or she signed (or asked another to sign for him or her) this document in my presence. I am not the person appointed as proxy by this document.

YOUR WITNESSES MUST SIGN AND PRINT THEIR ADDRESSES

Witness 1 _____

Address _____

Witness 2 _____

Address _____

2.56

Florida Living Will

INSTRUCTIONS

PRINT THE DATE

PRINT YOUR NAME

Declaration made this _____ day of _____, 19 ____.

I,_____, willfully and voluntarily make known my desire that my dying not be artificially prolonged under the circumstances set forth below, and I do hereby declare:

If at any time I have a terminal condition and if my attending or treating physician and another consulting physician have determined that there is no medical probability of my recovery from such condition, I direct that life-prolonging procedures be withheld or withdrawn when the application of such procedures would serve only to prolong artificially the process of dying, and that I be permitted to die naturally with only the administration of medication or the performance of any medical procedure deemed necessary to provide me with comfort care or to alleviate pain.

It is my intention that this declaration be honored by my family and physician as the final expression of my legal right to refuse medical or surgical treatment and to accept the consequences for such refusal.

In the event that I have been determined to be unable to provide express and informed consent regarding the withholding, withdrawal, or continuation of life-prolonging procedures, I wish to designate, as my surrogate to carry out the provisions of this declaration:

PRINT THE NAME, HOME ADDRESS AND TELEPHONE NUMBER OF YOUR SURROGATE

Name: _____

Address: _____

_____Zip Code: _____

Phone: _____

FLORIDA LIVING WILL—PAGE 2 OF 2

I wish to designate the following person as my alternate surrogate, to carry out the provisions of this declaration should my surrogate be unwilling or unable to act on my behalf:

PRINT NAME, HOME ADDRESS AND TELEPHONE NUMBER OF YOUR ALTERNATE SURROGATE

Name: _____

Address: _____

_____ Zip Code: _____

Phone: _____

ADD PERSONAL INSTRUCTIONS (IF ANY)

Additional instructions (optional):

I understand the full import of this declaration, and I am emotionally and mentally competent to make this declaration.

SIGN THE DOCUMENT

Signed: _____

WITNESSING PROCEDURE

TWO WITNESSES MUST SIGN AND PRINT THEIR ADDRESSES

Witness 1:
   Signed: _____

   Address: _____

Witness 2:
   Signed: _____

   Address: _____

EXHIBIT 1[*]
Organ Donor Declaration

This is to inform you that I want to be an organ and tissue donor if the occasion ever arises. Please see that my wishes are carried out by informing the attending medical personnel that I am a donor. My desires are indicated below:

In the hopes that I may help others, I hereby make this gift for the purpose of transplant, medical study, or education, to take effect upon my death. I give:

/ / Any needed organs/tissues
/ / Only the following organs/tissues

_____
Specify the organ(s)/tissue(s)

_____

_____
Limitation or special wishes, if any

_____

This is a legal document under the Uniform Anatomical Gift Act or similar laws, signed by the donor and the following two witnesses in the presence of each other.

_____
Donor's signature

_____
Donor's date of birth   City and state

_____
Witness   Witness

_____
Next of kin   Telephone

---

[*] Reprinted with permission of Warren, Gorham & Lamont of the RIA Group.

VOLUNTARY UNIFORM ANATOMICAL DONOR CARD

Signed by the donor and two witnesses (preferably next of kin)

_____
Signature of ☐ Donor ☐ Parent ☐ Guardian   Date of Birth of Donor

_____
Street, City, State   Date Signed

Signature of witnesses (next of kin preferable, but not necessary)

1. _____
   Witness (Age 18 or older)   Relationship   Date

2. _____
   Witness (Age 18 or older)   Relationship   Date

THIS IS A LEGAL DOCUMENT UNDER THE PENNSYLVANIA UNIFORM GIFT ACT.

- - - - - - - - - - - - - - FOLD - - - - - - - - - - - - - -

FOR MORE INFORMATION

If you have further questions regarding organ donation, consult your physician, your local kidney foundation, eye bank, county medical society or the Pennsylvania Department of Health, P.O. Box 90, Harrisburg, Pa. 17108, or call toll-free 1-800-692-7254. For total body donations, call the Humanity Gifts Registry 215-922-4440.

If you have further questions regarding emergency health information contact your physician.

PENNSYLVANIA DEPARTMENT OF HEALTH

TOM RIDGE, GOVERNOR

H507.001.1P (Rev. 8/95)

(Front)

Pennsylvania Department of Health
Voluntary Uniform Anatomical
DONOR CARD

_____
Print or type name of donor

I hereby voluntarily make this anatomical gift, if medically acceptable, to take effect upon my death. The words and marks below indicate my desire.

I give (A) ☐ Any needed organs or tissues

(B) ☐ Only the organs(s) or tissue(s) specified below:

☐ Eyes   ☐ Kidneys   ☐ Skin   ☐ Liver

☐ Heart   ☐ Pancreas   ☐ Ear bones   ☐ Lungs

(C) ☐ My body for anatomical study, if needed.

Limitations or
Special Wishes _____

For the purpose of Transplantation, therapy, medical research or education.

- -

EMERGENCY HEALTH INFORMATION

Known Medical Problems

_____   Allergies (Type) _____   Heart Related _____
_____   Diabetes _____   Epilepsy _____
_____   Other _____

Medication Taken Regularly

_____
_____
_____

Physician _____   Dr.'s Phone No. _____

(Back)

2.60

BUSINESS PLANNING

New Rules Make S Corporations More Flexible Planning Tools
Thomas P. Langdon

While S corporations enjoy many of the attributes of the corporate form of business—such as limited liability, centralized management, and free transferability of ownership—S corporations are pass-through entities, and are therefore taxed somewhat like partnerships. Because S corporations pass through all of their income to their shareholders, the double-tax problem associated with C corporations is avoided.

S corporations made their debut in the 1950s, when Congress determined that it was appropriate to give limited liability protection to small companies while at the same time allowing small and start-up businesses to enjoy the favorable tax treatment typically associated with partnerships. This compromise was accomplished by allowing businesses that were set up as corporations under state law to elect S corporation status if certain requirements were met. In 1982, the S corporation rules were substantially overhauled, and have remained relatively the same ever since.

The early 1990s brought in a new form of business entity: the *limited liability company (LLC)*. This new business form took advantage of regulations adopted by the IRS in the 1950s which had a built-in bias favoring partnership tax treatment. While an LLC is treated as a partnership for federal tax purposes, for state law purposes it is treated as a corporation that extends limited liability to its members. The LLC offers an advantage that the S corporation does not—pure partnership tax treatment. Even though an S corporation is a pass-through entity, certain of the S corporation rules are less favorable than partnership treatment.

Over the past 3 to 4 years, LLCs have grown in popularity, and in many cases have replaced S corporations as the preferred business and estate planning tool. During this period, Congress has also become sensitive to the plight of the small business owner in transferring control of his or her business. As a result, Congress recognized that the restrictions imposed by the Internal Revenue Code to achieve S corporation status were quickly making S corporations unpopular. While several proposals to ease these restrictions were advanced over the last few years, it was not until August 1996 that Congress finally made some changes. Most of the changes affecting S corporations are effective for tax years beginning after December 31, 1996.

This chapter explores the most significant changes in S corporation requirements and the impact of those changes on the business owner.

Increase in the Number of Permissible S Corporation Shareholders
Thomas P. Langdon

What Was the Situation Before?

In order to qualify for S corporation status, all shareholders of the S corporation must file a valid and timely Form 2553, and various statutory requirements must be met. If the statutory requirements are not met, S corporation status is terminated, and the corporation becomes a C corporation for federal tax purposes.

The first requirement for electing S corporation status sets a limit on the number of permissible shareholders in the corporation. Prior law held that the maximum number of shareholders allowed in an S corporation was 35. For purposes of meeting this test, however, a husband and wife are counted as one shareholder. Therefore, if all shareholders of the S corporation are married, there could be a total of 70 shareholders under prior law. While it appears that being married allows the number of permissible shareholders to double, if an S corporation shareholder marries a nonresident alien and, under the terms of local law, that nonresident alien spouse owns an interest in the S corporation (due to the application of community property laws, for example), the S corporation status is terminated because a nonresident alien is not an eligible shareholder in an S corporation (this topic will be discussed further in a later section).

An additional provision which became effective in 1995 eased the number-of-shareholders requirement as it relates to *qualified Subchapter S trusts (QSSTs)*. If an individual owns an interest in a QSST, that individual is counted as a shareholder for purposes of meeting the 35 shareholder test. If an individual owning an interest in a QSST also owns S corporation stock directly, that person will be treated as one shareholder, even though the form in which the shareholder possesses the stock (outright and as a trust beneficiary) is different.

What Is the Nature of the Change?

Pursuant to the provisions of the Small Business Job Protection Act, the number of permissible shareholders in an S corporation has been increased from 35 to 75. Applying the same rule as above, if all the shareholders are married, there can be up to 150 permissible shareholders in an S corporation. As under prior law, if an individual holds S corporation stock and is also a beneficiary under a QSST, that individual will be counted as one shareholder for purposes of the 75 shareholder test.

When Does This Change Affect Clients?

The 75 shareholder limit is effective for tax years beginning after December 31, 1996.

What Should Be Done?

No affirmative actions need be taken by the taxpayer. Both existing S corporations and newly organized companies will be eligible for the 75 shareholder limit effective for tax years beginning after December 31, 1996.

Where Can I Find Out More?

- HS 331 Planning for Business Owners and Professionals. The American College.
- GS 836 Business Succession Planning I. The American College.
- IRC Sec. 1361.
- Thomas P. Langdon. "IRS Hands Greater Flexibility to S Corporations." *Best's Review,* Life/Health Edition (February 1997), p. 74.
- Laura Saunders. "The Family Business Preservation Act." *Forbes* (November 18, 1996), pp. 268–270.

Permissible Shareholders
Thomas P. Langdon

What Was the Situation Before?

While the number of permissible shareholders is limited to 75, a second requirement dictated by Subchapter S of the Internal Revenue Code defines who can be a shareholder of an S corporation. Under prior law, only certain types of individuals and trusts are permitted shareholders of an S corporation. An S corporation cannot have shareholders (other than estates or qualified trusts) who are not individuals.[1] Partnerships and C corporations are not permissible shareholders in an S corporation. However, one exception to this general rule for partnerships is found in the final regulations under Code Sec. 1361, which became effective July 21, 1995.[2] This exception states that when a partnership holds S corporation stock as a nominee for a person, that person (not the partnership) will be deemed to be the shareholder for purposes of meeting the qualified shareholder test. If the partnership is the beneficial owner of the stock, the partnership will be treated as the shareholder, which will terminate S corporation status.

---

1. IRC Sec. 1361(b)(1)(B).
2. Treas. Reg. Sec. 1.1361-1(e)(2).

While individuals are eligible to hold S corporation stock, a nonresident alien is not a permissible shareholder. Furthermore, final regulations which became effective in 1995 state that a U.S. citizen married to a nonresident alien who, under local law (for example, the law of a community property state), has an interest in the U.S. citizen's stock cannot be an S corporation shareholder.[3]

What Is the Nature of the Change?

The 1996 Small Business Job Protection Act broadened the definition of permissible shareholder by adding persons and organizations previously prohibited from holding S corporation stock. One new rule regarding qualifying shareholders of S corporations will provide several opportunities for planning. Organizations that are exempt from tax under Sec. 401(a) of the Code (qualified retirement plans) or Sec. 501(c)(3) (charitable organizations) may qualify as S corporation shareholders. Each qualifying exempt organization that holds S corporation stock will be counted as one shareholder for purposes of the 75 shareholder limit.

When Does This Change Affect Clients?

These provisions are effective for tax years beginning after December 31, 1997, presumably to give the IRS the opportunity to offer guidance on this issue.

What Should Be Done?

In order to avoid termination of the S corporation election in such a situation, proper planning is required. Premarital agreements and trust arrangements could be employed to ensure that a nonresident alien spouse has no interest in the S corporation stock. Because sale of S corporation stock to an ineligible shareholder will terminate the election, transfer restrictions should be employed, and a legend should be placed on the stock stating that transfer is restricted to "eligible shareholders."

For tax years beginning after December 31, 1997, charitable organizations qualifying under Sec. 501(c)(3) of the Internal Revenue Code are eligible holders of S corporation stock. This provision has sparked heightened interest from financial planners who are interested in making charitable giving techniques available to owners of S corporations. Planners should, however, proceed with caution in this area.

The 1996 Small Business Job Protection Act made it clear that charitable organizations are eligible to hold contingent remainder interests in an *electing small business trust* (or *ESBT*, discussed below). One question that arises is whether or not a *charitable remainder trust (CRT)* will be a permissible shareholder of S corporation stock. Arguably, since part of the trust (the

---

3. Treas. Reg. Sec. 1.1361-1(e)(2), Treas. Reg. Sec. 1.1361-1(e)(g).

income portion retained) is owned by the grantor and the remainder is owned by a charitable organization (both of which are eligible shareholders of S corporation stock for tax years beginning after December 31, 1997), a CRT should be an eligible shareholder. IRS rules, however, provide that a CRT's tax exemption is revoked if the trust has any unrelated business taxable income. By definition, allocations of income and deductions from an S corporation to a charity, as well as the gain on the sale of the S corporation stock by a charity, are *unrelated business taxable income (UBTI)*. The presence of UBTI in a charitable trust "taints" all of the income of the trust, subjecting the income to taxation. A CRT, by definition, is not a grantor trust, and therefore cannot qualify under the grantor trust permissible shareholder provision. (See chapter 14, "Charitable Giving.")

The IRS has announced that a bill providing technical corrections to the Small Business Job Protection Act will be drafted in 1997. One of the items included in the bill will clarify that a charitable remainder trust does not qualify as an ESBT, regardless of its tax status. The IRS feels the correction is needed to straighten out the relationship of the new law, which provides that the ESBT cannot be tax exempt, and IRS rules regarding CRTs.[4] Based on this announcement, it appears the IRS is of the opinion that a CRT will not be a permissible holder of S corporation stock.

While technically correct under current IRS rules, this conclusion seems to thwart the intent of Congress in enacting the Small Business Job Protection Act. Congress' intent was clear—to ease the requirements necessary to make the S corporation election, and to provide more flexibility to S corporation owners in disposing of or transferring control of their businesses. Owners of C corporations may donate appreciated stock to a CRT, take a charitable deduction for the contribution based on the fair market value of the stock, receive an income stream, and make a gift to charity. Due to UBTI problems, however, existing IRS rules stipulate that owners of S corporations cannot make a gift of appreciated stock to a CRT even though a charitable organization is an eligible shareholder in an S corporation. However, if an S corporation shareholder wanted to make an outright gift of S corporation stock to a charity, the gift is permissible. UBTI problems aside (it is settled that even the charity will be taxed on UBTI), if all persons or organizations having an interest in a CRT are eligible shareholders of S corporation stock, it would seem that a CRT should be an eligible shareholder. If this is not the case, owners of S corporation stock are at a serious disadvantage when compared to owners of C corporation stock. During 1997, Congress and the IRS will have the opportunity to clarify this issue, since charitable organizations will not be eligible shareholders of S corporation stock until tax years beginning after December 31, 1997. This is one area where Congress can provide owners of S corporations with a benefit that is not available to owners of partnerships or LLCs.

---

4. See *Daily Tax Report,* Bureau of National Affairs, no. 11 (January 16, 1997), p. G-2.

With respect to S corporation ownership, see discussion in Appendix, Act Section 1316(a)(2).

Where Can I Find Out More?

- HS 331 Planning for Business Owners and Professionals. The American College.
- GS 838 Business Succession Planning II. The American College.
- IRC Sec. 1361.
- Thomas P. Langdon. "IRS Hands Greater Flexibility to S Corporations." *Best's Review,* Life/Health Edition (February 1997), p. 74.
- Tom Ochsenschlager. "S Corps Finally Get in Shape to Compete." *Family Business* (August 1996), p. 52.
- Laura Saunders. "The Family Business Preservation Act." *Forbes,* (November 18, 1996), pp. 268–270.

Affiliated Groups
Thomas P. Langdon

What Was the Situation Before?

Under prior law, in order to elect S corporation status a company had to be a domestic corporation, and could not be an insurance company, a foreign corporation, a *possessions corporation* (a company that does business in a possession of the United States and has a Sec. 936 election in effect), or a *domestic international sales corporation (DISC)*. Also included in this list for tax years beginning prior to December 31, 1996, were affiliated groups and all financial institutions. The affiliated group restriction imposed planning stipulations on the owners of S corporations because, unlike owners of C corporations, S corporation owners could not organize subsidiaries to further limit their liability for specific business practices.

What Is the Nature of the Change?

The 1996 Small Business Job Protection Act allows domestic building and loan associations, mutual savings banks, and cooperative banks without capital stock organized and operated for mutual purposes and without profit to qualify for S corporation status, provided they do not use the reserve method of accounting for bad debts.[5] In addition, the act allows an S corporation to hold 80 percent or more of the stock of a C corporation or a *qualified Subchapter S subsidiary (QSSS)*.[6] The creation of a QSSS mitigates the prior

---

5. Small Business Job Protection Act, Sec. 1215, amending IRC Sec. 1361(b)(2)(A).
6. Small Business Job Protection Act, Sec. 1308(a).

prohibition on affiliated groups and opens up a new planning opportunity for S corporation owners.

When Does This Change Affect Clients?

Qualified Subchapter S subsidiaries are available to S corporation owners for taxable years beginning after December 31, 1996.

What Should Be Done?

While these changes represent a substantial loosening of the S corporation requirements and may provide some opportunity for business planning, they are of little consequence to the small or family business owner who is concerned with optimal daily efficiency, and ultimately with transferring control of the business to future generations of family members.

Where Can I Find Out More?

- GS 836 Business Succession Planning. The American College.
- Thomas P. Langdon. "IRS Hands Greater Flexibility to S Corporations." *Best's Review,* Life/Health Edition (February 1997), p. 74.
- Tom Ochsenschlager. "S Corps Finally Get in Shape to Compete." *Family Business* (August 1996), p. 52.
- Laura Saunders. "The Family Business Preservation Act." *Forbes* (November 18, 1996), pp. 268–270.
- Stephanie Rapkin. "The Basics of the S Corporation for the Estate Planner." *Trusts & Estates* (September 1996), pp. 38–44.

1995 Final Regulations and Qualified Subchapter S Trusts (QSSTs)
Thomas P. Langdon

What Was the Situation Before?

Before the enactment of the final regulations in 1995, many questions regarding the use of trusts as S corporation shareholders prevented practitioners from utilizing such vehicles. Recall that only individuals and qualifying trusts were eligible shareholders in an S corporation prior to 1997.

What Is the Nature of the Change?

In 1995, the IRS made the use of trusts to hold S corporation stock more flexible by clarifying the requirements for qualified Subchapter S trusts (QSSTs). Only individuals and qualifying trusts and estates are permissible shareholders of S corporation stock. Trusts that qualify to hold S corporation stock include grantor trusts (Subpart E trusts) for a 2-year period,[7] voting

---

7. IRC Sec. 1361(c)(2)(A)(ii).

trusts (if the trust is created by a written instrument containing specific provisions set forth in the regulations), and testamentary trusts to the earlier of the disposition of the stock or 60 days[8] after the stock is transferred to the trust. Grantor trusts permit the settlor of the trust to retain sufficient control or enjoyment of the property so that he or she is still considered to be the "owner" of the property for tax purposes. Grantor trusts are governed by Sec. 671 of the Internal Revenue Code. If a grantor trust is used to hold S corporation stock, at the expiration of the 2-year period provided for by Code Sec. 1361(c)(2)(A)(ii), the trust ceases to be an eligible S corporation shareholder unless the income beneficiary makes a valid QSST election under Code Sec. 1361(d)(2). Failure to make the proper election can result in termination of the S corporation election.[9]

QSSTs are defined in Code Sec. 1361(d)(3). In order to qualify as a QSST, the trust must have only one income beneficiary during the life of the current income beneficiary.[10] A trust with a single surviving income beneficiary meets the definition of a QSST, assuming that there is only one income beneficiary at the time the trust receives the S corporation stock.[11] The trust must stipulate that any corpus of the trust that is distributed during the life of the current income beneficiary must be distributed only to that beneficiary.[12] No sprinkle powers over a class of beneficiaries are permitted. The income interest of the current beneficiary must terminate on the earlier of the beneficiary's death or the termination of the trust,[13] and upon termination of the trust during the current beneficiary's lifetime, all assets must be distributed to that beneficiary.[14] Furthermore, all income of the trust must be distributed (or is required to be distributed) currently to one individual who is a citizen of the United States.[15] If a court order awards an interest in the trust to a person other than the income beneficiary, QSST status is lost, resulting in termination of the S corporation election. Flexibility as to non-Subchapter S income can be achieved by structuring the trust so that S corporation stock is held in a separate trust (sub trust) that meets the QSST requirements.[16] These requirements apply from the date the QSST election is made through the term of the trust. The requirements need not be met during any period prior to the acquisition of S corporation stock by the trust, but once the requirements are in

---

8. For tax years beginning after December 31, 1996, the 60-day period for testamentary trusts is extended to 2 years. This change puts testamentary and subpart E trusts on equal footing with respect to the period during which they can hold S corporation stock.
9. PLR 9533006.
10. IRC Sec. 1361(d)(3)(A)(i).
11. PLR 9543024.
12. IRC Sec. 1361(d)(3)(A)(ii).
13. IRC Sec. 1361(d)(3)(A)(iii).
14. IRC Sec. 1361(d)(3)(A)(iv).
15. IRC Sec. 1361(d)(3)(B).
16. Rev. Rul. 92-20, 1992-1 C.B. 685.

place and the trust qualifies as a QSST, the requirements cannot be ignored when the trust no longer holds S corporation stock.[17]

When a QSST is established, the beneficiary of the trust is treated as the owner of the trust's S corporation stock. Whether or not a distribution of income is made from the trust, the beneficiary will be taxed as if he or she owned the shares in the S corporation outright. The S corporation will pass through all items of income and loss to the beneficiary through the trust regardless of whether the beneficiary ever receives a distribution from the corporation through the trust.[18] A QSST must recognize any gain on the sale of S corporation stock by the trust. This overturns the position taken by the IRS in Rev. Rul. 92-84, which required a QSST's current income beneficiary to recognize the gain on the sale of stock by the trust.[19]

When Does This Change Affect Clients?

The final regulations became effective in 1995.

What Should Be Done?

The final regulations to Code Sec. 1361 include provisions that make the QSST a more flexible planning mechanism. For example, if a husband and wife are both beneficiaries of a trust, are both U.S. citizens, and file a joint income tax return, they will be treated as a single beneficiary for purposes of meeting the QSST requirements.[20] If a trust is established to satisfy the grantor's legal obligation to support the income beneficiary, however, the trust will not qualify as, or will cease to be, a QSST as of the date of the disqualifying distribution.[21] Therefore, care should be exercised in setting up a QSST to ensure that the trust will not be disqualified because it meets a support obligation. In such a case, termination of QSST status occurs because the grantor would be treated as the owner of the income interest of the trust or, alternatively, would be treated as the beneficiary of the trust under Code Sec. 662 and Treas. Reg. Sec. 1.662(a)-4. In fact, to elect QSST status, the election statement must include sufficient information to show that "no distribution of income or corpus by the trust will be in satisfaction of the grantor's legal obligation to support or maintain the income beneficiary."[22]

The final regulations under Sec. 1361 also make it clear that a *qualified terminable interest property trust (QTIP trust)* that qualifies under Code Sec. 2056(b)(7) can qualify as a QSST and be a permitted S corporation shareholder. This may be an important provision for the owners of S corporation

---

17. Treas. Reg. Sec. 1.1361-1(h)(1)(i).
18. IRC Sec. 1361(d)(1)(B).
19. Treas. Reg. Sec. 1.1361-1(j)(8).
20. Treas. Reg. Sec. 1.1361-1(j)(2)(i).
21. IRC Sec. 667(b) and Treas. Reg. Sec. 1.677(b)-1.
22. Treas. Reg. Sec. 1.1361-1(j)(6)(ii)(E)(3).

stock. A trust that qualifies as a QTIP trust for gift tax purposes under Code Sec. 2523(f) cannot qualify as a QSST because the grantor would be treated as the owner of the income portion of the trust pursuant to the provisions of Code Sec. 677.

Example: William and Ellen are the sole owners of XYZ Closely Held Corporation. XYZ is currently organized as an S corporation and has made all appropriate filings and elections. William owns 80 percent of the stock, and Ellen owns 20 percent. William's 80 percent share is valued at $2 million at his death.

Pursuant to the terms of William's will, his interest in the S corporation is to be divided into two separate trusts; both trusts have Ellen as the sole income beneficiary for life. One trust, the credit shelter trust, is to be funded with an amount that can pass free of estate tax under William's unified credit. The terms of the credit shelter trust meet the requirements of IRC Sec. 1361(d)(3) as a QSST. The balance of the property passes to a marital trust, whose terms satisfy the requirements of Sec. 1361(d)(3) as a QSST and Sec. 2056(b)(7) as a QTIP.

In order to qualify the trusts as QSSTs, Ellen must file an election within the 16-day and 2-month period beginning on the date the stock is transferred to the trust. The election is made by signing and filing with the service center with which the S corporation files its income tax return an applicable form or statement that

- contains the name, address, and taxpayer identification number of the current income beneficiary, the trust, and the corporation
- identifies the election as an election made under Sec. 1361(d)(2)
- specifies the date on which the election is to become effective
- specifies the date on which the stock of the corporation was transferred to the trust
- provides all information and representations necessary to show that the trust meets the definition of a QSST

Once Ellen files the appropriate election, both the credit shelter and marital deduction trusts qualify as QSSTs.[23]

As long as a client is willing to comply with the restrictive provisions found in the regulations, QSSTs can be helpful in business and estate planning.

---

23. Treas. Reg. Secs. 1.1361-1(j)(4), 1.1361-1(j)(6)(ii), and 1.1361-1(k)(1).

Where Can I Find Out More?

- GS 836 Business Succession Planning I. The American College.
- IRC Sec. 1361(d).
- Thomas P. Langdon. "IRS Hands Greater Flexibility to S Corporations." *Best's Review,* Life/Health Edition (February 1997), p. 74.
- Tom Ochsenschlager. "S Corps Finally Get in Shape to Compete." *Family Business* (August 1996), p. 52.
- Laura Saunders. "The Family Business Preservation Act." *Forbes* (November 18, 1996), pp. 268–270.
- Stephanie Rapkin. "The Basics of the S Corporation for the Estate Planner." *Trusts & Estates* (September 1996), pp. 38–44.

Electing Small Business Trusts (ESBTs)
Thomas P. Langdon

What Was the Situation Before?

Prior to the enactment of the 1996 Small Business Job Protection Act, the only types of trusts eligible to hold S corporation stock were grantor trusts (for a period of 2 years), testamentary trusts (for a period of 60 days), and QSSTs.

What Is the Nature of the Change?

The 1996 Small Business Job Protection Act creates a more flexible option for trust ownership of S corporation stock, the *electing small business trust (ESBT)*. Unlike the QSST, the ESBT has virtually no restrictions on dispositive terms, and allows the trust to have multiple beneficiaries. All beneficiaries must be individuals or eligible estates, or charitable organizations with contingent remainder interests. Because an ESBT may have more than one current income beneficiary, a unified credit shelter trust that allows the trustee to sprinkle income among a class of beneficiaries or to distribute principal among several beneficiaries could qualify as an ESBT. No interest in the trust can be acquired by purchase, and each potential current beneficiary is counted as a shareholder. This additional flexibility, as compared to the QSST, comes at a cost, however. All S corporation income and the proceeds from sales of S corporation stock are taxed at the highest marginal rate imposed on estates and trusts—currently 39.6 percent, regardless of whether the income is accumulated or distributed. No deductions are allowed from this income except state and local taxes, and administration expenses.

When Does This Change Affect Clients?

ESBTs are available for use for tax years beginning after December 31, 1996.

What Should Be Done?

Due to the compressed rate schedule for trusts, the ESBT will not be useful unless all of the beneficiaries of the proposed trust are already in the highest marginal tax brackets. Under current law, a trust is taxed at its highest marginal rate once it reaches $7,500 in income.

If the beneficiaries of the proposed ESBT are already in the highest marginal tax bracket, the taxation of the trust does not impose an additional burden. Under these circumstances, an ESBT can be used for business planning purposes for a minimal incremental cost (administration fees) to the beneficiaries. Furthermore, if investment income earned in an S corporation owned by an ESBT avoids or defers local taxes until actual distribution, the ESBT can be used as a tax planning tool beyond standard estate planning needs.[24]

Where Can I Find Out More?

- GS 836 Business Succession Planning I. The American College.
- IRC Secs. 1361(c)(2)(A)(v), 1361(c)(2)(B)(v), 1361(e), and 641(d).
- Thomas P. Langdon. "IRS Hands Greater Flexibility to S Corporations." *Best's Review,* Life/Health Edition (February 1997), p. 74.
- Gerald S. Susman. "New, More Flexible S Corporation Trust Comes Out of Small Business [sic] Act." *The Legal Intelligencer* (September 10, 1996), p. 10.
- "New S Trust Offers Flexibility But at a Price." *Federal Taxes Weekly Alert* (August 22, 1996), p. 408.

Changes to Safe Harbor Debt Rules
Thomas P. Langdon

What Was the Situation Before?

One of the difficult problems facing an S corporation prior to the Subchapter S Revision Act of 1982 was whether certain shareholder loans to the corporation would be regarded as bona fide debt or as equity interest. If the debt was classified as an equity interest, the IRS could then reclassify the debt as a disqualifying second class of stock.

Straight debt will not be treated as a second class of stock. Straight debt is defined as any written unconditional promise to pay on demand or on a specified date a certain sum of money if

---

24. Gerald S. Susman, "New, More Flexible S Corporation Trust Comes Out of Small Business [sic] Act," *The Legal Intelligencer*, (September 10, 1996), p. 10.

- the interest rate and the dates are not contingent on corporate profits, the borrower's discretion, or similar factors
- the debt is not convertible into stock.
- the creditor is an individual, estate, or trust eligible to hold stock in an S corporation

Note that under the old rules, the only safe harbor debt available was debt held by an eligible shareholder of S corporation stock.

What Is the Nature of the Change?

Congress recognized that it is often beneficial for business owners to obtain commercial financing for business operations. For S corporations, however, the only debt meeting the safe harbor requirements of straight debt is that owned by an individual, estate, or trust eligible to hold S corporation stock. The 1996 Small Business Job Protection Act expands the definition of straight debt to include debt held by individuals and institutions that are regularly engaged in the business of extending credit.

When Does This Change Affect Clients?

The expanded definition of straight debt is effective for tax years beginning after December 31, 1996.

What Should Be Done?

No affirmative actions need be taken by the taxpayer. Both existing S corporations and newly organized companies will be eligible to treat debt issued to individuals and institutions that are regularly engaged in the business of extending credit as straight debt for tax years beginning after December 31, 1996.

Where Can I Find Out More?

- GS 836 Business Succession Planning I. The American College.
- 1996 Small Business Job Protection Act, Sec. 1304 amending IRC Sec. 1361(c)(5)(B)(iii).

S Corporation Stock and Sec. 1014 Step Up in Basis
Thomas P. Langdon

What Was the Situation Before?

Under prior law, an individual who inherited S corporation stock from a deceased shareholder received the stock with a basis equal to its fair market value on the date of the decedent's death or, if elected, on the alternative valuation date. No adjustment was made for the proportionate share of income of the corporation that would have been *income in respect of a decedent (IRD)* if the income had been acquired directly from the decedent.

What Is the Nature of the Change?

A person who inherits S corporation stock must treat as IRD the pro rata share of income of the corporation that would have been IRD if the income had been acquired directly from the decedent. The purpose of this provision is to equate the treatment of IRD for S corporation owners with the treatment of IRD for members of partnerships.

When Does This Change Affect Clients?

This change is effective with respect to decedents dying after August 20, 1996.

What Should Be Done?

No affirmative action is required on the planner's part. Administrators and executors of the estates of decedents holding S corporation stock must, however, comply with this new provision in administering the estate and filing the appropriate tax forms.

Where Can I Find Out More?

- GS 836 Business Succession Planning I. The American College.
- 1996 Small Business Job Protection Act, Sec. 1313(a), adding IRC Sec. 1367(b)(4)(A) and (B).

Limited Liability Companies (LLCs) and the New Entity Classification Scheme
Thomas P. Langdon

Introduction

Limited Liability Companies Defined. Limited liability companies (LLCs) are hybrid entities. They combine the best attributes of both partnerships and corporations. Legally, an LLC is an unincorporated business entity that provides limited liability for all its members. Prior to the advent of LLCs, the only way to obtain limited liability for all members of the business entity was to incorporate and be classified as either a *C corporation* (a regular corporation subject to double taxation) or an *S corporation* (a corporation under state law that attains pass-through taxation at the federal level). While limited partnerships were able to extend limited liability to some of their members, called *limited partners*, the general partners of a limited partnership had unlimited liability for business debts. The principal difference between an LLC and an S corporation, aside from the fact that the S corporation is incorporated and the LLC is not, is that an LLC is taxed according to the provisions of Subchapter K of the Internal Revenue Code (the partnership tax provisions), while the S corporation is taxed in accordance with Subchapter S. S corporations are pass-through entities, like partnerships, but, because they are incorporated, some elements of corporate taxation still apply.

Advantages and Disadvantages of Limited Liability Companies. The primary advantages of LLCs are inherent in their description—they offer limited liability to all their members, yet qualify for Subchapter K tax treatment. LLCs are superb estate and business succession planning vehicles because control of the LLC can be maintained by a senior generation while substantial interests in the business entity are transferred to younger-generation family members.

Counterbalancing these advantages is the fact that the LLC is a new business entity, and some uncertainty exists regarding how a domestic LLC will be treated outside the state boundaries. As of June 1996, every state has enacted an LLC statute, and about half the states have enacted *LLP (limited liability partnership)* statutes. Each state statute differs, and some concern has been expressed as to whether the limited liability conferred by one state will be respected by another state when the business entity is sued outside of its state of origin. While uncertainly still exits, principles of comity should ensure that the liability shield will be respected. Now that all states have LLC statutes, it is likely that efforts will be made to propose a uniform statute that can be tailored to each state's individual needs. The new IRS regulations that change the entity classification rules will give many states the opportunity to review their statutes and bring them into line with federal tax standards and the laws of other states.

Classification of Business Entities for Federal Tax Purposes

What Was the Situation Before?

When individuals organize a business, they must look to state law to determine how that business will be formed. State law defines the requirements for incorporation, limited partnerships, general partnerships, and LLCs. While state law determines the form in which a business operates, the state law characterization of that business is not binding for federal tax purposes. For purposes of federal taxation, if a business entity was organized as a corporation under state or federal law, it would be treated as such. A corporation organized under state law that meets the Subchapter S requirements may file an election to change the manner in which it is taxed (for federal tax purposes) from the normal rules under Subchapter C to the pass-through rules under Subchapter S.

Under the old entity classification scheme, the fact that a business entity (with two or more owners or members) was an unincorporated entity under state law did not mean that it automatically qualified for partnership tax treatment under federal law. The old rules may have classified the business as an association taxable as a corporation for federal tax purposes. In order to determine how an unincorporated business entity is taxed, the IRS used to examine traditional corporate attributes.

As discussed above, an LLC offers limited liability for all its members, yet is taxed as a partnership for federal tax purposes. The reason an LLC was able to achieve limited liability for its members while avoiding double taxation comes from a 1935 Supreme Court case called *Morrissey*.[25] In the Morrissey case, the Supreme Court set forth the corporate characteristics that determine whether an entity is taxed as a corporation or a partnership for federal tax purposes. These characteristics are *limited liability*, *centralized management*, *continuity of life*, and *free transferability of interest*. If an organization possesses three or more of these characteristics, it is taxed as a corporation. If, however, the organization avoids two of these characteristics, it is taxed as a partnership. Because this test required a delicate balancing between corporate and non-corporate characteristics, individuals setting up LLCs prior to the proposal of the check-the-box regulations had to engage in very careful (and expensive) planning with their advisers and attorneys.

One of the reasons LLCs were able to be classified as partnerships for federal income tax purposes is that the IRS, in developing entity classification regulations to implement the Morrissey test, worked in a bias that favored the partnership form of taxation over the corporate form. Subsequent to the Morrissey case, many professional practices (involving doctors and lawyers) which were forbidden from establishing corporations under state law, sought to classify their business entities as corporations for federal tax purposes in order to take advantage of qualified retirement plan benefits which, at that time, were only available to corporations. At least one group of doctors was successful in accomplishing this objective.[26] After losing a hotly contested court case in which the IRS argued that partnership taxation should apply (thereby denying eligibility for the qualified retirement plan benefits) the IRS issued entity classification regulations which favored partnership taxation over corporate taxation.[27]

Now that unincorporated business entities are essentially in parity with incorporated entities for qualified retirement plan purposes, business owners are not inclined to incorporate solely to take advantage of pension benefits. Furthermore, the General Utilities doctrine (which held that a corporate distribution of property was subject to only one level of tax) was legislatively repealed by the Tax Reform Act of 1986, requiring double taxation on corporate distributions of property. For these and other reasons, it is now generally preferable to be subject to the partnership tax rules at the federal

---

25. *Morrissey v. Comm'r.*, 296 U.S. 344, 16 AFTR 1247, 36-1 USTC Par. 9020 (S.Ct., 1935).
26. *Kinter v. Comm'r.*, 216 F.2d 418, 46 AFTR 995, 54-2 USTC Par. 9626 (CA-9, 1954).
27. Treas. Reg. Sec. 301.7701-1 through 301.7701-3.

level. Taking advantage of the test set forth in Morrissey, and the bias for partnership taxation which the IRS wrote into the entity classification regulations, the states enacted LLC statutes which allowed entities to structure themselves as partnerships for tax purposes while at the same time achieving limited liability for all members of the entity. While the IRS was successful in achieving a preference for partnership taxation at the time it wrote the regulations (thereby minimizing deductions allowable for qualified plan benefits), when the tax situation changed, the regulations intended to favor the IRS now favor the taxpayer.

What Is the Nature of the Change?

Newly adopted regulations (the *check-the-box regulations*) have greatly simplified the old entity classification test for unincorporated entities. The check-the-box regulations, as adopted, change the entity classification scheme from the balancing approach set forth by the Morrissey case and the Treasury regulations to a right to choose. As the IRS recognized in its explanation of the proposed revisions, "The existing regulations for classifying business organizations as associations (which are taxable as corporations...) or as partnerships...are based on the historical differences under local law between partnerships and corporations. However, many states have revised their statutes to provide that partnerships and other unincorporated organizations may possess characteristics that traditionally have been associated with corporations, thereby narrowing considerably the traditional distinctions between corporations and partnerships under local law." Since 1988 the IRS has invested considerable time in interpreting state LLC statutes and issuing rulings on specific transactions proposed by taxpayers. In response to these developments, the "Treasury and IRS believe that it is appropriate to replace the increasingly formalistic rules under the current regulations with a much simpler approach that generally is elective."[28]

The first step in the new classification process is to determine whether there is a separate entity for federal tax purposes. A business entity is any entity recognized for federal tax purposes that is not properly classified as a trust. (The proposed regulations are not intended to change the federal tax scheme for trusts, and therefore the Morrissey test still applies in this area.)

The second step looks to see how many members own the business entity. A business entity with two or more members is classified for tax purposes as either a corporation or a partnership. In general, business entities incorporated under state or federal law, joint-stock companies or joint stock associations, insurance companies and banks, business entities owned wholly by a state or political subdivision of a state, publicly traded partnerships, and certain enumerated foreign entities are considered per se corporations under the new regulation. These organizations are taxed as corporations and are not be

---

28. IRS explanation of provisions to the proposed regulations, issued May 13, 1996.

permitted to elect partnership taxation. Unincorporated businesses and entities with two or more members that are not per se corporations are eligible to choose corporate or partnership taxation for federal tax purposes. A business entity with only one member is classified as a corporation or is disregarded and is treated in the same manner as a sole proprietorship, branch, or division of the owner. Special classification provisions are included for foreign business entities.

While the new regulation speaks of an election, the current classification of existing entities will be respected if there was a reasonable basis for the classification, the same classification was claimed on all prior tax returns, and neither the entity nor any of its members was advised that the IRS was auditing the classification of the entity prior to May 8, 1996. Newly formed entities are not required to make an election. Instead, default rules apply. The default rules are designed to make the choice the entity would have made had an election been filed. Under the default rule, a domestic business entity with two or more members will automatically be classified as a partnership for federal tax purposes. For domestic business entities with only one member, the default rule disregards the entity, requiring treatment as a sole proprietorship. If the default classification is not desired, an election out of that classification is effective on either the date specified in the election if that date is within 75 days of the date the election is filed, or, if no date is specified, on the date the election is filed. Once an entity elects to change its classification it must wait 60 months (5 years) before it is able to change its classification again.

When Does This Change Affect Clients?

The check-the-box regulations became effective January 1, 1997. For entities formed before May 8, 1996 (the publication date of the proposed check-the-box regulations), a special provision applies. As noted above, if the IRS had failed to challenge (by way of an audit) the classification of a business entity prior to May 8, 1996, the entity had a reasonable basis for the classification, and the same classification was claimed on all prior tax returns, the entity has met the safe harbor provisions in the regulation, and its status will not be challenged by the IRS.

What Should Be Done?

The effect of the new regulations is to reduce the federal tax uncertainty faced by the client when forming an LLC under state law. Planners must proceed with caution, however. Many states based their LLC statutes on the 4 factor balancing test set forth by the Morrissey case. In those states, compliance with the balancing test may still be required to form an LLC. It is likely, however, that most states will revise their LLC statutes to bring them in line with the new regulations. Furthermore, be aware that if an entity, currently taxed as a corporation, elects to be taxed as a partnership, the election causes a liquidation of the corporation, triggering potentially huge tax liabilities at both the corporate and shareholder levels. While the regulations represent a step in the right direction, planners should not be too hasty to employ them without first considering the impact of an election on the business entity and client.

Conclusion

The IRS, in adopting the check-the-box regulations, has simplified the entity classification scheme and, by doing so, has made it easier for clients to choose the LLC as the preferred form of business. Because an LLC is more flexible than an S corporation with respect to planning opportunities, in almost all cases where a client is setting up a new business, the LLC will be preferred to an S corporation. The next article explores the tax advantages and disadvantages of the LLC versus the S corporation.

Where Can I Find Out More?

- HS 331 Planning for Business Owners and Professionals. The American College.
- GS 836 Business Succession Planning I. The American College.
- GS 838 Business Succession Planning II. The American College.
- Thomas P. Langdon. "Will Proposed IRS Rules Simplify Client Planning?" *Best's Review*, Life/Health Edition (October 1996), p. 98.
- Lewis J. Saret and Lewis D. Solomon. "New IRS 'Check the Box' Regulations." *Journal of Asset Protection,* Vol. 1, No. 6 (July/August 1996), pp. 67–72.
- Francis J. Wirtz. "Check-the-Box: The Proposed Regulations on Entity Classification." *Taxes*, Vol. 74, No. 6 (June 1996), pp. 355–364.

A Comparison of Limited Liability Companies and S Corporations in Planning for Closely Held or Family-Owned Businesses
Thomas P. Langdon

Given the substantial changes in S corporation rules and the enactment of the check-the-box regulations discussed in previous articles, the planner should carefully compare the advantages and disadvantages of the two forms of business to make appropriate choices for clients. The purpose of this article is to summarize the advantages and disadvantages of S corporations and limited liability companies (LLCs) in light of recent legislative and regulatory changes. Here is a summary of the topics covered in this article:

> **Planning Issues: Comparison of S Corporations and LLCs**
>
> 1. Asset Protection Aspects
> 2. Business Planning Considerations
> 3. Retirement Planning Considerations
> 4. Estate Planning Considerations
>
> **Comparison of S Corporation Taxation to Partnership Taxation**
>
> 1. Special Allocations
> 2. Effect of the Business Entity Incurring Debt
> 3. Basis Change upon Transfer of Interest
> 4. Contribution of Appreciated Property
> 5. Distributions of Property to the Owners
> 6. Special Taxes for S Corporations
> 7. Summary

Planning Issues

1. Asset Protection Aspects

S Corporations. Because S corporations are formed under state law, they possess the desirable characteristic of *limited liability*. Limited liability shields the owner of the business (the stockholder) from liability for business debts in excess of his or her investment. Creditors of the business do, however, have access to the business assets to satisfy their claims. If a creditor attaches and sells an asset vital to the continued operation of the S corporation, the business may fail.

For closely held and family businesses, protection from the claims of the owners' creditors, as well as the business's creditors, is an important planning goal. If an owner of S corporation stock experiences financial difficulty and files for bankruptcy, the S corporation stock is part of the bankruptcy estate, and is available to creditors to satisfy their claims. If creditors receive the stock in satisfaction of the shareholder's debt, outsiders now have voting power in the closely held or family business. Worse yet, if creditors sell the S corporation stock to an ineligible shareholder, the S corporation election is terminated, and the business is subject to the double-level tax assessed on C corporations.

These issues require careful planning on the part of S corporation owners. Buy-sell agreements can be structured to become effective on the death, disability, bankruptcy, or incapacity of any shareholder. Entering into a buy-sell agreement of this type will protect against outsiders obtaining a stake in the business and inadvertent termination of the S corporation election if the stock is sold to an ineligible shareholder. However, the buy-sell agreement itself will not protect individual shareholders from the claims of creditors because the value of the business interest will be available to satisfy creditor claims.

Limited Liability Companies. LLCs, like corporations, offer limited liability to all of their members. As such, an individual member's liability for business debts is limited to his or her investment in the LLC.

When a shareholder in an S corporation declares bankruptcy, the S corporation stock is generally available to the shareholder's creditors for satisfaction of the debt. Unless a buy-sell agreement is in place that takes effect upon bankruptcy or similar contingencies, it is possible that the creditor of an S corporation shareholder will acquire a voting interest in the corporation, or the stock will be sold to an ineligible shareholder, thereby terminating the S corporation election.

An LLC provides additional creditor protection to its members as compared with a shareholder in an S corporation. Most LLC statutes stipulate that a *charging order* is the exclusive remedy for creditors seeking to attach a member's interest in an LLC. A charging order is "a statutorily created means for a creditor of a judgment debtor who is a partner of others to reach the debtor's beneficial interest in the partnership, without risking dissolution of the partnership."[29] Under Sec. 25(2)(c) of the Uniform Partnership Act, partnership property may not be seized to satisfy a partner's obligation. The creditor may only seize the right to receive distributions from the partnership or LLC until the obligation is satisfied. The holder of a charging order is treated as an assignee entitled to distributions under state law, but is treated as a partner for federal tax purposes.[30] Because the creditor is treated as a partner or member of an LLC for federal tax purposes, phantom income results to the extent that the business earned more than it distributed during the taxable year. Faced with the prospect of reporting and paying tax on phantom income, creditors will be more amenable to settling their claim for a reasonable amount. Furthermore, because the creditor is only an assignee for state law purposes, he or she does not obtain the right to vote on LLC matters, and, as a result, there is no dilution of control of the family business.

2. *Business Planning Considerations*

S Corporations. For many years, the only way to obtain limited liability for all owners of a business was to incorporate. Incorporation carried with it undesirable tax consequences, however, since a double-level tax is imposed on the earnings of regular corporations. The corporation, as a legal person in its own right, is taxed on its earnings. In addition, when the corporation passes its earnings out to its owners in the form of dividends, the owners are taxed on the dividend income. In order to provide relief for smaller businesses while

---

29. Uniform Partnership Act, Sec. 28.
30. Rev. Rul. 77-137, 1977-1 C.B. 178; *Evans v. Comm'r*, 477 F.2d 547 (7th Cir. 1971).

allowing them to be organized as corporations, Congress passed Subchapter S of the Internal Revenue Code, allowing C corporations that meet certain requirements to elect *pass-through treatment* for federal tax purposes. Pass-through treatment results in a single-level tax on corporate earnings for federal tax purposes.

Obtaining pass-through treatment of corporate earnings comes at a significant cost, however. In order to get favorable pass-through treatment, the corporation must comply with the many requirements and restrictions discussed in a previous article. Not all corporations are eligible to make a Subchapter S election, and the limitation on the number and type of eligible shareholders often results in difficulty attracting investors. While recent legislative and regulatory changes have loosened the rules, the rules still demand compliance, thereby restricting the ability of the business to grow and compete with other businesses that are not subject to the litany of complex requirements under Subchapter S. New business entities must carefully consider the restrictions imposed by Subchapter S before deciding to organize as S corporations.

Limited Liability Companies. Unlike the situation with S corporations, there are no statutory restrictions on LLCs. An LLC may have an unlimited number of members, and there are no restrictions on the type of individuals or trusts eligible to hold an interest in the LLC. An LLC, like a partnership, may have both profits and capital interests in the entity and may structure ownership interests unequally between rights to distribution and rights to liquidation proceeds. Like a family limited partnership, an LLC can grant an interest only in profits to an important member of the management team. For example, the LLC could grant to its president or managing member a 5 percent interest in the profits of the LLC, even though no right to the underlying capital has been given away. If an S corporation tried to do this, it would terminate its S corporation status due to the "one class of stock" rule.

3. *Retirement Planning Considerations*

S Corporations. A significant planning opportunity available to owners of S corporation stock beginning in tax years after December 31, 1997 involves the use of S corporation stock to fund qualified retirement plans. Beginning in 1998, qualified retirement plans organized under Sec. 401(a) of the IRC will be eligible to hold S corporation stock. This means that *employee stock ownership plans (ESOPs)* can now be established for S corporations. Among the benefits of the ESOP is the ability to allow employees to participate in the ownership of the company, and to create a market for the S corporation stock. Use of S corporation stock in qualified retirement plans can serve many business and succession planning objectives, and should be explored by current S corporation owners. Because qualified plans are permissible shareholders beginning in 1998, the IRS will have the opportunity to issue guidance on the use of S corporation stock in qualified plans this year.

Limited Liability Companies. Because the members of LLCs are treated as partners for federal tax purposes, the restrictions encountered with retirement planning for partners are also present for members of LLCs.

4. Estate Planning Considerations

S Corporations. Owners of S corporation stock must also comply with the rules and restrictions of Subchapter S when engaged in estate planning. The most obvious restriction is that S corporation stock may not be left to an ineligible shareholder.

Trusts often play an important role in the estate planning process, yet only three types of trusts are eligible to hold S corporation stock. *Grantor trusts* are permitted to hold S corporation stock only for a 2-year period, which puts severe restrictions on the use of these trusts for estate planning purposes. This 2-year restriction can be overcome by electing qualified Subchapter S trust (QSST) status, but only if the grantor is willing to comply with another set of complex restrictions, the most significant being that these trusts can have only one current income beneficiary. Under the new provisions of the Small Business Job Protection Act of 1996, an *electing small business trust (ESBT)* is allowed to hold S corporation stock and have multiple beneficiaries, but only at a significant cost: all S corporation income is taxed at the highest marginal rate for estates and trusts. Furthermore, it is not yet clear whether *charitable remainder trusts (CRTs)* will be permitted to hold S corporation stock. Even if a CRT can hold S corporation stock, income attributed to the S corporation earnings, as well as gain realized on the sale of S corporation stock, will be taxed to the trust. (The taxation of S corporation earnings is presumably based on the premise that the trust, as a shareholder in a pass-through business entity, has *unrelated business taxable income [UBTI]*.) Every trust permitted to hold S corporation stock has significant restrictions, thereby limiting the estate planning opportunities for S corporation owners.

For estate planning purposes, S corporations, like other business entities, may qualify for minority and lack of marketability discounts. These discounts allow individuals to leverage their unified credit and annual gift tax exclusion. For example, if an individual holds a 40 percent minority interest in an S corporation valued at $2,250,000, the shareholder's proportional interest in the corporation is worth $900,000. If a 35 percent discount applies for the minority interest and lack of marketability, the 40 percent interest is worth only $585,000. This shareholder could pass the $900,000 proportional interest in the corporation to his or her heirs fully shielded by his or her unified credit of $600,000. In S corporations owned by families, this offers attractive wealth transfer opportunities.

The corporate form also makes transfer of control of the business relatively simple, since a transfer of a simple majority of the shares will transfer control. Often, this ability is limited by transfer restrictions placed in a buy-sell agreement to ensure that stock is not transferred to an ineligible shareholder. This serves as yet another example of how the rules complicate matters for owners of S corporations.

Overall, estate planning for S corporation owners is more intricate than planning for the owners of other business entities due to the myriad of complex rules that apply. Increased complexity in turn increases the cost of such planning, both in terms of time and money.

Limited Liability Companies. Unlike the case with S corporations, there are no restrictions on the types of individuals or trusts which can hold an interest in an LLC. By setting up a business as an LLC, it is possible to transfer a significant amount of the business interest to junior members of the family without losing any control. In fact, if the business owner makes full use of annual exclusion gifting, he or she can often transfer most of the value of the business to successive generations throughout his or her lifetime and still be in control. For business owners who wish to maximize their estate planning opportunities, therefore, the LLC is a more flexible tool than the S corporation.

Comparison of S Corporation Taxation to Partnership Taxation

Although an S corporation is taxed as a pass-through entity, it is not taxed under the provisions of the Internal Revenue Code dealing with partnerships. S corporations have their own set of rules, located in Subchapter S of the Code. The tax treatment of S corporations and partnerships is similar, but is not exactly the same; S corporation requirements and certain corporate tax attributes impose additional restrictions and requirements on the taxation of S corporations that are not found in the taxation of partnerships. While Subchapter K of the Code, dealing with partnership taxation, is arguably the most complex area of federal taxation, it provides more flexibility for business owners than Subchapter S. Some of the differences between partnership and S corporation taxation are discussed below.

1. Special Allocations

A partnership is permitted to make special allocations of tax items to its partners, provided that the allocation has *substantial economic effect*.[31] Substantial economic effect generally means that the allocations of the tax items made among the partners are actually reflected in the partners' capital accounts. An S corporation is not permitted to make special allocations. Making special allocations of tax items to S corporation shareholders would mean that the shareholders do not have identical rights to distributions and liquidation proceeds, thereby violating the "one class of stock" rule. Partnership tax treatment is therefore more flexible than S corporation tax treatment because the owners can tailor allocations of tax items in the most efficient fashion.

---

31. IRC Sec. 704(b).

2. Effect of the Business Entity Incurring Debt

While a partnership is itself a separate entity from its owners for state law purposes, it is not treated as such for federal tax purposes. Therefore, when a partnership incurs debt, for tax purposes the transaction is treated as though the partner contributed an amount of cash to the partnership equal to the partner's pro rata share of the debt.[32] When a partner makes a contribution of property to a partnership, the partner's basis in the partnership is increased by the amount of the contribution.[33] The increase in basis increases the amount of partnership distributions that can be received tax free. The reason for this treatment may be that, traditionally, because a partnership does not offer limited liability to its members, an increase in partnership debt equates to an increased investment in the partnership, since the partner could be personally liable for that debt. While a member of an LLC, which is taxed as a partnership, will receive an increase in basis when the entity takes on debt, no personal liability for that amount results. This is an illustration of one area where the partnership tax rules favor an LLC over a partnership.

When an S corporation incurs debt, the corporation is liable for the debt, not the shareholder. Consequently, no basis step up is permitted for S corporation shareholders when the entity incurs debt. Practically speaking, owners of S corporations frequently have to personally guarantee corporate debts, which places them on a par with partners when a partnership incurs debt. Regardless of personal guarantees, no basis step up is permitted for S corporation owners when the corporation incurs debt.

3. Basis Change upon Transfer of Interest

Once an entity is formed, the basis of the entity's assets in the entity's hands (*inside basis*), and the basis of the owner's interest in the owner's hands (*outside basis*) begins to change, so that the inside basis does not equal the outside basis. Under Code Sec. 754, a partner is permitted to elect to equate or *step up* the inside and outside bases of the partnership interest upon transfer. This gives an advantage to the acquiring partner because, when the asset is sold, the acquiring partner will only recognize gain to the extent of the partner's pro-rata share of the amount realized, less the section 754 stepped-up basis.

Owners of S corporation stock do not have the opportunity to equate inside and outside bases upon sale of an interest in the entity. As a result, when the underlying corporate assets are sold at a gain, this gain increases the shareholder's basis and often places the shareholder in a loss position, because the basis of the stock (including the step up) may exceed the stock's fair market value.

---

32. IRC Sec. 752.
33. IRC Sec. 705(a).

4. Contribution of Appreciated Property

When a partner contributes property to a partnership, no gain or loss is recognized.[34] When an S corporation owner contributes property to the corporation, gain or loss on the contributed property is recognized to the extent that the contributor owns less than 80 percent of the combined voting power of all classes of stock eligible to vote or less than 80 percent of all other shares of stock in the corporation immediately following the transfer.[35] Unless the owner of the S corporation stock can meet the 80 percent test, he or she will be discouraged from making additional contributions of capital to the business entity. This can minimize both business and estate planning opportunities for the affected business owners.

5. Distributions of Property to the Owners

When property is distributed from a partnership to a partner, no gain or loss is recognized.[36] The partner takes a carryover basis in the property received from the partnership, provided the basis in the asset distributed is not in excess of the partner's basis in the aggregate partnership interest.[37]

When an S corporation distributes property to a shareholder, a gain equal to the difference between the asset's fair market value and the corporation's adjusted basis is recognized at the corporate level.[38] The gain is passed through to the shareholders on the K-1, and is therefore taxed only once, at the individual shareholder level. Because there has been a recognition of gain on the transfer of the asset, the basis of the asset in the hands of the shareholder is the asset's fair market value. If the S corporation realizes a loss on the disposition of the asset, however, the loss is not recognized.[39]

Because Subchapter S requires gain to be recognized on the disposition of property and Subchapter K does not, partnership taxation again holds advantages over S corporation taxation.

6. Special Taxes for S Corporations

In order to discourage abuse, Subchapter S imposes special taxes on S corporations. The *built-in gains tax (BIG tax)* is imposed on the sale of corporate assets within 10 years of the time when the corporation converted from a Subchapter C taxpayer to a Subchapter S taxpayer. The purpose of this tax is to prevent taxpayers from electing Subchapter S status simply to avoid a second-level tax on the sale of corporate assets. Furthermore, if the S corporation has excessive passive income, a special tax is imposed on the corpo-

---

34. IRC Sec. 721(a).
35. IRC Secs. 351(a), 368(c).
36. IRC Sec. 731(a).
37. IRC Sec. 732 (a) and (b).
38. IRC Sec. 311(b).
39. IRC Sec. 311(a).

ration at the corporate level, which, in essence, effectuates a reversion back to a double-tax system. Neither of these taxes is imposed on partnerships or LLCs.

7. Summary

The following table summarizes the major differences between Subchapter K and Subchapter S taxation:

	PARTNERSHIP	S CORPORATION
Special allocations available	Yes	No
Effect of entity taking on debt	Increase in partner's basis	No change in shareholder's basis
Basis change on transfer of an interest	Election can be made to equate inside and outside bases	No election available
Contribution of appreciated property	Tax free	Tax free if contributors own, both before and after the contribution, 80% of the entity's stock
Distribution of property	No gain or loss recognized	Gain recognized at the corporate level and passed through to shareholders; no loss recognized unless complete liquidation
Built-in gains tax	No	Yes
Excess passive income tax	No	Yes

Conclusion

Although LLCs are new entities, they are quickly taking center stage in the business planning arena. LLCs provide limited liability for all their members, enhanced creditor protection of business interests, and favorable tax treatment when compared to S corporations. While complex, the partnership tax rules are more flexible than the rigid requirements and extra taxes imbedded in Subchapter S of the Code. LLCs include all of the benefits of S corporations with few of the headaches or costs. Now that all 50 states have enacted LLC legislation, it is likely that there will be some effort to propose model legislation based on the newly enacted check-the-box regulations, which will help standardize the treatment of these vehicles across the states. The IRS, grudgingly, has recognized the validity of these entities and, by adopting the check-the-box regulations, has provided the catalyst for increased use of LLCs in the future. For new businesses, the LLC will almost always be preferable to the S corporation.

Recent regulatory and legislative enactments have made the S corporation rules more flexible, but these changes are probably too late to save the S corporation as a business entity. The 1995 and 1996 enhancements will certainly ease the burden for existing S corporations which find it too costly to liquidate, but will not be likely to encourage new businesses to elect Subchapter S status. The advent of the LLC and its growing acceptance has prompted some commentators to call for repeal of Subchapter S, allowing existing S corporations to become either LLCs or C corporations without penalty.[40] "When statutes that have outlived their usefulness remain on the books, they create inefficiencies that neither the country nor the economy needs."[41] Perhaps Congress should consider enacting major reforms to the Code provisions dealing with S corporations instead of toying with minor changes that will impact fewer and fewer businesses as we move into the 21st century.

Where Can I Find Out More?

- GS 836 Business Succession Planning I. The American College.
- Walter D. Schwidetzky. "Is It Time to Give the S Corporation a Proper Burial?" *Virginia Tax Review*, Vol. 15, No. 4 (Spring 1996), pp. 593–651.

Interest Deduction Limitations for COLI
James F. Ivers III, Ted Kurlowicz, and Stephan R. Leimberg

What Was the Situation Before?

The Internal Revenue Service (IRS) has shown an increasing tendency to view interest deductions for company-owned life insurance (COLI) as abusive in certain cases. In 1995, the national office of the IRS requested information from all district and regional counsel attorneys regarding the deduction of interest payments on indebtedness incurred in connection with an insurance policy where a corporation is the policyowner and beneficiary.[42] This notice stated that leveraged COLI—that is, policies purchased in part through borrowing against their cash values—"may present an abuse under Sec. 264."[43]

COLI may take one of two forms.[44] A company may purchase insurance on the lives of its most valuable employees (*key person coverage*). However, when the company insures the lives of a large number of employees regardless

---

40. Walter D. Schwidetzky. "Is It Time to Give the S Corporation a Proper Burial?" *Virginia Tax Review,* Vol. 15, No. 4 (Spring 1996), p. 593.
41. Schwidetzky, p. 651.
42. IRS Notice N(35).
43. IRC Sec. 264 covers the rules for the income tax deduction for interest incurred on policy loans from a life insurance policy.
44. Another valuable use of COLI not mentioned in Notice N(35) is coverage on the life of shareholders of a corporation to fund the corporation's obligation under a stock redemption agreement or redemptions prescribed under IRC Sec. 303.

of their compensation or relative value to the business (*janitor insurance*), the IRS has viewed COLI as a tax abuse.

What the notice clearly ignores is that regardless of which employees are insured, COLI serves a business purpose in that the policies will be used by the company to meet certain financial needs, such as post-retirement medical coverage. The perceived benefits of COLI plans include relatively low out-of-pocket after-tax costs and tax-free income to the company upon the death of an insured employee. In some cases, the amount of interest paid on the policy loan is only slightly less than the rate of return credited to the policy's cash surrender value. Thus, the availability of an income tax deduction for interest paid on the policy loan might permit the corporation to profit on the tax-free buildup in the policy and receive a net cash influx as a result of the policy loan.

The IRS recognized that the business purpose for leveraged COLI may be valid. However, its position was that Sec. 264 was intended by Congress to prevent the financing of insurance purchases through tax benefits associated with the policy. Accordingly, the IRS examinations division was refusing to close cases involving COLI until formalized instructions on what specific grounds an interest deduction could be denied were issued from the national office.

What Is the Nature of the Change?

Congress enacted legislative changes related to the COLI issue in the Health Insurance Portability and Accountability Act of 1996.[45] These changes limit interest deductibility on COLI policies and can be summarized as follows:

- *Policies Purchased before 6/21/86.* These contracts are "grandfathered" for full interest deductibility based on rules in effect at that time. However, the interest rate that will be deductible is capped based on the applicable Moody's interest rate (discussed later).
- *"Key Person" Policies Purchased after 6/20/86.* Policies that meet the definition of *key person contracts* are permitted interest deductibility (based on the Moody's rate) for up to the first $50,000 of aggregate policy loans for COLI covering the life of a key person. Thus, COLI for (1) key-person coverage or (2) funding a stock-redemption agreement in a closely held corporation is largely unaffected.
- *Policies Not Covering Key Persons*
  - *Purchased between 6/21/86 and 12/31/95.* Transitional rules permit a phase-out of deductibility (based on the Moody's rate) for up to the first $50,000 of aggregate policy loans for COLI covering the life of a nonkey employee. The deduction is limited to 100 percent for 1996, 90 percent for 1997, and 80 percent for 1998,

---

45. Health Insurance Portability and Accountability Act of 1996, Sec. 501.

with no deduction thereafter. (Note that the transitional relief does not apply if the number of insured individuals exceeds 20,000.)
- *Purchased after 12/31/95.* Interest on such COLI is wholly nondeductible.

Basic Rule of Disallowance. Under the 1996 legislation, the basic rule for leveraged COLI is that no deduction will be allowed for interest paid on loans from company-owned life insurance, annuity, or endowment contracts that cover the life of an officer, employee, or other person financially interested in the business of the policyowner/taxpayer. The provision covers both incorporated and unincorporated businesses.[46]

The "Key Person" Rule. The most significant exception to the basic rule of disallowance is the key person rule. This exception applies to interest that is not subject to either the grandfather rule or the transitional rules. Deductions under the key person rule are subject to the $50,000 of indebtedness per insured limitation. This exception preserves the interest deduction on the traditional COLI uses, such as key person coverage or stock-redemption funding.

Interest deductions are allowable under the key person rule if the "covered" person under a life insurance, annuity, or endowment contract is a "key person." What is a *key person* for purposes of the rule? First, the person must be either an "officer" or a "20 percent owner" of the business to be a key person.[47] A *20 percent owner* is a person who owns 20 percent or more of the outstanding stock of the corporation, or one who owns stock possessing 20 percent or more of the voting power in the corporation. If the business is unincorporated, a *20 percent owner* is a person who owns 20 percent or more of the capital or income interests in the business entity.[48]

The number of persons who can qualify as key persons is limited by the new rules. That number cannot exceed 5 individuals unless the business has more than 100 total officers and employees.[49] If the business has more than 100 total officers and employees, then the total number of key persons cannot exceed the lesser of 5 percent of those officers and employees, or 20 individuals.[50] Therefore, the maximum number of key persons for any business is 20, and only businesses with officers and employees of 400 or more may have the maximum of 20 key persons.

---

46. Thus, the new rules apply to insurance purchased by a partnership on a partner's life or by a limited liability company on a member's life. Insurance on the life of a sole proprietor is treated as personally owned, and interest on such policy loans is treated under both Secs. 264 and 163 and is generally treated as personal interest.
47. IRC Sec. 264(d)(3).
48. IRC Sec. 264(d)(4).
49. IRC Sec. 264(d)(3)(A).
50. IRC Sec. 264(d)(3)(B).

New Limitation on Interest Deduction For COLI

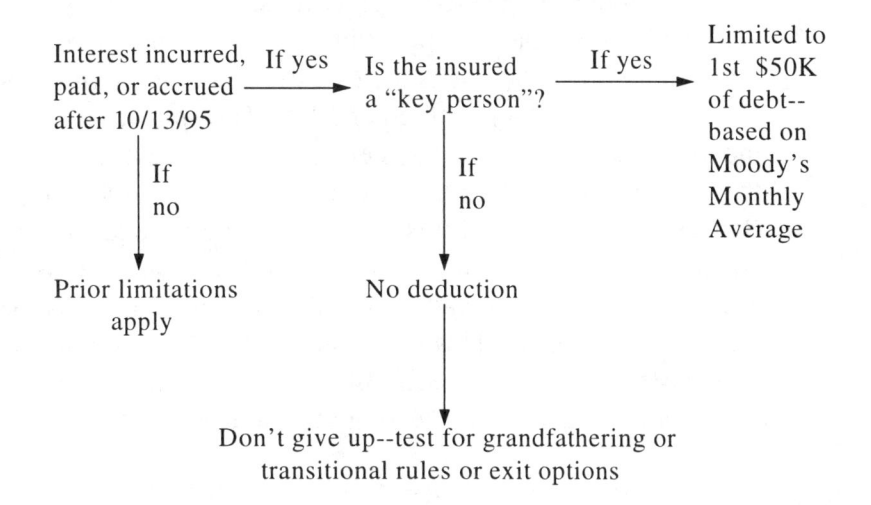

```
Interest incurred,  If yes   Is the insured   If yes    Limited to
paid, or accrued  ─────────▶ a "key person"? ─────────▶ 1st $50K
after 10/13/95                                          of debt--
     │                            │                     based on
     │ If                         │ If                  Moody's
     │ no                         │ no                  Monthly
     ▼                            ▼                     Average
Prior limitations            No deduction
apply
```

Don't give up--test for grandfathering or
transitional rules or exit options

There is also a limitation on the interest rate that may be used in calculating allowable deductions under the key person rule. The maximum allowable interest rate is the lesser of the actual interest rate under the contract or the monthly Moody's rate for the month the interest is paid or accrued.[51]

Aggregation rules apply for purposes of determining who is the "taxpayer" (business) in calculating the maximum number of allowable key persons as well as for purposes of applying the $50,000 limitation.[52] All members of a "controlled group" are treated as one taxpayer for these purposes. A *controlled group* includes all persons or entities treated as a single employer.[53]

When Does the Change Take Effect?

The Grandfather Rule. The general rule does not apply to interest on loans from contracts issued before June 21, 1986.[54] This interest is generally deductible, and it is not subject to the $50,000 of indebtedness per insured limitation. However, there is a limitation on the interest rate that may be used in calculating deductions for interest payments under the grandfather rule.

For loans with fixed rates of interest, deductions are limited by the applicable "Moody's Average" for the month in which the contract was

---

51. IRC Sec. 264(d)(2).
52. IRC Sec. 264(d)(5).
53. IRC Sec. 264(d)(5)(B). This includes those defined under IRC Sec. 52(a), Sec. 52(b), Sec. 414(m), and Sec. 414(o).
54. IRC Sec. 264(a)(4).

purchased.[55] The *Moody's Average* is a monthly corporate bond yield average published by Moody's Investors Services, Inc.[56]

If a contract subject to the grandfather rules has a loan that carries a variable interest rate, the applicable limiting interest rate is calculated somewhat differently. The rate is the Moody's rate for the third month before the first month in the "applicable period."[57] The *applicable period* is a period of months up to 12 months that is elected by the taxpayer owning the policy on the tax return for its first tax year ending on or after October 13, 1995.[58] Because of the timing of this rule, the tax return requiring the election of the applicable period has already have become due and may have been filed. If such a tax return has already been filed, it apparently must be amended to elect the applicable period. This period cannot be changed without IRS consent. The American Council on Life Insurance has asked the Treasury for guidance on the proper method for electing the applicable period.

The Transitional ("Phase-in") Rules. These rules apply to two specifically defined types of indebtedness: indebtedness incurred before 1997 with respect to contracts entered into in 1994 or 1995, and indebtedness incurred before 1996 with respect to contracts issued before 1994.

Deductions for "qualified interest"[59] on indebtedness subject to the transitional rules are limited with respect to the interest rate that can be used in calculating the deductions. Deductions are calculated by the lesser of two rates: the borrowing rate specified in the contract as of October 13, 1995, or the "applicable percentage" of the Moody's rate for the month the interest is paid or accrued.[60] The "applicable percentage" is 100 percent for 1996, 90 percent for 1997, and 80 percent for 1998.[61] Interest paid or accrued after 1998

---

55. IRC Sec. 264(d)(4)(1)(B)(ii)(I).
56. As a practical matter, it may create some compliance problems for the corporation to determine the appropriate rate. It is not known whether or not life insurance companies will pick up the burden of reporting the appropriate rate on such grandfathered policies.
57. IRC Sec. 264(d)(4)(1)(B)(ii)(II).
58. IRC Sec. 264(d)(4)(1)(B)(ii).
59. Health Insurance Portability and Accountability Act of 1996, Sec. 501(c)(2)(B).
60. Health Insurance Portability and Accountability Act of 1996, Sec. 501(c)(2)(B)(ii).
61. Health Insurance Portability and Accountability Act of 1996, Sec. 501(c)(2)(C). It is not clear how the taxpayer should determine the applicable phase-out percentages when the interest is reported by the insurer on a calendar or policy year that does not coincide with the corporation's fiscal year for tax purposes. For a discussion of a reasonable accounting compliance method, see Bradley K. Walton, "Corporate-Owned Life Insurance Takes a Hit," *Practical Accountant* (January 1997).

is not treated under the transitional rules. It is also important to note that interest can be deducted under the transitional rules only to the extent it would have been deductible prior to the 1996 legislation. For example, the $50,000 of indebtedness per insured limitation applies under the transitional rules.

"Qualified interest" under the transitional rules does not include interest paid or accrued after December 31, 1995, on borrowing by a taxpayer with respect to contracts on the lives of more than 20,000 persons.[62] For this purpose, the aggregation rules described under the key person rules for determining when more than one entity may be treated as a single taxpayer also apply.[63] This provision prevents the continuation of tax avoidance in certain insurance placements, which have been referred to as "janitor insurance."

"Spreadforward" of Income From Affected Contracts. There is further relief for taxpayers who are facing the immediate nondeductibility[64] or the near-term phase-out of COLI interest deductibility.[65] If a taxpayer surrenders a contract affected by these new rules in 1996, 1997, or 1998, gain resulting from the surrender can be spread over 4 taxable years, starting with the year in which full recognition of gain would otherwise have occurred.[66] This treatment applies to any surrender, redemption, or maturity of any contract affected by the new rules. In addition, such a surrender will not cause the contract to fail the "four-out-of-seven" test or to be treated as a single-premium contract.[67]

What Should Be Done?

Most closely held businesses will not be affected by these changes. Traditional uses of COLI, such as key person coverage or stock redemption funding, will probably qualify for the key person exception to the new rules; interest on such policies will continue to be deductible up to the first $50,000 of borrowing.

For taxpayers with COLI affected by the new law, some exit strategies could be suggested. First, policies on nonkey persons can be surrendered. The taxpayer may wish to wait until the end of 1998 to surrender the policies to take advantage of the continuing interest deduction during the phase-out

---

62. Health Insurance Portability and Accountability Act of 1996, Sec. 501(c)(2)(B)(i).
63. IRC Sec. 254(d)(5).
64. For example, taxpayers with COLI covering more than 20,000 individuals.
65. Taxpayers with post-6/20/1986 contracts covering 20,000 or fewer individuals.
66. Health Insurance Portability and Accountability Act of 1996, Sec. 501(d).
67. IRC Sec. 264(b).

COLI Interest--Grandfathering and Transitional Rules

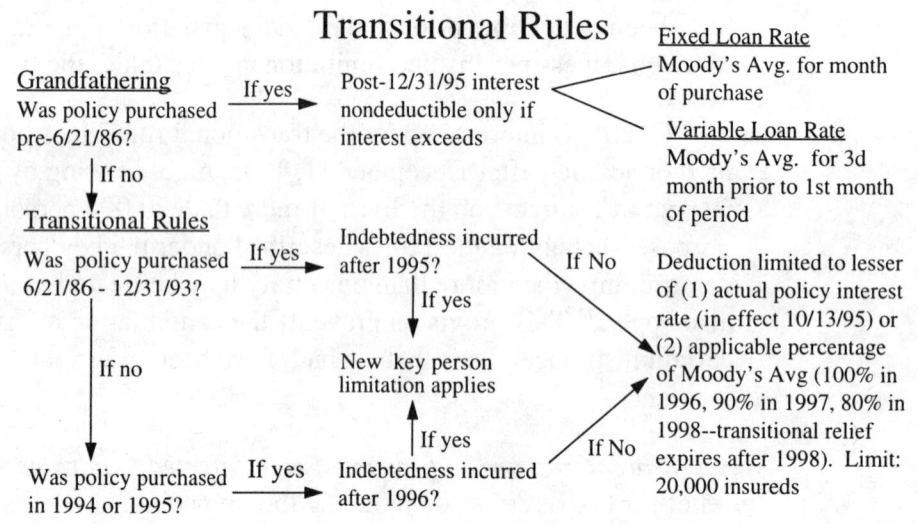

Grandfathering
Was policy purchased pre-6/21/86?

If yes → Post-12/31/95 interest nondeductible only if interest exceeds

If no ↓

Transitional Rules
Was policy purchased 6/21/86 - 12/31/93?

If yes → Indebtedness incurred after 1995?
If No →
If yes ↓
New key person limitation applies
↑ If yes
Indebtedness incurred after 1996?
If No →

If no ↓
Was policy purchased in 1994 or 1995? If yes →

Fixed Loan Rate
Moody's Avg. for month of purchase

Variable Loan Rate
Moody's Avg. for 3d month prior to 1st month of period

Deduction limited to lesser of (1) actual policy interest rate (in effect 10/13/95) or (2) applicable percentage of Moody's Avg (100% in 1996, 90% in 1997, 80% in 1998--transitional relief expires after 1998). Limit: 20,000 insureds

period.[68] With the partial deductions in 1997 and 1998, it may still be economically profitable to retain the COLI subject to the loans for the remainder of the transitional period.

When the contracts are surrendered, this will not create a taxable event if no gain exists. If gain exists, the gain can be spread over 4 tax years, beginning with the year of disposition.

Where Can I Find Out More?

- HS 321 Income Taxation. The American College.
- IRC Sec. 264(d).

---

68. Only applicable to taxpayers with COLI covering 20,000 or fewer individuals.

4

SPLIT-DOLLAR LIFE INSURANCE ARRANGEMENTS

Stephan R. Leimberg

The Importance of Documentation

What Was the Situation Before?

The apparent lack of IRS attention to split-dollar documentation in past years has made many planners and advisers complacent, sloppy, or even negligent. Hundreds of split-dollar agreements were established without the requisite paperwork.

What Is the Nature of the Change?

Recent cases have emphasized the importance of careful and full documentation of the split-dollar arrangement. For example, in one case, a court ruled against the taxpayer who claimed he should be taxed under split-dollar rules because of the taxpayer's lack of any supporting documentation. The insured employee-shareholder was required to recognize income to the extent of the entire amount of premiums paid by the employer (over $700,000) instead of the (much lower) economic benefit measurement. So regardless of the policy ownership and the structure of the split-dollar arrangement, separate documentation must be created and maintained to evidence the "at arm's length" transaction between the employer and the employee (or a third-party owner).[1]

First, a corporate resolution should state that the Board of Directors has authorized the establishment of a split-dollar arrangement. That resolution should identify the officer(s) who is (are) authorized to execute the necessary documents on behalf of the corporation and state the corporate purpose served by the agreement.[2]

---

1. *Goos vs. Comm'r.,* TC Memo 1991-146. For more detailed information, readers are encouraged to obtain the author's article titled "Split Dollar, the Bifurcated Peso: Split, Rip, or Tear?" published by Matthew Bender as part of the proceedings of the 31st Philip E. Heckerling Institute on Estate Planning. Also consult *Tax Planning with Life Insurance,* Financial Professional's Edition, published by the RIA Group.
2. Whenever there is a change to the arrangement, there should be a corporate resolution documenting such a change. Likewise, if the

Second, there must be a contractual agreement, and the parties should consider the following:

- This contract may (or may not) require that the agreement be submitted to the insurer or that it be filed in its records (depending on the standard practices or procedures of the insurer that issued the policy).
- The document should identify the parties. It should establish the relationship between the parties, for example., an employer-employee relationship.
- If the policy is to be owned by a third party, such as a trust or an adult child of the insured, it is important that the facts show that the policyowner and not the insured employee entered into the agreement with the employer.[3]
- The agreement should fully spell out the rights and obligations of the parties.
- The provisions of the agreement should include such issues as whether the plan is contributory or noncontributory, how the premium "split" is determined, and whether the employee (or a third-party owner) contributes an amount equal to the economic benefit cost, or a levelized amount[4]
- The document should also address the division of, and rights to, the policy's cash value. Specifically, while the agreement is in effect, the document should state how cash value should be "split" between the parties, how each party's share is to be determined, and the extent to which each party controls or can access the cash value. Generally, the policyowner controls the cash value—as in the case of an employer under an endorsement split-dollar plan. In the contract, the rights of the employee (or a third-party owner) are subject to the employer's assignee rights if the arrangement is cast under a collateral-assignment method. In this case, the extent of the parties' rights should be predicated upon the planning and tax objectives.[5] (If the employee (or a

---

agreement is terminated or when an employer-owned policy is transferred to the employee, the minutes should document the transaction.
3. Care should be taken if estate tax exclusion is to be achieved that the insured is not a party to the agreement.
4. Under a contributory plan, the employee's share of the premium may be handled through a bonus from the employer. However, the bonus arrangement should not be made part of the agreement; otherwise, the IRS could argue that the entire premium (including the employer's share) is taxable to the employee under IRC Sec. 162.
5. If the insured is a controlling (51 percent or greater) shareholder and the policy is owned by a third party (for estate planning purposes), the employer's assignee rights should be restricted such that it should not be allowed to borrow against or withdraw from the policy cash value.

third-party owner) has or gains an equity position in the cash value, there could be income, gift, or generation-skipping transfer tax implications).

- The agreement should specify repayment terms. For example, when the policy is surrendered or the arrangement is terminated, is the cash value used to "repay" the employer for its premium outlay? If so, what must be done if the available cash value is less than the employer's interest?[6]

- The division of the death benefit must be addressed. The amount of the death benefit payable to each of the parties to the arrangement typically should be the same as their respective interests in the cash value. However, in instances where the employer's interest in the cash value is less than its share of the death benefit, the disparity could create uncertainties with respect to the employee's taxation.[7]

- The policyowner's retained rights should be noted. The owner generally retains all policy ownership rights—except for the assignee rights granted the employer (under a collateral-assignment split-dollar arrangement) or the right of the employee to name his or her personal beneficiary(ies) for a specific amount or an amount in excess of the employer's share of the benefit (under an endorsement split-dollar plan). Each party should be allowed to designate or change the beneficiary(ies) for the portion of his or her (or its) death benefit, or to assign his or her (or its) interest in the policy.[8] Any such beneficiary or assignee should be bound to abide by and be subject to the terms of the split-dollar agreement.

- Termination of the arrangement should be considered. The provisions of the agreement should specify the circumstances under which the split-dollar arrangement will be terminated. Issues that should be addressed include events that will trigger involuntary termination, such as termination of the employee's employment (for example, retirement or involuntary termination for cause), dissolution of the corporation, death of the insured, and so forth. The document must also consider, in the event of a voluntary termination, who may initiate the process, and

---

Similarly, the ability of the employee (or a third-party owner) to access the cash value may also be restricted if income and gift taxation on "additional benefits" is to be avoided.

6. If the cash value received by the employer is less than the amount it is entitled to, the difference may be taxable to the employee as ordinary income under Sec. 83 (and deductible by the employer—unless the amount is deemed unreasonable).

7. See the discussion of "Equity Split Dollar," *infra*.

8. The employer's assignee rights (including the right to assign or pledge its interest) should be limited if the insured is a majority (51 percent or greater) shareholder (but the owner is a third party), and estate tax exclusion of the death proceeds is desired.

the procedure for notification.[9] It should also cover the disposition of the policy when the agreement terminates during the insured's lifetime so that it is clear which party gets the policy. In other words, the terms of the contract should spell out whether there will be a "roll-out" (transfer to the employee) or a "roll-in" (transfer to the employer) of the policy.[10]

- Split-dollar agreements must include certain provisions to comply with ERISA rules.[11] The document must name a fiduciary and plan administrator, contain a claims procedure, include a process for review in the event that a claim is wholly or partially denied, provide for funding and the basis of payments and benefits, and contain amendment provisions. (In most cases the document should allow the employer to make amendments at any time or the parties involved to do so from time to time and should specify that the agreement is binding upon the parties to it, their successors, assigns, and representatives).
- In certain situations, additional documentation (other than the split-dollar agreement) may be required by the insurer.[12]
- Some insurers have developed collateral-assignment or endorsement forms for split-dollar arrangements. The provisions of the split-dollar agreement must conform to any assignment forms offered by the insurer.

Where Can I Find Out More?

- HS 331 Planning for Business Owners and Professionals. The American College.
- *Tax Planning with Life Insurance*, Financial Professional's Edition. RIA Group. Phone (800) 950-1210.
- *Tools & Techniques of Life Insurance Planning*. National Underwriter Company. Phone (800) 543-0874.

---

9. Generally, either party may terminate the arrangement by giving written notice to the other. However, for estate planning purposes, the employer's right to terminate the agreement could be a *de facto* ability to access the cash value, such that the proceeds could be includible in the insured employee's gross estate if he or she is a majority shareholder.
10. For more detail, see "Termination of Split-dollar Arrangements," Leimberg, "Split Dollar, the Bifurcated Peso: Split, Rip, or Tear?" published by Matthew Bender as part of the proceedings of the 31st Philip E. Heckerling Institute on Estate Planning
11. There are exceptions under which ERISA does not apply: when the insured employee owns (alone or with his or her spouse) 100 percent of the corporation, and he or she is the only participant in the plan.
12. The insurer may take the position that since it is not a party to the split-dollar arrangement, it is inappropriate for it to accept the agreement for documentation and administrative purposes.

- Stephan R. Leimberg. "Split Dollar, the Bifurcated Peso: Split, Rip, or Tear?" published by Matthew Bender as part of the proceedings of the 31st Philip E. Heckerling Institute on Estate Planning.

Rules for Use of Insurer's One-Year Term Rates Have Tightened

What Was the Situation Before?

Prior cases and rulings have helped us understand how far the IRS was willing to allow taxpayers to go—and how far the Service itself would go in holding to the precise letter of the law.

What Is the Nature of the Change?

A number of recent cases and rulings have shown that the IRS will strictly construe the rules pertaining to the insured's privilege of using yearly renewable term (YRT) rates when reporting the taxable economic benefit under a split-dollar plan.

When an employee is provided life insurance by an employer through a split-dollar arrangement, according to Rev. Rul. 64-328, the insured employee is deemed to have received reportable income by virtue of the employer's premium payment under the economic benefit theory. (Note that before 1964, under Rev. Rul. 55-713, premium payments by an employer on a policy for the benefit of an employee were considered to be interest-free loans, and not taxable.[13] But the IRS changed its position in Rev. Rul. 64-328 and held that the employee was taxable each year for the life insurance protection received as a result of the employer's premium payment.)

---

13. A split-dollar agreement between an employer and an employee entered into on or before November 13, 1964, is not subject to the economic benefit theory, and the employee's insurance coverage is income tax free. *Bagley vs. United States,* 348 F.Supp. 418 (D. Minn. 1972). Rev. Rul. 64-328, 1964-2, CB 11. However, if a "significant change" is made to the plan, it may cause the arrangement to be considered a new plan, and thus become subject to taxation under the economic benefit theory. *Sercl vs. United States,* 684 F.2d 597 (8th Cir. 1982), rev'g and remanding 538 F. Supp. 460 (D.S.D 1981); and Ltr. Rul. 7832012.

    Current split-dollar arrangements are not considered to be interest-free loans but rather as an employee benefit under which the covered employee must realize taxable income each year. Even if the arrangement is technically a "collateralized" loan from an employer to an employee, and even though an interest-free loan now generates taxable income to the employee under IRC Sec. 7872, the IRS is still adhering to the economic benefit theory of Rev. Ruls. 64-328 and 66-110.

According to Rev. Rul. 64-328, the amount of the reportable ordinary income is equal to the one-year term insurance benefit received by the insured. This amount is based on the "net amount at risk," that is, the "pure death benefit" payable to the employee's beneficiary, which is then multiplied by the applicable rate under the PS 58 table,[14] and then offset by any premium payment provided by the employee.[15]

The 1964 ruling anticipated other design variations and stated that the same income tax result (that is, income taxation of the employee based on the pure insurance payable to his or her named beneficiary) would occur regardless of the form (for example, collateral-assignment or endorsement method) in which the transaction was cast if it resulted in a similar benefit to the employee.[16]

Rev. Rul. 66-110, 1966-1 CB 12 expanded on the 1964 ruling by addressing the taxation of dividends, additional benefits, and the use of the insurer's annual renewable term rates in lieu of the PS 58 rates. According to the 1966 ruling, based on the concept that employer dollars are generating policy values, dividends used for the benefit of the employee are taxable and currently reportable as ordinary income.[17] For instance, when income is paid to the employee in cash or used to purchase one-year term insurance payable to the employee's beneficiary, the actual amount of the dividend is includible in the employee's income. This ruling also states that if an employer provides benefits in addition to the "net amount at risk," those additional benefits are also currently taxable. The most obvious examples are employer-paid waiver of premium, the cost for accidental death benefit, or term riders. The employer-paid premiums would be additional reportable income by the employee—assuming the employee has the right to name his or her beneficiary(ies).

---

14. This is the government's schedule of term insurance rates (also used to compute the reportable economic benefit received when permanent life insurance is purchased inside a qualified plan), which is based on the probability of death. Thus the rates (and therefore reportable income) increase as the insured grows older.
15. This ruling is important because it recognizes a split-dollar arrangement as something other than a loan from the employer to the employee. The employee is not contractually bound to repay the employer from any asset other than the cash values or policy proceeds, so the employer's premium payment is a form of an "investment."
    Although not mentioned in the ruling, if an employer provides benefits other than the "net amount at risk" insurance coverage, those additional benefits are also taxable (presumably measured by the extra premium cost). For example, employer-paid waiver-of-premium, accidental-death benefit, or term riders costs would be reportable by the insured as additional income.
16. See also Rev. Rul. 76-274, 1976-2 CB 278.

This 1966 ruling anticipated that the IRS might not keep its PS 58 rates either current or realistic and provided that in calculating the economic benefit cost, the employee may use either the PS 58 rates or the insurer's yearly renewable term rates, if lower. In fact, the insurer's YRT rates are almost always significantly lower than the government's PS 58 table rates. But Rev. Rul. 66-110 required that certain tests must be met for an insured to use the substituted lower rates.

Recent cases have focused on these anti-abuse rules:

- The substituted rates must be initial issue rates of the insurer. This rule has been interpreted to mean that the rates must be issued by the same insurer as that of the policy subject to the split-dollar arrangement, and that rates of the insurer's subsidiary or affiliates cannot be used.
- The one-year term policy must be sold on an individual policy basis. This eliminates the use of the insurer's one-year term rates available only under its dividend options.
- The rates must be annually renewable term rates. So rates of a limited (such as a 5-year) renewable term contract will not be allowed.
- The rates must be available to all standard risks. This rule has been interpreted as meaning that the contract must be issued without any distinction based on health condition, smoking status, or other underwriting criterion.
- The type of individual contract being sold by the insurer in question must be available in all policy sizes. For example, rates available only in high face amount policies cannot be used—for instance, if the contract could only be purchased in amounts of $1 million or more.[18]
- The rates in question must be "published." "Published" implies that the rates have been made known officially to the insurer's licensed agents, brokers, and employees.

When a split-dollar arrangement is between an employer and a third-party owner (such as a spouse, an adult child, or an irrevocable life insurance trust), the insured employee (and not the third-party owner) is subject to income tax on the value of the economic benefit.[19]

---

18. See the favorable result in *Healy vs. United States,* 843 F.Supp. 562 (D.C.S.D. 1994) and S. Simmons' discussion of this case in *Tax Notes,* vol. 62, no. 11, March 14, 1994, p. 1445. See also PLR 8547006 and PLR 9452004, in which the IRS ruled against the taxpayers.
19. Rev. Rul. 78-420, 1978-2 CB 67 (situation 2); Ltr. Rul. 8003094. But see Rev. Rul. 79-50, 1979-1 CB 138, which involved a corporation and a nonemployee shareholder. In this situation, the value of the insurance protection was treated as a dividend to the shareholder under IRC Sec. 301(C).

If a life insurance policy on a third-party nonemployee (such as an employee's spouse) is subject to a split-dollar arrangement between a corporate employer and an employee policyowner, the economic benefit is attributable to the employee.[20]

Taxation of a survivorship (second-to-die) policy is not specifically covered in any IRS rulings. When both insureds are alive, the calculation of the economic benefit is (probably) based on the so-called PS 38 rates instead of the PS 58 rates.[21] These rates are much lower than the individual PS 58 rates, because they are based on the probability that both insureds would die within a 12-month period. After the first death of the joint insureds,[22] while there is no authority on point, if one of the insureds under a survivorship or second-to-die policy dies, the PS 58 rate (or the insurer's single-life individual annual renewable term rate, if lower) probably should be used in calculating the economic benefit.

---

20. See Rev. Rul. 78-420, 1978-2 CB 67, TAM 7832012, and *Sercl vs. United States,* 684 F.2d 597 (8th Cir. 1982). The same result occurs when the policy is used to fund a cross-purchase buy-sell arrangement. The shareholder-employee who owns the policy on his or her coshareholder's life will be taxed on the economic benefit—because he or she is relieved of the obligation of having to pay the entire premium.
21. Although technically there are no PS 38 rates or PS 38 Table, there is a U.S. Life Table 38 based on a 1938 CSO (Commissioner's Standard Ordinary) Table. U. S. Life Table is a mortality table, and it is the basis for interpolation commonly referred to as the PS 38 rates. This mortality table was used by the IRS actuary Norman Greenberg (in response to a request from Morton Greenberg, Counsel and Director of Advanced Underwriting, Manufacturer's Life) in converting individual PS 58 rates to what is now known as the PS 38 rates (but should technically be referred to as the "Survivorship PS 58 Rates").

    While there are no published rulings or cases providing guidance in the area, the prevailing (and accepted) practice is to use the PS 38 rates and the rules outlined in the "Greenberg-to-Greenberg" letter in computing the economic benefit measurement of a survivorship-type policy subject to a split-dollar plan. PLR 9709027 seems to sanction the use of U.S. Life Table 38 (which is often called PS 38). It should be noted that the survivorship computation is not based on the "joint equal age" of the insureds, but on the age of each of the insureds.
22. It is probably best to plan on rolling out the policy after the first insured dies. The substantially increased cash values in the policy after that event would help the new sole insured carry the policy. (Some authorities suggest a provision that automatically terminates the split-dollar agreement—prior to the first death.) At roll-out, if there is a transfer for value and the partnership exception to that tax trap is used, must both insureds be partners?

"Rated" insureds— individuals who must pay an additional premium beyond the standard because of health, occupation, or avocation—present a very special tax planning opportunity. Regardless of whether the insured is in the preferred, standard, or rated class, the reportable economic benefit is unaffected. In other words, the reportable economic benefit under split-dollar is the same for all risk classifications. An insured employee who is highly rated can (and must) use the same PS 58 rate (or the insurer's alternate one-year renewable term rates) in calculating the economic benefit as that of a preferred or standard risk insured of the same age. This circumstance creates a highly favorable tax result where the insured is for any reason classified by the insurer in a category that results in a higher-than-standard premium.

When premiums on a policy are no longer payable by either party (such as when the policy is paid up, or premiums have vanished), the employee continues to incur income taxation on the annual economic benefit received by virtue of his or her employer's outlay—as long as the split-dollar agreement is in effect.[23] Likewise, if the policy is owned by a third party such as a spouse or an irrevocable trust, the constructive gift continues to be made by the insured employee each year to the third party in the same amount and at the same time as the reportable economic benefit.

Where Can I Find Out More?

- HS 331 Planning for Business Owners and Professionals. The American College.
- *Tax Planning with Life Insurance*, Financial Professional's Edition. RIA Group. Phone (800) 950-1210.
- *Tools & Techniques of Life Insurance Planning*. National Underwriter Company. Phone (800) 543-0874.
- Stephan R. Leimberg. "Split Dollar, the Bifurcated Peso: Split, Rip, or Tear?" published by Matthew Bender as part of the proceedings of the 31st Philip E. Heckerling Institute on Estate Planning.

---

23. Rev. Rul. 64-328 contains an example of a policy on an abbreviated premium payment basis (ten-pay). The ruling concluded that even after the premium payment period ended, the economic benefit to the covered employee continued. Some commentators have suggested that the employee should give the employer a promissory note payable at death. Even assuming the employer would or properly could accept such a long-term note as payment for its interest in the policy, the impact of below-market or interest-free loan rules should be considered. IRC Sec. 7872.

Sec. 83 Has Been Applied to Equity Split-Dollar

What Was the Situation Before?

Although a few highly respected authorities had stated that the employee's cash value build-up in an employer-sponsored equity split-dollar plan would result in current income tax, most attorneys and CPAs have either not believed that would occur, were silent, or ignored the problem.

What Is the Nature of the Change?

Equity split-dollar is essentially an arrangement in which the agreement limits the employer's interest in the policy cash value and death proceeds to an amount equal to its premium contributions. Thus the balance of the cash value inures to or is controlled by the employee. The employee accumulates equity in the policy as the cash values exceed the amount repayable to the employer.

Why provide an employee with equity (aside from the obvious shift of wealth)? The answer is that split-dollar is a time-limited solution: At some point there must be a financing mechanism for the insured or other third-party owner to buy out the employer and pay premiums. Equity split-dollar was designed from inception to provide the employee or third-party policyowner with sufficient cash to finance the termination of the split-dollar arrangement. Cash to repay the employer comes from the policy itself. At the point where there's enough cash in the cash value of the contract, the employee or third-party owner can use the policy's equity to buy out the employer and continue the policy.

Equity split-dollar is typically established by using the collateral-assignment method.[24] Under this ownership method, the employee is the original applicant and owner of the policy and then makes a collateral-assignment of the contract to protect the interest of the employer. If anything, the employee contributes an amount equal to the economic benefit cost. The employer contributes the balance. In many cases there is an "employer-pay-all" arrangement, in which the employee makes no contribution. The net result is that the employee has very little (if any) out-of-pocket outlay and yet reaps

---

24. A split-ownership or sole-ownership method may also be used. The endorsement method is not used because the employer is the owner of the policy and the employee generally has no rights to the cash value. (Under certain endorsement split-dollar plans, the employee may have some rights to the cash value—for example, if the employer's interest is limited to the lesser of its premium payments or the cash value—but such designs are exceptions rather than the norm.)

the equity— the benefit of any increase in the cash value over and above the employer's interest in the policy.[25]

Although there is no good reason (and never was) why the basic rules regarding the income taxation of an equity split-dollar plan should be ignored or differ from other split-dollar plans, there have been many issues that remain unsettled.[26] The key issue is the taxation of the equity build-up that inures for the benefit of, and/or is controlled by, the employee (or a third-party owner). The pivotal questions are as follows:

- "Is the equity currently taxable to the insured or third-party policyowner?"
- "If the equity is currently taxable, to what extent?"
- "When, if at all, does the employee's or third party's equity become taxable?"
- "What, if any, basis does the employee receive if taxed on the equity build-up?"
- "Can the employer take a tax deduction for amounts the employee is taxable on and, if so, to what extent and when?"

Commentators on both sides of the issue continue to advance their theories (and counterarguments) regarding the taxation of the equity. The three most frequently presented theories are based on Code Secs. 61, 83, and 72 and are discussed below in detail.

Code Sec. 61 defines gross income as "all income from whatever source derived." If it is not elsewhere specifically excluded or the tax is not specifically deferred, it is both includible and currently reportable. Sec. 61

---

25. For purposes of this discussion, the term *equity* or *equity build-up* refers to any increase in the policy cash value that is in excess of the employer's share of the cash value under the split-dollar plan, and *not* the cash value increase (that is, the inside build-up) of a policy.

26. In spite of the unresolved issues, this concept has gained so much popularity—due to the benefit of the equity inuring to, or controlled by the employee (or a third-party owner)—that a significant number, if not most, current collateral-assignment split-dollar plans, were being structured under the equity approach prior to TAM 9604001.

    Some tax authorities have expressed their concerns with respect to the widespread disregard for the potential income tax fallout in the event that the IRS were to look closely at nontraditional split-dollar plans in general and equity split-dollar plans in particular. For example, see Connolly, "Split-Dollar Reckoning in the Offing?" *National Underwriter,* August 8, 1975, p. 7; Raby, "Split-Dollar Life Insurance," *Tax Notes,* August 24, 1995; and W. Patrick Cunningham, "The Taxation of Equity Split-Dollar Plans," *Journal of the American Society of CLU & ChFC,* Vol. LI, No. 1, January 1997, p. 67.

encompasses the concept of constructive receipt, which holds that income does not have to be actually received before it must be includible in income—if nothing stands between the taxpayer and the incomeand the taxpayer can get it when he or she wants it.

Sec. 61 also is the father of the economic benefit or cash equivalency theory: namely, that any measurable economic or financial benefit conferred upon an employee as compensation, whatever the form or mode, is currently includible in the recipient's income.

When applied to equity split-dollar, Code Sec. 61 implies that the equity build-up in excess of (and attributable to) employer-paid premiums is the equivalent of compensation and should be included in the employee's gross income as it accrues (absent—or at the point where there is no longer—a substantial risk of forfeiture). The authority for that statement rests in Rev. Rul. 64-328, which states that the employer owns the cash value interest, which provides an economic benefit to the employee even if the arrangement is cast in the form of a collateral-assignment. So even if the employee or third party is the legal contract owner from inception, in the classic split-dollar arrangement, cash values are considered employer money. Under Code Sec. 61 and Rev. Rul. 64-328, the Service could argue that the earnings on the portion of the cash value owned by the employer are, in an equity split-dollar arrangement, property that is transferred to the employee and taxable under Sec. 83.

Rev. Rul. 66-110, another of the key split-dollar rulings, is also based on Code Sec. 61. Rev. Rul. 66-110 states specifically that "additional benefits," meaning any other benefits received by the employee besides the term coverage, are currently taxable, presumably because other benefits were also generated by employer cash values. This is an argument the IRS could still use to tax an employee's year-by-year employer-paid enhancement in wealth.

The counterpoints to this Sec. 61 theory are these claims: First, Rev. Rul. 66-110 merely amplified Rev. Rul. 64-328 by addressing the taxation of incidental benefits costs for waiver-of-premium benefits, accidental-death benefits, and so on. So it should have no application to the income tax treatment of equity.[27] Second, Rev. Rul. 64-328 more directly addressed the

---

27. Cash value increases are arguably not "incidental benefits" under the policy, but rather are an integral part of the basic policy element that provides the underlying death benefit of a life insurance policy. Proponents of this position argue that "the theoretical basis for the rule announced in Rev. Rul. 64-328 (as explained in General Counsel Memorandum 32941, November 20, 1964) does not allow for the taxation of equity cash value which makes up part of the insured's share of the death benefit on any basis other than under the economic benefit formula. To do so amounts to the unauthorized taxation of cash value inside build-up." They argue that "Code sections enacted after Rev. Rul. 64-328 was

taxation of the basic elements of a life insurance policy subject to a split-dollar arrangement. Thus taxation should be based on this ruling.[28]

Code Sec. 83 is a very broadly drafted Code section that provides rules for the taxation of property transferred to a "service provider"[29] in connection with the performance of past, future, or current services. The regulations under Sec. 61 provide that Sec. 83 applies to all compensatory transfers of property made after June 30, 1969. The presumption is that every transfer of property arising out of a direct employment relationship is compensatory. If services are performed generating a transfer of property, the cause and effect triggers Sec. 83. There need not be a direct quid pro quo. The burden of proof rests on the taxpayer. The services in question can be past, present, or future.

"Property" is broadly defined under Sec. 83 to include both real and personal property. But the term "property" excludes money—or an unfunded and unsecured promise to pay money or property in the future. Money is excluded because transfers of money are already encompassed in Code Sec. 61(a)(1), which provides for taxation of compensation for services. So reference in Sec. 83 to transfers of money for services would be redundant. The exclusion of the later is to protect nonqualified deferred compensation, which is already governed by the interplay of Secs. 61 and 451.

Sec. 83 is very specific with respect to what it calls the receipt of a "beneficial interest" in assets transferred or set aside beyond the claims of the transferor's creditors. Money is included in the definition of a beneficial interest. So if a service provider receives as a quid pro quo of services a vested beneficial interest in property—including money—that income is currently reportable, that is, it's both realized and recognized. The only thing that would

---

    issued—such as Sec. 83 (transfer of property) and Sec. 7872 (below market loans)—don't apply to split-dollar arrangements, and if they did, would not apply in the way suggested by TAM 9604001." See Report by Association of Advanced Life Underwriters to members, November 1996.

28. In Rev. Rul. 64-328, the IRS conclusion seems to add weight to the argument for nontaxation of the "equity" because the policy at issue actually developed cash value in excess of the amount to which the employer was entitled. The ruling states that " . . . the employer is entitled to receive, out of the proceeds of the policy, an amount equal to the cash surrender value, or at least a sufficient part thereof to equal the funds it has provided for premium payments." This statement seems to indicate the recognition by the IRS of the equity build-up in the policy. See Brody, "Using Split-Dollar Life Insurance," *Trusts & Estates,* June 1990, p. 65; Brody and Althauser, "An Update on Business Split-Dollar Insurance," *Trusts & Estates,* April 1994, p. 10.

29. Note that the scope of Code Sec. 83 goes beyond employer-employee relationships and could apply between a corporation and its nonemployee director or independent contractor.

defer immediate taxation is if the assets or funds involved were not irrevocably set aside from the claims of the transferor's creditors. Sec. 83 is therefore a codification of the economic benefit doctrine: Once an asset is nonforfeitable by a service provider and set apart from the transferor's creditors, it is Sec. 83 property and currently taxable.

What of the requirement that there must in fact be a "transfer"? Sec. 83 Regulations[30] define the term "transfer" as a transaction in which a person acquires a beneficial ownership in property. A transfer of property does not require a physical handing over of an asset or a traceable paper trail. The key questions are, "Did the service provider receive absolute ownership rights this year that he or she didn't have in a prior year?" and "Because of services performed, did the service provider become richer?" If so, there has been a transfer. The amount that is taxable is the excess of the value received over the value of what has been paid.

The recipient's basis in Sec. 83 property is the amount paid, that is, the value of any money or property he or she paid for the transfer plus any amounts upon which the service provider has paid tax in a prior year— the amount included in gross income.

Sec. 83(b) allows the service provider to elect to accelerate the taxable event to the date of the transfer. This action closes the transaction as to that transfer. The employee is treated as owner of that property from then on. Any subsequent appreciation of the subject of that transaction is not considered compensation but, rather, growth in the service provider's investment.

If Sec. 83 applies and causes a service provider to be currently subject to income tax, the employer may receive a corresponding deduction. Sec. 83(h) controls the allowability, amount, and timing of that deduction. The party to whom services are provided receives a deduction equal to the amount included in the service provider's income. The amount of that deduction is based on Sec. 162 or 212 rules. So the deduction is limited to the extent that the payment is reasonable.

Sec. 83 performs three major functions. It determines

- whether the service provider is taxable
- when that income is reportable
- how much is taxable

That service provider is generally taxed on the value of such property at the time of its receipt. An exception under Sec. 83 delays that taxation if the recipient's interest in the property is subject to a substantial risk of forfeiture. In such a case, tax does not occur until and unless the risk of forfeiture is removed. When the property is substantially vested, that is, when the recipient

---

30. Reg. Sec. 1.83-3(a)(1).

can take the property and run without fear of losing it, in that tax year he or she must report the entire value of the property at that time (reduced by any amount he or she paid for the property or previously reported as income).

How does Sec. 83 relate to equity type split-dollar agreements? As noted, Sec. 83 deals with property transferred in connection with the performance of services.[31] Application of the pertinent parts of Sec. 83 means that the employee would be taxable each year when and to the extent that there is an increase in his or her equity, or entirely on the amount of the equity when the split-dollar is terminated and the policy is rolled out to him or her. The taxation of the equity occurs when the employee's rights to the cash value are no longer subject to a "substantial risk of forfeiture," or when the employee can freely transfer his or her interest to a third party (without any risk of forfeiture).[32] Therefore the employee is subject to taxation on the increase in his or her equity at the crossover point where the policy cash values exceed the amount repayable to the employer and the service provider begins to accumulate equity.

To the great surprise of many practitioners, this application of Sec. 83 to split-dollar is not new. In two private letter rulings, the IRS used this theory to tax the employees when the employers released their interests and rolled out the policies to the employees (albeit under some atypical fact situations).[33]

Some commentators have countered the IRS holdings in the above letter rulings by pointing out that under a collateral-assignment split-dollar plan, the employee owns the policy from its inception. Therefore, they argue, Sec. 83 is not applicable since neither the policy nor the cash value increase is being transferred from the employer to the employee. They point out that the employee owned the policy from inception and has not received from the employer property that was not already owned. Instead, they insist, the principles under Rev. Rul. 64-328 should apply.[34] In support of their position,

---

31. In order for personal property to be considered property for purposes of Sec. 83, it must be "funded" or "secured," that is, there must be no further action required by the employer for the income to be distributed or distributable to the employee. So the employee must have a nonforfeitable economic or financial benefit that is no longer subject to the rights of general creditors of the employer. See *Minor v. U.S.*, 772 F.2d 1472 (9th Cir. 1985) and *Childs v. Comm'r*, __F.3d.__ (11th Cir. 6/11/96), aff'g 103 T.C. 634 (1994). See also Chasman, "Life Insurance: A Sophisticated Estate and Financial Planning Tool," University of Miami 22nd Institute. on Estate Planning, Chapter 4 (1988).
32. IRC Sec. 83(a), and Treas. Reg. 1.83-3(e).
33. See PLR 7916029 and PLR 8310027.
34. But it might be argued that the above-mentioned private letter rulings are more on point although (technically), a private letter ruling (unlike a revenue ruling) lacks any precedential authority and is applicable only to the taxpayer who requested it. Additionally, they were issued many years

they have suggested that the employer's premium payment is like a loan to the employee. That is, if an employer were to lend funds to an employee to acquire an asset (for example, a residence), the appreciation in the asset would not be taxed until the asset was sold or disposed of. In other words, the employer has merely advanced money (premium) to the employee to purchase a life insurance policy; therefore any cash value increases are not "employer-provided," but result from an investment by the employee of the employer advances in an appreciating asset.[35] Further, they contend that even though split-dollar plans are not considered interest-free loans for tax purposes, the analogy should still pertain to the appreciation element (that is, the cash value increases) of the policy.[36]

Sec. 72 pertains to the timing of income. It states when the lifetime benefits received from a life insurance contract become taxable. This Code section governs the income taxation of all amounts received under life insurance contracts as "living" benefits, that is, cash values, dividends, premium returns, and proceeds paid during the insured's lifetime. Under Sec. 72(e)(2)(B) (Amounts Not Received As Annuities),[37] only amounts in excess

---

after Rev. Rul. 64-328; in fact, Sec. 83 was enacted 5 years after the 1964 ruling. Therefore the IRS could not possibly have considered or addressed the impact of Sec. 83 on equity split-dollar plans when it issued its "landmark" revenue ruling. But see discussion on TAM 9604001, *infra*.

35. It appears that this position for nontaxability can be sustained only if the money advanced by the employer is considered either as compensation (which is taxable to the employee as current income), or as a loan (which is subject to a reasonable interest rate; Sec. 7872 taxation will apply if it is below market or interest-free). But when the employer's advances (premium payments) are subject to a split-dollar arrangement (regardless of whether it is based on a collateral-assignment, split-ownership or sole-ownership method), part or all of the policy cash value increase each year is attributable to the funds provided by the employer. Therefore the employee should be taxable when he or she is enriched (in terms of the equity) by the employer's premium payments.

36. See Brody, *supra*. But this argument begs the following question: Are the employer-paid premiums interest-free loans (as opposed to being treated as advances subject to the economic benefit theory for taxation under Rev. Rul. 64-328)? If so, IRC Sec. 7872 should apply. In other words, should the employee be able to "pick and choose" among the various theories of taxation for the one(s) that would bolster (and successfully defend) his or her position for nontaxation?

37. "Amounts not received as an annuity" include policy dividends, lump-sum cash settlements of cash surrender values, cash withdrawals, and amounts received upon a partial surrender of the contract. This "invisible shield" applies only "if no provision of this subtitle (other than this subsection) applies with respect to such amount." See Sec.

of the consideration (premiums) paid by the policyowner for the life insurance contract would be taxed—and then only when actually received (that is, via surrender, withdrawal, or an MEC loan).

By inference, we assume—because it would be unfair to tax the same income twice—that income earned inside the policy is not taxable to the policyowner during the build-up phase. Therefore, if this section is applied to equity split-dollar arrangements, any cash value (while it is accruing) should not be subject to income taxation until such time when the employee is in receipt of the cash value, and then only to the extent of the excess cash value over his or her cost basis. It is like a magic glass: income earned on the capital inside the glass will not be taxed until the owner of the glass decides to take a drink. Code Sec. 72 is therefore the law used to justify the tax deferral on the income accruing to the policyowner's benefit inside a life insurance contract. But Sec. 72 does not specifically state that the internal build-up in a life insurance policy grows tax free. Furthermore, Sec. 72 expressly provides that Sec. 72 applies only if some other Code section does not.

This Sec. 72 theory for nontaxation is often used to refute the taxation theories based on Secs. 61 and 83 of the Code. Under standard principles of statutory construction, more specific statutory provisions take precedence over more general provisions when they overlap. Consequently it has been argued that Sec. 72 should take precedence over Secs. 61 and 83, and that any excess cash value should not be taxed until there is a surrender, a withdrawal, or an MEC loan.[38]

The major flaw in this line of argument is that the issue at hand is not the taxation of the "inside build-up" of a policy, or the "excess cash value" over the policyowner's basis to which Sec. 72 is definitely applicable. Indeed, at no point does the IRS in the TAM discussed below refute the concept of the tax-deferred build-up—once money is inside the policy. The issue revolves around the taxability of the property transferred by the employer to the service

---

72(e)(1)(A)(ii). Readers of this Code section will not find a clear statement of protection of the tax-free build-up of cash values. Instead, Sec. 72 provides, in essence, that "this is when we are going to tax," and only by assuming that the same income will not be taxed twice can the reader come to the conclusion that Congress meant to provide a tax-deferred "shell" around the policy until it is "cracked open" at surrender.

38. In contrast to Sec. 72, Secs. 61 and 83 contain much more general provisions with respect to income taxation. The former refers to all types of "restricted property," while the latter encompasses income "from whatever source derived." See Leimberg, et. al., *The Federal Income Tax Law,* RIA Group. Note also that the Sec. 72(e)(1) statement that provides that the internal build-up (income) is taxable when the policyowner surrenders the policy or takes an annuity applies only "if no other provision applies."

provider (in most cases, the employee) as compensation for past, present, or future services. The measure of that property's worth is the equity, that is, the excess amount of cash value over and above the employer's interest under the split-dollar plan, which inures to, or is controlled by, the employee.

But the point of taxation is at the pour-over of employer dollars under its (split-dollar) contract with the service provider. This is an event that occurs before—and independent of—the internal build-up of cash values within the life insurance contract. For this reason, Sec. 72 has no application to income tax aspects of equity split-dollar arrangements. Instead, the taxation of the employee should be in accordance with the principles set forth in Rev. Ruls. 64-328 and 66-110. Therefore, the equity is taxable to the employee under Secs. 61 and 83.[39] Stated in another way, since all cash values are originally generated by employer dollars, "any portion of the employer's cash value set aside for the benefit of the employee and beyond control of the employer may be an additional economic benefit taxable currently to the employee if his or her right is not subject to a substantial risk of forfeiture."[40]

Technical Advice Memorandum 9604001 brought all these theories to a boil. Here, the IRS clearly stated its position on the taxation of equity split-dollar arrangements.[41] It concluded that the insured employee must recognize

---

39. Substantial risk of forfeiture must be determined under a "facts and circumstances" test: Will the restriction impose a real risk such that the employee will forfeit the property if the specified condition (for example, the performance of services) are not met?

40. Chasman, "Life Insurance: A Sophisticated Estate and Financial Planning Tool," University of Miami 22nd Institute on Estate Planning, Chapter 22 (1988). Mr. Chasman feels that double counting of the employee's contributions as basis against both the net amount at risk and the cash value would be allowed.

41. The TAM (dated September 8, 1995) was issued by the IRS National Office. Since its release (on January 26, 1996), it has generated much concern in the insurance world. The American Council of Life Insurance (ACLI) and the Association for Advanced Life Underwriting (AALU) have submitted their comments on the findings in the TAM to the IRS and Treasury, and requested that the TAM be withdrawn or modified.

    To date, there has been no clarification or guidance from the IRS or the Treasury and there is certainly no consensus among industry experts and tax and legal professionals in their analysis of the TAM's impact on split-dollar plans. For example, see W. Raby, "Split-Dollar Life Insurance," *Tax Notes,* August 28, 1995, p. 1099; "Equity Split-Dollar TAM Has Insurers Shifting Gears," *National Underwriter,* (September 2, 1996, p. 7; D. West, "How to Deal with the Split-Dollar TAM," *National Underwriter,* October 21, 1996, p. 7; H. Saks, "New TAM Will Likely Lead to Changes in Tax Results of Collateral Assignment Split Dollar," *Estate Planning,* Vol. 23, No. 4, May 1996, p. 186; H. Chasman, "Equity Split-Dollar Life Insurance under Attack by IRS," *Journal of the*

income each year to the extent of the cost of the insurance protection, plus any equity—that is, the cash value in excess of the amount needed to repay the employer for its premium payments. As a corollary, it also ruled that when the employee was taxable, there would be a gift in a corresponding amount to a third-party policyowner.

According to the facts of the ruling, A was the chairman, CEO and a controlling (51 percent) shareholder of a holding company that owned 98 percent of a subsidiary (S). S purchased two $500,000 policies with single premium payments on A's life. The policies were issued to a trust (T) established by A as owner. T entered into an arrangement with S to split the policy benefits, and collaterally assigned the policies to S for T's obligation to repay S for its premium payments in the event of A's death, termination of A's employment, termination of the split-dollar arrangement, or surrender of the policy(ies). T would continue as owner and beneficiary of each policy (subject to the collateral assignee interest held by S), and hold all incidents of ownership. The policy dividends would be used to purchase paid-up additional insurance on A's life. Furthermore, T would be able to borrow from the policies or pledge or assign either policy, but only to the extent that the cash value of a policy exceeded the premium amount paid by S.

Relying on Rev. Rul. 64-328 as amplified by Rev. Rul. 66-110, the IRS determined that the amount included in income by A each year the split-dollar arrangement remained effective was "the annual value of the benefit" received. This amount would be equal to the one-year term cost of the insurance protection.[42] However, the IRS did not stop there. Pursuant to Rev. Rul. 66-110, any additional benefits (such as policy dividends or additional term insurance) also would be includible in A's gross income.

The IRS applied Code Secs. 61 and 83 in determining the value of the benefit received by A. First, Rev. Rul. 64-328 clearly indicates that the one-year term insurance provided to A would be includible as current income under Sec. 61. Second, the IRS applied Sec. 451(a) of the Code, which requires that income be included in the tax year compensation or that other income is received by a taxpayer unless it should be reported in a different year because of the accounting method used. It determined that A would have to recognize taxable income each year. Third, Sec. 83 was applied to the facts described in the TAM, and the IRS ruled that until the cash values in the

---

American Society of CLU & ChFC, November 1996, p. 76; and A. Kraus, "Is There Life after Equity Split Dollar?" *Personal Financial Planning,* September/October 1996, p. 56.

42. The IRS considered the single premium payment aspect of this arrangement to be an "insignificant" difference from the typical collateral-assignment split-dollar plans. It noted that A was "in the same position as the employee in the revenue ruling [64-328] after the employer has paid the premiums on the policy for a period of 3 years."

policies exceed the amounts that must be repaid to S, the only taxable income to A was the term insurance cost (based on the PS 58 table or the insurer's one-year term rates, if lower).

However, A would report income "... in later years under Sec. 83 to the extent that the cash surrender values of the policies exceed the premiums paid by S[ubsidiary] because this is the amount that is returnable to S[ubsidiary]." The IRS explained its position for the application of Sec. 83 in its analysis by stating that the provisions of Sec. 83 and Sec. 61 do not alter the application of the holdings of Rev. Ruls. 64-328 and 66-110, since Sec. 83 was enacted after the revenue rulings were published.[43]

Assuming a worst-case situation, full enforcement of the TAM, aside from the additional reportable income and the consequent income tax, some taxpayers would be exposed to interest charges on unpaid taxes. There is the potential for penalties charged both to clients and practitioners if the income wasn't reported and there is no substantial authority for not reporting equity build-ups. Practitioners should be asking the following questions:

"What 1099 obligation does a corporation have?"

- "What about withholding and social security taxes?"
- "How should we advise the business?"

---

43. This position is consistent with the IRS findings in PLRs 7916029 and 8310027. The same rationale, enrichment of an employee through employer dollars equals current taxation even though the enrichment was in the form of increased life insurance policy cash values and the policyowner did not surrender the policy, was reflected in *Young et ux. et al. vs Comm'r.*, T. C. Memo. 1995-379. See also "Corporation's Payment on Shareholder's Life Insurance Policies Were Constructive Dividends," *The Insurance Tax Review*, September 1995, p. 1359

   In the *Young* case, the Tax Court held that the employee-shareholder, covered under a plan that enriched him through employer-provided premiums, received currently taxable income. Specifically, the Court noted that each time the employer made a premium payment, the insured employee-shareholder was enriched (through the increasing policy cash value), while the employer received no economic return whatsoever on its outlay. Although this case technically did not involve a split-dollar arrangement, there is no reason to preclude the application of the rationale to such arrangements. Incidentally, Judge Armen in *Young* concluded that if an employer has no right to recover any part of the payments it made and no claim to any part of the policy proceeds, the arrangement cannot be classified as a split-dollar insurance arrangement (and therefore in *Young* the entire amount of premium payment constituted a dividend to the insured shareholder-employees).

Most authorities feel that the income tax cost of the TAM is a price that business clients would be willing to pay. But the gift and generation-skipping tax cost could be prohibitive. Prior to the TAM, the economic benefit of the term insurance was thought by many to be the only measure of the gift and GST transfer of equity split dollar. That made incredible gift and GST leverage possible. For example, compare the gift tax cost of making a $1million gift in the form of cash, stocks, bonds, or real estate to making a gift of the same value, $1million of life insurance, in the form of sufficient premiums for the donee to purchase and maintain a $1 million policy on the donor's life. For an annual outlay of slightly more than $15,000 a year, a 40-year-old could support that much permanent coverage.

On a split-dollared basis, the gift tax cost is not based on $1 million or even $15,000 a year. It's based only on the economic benefit reportable as income by the employee. In a worst-case scenario, in this example, that translates to less than $5,000 a year, an amount that could be totally sheltered by the donor's annual exclusion. On a joint-and-survivor policy, the gift or GST transfer tax is even less. The point is that split-dollar provides tremendous gift and GST leverage!

After the TAM, the gift tax cost may be the term cost plus all or a portion of the build-up in the policyowner's wealth. That would diminish the gift and GST tax leverage and turn an incredible technique into something that's just really good or perhaps only adequate compared to alternatives. To repeat, the biggest loss if the TAM is both correct and enforced is that the same degree of "tax-leveraged trust packing" possible in the past may not be possible in the future. The ability to shift wealth essentially at both an economic and tax discount will still be possible but not to the same extent.

Those who argue against a Sec. 83 imposition claim the following:

The holding of TAM 9604001 misapplies Sec. 83 and announces a result inconsistent with the Service's own published rulings regarding split-dollar life insurance. To leave the TAM unmodified would continue uncertainty in an area that is much used by taxpayers in the expectation of continued constancy by the Service with regard to these agreements. It is unfair to insinuate change in established and long standing administrative precedent by a technical advice memorandum that is flawed in its analysis and disregards substantial judicial precedent in the area of constructive receipt. The *Cohen*[44] and *Nesbitt*[45] cases hold that with regard to the taxation of cash build-up within a whole life policy, the owner realizes income not by the mere existence of an option to receive cash but only if the owner acts to

---

44. *Cohen v. Comm'r,* 39 T.C. 1055 (1963).
45. *Nesbitt v. Comm'r,* 43 T. C. 629 (1965).

reduce the option to cash and extracts it from the policy. So long as the cash remains in the policy, it will not be taxed.[46]

The major arguments made by those who feel the TAM is wrong can be broken down into

1. The "technical imperfection" argument
2. The "unfair-to-tax" argument
3. The "Sec. 72 applies" argument
4. The "there-was-no-transfer" ("the employee always owned the contract") argument.

The "Technical Imperfection" Argument

According to the technical imperfection (and "lower-level author") argument, sloppy or less-than-comprehensive drafting—or the fact that a senior-level official did not write it—flaws the TAM. Typical comments include, "To be charitable, TAM was not really well thought out or well written." "It lacked detailed analysis." "It goes on for pages but the key statement, equity is subject to income tax under Sec. 83 of the Code, is contained in one sentence." "There is no amplification, no rationale why Sec. 83 is applied." "There's no mention of any of the counterarguments against income taxation, particularly Sec. 72." "The reliance upon Sec. 83 is puzzling, probably misplaced" "The TAM was written by a lower-level author and not coordinated with higher-ups or other ruling branches of the IRS, particularly those who have been prominent in previous informal split-dollar discussions in the past." "The discussion of equity in the TAM was premature; there was no equity in the policy in question. During the tax years subject to audit, the policy illustration showed no equity." "The TAM doesn't discuss the impact of the employee's basis in the computation of taxation of future equity."

These are all accurate statements but true as they may be, none of these criticisms is very persuasive in countering the appropriateness of Sec. 83. Certainly, none rises to the level of a defensible legal argument. The key issue is, "Is the central conclusion of the TAM—that Sec. 83 applies to make the service provider currently taxable on income when equity begins to accrue—correct?"

The "Unfair to Tax" Argument

According to the "unfair to tax" argument, the IRS should be estopped from using Sec. 83 because for a long time they've allowed taxpayers to their detriment to rely on IRS inaction. Typical quotes include "In spite of over 30 years of change in life insurance product marketing, the IRS has been silent

---

46. J. Jensen, "Equity Split-Dollar Life Insurance and TAM 9604001," Outline presented to The American College of Trust and Estate Council, Fall Meeting, Cincinnati, Ohio, Oct. 12, 1996.

with respect to equity split-dollar. It would be inherently unfair, a breach of taxpayer rights, to retroactively go back on that position now. Many taxpayers have relied on the rulings and the IRS's silence," and "The TAM ignores the marketplace impact. It was issued without any consideration of the impact upon literally tens of thousands of equity split-dollar arrangements that are in existence."

It is true that political and economic considerations often influence tax law decisions. And tax law should be fair. Planning is impossible when tax law made today is implemented retroactively. But few true authorities in this area should have been shocked by the holdings of the TAM. One noted attorney said, "Why were they surprised?" This cloud didn't suddenly appear on the horizon. It's been there for years. Sec. 83 has been in place for almost all that time.

Reread Rev. Ruls. 64-328 and 66-110 and it will be obvious that the IRS didn't suddenly change its position. Rev. Rul. 64-328 doesn't have to be refuted by the IRS for the TAM's principles to apply. To the contrary, the IRS could easily refer back to it to argue that it is the employer's cash value that generates the employee's or third party's equity. The question that should be asked is, "Who was the real source of the cash in the cash value—and why was that cash paid over to the employee-insured?"

Rev. Rul. 66-110 noted that the employee is subject to tax—not only on the value of the term insurance but also on any additional benefit received in the split-dollar arrangement. Equity the insured has this year that she didn't have last year is certainly "another benefit." If it isn't another benefit, what is it? Sec. 61 applies even if for some reason Sec. 83 did not.

The "Sec. 72 (It Can't Be Taxed until Taken)" Argument

If Sec. 72 applies, as a natural corollary, Sec. 83 cannot apply. Proponents have stated, "The TAM completely ignores the previous government policy against taxing cash value of insurance policies. The original revenue ruling in this area, 64-328, did not raise the issue of taxing equity although it could have done so." "The General Counsel's memorandum (GCM 32941) said that it was against Congressional policy to ever tax the income build-up in the cash value of insurance" "The TAM essentially would tax life insurance cash value build-up currently and that would definitely appear to be a contradiction to Sec. 72."

Code Sec. 72 expressly provides that it applies only if no other Code section does. But the zealous defense of Sec. 72 is irrelevant. It misses the point. *The taxable event doesn't occur inside the life insurance contract. Nor does the TAM adversely affect Code Sec. 72's protection in any way. The IRS didn't think it needed to attack the tax-deferred build-up because the taxable event occurred outside the policy itself and before the protection of Sec. 72 takes over.* What is being taxed is the economic value the service provider receives each year as compensation. It is the benefit under the contract with the employer and not the life insurance contract or its cash values that is being taxed!

The protection of Code Sec. 72 remains intact—even if the TAM is correct and enforced. The IRS is arguing that the taxable event is the pouring of employer dollars into the magic glass owned by the service provider. When Congress wrote Sec. 72 into the Code, it presumed that the money inside a life insurance policy would be the employee's aftertax money. Basis, the employee's investment, should be recovered income tax free. Sec. 72 enables a deferral of taxation on income earned by what was assumed to be employee aftertax investment. Sec. 72 didn't anticipate—and certainly doesn't directly or even indirectly permit—the tax-free or tax-deferred receipt of compensatory income from an employer.

The "There Was No Transfer" Critique

"If you look at the typical collateral-assignment equity split-dollar arrangement, there would appear to be no transfer from the employer to the employee of the life insurance or of the entire insurance policy. On the surface the employee or his trust already owns everything in the policy and any future growth of equity." "The employee has owned the policy all along so nothing can be transferred. There is no transfer when equity appears. (Yet the same person stated, "If this were an endorsement arrangement—with the employer owning the policy, then equity ownership accruing to the employee or third party may very well be a transfer)."

According to this "there-was-no-transfer" argument, the form of the transaction governs. Presumably, a court would be asked to believe that since the insured or third party technically purchased the policy and was its original owner, all the future growth in that policy, no matter what the real source, should be assumed to be the employee's aftertax dollars. Would these same authorities argue that if an insured opened a bank account in her name and her employer put cash into the account as compensation for services she rendered, she had no reportable income? It's hard to believe a court could or would be so persuaded.

The "employee-always-owned-the-contract" argument is a mere extension of the "there-was-no-transfer" argument. "Under equity split-dollar, the employee or third party is almost always substantially vested from inception. So if Sec. 83 does apply, it would be a one-time event and have to be at the date of transfer. That would be either the date the split-dollar agreement was signed or the date the first equity appears. From then on, everything has already been transferred. The employee or third party would own the property. All future equity build-up should be protected from income taxation under Sec. 72."

Again, this "employee-owned-the-contract-from-inception" argument is an example of form without substance. Assume an individual fills out the form to purchase a mutual fund and that person's employer makes the one and only payment to that fund this year on his behalf. How can it be argued that all future payments made by the employer to that mutual fund account were the employee's ab initio? All future build-up inside that mutual fund account has already been transferred merely because the employee was always the owner of the account? Would a court believe that, next year, when the employer compensates that employee—by putting more money in the fund—the employee has no reportable income in that year?

There are many unresolved issues with respect to equity split-dollar agreements. One such issue is the impact of the TAM, if enforced, on types of split-dollar other than equity arrangements. In the TAM, the IRS focused on an arrangement established by a collateral-assignment method under which the policyowner (a trust) risked no forfeiture of its rights to the "equity."[47] The findings in the TAM should not have any impact on split-dollar plans structured under either the endorsement method[48] or the collateral-assignment method if the employee has no equityposition in the policy cash value.[49]

Basis is another issue the TAM did not address. Does the employee's contribution for the term insurance protection (for example, in a "PS 58 offset" plan) provide a tax basis in the policy that would reduce (or offset) the income taxation to him or her on the equityin the policy? Arguably, the IRS will not allow the employee contribution to serve double duty (that is, to offset the economic benefit cost and provide a tax basis for the employee in the policy).[50]

---

47. It should be repeated that a TAM is a private ruling such that, technically, it does not apply to other taxpayers. In spite of the fact that there are issues that remain unresolved (or not even raised) by the TAM, some tax authorities are of the opinion that the IRS conclusions are basically sound and should be sustainable if tested. Others feel that the IRS will withdraw or modify the TAM.
48. Obviously, if the policy is transferred from the employer to the employee, the employee will have to recognize income (either as compensation or dividend) in an amount equal to the policy cash value at the time of the transfer. See PLRs 7916029 and 8310027.
49. It is very likely that reverse split-dollar arrangements will be affected by the essential principles of this TAM. See discussion on "Reverse Split Dollar," *infra*.
50. The rationale is based on the fact that the economic benefit cost that is taxable to the employee is solely a measure of the term insurance; is "exhausted" in providing that protection; and has no connection with the tax basis or the policy cash value increase. See PLR 7916029. An employee's contribution under a split-dollar arrangement cannot be counted twice. But see PLR 8310027, in which the employee's taxable

A related issue to the question regarding the employee's tax basis is, "How should the amount of equity taxable to him or her be determined?" "Should it be all or a portion of the annual increases?" First, if the employee is taxed on the "equity," should the increase attributable to that portion of the equity be taxable in subsequent years? In other words, does the employee have a tax basis as a result of his or her recognition of income (to the extent of the yearly equity build-up)? It is likely that the employee will be credited with basis to the extent of taxability. Second, how is the taxable income determined if the employee contributes an amount in excess of the PS 58 cost?

Yet another unanswered issue is the extent, if any, to which an employer who is deemed to have made a Sec. 83 transfer of property under an equity split-dollar arrangement will be allowed a deduction. If the employee is taxed under Sec. 83, then the employer should be entitled to a corresponding deduction.[51] It should be noted that any amount in excess of the employer's premium payments recovered by the employer at the termination of the split-dollar arrangement would be includible as gain from appreciated property in its gross income. This would give the employer the potential for many years of deductions, albeit offset by taxable income at the conclusion of the arrangement but at a time largely in the employer's control (or in a year that the employer could predict and plan for). At worst, the net result would be a wash for the employer—unless the taxable income to the employee is deemed unreasonable or treated as dividend (if the employee is a shareholder).

Counsel should be prepared to assist clients who have established equity split-dollar plans in assessing the potential tax consequences based on the results of the TAM. Obviously, clients should seek advice from tax counsel before they enter into split-dollar arrangements (including equity type plans). The potential impact of the TAM should be considered with respect to their prospective split-dollar plans.[52] The following are some suggestions for counsel's consideration. They are not all inclusive and should not be viewed as such:

- Consider a worst-case scenario. A TAM is not law, nor does it have any precedential authority. But this TAM does reflect the IRS position

---

income was offset by his "PS 58 cost" contributions. Is the secret "allocation"?
51. Treas. Reg. 1.83-6.
52. When the TAM was first released, most (if not all) of the insurers that support their sales force in marketing the split-dollar concept made their producers aware of the TAM. Many required (and still require) that the producers notify their clients who have existing split-dollar arrangements of the TAM, and fully disclose the TAM to clients who contemplate establishing such plans. Some companies have halted sales of equity split-dollar until the issue is resolved.

with respect to equity split-dollar plans. From a conservative viewpoint, the consequences of the "worst-case" scenario should be considered. If the results in the TAM were to be applied to other taxpayers, the IRS probably could make retroactive adjustments to the insured employee's income and gift (if any) tax returns for 3 years. But if the employee made gifts within the annual exclusion or, for some other reason, never filed a gift tax return, all tax years in which the employee was deemed to have received income and made gifts under an equity split-dollar arrangement are vulnerable to adjustments.

- Consider maintaining any current equity split-dollar arrangement. It is important to remember that this TAM increases the income recognition of the insured employee only after the policy cash value exceeds the amount that is repayable to the employer. Until that point, the employee will not be subject to any more income taxation than he or she is currently incurring under the split-dollar plan. Therefore some commentators advise against acting too hastily in abandoning existing equity split-dollar plans or even forgoing the implementation of new plans.

- Many clients may be better off by waiting for further guidance or clarification from the IRS before taking any action. This wait-and-see approach allows some time for the client's advisers to carefully assess the additional tax exposure the client may incur and to weigh them against the benefits of the arrangement. For example, the additional tax might be a fair price to pay for the leveraged estate-tax-free death benefit payable to an irrevocable trust.

- Obviously, the viability of this approach is dependent upon the terms of the trust, the number of beneficiaries, and the availability of the client's unified credit. It might be preferable for the insured employee to recognize income on a yearly basis and be treated as making annual gifts (perhaps totally or partially sheltered by the annual exclusion) to a trust than to include in income a much larger amount later on at the termination of the split-dollar arrangement, when a large amount would simultaneously become subject to both a large income tax and significantly higher gift taxes (or might exhaust his or her unified credit). There is also a possibility that an employer may assist an employee in continuing the split-dollar arrangement. The employer might be willing to award a bonus to the employee to cover a part or all of the additional tax liability. This would basically remove any additional tax burden placed on the employee.

- Consider an amendment of the existing agreement. If the client's objective is to delay taxation on the annual cash value increases, the agreement could be amended so that policy cash values would be subject to "substantial risks of forfeiture" under certain conditions[53] or

---

53. For instance, the agreement could provide a 100 percent forfeiture to the employer of all cash values should the employee voluntarily terminate employment within one year of the first year in which cash values

the policyowner would agree not to have any access to the cash value except at the termination of the agreement or the employer would own all of the cash value. It is not likely that the IRS will give credibility to a substantial risk of forfeiture imposed on the sole or majority shareholder of a closely-held corporation. But if the employer were willing to forgo cash values and a nonmajority shareholder or nonowner employee was realistically willing to risk forfeiture, an effective "condition subsequent" might serve to delay and defer the taxability of the employee. Counsel would have to determine if any of these amendments would eliminate or delay recognition of income under the TAM. Counsel must further ascertain the appropriateness of such a course of action for the client's particular situation.

- Terminate the arrangement. The arrangement could be terminated at the point when the cash value is equal to the employer's total premium contribution. Then, another type of plan, such as a bonus of the annual premium (a so-called Sec. 162 bonus plan), could be established in place of the split-dollar arrangement. Some split-dollar arrangements may be created with a "self-destruct" mechanism that terminates the agreement at the crossover point where cash values exceed premiums.
- Consider alternative planning techniques. Depending upon the employee's relationship to the employer and his or her objectives, other executive perks could provide equally valuable benefits. These include such arrangements as executive bonus plans, endorsement nonequity split-dollar, nonqualified deferred compensation (NQDC), or death-benefit-only (DBO) plans.
- New types of policies may be designed to push back the date of reckoning. Insurers will probably develop or utilize new types of policies that delay cash value build-up. Even if the employee becomes taxable on equity, the number of years before that equity is taxable will be greater. Thus the wealth-shifting annual exclusion/unified credit leverage of split-dollar life insurance will be extended.
- Consider a rollout to the employee. This presents the problem of how the employee will reimburse the employer for its outlay. Policy loans are the obvious answer but may result in both a lower death benefit and annual nondeductible interest charges in addition to premium payments that would then be the total burden of the policyowner. A partial surrender of the policy by the employee following the rollout can trigger unexpected income taxation; if the partial surrender results

---

exceeded premiums. In the second year, the forfeiture would drop to 90 percent, and so on until the employee was completely vested after 10 years. This technique should result in only 10 percent of the available cash values being taxable to the employee each year. See H. Chasman, "Equity Split-Dollar Life Insurance under Attack by IRS," *Journal of the American Society of CLU & ChFC,* November 1996, p. 82.

in a reduction of the death benefit and the policy was issued after 1984, Code Sec. 7702(f)(7) may trigger ordinary income taxation.[54]
- Consider financing the purchase through interest-free or low-interest loans. The use of an actual cash loan by the employer subject to a personal demand loan signed by the employee would provide cash to finance life insurance. This alternative route should remove the transaction from the ambit of split-dollar rules and into Code Sec. 7872 but would result in annually increasing imputed income to the employee in an amount equal to the interest that should have been paid but was not. That imputed interest would be nondeductible. The employer would be deemed to receive imputed interest income from the employee—which fortunately would be offset by its compensation deduction in the same amount. The employee, as sole owner of the policy, would be able to pay off the employer from the policy cash values, most likely through a combination of policy withdrawals (up to but not in excess of basis) and policy loans. This approach in certain circumstances might be more advantageous than current taxation of the employee on the equity.

Tax preparers must be concerned that the position they take has "substantial authority." Substantial authority is a degree of confidence in a tax position so high that if the taxpayer is wrong and his or her position is not sustained, the Internal Revenue Service cannot impose negligence penalties. If a position is taken that does not have substantial authority and that position is not sustained, negligence penalties could apply to both the taxpayer and tax preparer. Substantial authority is the minimum comfort level that most advisers adhere to. Whether or not there is a substantial authority position is a qualitative rather than quantitative issue. It is even possible to have substantial authority for directly conflicting positions—such as those on either side of this discussion.

"Safety" lies in a position more likely than not to be sustained on its merits. This is generally understood to be present where there is a greater than 50 percent chance of prevailing. Another standard used balances the weight of authorities for one position against the weight of authorities that support the opposite stance. Here, it's not necessary to prove a 50 percent preponderance. In either case a mistake results in an underreporting of income or gift—and may result in an understatement of tax. In determining whether or not there is substantial authority one considers the Code, regulations, published rulings, PLRs, TAMs, and, in the appropriate situation, a well-constructed argument.

---

54. The severity of the problem will depend on how long the policy has been in force prior to the partial surrender. If the policy has not been in force for 15 years, the insured may be taxable even if the amount he or she withdraws does not exceed basis (net premiums paid). The solution may be a combination of partial surrender (up to the point of taxable gain) and policy loan.

Even a well-reasoned construction of the applicable Code section is placed on the scales when the Code or lower levels of authority are silent on a given point.[55]

Some authorities believe there is clearly substantial authority for not reporting the employee's buildup of equity currently—enough, in their words, and probably in most cases, to get to take a more-likely-than-not tax position. That is what a number of major accounting firms are advising their field offices in terms of how they prepare client returns and how they should advise their clients. This is also the position of counsel to the Association of Advanced Life Underwriters (AALU), who, in a letter to the president of that organization, stated, "There is no question of appropriate compliance with substantial authority." "Subject to special facts of which we are unaware, we conclude not only that federal income and gift tax returns may take the position that cash surrender value accretion does not, in an equity split-dollar arrangement of the type considered in TAM 9604001, generate taxable income or gift as there articulated, but that such position is the better one to be so reflected on such tax returns."

Is it worthwhile to create an equity split-dollar arrangement even if the TAM is both correct and enforced? A fully informed sophisticated client may look at the downsides and feel, with a proper exit strategy in place, that equity split-dollar, perhaps for some predetermined limited period of time, remains quite viable. Certainly, it can still deliver incredible leverage up to the point where it becomes taxable and even past that point for a number of years! To reiterate, at worst, all is not lost; just not quite as good as it was.

Where Can I Find Out More?

- HS 331 Planning for Business Owners and Professionals. The American College.
- *Tax Planning with Life Insurance*, Financial Professional's Edition. RIA Group. Phone (800) 950-1210.
- *Tools & Techniques of Life Insurance Planning*. National Underwriter Company. Phone (800) 543-0874.
- Stephan R. Leimberg. "Split Dollar, the Bifurcated Peso: Split, Rip, or Tear?" published by Matthew Bender as part of the proceedings of the 31st Philip E. Heckerling Institute on Estate Planning.

The Impact of Sec. 83 on Reverse Split-Dollar

What Was the Situation before the Change?

As is the case with split-dollar arrangments, many proponents of reverse split-dollar have either ignored basic tax principles; believe that in spite of

---

55. Reg. Sec. 1.6662-4(d).

employer enrichment of the employee, no current income is reportable; or proceed with the premise that their clients will not be "caught because of IRS ignorance or inattention."

What Is the Nature of the Change?

Reverse split-dollar (RSD) reverses the classic roles of split-dollar ownership. In the classic reverse split-dollar arrangement, the employee (policyowner) either endorses or assigns a portion of the death benefit to the employer. The two parties share the premium cost and death benefit of a cash value policy.[56] Upon termination of the agreement, usually when the employee retires, the employer's share of the death benefit reverts to the employee, who regains full control of the policy.

The RSD agreement usually provides that during the term of the agreement, the employer will pay for the cost of the insurance it "receives." Typically, the amount is equal to the "net amount at risk" or the pure term protection under the policy. However, its share of the death benefit may also be a stated amount, or based on a schedule (either increasing or decreasing) agreed to by the parties. The employer's premium share is typically based on the higher of the government's PS 58 rates or the one-year renewable term rates charged by the insurer. The insured employee pays the balance.[57]

Unfortunately, RSD is too often marketed solely as a tax-savings device, while the nontax and economic reasons for and implications of such plans are often ignored or understated. For example, the employer usually has various needs for life insurance on the employee during his or her working years, such as coverage for key person indemnification, credit obligation, and so forth. Or, it may combine the key person coverage with a death-benefit-only (DBO) plan to provide the covered employee's survivors with a substantial benefit.[58] On the other hand, the employee may need permanent insurance protection after retirement, or supplemental retirement income.

---

56. In the rare instance where the employee is not a shareholder or officer of the corporate employer, the endorsement method could violate the transfer-for-value rule—since there is a transfer of an interest in the policy to a nonexempt party in return for its premium payment (that is, a valuable consideration). Therefore the assignment method is preferable. See discussions on "Transfer for value concerns" in this section, *supra*; and "Additional documentation," *supra*.
57. Since the insurers' term rates are substantially lower than the PS 58 rates, this means that the employer is invariably overpaying for the term insurance coverage. Proponents of this approach use as their authority for the employer's payment of the higher PS 58 rates or the insurer's standard year term costs the word "may" in the classic split-dollar ruling, 66-110, allowing a taxpayer-employee to select the lower of the two.
58. See Leimberg and McFadden, *Tools and Techniques of Employee Benefit and Retirement Planning* (800-543-0874).

If properly structured, an RSD plan may be an excellent solution to meeting the planning objectives of both the employer and the employee. But many RSD plans are established not merely to fairly share in the costs and benefits of the underlying life insurance policy, but with the major intent to benefit one party (the insured employee in the classic case) through the overly generous premium payments of another party (typically the employer) and escape income taxation on that generosity.

There have been no rulings or guidance from the IRS directly relating to the income tax issues associated with RSD.[59] The main issue concerns the taxation of the employee on the cash values the employee gains each year under the arrangement. Commentators on both sides of the issue have advanced arguments in support of their respective positions. The most prevalent alternative income tax treatments of RSD are presented in the following discussion:[60]

Proponents for no current taxation of the employee base their arguments for nontaxation on Rev. Ruls. 64-328 and 66-110, as well as IRC Sec. 72. They claim RSD is similar to a classic arrangement, except the positions of the parties are reversed. They point to Rev. Rul. 64-328, which provides that the same tax treatment will apply " . . . if the transaction is cast in some other form resulting in a similar benefit to the employee." Therefore it could be argued that since the employer realized no income in the ruling, the employee should not realize income when their roles are reversed in an RSD plan.[61]

They also argue that the employee is entitled to the cash value of the contract. According to these proponents, in Rev. Rul. 64-328, the IRS stated that "the employer provides the funds representing the investment element in the life insurance contract, which would, in an arm's-length transaction, entitle it to the earnings accruing to that element." It also ruled that the employee in the split-dollar arrangement is provided an economic benefit that is measured by "the annual premium cost he should bear and of which he is relieved." When the employer in an RSD arrangement pays the annual cost for its term protection, and the employee pays the balance of the premium, each party's share of the premium is the same as that which he, she, or it would pay under an arm's-length transaction (as described in the ruling). Therefore the employee should be entitled to the "investment element in the life insurance contract" plus the "earnings accruing to that element."

The pivotal arguement made by proponents of the RSD arrangement is that the IRS has specifically sanctioned the use of its admittedly high PS 58 rates. The employer in an RSD pays the term insurance cost based on the government's PS 58 rates, which are generally much higher than the insurer's

---

59. But see "Equity Split Dollar," *supra*.
60. See "Reverse Split-dollar Arrangement," *supra*.
61. If the roles of the parties are reversed, would the IRS conclusions in its revenue rulings still apply to RSD?

one-year term rates. Rev. Rul. 66-110 provides that it is permissible to use either the PS 58 rates or the insurer's term rates. Therefore the use of the PS 58 rates is appropriate. Furthermore, it is argued that the PS 58 rates have long been used to value the insurance protection furnished to a taxpayer.[62]

Coupling these arguments with the same type of Sec. 72 argument used in equity split-dollar plans, RSD proponents claim that since the employee owns the policy, taxation is governed by IRC Sec. 72. The policyowner is taxable only when he or she accesses the policy cash value—and then only to the extent of the gain in excess of his or her cost basis.[63]

The better position is that taxation of the employee should be based on the fact situation of the RSD plan and its actual economic results. RSD is not similar to a classic arrangement since, by definition and plan design, RSD is not among the types of transactions on which the IRS based its findings in the above-mentioned revenue rulings, and the employee does not receive the same or a similar benefit. The employee in a classic split-dollar arrangement receives a large amount of death benefit at a relatively low cost, whereas, the employee in a typical RSD arrangement is provided with cash value in addition to a portion of the death benefit. In fact, the employee in Rev. Rul. 64-328 received term insurance coverage only and had no rights to the policy cash value. Furthermore, some of the RSD plans being marketed do not resemble the arrangement in the ruling. So the ruling should provide no comfort or protection.

Proponents of RSD, relying on Rev. Rul. 66-110, claim that the employer's term cost in an RSD plan should be based on the *higher* of the PS 58 rates or the insurer's one-year renewable term rates.[64] It may be argued that the purpose for using the higher rates is to (artificially) reduce the employee's premium share—especially when the majority of the death benefit is payable to the employer.

In Rev. Rul. 64-328, the employer contributed an amount equal to the cash value increase each year (not to exceed the total premium), and was entitled to the policy cash value; the balance was paid by the employee. However, in a typical RSD, the employer pays the term cost and the balance is paid by the employee. If the argument that the parties' roles are merely reversed is carried

---

62. Rev. Rul. 64-328.
63. IRC Sec. 72(e)(5). What is the employee's cost basis? Should it be his or her share of the premium, or the entire amount (including the employer's contribution)? If the employee has contributed neither actual dollars nor dollars paid for by the employer but taxed to the employee, there is no justification for giving the employee basis.
64. The operative word in the ruling is "may." As a practical matter, would the employer intentionally overpay for its term insurance coverage if it is solely for key person protection?

to its logical conclusion, shouldn't the employee's share be equal to the cash value increase if he or she were to be entitled to the cash value?[65]

It is logical that the IRS will conclude that the true measure of the term cost to the employer should be based on the *lower* (instead of the higher) of the PS 58 rates or the insurer's term rates. Consequently the difference between the term cost (based on the insurer's rates) and the employer's actual premium outlay would be currently taxed to the employee under IRC Sec. 61 as "income from whatever source derived."[66] The employee should be taxed if his or her share of the cash value is disproportionate to his or her premium payment. IRC Sec. 83 may be applied—that is, the cash value to which the employee is entitled is directly attributable to the employer's contribution.[67] Should the employee's rights or access to the cash value be restricted, he or she would be taxable when such restrictions are terminated.[68]

TAM 9604001 does not specifically address a reverse split-dollar arrangement. However, it is likely that the IRS would take the position that the cash value inuring for the benefit of, or controlled by the employee (but generated by employer-provided premium) would be taxable to the employee (absent a substantial risk of forfeiture). The rationale is that the employee's (unrestricted) equity position in the policy is a result of the employer's premium payments.

Where Can I Find Out More?

- HS 331 Planning for Business Owners and Professionals. The American College.
- *Tax Planning with Life Insurance*, Financial Professional's Edition. RIA Group. Phone (800) 950-1210.
- *Tools & Techniques of Life Insurance Planning*. National Underwriter Company. Phone (800) 543-0874.
- Stephan R. Leimberg. "Split Dollar, the Bifurcated Peso: Split, Rip, or Tear?" published by Matthew Bender as part of the proceedings of the 31st Philip E. Heckerling Institute on Estate Planning.

---

65. Some RSD plan designs require the employer to pay a levelized premium (that is, an average of its total costs) over the term of the agreement. As a result, the employee has little (if any) premium outlay. It is difficult for tax purposes to justify the employer's payments in excess of the economic benefit costs—especially in the early years.
66. See *supra*.
67. See *Young et ux. et a. vs. Comm'r., supra.*
68. PLRs 7916029 and 8310027.

More Favorable Controlling and Sole Shareholder Estate Tax Implications

What Was the Situation Before?

Many authorities had said it was possible to remove a split-dollared contract on the life of a majority or controlling shareholder from the insured's gross estate. But the IRS had not issued any favorable rulings to this effect.

What Is the Nature of the Change?

Generally, the same rules for estate taxation of life insurance apply to split-dollar policies so that Code Secs. 2042 and 2035 are the central focus for estate tax avoidance. Under IRC Sec. 2042, the insured's gross estate includes the amount of proceeds paid to, or for the benefit of, the insured's estate. Proceeds are also included in the gross estate if the amount is payable to a designated beneficiary and the insured holds one or more incidents of ownership at the time of death.[69]

In a split-dollar arrangement, the employee is deemed to have an incident of ownership—such as the right to name or change a beneficiary or to cancel the policy—even if such a right is exercisable only in conjunction with the employer. Thus all the proceeds payable under a life insurance policy should generally be includible in the insured employee's gross estate.[70]

An insured may remove the proceeds from his or her estate by transferring the policy ownership to a third party (for example, an adult child or an irrevocable trust). Likewise, an employee (who is not a shareholder, or who owns less than 51 percent of the corporation) in a split-dollar plan may also assign all of his or her interest under the arrangement.[71] However, the insured must survive for 3 years after he or she has divested all incidents of

---

69. See D. Jansen, "Sec. 2042—From Soup to Nuts," University of Miami 29th Institute on Estate Planning, Chapter 14 (1995).
70. Treas. Reg. 20.2042-1(c)(2). See "Endorsement Split Dollar," under section II, *supra*. Also, this is a major disadvantage of a reverse split-dollar arrangement; the insured employee's policy ownership will cause the proceeds to be includible in his or her gross estate even though the bulk of the proceeds is payable to the employer. Therefore the estate could be saddled with a tax liability without sufficient liquidity to pay for it (unless there is an offsetting deduction). See discussion on "Reverse Split Dollar," *supra*.
71. See discussion on "Controlling Shareholder Situation" in Leimberg, "Split Dollar, the Bifurcated Peso: Split, Rip, or Tear?" published by Matthew Bender as part of the proceedings of the 31st Philip E. Heckerling Institute on Estate Planning for different treatment when the insured is a majority or controlling shareholder.

ownership; otherwise the entire proceeds will be includible in his or her gross estate for federal estate tax purposes.[72]

Proceeds may not generate a tax in the insured's estate if the total taxable estate (including the life insurance proceeds) does not exceed the insured's available unified credit,[73] the proceeds are payable to a spouse who is a U.S. citizen or to certain trusts for a surviving spouse in a manner qualifying for the estate tax marital deduction, or the proceeds are payable to a qualified charity in a manner qualifying for the estate tax charitable deduction.

If an insured employee owns 51 percent or more of a closely held corporation (at or within 3 years of death),[74] he or she is considered a "controlling" shareholder such that the corporation's ownership over a policy will be attributable to him or her under IRC Sec. 2042. To the extent that proceeds of a life insurance policy are payable to a party other than the corporation (or its creditors), the amount is includible in the insured's estate rather than in the value of his or her interest in the corporation.[75]

The IRS ruled on the estate tax inclusion issues in the split-dollar context on a number of occasions. Rev. Rul. 76-274, 1976-2 CB 278 considered three situations involving the insured, his controlled corporation, and a third party. In the first situation, the IRS found that the insured had incidents of ownership, and the employer's rights (including the right to surrender and assign the policy) were of substantial importance and affected the entire policy. Consequently the proceeds were included in the insured's estate. The employer's rights in the second situation were restricted to borrowing against the policy up to the amount of the cash value (not to exceed its premium payments), but it was prohibited from surrendering or assigning the policy (except to the insured). The proceeds were included in the insured's estate because of his direct ownership; but the employer's "restricted" rights were not attributed to him. In the third situation, the employer's rights were the same as in situation two, but the policyowner was a third party. The IRS ruled that the insured held no incidents of ownership either directly or indirectly (held by the employer, but attributed to him). Therefore none of the proceeds was included in his estate.

Rev. Rul. 79-129, 1979-1 CB 306 pertained to a "private" split-dollar arrangement between the insured and a trust that owned the policy. The

---

72. See generally, *Lumpkin vs. Comm'r.*, 474 F.2d, 1092 (5th Cir. 1973), and PLR 9026041.
73. In addition to the life insurance proceeds, any gift tax paid within 3 years of death will be includible in the decedent's estate.
74. See Rev. Rul. 90-21, 1990-9 IRB 13. The IRS based its conclusion not on whether the deceased held more than a 50 percent interest in the corporation at death, but rather on the interest held at *any* time within 3 years of death.
75. Treas. Reg. 20.2042-1(c)(6).

insured had the right to borrow against the cash value to the extent of his premium contribution, and all other ownership rights were retained by the trust. The conclusion reached by the IRS was that the insured's right to borrow was an incident of ownership, which caused the proceeds payable to the trust to be included in his estate.

Rev. Rul. 82-145, 1982-2 CB 213 was used by the IRS to clarify the inconsistency in its findings between the two prior rulings. It noted that the right to obtain loans against the policy is a key incident of ownership (even when it is limited in amount), which would cause the proceeds to be includible in the insured's estate. In essence, it reversed its favorable finding under situation three of the 1976 ruling and attributed the corporation's right to borrow as an incident of ownership to the insured.[76]

It appears that now, with careful planning and proper documentation of the split-dollar arrangement, estate tax exclusion may be achieved.[77] The IRS should not automatically include the split-dollar life insurance proceeds in the insured's estate merely because the insured's controlled corporation is a party to the arrangement. For example, the death benefit from a life insurance policy on a sole shareholder was not includible in his gross estate in a fact pattern similar to a typical collateral-assignment split-dollar arrangement—except the policy was owned by the insured's two adult sons and the repayment to the corporation was not limited to the policy cash value. The sons were personally liable to repay the corporation for its premium contribution. Alternatively, they could surrender the policy to the corporation in discharging their obligation. The IRS held that the corporation did not possess any incidents of ownership. But the IRS indicated that it might have reached a different conclusion had the policy been owned by an irrevocable trust.[78]

PLR 9511046 involved a controlling shareholder situation. Here, the IRS ruled that the proceeds from a survivorship life insurance policy were not includible in the second-to-die insured's estate when the policy was subject to

---

76. See also PLR 9037012. The unfortunate term used in the taxpayer's submission to the IRS for the ruling was that the corporation *"owned"* the cash value.
77. See S. Schlesinger and S. Ball, "Life Insurance: Taxation and Products," 52nd N.Y.U. Institute on Federal Taxation, Chapter 9.
78. The difference could be that in the case of a trust-owned policy, the only resource to the trust for repayment to the corporation would be the policy cash value or death proceeds. Therefore the IRS could argue that there was a "link" between the corporation and the policy—that is, an incident of ownership—which could be attributable to the insured sole shareholder.

    It is interesting to note that the National Office never issued a formal technical advice memorandum on this particular situation. Could it be that it did not want to publish the favorable results that might encourage other taxpayers to use the similar techniques as described in the fact pattern?

a restricted collateral assignment under a split-dollar plan. An irrevocable trust owned a second-to-die policy on Taxpayer (T) and his spouse (S). The trustee was a third party who entered into a split-dollar arrangement with a closely-held corporation of which T and S were shareholders. Neither T nor S had any powers with respect to the trust that would be considered incidents of ownership (as defined by IRC 2042). Both spouses' corporate interests were held in their respective revocable living trust—which upon the grantor's death would become irrevocable and would be for the benefit of the survivor.

The split-dollar agreement provided that the corporation would be required to pay the premiums due (less any amount paid by the trust) on the policy while the arrangement was in effect. It further provided that only the trustee was permitted to obtain loans against the policy or pledge the policy for a loan, and that the corporation was prohibited from borrowing. The trustee retained all ownership rights granted by the policy. Only the trustee could surrender the policy or terminate the agreement. If the policy was surrendered or the agreement was terminated, the corporation had a security interest in the policy cash value in an amount equal to the lesser of its premium payments or the net cash value. Upon the death of the second to die of the insureds, the corporation would receive an amount of the proceeds equal to its total premium contribution. To secure the corporation's interest, the trustee executed a collateral assignment in its favor, but the corporation could not assign its interest to anybody except the trustee (or his nominee).

The IRS conclusion was that since the corporation held no incidents of ownership in the policy or ". . . its proceeds that are paid to the trustee under Sec. 2042," or any *de facto* ability to force the trustee to borrow against the policy cash value, there was no attribution of ownership to the last to die of the insureds—even though the survivor would control the corporation at the time of his or her death. Consequently, the proceeds payable to the trust would not be includible in the gross estate of the last to die of the insureds.[79]

---

79. See also See also PLR 961017, in which a husband and wife created an irrevocable trust for the benefit of the husband's children from a prior marriage. The trustee, a bank, purchased a survivorship policy on the couple's lives and named the trust as beneficiary of the proceeds. An S corporation in which the husband held majority interest agreed to split premium dollars with the trust. The couple—through contributions they made to the trust—were to pay an amount equal to the term insurance cost of the coverage to the corporation. The couple, both shareholders of the corporation, agreed, in the event that they did not make payments directly to the trust, which was to pay the money over to the corporation, to reimburse the corporation personally to the extent that it paid their share of the premium. As an additional assurance, the agreement provides that the corporation can make payments on the insured husband's behalf and charge him with compensation income equal to the couples' share of the premium. As an additional fail-safe, the agreement provides that if neither

So a split-dollar agreement—well drafted and administered—could be a device to avoid estate inclusion in a controlling shareholder situation. The key factor is the restriction placed on the corporation's rights in the policy. To warrant inclusion, the corporation must hold incidents of ownership in the portion of the proceeds payable to a third party. In other words, the Treasury Regulations should be interpreted as meaning what they state: any incidents of ownership held by the corporation as to *that* part of the proceeds (that is, the part not payable to or for the benefit of the corporation) will be attributable to the decedent through his or her stock ownership. If incidents of ownership extend only to the portion of the proceeds held by or payable to the corporation, there should be no inclusion of the amount payable to a third party.[80]

The key to estate tax exclusion success is to specifically prohibit the corporation from borrowing against the policy and limit the corporation's

---

the husband nor wife are employed by the corporation, then they must personally pay their share of the premium. These reimbursement promises were sufficient to prevent a second class of stock under Code Sec. 1361(b)(1)(D). See also PLR 9709027.

The IRS held that the corporation held no incidents of ownership in the policy—and so the majority shareholder held no incidents through his control of the corporation. Nor would the policy proceeds be included in the gross estate of the survivor of the insureds. In arriving at the "no inclusion" result, the IRS noted that the corporation could not assign its interest to anyone other than the trust and could not borrow against the policy or use it as collateral for a loan. Nor could the corporation terminate the agreement unilaterally or cancel or surrender the contract or change the beneficiary. Likewise, in PLR 9651030, the IRS held that the proceeds of collaterally assigned split-dollar policies would not be included in the insured's gross estate. There, an irrevocable trust owned three split-dollared contracts. The IRS again noted that the corporation's sole interest was to recover its outlay (or the policy cash value, if lower) and was expressly prohibited from borrowing against any part of the policies, and that the trust had the sole power to surrender or cancel the policy, change the beneficiary, revoke an assignment, pledge the policy for a loan, or borrow on the policy's cash values. It was important that all those rights were vested solely in the trustee and that the insured could not be appointed trustee.

80. See T. Commito, "Majority Shareholder Estate Taxation and Split-Dollar Plans," 42 *Journal of the American Society of CLU & ChFC* (January 1995); M. Weinberg, "29 Years of Sunshine, Stone Crabs, and Estate Planning Strategies," University of Miami 29th Institute on Estate Planning, Chapter 8 (1995). Although seldom appealing or practical, in some cases a reduction of ownership so that the insured is no longer a controlling shareholder should be considered.

rights to merely the recovery of its premiums from the policy at the insured's death, the surrender of the policy, or the termination of the agreement. A viable alternative is to remove all incidents of ownership from the corporation by securing its interest only by the promise of the third-party owner.[81]

Where Can I Find Out More?

- HS 331 Planning for Business Owners and Professionals. The American College.
- *Tax Planning with Life Insurance*, Financial Professional's Edition. RIA Group. Phone (800) 950-1210.
- *Tools & Techniques of Life Insurance Planning*. National Underwriter Company. Phone (800) 543-0874.
- Stephan R. Leimberg. "Split Dollar, the Bifurcated Peso: Split, Rip, or Tear?" published by Matthew Bender as part of the proceedings of the 31st Philip E. Heckerling Institute on Estate Planning.

More Guidance on the Tax Implications of Private (Family) Split-Dollar

What Was the Situation Before?

Family split-dollar has been used almost since the concept of splitting premium dollars was first conceived. But there has been little formal guidance as to how the IRS would tax the typical intrafamily arrangement.

What Is the Nature of the Change?

Although there is still no formal guidance, recent private rulings give advisers more information on probable IRS positions.

A split-dollar arrangement may be established between family members, between a trust and a family member, or between any two parties who agree to split the costs and benefits of a life insurance policy (assuming there are no prohibitions under either state law or the insurance contract itself).[82] For

---

81. See D. Jansen, "Sec. 2042—From Soup to Nuts," University of Miami 29th Institute on Estate Planning, Chapter 14 (1995). Mr. Jansen discusses "sole-owner" split-dollar arrangement, under which the insurance policy is completely owned by the third party and the corporation has no ownership, endorsement, or collateral-assignment interest in the policy. He points out that the advantage of this approach is that it creates strong arguments against the controlling shareholder estate tax problems but contains the inherent potential disadvantage of an IRS attack that there is a "forgone interest" issue.
82. See G. Slade, "Some Advanced Uses of Life Insurance in Financial and Estate Planning," N.Y.U. 53rd Institute on Federal Taxation (1994), Chapter 18.

example, a father purchases policy on son's life and endorses the right to name the beneficiary(ies) for an amount of the death benefit in excess of the father's premium outlay (or outlay plus a specified rate of interest). The father continues to control the policy cash value. In this case, Father is deemed to be making a gift of the "at risk" portion of the policy. The value of each year's gift should be measured by the PS 58 rates (or the insurer's lower term rates), and then that amount may be offset by the insured's premium contribution.

Is the premium payment by Father a gift or a loan? Some commentators are of the opinion that the insured should have no reportable income from the parent's premium payment—unless Sec. 7872 applies to the transaction. For instance, W purchases a policy on the life of H but immediately transfers the entire "net amount at risk" portion to an irrevocable trust she previously created for her children. She retains the cash value portion of the policy and thus she (and, indirectly, her husband, the insured) has access to those funds for an emergency or opportunity. Under a private (family) split-dollar agreement, the trustee pays the portion of the premium equal to the economic benefit that would have been reportable had the relationship been between an employer and an employee. At the death of the insured, the trustee will receive the death proceeds in excess of an amount equal to the policy's cash value at that time. W will receive any balance, an amount designed to equate to the immediate predeath cash value. H could make gift-tax-free gifts (through the marital deduction) to W, which she could use to pay the one-year term cost portion of the premium. Assuming W in this "direct spousal split-dollar" example is not in any way a beneficiary of the trust, there should be no estate tax inclusion of the trust's assets in her estate. If she is a beneficiary, gifts she makes, directly or indirectly, could be considered contributions to the trust, which in turn would cause her to be treated as a grantor and thus result in estate tax inclusion. The solution is for the insured to make gifts to the trust that are at least sufficient for the trustee to pay its share of the premium.

A drawback of the direct spousal split-dollar arrangement is that the presumably wealthy insured spouse's lifetime access to cash values is dependent on continued marital harmony. Consider a "spousal trust" alternative, the creation of a QTIP trust—an irrevocable trust split-dollar arrangement with the third-party trustee of the QTIP trust authorized to invade principal for the benefit of the spouse. Although not a perfect solution, this method removes policy cash values from the absolute control of the insured's spouse.[83]

In PLR 9636033, the IRS examined a "traditional" split-dollar arrangement between an irrevocable trust created by the insured and his

---

83. See G. Slade, "Some Advanced Uses of Life Insurance in Financial and Estate Planning," N.Y.U. 53rd Institute on Federal Taxation (1994), Chapter 18 for a discussion of the community property implications of this technique and creative solutions to the marital discord potential.

spouse.[84] The insured established an irrevocable trust and contributed cash to it at its inception. The trustee purchased a life insurance policy on the insured-grantor and entered into a collateral-assignment split-dollar arrangement with the grantor's spouse. The parties shared in the premium payment, with the trust paying an amount equal to the cost for term insurance; the spouse paid the balance due from her separate property. If the agreement terminated while the insured was alive, the spouse would receive the net policy cash value; at the insured's death, she would be entitled to an amount of the death benefit equal to the *greater* of the cash value or her total premium outlay.

This technique provides a way for a spouse, as collateral assignee, to access the cash value of a policy owned by the other spouse's irrevocable trust.[85] The issue was whether the premium payments made by the trustee and the spouse resulted in a gift to the trust by either the insured or his spouse.[86] The IRS conclusion was that no gifts were made because there was no employment relationship between the insured and the trust; hence the trustee's premium payments were not compensatory in nature. The insured's initial transfer to the trust was subject to gift tax; however, the insured received nothing of value, compensatory or otherwise, when the trustee made the premium payments. Thus the insured is not deemed to have made a second gift of the premium to the trust. The spouse's consideration for paying a portion of the premium was that she would receive the cash value (or the death benefit in an amount equal to the cash value) under the policy. Since she would be reimbursed for her premium payments, they would not be deemed as gifts to the trust.

In addition, the IRS determined that the portions of the death benefit payable to the trust and the spouse would not be includible in the insured's gross estate since he had no incidents of ownership. The ruling repeated the typical IRS warning that no opinion was expressed as to IRC 7872 below-market interest rate loan issues. It is important to note that in order to achieve this dual favorable transfer tax result, the insured's spouse used her separate funds to pay premiums on the trust-owned property.

---

84. See W. Wagner, "Favorable PLR on Private Split-dollar Arrangement," *National Underwriter Life & Health Edition,* Nov. 4, 1996, p. 8; "Payments under Private Split-Dollar Arrangement Are Not Gifts," *The Insurance Tax Review,* October 1996, p. 849; and "Private Reverse Split-Dollar Agreement Receives Favorable Gift and Estate Tax Ruling," *Tax Management Memorandum,* Vol. 37, No. 21, October 14, 1996, p. 331.
85. "Gift Tax Consequences of Private Split Dollar," *Keeping Current,* American Society of CLU & ChFC, Vol. 27, No. 1, December 1996, p. 53.
86. Even though the IRS applied the principles of Rev. Rul. 64-328 in reaching its favorable conclusion in this private split-dollar arrangement, it is doubtful that the result could be applied to an employment-related equity split-dollar plan such that the insured would not be deemed to make gifts of the equity to a third-party owner. See TAM 9604001, *supra.*

Where Can I Find Out More?

- HS 331 Planning for Business Owners and Professionals. The American College.
- *Tax Planning with Life Insurance*, Financial Professional's Edition. RIA Group. Phone (800) 950-1210.
- *Tools & Techniques of Life Insurance Planning*. National Underwriter Company. Phone (800) 543-0874.
- Stephan R. Leimberg. "Split Dollar, the Bifurcated Peso: Split, Rip, or Tear?" published by Matthew Bender as part of the proceedings of the 31st Philip E. Heckerling Institute on Estate Planning.

S Corporations and Second Class of Stock Issues

What Was the Situation before the Change?

The IRS has always taken a reasonable view of split-dollar as an employee benefit but not a second class of stock.

What Is the Situation after the Change?

It is comforting to taxpayers that the Service has continued this trend.

At first glance, split-dollar financing of life insurance appears inappropriate as a tool for shareholders of S corporations (or other pass-through entities such as partnerships or LLCs) because they are taxed directly and therefore immediately and fully on the corporation's earnings.[87] This could mean "double" taxation for a shareholder in such an arrangement. First, he or she is taxed on the corporate income used to pay the corporation's share of the premium, and second, the insured shareholder will be taxed on the economic benefit value received under the split-dollar plan.

Yet another potential problem is the risk that the value of the arrangement might be considered a second class of stock and terminate the S election. This risk may be overcome with careful drafting.[88] The IRS has privately stated

---

87. Split-dollar arrangements are often established for key employees (nonshareholders) of an S corporation as a fringe benefit.
88. See *Howard Johnson v. Comm'r,* 74 T.C. 1316 (1980) and PLRs 9709027, 9651017, 9318007, 9331009, and 9309046. It is important that the third-party owners be required to reimburse the employer for the economic benefit under the policies—even after premiums end. See PLR 9651017, which held that a collateral-assignment split-dollar agreement between an S corporation and a trust does not result in a second class of stock because it does not alter the shareholders' rights to corporate distributions or liquidation proceeds. There a couple proposed to create an irrevocable trust that would hold second-to-die policies on their lives.

that—under proper circumstances and with careful drafting—a split-dollar arrangement (even when the insured was a shareholder, and thus received a benefit that might not be provided to other shareholders)—would not be considered a "second class of stock" that would trigger a termination of the corporation's S election.[89]

But practitioners are urged to read PLRs 9331009, 9318007, and 9235020 carefully. Note that the agreements in all three of the rulings required employee-shareholder contributions to the premium, as well as reimbursement to the corporation of "any benefit derived from the corporation's outlay." The IRS may not reach the same conclusion in the absence of that language. The results may not be favorable if, in fact, the insureds do not actually reimburse the corporation.

Split-dollar should be considered in an S corporation as an employee benefit for nonshareholder-employees and even for shareholder-employees if gift taxes become a major consideration in their overall estate planning process. For example, if the policy is owned by a third party (for example, an irrevocable trust) for estate planning purposes, a split-dollar arrangement can

---

Once the policies were in force, the corporation would pay all premiums but the couple would contribute to the trust an amount equal to the economic benefit under the policy, which would then be paid over by the trustee to the corporation. If for any reason the corporation didn't receive reimbursement from the trust, the agreement required the husband and wife personally to pay that amount to the corporation or, failing that, the husband, an employee of the corporation, was to be charged with income in the amount of the economic benefit, which would be paid by the corporation on his behalf. The Service held that the shareholders' rights to distribution and liquidation proceeds were not altered by this arrangement. (The IRS also held that since all incidents of ownership were held from the inception of the policy by the trust that the life insurance would be includible in neither insured's estate even though the husband was a controlling shareholder.

89. Read PLRs 9331009, 9318007, and 9235020 carefully. Note that the agreements required employee-shareholder contributions to the premium as well as reimbursement to the corporation of "any benefit derived from the corporation's outlay." Would the IRS still reach the same conclusion in the absence of the unusual language, or if, in fact, the insureds had not actually reimbursed the corporation? Could the IRS have then determined that the insured shareholder indeed received distribution rights that were not given to the other(s) such that the distinction between (or among) them was essentially a second class of stock?

reduce (or eliminate) the amount of the gift tax.[90] The reason is that the gift is based on the economic value (term cost) rather than the full premium. Under this logic, if a third-party owner enters into a split-dollar agreement with the S corporation and the plan is contributory, the insured-grantor employee-shareholder can gift to the trust an amount equal to (or in excess of) the economic benefit value, which the trustee will use to pay for the trust's share of the premium. This amount will most likely be substantially less than the entire premium due on the policy and, as such, should create little or no gift tax (assuming the availability of the annual exclusion and/or unified credit).

Where Can I Find Out More?

- HS 331 Planning for Business Owners and Professionals. The American College.
- *Tax Planning with Life Insurance*, Financial Professional's Edition. RIA Group. Phone (800) 950-1210.
- *Tools & Techniques of Life Insurance Planning*. National Underwriter Company. Phone (800) 543-0874.
- Stephan R. Leimberg. "Split Dollar, the Bifurcated Peso: Split, Rip, or Tear?" published by Matthew Bender as part of the proceedings of the 31st Philip E. Heckerling Institute on Estate Planning.

Partnerships, LLCs, and Split-Dollar Arrangements

What Was the Situation before the Change?

Even though the same income tax issues that pertain to shareholders of S corporations using split-dollar arrangements should also apply to partners in partnerships and members of LLCs, it was uncertain how the IRS would treat split-dollar in such entities.

What Is the Situation after the Change?

Taxpayers have more guidance as to how the IRS will treat partnerships and their partners and LLCs and their members with respect to the income and estate taxation of split-dollar arrangments. Essentially, as is the case with equity split-dollar, the IRS trend is to apply basic tax principles to new situations. Once again, the past provides good guidance as to the future.

For instance, in a private letter ruling,[91] the IRS approved a split-dollar arrangement between a family limited partnership and its general partner—a revocable trust that owned a policy on the life of the grantor/trustee. The trust

---

90. See "Gift Tax Implications" in Leimberg, "Split Dollar, the Bifurcated Peso: Split, Rip, or Tear?" published by Matthew Bender as part of the proceedings of the 31st Philip E. Heckerling Institute on Estate Planning.
91. PLR 9639053.

entered into a split-dollar arrangement with the partnership, under which the trust would be the owner and could exercise all ownership rights, but could not sell, assign, transfer, borrow against the policy cash value, surrender or cancel the policy, change the beneficiary designation, or change the death benefit option without the express written consent of the partnership. The premium on the policy was "split" between the parties. The trust reimbursed to the partnership an amount equal to the term cost of the insurance protection (measured by the insurer's one-year term rates) it received, and the partnership paid the balance. In return for the partnership's premium payments, the trust assigned the policy in its favor. As collateral assignee, the partnership would have the sole right to borrow against the policy. It also would have the right to receive a portion of the death benefit in an amount equal to the *greater* of the premiums paid or the cash surrender value.

The IRS extended the rationale of Rev. Rul. 64-328 (employer/employee arrangement) and Rev. 79-50 (corporation/shareholder plan) to the partnership/ general partner situation, and stated that "[w]hile [the partnership/partner situation] differs from the relationships that were present in Rev. Rul. 64-328 and Rev. Rul. 79-50, the principles of those Rev. Ruls. are applicable." The IRS ruled that, since the trust contributed to the partnership an amount equal to the cost of the term insurance coverage, it would be treated as deriving no economic benefit from the split-dollar arrangement. Therefore the trust (the general partner) would not be deemed to have received a distribution from the partnership when the partnership paid the premiums.

From an estate tax perspective, there is only one private letter ruling and no cases or other direct authorities concerning split-dollar arrangements between a partnership and a third party involving life insurance on a partner's life. The estate tax result turns on whether or not the "partnership entity theory" is strictly applied. If so, even if a partner is a managing or controlling partner, incidents of ownership should not be automatically imputed.[92]

---

92. See PLR 9623024, which held that life insurance proceeds will not automatically be includible in the gross estate of an insured partner. To keep the proceeds out of the insured's estate, this ruling implies that it is important to be sure the proceeds are not subject to the debts or other obligations of the insured's estate, that the policies were not pledged as collateral by the partner, that the deceased partner's estate would include the value of his or her proportionate share of the partnership (which itself received the insurance proceeds), and that the insurance was purchased and held for a partnership purpose. The IRS referred to controlling shareholder regulations for guidance.

Practitioners should assure that the firm has significant business or investment activities apart from and unconnected with the ownership of the life insurance or the IRS may use a "pass-through" or "aggregate" rather than entity level approach, thus viewing proceeds as having been

Where Can I Find Out More?

- HS 331 Planning for Business Owners and Professionals. The American College.
- *Tax Planning with Life Insurance*, Financial Professional's Edition. RIA Group. Phone (800) 950-1210.
- *Tools & Techniques of Life Insurance Planning*. National Underwriter Company. Phone (800) 543-0874.
- Stephan R. Leimberg. "Split Dollar, the Bifurcated Peso: Split, Rip, or Tear?" published by Matthew Bender as part of the proceedings of the 31st Philip E. Heckerling Institute on Estate Planning.

A Warning and a Conclusion

The January 2, 1997, issue of the Daily Tax Report, Taxation, Budget and Accounting, *stated that according to Treasury Department Benefits Tax Counsel Mark Lwry, "The IRS is considering issuing guidance on split-dollar arrangements in response to an increasing number of inquiries by tax attorneys and CPAs. The IRS is concerned with a wide variety of abusive practices and inappropriately aggressive sales practices that create a competitive disadvantage for those unwilling to engage in them."*

Although some practitioners have asked that the IRS be lenient on past and current transactions, others have urged the government not to be lenient on aggressive transactions that have "pushed the edge." Lwry stated, "In developing any guidelines, we will of course carefully consider the extent to which it may or may not be appropriate to provide retroactive or transitional relief for past or existing transactions or arrangements that are not abusive and that reflect a reasonable interpretation of the law."

Lwry didn't state when the guidance might be released. Nancy Marks, IRS deputy associate chief counsel of Employee Benefits and Exempt Organizations, stated that nothing may be released until later in 1997, or possibly 1998, because of the complexity of the issue and the IRS's desire to act in as neutral a manner as possible. Marks is quoted as saying that "the IRS will not rush the issue to avoid creating inadvertent constraints by the way the guidance is phrased." She said, "This is something we would like to accomplish in 1997, but I am not sure if that is possible."

---

constructively distributed to the individual partners (and, in the case of a deceased partner, to his or her estate). See D. Jansen, "Sec. 2042—From Soup to Nuts," University of Miami 29th Institute on Estate Planning, Chapter 14 (1995), and D. Cornfeld, "Partnership as a Panacea for Life Insurance Problems (Penicillin or Placebo?)," University of Miami 29th Institute on Estate Planning, Chapter 15 (1995).

There is no more cost-effective and certain means of creating and shifting large amounts of wealth than life insurance. For many of our clients, life insurance is an unequaled means of providing liquidity, leveraging the annual gift tax exclusion and unified credits, and replacing wealth. It is a vehicle that provides the psychological freedom for an individual to spend and enjoy more of his or her other wealth currently.

Split-dollar arrangements often meet an estate liquidity problem of a shareholder-employee with corporate rather than personal dollars used to provide life insurance premiums. Aside from this obvious and highly important "premium assist," split-dollar's major advantage as an estate planning tool is its incomparable income, gift, and generation-skipping transfer tax leverage:

- Life insurance proceeds are income tax free. This should be compared to a lifetime gift of appreciated property in which the donees carry over the donor's basis and must therefore report capital gain upon a sale in excess of that basis.
- Although the wealth shift made possible by a given amount of cash gift shifts only that amount, the same value of gift, if given in the form of cash used by the donee as life insurance premiums, can provide wealth to the same donees in an amount equal to many times the cash gift, but at the same gift tax cost to the donor.
- Gift and generation-skipping costs in a split-dollar life insurance policy are based on a "discounted" basis (the insured's gift and/or generation-skipping cost is computed on the reportable economic benefit, that is, the PS 58 or, if lower, the one year term cost)[93] rather than on the gross premium or even on the insured employee's aliquot share of the premium.

Viewed in this sense, split-dollar can be thought of as a supercharged wealth transfer vehicle for enriching a future generation at the lowest possible overall cost. (There are no probate, administrative, or other transfer costs associated with split-dollar).

It is precisely because the benefits of split-dollar arrangements are so very appealing that we must be sure our clients understand the downsides and make their decisions about life insurance without illusions as to the tax and economic aspects of the transaction.

---

93. See Rev. Rul. 64-328, 1964-2 CB 11; Rev. Rul. 66-110, 1961 CB 12; Rev. Rul. 78-420, 1978-2 CB 67; PLR 8003094; Rev. Rul. 81-198, 1981-2 CB 188; Reg. Sec. 25.2511-1(h)(3). See also R. Adler, "Beyond Leverage: Split-dollar Funding of the GST-Exempt Trust," *Trusts and Estates,* Vol. 135, No. 5, p. 66 and R. Covey, "Practical Drafting: Split-dollar Life Insurance," *Tax Notes,* Oct. 1996, p. 4660.

> Determining the edge of the split-dollar envelope is much like the study of geometry; they both start with theorems of pristine simplicity—and gradually progress to caverns of complexity. The trick, in analyzing any complex transaction, however, is to reduce it to its basic components—and attempt to reconcile the results with fundamental principles. If dollars seem to move in circles, or if benefits appear to shift—without tax consequences, one had better illuminate the transaction with traditional tax tenets and common sense, because, if for no better reason, this is the crucible that the service and the courts will apply.[94]

The TAM's IRS Sec. 83 argument is sound; if it were tested in court, the IRS would prevail in both equity and reverse split-dollar situations. Therefore we must not let our clients go into a split-dollar arrangement if we don't know how we are going to get them out.

Having given these warnings, it is important to remember that the concept of split-dollar, used judiciously, remains a sound, creative, and cost-effective way to help clients pay large life insurance premiums—and shift huge amounts of wealth at the least possible gift, estate, and GST tax cost. Even equity and reverse split-dollar, used properly, will continue to have their place in the planning process.

Planners should apply a three-question, dispassionately objective acid test to split-dollar in general, equity split-dollar in particular—and to every other estate planning tool or technique:

First, ask, **"What are the pros and cons of the viable alternatives?"** Split-dollar, for example, is not the only way to finance needed life insurance—and certainly not a reason, by itself, to purchase it. So the question that must be asked is, "In my client's situation, is split-dollar better, just as good as, or worse than other ways to finance the needed coverage?

Second, ask, **"Which tool or technique—or combination of alternatives—will provide the most for the client and the client's family—at the least possible cost—and is most certain to actually work?"** What will the client implement and be comfortable with?

Third, ask, **"What if . . . ?" "What if the client does nothing?"** How important is the need for liquidity, leveraging, or wealth replacement? Who will lose—and how much will be lost—if nothing is done and no life insurance is purchased?

---

94. "The Evolving Edge of the Split-dollar Envelope," G. Quintiere & G. Needles, *Benefits Law Journal,* Vol. 9, No. 1, Spring 1996.

Where Can I Find Out More?

- HS 331 Planning for Business Owners and Professionals. The American College.
- *Tax Planning with Life Insurance*, Financial Professional's Edition. RIA Group. Phone (800) 950-1210.
- *Tools & Techniques of Life Insurance Planning*. National Underwriter Company. Phone (800) 543-0874.
- Stephan R. Leimberg. "Split Dollar, the Bifurcated Peso: Split, Rip, or Tear?" published by Matthew Bender as part of the proceedings of the 31st Philip E. Heckerling Institute on Estate Planning.

QUALIFIED PLANS

SIMPLEs: Will They Fly?
David A. Littell

What Was the Situation Before?

Since their inception in the early 1980s 401(k) plans have experienced phenomenal growth in popularity. However, much of the boom has been limited to the large- and medium-sized plan market.[1] To bolster plan participation in smaller markets, Congress instituted salary reduction simplified employee pensions (SARSEPs), but these plans did not provide employer matching contributions and required significant annual discrimination testing, so they never really caught on in a big way.

What Is the Nature of the Change?

Under the recently passed Small Business Job Protection Act, Congress made a second attempt to fit a 401(k) knockoff into the small plan market. The new plan is called a SIMPLE—derived from the acronym for the phrase *savings incentive match plan for employees*. SIMPLEs are administratively convenient salary deferral plans that also allow employer matching or nonelective contributions. Employers can begin sponsoring SIMPLEs in 1997, and after December 31, 1996, employers will no longer be able to establish a new SARSEP (although existing SARSEPs were grandfathered).

Congress actually provided for two new plans, both of which are referred to as SIMPLEs. One type of plan is a SIMPLE that is funded with IRAs, making it similar to the SEP. This version is referred to as either a SIMPLE or SIMPLE IRA—and most experts expect this to be the one that employers will use most commonly. However, the law also allows traditional 401(k) plans to avoid certain requirements by adopting certain SIMPLE provisions. This is generally referred to as a 401(k) SIMPLE. Except where specifically noted, the term SIMPLE below describes the IRA-funded plan. Later in the discussion, the 401(k) SIMPLE will be described and contrasted.

The tax advantages for the SIMPLE are essentially the same as for a 401(k) plan. Employee salary deferral contributions are not subject to income tax, even though they are subject to FICA and FUTA taxes. Employer

---

1. The focus of this section will be on the small plan market.

contributions are not subject to any taxes at the time they are contributed to the plan. Trust income is not taxed, and employees are taxed on their benefits only at the time of distribution.

Eligible Employers. Any type of organization, including any nonprofit organization or state or local government, can establish a SIMPLE. However, in the prior year, the entity cannot have had more than 100 employees with $5,000 or more of compensation. If the employer grows beyond the 100-employee limit, the law does allow the employer to sponsor the plan for an additional 2-year grace period. Note that that the 100-employee rule is determined by taking into consideration all employers that are required to be aggregated under controlled group, affiliated service, and leased employee rules of Code Secs. 414(b), (c), (m) and (n).

Also note that to be eligible, the sponsoring employer cannot maintain any other qualified plan, 403(b), or SEP during any part of a plan year that it maintains a SIMPLE. In other words, the SIMPLE must be the sponsor's only tax-sheltered retirement plan. The IRS has clarified that sponsoring an inactive or frozen plan (meaning a plan in which no benefits are currently accruing[2]) will not disqualify the sponsor from maintaining a SIMPLE.

Contributions. In a SIMPLE, all eligible employees have the opportunity to make elective pretax contributions of up to $6,000 (subject to cost-of-living adjustments). Unlike the 401(k) plan (or the old SARSEP), there is no nondiscrimination testing, so highly compensated employees can make contributions without regard to the salary deferral elections of the nonhighly compensated employees. Similarly the SIMPLE is not subject to the Code Sec. 415 limits (which limit contributions to the lesser of 25 percent of compensation or $30,000). This means that an employee can defer up to 100 percent of his or her compensation. The only other limit that can apply occurs if an individual participates both in a SIMPLE and in a salary-reduction-type retirement plan (401(k), SARSEP, SIMPLE, or 403(b) plan) with an unrelated employer. In this case the $9,500 salary deferral limit applies to all pretax salary deferral type contributions.

In addition to the employee elective deferrals, a SIMPLE sponsor is required to make a mandatory employer contribution. This contribution can be made in one of two ways:

- The employer can make a dollar-for-dollar matching contribution on the first 3 percent of compensation that the individual elects to defer.

---

2. IRS Notice 97-6 clarifies that a defined-contribution plan is not disqualifying if no contributions are allocated to participants. Transfers, rollovers, and even reallocated forfeitures are not treated as allocated contributions. A defined-benefit plan is not disqualifying if no participant receives a benefit accrual for the year.

- The employer can make a 2 percent nonelective contribution for all eligible employees.

If the employer elects the matching contribution, it has one other option. Periodically the employer can elect a lower match as long as the matching contribution is not less than one percent of compensation and participants are notified 60 days before the beginning of the plan year. The employer can elect the lower percentage for up to 2 years in any 5-year period, which can even include the first 2 years that the plan is in force.

The employer contribution amount just described is both the minimum required and the maximum employer contribution allowed. In other words, if the employer elects the matching contribution, 3 percent is the maximum match, and nonelective contributions are not allowed. If the employer elects the nonelective contributions, then the 2 percent contribution is the maximum, and matching contributions are not allowed. This means that the maximum amount that can be contributed for an owner or other highly compensated employee in a SIMPLE is $12,000 (table 5-1). This amount includes the $6,000 salary deferral and $6,000 for the dollar-for-dollar match, up to 3 percent of compensation. To contribute the full $12,000, the employee must earn $200,000 of compensation or more (3 percent of $200,000 equals $6,000). For the individual earning less, the maximum matching contribution is limited by the 3 percent rule (see table 5-1). As you can see, the 3 percent matching contribution—unlike in qualified plans or SEPs—is *not* subject to the $160,000 (in 1997) compensation cap. However, the compensation cap does apply if the employer elects the 2 percent nonelective contribution. This means that the 2 percent nonelective contribution for an individual who earns $160,000 or more is limited to $3,200.

TABLE 5-1
Maximum SIMPLE Contribution

Salary	Maximum Salary Deferral	Matching Contribution	Total Contribution
$ 50,000	$6,000	$1,500	$ 7,500
$ 75,000	$6,000	$2,250	$ 8,250
$ 100,000	$6,000	$3,000	$ 9,000
$ 125,000	$6,000	$3,750	$ 9,750
$ 150,000	$6,000	$4,500	$10,500
$ 175,000	$6,000	$5,250	$11,250
$ 200,000 or more	$6,000	$6,000	$12,000

Eligibility Requirements. The SIMPLE has eligibility requirements that are different from those of both the SEP and the qualified plan. The plan must cover any employee who earned $5,000 in any 2 previous years and is reasonably expected to earn $5,000 again in the current year. Employees subject to a collectively bargained agreement do not have to be covered (however, they do have to be counted when determining whether the employer has 100 or fewer employees). Eligible employees must be given the right to make the salary deferral and receive either an employer matching or nonelective contribution. For determining eligibility, compensation is essentially taxable income plus pretax salary deferrals. For a self-employed person, compensation is net earnings (not reduced by salary deferral elections). SIMPLEs can be maintained only on a calendar-year basis, and all employees become eligible to participate as of January 1.

The plan can have less restrictive eligibility provisions—for example, allowing immediate eligibility, reducing the number of years required prior to entry, or reducing the $5,000 compensation requirement. These options are clearly identified in the IRS model plan document, IRS Form 5304-SIMPLE.

Funding Vehicles. Like SEPs and SARSEPs, the SIMPLE plan is funded with individual retirement accounts, which means that the following requirements apply to the SIMPLE:

- Participants must be fully vested in all benefits at all times.
- Assets cannot be invested in life insurance or collectibles.
- No participant loans are allowed.
- No limitations can be placed on participant withdrawals.

Even though these accounts are essentially IRAs, accounts established under a SIMPLE will be referred to as SIMPLE IRAs and will differ from regular IRAs in one regard discussed further below. Due to a special 25 percent early distribution penalty tax that applies to distributions in the first 2 years of participation, there is a prohibition on the transfer out of a SIMPLE IRA and into a regular IRA in the first 2 years of participation. Otherwise, participants can circumvent the 25 percent tax.

Adopting a Plan. Although a plan must be maintained on a calendar-year basis, a plan can be established beginning on any date between January 1 and October 1 of the year, with two exceptions. First, if an employer previously sponsored a SIMPLE, then the effective date for the new plan can only be January 1. Second, if a new business entity is formed after October 1, it can establish a plan as soon as the entity is formed.

The adopting employer can establish a plan by adopting one of two IRS-provided model documents, Form 5305 SIMPLE or IRS Form 5304 SIMPLE. These documents do not need an IRS approval letter and are only two pages long. In addition, a SIMPLE IRA must be established for each participating employee before the date of the first required contribution. IRS form 5305-S can be used to establish a trust account, and form 5305-SA can be used to establish a custodial account.

Form 5305 SIMPLE is used when the plan has what is referred to as a *designated financial institution*. This is a financial institution (bank, insurance company, or mutual fund group) that agrees to be the sole recipient of all plan contributions. At first blush it might seem that most financial services providers would want to have this status so that they would be the exclusive agent for all IRA accounts. However, in reality most will probably not want this status. The problem is that if an entity is a designated financial institution, it must give participants the right to freely transfer their benefits to another SIMPLE IRA, or after 2 years of participation to any IRA, without cost or penalty. Even though the IRS has provided guidance allowing the institution to limit when such transfers can occur, it has defined the term *cost or penalty* broadly to include any liquidation, transaction, redemption, or termination fee; any commission, load (whether front-end or back-end), or surrender charge; or similar fee or charge imposed with respect to the balance being transferred. However, it is permissible for a designated financial institution to charge such transaction fees to the employer.

Because of this penalty most plans will probably be established with Form 5304 SIMPLE. Since this form does not require a designated financial institution, the SIMPLE IRA trustee or custodian will not have to be concerned about the "no charge or penalty" provision if a participant wants to transfer assets to another trustee. The IRS has clarified that the plan sponsor can still work with one primary service provider, as long as participants are made aware of their right to establish a SIMPLE IRA with another trustee.

Plan Operations. After establishing a plan, the sponsoring employer must notify participants that they have the 60-day election period just prior to the calendar year to make a salary deferral election or modify a previous election for the following year. This means that once the plan is operational, the election period is November 2 to December 31. For a new plan the first election period can be somewhat later and can comprise any 60-day period that includes either the day of or the day before the effective date of the plan. For example, if the plan begins on July 1, 1997, the election period can be June 30, 1997, to August 29, 1997. After the election period is over, employees who have made a salary deferral election must still be given the option to stop making deferrals at any time during the year. The sponsor can require that the participant wait until the following year to elect back in, or it may have a more liberal election modification provision—for example, allowing participants to modify their election at any time.

Every year, prior to the 60-day election period, the trustee (or custodian) must prepare and the employer must distribute a summary plan description (SPD) that includes employer-identifying data, a description of eligibility under the plan, benefits provided, terms of the salary election, and description of the procedures for and effects (tax results) of making a withdrawal. Also 30 days after the calendar year ends, the trustee must give participants a statement of the year's activity and the closing account balance.[3]

The clear and precise disclosure requirements are accompanied by clear penalties for failure to comply. The trustee is fined $50 a day for late distribution of participant statements or the annual summary plan description, and the employer is fined $50 a day for late notification to participants of their right to make salary deferral elections.[4] The disclosure requirements and penalty system were probably deemed necessary, since there is no direct incentive for the employer to encourage SIMPLE participation (unlike the 401(k) plan, in which highly compensated contribution levels are tied to nonhighly compensated contributions under the ADP nondiscrimination test).

Administrative costs for a SIMPLE should be quite low. At the present time, no annual reporting with the IRS or DOL is required. Also, unlike the 401(k) plan, no ADP test or other nondiscrimination tests must be performed.

Withdrawals. Like SEPs, the plan cannot put any limitations on participant withdrawals, which means that participants have access to funds at any time to spend them or roll them over into another IRA. If an individual takes a distribution, the entire amount of the distribution will be subject to income tax as ordinary income. If the participant is under age 59 1/2, the distribution will also be subject to the 10 percent early-distribution excise tax (unless one of the exceptions applicable to IRAs applies). Since participants have such easy access to funds, Congress decided to add an additional penalty. The 10 percent penalty tax becomes 25 percent for amounts withdrawn within 2 years of the date of first participation.

This special rule complicates SIMPLE IRA rollovers somewhat. The general rule is that amounts in a SIMPLE IRA can be rolled over (or transferred) to either another SIMPLE IRA or regular IRA under the rollover rules that apply to regular IRAs. However, individuals in the first 2 years of SIMPLE participation can only roll a distribution into another SIMPLE IRA.

401(k) SIMPLE. The new SIMPLE described above is sometimes referred to as the IRA SIMPLE, since the Small Business Job Protection Act of 1996 also allows for a similar alternative for 401(k) plans, which is referred to as a 401(k) SIMPLE. A 401(k) plan that adopts the principal provisions of the IRA SIMPLE will not be required to satisfy the ADP or ACP test (for matching contributions). Equally as important is that such a plan will not have to satisfy the qualified plan top-heavy requirements.

In order for the employer to sponsor a 401(k) SIMPLE, it cannot have more than 100 employees (applying the same rules that apply to SIMPLEs).

---

3. Code Sec. 408(l).
4. Code Sec. 6693(c)(1).

Similarly state and local government organizations that cannot sponsor a 401(k) plan cannot sponsor a 401(k) SIMPLE.

In order for a 401(k) plan to be treated as a 401(k) SIMPLE, the 401(k) plan must meet the following requirements:

- It must be maintained on a calendar year.
- Employee pretax salary deferrals cannot exceed $6,000.
- Employer contributions must be limited to either a 3 percent matching contribution for eligible employees or a 2 percent nonelective contribution for all eligible employees who earn more than $5,000 for the year.
- It must provide for full and immediate vesting.
- It must prohibit contributions for participants in the 401(k) SIMPLE from receiving contributions to any other qualified plan, SEP, SIMPLE, or 403(b) plan sponsored by the employer.

Note that in contrast to the SIMPLE IRA, in this plan if the employer makes the 3 percent matching contribution, the $160,000 compensation cap does apply. Consequently the maximum matching contribution for an individual earning $160,000 or more is $4,800.

Beginning in 1997, any 401(k) plan that is currently maintained can be converted to a 401(k) SIMPLE by adopting the model amendment provided in Rev. Proc. 97-9. To adopt the SIMPLE provisions for the year, the amendment and participant notification must occur more than 60 days prior to the beginning of the plan year. Also employees must be given a 60-day election period in which to make salary deferral elections in the following year. For 1997, however, the amendment can be adopted any time before July 1, 1997, as long as certain requirements are satisfied.

To fully understand the 401(k) SIMPLE, it is important to understand that except for the special requirements described above, this plan is still a 401(k) plan, so it is subject to the flexible qualified plan coverage requirements and the plan must file annual Form 5500s and meet other reporting and disclosure requirements. All qualified plan contribution limits and distribution requirements apply as well.

What Should Be Done?

All eligible plan sponsors (employers with 100 or fewer employees that do not sponsor another retirement plan) should consider their new options under the Small Business Job Opportunity Act of 1996. Under the new law beginning in 1997, the private for-profit employer interested in a tax-advantaged salary savings plan now has three choices: the traditional 401(k) plan, the 401(k) SIMPLE, or the SIMPLE funded with IRA accounts. First we will compare the traditional 401(k) to the SIMPLE and then discuss the uses of the 401(k) SIMPLE.

For those employers familiar and comfortable with the 401(k) plan, the SIMPLE appears incredibly rigid. With strict contribution requirements, the single plan requirement, and limited tax-shelter potential, at first glance it seems hard to see why an employer would choose a SIMPLE over the 401(k) plan. Feature by feature, the advantage almost always goes to 401(k) plans, which are better for maximizing contributions and skewing employer contributions to a targeted group of employees—typically two common goals of small-plan sponsors. In addition, a 401(k) plan is much more flexible. The plan can be limited to part of the workforce as long as the minimum coverage requirements are met, and matching and profit-sharing contributions can be designed to meet a variety of goals. Finally, employer contributions can increase or decrease over time. The features that make the 401(k) plan the more useful retirement planning vehicle are as follows:

- *Salary deferrals*—The maximum salary deferral amount of $9,500 is substantially higher than in the SIMPLE.
- *Maximum tax shelter*—The total maximum contribution on behalf of a highly compensated employee is $12,000 in a SIMPLE and as high as $30,000 in a 401(k) plan.
- *Matching contributions*—The matching contribution in a 401(k) plan can match both the employer's goals and the budget. Matching contributions can be subject to a vesting schedule and may even be made on a discretionary basis.
- *Profit-sharing contributions*—Nonelective contributions can be allocated using a cross-testing method in which the lion's share of the contribution is on behalf of the highly compensated employees.
- *Coverage*—The qualified plan coverage requirements are more flexible and allow the employer to keep part-time employees out of the plan.
- *Loans*—Participant loan programs are an important feature in the 401(k) plan. Participants are less reluctant to make salary deferral contributions if they feel that they will have access to these funds without adverse tax consequences.

There are, however, a few clear advantages to the SIMPLE. First, establishing and maintaining a SIMPLE is considerably less complicated than a 401(k) plan. The plan document is short and easy to read, and no IRS determination letter is involved. The employer's responsibilities are limited to establishing the plan, giving participants the opportunity to make a salary deferral election, distributing the trustee-provided summary plan document, and directing contributions to the IRA trustee. The sponsor does not even have to reach out to any specific service provider; it can require that the participants take the step of establishing their own SIMPLE IRA. The employer does not have to worry about annual administrative tasks, such as completing annual Form 5500s, nondiscrimination testing, or calculating the various contribution limits that apply to 401(k) plans. In those plans, the paperwork involved in distribution planning has become quite complicated. Spousal elections, mandatory withholding, and direct transfer options are costly. In the SIMPLE, none of these is a concern. Distributions can occur at any time and require no involvement by a plan administrator. The distribution transaction is between the participant, the trustee, and the tax collector. All these factors translate into significantly lower operating costs than for a 401(k) plan. In addition, less administration means less exposure to plan noncompliance problems that can have a negative impact for the sponsor, service providers, and/or plan participants.

For the employer looking to contribute the smallest amount to the plan, the advantage in most cases will go to the SIMPLE. Theoretically, a small employer-sponsored 401(k) plan can provide for employee salary deferral contributions only. When this is the case, the employer's only cost is for administration (and some of those costs can be passed on to the participants). However, if the plan is top-heavy[5]—which is often the case for the small-employer plan—the employer is required to make a 3 percent contribution for nonkey employees.[6] Unfortunately, the top-heavy contribution requirement generally cannot be satisfied with matching contributions, so the employer who has a match must still make the additional 3 percent contribution. In comparison, the 3 percent SIMPLE contribution only has to be made for those employees who make salary deferral elections. If the employer is on a tight budget and expects full participation, then the employer can elect the 2 percent nonelective contribution instead or periodically lower the matching contribution to as low as 1 percent. Even when comparing the SIMPLE to a non-top-heavy 401(k) plan, the sponsor with a small budget is still going to be more interested in spending its limited plan dollars on employee benefits and not on administrative expenses.

The strengths of the SIMPLE make it an interesting option for the small employer with a small benefit budget that is shopping for its first retirement plan. It's hard to imagine that the employer currently maintaining a 401(k) plan will want to give up its design flexibility. But to the small employer, the SIMPLE is an inexpensive, easy-to-administer plan that can give the company a competitive edge by providing a 401(k) lookalike retirement program. It's too early to tell how well this plan will catch on, and its success will depend in part on the types of products service providers make available and the aggressiveness with which the SIMPLE is marketed. But if the SIMPLE does become popular, this should be good news for employees and for employee benefits service providers. Hopefully the SIMPLE will open up a whole new market of retirement plan sponsors.

---

5. In top-heavy plans the aggregate of the accounts of key employees under the plan exceeds 60 percent of the aggregate of the accounts of all employees.
6. IRC Sec. 416(c). Note that most employers required to make a 3 percent contribution for nonkey employees will end up choosing to contribute the same amount for key employees as well.

Remember that the SIMPLE can also be sponsored by nonprofit organizations and government entities, but governments will not be adopting them because they have other retirement plans. On the other hand, the nonprofit sector could be the largest potential market for the SIMPLE because many nonprofit organizations fit the appropriate profile: fewer than one hundred employees, no current retirement plan, a small budget, and a concern for the retirement security of employees. For these organizations, if the employer can afford the contribution, the SIMPLE can look quite attractive. Low administrative expenses mean that most of the money spent goes towards providing benefits. Even 501(c)(3) organizations that are eligible to sponsor 403(b) plans should consider the SIMPLE. The 403(b) plan is generally the appropriate choice if the employer does not make any contributions (salary deferral only), since this type of plan is generally exempt from ERISA and many of the income tax rules as well. However, if the employer is going to make a modest contribution, maintaining a 403(b) plan becomes almost as complex as a 401(k) plan. Here the employer should seriously consider the SIMPLE.

For example, a small nonprofit organization with 10 employees has an interest in sponsoring a retirement plan. They have a budget of 3 percent of compensation and also want to allow employee pretax salary deferrals. They have already explored the 403(b) and 401(k) options and are discouraged by the administrative costs of maintaining either plan. For them the SIMPLE is by far the superior choice, and they are excited about setting one up as soon as possible.

In contrast to the SIMPLE, the 401(k) SIMPLE is a whole different story. Here, it is hard to see just who will benefit from this plan design option. The employer is subject to the rigid design restrictions of the SIMPLE without the benefit of significant simplification. The 401(k) SIMPLE does eliminate nondiscrimination testing as well as the top-heavy problem, but the employer must adopt and maintain a 401(k) plan document, meet qualified plan reporting and disclosure requirements, and comply with the various distribution requirements. This option might make sense for the employer who is already sponsoring a 401(k) plan but has been frustrated by either the top-heavy test or has had to significantly limit contributions for highly compensated employees because of the nondiscrimination tests. This employer might be interested in sponsoring a SIMPLE, but making a transition would require terminating the 401(k) plan, distributing benefits, and establishing the SIMPLE with individual IRAs. Instead, the employer could amend the plan into a 401(k) SIMPLE, while retaining the same funding vehicle and avoiding the plan termination. Also if the company later outgrows the 401(k) SIMPLE, the SIMPLE provisions can be revoked, allowing a seamless transition into a more complex 401(k) plan design.

Other features that can make the 401(k) SIMPLE more attractive than the SIMPLE with IRAs include

- participant loans—Like other 401(k) plans this plan can offer a participant loan program.
- flexible coverage requirements—One advantage of the qualified plan rules that is helpful to the employer with a large number of part-time employees is the ability to exclude employees with fewer than 1,000 hours of service.
- other plans—Even though employees in the 401(k) SIMPLE cannot be covered in another retirement plan, the sponsor can maintain another plan for other employees. This might be helpful if the employer has, for example, two work sites and wants a different plan for each group.

At the present time, no one knows whether the SIMPLE (or the 401(k) SIMPLE) will be a hit, or like the SARSEP, another flop. The SIMPLE solves some of the SARSEP's problems but also sets up some new roadblocks for the sponsor. The benefits professional who is turned off by the lack of flexibility should stay open to the possibility that this plan may look good to the small, struggling business or nonprofit organization. To this group a plan that is easy to understand, explain, and administer may look quite attractive—spawning a whole new generation of retirement plan sponsors.

Where Can I Find Out More?

- HS 326 Planning for Retirement Needs. The American College.
- HS 341 Selected Retirement Plan Topics. The American College.
- GS 814 Advanced Pension and Retirement Planning I. The American College.
- IRS Model SIMPLE plan documents. Form 5305-SIMPLE, to be used with a designated financial adviser, and Form 5304-SIMPLE, to be used when there is not a designated financial adviser.
- IRS Model SIMPLE IRA forms. Form 5305-S: SIMPLE individual retirement trust account and Form 5305-SA: SIMPLE individual retirement custodial account.
- IRS Notice 97-6, which provides guidance in a question-and-answer format regarding SIMPLEs.
- IRS Rev. Proc. 97-9, which contains a model amendment for 401(k) plan sponsors that want to adopt the 401(k) SIMPLE provisions.
- Internal Revenue Code Sec. 408(p), which lists the SIMPLE requirements.

401(k) Plans after the Small Business Job Protection Act of 1996
David A. Littell

What Was the Situation Before?

In the 1990s, 401(k) plans have taken the pension market by storm. In 1995, for example, 70 percent of all newly adopted qualified plans were

401(k) plans. The Profit Sharing/401(k) Council of America's 1995 survey showed that the average 401(k) participation level was 86 percent and that the average participant account balance stood at $65,294. This represents an increase from 80 percent in 1994, and a doubling of the 1990 account figure of $31,246. The primary dissatisfaction with these plans has been their administrative complexity. Also as workers have become used to—and attached to—their 401(k) plans, nonprofit organizations, which couldn't sponsor 401(k)s, were at a competitive disadvantage with for-profit organizations.

What Is the Nature of the Change?

The Small Job Protection Act of 1996 responded to both these concerns by expanding access to the 401(k) plan and by simplifying plan administration. Some simplification provisions directly focused on 401(k) concerns, while others had an impact on a broader spectrum of plans.

Broader Access. Beginning in 1997, nonprofit organizations (and Indian tribal governments) can now sponsor 401(k) plans.[7] This should be very good news for those nonprofit organizations that have not been eligible to sponsor either 401(k) or 403(b) plans (organizations that are not 501(c)(3) nonprofit organizations). These employers—which include business associations, private clubs, labor unions, credit unions, and civic leagues—could not previously sponsor any type of tax-sheltered plan. Under the new law, 501(c)(3) charitable organizations are now able to choose between 401(k) and 403(b). Even though the 403(b) plan is still the appropriate choice in most situations, some employers will want the ability to have a vesting schedule or to invest in a broader range of investments than is afforded by the 401(k) plan.

Changes to ADP and ACP Testing. 401(k) plans continue to have to satisfy a nondiscrimination test for employee elective salary deferrals (called the ADP test) and a nondiscrimination test for employer-matching contributions as well as participant after-tax contributions (called the ACP test). In most ways the methodology remains the same, and the objective of the tests remains the same, as well—to limit contributions for the highly compensated employees (HCEs) based on the level of contributions made for the nonhighly compensated employees (NHCEs). However, there are several welcome changes that will make it easier to perform and satisfy the tests. One change is the timing of the testing. Under the prior law, the maximum average deferral percentage for the HCEs for the current plan year was based on the average deferrals of the NHCEs for the current year, so it could not be determined with certainty how much the HCEs could contribute to the plan until the close of the plan year.

---

7. This extension does not apply to state and local government entities, which are still prohibited from maintaining 401(k) plans.

Under the new law, determining the maximum average deferral percentage for the HCEs for the current year is based on the previous year's results for the NHCEs, which means that the employer knows for certain at (or near) the beginning of the year how much the HCEs can elect to defer. Now it is much more likely that the plan will satisfy the ADP test. This new methodology applies to the ACP test as well.

The IRS has clarified[8] that the new law really means using the deferral percentages for the NHCEs for the previous year, applying law in effect during that year and deferral percentages for that year. For example, this means that in 1997, the NHCE percentage is the same as was used to calculate the 1996 ADP test. Also note that the law provides that for the first year that the plan allows employee salary deferrals, the deferral percentage for the NHCEs is deemed to be 3 percent (meaning that the ADP for the HCEs can be up to 5 percent).

The new law also gives the employer the right to elect to continue performing the tests using current-year numbers—as under the old rules. The IRS has clarified that for 1997, no special election needs to be made in order to elect the current-year numbers in 1997 and that an employer electing to use the current-year numbers in 1997 can elect back in 1998. The IRS has not yet provided guidance on the ability to go back and forth between the two methods for years after 1997. In the average case, employers will welcome the new law and will not make the election. However, the decision to use current-year salary ADP will be made in situations where NHCE deferral contributions tend to be volatile from year to year.

Highly Compensated Employees. Another welcome change under the new law is a simplified definition of highly compensated employee. Beginning in 1997, highly compensated employees include only individuals who are 5 percent owners during the current or previous year and individuals who in the previous year earned at least $80,000 (as indexed in 1997). The employer has the option to limit the second category to only those employees who are in the top-paid group. The top-paid group includes those employees whose earning are in the highest-paid 20 percent of the employees. IRS has not yet provided any guidance regarding top-paid group election.

Under the old rules, the highly compensated employee determination was quite complex, and employees with compensation as low as $66,000 (in 1996) could be considered highly compensated. Also under the old rules, the highest-paid officer was considered an HCE regardless of salary. Under the new rules, the floor is raised, the determination is less complicated, and the one-officer rule no longer applies.

There are few complications under the new rules. Still note that certain attribution rules apply for determining 5 percent ownership. A participant is

---

8. IRS Notice 97-2.

considered owning any stock owned by his or her spouse, children, parents, and grandparents. It's also interesting to note that under the new rules, newly hired executives (who are not 5 percent owners) may not become highly compensated employees for several years. For example, take an individual hired at a company with a calendar plan year. The employee is hired on July 1, 1997, with an annualized salary of $100,000 but earns only $50,000 in 1997. This individual does not become highly compensated until 1999.

Employers with more than 20 percent of the workforce earning more than $80,000 (such as law firms and medical practices) will have to decide whether or not to make the "top-paid group" election. Unfortunately, no general rule can be given; the decision will be based upon the specific facts and objectives of the employer.

Family Aggregation Rules. Under the old law, the family aggregation rules significantly complicated 401(k) administration. The old law actually had two aggregation rules. One treated all members of one family (parents, grandparents, children, and grandchildren) as one highly compensated employee. This treatment particularly had an impact when performing the ADP test. The second—and more onerous—rule limited compensation to a total of $150,000 (the compensation cap in 1996) for married couples and children under age 19 when one partner was either a 5 percent owner or one of the 10 highest-compensated employees. Effective for plan years beginning in 1997, both of these rules were repealed. Now families are no longer penalized, and performing the tests is less complicated.

New Correction Method for Plans That Fail the ADP Test. Under the old rules, if a plan did not satisfy the ADP or ACP test at the end of the year, the plan had to take corrective action. This meant distributing or recharacterizing salary deferrals of specified HCEs. Under the old rules, the HCEs with the highest deferral were the first to have their deferral amounts reduced. However, the individuals with the highest deferral percentages were often the lowest-paid HCEs. In most cases, employers would prefer to have the owners or others with the highest contributions be corrected first. Effective for 1997, the law requires that the HCE with the largest dollar deferral be corrected first.[9] Hopefully, however, correction of failed tests will occur much less often under the new testing rules.

Special Testing Rules for 401(k) Plans That Allow Early Participation. Under previous law, Code Sec. 410(b) allowed plans that included individuals who did not meet the statutory minimum age and service requirements (one year of service and age 21) to separately test whether that group of employees satisfied the minimum coverage requirements. The rule was intended to make sure that plans were not punished for including those individuals. Although there was no similar statutory provision under the ADP and ACP tests for

---

9. IRS Notice 97-2 provides a specific methodology for making correction calculations.

401(k) plans, IRS guidance had permitted separating this group and testing it separately under both tests. The new statutory provision goes a bit further. Now, in any case where the employer separately tests such employees for coverage under the minimum coverage requirements, when performing either the ADP or ACP test, such individuals (except highly compensated employees) can simply be removed from the testing group. Note that this law does not go into effect until plan years that begin in 1999.

New Definition of Compensation under Code Sec. 415. Under the old law, compensation for purposes of determining the 25 percent or $30,000 maximum allocation limit was reduced by pretax contributions to a 401(k) or other tax-sheltered plan. Under the new rule, effective for plan years beginning after December 31, 1997, contributions to 401(k), 403(b), 457, cafeteria, and SIMPLE plans do not reduce compensation for Sec. 415 purposes. The old rule created a trap, especially for the second wage earner with low wages and high contributions to the plan. For example, an individual with $20,000 in compensation who deferred $5,000 had deferred too much. The new law removes the trap beginning in 1998. However, note that the problem still exists under the 15 percent maximum deduction rules for a profit-sharing (including 401(k)) or stock bonus plan. Here compensation is still reduced by the above-mentioned salary deferral amounts.

Other Related Changes. In addition to those rule changes mentioned above, other issues discussed in this chapter affect 401(k) plans. Because the 401(k) is a qualified plan, the distribution rule changes discussed in the Appendix apply to 401(k) distributions. Also employers eligible to sponsor a traditional 401(k) plan now have the opportunity to choose instead a SIMPLE, a 401(k) SIMPLE, or, beginning in 1999, the safe harbor 401(k) plan. The discussion of the SIMPLE in this chapter reviews the plan sponsor's new options. See those sections for a discussion of these issues. Also review the Appendix for other issues that have an impact on qualified plans.

What Should Be Done?

The first step for the financial adviser—and those involved in plan administration—is to learn the rules. Most of the new rules are effective in 1997, and plans must administered in compliance with the new law. Generally plans need not be amended for the new law until 1998; however, the IRS has indicated that plans with family aggregation concerns should be amended to eliminate the family aggregation rules in 1997.

It's also important to learn how the new law can help clients. The new rules repealing family aggregation and limiting the group of employees who are considered HCEs may allow the plan to better meet the objectives of the owners and the highly compensated, especially for businesses in which both spouses are working. In addition, plans that have had discrimination concerns should be relieved, because it is now easier to ensure plan compliance. Plan sponsors will want to review the new plan options to see if any of them are helpful (see discussion of SIMPLE).

Finally, consider whether the law changes can open up new markets. The most important development is the opportunity to install 401(k) plans in the nonprofit marketplace. In addition, the simplified rules, which make it easier to test and ensure compliance, may persuade more small businesses to sponsor a 401(k) plan.

Where Can I Find Out More?

- HS 326 Planning for Retirement Needs. The American College.
- GS 814 Advanced Pension and Retirement Planning I. The American College.
- IRC Secs. 401(k), 414(q), 410(a)(17)(A), 415(c)(3)(D)
- Kenn Beam Tacchino and David A Littell. *Planning for Retirement Needs.* Used in The American College's HS 326 course.
- David A. Littell, Kenn Beam Tacchino, and David W. Cordell, eds. *Financial Decision Making at Retirement.* Used in The American College's HS 336 course.
- David A. Littell et al. *Retirement Savings Plans: Design, Regulation, and Administration of Cash or Deferred Arrangements* and *Retirement Savings Plans Supplement.* Used in The American College's HS 341 course.

The 15 Percent Excise Tax Moratorium—Should You Bite?
John J. McFadden

What Was the Situation Before?

Congress has long been concerned that the substantial tax incentives included in the qualified plan provisions will be used disproportionately by highly compensated employees (HCEs) who in their view need no government help in saving for retirement. Code Sec. 415 (enacted as part of ERISA in 1974) sets limits on annual additions to a defined-contribution plan (the lesser of 25 percent of compensation or $30,000, as indexed) and on benefits under a defined-benefit plan (the lesser of 100 percent of average compensation or $125,000, as indexed). Under Sec. 415(e), if a participant was covered under both a defined-benefit plan and a defined-contribution plan of the same employer, a complex computation involving a *combination fraction* had to be made each year to limit total benefits so that it was not possible to maximize both the defined-benefit and defined-contribution amounts.

The Tax Reform Act of 1986 added another provision aimed at preventing excessive qualified plan accumulations by HCEs, the 15 percent excess distribution tax. Under this provision, an excise tax of 15 percent is enacted on annual plan distributions exceeding $160,000 (indexed), in addition to the regular income tax. There are provisions exempting accrued benefits in excess of $562,500 as of August 1, 1986 (the grandfathered amount). There is also an additional 15 percent estate tax on excess accumulations at death.

What Is the Nature of the Change?

Congress has apparently determined that the existence of all the provisions described above constitutes overkill, and has repealed the combination-fraction computation of Section 415(e).

When Does This Change Affect Clients?

The combination-fraction repeal becomes effective after 1999. To provide relief during the interim period, the 15 percent excess distribution tax (but not the excess accumulation tax) is suspended for years beginning after December 31, 1996 and before January 1, 2000. Distributions during this period are deemed to be made first from non-grandfathered amounts.

What Should Be Done?

The repeal of Section 415(e) is welcome and will simplify administration of plans covering owners and executives, as well as open new opportunities for creative plan design after 1999. In the interim, however, the question is whether the moratorium on the 15 percent excess distribution tax should eagerly be taken advantage of.

Should clients accelerate distributions—that is, take distributions in excess of $160,000 (as indexed) each year? Note that 5-year averaging expires after 1999, seemingly adding urgency to this possibility.

However, clients should do some sober reflecting (and calculating) before rushing to withdraw more from their qualified plans than they ordinarily would. Accelerating distributions means that the benefits of deferring income taxes are lost. In fact, from the Treasury's point of view, the suspension of excise taxes is a Trojan horse; this purported benefit to taxpayers will actually increase income tax revenues during the 3- year period as taxpayers rush to take advantage of the opportunity to pay their income taxes early.

When is it really beneficial to take distributions during the 3-year moratorium to avoid the 15 percent excess distribution tax? Apparently not very often. Consider these points:

- If the participant's account is not large enough ever to attract any significant 15 percent excess distribution taxes, the moratorium is of no use. Account balances as large as $1 million may be subject to little or no 15 percent tax if the participant and spouse live out their normal life expectancy.

- Pension distribution software that shows various payout scenarios is indispensable in advising clients on this issue. In general, the *crossover point* (number of years of survival after a lump-sum distribution when deferring taxes becomes more advantageous than taking a lump sum under the moratorium) comes quite soon in most scenarios.
- For very large distributions, the crossover point comes later because the moratorium saves large amounts of 15 percent taxes. However, in one scenario run on a popular pension distribution software package, even an $8 million pension accumulation had a crossover point that came sooner than the joint life expectancy of the 70-year-old participant and spouse.
- The larger the grandfathered amount, the sooner the crossover (because the grandfathered amount itself avoids a considerable portion of the 15 percent tax).
- The crossover point depends heavily on projected rates of return and projected tax rates. These are difficult to predict with accuracy and probably are best addressed using best-case and worst-case scenarios.

In short, running the numbers with pension software provides an important reference point in making this decision, but ultimately planners and clients must use their best judgment. Factors include

- health status of participant and spouse
- age of participant and spouse
- need for money
- charitable intentions (A charitable gift gets income/estate tax deductions but is subject to 15 percent excess distribution tax. This includes charitable remainder gifts. See chapter 15 for further discussion.)

Where Can I Find Out More?

- Stephan R. Leimberg. *Pension and Excise Tax Planner* software. Phone (610) 527-5216.

Qualified Plan Options for Nonprofits
John J. McFadden

What Was the Situation Before?

Nonprofit organizations (private corporations or other entities entitled to federal tax exemption under Code Sec. 501) were entitled to adopt qualified plans for their employees, except that Sec. 401(k) plans and salary reduction SEPs were not available. For organizations qualifying under Sec. 501(c)(3) (religious, charitable, educational and similar organizations) Sec. 403(b) annuity plans were available as an alternative. However, for other types of nonprofit organizations such as business leagues, lobbying organizations, and credit unions there was no way to design a practical salary-reduction (elective-deferral) plan for a broad group of regular employees. Code Sec. 457 permitted a limited form of salary-reduction deferred-compensation plan, but this was effectively available only to a select group of management or highly compensated employees.

What Is the Nature of the Change?

Repeal (as part of the Small Business Act of 1996) of the prohibition on 401(k) plans for tax-exempts expands the options for tax-advantaged salary-reduction (elective-deferral) plans for nonprofit employers. Here are the current options for salary-reduction plans, reflecting the new SIMPLE provisions and the repeal of SARSEPs:

- *501(c)(3) organizations*—401(k) plan, 403(b) plan, SIMPLE (if 100 or fewer employees and no other qualified plan, etc.), 457 plan for select group of management or highly compensated employees
- *other 501 tax-exempts*—401(k) plan, SIMPLE (if 100 or fewer employees and no other qualified plan, etc.), 457 plan for select group of management or highly compensated employees

When Does This Change Affect Clients?

These provisions of the Small Business Act take effect for plan years beginning after December 31, 1996.

What Should Be Done?

For 501 organizations other than 501(c)(3)s, the new provisions will prove a boon for benefit plan design for regular employees. Many such organizations were frustrated by their inability to meet their employees' demands for a 401(k) plan or alternative, and the new provisions will make it much easier for these organizations to provide retirement benefits that attract and retain employees.

For 501(c)(3) organizations, the new provisions will require the organization to review its current plans and in many cases choose between a 401(k) plan and a new or existing 403(b) plan. There generally is little or no advantage in maintaining both types of plan since the elective-deferral limit is $9,500 (indexed) per employee effectively on an aggregate basis—that is, having both plans does not generally allow an employee to make additional elective deferrals.

In the current state of limited experience with this issue, most practitioners believe that 403(b) plans are generally more favorable as an option. The advantages of 403(b) plans include the following:

- no ADP testing (although employer contributions are subject to 401(m) tests)
- no ERISA applicability for salary-reduction-only plans
- entire plan not disqualified for exceeding $9,500 limit for one employee
- Sec. 415 limitation more favorable (403(b) plan not aggregated with other plans)
- top-heavy rules don't apply

By contrast, 401(k) plans have only a few advantages over 403(b) plans, including the following:

- somewhat broader investment flexibility—not limited like 403(b) plans to annuity contracts and mutual funds
- the ability to accept rollover contributions from qualified plans
- 5-year and 10-year averaging on lump-sum distributions

Because of potential complexities in actual situations, however, this choice should always be carefully studied for the individual case at issue.

Where Can I Find Out More?

- GS 814 Advanced Pension and Retirement Planning I. The American College.
- IRC Sec. 401(k)(4)
- Stephan R. Leimberg and John J. McFadden, *Tools and Techniques of Employee Benefit and Retirement Planning,* 5th edition, The National Underwriter Company. Phone (800) 543-0874.

6

LIFE INSURANCE PRODUCTS AND SERVICES

Edward E. Graves

Equity-indexed Annuities

What Was the Situation Before?

Annuity contracts were either variable contracts or fixed-dollar contracts relying primarily on bonds and mortgages for investment income. The fixed annuity contracts were very popular during the era of high interest rates (the 1980s and early 1990s). However, as interest rates dropped and stock market returns strengthened, the demand for fixed annuity contracts dropped off. Many purchasers of annuities selected variable annuity contracts, but the insurers were aware that some potential purchasers were reluctant to select variable annuities because they were not willing to assume all the investment risk.

What Is the Nature of the Change?

As a result of the reluctance of some potential purchasers, some insurers have designed new annuity products to enhance the investment return on the fixed annuity contract while maintaining the guaranteed minimum interest rates. These products, called *equity-indexed annuities,* are fixed, deferred-annuity products. They were introduced in the mid-1990s to enhance the appeal of fixed annuities.

Product Evolution. Some insurance companies have introduced equity-indexed annuities as a product that still offers guaranteed minimum interest rates and at the same time will pay a higher return if the specified stock index increases enough to provide a higher yield. These products are promoted as offering the best of both worlds—fixed-interest debt investments (bonds and mortgages) and equities (stocks). They are designed to appeal to persons who want to participate in high-equity investment yields without bearing the full investment risk that must be assumed in the purchase of a variable annuity. Variable annuities are still the only annuity products that provide most of the full yield of the equity investments to the owner/annuitant.

The equity-indexed annuity provides only a portion of the capital gain of the stocks making up the applicable index (commonly the Standard & Poor's 500 Composite Stock Price Index). Since the formulas look at the value of the index only at anniversary dates, there is no way to capture the dividend income (if any) of those stocks in the formula approach used in the equity-indexed annuities. It is difficult for prospective purchasers of these annuities to find accurate information about past performance of the capital-gain portion of the index because most sources report the combined total return—both capital gain and income from dividends. Over the past 20 years, about 20 percent of the total return of the Standard & Poor's 500 Index (S&P 500) has been from the income portion.

Participation Rate Formula. Prospective purchasers of equity-indexed annuities need to understand that their potential return based on increases in the value of the index is determined by the actual formula approach set forth in the contract. Generally this formula includes a participation rate as well as an increase in the index from the beginning of the term to the acceptable anniversary-date value of the index. Some contracts use the increase in the index to the anniversary date during the specified term period (ranging from one year to 8 years, depending on the specific contract) when the index reached its highest value. The participation rate is a percentage (always less than 100 percent) of the defined increase that will be used to calculate the crediting amount. This participation rate is set by the insurer and is subject to change. Some companies do not even specify the current participation rate in their promotional materials. Often the rate is guaranteed for a specified first term, such as 5 or 7 years. The insurance company reserves the right to change the participation rate at the expiration of each term but usually guarantees the then-current rate for the subsequent term.

Most contracts anticipate a series of terms of uniform length, much like renewals of 5-year term life insurance. However, some contracts reserve the insurer's right to modify the term period available for continuation at the expiration of any existing term. In most designs, the higher increase from the index calculation is available only at the end of the applicable term unless the owner dies or the contract is converted to benefit-payout status (annuitized) before the end of the term. The higher value based on the index will not apply if the contract is terminated before the end of the term.

The participation rate is very important in that it restricts the amount of the index gain (if any) that can be applied to get more than the guaranteed yield. There is also a link between the participation rate and the guaranteed interest rate. Higher participation rates may be available from some insurers if the purchaser will accept a lower guaranteed interest rate. For instance, one company guarantees that the participation rate will never be lower than 25 percent. Illustrations are often based on 80 or 90 percent participation rates. It is reasonable to assume that participation rates range from 25 to 90 percent. Under most contracts, the participation rate cannot be changed more than once a year.

Another aspect of the indexed benefit is that some contracts include a cap on the crediting rate that can be applied to the accumulated value of the contract. This cap may be a single stated percentage applicable to the whole participation period (contract term). It can be stated as an annual equivalent that, in turn, determines the aggregate limit for the full participation period. The existence of such a cap prevents even the full formula participation in times of very rapid index increases.

As a protection on the down side, most contracts specify a floor of zero percent as the minimum interest crediting rate applicable to the accumulated value. This prevents the application of a negative percentage in the formula to reflect plunges in the index value.

The intent is that the fixed-interest-rate guarantee is the worst possible outcome, and if the equity index does better, the accumulation may be even better than the guaranteed accumulation. The marketing material touts this feature as presenting the best of both worlds. Equity-indexed annuities are clearly designed to appeal to purchasers who want higher yields than bonds have provided in the mid-1990s.

No Securities and Exchange Commission Regulation. Equity-indexed annuities satisfy another objective of the insurance companies: they are classified as fixed annuities and can be sold by agents who are not licensed to sell variable products. Thus the agent has a product that is partly influenced by equity performance and that offers a minimum-accumulation guarantee. The agent can sell the product without having to acquire a new license and thus avoids the training requirement and commitment necessary to enter the variable-annuity market.

It is worthy of note that the Securities and Exchange Commission (SEC), which is currently examining insurance products, could decide that equity-indexed annuities really are a variable product rather than a fixed product. Many experts argue that the current definitions of terms adhered to by the SEC are broad enough for such an interpretation without changing any existing authorizations or guidelines. Others believe that equity-indexed annuities cannot be classified as variable products without some action to change the SEC definitions.

In early 1997, one insurance company introduced an equity-indexed annuity contract that it describes as an investment product. The product is registered with the SEC and is sold by registered agents using a prospectus.

The Guarantees. The minimum guarantees under equity-indexed annuities are lower than those for traditional fixed annuities. In fact, the rates that are actually guaranteed apply to less than the full amount paid as a premium. It is common to apply the guaranteed rate to 90 percent of the amount paid to purchase the annuity. That percentage (often 10 percent) not included in the guarantees can be used to cover insurer expenses. With this approach it usually takes 3 or 4 years before the guaranteed amount equals or exceeds the initial purchase amount. The guaranteed rate may result in only a 10 percent gain over a 7-year term when calculated on the full original purchase price. The specified interest rate applied each year to the contract value is set forth in the contract and remains fixed unless a negotiated change is later agreed to by both the contract owner and the insurance company. Many of the existing equity-indexed annuities' guaranteed rates are in the range of 3 to 3.5 percent.

Value of the Contract at End of Term. At the end of each term, or participation period, the value of the annuity will be the greater of the following three amounts:

- the contract value based on the minimum interest-rate guarantees
- the accumulated value derived by applying the participation rate to the increase in the index on the applicable anniversary. This amount will be subject to any cap on maximum crediting rate and to any floor on minimum crediting rate.
- the purchase premiums paid up though the end of the term. (Partial withdrawals will be deducted from the premium amount.)

In many contracts the same procedure will be used to calculate the death benefit payable if the owner dies during the deferral phase of the contract.

Terminating an equity-indexed annuity before the end of a specified term will usually result in loss of the index-crediting option. The termination benefit will usually be the greater of the following two amounts:

- the guaranteed-interest contract value
- the aggregate purchase amount less adjustments for any partial withdrawals previously taken

Annuitization. The equity-indexed annuity can be converted to benefit-paying status at any time prior to the maximum age specified for mandatory benefit payout. For qualified annuity contracts, the benefit payout must meet the minimum distribution requirements of the tax law. For nonqualified annuities, the benefit payout does not have to begin before age 85 with some insurers and may be pushed beyond that by an insurer in the future.

Tax law forces payout of qualified annuity contracts starting at whichever of the following times is later:

- April 1st of the year following the year in which the annuitant reaches age 70 1/2
- April 1st of the year following the year the annuitant retires

Most equity-indexed annuities in force were issued before the 1996 tax law change that permits delay of annuitization until retirement if that is later than age 70 1/2. Consequently many equity-indexed annuity contracts used for IRA purposes or other qualified plans will force the start of benefits before retirement for people working beyond age 70 1/2.

The tax law does not mandate a maximum age for distributions to start for nonqualified annuities (those purchased with after-tax dollars). It is the insurer that imposes the maximum age constraints on nonqualified annuities.

The benefits-payout options are the same as those for any other type of fixed annuity contract, as is the taxation of equity-indexed annuities.

Indexes. Although the most commonly used index is The Standard & Poor's 500 Composite Stock Price Index, some insurers use another index specified in the contract. These are generally established indexes that are regularly published in financial publications such as the *Wall Street Journal*. However, some insurers have chosen to use international indexes or a composite of two or more established indexes. This puts the definition of the index under the insurance company's control, and theoretically the company could change the definition of the index after the contract is created, leaving open the possibility of intentional manipulation of the index in the future.

The contracts often set forth an alternative index to be used in case the primary index ceases to exist in the future.

Asset Match. All financial products involve risks, and the equity-indexed annuity is no exception. The issuer needs to invest in assets that will provide an adequate return to honor the contractual promises.

Since the index participation promises some results that are above those of bond returns when the stock index outperforms the bond market, how will a company invest assets to produce the higher increment? The closest match will come by investing some funds in the same stocks that make up the index. However, some insurers have chosen to invest in derivatives and other financial assets that they feel will track well with the index even though these choices are not a composite of the items that make up the index. Over the long run there could be a significant difference between investment results and contractual obligations. If the investment results exceed the contractual obligations, there will be no problem honoring the annuity contract terms. On the other side, though, underperformance of asset returns relative to obligations could threaten the insurer's financial viability. Purchasers should feel more comfortable with issuing companies whose investments more closely resemble the index the benefits are related to.

The equity-indexed annuity concept is an acceptable composite approach to fixed annuities. It needs much more explanation than the traditional fixed annuity contract. If purchasers do not fully understand the features and the very limited extent to which these annuities participate in the index, they may later be extremely disappointed and revert to class action suits to seek redress. A small number of insurance companies are taking an aggressive stance on both indexes and investments that could potentially tarnish this product, which would be unfortunate because the concept is a sound one and many insurers seem to be taking a responsible approach to both the choice of the index and the offsetting asset portfolio mix.

Equity-indexed annuities have become highly visible in the market since 1996. In fact, new equity-indexed life insurance policies are now available in the marketplace. Time will tell how successfully equity-indexed products satisfy the needs and desires of the purchasing public.

When Does This Change Take Effect?

This product, which was first introduced in 1995 and is quickly gaining market acceptance, is already available from nearly 20 insurance companies. No doubt there will be more insurance companies introducing the product in the future. If it is considered a success within the insurance industry, it may be available from nearly all life insurers within a few years. Some insurers— usually the more cautious ones—are always willing to let other companies try new ideas and work out some of the problems before adopting the product.

What Should Be Done?

Financial services professionals can become aware of this product and how it is being promoted by getting copies of the promotional materials and reading them thoroughly, and by comparing the differences between different insurer contracts.

It is important to learn what you can about the investment strategy being used to enhance the portfolio yield, assess the strategy, and decide whether you think it is viable for any and all market conditions.

If you market the product, take care to explain it thoroughly. Purchasers need to know that they are not getting to participate in dividend income of the index and that the participation rate is less than 100 percent and can change from what is set forth in the contract. Purchasers should also be aware of how low the participation rate is permitted to go according to the contract.

Furthermore, purchasers of equity-indexed annuities should be informed about how the insurer intends to invest funds to enhance yields above those from debt instruments such as bonds and mortgages. Some insurers are investing in derivatives and highly volatile, high-risk assets.

The index used in the formula is very important. It should be readily available from sources outside the insurance company so it is not subject to internal manipulation.

Indexes based on foreign stock exchanges introduce an additional element of risk due to currency fluctuations against the dollar. Purchasers need to be aware of these factors up front in order not to be surprised by them when they manifest themselves in the market.

This product has the potential to create expectations beyond what it may deliver. Unbridled optimism tied to recent high yields in the stock market may create unrealistically high expectations. There could be negative effects in the future if actual results are significantly lower than expectations.

Where Can I Find Out More?

- HS 323 Individual Life Insurance. TheAmerican College.
- *National Underwriter, Life/Health,* March 3, 1997, p. 1, and March 24, 1997, p. 14.

Criminalization of Donors

What Was the Situation Before?

Prior to 1997, the only deterrent to giving away assets for the purpose of qualifying for medicaid benefits was a delay in the start of benefit payments. In essence, the delay was equal to the period it would take for medicaid benefits to equal the value of the assets given away. The law applied the delay to gifts made within the 36 months prior to applying for medicaid benefits (The look-back window was increased to 60 months if the gifts involved any trust[s].)

> *Example:* If there is a $60,000 gift in a state where the medicaid payment is $3,000 per month, this formula would result in a 20-month delay of benefit eligibility. That is the period of time that the gifted assets would have supported the individual at the medicaid rate. In that particular state a gift in excess of $108,000 would delay benefits for 36 months.

The intention of the government is that people should exhaust their own assets for their own care before they are eligible for medicaid (welfare) benefits. Congress has always intended to discourage any transfers of assets to other individuals or tax entities to preserve those assets and accelerate access to public welfare benefits.

The widespread practice of attorneys advising elderly clients who needed custodial nursing home care to either give away or rearrange their assets so they could qualify for medicaid prompted Congress to strengthen the discouragement.

What Is the Nature of the Change?

Congress strengthened the penalty for giving away assets to qualify for medicaid benefits by making it a criminal offense. The punishment for violation can be up to one year in prison and up to $10,000 in fines to the donor. This change in the law (Sec. 217 of the Health Insurance Portability and Accountability Act, also known as Kennedy-Kassebaum) simply states that any transfers that would trigger a delay in benefits under the prior law are illegal. There was no attempt to modify the prior statute specifying the delay. This is important because the original statute was never intended to impose criminal penalties. There is a lack of detail in the existing law that makes it less than clear what the dividing line is between legal transfers and illegal transfers. The wording is that knowingly and willfully disposing of assets to become eligible for medicaid is illegal.

Legal scholars are divided in their interpretations. Some believe that any transfer that *could* trigger a delay in benefits is illegal. Others argue that only those transfers that actually result in the imposition of a delay in benefits are illegal. The first interpretation could turn anyone who has given away assets into a criminal if he or she ever subsequently applies for medicaid benefits.

When Does This Change Take Effect?

The new law makes criminal penalties applicable to gifts made after December 31, 1996. Those who interpret the law to apply only to actual delays in benefits suggest that the law is easily circumvented. They advise that no application for benefits be made until 36 months after a transfer (60 months if a trust is involved). Following that same interpretation, they advise postponing the application for benefits to some point after the end of any potential delay if the gift is small enough that the delay would be less than 36 months (60 months for trusts).

The stricter interpretation would make the transfer itself a crime if the donor *ever* applies for benefits; the time of application for benefits would be irrelevant. This could be a shock to persons who gave away assets before they were forced into early retirement or otherwise lost their income and subsequently became destitute.

There is no question that Congress wants to curb giving that is motivated by a desire to qualify for medicaid benefits. The financial pressure on medicaid is already exhausting both federal and state funds, and the future increases in demand due to an aging population will worsen the situation. It is conceivable that Congress will get even more aggressive and expand the scope of what are classified as illegal transfers.

What Should Be Done?

Anyone considering gifts of assets in order to qualify for medicaid benefits should consult an elder law attorney as to the advisability of such actions. To some extent, the decision will be influenced by the expected interpretation of the less-than-clear law.

Attorneys are less likely to suggest a giving program to qualify for medicaid because there are also criminal penalties applicable to advisers who recommend gifts to accelerate benefit eligibility (up to 5 years' imprisonment and up to $25,000 in fines).

Those who have enough assets to want to preserve them for other family members may well be advised to purchase long-term care insurance while they are healthy, thus giving them insurance benefits to cover custodial care if it is needed. Such coverage provides many options not available to medicaid beneficiaries.

The benefits are payable even in upscale facilities that are not certified for medicaid benefit eligibility. Many long-term care policies provide benefits for home care and other circumstances outside of a nursing home. The protection of a long-term care policy allows the insured to maintain dignity and avoid the stigma of taking welfare benefits. It also allows the insured to avoid becoming dependent on his or her children to help pay for nursing home care. This protection may also enable persons with long nursing home stays to preserve assets for bequests to family or charities.

Long-term care policies are not appropriate for persons who are already eligible for medicaid or whose assets will quickly be diminished to the level of medicaid eligibility. With the average cost of nursing home care exceeding $36,000 per year ($3,000/month), it does not take long to exhaust most people's accumulated assets once they enter a nursing home. These people have fewer choices and may have to wait for an opening in a facility after they need care.

Gifts of assets should be made at least 36 months before applying for medicaid benefits.

Where Can I Find Out More?

- HS 323 Individual Life Insurance. The American College.
- *Eldercare News.*
- "All About Medicaid," *National Underwriter.*
- "Tax Line," *National Underwriter,* March 1997, p. 4 (vol. 97, no. 3).

Life Insurance Policy Illustrations

What Was the Situation Before?

Prior to January 1, 1997, there were no standards for life insurance illustrations. Since the 1980s, life insurance sales have frequently been based on computer-generated illustrations. Many of these illustrations were created on personal computers using software that allowed the agent to change some factors, such as interest. In some instances these illustrations were based on unrealistically high interest assumptions.

The purchasers of life insurance relying on these illustrations became very dissatisfied; in fact, in some of the more blatant cases, policyowners have actually sought damages through litigation.

The most problematic illustrations were those depicting the use of policy dividends to pay policy premiums and grossly overestimating dividend levels. These policies were sold as "vanishing premium" products. The purchasers claim they were never told that the policy still had premiums after the target vanish date. They maintain that they did not realize the dividends were the key to paying subsequent premiums and that dividends could decrease.

This situation resulted in many class action suits against insurers and agents after numerous unhappy policyowners found out that they still needed to pay premiums after the expected vanish date.

There has been much criticism of illustrations, resulting in various actions. A study was done by the Society of Actuaries and the Board of Actuarial Standards. The American Society of CLU & ChFC created a Professional Practice Guideline for illustrations and supplanted that with a life insurance illustration questionnaire. This questionnaire is intended to be filled out by the insurer's home office staff to describe the assumptions used to generate illustrations. The questionnaire was designed for use by agents and other financial services professionals.

The litigation and other activities dealing with illustrations prompted the National Association of Insurance Commissioners (NAIC) to appoint a task force and develop a model regulation.

What Is the Nature of the Change?

With the stated purpose of protecting consumers and fostering consumer education, in 1996 the NAIC adopted a model regulation pertaining to life insurance illustrations. This is the NAIC's first attempt to set standards for policy illustrations. By January 1, 1997, two states (North Carolina and Utah) had already adopted the model regulation, and additional states are expected to adopt some form of the regulation in 1997. The regulation will probably be effective by January 1, 1998, or later in California, Iowa, Louisiana, North Dakota, New York, and Pennsylvania.

The new model regulation is already having an impact on illustrations in all states because many life insurance companies are moving toward using the same illustration model in every state so they do not need different software systems for each state. Within companies seeking uniformity in all states, all the illustrations are being made to conform to the most stringent state's requirements.

The new regulation does not apply to variable life, credit life, or life insurance with a face amount of less than $10,000, nor does it apply to either individual or group *annuity* contracts. The new regulation *does* apply to all nonvariable group and individual *life insurance* policies and certificates for more than $10,000 of death benefit.

The regulation requires the insurance company to declare to the state insurance department for each policy form whether or not it intends to use illustrations to market that form of coverage. A copy of each illustration the insurer intends to use must be forwarded to the state insurance department. Each illustration used in the sale of a life insurance policy covered by the new regulation must be clearly labeled "life insurance illustration" and must include the following:

- name, age, and sex of the proposed insured
- the underwriting or rating classification upon which the illustration is based
- the generic name of the policy (for example, whole life, universal life, and so forth)
- the initial death benefit amount
- the dividend option election or application of nonguaranteed elements, if applicable

The NAIC model regulation prohibits insurers and their agents from the following:

- representing the policy as anything other than a life insurance policy
- using or describing nonguaranteed elements in a manner that is misleading or has the capacity or tendency to mislead
- stating or implying that the payment or amount of nonguaranteed elements is guaranteed
- using an illustration that does not comply with the illustration regulation
- using an illustration that is more favorable to the policyowner than the illustration based on the illustrated scale of the insurer
- providing an applicant with an incomplete illustration
- representing in any way that premium payments will not be required for each year of the policy in order to maintain the illustrated death benefits, unless that is the fact
- using the terms "vanish," "vanishing premium," or any similar term that implies that the policy becomes paid up to describe a plan for using nonguaranteed elements to pay a portion of future premiums
- using an illustration that is not "self-supporting"

The NAIC model illustration regulation specifies that all illustrations must be dated as of the date prepared. All pages must be marked to indicate both the individual page number and the total number of pages in the illustration (for example, "page 3 of 7"). The illustration must clearly indicate which elements are guaranteed and which are nonguaranteed. Any amount available upon surrender shall be the amount after deduction of surrender charges. Items presented in illustrations can be in the form of charts, graphs, or tabular values.

Each illustration must be accompanied by a narrative summary that describes the policy, premiums, and features and defines column headings used in the illustration. The summary should also state that actual results may be more or less favorable than those shown in the illustration.

Universal Life Policies

The regulation states that illustrations for universal life policies must comply with the regulation requirements and additionally that the insurance company must issue annual reports to policyowners after the policy is issued. These annual reports must specify the beginning and ending dates for the reporting period.

The content of the annual reports is specified in the NAIC model regulation as follows:

- all transactions affecting the policy during the reporting period (debits and credits) and a description of each (for example, premiums paid, interest credited, loan interest debited, mortality charges, expenses debited, rider transactions, and so forth)
- cash values at the beginning and end of the period
- death benefit at the end of the reporting period (for each life covered)
- the cash surrender value at the end of the period after deduction of surrender charge (if any)
- the amount of outstanding policy loans, if any, at the end of the report period
- a special notice to policyowners if the policy will not maintain insurance in force until the end of the next reporting period unless further premium payments are made

The regulation further stipulates that policyowners have the right to request an in-force illustration annually without charge. The insurer must provide information regarding where and how to direct such requests and must supply a current illustration within 30 days of the request. Such illustrations are to be based on the insurer's present illustrated scale.

Annual Certifications

Each insurer's board of directors must appoint at least one illustration actuary, who will certify that the illustrations are in compliance with the illustration regulation and are insurer-authorized. The regulation states the qualifications of an illustration actuary, including membership in good standing of the American Academy of Actuaries.

The illustration actuary must annually certify the method used to allocate overhead and expenses for all illustrations and must file such certification with the insurance commissioner and with the insurer's board of directors. Further, the illustration actuary is required to report any mistakes found in previous certifications to both the commissioner and the board of directors. Also the insurance commissioner must be notified of any change in the illustration actuary and the reasons for the change.

The model regulation sets forth limits on the methodology for calculating illustrations. These limits are intended to curb some of the overly optimistic projections that a few insurers were utilizing in recent years in the absence of any standards or constraints. Most of the new constraints are contained in the definitions of *currently payable scale*, *disciplined current scale*, and *illustrated scale*.

These definitions are as follows:[1]

- *currently payable scale*: a scale of nonguaranteed elements in effect for a policy form as of the preparation date of the illustration or declared to become effective within the next 95 days
- *disciplined current scale*: a scale of nonguaranteed elements constituting a limit on illustrations currently being used by an insurer that is reasonably based on actual recent historical experience, as certified annually by an illustration actuary designated by the insurer. Further guidance in determining the disciplined current scale as contained in standards established by the Actuarial Standards Board may be relied upon if the standards

    (1) are consistent with all provisions of this regulation,
    (2) limit a disciplined current scale to reflect only actions that have already been taken or events that have already occurred,
    (3) do not permit a disciplined current scale to include any projected trends of improvements in experience or any assumed improvements in experience beyond the illustration date, and
    (4) do not permit assumed expenses to be less than minimum assumed expenses.

- *illustrated scale*: a scale of nonguaranteed elements currently being illustrated that is not more favorable to the policyowner than the lesser of

    (1) the disciplined current scale, or
    (2) the currently payable scale.

---

1. From section 4, Life Insurance Illustrations Model Regulation.

Outlook

It is important to note that even if all states adopt the model regulation, there will still be wide variation in acceptable underlying assumptions. (Texas has already deviated significantly by adopting an incompatible regulation.) Illustrations will never be an accurate prediction of future results or policy performance. Actual future situations will be heavily influenced by the economy and by the investment performance of the specific insurance company's actual portfolio.

Illustrations are useful for showing how a policy works and how sensitive a policy is to given changes in factors such as interest, mortality, or expenses. However, illustrations are of limited value for comparing different policies (whether from the same insurer or from different insurers).

The new regulation will no doubt eliminate some of the past abuses in illustrations where the assumptions were based on unfettered pie-in-the-sky optimism. The new restrictions do *not* constrain illustrations to such an extent that apples are being compared to apples. It is still important to study all the questions about the underlying assumptions. Those questions are set forth in the Life Insurance Illustration Questionnaire (IQ) developed by the American Society of CLU & ChFC and included at the end of this chapter, beginning on page 6.18.

When Does This Change Take Effect?

The NAIC model regulation became effective on January 1, 1997, in at least two states. Each subsequent adoption will have an individual effective date for each specific state. If the model regulation or some variation of it is not adopted within a particular state, there will not be an effective date for that state with respect to constraints and enforcement.

However, large insurers trying to comply with the new regulation everywhere they conduct business have already been taking steps to comply. In many companies the implementation is being phased in as quickly as possible. The actual illustrations from most large insurers doing business in all states are already in compliance. However, the computer systems to support the new illustrations are being massively revised. Short-term steps were taken quickly to comply, but better-integrated incorporation requires longer-term system programming developments. Large home office computing systems are not as flexible as personal computers and require very careful coordination with all the other ongoing computing requirements. These systems are already running around the clock 7 days a week to process a myriad of transactions and generate reports. Compliance with the new illustration regulation shifts to the centralized system a major processing burden that had been performed at the agency or agent level, creating some logistic nightmares for home office systems. They are modifying their programs as rapidly as possible while still providing the daily processing and support for all home office functions. The phase-in should not disrupt the regular processing but has the potential of delaying or disrupting everything on the system. Full integration of centralized illustrations may take a few years as desirable features and enhancements are developed and implemented.

There will be much frustration in the field force as this new approach to illustrations evolves. Their hands have been tied with respect to generating customized illustrations. Agents understandably perceive the change as a reduction in support resources and a development that makes their job much harder.

What Should Be Done?

Financial services professionals should familiarize themselves with both the nature and the spirit of the illustration regulations so they know what is prohibited and what is required. Knowing the new constraints will help practitioners understand insurer reactions and changes in company procedures. It will also make it clearer to know how to always be safely in compliance.

Agents and prospects need to sign the illustrations. Every page of an illustration must be presented to the prospect. Agents need to maintain adequate records to verify that their illustrations are in compliance. It is appropriate to remember that the judicial system still relies heavily on paper documentation as convincing evidence. Preserving a collection of memos will make it possible to convince a court that oral testimony is credible.

Where Can I Find Out More?

- HS 323 Individual Life Insurance. The American College.
- Insurance company materials.
- The Official N.A.I.C. Model Insurance Laws, Regulations and Guidelines. NIARS Corporation, 8120 Penn Avenue South, Minneapolis, MN 55431.
- *Life Association News.*
- *Life Insurance Selling.*

Replacement Questionnaire

What Was the Situation Before?

Prior to the 1980s insurance companies universally discouraged replacement of one life insurance policy with another. However, with the premium reductions of the 1980s and the introduction of universal life policies, many insurers eliminated their objections to policy replacements. Now that insurance regulators are focusing on agent conduct, there is renewed interest in discouraging replacements. The American Society of CLU & ChFC was the first independent organization to create any document addressing the issues of replacement. Up until that action the only materials addressing the issue came from insurance companies. There are state statutes and regulations requiring that the policyowner be supplied with adequate information from both the existing insurer and the proposing insurer to make a meaningful comparison. There was no uniform approach to replacement evaluation.

What Is the Nature of the Change?

A task force was convened by the American Society of CLU & ChFC to create a questionnaire to help agents and other financial services professionals evaluate replacement proposals. The task force included actuaries, agents, professional organizations, insurance company representatives, educators, and consultants. Their efforts produced a six-page questionnaire intended to be an educational resource for insurance professionals. It was completed in 1995 and approved by the officers and directors of the American Society of CLU & ChFC.

The questionnaire asks for the reason and justification for the proposed change. It states in bold print twice on the cover that replacement is generally *not* in the policyholder's best interest. There are questions to determine whether illustration questionnaires have been obtained for both the existing policy and the proposed policy. The evaluator is asked whether the underlying assumptions are comparable and to describe any significant differences. He or she is further asked how long it will take before the policyowner will be in the same or improved position after the replacement with respect to cash surrender values and death benefits (both on a guaranteed basis and an illustrated basis).

Most of the replacement questionnaire is devoted to identifying the similarities in and differences between the two policies. It provides a systematic format for comparison. These factors include term insurance component, interest rate on cash values, interest rates on loans, death benefits, tax treatment of replacement, grandfathered protections that may be applicable to the existing policy, and insurer financial strength ratings.

The intent of the replacement questionnaire is to discourage replacements unless there is a strong and significant advantage to the policyowner for making the replacement. The questionnaire prompts the agent to document the purported strengths and weaknesses of both policies. Use of the replacement questionnaire will prompt evaluation of all significant factors.

When Does This Change Take Effect?

Replacement questionnaires can be used by both the agent representing the existing coverage and the agent proposing the new policy. It is appropriate whenever a replacement is being proposed because it provides a checklist of important factors to be evaluated and compared before a change in coverage is made. The evaluations may become important evidence if the agent is even asked to defend his or her actions with respect to the attempted replacement.

What Should Be Done?

Insurance professionals should become familiar with the replacement questionnaire (included at the end of this chapter) and use it as a basis for evaluating replacement proposals. A report can be composed based on the responses to the specific questions. This report can be preserved in the client files in case it is ever needed in the future to justify actions taken.

Since it is likely that new versions of the replacement questionnaire will be introduced in the future, updated versions should be obtained when they become available (a revision is expected later in 1997). A record should be kept of which version was used between which dates, and file copies of each version used should be maintained.

Insurance professionals who are not members of the American Society of CLU & ChFC may want to consider joining if they are eligible for membership. The Society generally requires that you have either a CLU or a ChFC designation to join. If you want information on pursuing the designations, contact The American College.

Where Can I Find Out More?

- HS 323 Individual Life Insurance. The American College.
- Contact the American Society of CLU & ChFC directly at 270 S. Bryn Mawr Ave., Bryn Mawr, PA 19010-2195. Phone (610) 526-2500. Contact The American College at the same address or by phone at 610-526-1000.
- Check with your insurance company or state insurance regulator to get information on the statutes and regulations applicable to policy replacements in your state.

Reprinted with permission of the American Society of CLU & ChFC.

Introduction to the Life Insurance Illustration Questionnaire (IQ)

The Life Insurance Illustration Questionnaire (IQ) is an educational tool; its use by companies or agents is entirely voluntary.

The purpose of the IQ is to help the reader understand the different non-guaranteed performance assumptions which insurance companies use to design and create sales illustrations. The IQ may be particularly useful to agents, their clients (under the agent's guidance) and the clients' other advisors.

It has been developed for non-SEC regulated products. The reader should understand that sales illustrations are useful in developing the best combination of policy specifications to achieve the buyer's objective. However, illustrations have little value in predicting actual performance or in comparing products and companies.

Most life insurance products sold today have adjustable pricing. This can be accomplished either as a traditional "participating" product or as a product with "non-guaranteed pricing elements" such as changeable interest crediting rates, mortality charges, expense charges, etc. All adjustable pricing products incorporate some guarantees. However, the sales illustrations are usually designed to present potential benefits and costs under a set of non-guaranteed assumptions more optimistic than the guarantees. The insurance company generally limits its responsibility to the guarantees. So the risks associated with the possible inability of a product to achieve the higher illustrated benefits, or lower illustrated costs, than those generated by the guarantees are borne by the policyholder. A study of the responses to the IQ should help the reader better understand those risks.

Life Insurance Illustration Questionnaire

Information about this response:

Contact Person: _____   Date Completed: _____

Policy(ies) Covered: _____

Are there any more IQs that cover other policies of this Company?
☐ No   ☐ Yes _____
(how many)

Do the illustration(s) covered by this IQ response comply with the NAIC Life Insurance Illustrations Model Regulation?
☐ No   ☐ Yes

In the following responses, "scale" means the scale of dividends or other non-guaranteed elements used in the illustrations.

American Society of CLU & ChFC®
A National Organization of Insurance and Financial Service Professionals

I. General

1. With respect to participating policies, does the company employ the contribution principle*? If not how do practices differ?
   *The contribution principle calls for the aggregate divisible surplus to be distributed in the same proportion as the policies are considered to have contributed to the divisible surplus.

2. With respect to non-participating policies:

   a) Describe the non-guaranteed elements.

   b) What is the company's policy and discretion with respect to the determination and redetermination of non-guaranteed pricing elements?

3. Do any of the experience factor(s) underlying the scales of dividends or other non-guaranteed elements used in the illustration differ from actual recent historical experience? If so, describe.

4. Is there a substantial probability that the current illustrative values will change if actual recent historical experience continues unchanged?

5. Is it company policy to treat new and existing policyholders of the same class the same or consistently with respect to the underlying factors used in pricing? Please elaborate.

6. With respect to joint and survivor policies, describe all the effects of the first death on the policy and any riders (e.g., change in cash values, mortality charges, premiums).

II. Mortality

1. Do the mortality rates underlying the scale used in the illustration differ from actual recent historical company experience? If so, describe. Define actual recent historical experience (e.g., company experience for the last 5 years).

2. Does the illustration assume mortality improvements in the future? If so, describe.

3. Do the mortality or cost of insurance charges used in the illustration include some expense charge? If so, describe.

4. Do the underlying mortality rates vary by product (e.g., whole life, universal life, survivorship life), policy size or by any other feature (e.g., term riders)? If so, specify. (Provide general description of differences - not the actual rates used).

5. Indicate the approximate duration, if any, when all underlying mortality rates vary only by attained age (i.e., when does select become ultimate?).

III. Interest or Crediting Rates

1. The interest rate used in the dividend scale or credited in the illustration is (does):

    a) ☐ a Portfolio rate ☐ an Investment Generation ☐ Other (Describe)
       (Describe)   ("New Money") rate (Describe)

    b) ☐ a Gross rate ☐ a Net rate, which is net of ☐ investment expenses
                                                      ☐ income taxes
                                                      ☐ profit or expense charges
                                                      ☐ other _____

    c) Include ☐ Realized ☐ Unrealized ☐ No Capital Gains.

    If capital gains are included, describe the general method (e.g., smoothed over ___ years).

2. Do the interest rate(s) reflect the earnings on all invested assets? A portion of the assets? New investments over certain number of years? (If so, specify number of years.) An index? (If so, briefly describe.)

3. At any policy duration, do the company investment earnings rates required to support the scale used in the illustration exceed the company's actual recent historical earnings rate on the investment segment backing that block of policies?

4. Does the interest rate used in the underlying scale reflected in the illustration vary between new and existing policies? Describe.

5. Except for any impact of using an investment generation approach, do the interest rates used in the scale reflected in the illustration vary by policy duration? Describe.

6. Do the illustrated interest rates vary by product, class or otherwise? Describe.

7. How does individual policy loan activity affect the illustrated interest rates? Describe.

IV. Expenses

1. Do the expense factors used in the scale reflected in the illustration represent actual recent historical company experience? If so, what is the experience period? If not, describe the basis under which the experience factors are determined.

2. Are the expense factors based on a ☐ fully allocated ☐ marginal or ☐ generally recognized approach, as defined in the NAIC Model Regulations?

3. Are the expense charges used in the underlying scale reflected in the illustration adequate to cover the expenses incurred in sales and administration? If not, how are remaining expenses covered (e.g., charges against interest rate, increased mortality charges)?

4. How are investment expenses and all taxes assessed?

5. Are expense factors used in the scale reflected in the illustration different for new and existing policies? If so, describe.

6. Do the expense factors underlying the scale reflected in the illustration vary by product, class or otherwise? If so, describe.

7. Do the expense charges used in the dividend scale or charged in the illustration vary by duration after the initial expenses are amortized? If so, describe.

V. Persistency

1. If the actual persistency is better than that assumed, would that negatively affect illustrated values?

2. Persistency bonuses are generally amounts illustrated as being paid or credited to all policyholders who pay premiums for a specified number of years. Does the illustration involve such a bonus?

   a. If so, is it ☐ non-guaranteed or ☐ guaranteed?

   b. Is there any limitation on company discretion in deciding whether to pay or credit the bonus?

   c. What conditions must be met to pay or credit the bonus?

   d. What is its form (e.g. cash amount, additional interest credit, refund of mortality and/or loading charges)?

   e. Does the company set aside any reserve or other liability earmarked for future bonuses?

This IQ was developed as an educational resource for insurance professionals by the American Society of CLU & ChFC, 270 S. Bryn Mawr Avenue, Bryn Mawr, Pa. 19010

Reprinted with permission. Copyright © 1997 by the American Society of CLU & ChFC. All rights reserved.

Replacement Questionnaire (RQ)
A Policy Replacement Evaluation Form

To CLUs/ChFCs:

Replacing an existing life insurance policy with a new one generally is not in the policyholder's best interest. New sales loads and other expenses, the new company's right to challenge a death claim during the suicide and contestibility periods, changes in age or health and the loss of important grandfathered rights are some of the obvious reasons that **most replacements cannot be justified.** On the other hand, there may be circumstances where a replacement is in your client's best interest. The ethical agent will provide his or her client with the impartial information needed to make an informed decision, including reasons the client should not replace the current policy and/or how to modify the existing policy to accomplish their goals. The need for additional coverage is not, by itself, a justification for replacement.

This Form is designed to assist you in evaluating some of the facts and circumstances that a policyholder should take into consideration when addressing the possibility of replacing a life insurance policy. It can be used for both internal and external replacements. **The definition of "replacement" is much broader than the cancellation of one policy and the issuance of another.** The legal meaning of the word "replacement" is determined by state law and varies substantially by state. You should be familiar with your own state's definition of the word. However, for purposes of simplifying the definition, we may think of "replacement" in general terms as an action which eliminates the original policy or diminishes its benefits or values. Examples of this are policy loans, taking reduced paid-up insurance or withdrawing dividends. Since no form can cover every possible situation, you may need additional material to enable your client to make a truly informed decision.

Please note that "illustrated" results in this Form are always nonguaranteed. Also, keep in mind that different companies use different assumptions in preparing illustrations and that illustrations alone should never be used to compare policies. However, current in-force illustrations for the existing policy and current illustrations for the proposed policy must be provided to the client, showing the effects of applicable surrender charges. In situations where the current policy will be changed, but not terminated, comparisons should include in-force ledgers of the policy before and after the change, if available. Reduced scale illustrations (or illustrations with lower yield assumptions) should be provided on both existing and proposed policies to demonstrate volatility in the performance of nonguaranteed policy elements under different circumstances. The reduced scale illustrations should be consistent with those required by the NAIC model illustration regulations, when effective.

This Form is intended for evaluation purposes. It is not a substitute for state replacement requirements. This Form is not designed for direct use with clients. Further, if either the existing or proposed policy is variable life insurance, use of this Form with the client must be approved by your broker-dealer.

Copyright © 1997
American Society of CLU & ChFC
All rights reserved.

American Society of CLU & ChFC®
A National Organization of Insurance and Financial Service Professionals

Replacement Questionnaire (RQ)
A Policy Replacement Evaluation Form

A. 1. What does the policyholder want to achieve that the existing policy cannot provide?

   _____
   _____
   _____

   2. Has the current carrier been contacted to see if the policy can be modified to meet the policyholder's objectives?

   _____

B. 1. Recognizing that the replacement of an existing policy generally results in the reduction of cash surrender value as a result of new acquisition costs, what is the cash surrender value of:

   a. The original policy **immediately** before replacement _____
   b. The original policy **immediately** after the replacement _____
   c. The proposed policy **immediately** after the replacement _____

   These cash surrender values should be obtained directly from the insurance carrier's policyowner service department and not from an illustration, since illustrations typically reflect end of year values.

   2. Illustrations should **never** be the sole criteria for evaluating a replacement. Additionally, Illustrated Cash Values and Illustrated Death Benefits are **never** reliable predictions of future results. If these non-guaranteed values and benefits are the basis for considering a replacement, the agent should attempt to know and understand the underlying assumptions in both the inforce illustration for the current policy, as well as the sales illustration for the proposed policy. In addition to reviewing illustrations, the agent should attempt to obtain an Illustration Questionnaire (IQ), which may be available directly from the companies or may be requested through the client. The agent and the client should be aware that there may be differences in the assumptions used by each company which may render a comparison based upon such illustrations invalid.

   How many years from now before the proposed policy's cash surrender values and death benefits exceed those benefits in the current policy?

   a. Guaranteed Cash Surrender Values _____ years and subsequent.
   b. Guaranteed Death Benefits _____ years and subsequent.
   c. Illustrated Cash Surrender Values _____ years and subsequent.
   d. Illustrated Death Benefits _____ years and subsequent.

3. If the proposed policy is a variable life policy, what gross yield rate is being assumed? ____%

   What is your justification for that rate? _____

C. 1. Describe the differences in the plans of insurance. _____
   _____

   2. Describe any term riders or term elements (above the base policy). Include the ratio of the initial term amount to the total death benefit and any term rate guarantees which may or may not be included.
   Current policy: _____ _____
   Proposed policy: _____

   3. Other than term riders, what riders do the policies include?
   Current policy: _____
   Proposed policy: _____

   4. How long is the initial death benefit **guaranteed** to be in force at the **illustrated** premium?
   Current policy: _____ years.   Proposed policy: _____ years.

   5. What premium is necessary to **guarantee** coverage at initial/current levels for life?
   Current policy: $_____.   Proposed policy: $_____.

D. 1. Is there a potential taxable gain if the current policy is replaced?
   ❏ YES   ❏ NO   If yes, how is it to be managed?
   _____

   2. If there is a taxable gain, **and if there is a loan,** how is the loan to be managed?
   ❏ The new policy will assume the existing loan.
   ❏ The loan will be repaid.
   ❏ The policyowner will recognize taxable income.

E. Is an IRC Sec. 1035 exchange planned to preserve basis?   ❏ YES   ❏ NO

F. If a replacement is under consideration because a more favorable rate classification is available, has a reduction or removal of the rating on the existing policy been requested? If so, what was the result. If not, explain why such a request has not been made.
   _____

G. Does the proposed policy qualify as life insurance under IRC Section 7702?
   ❏ YES   ❏ NO

H. What is the issue date of the current policy? _____

The following "grandfathered" features will be lost if the policy is replaced.
(See Appendix for explanation of items 3-9.)

1. The current policy is incontestable by the insurance company. ☐ YES ☐ NO
2. The period has expired during which the insurance company can deny policy benefits in the event of the insured's suicide. ☐ YES ☐ NO

The current *life insurance policy* was issued on or before:			The current *annuity policy* was issued before:			The current *second to die policy* was issued before:		
	YES	NO		YES	NO		YES	NO
3. 8/06/63	☐	☐	6. 10/21/79	☐	☐	9. 9/14/89	☐	☐
4. 6/20/86	☐	☐	7. 8/14/82	☐	☐			
5. 6/20/88	☐	☐	8. 2/28/86	☐	☐			

I. If the current policy is term, is a conversion to permanent insurance available? ☐ YES ☐ NO
If so, other than the suicide and incontestable provisions would a conversion to permanent insurance be more advantageous?
☐ YES ☐ NO Explanation: _____
_____

J. Financial Strength Ratings. Much has been made of ratings in the last few years; financial strength is important, but it is not the sole determining factor in selecting a life insurance company. A drop in ratings alone generally is not a sufficient reason to replace a policy. It is also important to know that there can be differences of opinion among rating agencies and that small differences in ratings generally are not significant. Furthermore, financial strength ratings are not necessarily indicative of policy performance. If reviewed with the client, a detailed explanation of the ratings must be provided in accordance with state regulations.

	Current Company Rating (Rank)*	Proposed Company Rating (Rank)	Date & Source of Answer
A. M. Best (15 ranks)	_____	_____	_____
Duff & Phelps (18 ranks)	_____	_____	_____
Moody's (19 ranks)	_____	_____	_____
S & P Claims Paying Ability** (18 ranks)	_____	_____	_____

* For example, an AA rating from S & P is the third highest **rank** out of 18 possible ratings.
** S & P offers two rating services. Claims Paying Ability is on a par with the other services listed here; S & P's Qualified Solvency Rating is a much differently oriented rating and is inappropriate for use in this context.

K. Policy loans: Current Policy   Proposed Policy

   1. Gross rate   _____   _____

   2. Fixed or Variable?   _____   _____

   3. Permanent policies:
      Direct Recognition?   _____   _____

   4. Universal life, etc.
      a. Current spread?   _____   _____

      b. Is spread guaranteed?   ❏ YES ❏ NO   ❏ YES ❏ NO

L. Additional remarks:
_____
_____
_____
_____

This RQ was developed as an educational resource for insurance professionals by the
American Society of CLU & ChFC, 270 S. Bryn Mawr Avenue, Bryn Mawr, Pa. 19010
Copyright © 1997. All rights reserved.

Appendix
Grandfathered Features Explanation
(See question H.)

3. The current policy was purchased on or before 8/6/63, so IRC Section 264(a)(3) which limits deductions for interest indebtedness does not apply. If the current policy has met the "four out of seven" test of IRC Section 264(c)(1), interest on indebtedness is deductible to the extent otherwise allowed by law. Personal interest deductions are generally denied for tax years beginning after 1990, irrespective of when the policy was purchased. IRC Sec. 163(h)(1).

4. The current policy was purchased on or before June 20, 1986. Certain policies purchased for business purposes after this date have a $50,000 ceiling on the aggregate amount of indebtedness for which an interest deduction is allowed. IRC Sec. 264(a)(4).

5. Policy was issued on or before 6/20/88 and is not subject to Modified Endowment Contract rules. IRC Sec. 7702A. Substantial increases in the death benefits of grandfathered contracts after 10/20/88 may cause the imposition of the MEC rules. H.R. Conf. Rep. No. 1104, 100th Cong., 2d Sess. (TAMRA '88) reprinted in 1988-3 CB 595 - 596.

6. Variable annuity contracts purchased before 10/21/79 are eligible for a step-up in basis if the owner dies before the annuity starting date. IRC Sec. 72; Rev. Rul. 79-335, 1979-2 CB 292.

7. An annuity issued prior to 8/14/82 is subject to more favorable (basis out first) cost recovery rules for withdrawals. IRC Sec. 72(e). Such policies are not subject to the 10% penalty on withdrawals made prior to age 59 1/2. IRC Sec. 72(q)(2).

8. To the extent contributions are made after 2/28/86 to a deferred annuity held by a non-natural person (such as a business entity), the contract will not be entitled to tax treatment as an annuity. IRC Sec. 72(u).

9. A survivorship life policy issued prior to 9/14/89 is not subject to the 7-pay MEC test if there is a reduction in benefits. IRC Sec. 7702A(c)(6).

*This Appendix is provided for educational purposes only.
You should seek competent legal counsel before
applying this to any specific situation.*

American Society of CLU & ChFC®
A National Organization of Insurance and Financial Service Professionals

Model Regulation Service—January 1996

LIFE INSURANCE ILLUSTRATIONS MODEL REGULATION

Table of Contents

Section 1.　Purpose
Section 2.　Authority
Section 3.　Applicability and Scope
Section 4.　Definitions
Section 5.　Policies to Be Illustrated
Section 6.　General Rules and Prohibitions
Section 7.　Standards for Basic Illustrations
Section 8.　Standards for Supplemental Illustrations
Section 9.　Delivery of Illustrations and Record Retention
Section 10.　Annual Report; Notice to Policy Owners
Section 11.　Annual Certifications
Section 12.　Penalties
Section 13　Separability
Section 14.　Effective Date

Section 1.　Purpose

The purpose of this regulation is to provide rules for life insurance policy illustrations that will protect consumers and foster consumer education. The regulation provides illustration formats, prescribes standards to be followed when illustrations are used, and specifies the disclosures that are required in connection with illustrations. The goals of this regulation are to ensure that illustrations do not mislead purchasers of life insurance and to make illustrations more understandable. Insurers will, as far as possible, eliminate the use of footnotes and caveats and define terms used in the illustration in language that would be understood by a typical person within the segment of the public to which the illustration is directed.

Section 2.　Authority

This regulation is issued based upon the authority granted the commissioner under Section [cite any enabling legislation and state law corresponding to Section 4 of the NAIC Unfair Trade Practices Act].

Drafting Note: Insert the title of the chief insurance regulatory official whenever the term "commissioner" appears.

Section 3.　Applicability and Scope

This regulation applies to all group and individual life insurance policies and certificates except:

　　A.　Variable life insurance;

　　B.　Individual and group annuity contracts;

　　C.　Credit life insurance; or

　　D.　Life insurance policies with no illustrated death benefits on any individual exceeding $10,000.

Section 4.　Definitions

For the purposes of this regulation:

Reprinted from *Model Laws, Regulations and Guidelines* with permission from the Association of Insurance Commissioners. Copyright © January 1996.

Life Insurance Illustrations Model Regulation

A. "Actuarial Standards Board" means the board established by the American Academy of Actuaries to develop and promulgate standards of actuarial practice.

B. "Contract premium" means the gross premium that is required to be paid under a fixed premium policy, including the premium for a rider for which benefits are shown in the illustration.

C. "Currently payable scale" means a scale of non-guaranteed elements in effect for a policy form as of the preparation date of the illustration or declared to become effective within the next ninety-five (95) days.

D. "Disciplined current scale" means a scale of non-guaranteed elements constituting a limit on illustrations currently being illustrated by an insurer that is reasonably based on actual recent historical experience, as certified annually by an illustration actuary designated by the insurer. Further guidance in determining the disciplined current scale as contained in standards established by the Actuarial Standards Board may be relied upon if the standards:

   (1) Are consistent with all provisions of this regulation;

   (2) Limit a disciplined current scale to reflect only actions that have already been taken or events that have already occurred;

   (3) Do not permit a disciplined current scale to include any projected trends of improvements in experience or any assumed improvements in experience beyond the illustration date; and

   (4) Do not permit assumed expenses to be less than minimum assumed expenses.

E. "Generic name" means a short title descriptive of the policy being illustrated such as "whole life," "term life" or "flexible premium adjustable life."

F. "Guaranteed elements" and "non-guaranteed elements"

   (1) "Guaranteed elements" means the premiums, benefits, values, credits or charges under a policy of life insurance that are guaranteed and determined at issue.

   (2) "Non-guaranteed elements" means the premiums, benefits, values, credits or charges under a policy of life insurance that are not guaranteed or not determined at issue.

G. "Illustrated scale" means a scale of non-guaranteed elements currently being illustrated that is not more favorable to the policy owner than the lesser of:

   (1) The disciplined current scale; or

   (2) The currently payable scale.

H. "Illustration" means a presentation or depiction that includes non-guaranteed elements of a policy of life insurance over a period of years and that is one of the three (3) types defined below:

(1) "Basic illustration" means a ledger or proposal used in the sale of a life insurance policy that shows both guaranteed and non-guaranteed elements.

(2) "Supplemental illustration" means an illustration furnished in addition to a basic illustration that meets the applicable requirements of this regulation, and that may be presented in a format differing from the basic illustration, but may only depict a scale of non-guaranteed elements that is ~~not~~ permitted in a basic illustration.

(3) "In force illustration" means an illustration furnished at any time after the policy that it depicts has been in force for one year or more.

I. "Illustration actuary" means an actuary meeting the requirements of Section 11 who certifies to illustrations based on the standard of practice promulgated by the Actuarial Standards Board.

J. "Lapse-supported illustration" means an illustration of a policy form failing the test of self-supporting as defined in this regulation, under a modified persistency rate assumption using persistency rates underlying the disciplined current scale for the first five (5) years and 100 percent policy persistency thereafter.

K. (1) "Minimum assumed expenses" means the minimum expenses that may be used in the calculation of the disciplined current scale for a policy form. The insurer may choose to designate each year the method of determining assumed expenses for all policy forms from the following:

(a) Fully allocated expenses;

(b) Marginal expenses; and

(c) A generally recognized expense table based on fully allocated expenses representing a significant portion of insurance companies and approved by the [National Association of Insurance Commissioners or by the commissioner].

(2) Marginal expenses may be used only if greater than a generally recognized expense table. If no generally recognized expense table is approved, fully allocated expenses must be used.

L. "Non-term group life" means a group policy or individual policies of life insurance issued to members of an employer group or other permitted group where:

(1) Every plan of coverage was selected by the employer or other group representative;

(2) Some portion of the premium is paid by the group or through payroll deduction; and

(3) Group underwriting or simplified underwriting is used.

M. "Policy owner" means the owner named in the policy or the certificate holder in the case of a group policy.

N. "Premium outlay" means the amount of premium assumed to be paid by the policy owner or other premium payer out-of-pocket.

O. "Self-supporting illustration" means an illustration of a policy form for which it can be demonstrated that, when using experience assumptions underlying the disciplined current scale, for all illustrated points in time on or after the fifteenth policy anniversary or the twentieth policy anniversary for second-or-later-to-die policies (or upon policy expiration if sooner), the accumulated value of all policy cash flows equals or exceeds the total policy owner value available. For this purpose, policy owner value will include cash surrender values and any other illustrated benefit amounts available at the policy owner's election.

Section 5. Policies to Be Illustrated

A. Each insurer marketing policies to which this regulation is applicable shall notify the commissioner whether a policy form is to be marketed with or without an illustration. For all policy forms being actively marketed on the effective date of this regulation, the insurer shall identify in writing those forms and whether or not an illustration will be used with them. For policy forms filed after the effective date of this regulation, the identification shall be made at the time of filing. Any previous identification may be changed by notice to the commissioner.

B. If the insurer identifies a policy form as one to be marketed without an illustration, any use of an illustration for any policy using that form prior to the first policy anniversary is prohibited.

Drafting Note: The prohibition in Section 5B may need to be modified if required by the state's replacement regulation.

C. If a policy form is identified by the insurer as one to be marketed with an illustration, a basic illustration prepared and delivered in accordance with this regulation is required, except that a basic illustration need not be provided to individual members of a group or to individuals insured under multiple lives coverage issued to a single applicant unless the coverage is marketed to these individuals. The illustration furnished an applicant for a group life insurance policy or policies issued to a single applicant on multiple lives may be either an individual or composite illustration representative of the coverage on the lives of members of the group or the multiple lives covered.

D. Potential enrollees of non-term group life subject to this regulation shall be furnished a quotation with the enrollment materials. The quotation shall show potential policy values for sample ages and policy years on a guaranteed and non-guaranteed basis appropriate to the group and the coverage. This quotation shall not be considered an illustration for purposes of this regulation, but all information provided shall be consistent with the illustrated scale. A basic illustration shall be provided at delivery of the certificate to enrollees for non-term group life who enroll for more than the minimum premium necessary to provide pure death benefit protection. In addition, the insurer shall make a basic illustration available to any non-term group life enrollee who requests it.

Section 6. General Rules and Prohibitions

A. An illustration used in the sale of a life insurance policy shall satisfy the applicable requirements of this regulation, be clearly labeled "life insurance illustration" and contain the following basic information:

(1) Name of insurer;

(2) Name and business address of producer or insurer's authorized representative, if any;

(3) Name, age and sex of proposed insured, except where a composite illustration is permitted under this regulation;

(4) Underwriting or rating classification upon which the illustration is based;

(5) Generic name of policy, the company product name, if different, and form number;

(6) Initial death benefit; and

(7) Dividend option election or application of non-guaranteed elements, if applicable.

B. When using an illustration in the sale of a life insurance policy, an insurer or its producers or other authorized representatives shall not:

(1) Represent the policy as anything other than a life insurance policy;

(2) Use or describe non-guaranteed elements in a manner that is misleading or has the capacity or tendency to mislead;

(3) State or imply that the payment or amount of non-guaranteed elements is guaranteed;

(4) Use an illustration that does not comply with the requirements of this regulation;

(5) Use an illustration that at any policy duration depicts policy performance more favorable to the policy owner than that produced by the illustrated scale of the insurer whose policy is being illustrated;

(6) Provide an applicant with an incomplete illustration;

(7) Represent in any way that premium payments will not be required for each year of the policy in order to maintain the illustrated death benefits, unless that is the fact;

(8) Use the term "vanish" or "vanishing premium," or a similar term that implies the policy becomes paid up, to describe a plan for using non-guaranteed elements to pay a portion of future premiums;

(9) Except for policies that can never develop nonforfeiture values, use an illustration that is "lapse-supported"; or

(10) Use an illustration that is not "self-supporting."

C. If an interest rate used to determine the illustrated non-guaranteed elements is shown, it shall not be greater than the earned interest rate underlying the disciplined current scale.

Drafting Note: States may wish to replace disclosure requirements under the state's version of the Universal Life Insurance Model Regulation with the basic illustration as contained in this regulation.

Section 7. **Standards for Basic Illustrations**

    A.   Format. A basic illustration shall conform with the following requirements:

        (1)   The illustration shall be labeled with the date on which it was prepared.

        (2)   Each page, including any explanatory notes or pages, shall be numbered and show its relationship to the total number of pages in the illustration (*e.g.*, the fourth page of a seven-page illustration shall be labeled "page 4 of 7 pages").

        (3)   The assumed dates of payment receipt and benefit pay-out within a policy year shall be clearly identified.

        (4)   If the age of the proposed insured is shown as a component of the tabular detail, it shall be issue age plus the numbers of years the policy is assumed to have been in force.

        (5)   The assumed payments on which the illustrated benefits and values are based shall be identified as premium outlay or contract premium, as applicable. For policies that do not require a specific contract premium, the illustrated payments shall be identified as premium outlay.

        (6)   Guaranteed death benefits and values available upon surrender, if any, for the illustrated premium outlay or contract premium shall be shown and clearly labeled guaranteed.

        (7)   If the illustration shows any non-guaranteed elements, they cannot be based on a scale more favorable to the policy owner than the insurer's illustrated scale at any duration. These elements shall be clearly labeled non-guaranteed.

        (8)   The guaranteed elements, if any, shall be shown before corresponding non-guaranteed elements and shall be specifically referred to on any page of an illustration that shows or describes only the non-guaranteed elements (*e.g.*, "see page one for guaranteed elements.")

        (9)   The account or accumulation value of a policy, if shown, shall be identified by the name this value is given in the policy being illustrated and shown in close proximity to the corresponding value available upon surrender.

        (10)   The value available upon surrender shall be identified by the name this value is given in the policy being illustrated and shall be the amount available to the policy owner in a lump sum after deduction of surrender charges, policy loans and policy loan interest, as applicable.

        (11)   Illustrations may show policy benefits and values in graphic or chart form in addition to the tabular form.

        (12)   Any illustration of non-guaranteed elements shall be accompanied by a statement indicating that:

            (a)   The benefits and values are not guaranteed;

            (b)   The assumptions on which they are based are subject to change by the insurer; and

(c) Actual results may be more or less favorable.

(13) If the illustration shows that the premium payer may have the option to allow policy charges to be paid using non-guaranteed values, the illustration must clearly disclose that a charge continues to be required and that, depending on actual results, the premium payer may need to continue or resume premium outlays. Similar disclosure shall be made for premium outlay of lesser amounts or shorter durations than the contract premium. If a contract premium is due, the premium outlay display shall not be left blank or show zero unless accompanied by an asterisk or similar mark to draw attention to the fact that the policy is not paid up.

(14) If the applicant plans to use dividends or policy values, guaranteed or non-guaranteed, to pay all or a portion of the contract premium or policy charges, or for any other purpose, the illustration may reflect those plans and the impact on future policy benefits and values.

B. Narrative Summary. A basic illustration shall include the following:

(1) A brief description of the policy being illustrated, including a statement that it is a life insurance policy;

(2) A brief description of the premium outlay or contract premium, as applicable, for the policy. For a policy that does not require payment of a specific contract premium, the illustration shall show the premium outlay that must be paid to guarantee coverage for the term of the contract, subject to maximum premiums allowable to qualify as a life insurance policy under the applicable provisions of the Internal Revenue Code;

(3) A brief description of any policy features, riders or options, guaranteed or non-guaranteed, shown in the basic illustration and the impact they may have on the benefits and values of the policy;

(4) Identification and a brief definition of column headings and key terms used in the illustration; and

(5) A statement containing in substance the following: "This illustration assumes that the currently illustrated nonguaranteed elements will continue unchanged for all years shown. This is not likely to occur, and actual results may be more or less favorable than those shown."

C. Numeric Summary.

(1) Following the narrative summary, a basic illustration shall include a numeric summary of the death benefits and values and the premium outlay and contract premium, as applicable. For a policy that provides for a contract premium, the guaranteed death benefits and values shall be based on the contract premium. This summary shall be shown for at least policy years five (5), ten (10) and twenty (20) and at age 70, if applicable, on the three bases shown below. For multiple life policies the summary shall show policy years five (5), ten (10), twenty (20) and thirty (30).

(a) Policy guarantees;

(b) Insurer's illustrated scale;

(c) Insurer's illustrated scale used but with the non-guaranteed elements reduced as follows:

  (i) Dividends at fifty percent (50%) of the dividends contained in the illustrated scale used;

  (ii) Non-guaranteed credited interest at rates that are the average of the guaranteed rates and the rates contained in the illustrated scale used; and

  (iii) All non-guaranteed charges, including but not limited to, term insurance charges, mortality and expense charges, at rates that are the average of the guaranteed rates and the rates contained in the illustrated scale used.

(2) In addition, if coverage would cease prior to policy maturity or age 100, the year in which coverage ceases shall be identified for each of the three (3) bases.

D. Statements. Statements substantially similar to the following shall be included on the same page as the numeric summary and signed by the applicant, or the policy owner in the case of an illustration provided at time of delivery, as required in this regulation.

(1) A statement to be signed and dated by the applicant or policy owner reading as follows: "I have received a copy of this illustration and understand that any non-guaranteed elements illustrated are subject to change and could be either higher or lower. The agent has told me they are not guaranteed."

(2) A statement to be signed and dated by the insurance producer or other authorized representative of the insurer reading as follows: "I certify that this illustration has been presented to the applicant and that I have explained that any non-guaranteed elements illustrated are subject to change. I have made no statements that are inconsistent with the illustration."

E. Tabular Detail.

(1) A basic illustration shall include the following for at least each policy year from one (1) to ten (10) and for every fifth policy year thereafter ending at age 100, policy maturity or final expiration; and except for term insurance beyond the 20th year, for any year in which the premium outlay and contract premium, if applicable, is to change:

  (a) The premium outlay and mode the applicant plans to pay and the contract premium, as applicable;

  (b) The corresponding guaranteed death benefit, as provided in the policy; and

  (c) The corresponding guaranteed value available upon surrender, as provided in the policy.

(2) For a policy that provides for a contract premium, the guaranteed death benefit and value available upon surrender shall correspond to the contract premium.

(3) Non-guaranteed elements may be shown if described in the contract. In the case of an illustration for a policy on which the insurer intends to credit terminal dividends, they may be shown if the insurer's current practice is to pay terminal dividends. If any non-guaranteed elements are shown they must be shown at the same durations as the corresponding guaranteed elements, if any. If no guaranteed benefit or value is available at any duration for which a non-guaranteed benefit or value is shown, a zero shall be displayed in the guaranteed column.

Section 8. **Standards for Supplemental Illustrations**

    A. A supplemental illustration may be provided so long as:

        (1) It is appended to, accompanied by or preceded by a basic illustration that complies with this regulation;

        (2) The non-guaranteed elements shown are not more favorable to the policy owner than the corresponding elements based on the scale used in the basic illustration;

        (3) It contains the same statement required of a basic illustration that non-guaranteed elements are not guaranteed; and

        (4) For a policy that has a contract premium, the contract premium underlying the supplemental illustration is equal to the contract premium shown in the basic illustration. For policies that do not require a contract premium, the premium outlay underlying the supplemental illustration shall be equal to the premium outlay shown in the basic illustration.

    B. The supplemental illustration shall include a notice referring to the basic illustration for guaranteed elements and other important information.

Section 9. **Delivery of Illustration and Record Retention**

    A. (1) If a basic illustration is used by an insurance producer or other authorized representative of the insurer in the sale of a life insurance policy and the policy is applied for as illustrated, a copy of that illustration, signed in accordance with this regulation, shall be submitted to the insurer at the time of policy application. A copy also shall be provided to the applicant.

        (2) If the policy is issued other than as applied for, a revised basic illustration conforming to the policy as issued shall be sent with the policy. The revised illustration shall conform to the requirements of this regulation, shall be labeled "Revised Illustration" and shall be signed and dated by the applicant or policy owner and producer or other authorized representative of the insurer no later than the time the policy is delivered. A copy shall be provided to the insurer and the policy owner.

    B. (1) If no illustration is used by an insurance producer or other authorized representative in the sale of a life insurance policy or if the policy is applied for other than as illustrated, the producer or representative shall certify to that effect in writing on a form provided by the insurer. On the same form the applicant shall acknowledge that no illustration conforming to the policy applied for was provided and shall further acknowledge an understanding that an illustration conforming to the policy as issued will be provided no later than at the time of policy delivery. This form shall be submitted to the insurer at the time of policy application.

    (2) If the policy is issued, a basic illustration conforming to the policy as issued shall be sent with the policy and signed no later than the time the policy is delivered. A copy shall be provided to the insurer and the policy owner.

C. If the basic illustration or revised illustration is sent to the applicant or policy owner by mail from the insurer, it shall include instructions for the applicant or policy owner to sign the duplicate copy of the numeric summary page of the illustration for the policy issued and return the signed copy to the insurer. The insurer's obligation under this subsection shall be satisfied if it can demonstrate that it has made a diligent effort to secure a signed copy of the numeric summary page. The requirement to make a diligent effort shall be deemed satisfied if the insurer includes in the mailing a self-addressed postage prepaid envelope with instructions for the return of the signed numeric summary page.

D. A copy of the basic illustration and a revised basic illustration, if any, signed as applicable, along with any certification that either no illustration was used or that the policy was applied for other than as illustrated, shall be retained by the insurer until three (3) years after the policy is no longer in force. A copy need not be retained if no policy is issued.

Section 10. Annual Report; Notice to Policy Owners

A. In the case of a policy designated as one for which illustrations will be used, the insurer shall provide each policy owner with an annual report on the status of the policy that shall contain at least the following information:

    (1) For universal life policies, the report shall include the following:

        (a) The beginning and end date of the current report period;

        (b) The policy value at the end of the previous report period and at the end of the current report period;

        (c) The total amounts that have been credited or debited to the policy value during the current report period, identifying each by type (e.g., interest, mortality, expense and riders);

        (d) The current death benefit at the end of the current report period on each life covered by the policy;

        (e) The net cash surrender value of the policy as of the end of the current report period;

        (f) The amount of outstanding loans, if any, as of the end of the current report period; and

        (g) For fixed premium policies:

If, assuming guaranteed interest, mortality and expense loads and continued scheduled premium payments, the policy's net cash surrender value is such that it would not maintain insurance in force until the end of the next reporting period, a notice to this effect shall be included in the report; or

(h) For flexible premium policies:

If, assuming guaranteed interest, mortality and expense loads, the policy's net cash surrender value will not maintain insurance in force until the end of the next reporting period unless further premium payments are made, a notice to this effect shall be included in the report.

Drafting Note: For states that have adopted the NAIC Universal Life Model Regulation, this paragraph could be replaced with a reference to the equivalent of Section 9 of the model regulation.

(2) For all other policies, where applicable:

(a) Current death benefit;

(b) Annual contract premium;

(c) Current cash surrender value;

(d) Current dividend;

(e) Application of current dividend; and

(f) Amount of outstanding loan.

(3) Insurers writing life insurance policies that do not build nonforfeiture values shall only be required to provide an annual report with respect to these policies for those years when a change has been made to nonguaranteed policy elements by the insurer."

B. If the annual report does not include an in force illustration, it shall contain the following notice displayed prominently: "**IMPORTANT POLICY OWNER NOTICE:** You should consider requesting more detailed information about your policy to understand how it may perform in the future. You should not consider replacement of your policy or make changes in your coverage without requesting a current illustration. You may annually request, without charge, such an illustration by calling [insurer's phone number], writing to [insurer's name] at [insurer's address] or contacting your agent. If you do not receive a current illustration of your policy within 30 days from your request, you should contact your state insurance department." The insurer may vary the sequential order of the methods for obtaining an in force illustration.

C. Upon the request of the policy owner, the insurer shall furnish an in force illustration of current and future benefits and values based on the insurer's present illustrated scale. This illustration shall comply with the requirements of Section 6A, 6B, 7A and 7E. No signature or other acknowledgment of receipt of this illustration shall be required.

D. If an adverse change in non-guaranteed elements that could affect the policy has been made by the insurer since the last annual report, the annual report shall contain a notice of that fact and the nature of the change prominently displayed.

Section 11.   Annual Certifications

A. The board of directors of each insurer shall appoint one or more illustration actuaries.

B. The illustration actuary shall certify that the disciplined current scale used in illustrations is in conformity with the Actuarial Standard of Practice for Compliance with the NAIC Model Regulation on Life Insurance Illustrations promulgated by the Actuarial Standards Board, and that the illustrated scales used in insurer-authorized illustrations meet the requirements of this regulation.

C. The illustration actuary shall:

   (1) Be a member in good standing of the American Academy of Actuaries;

   (2) Be familiar with the standard of practice regarding life insurance policy illustrations;

   (3) Not have been found by the commissioner, following appropriate notice and hearing to have:

   (a) Violated any provision of, or any obligation imposed by, the insurance law or other law in the course of his or her dealings as an illustration actuary;

   (b) Been found guilty of fraudulent or dishonest practices;

   (c) Demonstrated his or her incompetence, lack of cooperation, or untrustworthiness to act as an illustration actuary; or

   (d) Resigned or been removed as an illustration actuary within the past five (5) years as a result of acts or omissions indicated in any adverse report on examination or as a result of a failure to adhere to generally acceptable actuarial standards;

   (4) Not fail to notify the commissioner of any action taken by a commissioner of another state similar to that under Paragraph (3) above;

   (5) Disclose in the annual certification whether, since the last certification, a currently payable scale applicable for business issued within the previous five (5) years and within the scope of the certification has been reduced for reasons other than changes in the experience factors underlying the disciplined current scale. If nonguaranteed elements illustrated for new policies are not consistent with those illustrated for similar in force policies, this must be disclosed in the annual certification. If nonguaranteed elements illustrated for both new and in force policies are not consistent with the nonguaranteed elements actually being paid, charged or credited to the same or similar forms, this must be disclosed in the annual certification; and

   (6) Disclose in the annual certification the method used to allocate overhead expenses for all illustrations:

   (a) Fully allocated expenses;

   (b) Marginal expenses; or

(c) A generally recognized expense table based on fully allocated expenses representing a significant portion of insurance companies and approved by the [National Association of Insurance Commissioners or by the commissioner].

D. (1) The illustration actuary shall file a certification with the board and with the commissioner:

(a) Annually for all policy forms for which illustrations are used; and

(b) Before a new policy form is illustrated.

(2) If an error in a previous certification is discovered, the illustration actuary shall notify the board of directors of the insurer and the commissioner promptly.

E. If an illustration actuary is unable to certify the scale for any policy form illustration the insurer intends to use, the actuary shall notify the board of directors of the insurer and the commissioner promptly of his or her inability to certify.

F. A responsible officer of the insurer, other than the illustration actuary, shall certify annually:

(1) That the illustration formats meet the requirements of this regulation and that the scales used in insurer-authorized illustrations are those scales certified by the illustration actuary; and

(2) That the company has provided its agents with information about the expense allocation method used by the company in its illustrations and disclosed as required in Subsection C(6) of this section.

G. The annual certifications shall be provided to the commissioner each year by a date determined by the insurer.

H. If an insurer changes the illustration actuary responsible for all or a portion of the company's policy forms, the insurer shall notify the commissioner of that fact promptly and disclose the reason for the change.

Section 12. Penalties

In addition to any other penalties provided by the laws of this state, an insurer or producer that violates a requirement of this regulation shall be guilty of a violation of Section [cite state's unfair trade practices act].

Section 13. Separability

If any provision of this regulation or its application to any person or circumstance is for any reason held to be invalid by any court of law, the remainder of the regulation and its application to other persons or circumstances shall not be affected.

Section 14. Effective Date

This regulation shall become effective [January 1, 1997 or effective date set in regulation, whichever is later] and shall apply to policies sold on or after the effective date.

Life Insurance Illustrations Model Regulation

Legislative History (all references are to the Proceedings of the NAIC).

1995 Proc. 4th Quarter (adopted).

7

GROUP BENEFITS

Burton T. Beam, Jr.

Increased Availability of Medical Expense Coverage

What Was the Situation Before?

Prior to the passage of the Health Insurance Portability and Accountability Act of 1996, there were few laws at the federal level that were aimed at making group insurance available to employers and their employees. Rather this was left to the states, and most of them have enacted small-group legislation.

What Is the Nature of the Change?

The Health Insurance Portability and Accountability Act of 1996 contains several provisions designed to help both employees and employers obtain medical expense coverage more easily. Portions of the act that deal with portability are covered in a later section of this chapter when the issue of eligibility is discussed. For now though, the focus is on the plans covered by the act and parts of the act that address nondiscrimination rules, special enrollment periods, renewability, and small groups.

Covered Plans. The act applies to *group health plans* that cover two or more employees, whether insured or self-funded. However, there is a long list of *excepted benefits,* including the following:

- coverage for accident or disability insurance, liability insurance or coverage issued as a supplement to liability insurance, workers' compensation insurance, automobile medical payments insurance, coverage for on-site medical clinics, and other similar insurance specified in regulations, under which benefits for medical care are secondary or incidental to other insurance benefits
- limited vision or dental benefits, long-term care insurance, nursing home insurance, home health care insurance, and insurance for community-based care if these benefits are offered separately rather than as an integral part of a medical expense plan
- coverage for a specific disease or illness, or hospital or other fixed indemnity insurance if the benefits are not coordinated with other coverage under a medical expense plan

- medicare supplement insurance or other similar supplemental coverage if the policy is offered as a separate insurance policy

With one exception, all employers—including the federal government—must comply with the act's provisions. Nonfederal government plans can elect to be excluded for a specific plan year.

Nondiscrimination Rules. The act prohibits the use of any of the following health-related factors as a reason to exclude an employee or dependent from coverage under a group health plan or to charge the individual or dependent a higher premium:

- health status
- medical condition including both physical and mental condition
- claims experience
- receipt of health care
- medical history
- genetic information
- evidence of insurability, including conditions caused by domestic violence
- disability

It is important to note that these factors relate to coverage for specific individuals under a plan. The overall plan itself (except for plans in the small-group market, as explained below) can still be subject to traditional underwriting standards. In addition, group health plans are not required to offer any specific benefits and can limit benefit levels as long as they do not discriminate on the basis of these health-related factors. The act does not restrict the amount an insurance company or other provider of health care coverage can charge an employer for coverage. The act does allow an employer or provider of medical expense coverage to establish premium discounts or rebates or to modify copayments or deductibles for persons who adhere to programs that promote good health or prevent disease. For example, a lower premium can be given to nonsmokers.

Special Enrollment Periods. For various reasons, employees and their dependents may elect not to enroll in an employer's plan when they are initially eligible for coverage. For example, a new employee may have coverage under a spouse's plan. The act requires employers to allow these employees and dependents to enroll in the employer's plan under any one of several specified circumstances as long as the employee had previously stated in writing that the original declination was because there was other coverage. However, the requirement of a written declination does not apply unless the employer requires it and notifies the employee that it is a requirement for future coverage. The following are the circumstances for special enrollment:

- The other coverage was lost because of loss of eligibility under the other plan. This loss of eligibility can result from circumstances such as divorce, the spouse's termination of employment, or death.
- The other coverage was lost because employer contributions for the coverage terminated.
- The other coverage was COBRA coverage that is exhausted.

The employee has 30 days following the loss of coverage to request enrollment in the employer's plan.

In addition, new dependents (including children placed for adoption) are also eligible for coverage under special enrollment rules. The employee must enroll the dependent within 30 days of his or her gaining dependent status. Coverage for a new spouse must become effective no later than the first month beginning after the employee's request. However, coverage for children must go into effect as of the date of birth, adoption, or placement for adoption.

Guaranteed Renewability. All group health insurers must renew existing health insurance coverage unless one of the following circumstances exists:

- The plan sponsor failed to pay premiums or the issuer of health insurance coverage failed to receive timely premiums.
- The plan sponsor performed an act of fraud or made an intentional misrepresentation of material fact under the terms of the coverage.
- The plan sponsor failed to comply with a material plan provision relating to employer contribution or group participation rules as long as these rules are permitted under applicable state or federal law. For example, an employer might fail to maintain a minimum required percentage of participation under a plan.
- There is no covered employee who lives or works in the service area of a network plan such as an HMO.
- The employer is no longer a member of the association that sponsors a plan.
- The issuer of coverage ceases to offer coverage in a particular market. The issuer must notify each plan sponsor, participant, and beneficiary at least 90 days prior to the discontinuation of coverage, and the issuer must offer each plan sponsor the option to purchase other health insurance coverage currently being offered by the issuer to a group health plan in the market. If the issuer exits the market entirely, the period of notice is 180 days, and the issuer cannot reenter the market and sell health insurance coverage for at least 5 years.

Similar rules require multiemployer plans and multiple-employer welfare arrangements to renew coverage for employers. It also establishes guaranteed-issue rules for the individual marketplace.

Guaranteed Issue for Small-Group Plans. With some exceptions, the act requires insurers, HMOs, and other providers of health care coverage that operate in the small-group market to accept all small employers—defined as employers with two to 50 employees—that apply for coverage. In addition, all employees of small employers and their dependents must be accepted for coverage as long as they enroll during the period in which they are first eligible. This rule is in line with the small-group legislation of many states. However, some states have similar rules for groups as small as one employee or have an upper limit of 25, above which the small-group legislation does not apply.

Exceptions to this guaranteed-issue requirement are allowed if a provider of coverage in the small-group market has inadequate network or financial capacity or if applicants are not in a plan's service area.

Minimum participation or employer contribution requirements are acceptable as long as they are permitted under applicable state law.

Interrelationship of State and Federal Legislation. For the most part, the new federal legislation does not preempt state laws pertaining to group health insurance except in those situations where any state standard or requirement would prevent the application of the federal law. To prevent any preemption, most states will need to make some modifications to their laws and regulations.

The act permits a state to enforce its provisions with respect to insurance companies and other medical expense providers. However, the federal government can take over enforcement if a state does not perform its duties. In that case enforcement will be by the secretary of health and human services. The secretary of labor has enforcement power for the act's provisions as they apply to group health plans themselves. When there is federal enforcement, the penalty for noncompliance can be up to $100 per day for each individual with respect to whom a plan or issuer is in noncompliance.

When Does This Change Affect Clients?

Employers, group health plans, and issuers of medical expense coverage are subject to the act's provisions. The provisions generally become effective for plan years beginning after June 30, 1997. The effective date for plans established under collective-bargaining agreements will vary, depending on the dates a collective-bargaining agreement was ratified and expires.

What Should Be Done?

Insurance companies and other issuers of group health plans need to examine their underwriting practices and determine what changes need to be made.

Employers and other plan sponsors need to do the following:

- Determine which group health plans are subject to the act's provisions.
- Make necessary changes to bring applicable group health plans into compliance with the act's provision. This includes making any necessary changes to plan documents.
- Prepare revised summary plan descriptions as necessary. See "ERISA Modification for Group Health Plans" later in this chapter.
- Establish a system for tracking any guidance issued by regulatory agencies with regard to the act. This includes changes that states will make to their rules and regulations.

Where Can I Find Out More?

- HS 325 Group Benefits. The American College.
- IRC Sec. 9802.
- The Health Insurance Portability and Accountability Act (Public Law No. 104-191).
- Many loose-leaf services and benefit consulting firms have prepared extensive materials on the act.
- Watch the trade press for information on the issuance of government guidelines and how other employers are reacting to the changes.

Portability of Group Medical Expense

What Was the Situation Before?

Prior to the passage of the Health Insurance Portability and Accountability Act of 1996, there was no federal legislation that regulated the use of preexisting-conditions provisions when an employee changed jobs or applied for coverage in the individual marketplace after having had group coverage.

What Is the Nature of the Change?

Group-to-Group Portability. Some of the most significant parts of the Health Insurance Portability and Accountability Act are the provisions dealing with "portability" of medical expense coverage. These provisions do not allow an employee to take specific insurance from one job to another. Rather, they put limitations on preexisting-conditions exclusions and allow an employee to use evidence of prior insurance coverage to reduce or eliminate the length of any preexisting-conditions exclusion when the employee moves to another medical expense plan. These provisions should minimize job lock for employees by eliminating the fear that medical expense coverage will be lost if an employee changes jobs.

The portability provisions apply to almost all group health insurance plans (either insured or self-funded) as long as they have at least two active participants on the first day of the plan year. Note that the same definition of *group health plan* mentioned in the prior discussion in this chapter (see "Increased Availability of Medical Expense Coverage") also applies to the portability provisions.

Limitations on Preexisting Conditions. A plan may limit or exclude benefits for preexisting conditions for a maximum of 12 months (18 months for late enrollees). In addition, the period for preexisting conditions must be reduced for prior creditable coverage as defined below. It should be noted that there is nothing in the act that prohibits an employer from imposing a waiting period before a new employee is eligible to enroll in a medical expense plan. However, any waiting period must be applied uniformly without regard for the health status of potential plan participants or beneficiaries. In addition, the waiting period must run concurrently with any preexisting-conditions period.

> *Example:* An employee might be subject to a preexisting-conditions period of 7 months because of prior coverage. If the employer's plan had a 3-month waiting period for enrollment, the length of the preexisting-conditions period after enrollment could be only 4 months.

An HMO is also permitted to have an affiliation period of up to 2 months (3 months for late enrollees) if the HMO does not impose a preexisting-conditions provision and if the affiliation period is applied without consideration of health status-related factors.

Under the act, a *preexisting condition* is defined as a mental or physical condition for which medical advice, diagnosis, care, or treatment was recommended or received within the 6-month period ending on the enrollment date. No preexisting-conditions exclusions can apply to pregnancy or to newborn children or, if under age 18, to newly adopted children or children newly placed for adoption as long as they become covered for creditable coverage within 30 days of birth, adoption, or placement. In addition, the use of genetic information as a preexisting condition is prohibited unless there is a diagnosis of a preexisting medical condition related to the information.

The 12-month limitation for preexisting conditions applies if an employee enrolls when he or she is initially eligible for coverage. It also applies in the case of special enrollment periods (discussed in the prior section of this chapter) that are required by the act for employees and dependents who lose other coverage and for new dependents. Anyone who does not enroll in an employer's plan during the first period he or she is eligible or during a special enrollment period is a late enrollee and can be subject to a preexisting-conditions period of 18 months.

Creditable Coverage. The act defines creditable coverage as coverage under an individual policy, an employer-provided group plan (either insured or self-funded), an HMO, medicare, medicaid, or various public plans, regardless of whether the coverage is provided to a person as an individual, an employee, or a dependent. However, coverage is not creditable if there has been a break in coverage of 63 days or more.

In determining the length of a person's preexisting-conditions period, the period of prior creditable coverage must be subtracted. Assume, for example, that an employer's plan has a preexisting-conditions period of 12 months. If a new employee has 12 months or more of creditable coverage, the preexisting-conditions period will be satisfied. If the period of creditable coverage is only 7 months, then the preexisting-conditions period will run 5 more months. Note, however, that if the employee has been without coverage for at least 63 days between jobs, the full preexisting-conditions period will apply.

Employers have two ways in which they can apply creditable coverage: on a blanket basis to all categories of medical expense coverage or on a benefit-specific basis.

> *Example:* If an employee had prior coverage that excluded prescription drugs, this particular coverage could be subject to the full preexisting-conditions period, while the period for other benefits would be reduced because creditable coverage had applied to them. However, for administrative ease, an employer would probably apply the creditable coverage to all categories of medical expense.

The act requires an employer to give persons losing group coverage a certificate that specifies the period of creditable coverage under the plan they are leaving, including any period of COBRA coverage.

State Options. The act's provisions on portability override state laws with some exceptions, including state laws that provide greater portability. For example, a look-back period of less than 6 months might be required, or the maximum preexisting-conditions period could be less than 12 months.

Group-to-Individual Portability. The Health Insurance Portability and Accountability Act makes it easier for individuals who use group medical expense coverage to find alternative coverage in the individual marketplace. The purpose of the federal legislation seems to be to encourage states to adopt their own mechanisms to achieve this goal. The federal rules will apply in a state only if the state fails to have its plan in effect by either January 1, 1998, or July 1, 1998, depending on which provisions of the act apply in a specific state.

It is assumed that most states will adopt their own plans so that the federal rules will not become effective. The state alternative must do all the following:

- provide a choice of health insurance coverage to all eligible individuals
- not impose any preexisting-conditions restrictions
- include at least one policy form of coverage that either
  - is comparable to comprehensive health coverage offered in the individual marketplace or
  - is comparable to (or is a standard option of coverage available under) the group or individual laws of the state

In addition, the state must implement one of the following:

- one of the NAIC model laws on individual market reform
- a qualified high-risk pool
- certain other mechanisms specified in the act

If a state fails to adopt an alternative to federal regulation, then insurance companies, HMOs, and other health plan providers in the individual marketplace will be required to make coverage available on a guaranteed-issue basis to individuals with 18 or more months of creditable coverage and whose most recent coverage was under a group health plan. However, coverage does not have to be provided to an individual who has other health insurance or who is eligible for COBRA coverage, medicare, or medicaid. No preexisting-conditions exclusions can be imposed. Health insurers have three options for providing coverage to eligible individuals:

- They may offer every health insurance policy they offer in the state.
- They may offer their two most popular policies in the state, based on premium volume.
- They may offer a low-level and a high-level coverage as long as they contain benefits that are similar to other coverage offered by the insurer in the state.

Rules similar to those described in the prior topic in this chapter require the renewal of individual coverage.

When Does This Change Affect Clients?

Employers, group health plans, and issuers of medical expense coverage are subject to the act's provisions. The provisions generally become effective for plan years beginning after June 30, 1997. The effective date for plans established under collective-bargaining agreements will vary, depending on the dates a collective-bargaining agreement was ratified and expires.

What Should Be Done?

Insurance companies and other issuers of group health plans need to examine their underwriting practices and determine what changes need to be made.

Employers and other plan sponsors need to do the following:

- Determine which group health plans are subject to the act's provisions.
- Make necessary changes to bring applicable group health plans into compliance with the act's provision. This includes making any necessary changes to plan documents.
- Design a system of tracking group health plan coverage of current employees and for issuing coverage certificates to eligible persons who terminate employment.
- Determine the method to use for applying creditable coverage.
- Prepare revised summary plan descriptions as necessary. See "ERISA Modification for Group Health Plans" later in this chapter.
- Establish a system for tracking any guidance issued by regulatory agencies with regard to the act. This includes changes that states will make to their rules and regulations.

Where Can I Find Out More?

- HS 325 Group Benefits. The American College.
- IRC Sec. 9801.
- See the Health Insurance Portability and Accountability Act (Public Law No. 104-191).
- Many loose-leaf services and benefit consulting firms have prepared extensive materials on the act.
- Watch the trade press for information on the issuance of government guidelines and how other employers are reacting to the changes.

COBRA Changes

What Was the Situation Before?

The continuation of group medical expense coverage under COBRA has been in effect since 1985. Until the passage of the Health Insurance Portability and Accountability Act of 1996, a qualified beneficiary has been defined as any employee, or the spouse or dependent child of the employee, who on the *day before the qualifying event* was covered under the employee's group health plan.

Qualified beneficiaries who were determined to have met the social security definition of total disability at the time of a qualifying event for COBRA coverage were able to extend COBRA coverage from 18 to 29 months.

What Is the Nature of the Change?

The Health Insurance Portability and Accountability Act of 1996 changed the definition of a qualified beneficiary to include any child who is born to or placed for adoption with the employee during the period of COBRA coverage. This change gives automatic coverage to the child and also gives the child the right to have his or her own election rights if a second qualifying event (such as the parent's death) occurs.

The right to extend COBRA coverage from 18 to 29 months now also applies to a qualified beneficiary who becomes disabled (using the Social Security Administra-tion definition) during the first 60 days of COBRA coverage.

When Does This Change Affect Clients?

Clients should have made each qualified beneficiary who had elected coverage aware of these changes by November 1, 1996. This could be done by mailing, first class, a copy of ERISA Technical Release No. 96-1 to the last known address of each qualified beneficiary.

What Should Be Done?

Employers and other plan sponsors should do the following:

- Send the previously described notification to qualified beneficiaries if it has not already been sent.
- Revise COBRA notices to comply with the act.
- Establish a system for tracking any guidance issued by regulatory agencies with regard to the act.

Where Can I Find Out More?

- HS 325 Group Benefits. The American College.
- IRC Sec. 4980B.
- The Health Insurance Portability and Accountability Act (Public Law No. 104-191)
- COBRA materials contained in loose-leaf services and prepared by a benefit consulting firm

ERISA Modification for Group Health Plans

What Was the Situation Before?

ERISA required a summary of material modification to be issued automatically to each plan participant and the Department of Labor within 210 days after the end of the plan year in which a material change was made to any welfare benefit plan.

What Is the Nature of the Change?

The Health Insurance Portability and Accountability Act of 1996 changes the 210-day requirement with respect to group health plans. (See the definition in the first section of this chapter.) If there is a material change in such plans, the plan administrator has two options. The first is to furnish the summary of material modification to participants and beneficiaries no later than 60 days after the change. As an alternative, plan administrators can elect to provide the notification at regular intervals no longer than 90 days. This option is probably useful only if a plan is expected to undergo frequent changes.

The summary plan description must identify any health insurance issuer (for example, an insurance company or HMO) that is responsible for the financing or the administration of the plan and provide its address.

When Does This Change Affect Clients?

Plan administrators must comply with these changes or face financial penalties under ERISA beginning in plan years starting after June 30, 1997.

What Should Be Done?

Plan administrators should establish procedures for monitoring changes to group health plans so that these changes can be incorporated into summaries of material modification in a timely manner.

Where Can I Find Out More?

- HS 325 Group Benefits. The American College.
- The Health Insurance Portability and Accountability Act (Public Law No. 104-91)
- ERISA material in loose-leaf services and prepared by benefit consulting firms

Favorable Tax Treatment for Medical Savings Accounts

What Was the Situation Before?

One suggested approach to making medical expense insurance more available and affordable is the use of medical savings accounts (MSAs). An MSA is an alternative to a medical expense plan, but it has few copayments. In this case an employee maintains a comprehensive medical plan with virtually total coverage for medical expenses to the extent that they exceed a high deductible, such as $2,000. The employer then contributes part of the savings in premium to an MSA, which is often an interest-bearing account. An employee can draw from the account to pay medical expenses not covered by the medical expense plan, such as charges for routine office visits or the cost of eyeglasses. At the end of the year any monies in the MSA are paid to the employee under plans that have been in existence.

The rationale for a medical savings account is that significant cost savings can occur for two primary reasons. First, the expensive cost of administering small claims is largely eliminated, as demonstrated by the fact that a major medical policy with a $2,500 deductible can often be purchased for about one-half the cost of a policy with a $250 deductible. Second, employees now have a direct financial incentive to avoid unnecessary care and to seek out the most cost-effective form of treatment.

A few employers have used medical savings accounts for some time with positive results. Costs have in fact been lowered or risen less rapidly than would otherwise be expected. Employee reaction has generally been favorable, but there has been one major drawback—contributions to an MSA have constituted taxable income to employees.

As with almost any approach to cost containment, medical savings accounts have had their critics. It is argued that MSAs may make sense when used with traditional indemnity plans, but long-term health care reform should focus on managed care. However, proponents counter that the concept could also work with HMOs or preferred provider organizations (PPOs). Another argument against MSAs is that employees will be more interested in receiving cash at the end of the year and therefore minimize treatment for minor medical expenses and preventive care that would have been covered under a plan without an MSA. This avoidance of medical care, contend the critics, may lead to major expenses that could have been avoided or minimized with earlier treatment. A final criticism of MSAs is that they do not focus on the uninsured's problem. However, proponents argue that any technique that lowers costs for employers will encourage some additional small employers to provide coverage that would have previously been unaffordable.

What Is the Nature of the Change?

The use of MSAs will undoubtedly increase as a result of the Health Insurance Portability and Accountability Act of 1996. The act provides favorable tax treatment for MSAs established under a pilot project that began on January 1, 1997, as long as prescribed rules are satisfied. The project, which runs through the end of the year 2000, allows the establishment of up to approximately 750,000 MSAs. At the end of the 4-year trial period, tax-favored MSAs cannot be established unless Congress expands the program. However, MSAs in existence at the end of the 4-year period can generally continue in force after that time under the current rules. During this 4-year period, the act calls for two studies to assist Congress in making its decision regarding MSAs. First, the Treasury Department will assess MSA participation and its effect on tax revenue. Second, the General Accounting Office will assess the effect of MSAs on the small-group market by looking at factors such as the effect of MSAs on health care costs and the use of preventive care.

It should be noted that MSAs, which existed on a non-tax-favored basis prior to 1997, will probably need to be revised to meet the act's requirements and receive favorable tax status.

General Nature. An MSA is a personal savings account from which unreimbursed medical expenses, including deductibles and copayments, can be paid. Coverage can either be limited to an individual or include dependents. An MSA must be in the form of a tax-exempt trust or custodial account established in conjunction with a high-deductible health (that is, medical expense) plan. An MSA is established with a qualified trustee or custodian in much the same way that an IRA is established. Any insurance company or bank (as well as certain other financial institutions) can be a trustee or custodian, as can any other person or entity already approved by the IRS as a trustee or custodian for IRAs. While there are some similarities between MSAs and IRAs, there are also differences. As a result, an IRA cannot be used as an MSA, and an IRA and MSA cannot be combined into a single account.

Even though employers can sponsor MSAs, these accounts are established for the benefit of individuals and are portable. If an employee changes employers or leaves the workforce, the MSA remains with the individual.

Eligibility for an MSA. Two types of individuals are eligible to establish MSAs:

- an employee (or spouse) of a *small employer* that maintains an individual or family *high-deductible health plan* covering that individual. These persons will establish their MSAs under an employer-sponsored plan.
- a self-employed person (or spouse) maintaining an individual or family high-deductible health plan covering that individual. These persons will need to seek out a custodian or trustee for their MSAs.

A *small employer* is defined as an employer who has an average of 50 or fewer employees (including employees of controlled group members and predecessor employers) on business days during either of the two preceding calendar years. In the case of a new employer, the number of employees is based on an estimate of the reasonably expected employment for the current year. After the initial qualification as a small employer is satisfied, an employer can continue to make contributions to employees' MSAs, and employees can continue to establish MSAs until the first year following the year in which the employer has more than 200 employees. At that time participating employees may take over contributions to their accounts, but no employer contributions can be made, and nonparticipating employees may not start new accounts.

A *high-deductible health plan,* for purposes of MSA participation, is a plan that has the following deductibles and annual out-of-pocket limitations, all of which will be adjusted for inflation after 1998:

- In the case of individual coverage, the deductible must be at least $1,500 and cannot exceed $2,500. The maximum annual out-of-pocket expenses cannot exceed $3,000.
- In the case of family coverage, the deductible must be at least $3,000 and cannot exceed $4,500. The maximum annual out-of-pocket expenses cannot exceed $5,500.

A high-deductible plan can be written by an insurance company or a managed care organization, such as an HMO. At the time this book was being prepared, the early high-deductible plans were being written primarily by insurance companies in the form of traditional major medical products but possibly with the requirement that covered persons use preferred-provider networks. No HMOs had established high-deductible plans.

A high-deductible plan can be part of a cafeteria plan, but the MSA must be established outside the cafeteria plan.

With some exceptions, a person who is covered under a high-deductible health plan is denied eligibility for an MSA if he or she is covered under another health plan that does not meet the definition of a high-deductible plan but provides any benefits that are covered under the high-deductible health plan. The exceptions include coverage for accident, disability, dental care, vision care, and long-term care as well as medicare supplement insurance, liability insurance, insurance for a specific disease or illness, and insurance paying a fixed amount per period of hospitalization.

The intent of Congress was that the number of MSAs be limited to approximately 750,000. There are lower statutory limits that, if reached at various specified cutoff dates, will close off the individual's ability to establish an MSA unless he or she is covered under an employer's high-deductible plan that existed prior to the cutoff date.

Contributions. Either the account holder of an MSA or the account holder's employer—but not both— may make a contribution to an MSA. If the employer makes a contribution, even one below the allowable limit, the account holder may not make a contribution. Contributions must be in the form of cash.

Contributions by an employer are tax deductible to the employer and are not included in an employee's gross income or subject to social security and other employment taxes. Employee contributions are deductible in computing adjusted gross income. As with IRAs, individuals' contributions must generally be made by April 15 of the year following the year for which the contributions are made.

The annual tax deduction for the contribution to an employee's account is limited to 65 percent of the deductible for the health coverage if the MSA is for an individual. The figure is 75 percent if an MSA covers a family. If each spouse has an MSA and if one or both of the MSAs provide family coverage, the aggregate deductible contribution is equal to 75 percent of the deductible for the family coverage with the lowest deductible. The deductible contribution is split equally between the two persons unless they agree to a different division.

The actual MSA contribution that can be deducted is limited to 1/12 of the annual amount, as described in the previous paragraph, times the number of months that an individual is eligible for MSA participation. For example, assume that the deductible under an individual's health plan is $1,800. The maximum annual contribution to the MSA is then 65 percent of this amount, which is $1,170, and the monthly amount is $97.50. If the individual is covered under a high-deductible plan only for the first 8 months of the year, then the annual deductible contribution is eight times $97.50, or $780. Note, however, that there are no requirements that contributions be made on a monthly basis or at any particular time. In this example, the full $1,170 could have been made early in the year. The excess over $780 would then be an excess contribution.

An excess contribution occurs to the extent that contributions to an MSA exceed the deductible limits or are made for an ineligible person. Any excess contribution made by the employer is included in the employee's gross income. In addition, account holders are subject to a 6 percent excise tax on excess contributions for each year these contributions are in an account. This excise tax can be avoided if the excess amount and any net income attributable to the excess amount are removed from the MSA prior to the last day prescribed by law, including extensions, for filing the account holder's income tax return. The net income attributable to the excess contributions is included in the account holder's gross income for the tax year in which the distribution is made.

An employer that makes contributions to MSAs is subject to a comparability rule that requires the employer to make comparable contributions for all employees who have MSAs. However, full-time employees and part-time employees (those working less than 30 hours per week) are treated separately. The comparability rules require that the employer contribute either the same dollar amount for each employee or the same percentage of each employee's deductible under the health plan. Failure to comply with this rule subjects the employer to an excise tax equal to 35 percent of the aggregate amount contributed to MSAs during the period when the comparability rule was not satisfied.

Growth of MSA Accounts. Unused MSA balances carry over from year to year, and there is no prescribed period in which they must be withdrawn. Earnings on amounts in an MSA are not subject to taxation as they accrue.

Distributions. An individual can take distributions from an MSA at any time. The amount of the distribution can be any part or all of the account balance. Subject to some exceptions, distributions of both contributions and earnings are excludible from an account holder's gross income if used to pay medical expenses of the account holder and the account holder's family as long as these expenses are not paid by other sources of insurance. For the most part, the eligible medical expenses are the same ones that would be deductible—ignoring the 7.5 percent of adjusted gross income limitation—if the account holder itemized his or her tax deductions. However, tax-free withdrawals are not permitted for the purchase of insurance other than long-term care insurance, COBRA continuation coverage, or premiums for health coverage while an individual receives unemployment compensation. In addition, in any year a contribution is made to an MSA, tax-free withdrawals can be made to pay the medical expenses of only those persons who were eligible for coverage under an MSA at the time the expenses were incurred. For example, MSA contributions could not be withdrawn tax free to pay the unreimbursed medical expenses of an account holder's spouse who was covered under a health plan of his or her employer that was not a high-deductible plan.

Expenses that are withdrawn for reasons other than paying eligible medical expenses are included in an account holder's gross income and are subject to a 15 percent penalty tax unless certain circumstances exist. The penalty tax is not levied if the distribution is made after the account holder turns 65 or because of the account holder's death or disability. In addition, the penalty tax does not apply to funds rolled over to a new MSA as long as the rollover is done within 60 days. Transfers of MSA accounts as a result of divorce are also tax free.

Estate Tax Treatment. Upon death, the remaining balance in an MSA is includible in the account holder's gross estate for estate tax purposes. If the beneficiary of the account is a surviving spouse, the MSA belongs to the spouse and he or she can deduct the account balance in determining the account holder's gross estate. The surviving spouse can then use the MSA for his or her medical expenses. If the beneficiary is anyone else, or if no beneficiary is named, the MSA ceases to exist.

Reporting and Disclosure Requirements. MSA trustees must report annually to the secretary of the treasury with information such as the number of MSAs for which they are a trustee and also must provide information about persons with MSAs, including the number who were previously uninsured.

Employers that sponsor MSAs must provide annual statements to employees that show amounts contributed to any MSA of the employee or the employee's spouse.

When Does This Change Affect Clients?

This change is now in effect.

What Should Be Done?

Employers interested in using medical expense accounts need to determine whether this is the preferable approach for providing medical expense coverage to employees. While this approach has the potential to save money in the short run, an employer cannot ignore the possibility that MSAs may also have the effect of minimizing preventive care. This might have a long-run negative effect on cost.

If an employer decides to use MSAs for employees, several issues need to be addressed.

- The employer must determine that it meets the definition of a small employer.
- The employer must decide whether to insure or self-fund the high-deductible health plan. If the employer self-funds, the employer must establish the MSA through a trust document and select the trustees. However, if the employer insures the health plan, the insurer may also provide and administer the MSA accounts.
- The employer must establish a system to comply with the reporting and disclosure requirements for MSAs.

Where Can I Find Out More?

- HS 325 Group Benefits. The American College.
- IRC Sec. 220.
- The Health Insurance Portability and Accountability Act (Public Law No. 104-91)
- Many loose-leaf services and benefit consulting firms have prepared extensive materials on the act.
- Insurers who intend to sell high-deductible medical expense plans have prepared materials on MSAs.
- Watch the trade press for information on how other employers are reacting to the availability of tax-favored medical savings accounts.

Expanded Coverage for Newborns and Mothers

What Was the Situation Before?

There were no federal rules that required minimum stays for newborns or mothers following birth. However, some states did have such legislation.

What Is the Nature of the Change?

Beginning with plan years on or after January 1, 1998, group health plans are subject to the provisions of the Newborns' and Mothers' Health Protection Act. This federal act is very broad and, with one exception, applies to all employers regardless of size and to self-funded plans as well as those written by health insurers and managed care plans. The exception is for plans subject to similar state legislation, which exist in over half the states. The impetus for such legislation at both the state and federal level arose from consumer backlash over the practice of an increasing number of HMOs and insurance companies limiting maternity benefits to 24 hours after a normal vaginal birth and 48 hours after a cesarean section. The act affects maternity benefits if they are provided. It does not mandate that such benefits be included in benefit plans. Of course, many employers are subject to other state and federal laws that do mandate maternity benefits.

The act prohibits a group health plan or insurer from restricting hospital benefits to less than 48 hours for both the mother and the newborn following a normal vaginal delivery and 96 hours following a cesarean section. In addition, a plan cannot require a provider to obtain authorization from the plan or insurer for a stay that is within these minimums. While a new mother, in consultation with her physician, might agree to a shorter stay, a plan or insurer cannot offer a monetary incentive to the mother for this purpose. In addition, the plan or insurer cannot limit provider reimbursement because care was provided within the minimum limits or make incentives available to providers to render care inconsistent with the minimum requirements.

If a plan has deductibles, coinsurance, or other cost-sharing requirements, these cannot be greater than those imposed on any preceding portion of the hospital stay.

When Does This Change Affect Clients?

Group health plans that provide maternity benefits must comply with the act for plan years beginning on or after January 1, 1998.

What Should Be Done?

Employers and providers of medical expense coverage should bring plans and practices within conformity with the act no later than the start of plan years beginning on or after January 1, 1998. However, many employers will already be in compliance because of similar state legislation.

The act treats the imposition of the minimum-stay requirement as a material modification for purposes of ERISA and requires each plan sponsor to provide a summary of material modification to plan participants and the Department of Labor within 60 days after the start of the plan year (rather than the usual 210 days after the end of the plan year) for which the requirements apply.

Where Can I Find Out More?

- HS 325 Group Benefits. The American College.
- The Newborns' and Mothers' Health Protection Act (Title VI of Public Law No. 104-204)
- Many loose-leaf services and benefit consulting firms have prepared extensive materials on the act.

Some Minor Changes in Mental Health Benefits

What Was the Situation Before?

It has been common for major medical plans to impose an annual maximum (such as $1,000) and/or an overall maximum lifetime limit (such as $25,000) on benefits for mental and nervous disorders, alcoholism, and drug addiction.

What Is the Nature of the Change?

At the time of the debate over the Health Insurance Portability and Accountability Act of 1996, there was considerable disagreement over the issue of requiring mental illness to be treated as any other illness for purposes of medical expense coverage. With estimates that complete parity would raise the cost of providing medical expense benefits by 4 to 10 percent (depending on whose estimate could be believed), Congress left the issue unresolved. The debate continued after the passage of the previously mentioned act and resulted in the passage of another act the following month—the Mental Health Parity Act. However, because of cost considerations, its provisions are limited, and the use of the term *parity* is probably a misnomer.

The provisions of the act are effective for plan years beginning on or after January 1, 1998, and apply only to employers that have more than 50 employees. The act prohibits a group health plan, insurance company, or HMO from setting annual or lifetime *dollar* limits on mental health benefits that are less than the limits applying to other medical and surgical benefits as follows:

- If there are no such dollar limitations for substantially all other (meaning two-thirds or more) medical and surgical benefits under a plan, there can be none for mental health benefits.
- If substantially all benefits are subject to an annual or lifetime limit, the parity requirements can be satisfied by either having separate dollar limits that are equal for mental health benefits and other medical and

surgical benefits or applying a uniform dollar limit to all benefits in the aggregate.
- If a plan has different limits for different categories of benefits, the act calls for the use of a weighted average of all the limits to be used for the mental health limitations.

The act imposes no parity rules on benefits for alcoholism or drug addiction. In addition, the act is noteworthy for other things it does not do. It does not require employers to make any benefits available for mental illness, and it does not impose any other restrictions on mental health benefits. Employers can still impose limitations such as an annual maximum on the number of visits or days of coverage and different cost-sharing provisions for mental health benefits than those that apply to other medical and surgical benefits.

Congressional advocates of the act estimate that overall medical costs to employers should not increase by more than .4 percent. Any employer who can prove that the act's provisions will increase its costs by more than one percent is exempt from the act.

The act is subject to a sunset provision of September 30, 2001. As of that date, any benefits required by the act can be eliminated unless Congress extends the date or removes the sunset provision prior to that time.

When Does This Change Affect Clients?

Clients whose medical expense plans have maximum annual or lifetime dollar limits for mental health benefits must amend their plans for plan years beginning on or after January 1, 1998.

What Should Be Done?

Employers need to determine if their medical expense plans are subject to the act's provisions and make any necessary changes.

Changes need to be communicated to employees; these changes probably should include the issuance of a summary of material modification.

Where Can I Find Out More?

- HS 325 Group Benefits. The American College.
- The Mental Health Parity Act (Title VII of Public Law No. 104-204)
- Many loose-leaf services and benefit consulting firms have prepared extensive materials on the act.

INVESTMENTS

Asset Allocation
George Alden

Meeting an investor's needs is more than a matter of finding the perfect financial product. The investor's short-term and long-term financial goals must be identified. Once this is done, the various investments can be analyzed for their risk and return and their impact on the investor's goals. An increasingly common method for developing an appropriate portfolio is referred to as *asset allocation.*

What Is Asset Allocation?

First, let us look at what asset allocation is. Ibbotson Associates defines it in part as "the process of developing a diversified investment portfolio by mixing different assets in varying proportions."[1] The mathematical process that calculates this mix was developed by Harry Markowitz in the early 1950s; he was later awarded a share of the 1990 Nobel Prize in Economics for this work. The actual process, called *mean-variance optimization (MVO),* calculates the security or asset class weights that give a portfolio the maximum expected return for a given level of risk or, conversely, the minimum risk for a given expected return. Although Markowitz first developed his model for individual stocks, the model also has numerous applications to bonds, mutual funds, and other asset classes as historical data have been tracked and measured.

Numerous studies have supported the importance of asset allocation. Brinson, Singer, and Barbower's famous study found that asset allocation accounted for 91.5 percent of the actual return and differences among the returns in the pension funds they studied. Their research also found that market timing adds only 1.8 percent to the true growth of a portfolio. This means that investors should devote the majority of their efforts to formulating an appropriate allocation policy.[2]

---

1. Ibbotson Associates, *The Asset Allocation Decision*, presentation materials, Chicago, 1995, p. 58.
2. Ibid., 46.

FIGURE 8-1
Importance of Asset Allocation

How do management decisions contribute to a portfolio's performance?

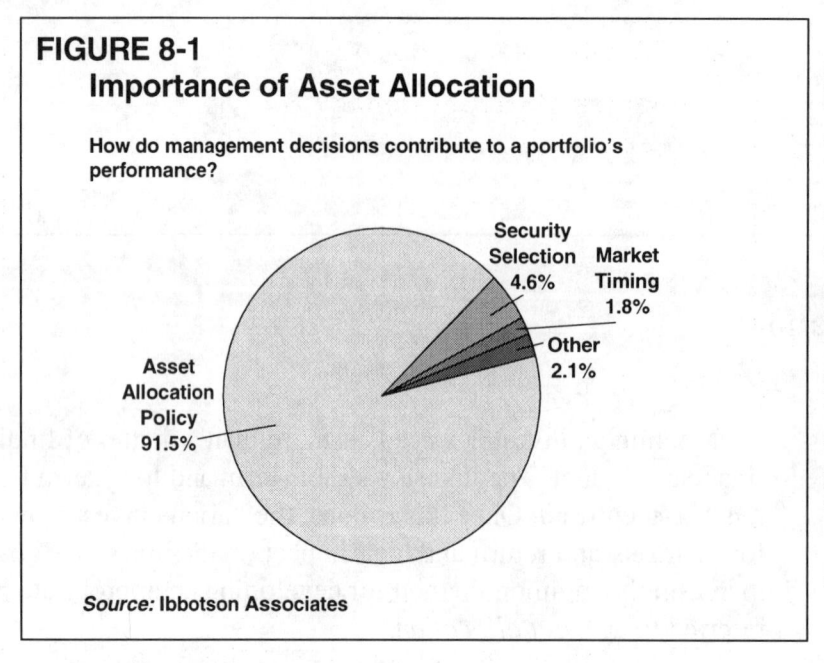

- Asset Allocation Policy 91.5%
- Security Selection 4.6%
- Market Timing 1.8%
- Other 2.1%

Source: Ibbotson Associates

Source: © *The Asset Allocation Decision* Presentation 1995, Ibbotson Associates, Chicago. Used with permission. All rights reserved.

The importance of asset allocation over market timing is further supported by looking at the dangers of market timing. Figures 8-2 and 8-3 illustrate the risks of attempting to time the stock market over the past 69 years and over the immediate 15-year period.[3]

FIGURE 8-2
Dangers of Market Timing

Value of $1 invested from year-end 1925-1996

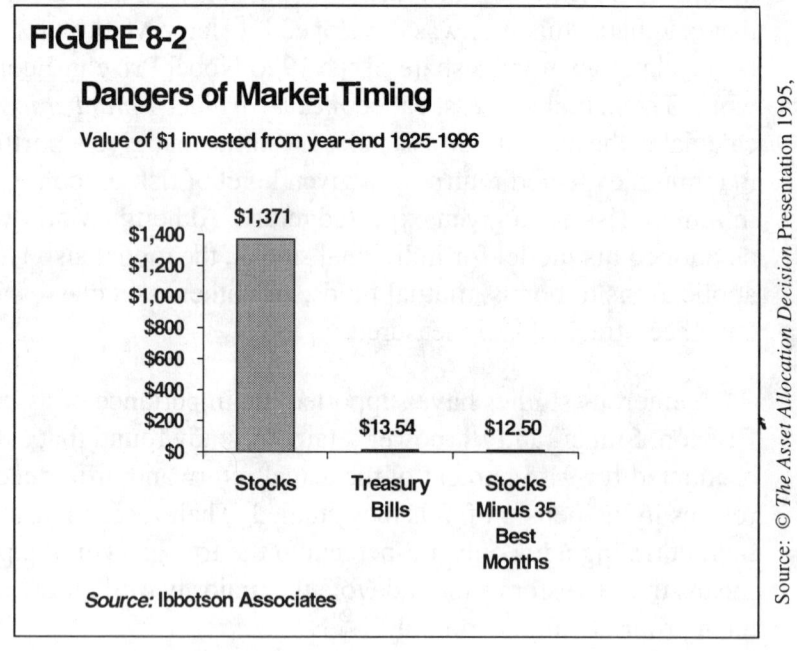

- Stocks: $1,371
- Treasury Bills: $13.54
- Stocks Minus 35 Best Months: $12.50

Source: Ibbotson Associates

Source: © *The Asset Allocation Decision* Presentation 1995, Ibbotson Associates, Chicago. Used with permission. All rights reserved.

---

3. *Asset Allocation Decision*, 29.

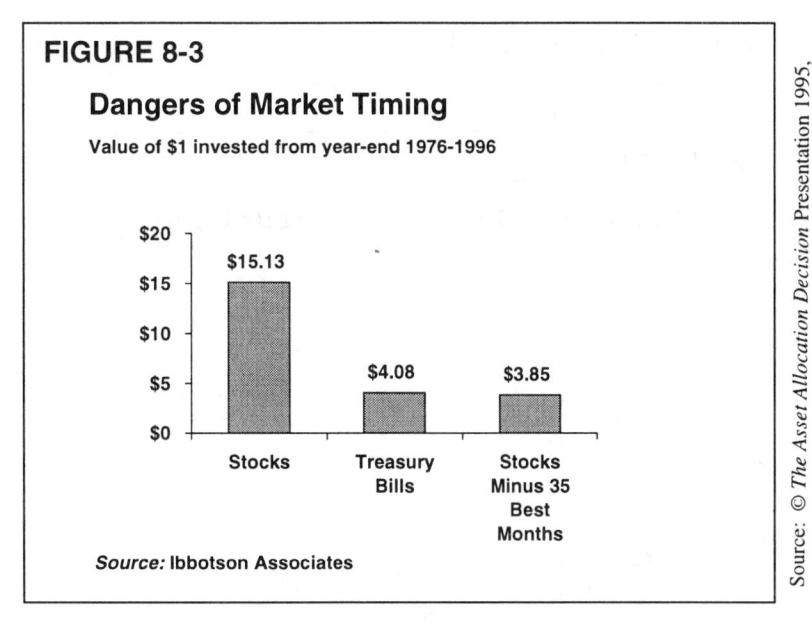

FIGURE 8-3

Dangers of Market Timing

Value of $1 invested from year-end 1976-1996

- Stocks: $15.13
- Treasury Bills: $4.08
- Stocks Minus 35 Best Months: $3.85

Source: Ibbotson Associates

Source: © *The Asset Allocation Decision* Presentation 1995, Ibbotson Associates, Chicago. Used with permission. All rights reserved.

The first step in developing an asset allocation policy with a client is making sure that the client has a working knowledge of the different investment alternatives (asset classes), their characteristics, and how they work together. Ibbotson's presentation material on investment principles and historical asset performance, for example, meets this need and also gives financial services professionals excellent written material to leave with investors.

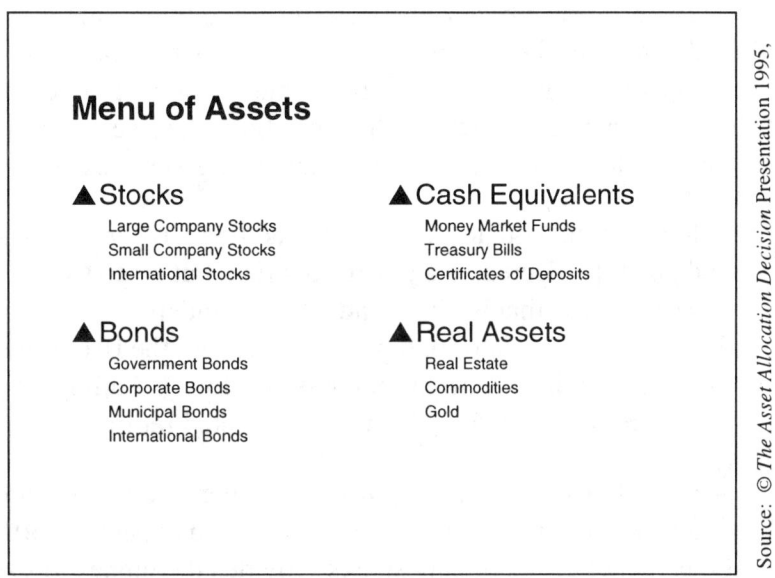

Menu of Assets

▲ **Stocks**
  Large Company Stocks
  Small Company Stocks
  International Stocks

▲ **Bonds**
  Government Bonds
  Corporate Bonds
  Municipal Bonds
  International Bonds

▲ **Cash Equivalents**
  Money Market Funds
  Treasury Bills
  Certificates of Deposits

▲ **Real Assets**
  Real Estate
  Commodities
  Gold

Source: © *The Asset Allocation Decision* Presentation 1995, Ibbotson Associates, Chicago. Used with permission. All rights reserved.

Once this is accomplished, financial advisers can use Ibbotson's portfolio optimization booklet to review and explain the asset allocation theory and its portfolio optimization software to supplement it. Whatever presentation material and software are used for this purpose, the goal is to further discussion of the client's given concerns and preferences in developing and selecting investments that can go in his or her model. This culminates with the adviser's and client's understanding of the *efficient frontier line* (see figure 8-4[4]).

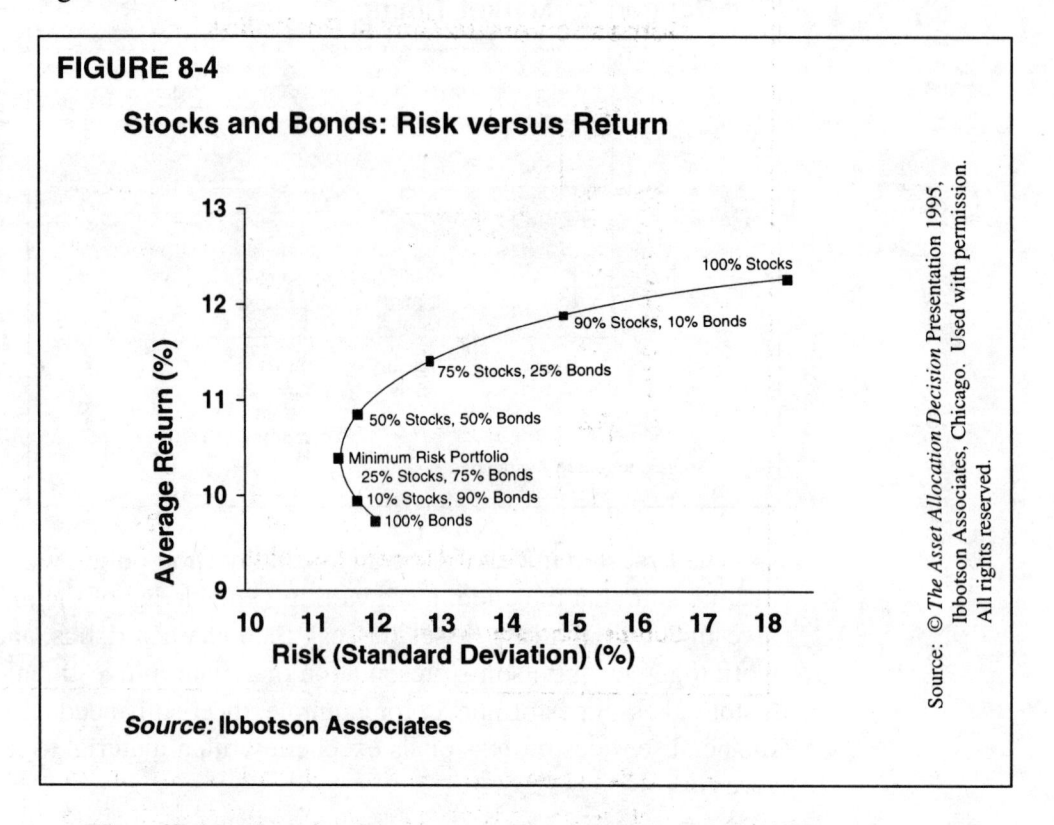

FIGURE 8-4

Stocks and Bonds: Risk versus Return

[Graph showing efficient frontier curve with Average Return (%) on y-axis (9 to 13) and Risk (Standard Deviation) (%) on x-axis (10 to 18). Points marked along the curve:
- 100% Stocks
- 90% Stocks, 10% Bonds
- 75% Stocks, 25% Bonds
- 50% Stocks, 50% Bonds
- Minimum Risk Portfolio 25% Stocks, 75% Bonds
- 10% Stocks, 90% Bonds
- 100% Bonds]

Source: Ibbotson Associates

Source: © *The Asset Allocation Decision* Presentation 1995, Ibbotson Associates, Chicago. Used with permission. All rights reserved.

The efficient frontier line was created to represent every possible combination of the two given asset classes: large company stocks and long-term government bonds. Only portfolios that lie on or below the efficient frontier can be constructed. The area above the line represents very high returns at low risk, which are unattainable, given these two asset classes.

It may seem counterintuitive that adding a risky asset—stocks—to an all-bond portfolio decreases a portfolio's risk, but since stocks and bonds have a low correlation (that is, they tend to move independently of each other), adding stocks to an all-bond portfolio *reduces* the risk of the portfolio—but only up to a point (the minimum risk portfolio). Adding stocks beyond this point increases both the risk and the expected return of the portfolio.

Portfolios in the upper right-hand corner of the graph are those with the highest returns and risk levels. As one would expect, a portfolio consisting of 100 percent large company stocks provides the highest possible returns as well as the highest risk on this given efficient frontier. An understanding of the model above forms the basis from which to explain how other asset classes can be used in diversifying and designing an even more efficient model.

---

4. *Asset Allocation Decision*, 48.

FIGURE 8-5

Domestic versus Global Portfolios

[Chart showing efficient frontier with Average Return (%) on y-axis ranging from 13 to 15.5, and Risk (Standard Deviation) (%) on x-axis ranging from 15 to 23. Points plotted: 100% U.S. (~13.5% return), Minimum Risk Portfolio 20% International, 80% U.S., 40% International, 60% U.S., 60% International, 40% U.S., 80% International, 20% U.S., and 100% International (~15% return).]

Source: Ibbotson Associates

Source: © *The Asset Allocation Decision* Presentation 1995, Ibbotson Associates, Chicago. Used with permission. All rights reserved.

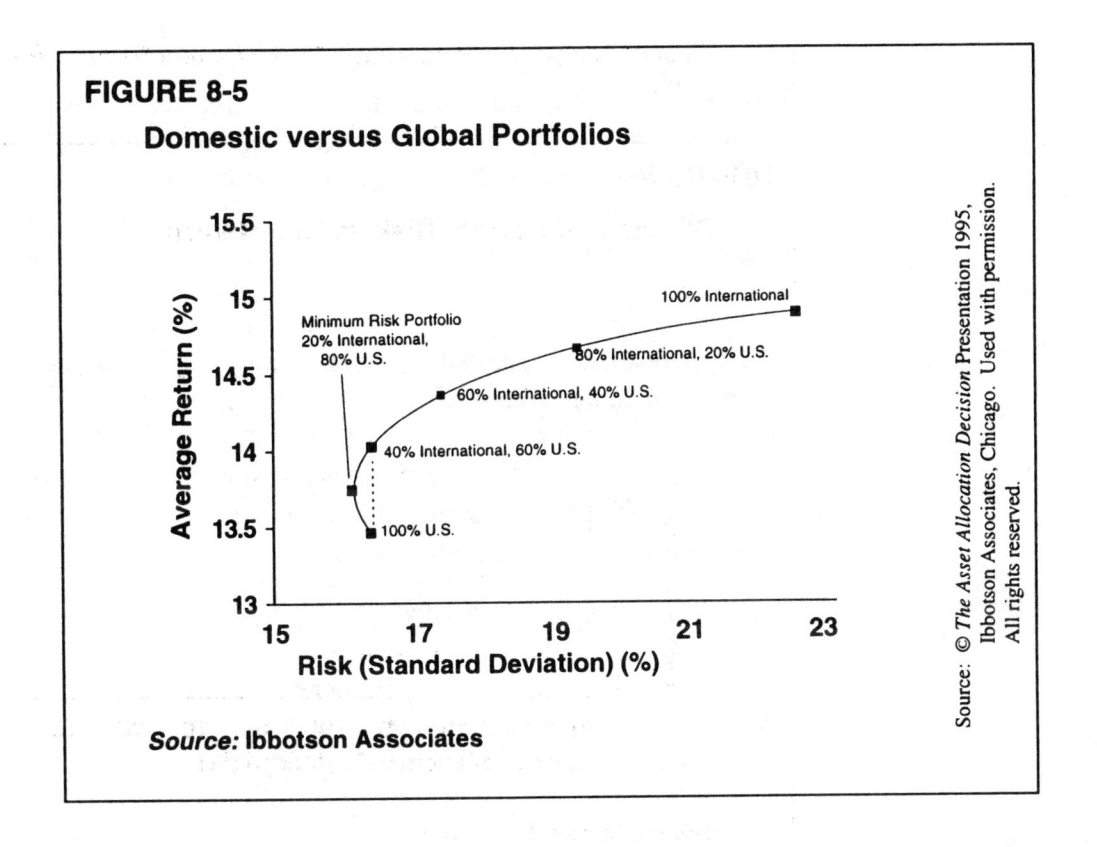

Figure 8-5 shows the benefit of global diversification when comparing the risk and return on a historical basis over the past 20 years.[5] Although international stocks have a higher risk than the U.S. stocks, combining the two in a portfolio may actually reduce the portfolio's risk. This is due to the low correlation of one to another, as explained earlier.[6]

What Optimization Software Should Be Selected?

Once the the investment professional and investor have a conceptual understanding of asset allocation and how mean-variance optimization models can be utilized to design a portfolio, the next major step is the actual selection of optimization software. There are three main players in this area—Ibbotson Associates, Frontier Analytics, and Wilson Associates International.

This brings us to our next topic: the definition of the financial adviser's role.

What Is the Financial Adviser's Role?

A financial adviser provides many services to his or her client. First, the adviser offers professional advice on the optimal strategic allocation of assets so that the investor can achieve his or her financial objectives. That is, the

---

5. *Asset Allocation Decision*, 45.
6. Ibbotson Associates, *Global Investing*, Presentation booklet, Chicago, 1995.

financial adviser helps to allocate the client's wealth across familiar and efficient asset classes and products so the client can achieve a specific return, given the client's risk tolerance, time frame, and tax and liability situation. The strategic allocation decision is based on attaining full diversification for the client and long-term results so that in the long run, the allocation will maximize expected returns subject to the client's risk tolerance and constraints.[7]

Since research suggests that on average tactical (short-run) deviations do not result in enhanced returns, the adviser should minimize short-term risk only through dollar-cost-averaging techniques and timing a trade or reallocation to the next or lower tax year to defer or minimize taxes.[8] Another added value is the coordination and timing of investments to minimize transaction costs and investor's fees.

What Is the Implementation Process in Building the Model?

First, we must set investor parameters. In this example, we will limit the investments in our model to mutual funds and like investments where money managers/investments have a track record.

The first step in the process is to break down the mutual fund universe into manageable sectors in which we can analyze and compare the actual performance of each fund and money manager to its own peer group or industry averages. To quote Peter Lynch, "As long as you are picking a fund, you might as well pick a good one." This type of analysis can be done by many of the mutual fund database providers—for example, Datamax. Datamax allows the financial adviser to break the mutual fund universe into 11 equity sectors, 9 bond sectors, and 3 money market sectors.

---

7. *Mutual Funds: Analysis, Allocation, and Performance Analysis,* The American College, 1995, p. 9.
8. Ibid.

Mutual Fund Sectors / Top Mutual Funds
FIGURE 8-6

Mutual Fund Sectors

- AGGRESSIVE GROWTH
- LONG TERM GROWTH
- GROWTH & INCOME
- INCOME
- TOTAL RETURN FUNDS
- GOLD & PRECIOUS METALS
- BALANCED
- FOREIGN EQUITY
- FOREIGN/U.S. EQUITY
- HIGH YIELD CORP BOND
- HIGH QUALITY CORP BOND
- FOREIGN/U.S. BOND
- GOVERNMENT SECURITIES
- GINNIE MAE
- HIGH QUALITY MUNI BOND
- HIGH YIELD MUNI BOND
- SINGLE STATE MUNI BOND
- MONEY MARKET TAXABLE
- MONEY MARKET TAX-FREE
- MONEY MARKET GOV SECURITIES

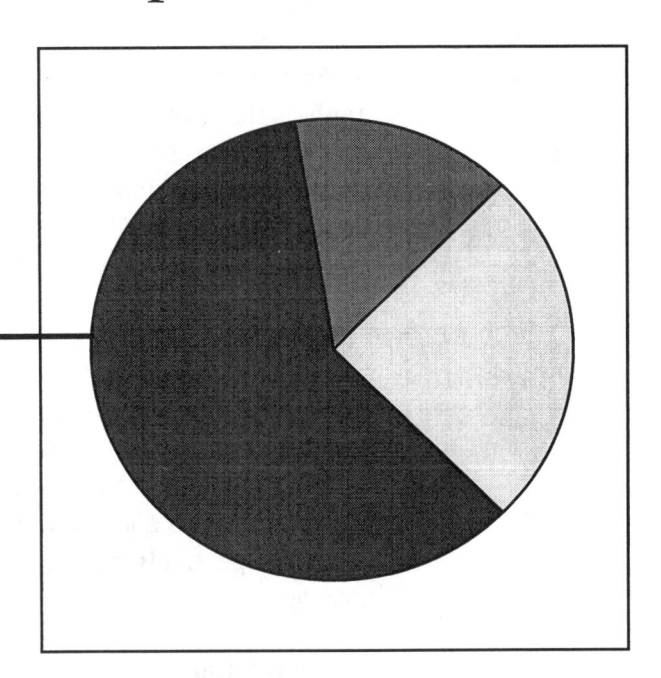

Top Mutual Funds

- STOCKS
- BONDS
- CASH

8.7

Datamax then enables the adviser to analyze a given fund to a sector or industry benchmark over various time frames. For the purpose of strategic allocation, we use the most recent 5-year returns to identify the best performers and money managers, taking note of any recent management changes. This is not to say that funds that have been in existence for fewer than 5 years are not in our model. With the high turnover of money managers, we can actually look at historical track records and arrive at a conclusion based on their abilities. Historical data can also be extrapolated to fill in benchmarks for these new funds to provide comparable—but not exact—standard deviation calculations.

The next step is to select a core of mutual fund families (normally six) that continually outperform their peers' returns on both a gross and net basis in fees, loads, and expenses. This also has some practical merit in that reallocating within a few given families keeps transaction costs to a minimum. Since front-end loads, no loads, contingent deferred sales charges, and investment breakpoints can dramatically reduce a fund's return, advisers and investors must take this practical step when building a model portfolio.

Another consideration in the selection process of a specific mutual fund family is the investor's actual investment selections in his or her 401(k) or retirement plan. In most cases, the financial adviser is able to find and account for these mutual funds in the overall management of the portfolio. The adviser can then efficiently constrain a certain amount of dollars to these funds and efficiently manage and account for these dollars. In a lot of cases, this is a major portion of the client's portfolio, and financial advisers would be remiss if they did not correctly allocate and account for these dollars.

The next consideration is to ensure that at least one of the families offers some indexed funds as an option. The adviser's position is to provide a given return with the least risk, taking the client's specific needs, risk, and other requirements into consideration. It is *not* the adviser's decision to select actively or passively managed funds. Both types of funds are compelling and have their own merits. Excluding one or the other would be a mistake.

The final step is to select at least one top mutual fund family that offers its funds and money managers through a variable annuity and a variable universal life (VUL) product. This would obviously add value and real return to a portfolio if all taxes were deferred. Another requirement is a fixed rate or guaranteed option. Because the risk (standard deviation) of a fixed-rate annuity or VUL is usually very low, including one in a portfolio has brought down many complete portfolios' standard deviation by 20 to 30 percent. Another added value of annuities and life insurance is that they are creditor and bankruptcy proof in some states—Texas, for example. That alone could sway an investor to use them, not to mention covering the typical mortality fee of 20 to 30 points that a mutual fund does not have.

Based on finding (1) the top mutual funds in our 20 fund sectors, (2) a crossover fund for variable annuities, and (3) a variable universal life product, we have identified the following mutual fund families:

- American
- Mainstay
- MFS
- Oppenheimer
- Putnam
- Templeton

The Mainstay Family of Funds—the proprietary mutual funds of NYLIFE Securities (New York Life)—gives us the crossover to a variable annuity and variable universal life product with a guaranteed rate/fixed-rate option, and an S&P 500 index option.

How Are Individual Mutual Funds Selected?

To narrow down our investment selection process the next step is to come up with, in essence, a dream team or all-star performers from the six fund families, spanning the 20 investment sectors.

This can be accomplished quantitatively, subjectively, or both. Some financial advisers prefer to use both, but in a given order with different objectives in mind. The following summarizes the five-step process:

Step 1: Analyze each sector on a 5-, 3-, and one-year basis net of all fees and expenses. This simply identifies the best-performing funds for each sector and time frame.

Step 2: Look for upward or downward trends in the performance of the fund.

Step 3: Identify any management changes or concerns.

Step 4: Cross-reference the findings with Morningstar (another software package, which gives a subjective opinion on each of the funds and reports how each fund did in its sector analysis along with the many standard modern portfolio theory components: alpha, beta, sharpe, and so on[9]).

Step 5: Select the top four to eight funds per sector, depending on the number available in each sector and actual return differences.

How Is the Asset Allocation Software Implemented?

The following are the steps involved in an *unconstrained allocation:*

---

9. Morningstar, Inc., "Mutual Funds."

TABLE 8-1
Asset Allocation/Top Mutual Funds

NYLIAC

★1. ☐ SPRA

Mainstay

★2. ☐ CAPITAL APPRECIATION
★3. ☐ VALUE
★4. ☐ EQUITY INDEX
★5. ☐ CONVERTIBLE
★6. ☒ TOTAL RETURN
★7. ☐ HIGH YIELD CORPORATE BOND
★8. ☐ GOVERNMENT
★9. ☐ TAX FREE BOND
★10. ☐ ALGER SMALL CAPITALIZATION
★11. ☐ FIDELITY CONTRAFUND
★12. ☐ FIDELITY EQUITY INCOME
★13. ☒ JANUS WORLDWIDE

American

★14. ☐ FUNDAMENTAL INVESTORS
★15. ☐ WASHINGTON MUTUAL INVESTORS FUND
★16. ☐ INCOME FUND OF AMERICA
★17. ☐ EUROPACIFIC GROWTH FUND
★18. ☒ SMALLCAP WORLD FUND
★19. ☒ NEW PERSPECTIVE
★20. ☐ BOND FUND OF AMERICA
★21. ☒ CAPITAL WORLD BOND FUND
★22. ☐ TAX EXEMPT BOND FUND OF AMERICA.

MFS

★23. ☐ EMERGING GROWTH FUND B
★24. ☐ RESEARCH FUND A
★25. ☐ VALUE FUND A
★26. ☐ MASSACHUSETTS INVESTORS TRUST A
★27. ☒ TOTAL RETURN FUND A
★28. ☒ WORLD EQUITY FUND A
★29. ☐ HIGH INCOME FUND A
★30. ☒ STRATEGIC INCOME FUND A
★31. ☐ GOVERNMENT SECURITIES FUND A
★32. ☐ MUNICIPAL BOND FUND A

Oppenheimer

★33. ☐ DISCOVERY FUND A
★34. ☐ MAIN STREET INCOME & GROWTH A
★35. ☐ QUEST OPPORTUNITY VALUE FUND A
★36. ☐ BOND FUND FOR GROWTH M
★37. ☐ CHAMPION HIGH YIELD FUND A
★38. ☒ STRATEGIC INCOME FUND A
★39. ☐ LIMITED TERM GOVERNMENT FUND

Putnam

★40. ☐ OTC EMERGING GROWTH FUND A
★41. ☐ VOYAGER FUND A
★42. ☐ NEW OPPORTUNITIES FUND A
★43. ☐ VISTA FUND A
★44. ☐ THE FUND FOR GROWTH & INCOME A
★45. ☐ EQUITY INCOME FUND A
★46. ☐ CONVERTIBLE INCOME-GROWTH TRUST A
★47. ☒ GEORGE PUTNAM FUND OF BOSTON A
★48. ☒ EUROPE GROWTH FUND A
★49. ☒ INTERNATIONAL GROWTH A
★50. ☐ HIGH YIELD ADVANTAGE FUND A
★51. ☐ HIGH YIELD TRUST A
★52. ☒ DIVERSIFIED INCOME TRUST A
★53. ☐ MUNICIPAL INCOME FUND A
★54. ☐ TAX-FREE HIGH YIELD FUND A

Templeton

★55. ☒ AMERICAN TR/2
★56. ☒ FOREIGN FUND
★57. ☒ WORLD FUND
★58. ☒ GROWTH FUND
★59. ☒ GLOBAL BOND FUND

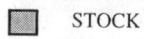

☐ STOCK   ☒ GLOBAL STOCK
☐ BOND   ☒ GLOBAL BOND

8.10

Step 1: Load the historical returns of the 59 funds on a quarterly basis—maximum of 60 quarters (15 years)—into the model. In our example, the returns loaded are from Morningstar and its database. Gross returns are loaded for all funds (due to separate classes of funds, A, B, C, and all of the various combination of fees, loads, and expenses). Note that the gross and net returns of a lot of these funds are the same because of their fund classes and their specific reporting procedures.

Step 2: Calculate what the gross returns of all tax-free municipal bonds would be (using 28 percent or the appropriate tax bracket). This allows the model to evaluate and calculate all numbers on an equal basis.

Step 3: Run an unconstrained model of the above 59 funds with their actual return capabilities.

Step 4: Review the correlation matrix of funds to ensure polarization of given funds. It may be necessary to revisit the 20 sectors at this point to obtain adequate diversification.

The steps for a *constrained allocation* are as follows:

Step 1: Determine what internal and external constraints are needed for the model, using the following checklist:

Internal Constraints (Limits or Caps Set by Investor or Adviser)

Individual fund limits:	% or $ of portfolio minimum/maximum
Sector fund limits:	% or $ of stocks/bonds/international stocks and bonds minimum/maximum
Fund family:	% or $ minimum or maximum and/or retirement plan investments (401(k) choices) % or $
Variable annuity:	Investment choices
Variable universal life:	Investment choices

External Constraints (Limits or Caps Set by Outside Source)

Fund family:	Retirement plan investments (401(k) choices) % or $
Variable annuity:	Investment choices
Variable universal life:	Investment choices
Taxation:	Regular/capital gains/tax deferred
Transaction costs:	Front-end loads, fees, contingent deferred sales charges
Market condition:	Current trend
Interest rates:	Current trend

Step 2: Run the constrained model within the return capabilities. If the model cannot solve for a given return, the financial adviser will be forced to amend constraints and rerun the model until there are acceptable results for each given return.

Examples of these procedures are included at the end of this article. Also included is an example of a 401(k) plan with an efficient frontier calculated for its investment choices.

What Are Some Practical Issues and Concerns in the Initial Allocation and Reallocation Process?

The initial allocation and the reallocation process of the given portfolio are very similar but are separate events. In fact, the recommendation to sell old and familiar investments in order to buy unfamiliar investments *will* generate client anxiety even though the changes may substantially improve the risk/return characteristic of the portfolio.[10]

There is a tendency for clients to view appreciated assets as bargains, because they think of them in terms of their low purchase prices. Of course, the historical cost has nothing to do with whether the stock will continue to perform based on its current market value and potential.[11]

The tax issues involved with the sale of an appreciated investment can often complicate the decision. Unless held to death, the income tax due on the gain of the asset will have to be paid sooner or later. For income tax purposes, the event should be timed, if possible, so tha it occurs in the first quarter of the next year if the end of the calendar year is approaching.[12]

Another complicating factor occurs when a highly appreciated asset has a good income yield. Although the government has a claim on the unrealized appreciation, the client nevertheless gets the entire income stream from the investment. Consider a stock or bond with a $10 per share tax basis that is now selling for $60 per share. If it currently pays $3.60 per year in dividends, its current income yield is 6 percent. Assume that upon the sale, 30 percent of the realized gain will be lost to income taxes. This leaves an after-tax proceeds of $45 available for repositioning. To generate the same $3.60 per share in income means finding a stock or bond with an 8 percent yield ($45.00 x 0.08 = $3.60). Clearly, this is a factor that must be carefully weighed in the retention/disposition decision.[13]

---

10. Roger C. Gibson. *Asset Allocation: Balancing Financial Risk,* Irwin Professional Publishing, 1990, p. 243.
11. Ibid.
12. Ibid., 244.
13. Ibid., 245.

A client's age and health also need to be considered. The current tax code provides for a stepped-up tax basis for appreciated assets upon the investor's death. Retaining these assets would be the obvious decision for a terminally ill client.[14]

Another potential problem arises when an investment could be sold that has an unusually large unrealized capital loss. The client may have to overcome the psychological problem—the paper loss syndrome—of feeling that no money is lost unless the position is sold. The investor and the adviser should make lemonade out of this sour event by checking with the investor's CPA to ensure that the investor enjoys the maximum tax benefits.[15]

To head off a lot of these problems the adviser and investor could hypothetically convert the client's entire portfolio to cash and base the analysis and returns on those numbers. The real question to the client would then be, would you buy the investment again?[16]

After all is said and done, if the investor mandates that a specific investment not be sold, the financial adviser is left with two options:

- Exclude the investment and its corresponding dollars from the model.
- Have the specific investment pinch-hit (substitute) for a fund and dollar amount in the model. (This can actually add value to some portfolios in which an asset-backed security with a high return pinch-hits for a government bond fund or like investment where a lower return is expected.)

Common sense is paramount. To implement the allocation process the adviser should use a dollar-cost-averaging technique over a 3- to 6-month period, giving consideration to all of the points above.

Reallocation Process (Rebalancing). The decision process for reallocating or rebalancing the model is basically the same as the initial process—but in reverse order. When a given fund is outside its accepted percentage—that is, ±5 percent—the rebalancing issue should be addressed.[17] An investment that is performing outside the ±5 percent range usually signals to clients and qualified plan sponsors that reallocation should be considered.

---

14. Ibid.
15. Ibid., 246.
16. Gibson. *Asset Allocation*, 247.
17. Jess Lederman and Robert A. Klein. *Global Asset Allocation Techniques for Optimizing Portfolio Management,* John Wiley and Sons, Inc., p. 57.

These round percentage numbers have an inherent simplicity and beauty. Clients, trustees, and fiduciaries understand percentages much more easily than standard deviations, variances, geometric means, and other statistical terms.[18]

Are there other techniques available to manage the asset allocation structure more efficiently? Studies by industry leaders Perold and Sharpe evaluated several rebalancing strategies for their potential payoff under different market conditions, including the buy-and-hold approach and the constant-proportion strategy. Their findings can be summarized as follows:

- A buy-and-hold approach is a completely passive strategy; no rebalancing of the portfolio occurs. In a constantly declining or rising market, this strategy will outperform a constant-mix strategy.[19]
- A constant-mix strategy keeps the exposure to each asset class at a constant proportion of the total portfolio. This is an active process that usually requires
    - the purchase of an asset class as it drops in relative value
    - the sale of an asset class as it rises in relative value

These adjustments are usually guided by a decision rule (for example, ±5 percent) that triggers the point at which to take the rebalancing action. The constant-mix strategy tends to outperform the buy-and-hold process in markets that oscillate and show some volatility but do not exhibit a major sustained movement in any one direction.[20]

The key point that Perold and Sharpe made was that no one type of rebalancing strategy is the best for all investors because the asset allocation decision (model) itself attempts to optimize return relative to risk (volatility). The result is that each investor brings to the reallocation process a different degree of fit and constraints between the investor's risk tolerance and the rebalancing strategy's payoff potential in different type of markets. Therefore the selection of an appropriate rebalancing strategy requires a clear understanding of who will enjoy the reward of return and who will bear the risk associated with not achieving that return. That brings us full circle to our original defined-return (defined-benefit) approach to achieve a specific benefit for our client.[21]

---

18. Ibid., 57.
19. Ibid.
20. Lederman and Klein. *Global Asset Allocation Techniques*, 57.
21. Ibid.

One last finding concerning portfolio rebalancing: Mark A. Hurrell, who evaluated various calendar period and percentage-of-portfolio rebalancing thresholds, indicates that of the calendar-based methods, quarterly rebalancing produces the best results. This study also suggests that the ideal range for percentage-of-portfolio variance bands ranges from ±5 percent to ±9 percent. This range, however, outperformed the annual rebalancing only by one-quarter of one percent (10 basis points). Investors should weigh that extra edge in return to the actual transaction costs and tax ramifications of making frequent changes on a quarterly basis.[22]

The obvious and final role of the adviser in the reallocation, rebalancing, and maintenance process is to maintain a steady vigil on the performance of the actual funds and asset classes themselves. He or she should make appropriate additions and subtractions of funds to or from the asset classes and thus help the client not only to reach his or her financial goal but also to maintain it over time.

Where Can I Find out More?

- GS 811 Security Analysis and Portfolio Management
- GS 819 Mutual Funds: Analysis, Allocation, and Performance Evaluation
- HS 320 Fundamentals of Financial Planning
- Roger C. Gibson. *Asset Allocation: Balancing Financial Risk.* Irwin Professional Publishing, 1990.
- Mark A. Hurrell. "Measuring Up." Yannie Bilkey Investment Consulting, 1991.
- *The Asset Allocation Decision*, Presentation materials. Ibbotson Associates. Chicago, 1995.
- *Global Investing*, Presentation booklet. Ibbotson Associates. Chicago, 1995.
- *Historical Asset Performance*, Presentation booklet. Ibbotson Associates. Chicago, 1995.
- *Investment Principles*, Presentation booklet. Ibbotson Associates. Chicago, 1995.
- Jess Lederman and Robert A. Klein. *Global Asset Allocation Techniques for Optimizing Portfolio Management.* John Wiley and Sons, Inc., 1994.
- "Mutual Funds." Morningstar, Inc. Chicago, 1995.
- "Mutual Fund Manager." National Datamax, Inc. San Diego, 1991.

---

22. Mark A. Hurrell. "Measuring Up," Yannie Bilkey Investment Consulting, 1991.

- "Dynamic Strategies for Asset Allocation." Andre F. Perold and William F. Sharpe. *Financial Analysts Journal*, 1988.
- *Personal Financial Risk Tolerance*. The American College, Bryn Mawr, PA, 1992.

Definition of Unconstrained Allocation: Where there are no Client-Specified Constraints, limits, or minimum allocations imposed on the solution of achieving a target return with minimum risk given a set of investments (mutual funds).

Unconstrained Results			Portfolio	A	B	C	D	E	F	G	H
			Target Return:	8.0	9.0	10.0	11.0	12.0	13.0	14.0	15.0
			Actual Return:	8.0	9.0	10.0	11.0	12.0	13.0	14.0	15.0
	Class	Return	Risk	Risk:	9.1	10.0	11.0	12.3	13.7	15.2	17.2	36.0
1	MCAPAPPB	15.26	44.04	Percent Wts:								74.2
2	MVALUEB	11.62	30.00		5.3							
3	MEQINDEX	14.27	17.80			15.9	29.8	43.6	57.5	71.3	93.7	25.8
4	MCONVERB	10.23	22.83									
5	MTOTRTNB	12.39	20.45									
6	MHYCBB	10.07	16.17		24.3	27.3	27.1	26.9	26.8	26.6	6.3	
7	MGOVTB	7.01	9.88		70.3	56.8	43.1	29.4	15.8	2.1		

Definition of Constrained Allocation: Where given the Client-Specified Constraints, limits, and minimum allocations **are** imposed on the solution of achieving a target return with minimum risk given a set of investments (mutual funds).

Constrained Results			Portfolio	A	B	C	D	E	F	G	H
			Target Return:	8.0	9.0	10.0	11.0	12.0	13.0	14.0	15.0
			Actual Return:	8.0	9.0	10.0	11.0	12.0	13.0	14.0	15.0
	Class	Return	Risk	Risk:	10.1	11.6	14.2	15.1	19.0	21.6	23.2	36.0
1	MCAPAPPB	15.26	44.04	Percent Wts:				0.7	20.0	25.0	35.0	75.0
2	MVALUEB	11.62	30.00		3.0	5.0		12.4	4.4			
3	MEQINDEX	14.27	17.80			25.0	4.1	20.0	20.0	25.0	35.0	25.0
4	MCONVERB	10.23	22.83		17.0		25.0	6.9				
5	MTOTRTNB	12.39	20.45				20.9	20.0	20.0	25.0	5.0	
6	MHYCBB	10.07	16.17		10.0	35.0	25.0	20.0	20.0	25.0	25.0	
7	MGOVTB	7.01	9.88		70.0	35.0	25.0	20.0	15.6			

Target Return	INDIVIDUAL FUND CONSTRAINTS/ CAPS		SECTOR CONSTRAINTS/CAPS	
	Stocks	Bonds	Stocks	Bonds
8%	≤25%	≤70%	≥20%	≤80%
9%	≤25%	≤35%	≥30%	≤70%
10%	≤25%	≤25%	≥25%	≥25% and ≤75%
11%	≤20%	≤20%	≥25%	≥25% and ≤75%
12%	≤20%	≤20%	≥25%	≥25% and ≤75%
13%	≤25%	≤25%	≥25%	≥25% and ≤75%
14%	≤35%	≤25%	≥25%	≥25% and ≤75%
15%	≤75%	≤25%	≥25%	≤75%

Footnotes:
- **Software:** C.A.M.P.
  Customized Asset Management Program
  The American College
- **Returns/Fund/Calculated Annually/Class B Funds**
  Source: Morningstar
- **Maximum Time Frame:** 60 Quarters=15 years (9/30/80-9/30/95)
  Minimum Time Frame: Inception date of mutual fund
  All mutual funds are a minimum of five years old.

FIGURE 8-7

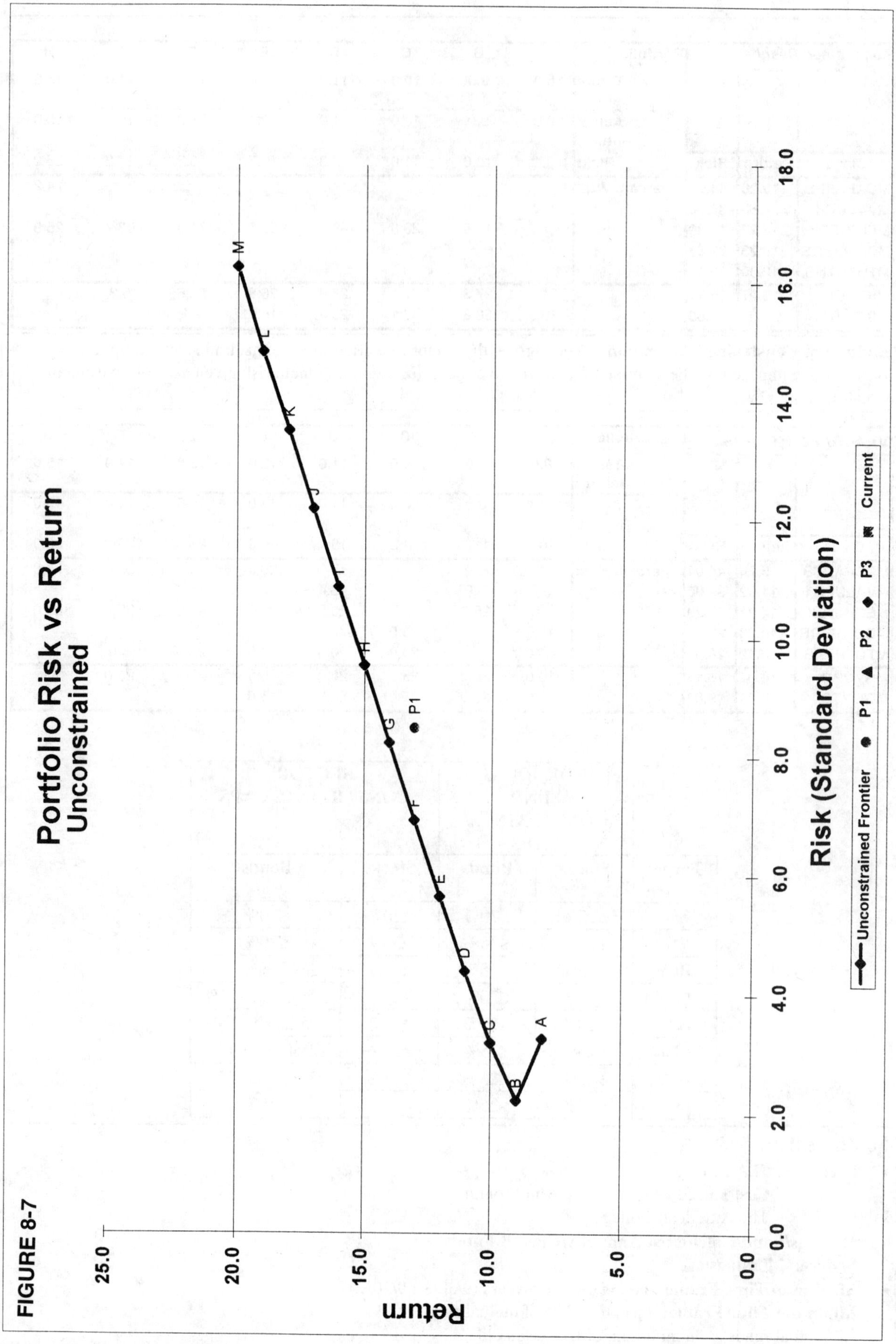

Portfolio Risk vs Return
Unconstrained
Return
25.0
20.0
15.0
10.0
5.0
0.0
0.0
2.0
4.0
6.0
8.0
10.0
12.0
14.0
16.0
18.0
Risk (Standard Deviation)
A
B
C
D
E
F
G
H
I
J
K
L
M
P1
Unconstrained Frontier
P1
P2
P3
Current

ALLOMAX Version 2.0

3/21/97

FIGURE 8-8

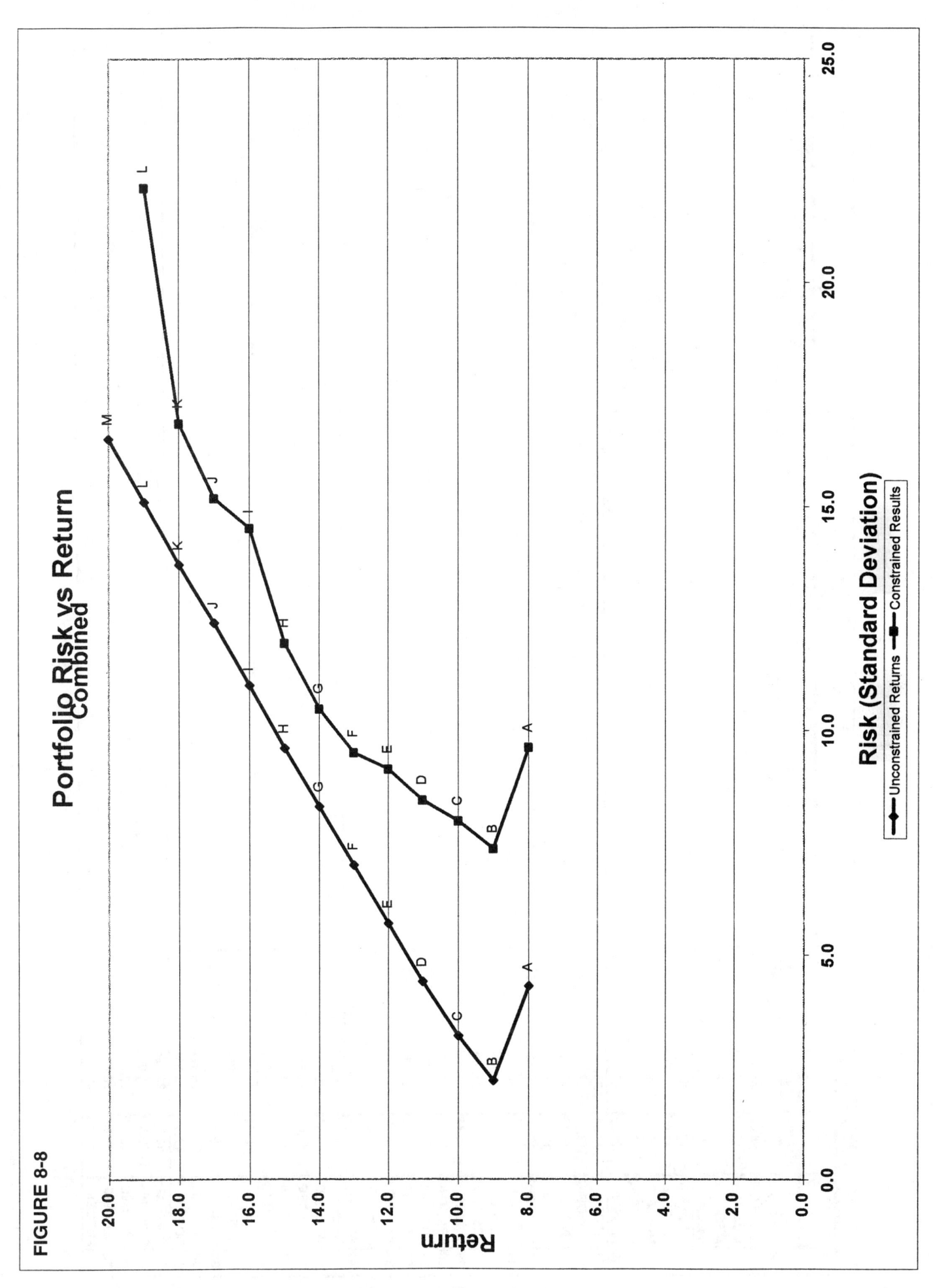

Portfolio Risk vs Return
Combined

8.19

Unconstrained Results

	Class	Return	Risk	Portfolio Target Return:	A 8.0	B 9.0	C 10.0	D 11.0	E 12.0	F 13.0	G 14.0	H 15.0	I 16.0	J 17.0	K 18.0	L 19.0	M 20.0	N	O
				Actual Return:	8.0	9.0	10.0	11.0	12.0	13.0	14.0	15.0	16.0	17.0	18.0	19.0	20.0		
				Risk:	3.3	2.2	3.2	4.4	5.7	6.9	8.2	9.5	10.9	12.2	13.5	14.8	16.3		
				Percent Wts:															
1	NYLSPRA	8.45	2.30		76.0	87.3	78.1	69.4	60.3	51.3	42.2	33.2	24.1	15.1	6.0				
2	MCAPAPP	15.50	41.88																
3	MVALUEB	11.92	28.57																
4	MEQINDE	14.92	16.26																
5	MCONVE	10.24	21.70																
6	MTOTRTN	12.38	19.28																
7	MHYCBB	10.45	15.40			0.8													
8	MGOVTB	6.57	9.93		24.0														
9	MTXFRBD	9.10	13.17																
10	ALGSMC	21.08	49.62																
11	FIDCONT	18.04	35.44																
12	FIDEQINC	16.67	27.31							1.5	3.3	5.2	7.0	8.8	10.7	12.5	14.0		
13	JANWLD	19.49	20.78																
14	AFUNDIN	16.51	29.20																
15	AWASHIN	17.00	26.70																
16	AINCFUN	14.33	20.45																
17	AEUROPG	16.59	26.03																
18	ASMALCA	15.36	27.06																
19	ANEWPE	15.45	25.73																
20	ABNDFUN	11.17	16.67																
21	ACAPWR	9.52	14.57																
22	ATXEXTB	12.25	23.08																
23	MEMGRO	22.92	56.06																
24	MRESEA	17.81	33.69																
25	MVALUEA	13.80	35.42																
26	MASSINV	15.38	29.56																
27	MTOTRTN	14.13	22.90																
28	MWLDEQ	11.84	26.78																
29	MHIINFUA	12.01	21.93																
30	MSTINCO	9.02	13.07																
31	MGVTSE	8.51	10.54																
32	MMUNIBD	14.24	22.28																
33	ODISCOV	20.08	42.59												0.0	0.1			
34	OMAINST	20.74	30.18			0.6													
35	OQESTOP	17.32	24.86																
36	OBDFDGR	10.99	22.16			2.0													
37	OCHMPIN	12.54	11.02			6.9	14.0	18.5	23.0	27.4	31.8	36.2	40.6	45.0	49.4	50.5	45.9		
38	OSTRINC	10.64	10.32																
39	OLGTMG	7.85	8.82																
40	POTCEM	22.38	46.35																

ALLOMAX Version 2.0

3/20/97

8.20

#	Name											
41	PVOYAGE	19.41	41.53									
42	PNEWOPP	32.71	38.38									
43	PVISTAA	18.05	35.19	3.0	6.1	9.1	11.7	14.2	16.6	19.1	21.6	24.0	27.2	31.7
44	PGRINCA	16.42	24.68									
45	PEQINCA	12.57	25.00									
46	PCNINCG	14.50	25.26									
47	PGRGBST	13.83	24.14	2.3								
48	PEURGRT	13.65	18.41	4.4	6.0	7.6	8.1	8.5	8.8	9.2	9.5	9.9	9.6	8.4
49	PINTLGR	12.54	18.70	0.1								
50	PHYADVA	10.47	18.51									
51	PHYTRUS	12.36	22.19									
52	PDIVINCA	9.77	10.54	0.5								
53	PMUNIINA	10.90	13.46									
54	PTXFRHY	11.33	14.52									
55	TAMERII	11.49	10.41									
56	TFOREIG	16.61	25.66									
57	TWORLD	15.23	29.41									
58	TGROWT	15.08	29.13									
59	TGLOBAL	8.33	10.40									

8.21

ALLOMAX Version 2.0   3/20/97

Constrained Results

			Portfolio	A	B	C	D	E	F	G	H	I	J	K	L	M	N	O
			Target Return:	8.0	9.0	10.0	11.0	12.0	13.0	14.0	15.0	16.0	17.0	18.0	19.0	20.0		
			Actual Return:			10.0	11.0	12.0	13.0	14.0	15.0	16.0	17.0	18.0				
			Risk:			6.9	7.0	7.6	8.5	9.8	11.5	13.0	15.1	17.8				
#	Class	Return	Risk	Percent Wts:														
1	NYLSPR	8.45	2.30				20.0	20.0	20.0	20.0	20.0	14.8	19.5	6.3				
2	MCAPAP	15.50	41.88															
3	MVALUE	11.92	28.57				2.0											
4	MEQIND	14.92	16.26				3.5	8.7	4.7	0.4		5.9	12.5	20.0	20.0			
5	MCONVE	10.24	21.70				0.7											
6	MTOTRT	12.38	19.28				2.3											
7	MHYCBE	10.45	15.40				6.9	6.1	4.9	3.8	1.0							
8	MGOVTE	6.57	9.93															
9	MTXFRB	9.10	13.17				8.5											
10	ALGSMC	21.08	49.62															
11	FIDCONT	18.04	35.44															
12	FIDEQIN	16.67	27.31															
13	JANWLD	19.49	20.78					3.4	5.0	5.0	5.0	5.0	5.0	5.0				
14	AFUNDIN	16.51	29.20															
15	AWASHII	17.00	26.70											2.8				
16	AINCFUN	14.33	20.45															
17	AEUROP	16.59	26.03										3.7	15.0				
18	ASMALC	15.36	27.06															
19	ANEWPE	15.45	25.73															
20	ABNDFU	11.17	16.67															
21	ACAPWF	9.52	14.57				5.0			0.4	5.0	5.0						
22	ATXEXT	12.25	23.08															
23	MEMGR	22.92	56.06															
24	MRESEA	17.81	33.69															
25	MVALUE	13.80	35.42															
26	MASSIN	15.38	29.56															
27	MTOTRT	14.13	22.90															
28	MWLDEC	11.84	26.78															
29	MHIINFU	12.01	21.93															
30	MSTINC	9.02	13.07															
31	MGVTSE	8.51	10.54				10.0	10.0	8.5	7.2								
32	MMUNIB	14.24	22.28									2.7	10.0	10.0	10.0			
33	ODISCO	20.08	42.59								3.6							
34	OMAINS	20.74	30.18									6.4	9.1	10.0	10.0			
35	OQESTC	17.32	24.86									5.2	8.9	10.0	10.0			
36	OBDFDG	10.99	22.16															
37	OCHMPI	12.54	11.02				10.0	10.0	10.0	10.0	10.0	10.0	10.0	10.0	10.0			
38	OSTRINC	10.64	10.32							5.0	5.0	5.0						
39	OLGTMC	7.85	8.82				10.0	10.0	10.0	10.0								
40	POTCEM	22.38	46.35											2.2				

ALLOMAX Version 2.0

3/20/97

41	PVOYAG	19.41	41.53						
42	PNEWOF	32.71	38.38		1.3	5.3	9.6	10.0	10.0	10.0	10.0
43	PVISTA	18.05	35.19						
44	PGRINC	16.42	24.68						
45	PEQINC	12.57	25.00	1.5					
46	PCNINC	14.50	25.26						
47	PGRGBS	13.83	24.14		2.6	5.0	5.0	5.0	5.0	5.0
48	PEURGR	13.65	18.41	4.6	4.4		1.6		5.0	5.0
49	PINTLGR	12.54	18.70						
50	PHYADV	10.47	18.51						
51	PHYTRU	12.36	22.19						
52	PDIVINC	9.77	10.54		8.5	10.0	10.0	10.0		
53	PMUNIN	10.90	13.46						
54	PTXFRH	11.33	14.52	10.0	10.0	10.0	10.0	10.0		
55	TAMERI	11.49	10.41			1.9	3.6	5.0	5.0	5.0
56	TFOREI	16.61	25.66						
57	TWORLD	15.23	29.41	5.0	5.0	4.7				
58	TGROW	15.08	29.13						
59	TGLOBA	8.33	10.40						

8.23

ALLOMAX Version 2.0   3/20/97

The Asset Allocation Decision

Plan Name: Sample Co. 401(k) Savings Plan

The Trustees of Sample Co. 401(k) Savings Plan have requested that we provide you with an **Asset Allocation Program** illustrating the **Efficient Frontier** of the mutual funds that were selected based on actual performance. Please see the attached brochures offering an explanation of these concepts: The Asset Allocation Decision, Understanding the Efficient Frontier, and Investment Alternatives.

Sample Co. and Alden Financial Services make no promises or guarantees about the future return or risk level of any individual security, asset class, or portfolio. Historical performance does not guarantee future results.

This **Asset Allocation Program** is intended for use only as a guideline for your own investment decision to integrate with your individual retirement objectives and risk tolerance.

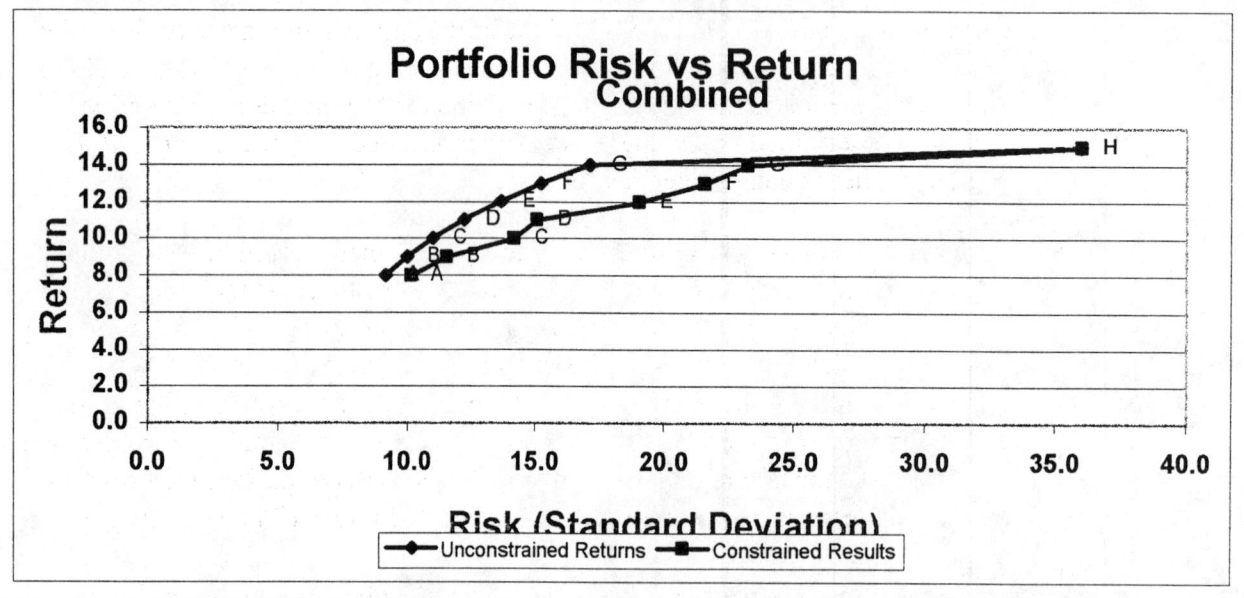

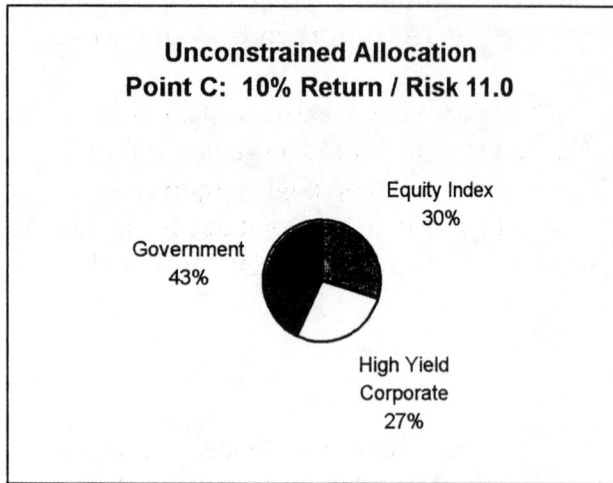

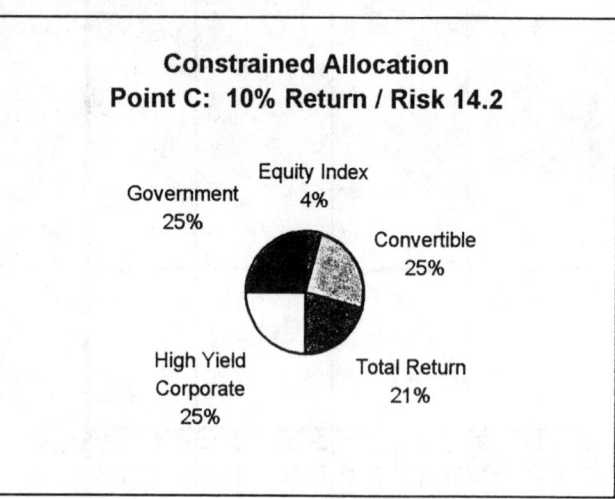

Portfolio Risk vs Return
Combined

(Chart: Return vs Risk (Standard Deviation), showing Unconstrained Returns and Constrained Results curves with points A–H)

Unconstrained Allocation
Point C: 10% Return / Risk 11.0

- Equity Index 30%
- Government 43%
- High Yield Corporate 27%

Constrained Allocation
Point C: 10% Return / Risk 14.2

- Equity Index 4%
- Government 25%
- Convertible 25%
- High Yield Corporate 25%
- Total Return 21%

This illustration is supplied by Alden Financial Services in response to the specific request of a client, and is to be used accordingly. It must be preceded or accompanied by the Fund's current prospectus. While the period covered by the illustration was, on the whole, one of generally rising common stock prices, it may have included some interim periods of substantial markets decline. Results shown should not be considered a representation of the dividend income or capital gain or loss which might be realized from an investment in the Funds today. Programs of regular investing cannot assure a profit nor protect against a loss in declining markets. The performance data quoted represents past performance and is no guarantee of future results. Investment return and principal value of an investment will fluctuate so that an investor's shares, when redeemed, may be worth more or less than their original cost. The format of this hypothetical illustration is adapted from the Cost Allocation Management Program (C.A.M.P.) illustration system.

3/24/97, h:/document/sampleco.doc

Revised Stock Market Circuit Breakers
William J. Ruckstuhl

What Was the Situation Before?

As a consequence of the sharp drop in the Dow Jones Industrial Average (and all other market indices) in October 1987, a system of trading halts, known as circuit breakers, was established and specified in terms of changes in the Dow Jones Industrial Average (DJIA).

The need for some moments of pause in trading was a consequence of changes that had occurred in the securities markets. Institutions then, as now, were a major factor in determining the number of transactions and shares traded, amounting to almost 90 percent of the daily trading activity. With the increase in performance bonuses, computer-driven trading decisions, and the use of competing money managers for segments of portfolios, conventional wisdom determined that some changes were needed after the October 1987 decline. These changes were as follows:

- If the market were to drop by 250 points, there would be a 30-minute stock trading halt and then trading could resume. At the time this policy was established, the DJIA was about 2080, and a 250-point drop translated into a 12 percent change in the index.
- After the 30-minute hiatus, if the market continued its decline, trading would be halted for one hour (or until the close of trading for the day if less than one hour remained) should the DJIA experience a 400-point decline. When established, this translated into a 19 percent drop for the day.
- A third major change was that a trading collar for computer-driven trades was established whenever the DJIA rose or fell 50 points above or below its previous close.
- Trading halts were established for other price measures when those measures experienced a change equivalent to those established for the DJIA. For example, eight points on the DJIA is roughly equivalent to one point on the S&P 500. Using this ratio, a 250-point decline in the DJIA was translated to a 30-point fall in the price of S&P 500 stock index future contracts.

What Has Been Occurring?

The DJIA has reached heights that most investors never thought would be seen in their lifetime. Today (February 14, 1997) the DJIA exceeds 7000, a more-than-threefold increase since the installation of the trading halts.

Due to this increase, these trading collars could be implemented for relatively small percentage changes. For example, the 250-point change for a 30-minute trading halt now represents a 3.5 percent change in the DJIA and the 400-point change a 5.7 percent decline. The intent was that these trading collars would take effect for drops in the DJIA that are really significant. Are these percentage changes significant? The SEC thought not.

What Is the Situation Now?

The limits for the trading collars have been increased to 350 for the half-hour trading halt and 550 for the hour halt. Even so, the percentage declines are 5 percent for the half-hour and 7.85 for the hour halt when the Dow is 7000. (Note: The trigger points for other measures have also been changed in line with the adjustments for the DJIA triggers.)

No change was made in the 50-point rise or fall limit for computer-generated trading collars despite their being triggered 24 times during the first 4 trading weeks of 1997.

Analysis

Only once since the original trading collars were put in place did the DJIA almost fall by 250 points (March 1996). Although the limit now is 350 points or 5 percent, a change of this magnitude could occur. More important than the 5 percent drop is the psychological effect of the market "shutting down" for 30 minutes. How would investors, money managers, 401(k) participants, and computer trading react to such a condition? This is an unknown and a prognostication would only be conjecture.

A Sample Prognostication. What would happen if a 30-minute halt in security trading, due to the sharp decline in prices, were to occur on the exchanges? Conventional wisdom holds that the stock market overreacts to both good and bad news. If so, then there is hope that less emotional, more rational decisions would be made and the market would reverse its downward movement. What actually occurs will be influenced by the precipitating cause of the halt. The answer to the question "What happened to change the expectations of stock market participants?" would profoundly influence how decision makers, professional money managers, and individuals react to the trading halt.

For example, from Friday, February 28, to Tuesday, March 4, 1997 (3 trading days), the market fell almost 200 points as a consequence of some relatively mild statements by the chairperson of the Federal Reserve (at least, so conventional wisdom explains this decline). Had the statements been stronger and been followed with actions that would lead to reducing the availability of credit and its consequential increase in interest rates, then the market could have declined by more than 350 points (less than a 4 percent decline). In this scenario, uncertainty as to the magnitude of the monetary policy change could indeed lead to a continued increase in selling pressures as investors sought to protect themselves from the interest rate risk and its consequences. Thus stock prices would continue their downward spiral and perhaps trigger the one-hour trading halt. If by good fortune this second halt started slightly less than one hour prior to the close of trading, investors would have time to assess the change prior to the market opening the next trading day. Coupling the Federal Reserve's actions with more financial information could lead to different trading behaviors. If expectations suggested that any change in interest rates would be insignificant and after-trading news provided favorable earnings and other corporate information, the market could largely ignore the Federal Reserve's comments and monetary changes. Should the opposite be the case (sharp interest rate increase and disappointing corporate profits), the market conditions could worsen.

Suppose for a moment that the cause of the decline was the President's heart attack (as occurred when Eisenhower was President) or the start of a war that impeded the flow of petroleum. Then the market could easily fall the 350 points, but when trading resumed, the overreaction might be reversed.

Conjecture of the above ilk is purely that, conjecture. Who can write today what will be the force that drives the market down sufficiently to have a trading halt implemented? The big drop in October 1987 was not immediately preceded by an earth-shattering event. The decline had started in August, and something happened between Friday and Monday in October that changed investor expectations. Certainly both trading halts would have occurred. The next day several stocks did not open for some time, and many investors continued to contact their brokers to unload their holdings. By the end of the week, some semblance of order was achieved. But one must wonder about investor reaction if a halt was imposed for the very first time.

Many variables have changed since October 1987. One such change is the greater use of defined-contribution pension plans where the investment decisions (timing and the investment security) are made by plan participants (self-directed plans). Participants have been advised for years that equities are the long-term instrument to beat inflation. Should participants elect to remain with their equity holdings, then the market could possibly avoid the kind of fall that is feared after a halt.

A second favorable change is that recently more money is being invested in mutual funds than in guaranteed investment contracts—again, a potential stabilizer.

One facet of this is certain. The 6-year bull market eventually will end, hopefully with a whimper.

Where Can I Find Out More?

- HS 328 Investments. TheAmerican College.
- Charles P. Jones. *Investments: Analysis and Management*, 5th ed., John Wiley & Sons., Inc., p. 121.
- *Financial Services Professional's Guide to the State of the Art,* 2d ed., The American College, pp. 9.10–9.14.

- Securities and Exchange Commission, Division of Market Regulations, 450 5th Street N.W., Washington, DC 20549. Phone (202) 272-7450.

New Twists on Corporate Dividend Reinvestment Plans (DRIPs)
William J. Ruckstuhl

What Was the Situation Before?

During the past 10 or more years, many publicly traded corporations have installed DRIPs. In these plans, dividends declared are used by some investors to acquire additional shares in a manner similar to the reinvestment of dividends in mutual funds. For the corporation, these plans are a way of (1) raising capital by selling newly issued or treasury stock shares, (2) supporting the market price by having the plan purchase shares on behalf of investors, and (3) increasing the number of shares held by investors who are favorably disposed to the corporation in case of an unfriendly tender offer. Currently more than 825 publicly traded corporations offer such plans.

Although variations exist among these firms, all require either a partial or full reinvestment of declared cash dividends. Other features of these plans, though not necessarily found in each and every DRIP, provide the investor with the following opportunities:

- to purchase the shares at a discount from the current market price
- to acquire the shares without any fees (if the corporation pays any brokerage commissions to acquire shares in the market, there is a taxable economic benefit to plan participants)
- to receive the share certificates when desired without any additional cost
- to periodically send, within limits of amount and time, funds with which to acquire additional shares through the plan
- to have financial record keeping for taxes and other purposes provided

What Is the Nature of the Changes?

Recently the IRS has permitted participating corporations to modify their plans and allow investors to do the following:

- purchase shares directly from the corporation and place these shares in the DRIP (currently 45 plans provide this option) without being an existing shareholder in the corporation
- establish an IRA account with the corporation
- hold new or existing investor shares in the DRIP with or without the reinvestment of dividends
- sell investor ownership interests directly (or by wire to their broker)

Why Were the Changes Made?

Several reasons can be advanced for these changes. The first is that several years ago the SEC reduced the time that investors have to settle with their broker for any transactions from 5 days to 3 days. Concurrent with this change, the brokerage firms heavily advocated leaving shares in "street name" for the convenience of both the investor's trading activities and dividend and tax record keeping. When shares are held in street name, the issuing corporation is handicapped in attempting to communicate with its shareholders and must rely on the brokerage firms to notify the issuer as to how many street-name shareholders they have and then to forward the issuer's quarterly and annual reports as well as other communications to the shareholders. This is a time-consuming process, and not all street-name shareholders receive this information flow that the issuing corporations and their shareholder relations departments view as desirable.

A second reason is cost to the investor. As more and more brokerage firms impose annual account fees and specific charges if the investor desires to receive the shares in certificate form, the issuing corporations have pointed out that these investment costs can be reduced by using their plans.

A third reason, only obliquely mentioned, is the advantage that a DRIP participant has for easily changing the brokerage firm with whom he or she has a relationship. This is accomplished by opening an account elsewhere and trading through that firm. Although brokerage firms can sell one's street-name or delivered stock the same day, it seems to take 4 to 6 weeks for street-name shares to be transferred to another broker (or delivered to the customer in certificate form).

How Can Financial Planners Use These Changes?

For fee-only planners, the changes provide a means of recommending investments that do not add to the client's total cost. For fee-with-commission-offset planners, they provide a means by which the planner can retain a larger percentage of the annual fee.

Of course, these plans should be recommended only when they are in the best interests of the client. Holding only one stock loses any benefits of diversification. However, if an investor currently possesses a diversified portfolio, these plans can add some additional diversification with little or no cost.

Are There Any Drawbacks?

Certainly. The first is that the firms providing DRIPs or these new variations tend to be concentrated in the noncyclical consumer goods, utility, service, and financial industries. A diversified portfolio could be difficult to construct given the limited number of firms and industries offering these plans.

In addition, being larger than nonproviders of these plans, these firms tend to have lower projected growth rates, P/Es, sales, and book values. But they do tend to have significantly higher market prices and dividend yields.

Where Can I Find Out More?

- HS 328 Investments. The American College.
- Charles P. Jones. *Investments: Analysis and Management*, 5th ed., John Wiley & Sons., Inc., pp. 112–113.
- John Bajkowski. "Investment Characteristics of Firms with Dividend Reinvestment Plans." *AAII Journal,* June 1996 (vol. 18, no. 5).
- American Association of Individual Investors."The Individual Investor's Guide to Dividend Reinvestment Plans" (4th annual ed.). *AAII Journal*, June1996.
- North Star Financial, Inc. *DRIP Investor* (newsletter).

Financial Planning 2000—What Will It Be Like?
William J. Ruckstuhl

What Is the Current Situation?

The DJIA exceeds 7000 and other indexes of the United States stock market performance are nearing or passing all-time highs. Consumers are optimistic about their future income as their use of consumer credit has risen sharply and retail sales reflect this spending. Economists, the practitioners of the dismal science, generally agree that inflation is under control (and probably has been overstated for years), the American economy's health is good, interest rates are within due bounds, and the recovery has at least 2 more years to run.

Having been around for threescore and seven years, I find my skepticism arises when the consensus has few if any dissenters. But let us remember the words of the eminent economist, Irving Fisher, who stated in early 1929 that "the economy is reaching a new level of prosperity." Indeed it did! Unfortunately within a few years it did again, but at a much reduced level than had been attained in 1929.

What Were the Conditions in 1997 and 1998?

The economy moved along, boosted by rising stock markets and benign Federal Reserve actions leading to a period of relatively stable interest rates. Corporate profits rose, wealthy taxpayers and homeowners obtained capital-gains tax relief, transfer taxes (inheritance and gift) were largely eliminated, and the balanced budget amendment including social security expenditures and unemployment compensation payments was passed and sent to the states for ratification. Employment remained at high levels, lowered CPI inflation reduced government expenditures and raised revenues since inflation-indexing of tax rates lessened. Life was good.

What Happened in 1999?

Scenario One

Following the Republican landslide in the 1998 elections that resulted in control of state legislatures, the balanced budget amendment rapidly received the approval of 38 states.

Small engagements over turf on distant continents had few worldwide economic spin-offs. There was widespread concern with the rising use of the petroleum reserves due to the prosperity of the world's nations, and energy prices started to inch upward. Simultaneous eruptions of dormant volcanoes in the North American and the South Pacific regions spewed voluminous amounts of dust, ash, and other impurities into the air, with the result that Earth's climate underwent a significant change. Less sunlight reached agricultural areas, the incidence of respiratory illnesses decimated world labor force participation rates, speculators acquired futures on every agricultural commodity, and then crops failed.

The resulting panic to stock the larder and freezers swelled consumer demand for food products and the prices of these goods responded as economists would predict. Available spending for other consumer nondurables, durables, and services sharply declined, resulting in widespread curtailment of production and rapid upward movement in the new claims for unemployment compensation.

Consumers, acting in their self-interest, curtailed spending beyond the price effect of food on their budgets, and savings rates rose beyond prior historical levels, further worsening the production and unemployment statistics. Private sector capital expenditures, except for the massive unplanned inventory buildups, virtually ceased worldwide. Government revenues plummeted, leading to massive reductions in spending to maintain the balanced budget.

The DJIA fell 4,000 points, and other broad-based indexes experienced equal relative declines. Small stock indexes lost almost 85 percent of their value. The Federal Reserve sought to stimulate investment by lowering interest rates to 1 and 2 percent to help the budget deficit by making short-term borrowing less expensive. Unfortunately, individuals and institutions wanted whatever could be salvaged from their debt instruments. EE bond redemptions soared, rollovers of T-bills became nonexistent, and refunding issues failed to sell. Corporations faced the same results. Money and capital debt markets collapsed. Confidence in the financial community disappeared as life insurance cash values and bank account balances were converted to currency.

Scenario Two

World opinion created an unpleasant environment for petty dictators and emotional factions that endangered world peace and human rights during the early 1990s. Additional petroleum reserves were located and alternative fuels showed the promise of economic feasibility, leading to sustained economic growth. Technological advances in agriculture and animal cloning produced bumper harvests. Food prices fell and consumers used these cost reductions to acquire more of the toys of the adult. Medical advances stopped the main killers dead in their tracks, and life expectancies increased by a decade or more.

Rising prosperity increased government receipts, resulting in significant reductions in the magnitude of the government debt. Freed accumulated savings sought other investment opportunities. As a consequence, interest rates fell sharply and the DJIA soared past 15,000. Other indexes did likewise. Dividend yield plummeted.

Prices, except for food, began a steep climb. The Federal Reserve was unable to pursue effective monetary restraint to stem this inflationary effect due to the huge government surplus and private sector saving. Bank interest paid on savings neared the rates that existed prior to the Accord of 1951. Congress was stymied, uncertain whether to raise taxes (more government saving that would drive interest rates down) or cut taxes (more consumer spending that would increase the rate of inflation).

Low interest rates in the United States precipitated large flights of capital to other parts of the world, thus having the effect of reducing interest rates across the industrial nations. World investment and then consumption expenditures rose, and inflation rates increased dramatically. Seeking to halt the upward price spiral, economic policy of most countries resulted in rapid increases in unemployment rivaling those of the 1930s. International trade ground to a halt except for needed raw materials. Tariffs on manufactured goods skyrocketed due to the collapse of GATT.

Scenario Three

The economy maintained its upward growth in employment and output while inflation remained at mid-1990s rates. The Federal Reserve was able, by jawboning, to contain some of the exuberance that drove the DJIA from 4000 in February 1995 to 7000 in February 1997 and to 8000 in late 1998. P/E ratios and dividend yields returned to more traditional levels as corporate profits and dividends increased as a result of the widespread prosperity. Modest increases in stock indexes were the rule. Partial relief on capital-gains taxation created many of the benefits stressed by its advocates.

The welfare program changes enacted in 1996 and 1997 reduced government spending to the point where, with increased tax revenues, draconian spending reductions were avoided and slight inroads were made on the magnitude of the federal debt. Confidence in government emerged as the citizenry realized that action could be taken if an economic collapse occurred, and the balanced budget amendment, although approved by 26 states, disappeared as a political issue as rapidly as did the Know-Nothing Party of the mid-1800s.

Worldwide events stabilized. Minor wars flourished, however, providing markets for defense contractors, although none of these excursions spread beyond small regions of Asia or Africa. Alternative fuels for petroleum began to be commercially viable, and world petroleum reserves increased because of successful exploration in previously undeveloped petroleum-producing areas. Weather conditions remained favorable for agricultural products, and technological advances from the American agricultural colleges continued to raise crop yields.

Economists, politicians, and businesspersons agreed that a continuation of the 1990s expansion would be the most likely scenario for the foreseeable future. Not only will the year 2000 be a numerical millennium, but it is being touted as the start of an economic millennium that should carry the United States and the world economies through an extended period of prosperity.

How Does the Financial Planner Advise Clients in the Year 2000?

For scenario one: Advise clients to buy gold, dig a bomb shelter, and shoot to kill. (Also open a direct hotline to Dr. Kevorkian.)

For scenario two: Advise clients to buy gold and escape to the north woods until the shakeout is over.

For scenario three: Advise clients to hire their own economist—they obviously bring good luck.

What Is the Benefit of These Scenarios to the Planner?

Economic and political events, coupled with human behavior, oft sink the plans of mice and humans. Planners must realize that changes will occur and that long-range planning faces undreamed-of uncertainties. For financial planning 2000, who knows? Unless you have a better crystal ball than the author, pick your scenario for the latter part of 1999 and then devise the appropriate strategies for your clients. Remember that you must also explain what happened in 1997 and 1998!

Mutual Fund Capital Gains—A Conduit Is Not Always a Conduit
William J. Ruckstuhl

In many applications associated with financial affairs, devices provide a conduit so that funds received hold their characteristics when flowing to the residual owners. And we think that mutual funds also have this characteristic since municipal bond interest flows to shareholders as tax-exempt income for federal tax purposes. U.S. Treasury flows are, for fund shareholders, exempt from state income taxation, and long-term capital gains retain this characteristic when passed to shareholders.

Where Does the Conduit Concept Not Apply?

Short-term capital-gains realized by mutual funds, unlike long-term capital gains, are not passed through as such. Rather they are used in a manner not consistent with the conduit concept. IRS regulations state that the long-term capital gain of the fund is determined by subtracting any realized short-term capital losses from the realized long-term gains. This becomes the amount of long-term capital gain that is distributable by the fund.

When Do These Tax Effects Work to the Disadvantage of the Fund Shareholder?

This procedure results in the fund performing the equivalent of the 1040 schedule D calculation for the shareholder before making its distribution for tax purposes. When the net long-term capital gain exceeds the net short-term capital loss, then the shareholder becomes indifferent to methodology, since the net result is a long-term capital gain.

In another scenario, suppose the fund realizes only short-term capital gains during its year. These gains flow to the shareholder as ordinary dividends and are subject to the shareholder's marginal income tax bracket. In this instance, the shareholder/taxpayer is unable to use these short-term gains to offset his or her other portfolio short- or long-term capital losses.

> *Example:* J. Investor's mutual fund had, for his ownership interest, $1,000 of short-term gain for the year. For the same year he realized $5,000 of long-term capital loss from his non-mutual fund investments. Had the short-term gains flowed through to him, he would have been able to reduce his taxable income by $4,000 of the long-term capital loss ($1,000 offset by the fund's short-term gains and the maximum $3,000 long-term capital gain [loss] deduction for any one year). Instead, he has a $1,000 higher ordinary income since the short-term gain from the fund was reported as a dividend, and he is able to deduct only $3,000 of the loss. Investor has a higher taxable income by $1,000, so in addition to paying income taxes on that sum in his highest tax bracket, it is also possible that,

because of the higher income, he could lose some of his itemized deductions and personal exemptions and be subject to additional income taxes.

If the fund's short-term capital gains exceed its long-term losses, the same result occurs, to the detriment of the fund's shareholder.

> *Example:* S. Investor's mutual fund had, for her ownership interest, $2,000 of short-term capital gains and $1,000 of long-term capital losses. For the same year she realized $7,000 of capital losses (either short- or long-term) from her non-mutual fund investments. Had the net short-term capital gain of the fund flowed as such, she would have been able to use it to offset some of her non-mutual fund capital losses, thereby reducing her total income tax (as well as possibly avoiding loss of some of the standard deductions and personal exemptions).

In these situations, the shareholder loses as a consequence of the manner prescribed by the IRS.

How Can the Investor Manage These Differences?

Certain types of mutual funds are more likely to have the majority of their capital gains in the form of long-term rather than short-term. Examples of these are the following:

- index funds—Their trading pattern is to retain the characteristics of the index being matched, and they do not seek to enhance shareholder return through either short- or long-term timing of trading activity.
- growth funds—With an emphasis on long-term returns, these funds should have little short-term timing trading and therefore should minimize short-term gains.

Where Can I Find Out More?

- IRC Sec. 852.
- Reg. Sec. 1.852-1 to 1.852-3.

Emergency Cash—Investment Alternatives
Thomas A. Dziadosz

Advice differs on how much clients should keep in emergency cash reserves and where the funds should be invested. Conventional wisdom holds that an emergency fund should be invested in cash instruments, such as savings accounts, NOW accounts, CDs, money market mutual funds, T-bills, and similar very low-risk, highly liquid assets. Generally, clients should not start an investment program to achieve various long-term goals until they feel comfortable with the level of their emergency cash holdings.

How Much Do Clients Need?

Ask five people and you will get five different answers. A popular rule of thumb suggests keeping 6 months' living expenses (estimated from the family budget) invested in cash-equivalent-type investments. (Note that this amount is closer to 6 months' take-home pay than to 6 months' gross salary before taxes and retirement plan contributions are deducted).

Realistically, it might take 4 to 5 years of saving a substantial amount from each paycheck to build up such a fund. The thought of having that amount of money invested in a low-earning cash-equivalent fund, subject to taxes on its meager earnings and inflation on its purchasing power, is not very appealing.

Many families, especially those that have two wage earners with steady employment prospects, can safely reduce the size of their cash reserves to about 3 months' living expenses.

What Are the Purposes of an Emergency Fund?

The first purpose is to provide liquid assets to cover minor disasters, such as the unexpected demise of a home appliance, postwarranty auto repairs, or the loss of extra income from a part-time job. Anything that presents people with an unanticipated bill or reduction in income requires a source of funds to handle the problem smoothly.

Second, major disasters—the temporary loss of employment for the client or spouse, damage to the client's home from an uninsured or underinsured loss caused by a flood or earthquake, or uncovered medical expenses—require ready access to funds for living expenses or substantial cash outlays on short notice.

What More Aggressive Approach Can Be Used?

Some people prefer not to keep a substantial emergency fund tied up in cash equivalents. For them, a well-diversified portfolio of mutual funds, both stock and short-term bond, is the investment of choice for most of their emergency funds.

Let's examine the pros and cons of this approach.

Emergency Funds versus Working Capital. An emergency fund is established to provide for events that are unlikely to happen. If a client is constantly tapping the emergency fund to handle ordinary day-to-day expenses, it is really a source of working capital rather than an emergency fund.

Opportunity Cost. The opportunity cost of keeping money in cash equivalents year after year rather than invested in a portfolio of stock and bond mutual funds is the reduction in after-tax returns earned over the extended period. Earning 3.5 percent after taxes versus 8 percent after taxes amounts to a substantial loss of income.

Inflation. The after-tax return on many cash equivalents fails to keep up with inflation. The real value of the emergency fund may be in a long-run decline, requiring the investor to periodically add funds to keep its purchasing power intact.

Bad Timing. What happens if an emergency requiring a large cash outlay arises at a time when the financial markets are going through a severe correction? The value of emergency fund investments could be hard hit and temporarily insufficient to cover one's needs; fund shares might have to be sold at the bottom of a bear market.

Borrowing Short-term. To avoid selling stock and bond mutual funds in a bear market, proponents of this strategy recommend temporary borrowing against assets, making unsecured loans, and tapping preestablished credit lines, such as

- borrowing against a home equity credit line
- borrowing from an unsecured line of credit previously established at a bank
- taking cash advances against credit cards
- borrowing against life insurance cash values
- borrowing from a qualified plan (401(k))

The amounts borrowed are to be paid back from future income or from the sale of assets when markets recover. Interest expense can be minimized by borrowing first from the lowest-cost loan sources. Recent steep market declines have been for relatively short durations; it is assumed that the length of future market declines will also be short.

Evaluation. This aggressive approach is certainly more risky than the traditional approach requiring an emergency fund invested in safe cash equivalents. The theory behind the aggressive approach is based on certain assumptions, many of which are not always clearly spelled out or clearly understood by its advocates.

The aggressive approach assumes the following:

- The need to tap emergency funds will be infrequent.
- The need for a substantial amount of emergency cash at a time when financial markets are in a serious correction phase is remote.
- Credit sources will be available when needed.
- The duration of borrowing at high interest rates will be short.

- Markets will recover in a reasonable time, and borrowing, for the most part, will be repaid from the sale of assets at favorable prices.
- The extra earnings on the mutual fund portfolios over time will more than compensate for the interest expense incurred on any required borrowing.

Are the Potential Returns Worth the Extra Risk?

Suppose that the extra after-tax return on the stock and bond mutual fund portfolios averaged 4.5 percent above the return on a portfolio of cash equivalents and that the average balance in the emergency fund over a 20-year period is $20,000.

Example:

$20,000 invested at 8 percent for 20 years	$93,219.14
$20,000 invested at 3.5 percent for 20 years	$39,795.78
The added value over 20 years	$53,423.36

You would have to borrow large amounts for extended periods to overcome the $53,423.36 potential earnings differential over the 20-year period.

What Should Be Done?

This approach is not for everyone, but it *is* worth thinking about. Clients with access to sufficient credit sources, especially sources with a low after-tax cost, are in a position to consider the more aggressive approach.

This is not an all-or-nothing proposition; clients with different risk profiles can select different mixes. The most risk-averse clients might be comfortable with the conventional approach—100 percent of the emergency fund invested in ultrasafe cash equivalents, regardless of the relatively low after-tax, after-inflation returns offered by such investments. Other clients with higher risk-tolerance levels might be willing to invest 20 to 80 percent of their emergency funds in a mix of equity funds and intermediate-term bond mutual funds.

The client must determine the relative mix of cash equivalents, intermediate-term bond funds, and equity funds as well as the estimated level of risk inherent in each specific investment chosen. The earnings gap between cash equivalents and the more risky investment alternatives over an extended period must be considered in making the decision.

Is the safety of the conventional approach worth the price? The client must decide.

Where Can I Find Out More?

- Jonathan Clements. "Saving for a Rainy Day is Smart, but Sitting on Buckets of Cash Isn't." *Wall Street Journal,* June 27, 1995.

- Elizabeth DeYoe. "How to Create a Financial Safety Net." *Working Woman,* September 1995.

ATM Cards, Debit Cards, and Credit Cards
Thomas A. Dziadosz

What Was the Situation Before?

Banks issue automated teller machine (ATM) cards that enable customers to make deposits and cash withdrawals "on-line" at ATMs. The cards can also be used at on-line point-of-sale (POS) terminals, typically in supermarkets, to make purchases and receive cash. In both cases, the customer has to supply a personal identification number (PIN) to ensure the legitimacy of the transaction. Withdrawals at ATMs and purchases at on-line POS terminals result in an immediate reduction in the customer's bank account balance.

The use of ATMs was encouraged as a convenience to customers and a low-cost alternative to a live teller. Typically, there was no charge for using an ATM owned by a customer's bank, and many banks did not charge for withdrawals made at ATMs owned by other banks in the same network.

What Is the Nature of the Change?

Recently, banks have initiated charges, typically $1 per withdrawal, imposed on their customers who use ATMs owned by other banks. In addition, a fee—often $2—is imposed by the bank owning the ATM. Paying $3 to withdraw funds is difficult to avoid when traveling away from home, and making withdrawals in small amounts has become very expensive. One way to avoid the transaction fee(s) is to make a small purchase at a supermarket with an ATM card and request cash. The maximum amount given in cash varies—some supermarkets set a limit of $50 or $100, whereas others will go as high as allowed by the bank that issued the card.

A more troubling innovation from the client's point of view is the move by banks to have customers accept a combination ATM/debit card (also referred to as a debit card or check card) in place of their ATM card. These new debit cards are touted in ads as being more "convenient" than the current ATM cards they are replacing, but this is a matter of interpretation.

For example, when using the new card on-line to withdraw funds from an ATM, a customer is still required to supply a PIN. However, the combination ATM/debit card can be used to make purchases "off-line" at retail establishments without supplying the PIN, simply by giving the merchant the debit card and receiving a receipt indicating the amount of the checking account debit. The payment is made either immediately or within several days. No credit is being extended because the funds come directly from the checking account.

Question: What are the advantages of paying for a retail transaction with the new debit card rather than with a credit card—especially one offering a grace period on new purchases?

Answer: None.

How Credit Cards Are Used. Credit cards are used for convenience by about 35 percent of cardholders (meaning they pay their balance in full each month) and as a source of credit by those who carry over an unpaid balance from the previous month.

When purchasing goods with a credit card, the customer's bank pays the merchant now, and the customer pays the bank several weeks after receiving a statement, or over an extended period if the customer elects to carry a balance.

Credit Cards versus Debit Cards. Those who pay their credit card balance in full each month effectively receive an interest-free loan from the date of purchase until the date the check is cleared. When making a purchase with a debit card, the amount of the purchase is taken directly from the buyer's checking account. In effect, the interest-free, short-term loan aspect of making convenience purchases with a credit card is lost.

Furthermore, when goods are paid for with a debit card rather than a credit card, the buyer does not have the same rights under consumer credit laws. For example, payment cannot be withheld until a dispute with the merchant is resolved. Since the funds are taken directly from the buyer's account, any problems must be settled directly with the merchant.

Fraudulent use of a debit card gives the thief direct access to the owner's checking account as well as any attached credit line. When a debit card is used off-line to pay for merchandise, only a signature identifies the cardholder, and a PIN is *not* required—the process is similar to presenting a credit card when purchasing goods. The customer, not the bank, is immediately hit with an out-of-pocket loss, and he or she will be in the position of having to convince the bank to replace the stolen funds. Failure to report promptly the fraudulent use of a debit card increases the cardholder's potential loss exposure. If the cardholder reports the card missing within 2 days *after noticing* its disappearance, the loss is limited to $50. Waiting longer than 2 days to report the card missing increases the potential liability to $500. And after 60 days, the bank is not obligated to restore *any* lost funds.

To make matters worse, during the attempt to resolve the fraudulent use problem, any checks written against the funds that the customer thought were in the account will be bouncing all over the place.

What Should Be Done?

It is difficult to find any advantages to paying for merchandise with a debit card rather than with a credit card, especially if the balance is paid in full each month to avoid being charged interest on new purchases. However, even if a balance is carried, many credit cards allow a grace period before charging interest on new purchases.

Those who typically carry an unpaid balance should check the terms of their current credit card to ensure that they are not incurring unnecessary interest changes on new purchases. There are plenty of other credit cards that can be acquired if the terms of the current card are unfavorable.

Generally, an ATM card is preferable to a debit card because the ATM card can only be used on-line by supplying a PIN. The debit card can also be used on-line—PIN required—and off-line without a PIN to pay for retail purchases. It is the off-line use that causes additional risk. Fraudulent off-line use of a lost or stolen debit card or the use of a counterfeit card with the cardholder's card number allows direct access to the checking account.

Paying for retail purchases with a credit card on which no previous balance is carried is preferable to paying with a debit card. The cardholder gets the float—the interest-free loan—during the grace period and retains all rights under consumer credit laws.

Where Can I Find Out More?

- Richard Mitchell. "Clearing Debit's Risk Hurdle." *U.S. Banker,* March 1997.
- Alexandra Alger. "Carte Blanche for Crooks." *Forbes Magazine,* December 1, 1996.

Recent Changes in Credit Card Terms
Thomas A. Dziadosz

Credit card offers are constantly changing. Clients receive a steady stream of mailings from card issuers; some offer lower regular interest rates, while others offer tempting "teaser" interest rates that provide a below-market interest rate for a limited time on transferred balances and, in some cases, on additional borrowing.

Let's examine some typical offers to compare the terms, avoid hidden surprises, examine fee structures, and find ways to take advantage of the better deals.

How Should Credit Card Offers Be Compared?

Compare the key features of two recent credit card offers from different banks. Each card has no annual fee and encourages the transfer of balances from other credit cards by offering a low introductory interest rate on transfers.

TABLE 8-2
Summary of Card Transactions

Transaction	ATM Card	Combination ATM/Debit Card	Credit Card
Withdraw $100 cash	• At your bank—no charge or nominal charge • At other bank—your bank may charge $1, other bank may charge $2 • Must supply PIN	• At your bank—no charge or nominal charge • At other bank—your bank may charge $1, other bank may charge $2 • Must supply PIN	• Considered a cash advance (loan); fee 2%–2.5% (possible $2 minimum, $20 maximum) • Interest of 5.9%–21% or higher charged from day of transaction
Purchase appliance for $300	• Cannot be done with ATM card	• Direct debit of your checking account for $300 • PIN *not* required • *No protection under consumer credit protection laws because this is not a credit transaction* • You must settle disputes directly with merchant	• Grace period on new purchases *or* interest charged immediately on some cards if balance is carried from previous month • Grace period is essentially an interest-free loan from date of purchase until check is cleared at your bank *or* finance charge is applied to unpaid balance • *Consumer credit protection laws apply in disputes with merchants*
Card lost or stolen and used fraudulently	• Card is useless without your PIN at on-line ATMs • Card *cannot* be used off-line • Notify issuer immediately after you discover the card is missing to limit potential loss	• Card is useless without your PIN at on-line ATMs • Card *can* be used off-line *without* supplying your PIN • Notify issuer immediately after you discover card is missing to limit potential loss • Thief has direct access to your bank account and any attached credit line until bank is notified.	• Fraudulent use does *not* allow thief direct access to your personal bank account • Notify issuer immediately after you discover card is missing to limit potential loss

Card A	Card B
• 5.9% on transferred balances, new purchases, and cash advances made after the transferred balances have been posted. After 1 year, the rate increases to 9.4% above the prime rate (currently 8.25%).	• 7.9% for the first 6 months, then rising to 2.9% above the prime rate (currently 8.25%).
• If no balances are transferred, the low 5.9% rate does *not* apply to new purchases and cash advances.	• The low introductory rate applies to new purchases and advances even if no balances are transferred.
• If the cardholder fails to keep all accounts with the bank in good standing, the rate (including the introductory rate) immediately rises to 12.9% above the prime rate.	• No penalty rate is imposed if the cardholder fails to keep all accounts with the bank in good standing.

Other features, such as a grace period for purchases, transaction fees for cash advances, and the method of computing the balance for purchases (average daily balance, including new purchases) are similar for each card.

Card A offers the lowest teaser rate, 5.9 percent, for the longer period, 1 year; Card B's rate, 7.9 percent, is good for 6 months. But Card A's 5.9 percent rate applies only if balances are transferred; otherwise, a rate of 17.65 percent (9.4 percent above the current prime rate) is charged on additional purchases and cash advances. Card B has no such requirement to get the 7.9 percent rate on additional purchases and cash advances.

Why not apply for both cards? Anyone who carries credit card balances and intends to add to them might transfer existing card balances to Card A and add new borrowings to Card B.

What Happens When the Introductory Rate Expires? Card A's rate rises after 1 year to 17.65 percent (9.4 percent above the prime rate). Card B's rate rises after 6 months to 11.15 percent (2.9 percent above the prime rate), which is a substantially better long-term rate for existing balances as well as new purchases and cash advances.

What Happens If All Accounts with the Issuing Bank Are Not Kept in Good Standing? Bank A, at its discretion, can immediately raise the rate to 21.15 percent (12.9 percent above the current prime rate). Note that this is a penalty rate—the regular rate on the card is 9.4 percent above prime. Bank B has no such penalty rate in its offer. This could be a real problem with Card A if a payment is received 1 day past its due date or any other accounts at the bank become even temporarily delinquent!

Therefore, beware of offers that allow the bank to unilaterally adjust the card's current interest rate to a higher penalty rate if any of the cardholder's accounts with the bank are no longer considered in good standing.

Also, some offers state in the fine print that the issuer can from time to time review the credit report of a cardholder and raise the interest rate without notice if there has been a decline in the individual's credit rating. The interest rate can be increased even though all accounts are in good standing.

What Should Be Done?

Every time a credit card offer arrives, compare its terms to the terms of credit card(s) currently held. If a large, unpaid balance typically is carried (not a good idea), the entire amount can be refinanced to save a tidy sum on the interest charges. Take advantage of the competition among lenders.

Above all, use the savings to pay down high-interest debt, as shown in the example below.

Example: Assume a consumer has the credit card debts and interest costs shown in the table below.

TABLE 8-3
Consumer Credit Cost Summary

Source of Credit	Average Annual Balance	Rate	Annual Interest Cost
Visa	$1500	17%	$255.00
MasterCard	$1250	18%	$225.00
Other national cards	$ 850	17.5%	$148.75
Department store credit cards	$ 500	21%	$105.00
Oil company credit cards	$ 300	18%	$ 54.00
	$4400		$787.75

If the above balances are transferred from high-interest rate credit cards to a credit card offering a 1-year teaser rate of 5.9 percent, the annual interest cost would drop to $259.60 ($4,400 x 5.9 percent).

The average annual amount of indebtedness, $4,400, is the same. But instead of paying $787.75 in interest charges, the

8.44

annual interest expense drops to $259.60, a saving of $528.15 ($787.75 − $259.60).

The out-of-pocket savings can be applied, along with other funds from current income, to pay down that expensive credit card debt before the teaser rate expires and the interest rate jumps to a higher level.

Note: Some credit card teaser rate offers apply only to balances transferred from a short list of other credit cards; for example, only balances transferred from Visa, MasterCard, Optima, or Discover cards qualify. One way around this is to pay off nonqualifying balances with a check or cash advance from a source that does qualify, effectively transferring the balance from, say, an oil company credit card or a local department store card to a Visa card. The balance on the Visa card qualifies for transfer to the credit card (another Visa or MasterCard) offering the teaser rate.

How Is Credit Card Interest Calculated?

The annual rate of interest charged on credit card balances is not the only factor determining the size of the finance charge. How the finance charges are calculated can make a big difference in the amount you pay. Also, the way new purchases are treated, the timing of new purchases, and the timing of payments can influence the result.

The *adjusted balance method* of financing calculation typically results in the lowest charge. The finance charge is applied to the amount outstanding at the beginning of the billing cycle minus payments and credits (returns) made during the month.

The *average daily balance method (excluding new purchases)* applies the finance charge to the amount outstanding each day, divided by the number of days in the month. Notice that new purchases during the month are not included in the amount on which the finance charge is applied. The grace period applies to new purchases even though a balance is carried.

The *average daily balance method (including new purchases)* calculates the finance charge in essentially the same way, except that new purchases during the month are included in the amount on which the finance charge is applied. Carrying a balance from the previous month eliminates the interest-free grace period on new purchases.

The *previous balance method* applies the finance charge to the balance outstanding at the beginning of the billing cycle.

The amount paid in finance charges for the month, with the same beginning balance and purchases and credits during the month, is fairly close with all of these methods except average daily balance (including new purchases). This method usually results in a moderately higher finance charge because new purchases during the month are included in the amount on which the finance charge is applied. Most credit cards use one of these four methods when calculating finance charges.

The *two-cycle average daily balance method* has been around for several years. Recently, more credit card offers have listed the *two-cycle average daily balance method (excluding new purchases)* or the *two-cycle average daily balance method (including new purchases)* for computing finance charges. Under these methods, the balance on which the finance charge is based is the sum of the average daily balances for *two* monthly cycles—the current month and the previous month, with new purchases either excluded or included.

Some credit cards apply the two-cycle method only when the borrower first carries an unpaid balance; then after the second month, the finance charge is calculated using the average daily balance for one month.

Credit card companies must state the method used to calculate finance charges, but they are not required to explain the details. Most people do not understand how a two-cycle average daily balance method actually works. If a credit card ad offers an unusually low regular interest rate, check the method used to calculate the finance charge. The two-cycle method can greatly increase the effective rate of interest and eliminate most or all of the expected savings from the lower advertised rate.

What Should Be Done?

Clients who typically carry a balance should avoid credit cards employing either of the two-cycle average daily balance methods to calculate the balance on which the finance charge applies.

Also, as previously mentioned, credit card issuers may review a cardholder's credit report periodically to determine if there has been any deterioration in the borrower's credit rating. This can result in an immediate increase in the finance charge to a punitive level, even though the cardholder's account balance is in good standing. In states that prohibit creditors from unilaterally changing the terms of the current credit agreement, cardholders will be notified by the card issuer that they have the right to close their account and pay off the balance under the terms of the original contract. Continued use of the card after a certain date means that the cardholder has agreed to accept the changes in the terms of the agreement, including the higher finance charge on the previous balance.

Cardholders who typically carry a balance should look for a card that *excludes new purchases* when calculating the finance charge. If new purchases are included, the grace period on new purchases is lost in any month that a balance is carried on the card.

Another way around this problem is to have two cards. Carry a balance on the card with the most favorable finance terms and use the second card for new purchases that will be paid in full each month.

Check the fees charged for cash advances, late payments, returned checks, and going over the credit limit.

Using the card for a small cash advance, such as $100, at an ATM may trigger an ATM fee by the bank owning the machine. The credit card agreement can impose additional charges, such as

- 2 percent of the amount of the advance, subject to a $10 minimum
- 2 percent of the amount of the advance, subject to a $2 minimum and a $10 maximum
- 2 percent of the amount of the advance, subject to a $2 minimum and a $20 maximum
- 2.5 percent of the amount of the advance, subject to a $3.50 minimum

Late payment fees are anywhere from $10 to $20. Currently, late payment fees are imposed by most issuers on the day after the payment is due. (Several years ago, late payment penalties were not imposed until about 2 weeks after the due date.) Returned check fees are in the $10 to $20 range. Over-the-credit-limit fees can be as high as $20, even if the purchase is preapproved over the phone.

Where Can I Find Out More?

- Frank Lalli. "Consumer Alert: Avoid the New Credit Penalties." *Money,* November 1996.
- Peter Pae. "Watching for 'Traps' on Lower Card Rates." *Wall Street Journal,* February 21, 1992.
- Recent credit card offers.

9

FINANCIAL PLANNING

David M. Cordell

Changes in Registration Requirements for Investment Advisers

What Was the Situation Before?

The number of investment advisers subject to regulation at the federal level has grown significantly. This regulation derives primarily from the Investment Advisers Act of 1940 as administered by the Securities and Exchange Commission (SEC). Prior to the passage of the Investment Advisers Supervision Coordination Act (IASCA) in October 1996, financial planners were with few exceptions required to register as investment advisers with the SEC. Most states also required financial planners to register as investment advisers at the state level.

Congress passed the Investment Advisers Act in the post-Depression era primarily to police and control discretionary money managers. This act and subsequent regulations exempted the following entities from the definition of *investment adviser:*

- any bank or holding company as defined in the Bank Holding Company Act of 1956 that is not an investment company
- any lawyer, accountant, engineer, or teacher if the performance of advisory services is solely incidental to the practice of his or her profession
- any broker, dealer, or registered representative thereof whose performance of advisory services is solely incidental to the conduct of his or her business as a broker or dealer and who receives no "special compensation" for his or her services
- the publisher of any newspaper, news magazine, or business or financial publication of general or regular circulation
- any person whose advice, analyses, or reports relate only to securities that are direct obligations of or obligations guaranteed as to principal or interest by the United States of America
- such other persons not within the intent of the law as the SEC may designate by rules and regulations or by order

The Investment Advisers Act and subsequent regulations exempted five other groups from registration although they fall within the definition of *investment adviser:*

- advisers whose clients are all residents of the state within which the investment adviser maintains the principal office and place of business and who do not furnish advice or issue analyses or reports with respect to listed securities or securities admitted to unlisted trading privileges
- advisers whose only clients are insurance companies
- advisers who, during the preceding 12 months, have had fewer than 15 clients and who neither present themselves to the general public as investment advisers nor act as investment advisers to any investment company registered under the Investment Company Act of 1940
- advisers that are charitable organizations and that provide advice only to other charitable organizations
- advisers that provide advice solely to church plans

Although these advisers are not required to register, they are still required to comply with the act's antifraud provisions.

In August 1981, the SEC's Release No. IA-770 specified three tests to apply when determining if a financial planner was required to register with the SEC as an investment adviser. If the planner answered each of these tests affirmatively, he or she was required to register with the SEC.

The first test asked whether the planner provided clients with "advice or analyses" concerning securities. Although some planners believe that they do not provide such services, they are often surprised to learn that Sec. 80b-22(a)(18) of the Investment Advisers Act of 1940 defines *security* as

> ...any note, stock, Treasury stock, bond, debenture, evidence of indebtedness, certificate of interest or participation in any profit-sharing agreement, collateral trust certificate, preorganization certificate or subscription, transferable share, investment contract, voting-trust certificate, certificate of deposit for a security, fractional undivided interest in oil, gas or other mineral rights, or in general, any instrument or interest commonly known as a *security*, or any certificate of interest or participation in, temporary or interim certificate for, receipt for, or guarantee of, or warrant or right to subscribe to or purchase any of the foregoing.

Because of the breadth of this definition, almost all financial planners must answer the first test affirmatively.

The second test specified by Release No. IA-770 concerned whether the planner holds himself or herself out to the public as being "in the business" of providing advice or analyses about securities. Indications that the planner must answer affirmatively to this "holding out" provision can be inferred from such things as the planner's business card, advertising, and letterhead as well as the way he or she describes his or her business activity.

The third test specified by Release No. IA-770 related to compensation. If the planner receives any compensation for services rendered, he or she must answer affirmatively to this test. Although commission-based planners often consider themselves excluded because of this test, the SEC makes no distinction between fee and commission compensation. The effect of this interpretation is that it is nearly impossible for a planner not to answer in the affirmative.

One effect of these inclusive definitions and the burgeoning financial planning field was the enormous growth in the number of registered investment advisers from 5,680 in 1980 to 22,500 in early 1997. The SEC's budget was woefully inadequate to supervise or examine such a large group on a regular basis. Furthermore, as already noted, regulation of investment advisers was not the exclusive purview of the SEC. Forty-six states mandated registration of investment advisers at the state level, although with widely varying requirements. Many states specified qualifications and/or requirements that were much more stringent than federal requirements. For example, many states specified capital requirements, and most required National Association of Securities Dealers (NASD) registration, such as series 63 (uniform state securities exam) or series 65 (investment adviser).

Two important factors were at work. First, there was concern about the cost associated with overlapping and duplicative federal and state regulatory bodies. Second, there was concern about whether it was reasonable to require investment advisers and financial planners to be regulated at both the state and federal level.

What Is the Nature of the Change?

The relationship between state and federal regulation of investment advisers has changed. After years of dispute about the direction of regulation of investment markets and investment advisers, the Congress passed and the president signed the National Securities Markets Improvement Act in October 1996 with an effective date of April 9, 1997. Title III of that act is the Investment Advisers Supervision Coordination Act (IASCA). The most important aspects of IASCA concern allocating the jurisdiction of investment advisers between the SEC and state authorities based primarily on the level of assets under an adviser's management. IASCA also authorizes appropriations for the SEC, prohibits felons from registering as investment advisers within 10 years of conviction, and mandates a consumer hotline (presumably via telephone and the Internet) for inquiry concerning disciplinary actions and proceedings against registered investment advisers and associated persons.

Under IASCA, investment advisers—and thus financial planners—need to register with either the SEC or state authorities, but not with both. The critical provisions of this law have the following effects:

- Amending the Investment Advisers Act of 1940 to exempt from SEC registration requirements investment advisers who are subject to a state securities regulator unless they (1) manage at least $25 million in assets, or (2) serve as advisers to certain federally registered investment companies. (Colorado, Iowa, Ohio, and Wyoming were the only states without securities regulations at the time this was written.)
- Exempting from state regulation advisers who are subject to SEC regulation or who are excepted from the SEC definition of investment adviser. IASCA permits states in such cases to (1) require the filing of documents for notice purposes, and (2) investigate fraud or deceit and bring enforcement actions.
- Prohibiting the enforcement of any state law or regulation that sets record-keeping or capital and bond requirements in addition to those of the state in which the adviser maintains its principal place of business as long as the adviser is in compliance with applicable requirements.
- Exempting from state registration, licensing, or qualification requirements certain investment advisers who (1) do not have a place of business located within the state, and (2) have had fewer than six clients who are residents of the state during the preceding 12-month period.
- Declaring that a state securities commission (or similar agency) can require the filing of any documents filed with the SEC pursuant to securities laws solely for notice purposes, together with consent to service of process and any required fee.
- Allowing states to continue collecting filing and registration fees that were in effect before the enactment of IASCA, until state law or regulation provides otherwise. For 3 years after IASCA's enactment, state securities commissions may require the state registration of advisers who fail to pay such fees.

When Does this Change Affect Clients?

IASCA was supposed to take effect on April 9, 1997; however, Congress subsequently recognized that regulators and advisers needed more time to comply with the law. Both houses of Congress passed and the president signed legislation to postpone the effective date of IASCA to July 8, 1997. Meanwhile, on December 20, 1996, the SEC issued Release No. IA-1601, which contained proposed regulations for implementing IASCA and requested public comment during a period that expired February 10, 1997. Also on December 20, 1996, the SEC issued Release No. IA-1602, which stayed the requirement of filing Form ADV-S that investment advisers must file within 90 days of the end of their fiscal year.

What Should Be Done?

Of course, when governmental regulations change, the only appropriate response is compliance. Unfortunately, until the SEC finalizes the regulations, it is impossible to know exactly what to do. Although the proposed regulations are apt to change before reaching their final form, we can review some of the major points for guidance because it is likely that most will survive intact. The critical provisions of these proposed regulations would have the following effects:

- Requiring all registered investment advisers to file a new Form ADV-T, the instructions for which help determine whether the adviser meets the criteria for SEC registration. Under proposed transition rule 203A-5, all advisers registered with the SEC on July 8, 1997, are required to file a completed Form ADV-T by that date.
- Refining the definition of *assets under management* as used in the Investment Advisers Act of 1940 for the purpose of determining whether advisers must register at the state or federal level. (See the Author's Note at the end of this topic section for the actual text used in instruction 7 of Form ADV-T.) Advisers would include only those accounts for which they provide "continuous and regular supervisory or management services" and 50 percent of the value of which consists of securities. Cash and cash equivalents must be excluded in the calculation of the percentage. If an account is determined to be a *securities portfolio*, the entire value of the account, including cash and other nonsecurities positions, must be included in calculating assets under management.
- Requiring that valuation of securities be calculated no more than 10 days prior to filing Form ADV-T.
- Creating a safe haven from SEC registration for an adviser that is registered with state securities authorities based on a reasonable belief that it is prohibited from registering with the SEC because it has insufficient assets under management.
- Increasing the level of assets under management for required SEC registration to $30 million, and making SEC registration optional for assets under management of $25 million to $30 million, thus lessening the likelihood that market volatility will force the adviser to move back and forth between state and federal registration.
- Requiring annual filing of a new Schedule I ("eye") to Form ADV to determine whether the adviser's assets under management have fallen below $25 million, requiring de-registration. It also provides a 90-day grace period for registering at the state level after a schedule I filing that forces federal de-registration.
- Exempting four types of advisers from the prohibition on SEC registration:
    - Nationally recognized statistical rating organizations, often referred to as rating agencies. These entities do not have assets under management, but the SEC believes they are better regulated at the federal level.
    - Pension consultants, defined as investment advisers that provide investment advice to certain employee benefit plans with respect to

assets having an aggregate value of at least $50 million during the
   adviser's last fiscal year.
   – Certain affiliated investment advisers, primarily including firms
   that conduct their advisory activities through separately registered
   advisers, not all of which meet the criteria for SEC registration.
   – Newly formed investment advisers that reasonably expect that they
   will, within 90 days of formation, have assets under management
   that will qualify for SEC registration.
- Defining the terms *principal office and place of business*, *supervised persons* (of SEC-registered investment advisers), *investment adviser representative*, and *solicitor* to further delineate whether state or federal registration is appropriate.
- Amending the Investment Advisers Act to make state investment adviser statutes inapplicable to advisers that do not have a place of business in that state and have fewer than six clients who are residents of that state ("national *de minimis* standard"), and defining as a single client for this purpose (1) any natural person and any relative or spouse of the natural person sharing the same principal residence, and (2) all accounts of which such persons are the sole primary beneficiaries. The proposed rule also treats as a single client a corporation, general partnership, limited partnership (meeting the safe harbor definition in rule 203(b)(3)-1 of the Investment Advisers Act), trust, or other legal organization that receives investment advice based on its investment objectives rather than the investment objectives of its shareholders, partners, members, or beneficial owners.
- Limiting the applicability of the book- and record-keeping requirements of rule 204-2 only to advisers registered with the SEC and requiring advisers registered with the SEC to preserve any books and records the adviser was previously required to preserve under state law.
- Extending to advisers who are not required to register with the SEC the exemption from the prohibition against performance fee arrangements. This exemption allows advisers to charge performance fees (also called incentive fees), but only if the adviser is managing $500,000 of the client's assets or reasonably believes that the client has a net worth of at least $1 million.
- Continuing to apply the antifraud provisions of the Investment Advisers Act to all advisers. However, four existing rules will no longer be applied to state-registered advisers because it is assumed that the states can more appropriately address these issues. These four rules prohibit certain abusive advertising practices, govern the adviser's custody of funds and securities of clients, address the payment of cash to persons soliciting on behalf of the adviser, and require certain disclosure to clients regarding the adviser's financial condition and disciplinary history.
- Continuing to apply the Investment Adviser Act's prohibitions against advisory contracts that (1) contain certain performance fee

arrangements, (2) permit an assignment of the advisory contract to be made without the consent of the client, and (3) fail to require an adviser that is a partnership to notify clients of a change in the membership of the partnership.
- Requiring advisers subject to state regulation to continue to be subject to the Investment Advisers Act's requirement to establish, maintain, and enforce written procedures reasonably designed to prevent the misuse of material nonpublic information.

A review of the responses sent to the SEC via the Internet and posted on the SEC's Web site suggests that respondents' concerns are numerous. State regulators have expressed concern about definitions, being usurped by federal law, and losing revenue from investment advisers who will no longer need to register with states (although IASCA specifically allows states to charge fees). Advisers and their representatives have also expressed numerous concerns. For example, advisers with assets under management near the $25 million mark fear that they will need to switch back and forth between federal and state registration if market conditions are volatile, even with the SEC's proposed $5 million buffer. Some small advisers with clients in several states complain that they must register in each state. Among the other controversial issues include the definitions of *assets under management, client, place of business,* and *investment adviser representative* and the registration of pension consultants at the federal level regardless of assets under management.

Despite all the uncertainty about the final form of the regulations, the effect on most advisers is clear. Instead of registering at both the state and federal level, relatively small advisers (with less than $25 million under management) will be regulated by the states while larger advisers will fall under SEC jurisdiction. Since SEC regulation may be easier and more predictable than state regulation, there is added reason to seek to increase the level of assets under management (as if there were not reason enough already).

Where Can I Find Out More?

- HS 318 Insurance and Financial Planning. The American College.
- HS 320 Fundamentals of Financial Planning. The American College.
- David M. Cordell, ed. *Readings in Financial Planning*, 2d ed., 1997. The American College. (This textbook is used in The American College's HS 318 course. See chapter on SEC registration and compliance for investment advisers.)
- David M. Cordell, ed. *Fundamentals of Financial Planning*, 3d ed., 1996. The American College. (This textbook is used in The American College's HS 320 course. See chapter on SEC registration and compliance for investment advisers.)
- For the most up-to-date information concerning regulatory requirements under the IASCA, contact the SEC's Web site on the Internet (http://www.sec.gov) and click "Current SEC Rule Making."

Review the sections "Proposed Rules" and "Final Rules." Electronically filed comments to proposed rules can be accessed from the "Proposed Rules" screen.

Author's Note

The full text of instruction 7 of proposed Form ADV-T is as follows:

In determining the amount of assets the registrant has under management, include the total value of securities portfolios with respect to which the registrant provides continuous and regular supervisory or management services.

a. An account is a securities portfolio if at least 50% of the total value of the account (less cash and cash equivalents) consists of securities. Include securities portfolios that are: (i) family or proprietary accounts (unless the registrant is a sole proprietor, in which case the personal assets of the sole proprietor should be excluded); (ii) accounts for which the registrant receives no compensation for its services; and (iii) accounts of clients who are not U.S. residents.

b. Include the entire value of each securities portfolio for which the registrant provides "continuous and regular supervisory or management services."

c. A registrant provides continuous and regular supervisory or management services with respect to a securities portfolio if the registrant (i) has discretionary authority over and (ii) provides ongoing management or supervisory services with respect to the portfolio.

Whether a registrant that provides ongoing management or supervisory services on a *non-discretionary* basis provides continuous and regular supervisory or management services is a question of fact. The greater the registrant's ongoing responsibilities, the more likely the adviser will be providing continuous and regular supervisory or management services.

To assist registrants, the Commission is providing examples of accounts that receive continuous and regular supervisory and management services. These examples are not exclusive.

Accounts that receive continuous and regular supervisory and management services:

- accounts for which the adviser provides traditional portfolio management services on a discretionary basis;
- accounts for which the adviser provides ongoing management services (*i.e.,* is responsible for the selection of which securities

to buy and sell and when to buy and sell them) without a grant of discretionary authority;
- accounts managed by other advisers (i) that the adviser has been given a grant of discretionary authority to hire and discharge on behalf of the client, and (ii) among which the adviser has the authority to allocate and reallocate account assets; and
- accounts for which the adviser provides asset allocation services by (i) continuously monitoring the needs of the clients and the markets in which account assets are invested, and (ii) allocating and reallocating account assets to meet client objectives under a grant of discretionary authority.

Accounts that do not receive continuous and regular supervisory and management services:

- accounts for which the adviser provides only periodic advice (no matter how frequent), *e.g.,* an account for which the adviser has prepared a financial plan which is periodically reviewed and updated;
- accounts for which the adviser provides advice only on a periodic basis or as a result of some market event or change in client circumstances (even if the adviser has discretionary authority), *e.g.,* an account that is reviewed and adjusted on a quarterly basis or upon client request;
- accounts for which the adviser provides market timing recommendations (to buy or sell) but does not manage on an ongoing basis;
- accounts for which the adviser provides impersonal advice, *e.g.,* market newsletters;
- accounts for which the adviser provides only an initial asset allocation, without continuous and regular monitoring and reallocation; and
- accounts for which the registrant undertakes to monitor the markets and apprise the client of any developments, or make recommendations as to the reallocation of client assets upon any developments.

d. Determine the total amount of assets under management based on the current market value as determined with 10 business days prior to the date of filing this Form. Current market value should be determined using the same methodology as the account value reported to clients or calculated to determine fees for investment advisory services.

e. Include only those accounts for which registrant provides continuous and regular supervisory and management services as of the date of filing this Form.

10

ECONOMICS

Roger C. Bird

Competition in Financial Services: Who Is Ahead?

What is the Current Situation?

- Insurance industry: 1/2 win, 4 losses; team breakdown—no unity on the bench
- Banking industry: 3 1/2 wins, 1 loss; potential turnaround champs
- Mutual funds: everybody's favorite
- Credit unions: dark horse players
- S&Ls: out of the game
- Finance companies: barbarians at the gate (players without rules)

What Is the Nature of the Change?

In brief, in the last 5 years we have seen the most remarkable apparent recovery of the stock market performance and public approval of the commercial banking industry compared with the dark days of 1989–1990. In the meantime, the insurance industry is assailed on all sides for poor management, poor teamwork, poor public relations, and mediocre results. Furthermore, the referees (the courts) keep calling fouls against it. The mutual-funds phenomenon is unstoppable, winning every contest in the public eye. Credit unions are in contest with the banking industry and are a dark horse to achieve an unassailable niche in personal finance markets. The savings and loan industry is finally quelled—some members will become banks—the rest will wither away or be merged. And finally the finance companies (including private insurers of asset-based securities and mortgage companies)—an unpredictable set of players without many rules—have been entering the financial services game in strength, and they are positioned to continue to avoid many regulations, yet still gain market advantage through technology and sheer muscle power. These few players are not the only subcomponents of the financial services industry, but they represent the major action involving recent changes and controversies.

Market Share. Market share of assets is one of the few numerical criteria of achievement that can be used for comparison purposes among financial services participants. If available, return on stockholder's equity would be another important measure, but it would leave out all of the *mutual style* organizations that are mainly found outside of commercial banking. Table 10-1 shows the latest available figures on shares of assets by industry segment, reflecting the relative decline in both banking and insurance since 1980 compared with mutual funds and pension funds. Thus far, life insurance companies at least have managed to avoid losing much share (strike one loss for banks and 1/2 win for insurance companies).

The insurance industry is under stress in several other arenas, however, including technology and innovation, regulation and litigation, public relations, and globalization. Banks are subject to some of the same stresses but appear to have coped better than the insurance industry in several respects. Moreover, in spite of potentially rancorous divisions among banks based on size and locale, as a group they have acted far more cohesively than have insurance companies when subject to these stresses.

TABLE 10-1
Financial Sector Assets: Percentage Distribution by Sector for Selected Years

	1980	1985	1990	1995	1996 .03
Commercial banks[1]	37.1	32.1	28.3	25.1	24.1
Savings institutions[2]	17.0	15.0	10.0	4.9	4.6
Credit unions	1.5	1.6	1.6	1.5	1.5
Insurance companies	13.9	12.9	13.9	13.6	13.3
Life	10.0	9.4	10.0	10.0	9.8
Property & casualty	3.9	3.5	3.9	3.6	3.5
Pension funds[3]	15.1	17.5	17.9	19.9	20.3
Mutual funds[4]	3.2	5.9	8.5	13.2	14.4
Securities brokers	1.0	1.8	1.9	2.7	2.6
Finance companies[5]	4.7	5.0	6.9	7.4	7.5
Other sectors[6]	6.6	8.2	11.9	11.9	11.7
Total	100.0	100.0	100.0	100.0	100.0
Addendum:					
Total financial Sector assets ($ Billions)	4656	8508	13647	20877	22389
Compound annual average growth rate (%)		12.8	9.9	8.5	9.8*
Ratio: Assets/GDP	1.67	2.03	2.38	2.88	2.94

Source: Board of Governors, Federal Reserve System. Flow of Funds Coded Tables L.1–L.131

[1] Including bank personal trusts and estates.
[2] Including savings and loan associations and mutual savings banks.
[3] Including private pension funds (not held by life insurance companies) plus state and local government retirement funds.
[4] Including mutual funds, money market funds, closed-end funds, and REITS.
[5] Including issuers of asset-based securities (ABS), and mortgage companies.
[6] Including government-sponsored enterprises (GSEs), federally related mortgage pools.
* Indicated annual rate.

Technology and Innovation. The interactive computer revolution and the use of computerized databases for marketing, distribution and analysis, and new product innovations threatens to leave the insurance industry in the dust. Banks, credit unions, mutual funds, the brokerage industry, and especially the major finance companies (for example, GMAC, GEC, etc.) have all automated their relationships with their clients at a much faster rate than have insurance companies through automated teller machines (ATMs), automated telemarketing systems, various proprietary on-line banking and brokerage services, and on-line marketing and delivery through the Internet. The result has been a booming set of new business opportunities in areas traditionally reserved for insurance companies and old-line retail brokerages. The use of systematized depositor databases coupled with credit application information, all coordinated with new globalized credit reporting systems has enabled explosive growth in credit use (especially credit cards) and interactive client account management. This innovation enables banks, finance companies, mutual funds, and credit unions to all increase their shares of household usage of financial services. Their management of household assets has of course grown relative to insurance companies as well. Banks also have rebounded from their loss of place in the business sector, with a rebirth of commercial and industrial lending. They are learning how to apply mass computerization techniques to small business loans as well, following their success in the household area.

Financial innovation in the form of securitization of credit card debt, mortgage debt, auto debt, and small business loans has only been possible because of the ability to use computers to *standardize* the problem of packaging and servicing myriad individual loans and debts. This has opened up new avenues for use in marketing and distribution of information derived from interactive on-line databases with sharing of massive amounts of information through credit agencies and other clearing houses. Insurance companies, in the meantime, are having trouble agreeing to share their company data among state regulators, (the NAIC) let alone among themselves through an industry clearing house. The great *potential* ability for insurance companies to use their collective knowledge about assets and liabilities, risk preferences, and financial needs of their clients is no less than the banks' current ability. But they appear to be late in the game. On this issue the score is probably banks, 1; insurance companies, 0.

Regulation and Litigation. The banks are clearly advancing in this arena as well. Following the *Barnett Bank* decision and its various interpretations in federal courts, national unlimited geographic sales of any and all kinds of insurance anywhere in the U.S. are effectively permitted as long as the operation is centered in *places* of less than 5,000 inhabitants. This is a loophole that a fleet of Brinks trucks could drive through. Some state legislatures (for example, Rhode Island and Pennsylvania) are attempting rear-guard action at the behest of the insurance agents' lobby, but the insurance companies themselves have conceded the field and many are rapidly designing marketing and distribution strategies for alliances (affiliations) with various banks and bank holding companies (BHCs). Even though the Barnett decision referred to national banks, state-chartered banks are following in train using the principle of reciprocity in the dual-banking system.

In the Congress, it is only a matter of time before the Glass-Steagall Act of 1933 is effectively repealed as regards banking powers. The act

- separated commercial banking from investment banking except for federal, state, and local government securities
- established by amendment the principal of deposit insurance
- generally prohibited banks from engaging in business activities unrelated to banking (such as insurance)

Most observers expect the repeal in this Congress in order to avoid controversy in the proximity to the next presidential election in the year 2000. Several versions of legislation effectively repealing the act are in play currently in the Congress. But one common thread among all parties is that banks or BHCs will be permitted to operate in every financial services field, including insurance and securities underwriting (with very few restrictions on the type or scope of entry). Relative to players already in the field, debate still lingers about the powers of nonfinancial entities (called *commercial firms*) to enter the fray and buy, be bought, or affiliate with, banks and BHCs. The finance companies are the major players here, since the main ones are owned and/or controlled by major industrial-type firms such as GM, GE, Ford Motor, and such. Microsoft is also in this act due to its alliance with Citibank, and its ambitions to facilitate financial transactions on the Internet. On this score, Intuit is a potential player as well.

The major issue with respect to conglomeration by banks is related to the implicit or explicit use of insured deposits (a publicly protected resource exclusive to banks and credit unions) to enter and/or operate in the new financial services arena. To the extent that the insured deposit funds (held in the Bank Insurance Fund or BIF) are regarded as a public good within the traditional function of banks as money-creating instruments of macroeconomic public policy, *natural monopoly* rules may apply. For this reason another major distinction among all of the major legislative proposals has to do with the degree of *firewalls* built between the various functions of banks and other financial institutions. Functional regulation is harder to achieve when *functions* correspond less and less to institutions or entities. Overall, this concern is unlikely to stop the legislation and some compromise will be reached soon.

On balance, the relative legislative gain for banks versus others in the financial services industry is clear. However, all financial services firms will gain something regarding their ability to more closely match their comparative advantage to the new and exciting markets of the future.

Insurance companies have one big disadvantage in the current legislative and regulatory arena—they have no single regulating body at the national level with the clout of the agencies who regulate the banks (whether federal or state chartered) or the securities firms. Such agencies frequently serve the role of advocates as much as regulators. Insurance companies' cherished regulators are all at the state level and are too independent to win contests at the national level. This disunity among regulators, even though patched together through the good offices of the National Association of Insurance Commissioners (NAIC), is evident in their missing voice at the referees' table when the Federal Reserve Board (FRB), the Office of Comptroller of the Currency (OCC), and the Federal Deposit Insurance Corporation (FDIC) are all looking out for their respective banking constituents, and the Securities and Exchange Commission (SEC) is looking out for the securities industry. Couple this with the disunity among and between insurance companies and insurance agents, and it is clear that lobbying efforts will be diffused. Consequently attempts to secure the position of the insurance industry are problematic, and attempts to obtain any new legislative ground are even more problematic.

Other examples of disunity are the lingering disputes *between* insurance commissioners over settlements in the *Prudential Insurance Company* cases dealing with past alleged sales force *churning* of client life insurance contracts. Another episode of disunity is the continuing saga of CIGNA's disputed creation of a run-off company to handle residual environmental and health-related (asbestos) claims under litigation. These cases not only illustrate the problem of unified action, but they also lower federal legislators' opinion about the regulatory environment of the insurance industry itself, whether life or property-casualty.

Finally, merger and acquisition activity among banks and BHCs has been positively encouraged by the FRB, OCC, and FDIC, with the full acquiescence of the antitrust division of the Justice Department. This is all part of a strategy to strengthen the banking sector and to avoid as many claims on the deposit insurance trust funds or the general budget as possible. The horrible federal budget experience of 1989–1992 when the savings and loan debacle caused massive spillover effects upon the commercial banks (most of which had to be picked up by the general public to the tune of more than $160 billion) has seared itself into the memories of Congress and the regulators. Even though Congress and the regulators now may be going too far in the other direction, strengthening the banking sector has been a clear policy goal of the Fed and the others since 1990. It is showing in merger and acquisition activity, as well as in stock prices of the banks themselves. Here, again, the relative position of the banks has been and will be strengthened vis à vis the insurance industry. Combining these regulation and litigation factors on our subjective scale of wins and losses would again show banks, 1; insurance industry, 0.

Public Relations. Coincidently, banks appear to be less prone to receiving bad press in the last 5 years compared with the insurance industry. The ongoing *Prudential* case as well as similar settled cases with regard to *New*

York Life and *Metropolitan Life* have been digested in endless detail in the popular press and on TV exposé shows. Insurance agents continue to get low marks in public polls about their performance. The move to managed health care systems under the aegis of several insurance companies has placed a whole new set of public relations issues in the sights of the press—HMOs are regularly seen as malign insurers (not benign as was more or less the case with most of the Blue Cross/Blue Shield system less than 10 years ago). The old lingering accusations about whole life insurance being a bad financial deal for the average household have not yet been put to rest (Jane Bryant Quinn of *Newsweek* magazine continues to beat this drum, for example). This impression persists in spite of the fact that the insurance industry has long since moved to emphasize other products and services (such as variable life, and universal life insurance). The public relations advertising of the industry leaders frequently seen on TV continues to stress security of savings and assets, rather than the fact that U.S. insurance companies and agents probably have the best training and the best personal and household financial planning skills in the world. The training of agents is far stronger than that found among banking staffs or mutual fund and securities brokers. Yet it is the latter that are gaining market share among households as a group, probably because (a) they are ahead of the insurance companies when it comes to utilizing the latest computerized marketing and distribution systems and (b) these latter groups also are regularly advertising the skills of their staffs rather than the size or safety of their assets. What prevents insurance companies from advertising their agents' skills at financial planning? We would guess fear of litigation *and* disunity between agents and companies. In the meantime, the industry suffers both relatively and absolutely.

The banks are not without their own public relations problems. There is vocal apprehension in the press about the impact of certain massive mergers and acquisitions on local economies. Consumers are noticing restructurings (downsizing of the workforce, in particular), and new and/or rapidly growing fees for services (ATM usage, teller usage, telephone access usage, overdrafts). The financial press has a growing sense that credit cards are being flogged to the public beyond prudence, at the same time that credit card interest rates remain high. Community development lending continues to be a sore point with minority groups as the mergers affect many local community banks, upset established relationships, and regularly appear to set the clock back as regards meeting of Community Reinvestment Act (CRA) goals. In fact, it is Allstate and Nationwide that receive the worst press from a minority relations point of view. The banks seem to keep most of their bad CRA news contained in the back pages of the *Federal Reserve Bulletins*. Moreover, all of these foul points against the banks have not slowed them down in the legislative or regulatory arenas. And bankers still appear to score higher in public opinion polls than insurance agents do. As a group, they are paying a dear price in terms of public perception for the shenanigans of a few.

Overall, the public relations score on our measure is banks, +1/2; insurance industry, 0.

Globalization. This overused term describes the process whereby firms and industries are (1) taking advantage of the blossoming opportunities for selling, and/or buying, and/or producing abroad in a globalized system of decisions; and (2) obtaining thereby economies of scale or other efficiencies that give them comparative advantages at home as well as abroad. The banks have always had clearer advantages here than the insurance industry, and they are using their new-found strength to prove it. The opportunity for international bank lending and the provision of myriad other international financial services is exploding for U.S. banks. This situation is occurring as the dollar strengthens in international financial markets and as most Japanese and some European banks pull back from their prior incursions, leaving the field to the rejuvenated U.S. commercial-banking sector. Cross-border trade in insurance has steadily grown along with the world economy, but these opportunities are nothing like the growth opportunities presented to bankers. Indeed, in the property-casualty area the global reinsurance market appears flat. While some merger and acquisition activity is regularly occurring among life and P&C companies, none of it appears to be driven by any new market opportunities based on geography, technology, or new products and services—unlike the banks. Again, the score would be something like banks, 1; insurance industry, 0.

Other Financial Service Sectors. We have already mentioned the looming demise of savings and loan banks (S&Ls) and mutual savings banks. The final death throes will occur when the Savings Association Insurance Fund (SAIF) is phased out in 1999, and the merger of the BIF and SAIF is finally accomplished as the last chapter of the savings and loan industry debacle. The *charters* of the banks and the S&Ls will then be *merged* and any remaining S&Ls will effectively be banks chartered under federal or state rules. If, as believed, the impediments of Glass-Steagall are removed in the next 2 years, then the remaining banks can turn their complete attention to expanding their businesses into the newer arenas of insurance, mutual funds, and annuities. Therefore the remaining S&Ls will effectively become competitors of the independent insurance agencies, if they are not already.

As noted above at several points, the mutual funds industry has the fastest growth rate of assets of all the major financial sectors. The combination of technology, public awareness, robust stock markets, and favorable legislation on tax deferral (especially with regard to 401(k) plans, 403(b) plans, and IRAs) has led to the booming growth of mutual fund assets. Every sector of the financial services industry wants to be aligned with the mutual funds industry. It is clearly the winning vehicle for long-term household savings in the United States.

Credit unions are an interesting case of an old-fashioned nonprofit cooperative arrangement between close-knit communities-of-interest (for example, employees of a company or union members) that have a *common bond.* Their tax-free status has made them extremely popular and the number of participants has grown steadily to over 70 million members, even as the number of credit unions has declined through consolidation and merger. The fact that interest paid on insured deposits (called *share accounts*) is higher than at commercial banks or S&Ls, and that net interest charged is at highly competitive rates (with share dividends declared annually), means that many consumers and household savers are members. Credit unions have steadily increased their share of consumer credit. Moreover, they offer very low-cost, convenient access to the stock, bond, and mutual fund markets. They are also technologically adept at keeping up with (and even surpassing) the skills and capabilities of the commercial banks in most respects. As further financial liberalization takes hold, they will be a recognizable force in offerings of new products and services. Insurance (life products, especially) is a currently underdeveloped area of potential credit-union interest.

The biggest risk to credit-union growth comes in the form of lawsuits over the issue of liberal interpretations of the *common-bond* requirement of the 1934 Federal Credit Union Act. A federal appeals court has slowed down the growth of credit unions significantly in the last half of 1996 pending an appeal to the Supreme Court. The issue will probably end up in the Congress where some compromise on permissible growth will be reached. On balance, even with some unfavorable ruling, credit-union assets will continue to grow in opposition to banks, which are seen as more and more distant from their small customers.

What Will Be the Effects upon the Industry?

Competition in financial services offerings has never been greater. Household and business clients are all finding new ways of borrowing and saving through the new modes and mechanisms of financial intermediation. The main sources of this development are technology, the push to deregulate, and the federal government's efforts to encourage tax-deferred savings. To the extent that diversity and competition are healthy, the public is being well-served in the current environment.

Appropriate safeguards are the issue. Rules make competition healthy. The addition of new ways of doing business, and the breakdown of previously established barriers can lead to free-for-all tactics that go well beyond the current ability of regulators to foresee. Thus, three key decisions yet to come are as follows:

1. Can deposit-taking institutions (banks and credit unions) with insured deposits be permitted to operate in any manner they choose with those deposits, or are there restrictions on use or capital requirements for use?
2. Can any firm own or control a bank, or only certain types of firms?
3. Except for government-insured deposits, and assuming financial disclosure to regulators is sufficient and available to investors, can the market be trusted to regularly cull out the weak and inefficient and potentially insolvent, among the new conglomerated financial

institutions, or will the old cycles of market euphoria and depression reappear?

These three questions—and there are many ancillary consumer-protection questions—have a remarkable similarity to the questions that have been raised over and over again as financial legislation has been considered throughout American history. Certainly, they were all considered at the time of the passage of the Glass-Steagall Act of 1933—which is now subject to repeal.

We expect that a consensus will emerge that makes incremental adjustments to the current regulatory regime. In other words, evolution not revolution will be the norm. In this scenario, the likely outcomes are already set and in most cases (discussed below) have already been allowed or implemented.

The banks' new *Barnett* decision powers will be confirmed. Securities and brokerage firms will be permitted to merge with bank holding companies. Bank holding companies will be permitted unrestricted engagement in investment banking through arms-length nonbank subsidiaries. All customer databases of banks and securities firms will be shared across all subsidiaries of the BHCs for any legitimate uses. Insurance companies will be permitted to merge with securities firms *and* to become BHCs. Finance companies will be permitted to become or merge with BHCs.

Insured deposit-taking powers will be tightly controlled with more, not fewer, *firewalls* between deposit-taking and other activities of banks and BHCs *except* for customer database sharing. The Bank Insurance Fund for insured deposits will continue to be regulated by the FDIC with new capital and risk-assessment requirements. However, the powers of the Federal Reserve board and the Office of Comptroller of the Currency will be realigned giving more power to the Fed over BHCs (mainly for reasons of continued macro-economic control over the creation of money and the conditions of credit availability) and less power to the OCC over the national banking subsidiaries of the BHCs with regard to charters and powers. The BHC form of organization will progressively win out both at the state and federal levels. While state regulation will continue as an anachronism of bygone days, mainly with regard to licensing and granting of state franchise, it will progressively recede in importance. Consolidations at the state level between banks, securities, and insurance regulators will increase, paralleling the other merger-acquisition-consolidation moves in the financial services industry.

How Does This Change Affect Clients?

How will the typical client of these new financial conglomerates be treated compared to today? The major differences will occur due to technology rather than the regulatory regime—in other words, substance, not form, will rule in determining what services are provided and in what packages they come. Cross-marketing and cross-selling of services—except for gross and illegal tying arrangements (for example, making a loan contingent upon purchase of insurance)—will be more commonplace than today, but the *mechanisms* of cross-selling and -marketing will be ever more sophisticated. Customer databases covering a household's actual or imputed (estimated) assets, liabilities, income, buying habits, and family-member biographies will all be integrated. Regular telephone or on-line interviews of household members to establish needs, goals, and risk-tolerance profiles as well as contingency plans will also be co-integrated with the basic data. Household financial planning (actually a form of lifetime portfolio management for each household) can then begin to be treated en masse with the latest software techniques of portfolio optimizers. The financial planning capabilities of financial services providers will be delivered via the Internet to those who prefer this mode. But, the main point is that financial planning can and will become a mass market through the immense information-processing capabilities of the comprehensive financial services firms.

What Should Be Done?

In this new world, there will be a premium on those financial planners who can best communicate the lifetime portfolio management process to clients, and yet still treat the clients as individuals with individual needs and goals. Success in the arena of financial services will go to those with such skills and training.

Herein, perhaps, lies the salvation of the life insurance industry and its agents. No other industry group has devoted as much time and energy to understanding client financial needs and assessing goals. With their superior institutionalized training and professional development programs, they are in a strong if not unique position to capitalize on their human skill base in this brave new world of financial services described above.

Where Can I Find Out More?

- David S. Kidwell, Richard L. Peterson, and David W. Blackwell. *Financial Institutions, Markets, and Money,* 1995. Dryden Press.
- Robert E. Litan. *The Revolution in U.S. Finance: Past, Present, and Future.* The American College, 1991.
- Clifford E. Kirsch, editor. *The Financial Services Revolution,* Irwin, 1997.
- Board of Governors of the Federal Reserve System. *Federal Reserve Bulletin,* Washington, DC, monthly, and *Flow of Funds,* quarterly.

Everything You Need To Know about Price Indices

Price indices of various types have found their way into the core of the financial planning toolkit because they are necessary to assess inflation. Applications of such indices are critical to forward-looking estimates of taxes, social security, health care, business valuations, insurance needs, and estate and annuity planning, all of which have an inflation component. This section will focus on measurement and selection of price indices rather than applications (except for illustrative purposes). It will be clear, however, that *correct application* is dependent upon knowing about such measurement and selection.

What Is the Current Situation?

The Basics. All price indices are calculated using weighted averages of price relatives. A price relative is the ratio of an item's (or group of items) price at one time to the same item (or group of items) price at another period of time. For some purposes the price relative may be composed of ratios across geographic areas rather than across time periods. Such indices are primarily used for state-by-state or international comparisons of prices and costs of living or costs of doing business. They will not be discussed in any detail here, but their principles of formation have many similarities to the period-to-period price indices.

Table 10-2 shows the price indices calculated for a variety of sets of items over a selection of periods. The sets shown for illustration are (1) consumer goods and services (CPI-U), (2) consumer goods at wholesale prices (PPI-C—actually defined as producer finished goods for consumers, (3) export goods (PDX—a chain-type price index), (4) all goods and services produced in the domestic economy (PDGDP—a chain-type price index), and (5) price of personal consumption expenditures (PDCE—a chain-type price index). This sample clearly illustrates the variety of indices available as well as the different stories about inflation that they tell. *Inflation* here is simply the annual average percentage rate of change of any one index between any two periods.

TABLE 10-2
Selected Price Indices

Measure	CPI-U[1]	PPI-C[2]	PDGDP[3]	PDX[4]	PDCE[5]
Reference period	1982-84	1982	1992	1992	1992
Value in 1995	152.4	127.5	107.6	104.1	107.6
Rates of growth (%) Selected periods*					
1960–70	2.7	1.5	2.7	2.1	2.4
1970–80	7.5	8.2	6.8	8.5	6.8
1980–1990	4.6	2.9	4.3	1.6	4.6
1990–1995	3.1	1.2	2.8	1.1	1.5
1995–1996	2.9	3.1	2.4	0.2	2.4

Source: Economic Report of the President, Washington, D.C., February 1997.

[1] Consumer price index for all items, all urban consumers.
[2] Producer price index for total finished consumer goods.
[3] Chain-type price index for gross domestic product.
[4] Chain-type price index for exports of goods and services.
[5] Chain-type price index for personal consumption expenditures.
* Compound annual average rate of growth between selected years.

The price relatives of the items which compose each index are generally calculated in the same manner, and several items (for example, trucks/autos) will appear as subcomponents in all five of the indices. In fact, the great majority of item price relatives for all of these indices are created by the statisticians at the Bureau of Labor Statistics (BLS). The difference in treatment will primarily be due to the treatment of the *weights* in each weighted average; and here lies the second choice facing the statisticians and practitioners, the first choice being which items should be in the *basket* of items whose price change (inflation) is to be measured.

Choice of Items. At first glance, this decision seems straightforward. If consumers are involved, one should choose those items (goods and services) that consumers buy (for example, cars and haircuts). But, these items in fact change more or less over time due to (1) technology, (2) tastes, and (3) new items (goods or services) being introduced and old items being withdrawn. Technology here encompasses all the changes in function and availability, frequently called *quality change,* that accompany new discoveries (inventions) and new ways of doing things (innovation), whether in packaging, delivery, marketing, quality control, distribution (for example, supermarkets versus corner groceries), or any of the other many ways in which change occurs in the marketplace aside from invention. Tastes change due to a variety of reasons which are often misunderstood. For example, choices of entertainment have dramatically changed through time and not simply because of technology (for example, video) or advertising. This means that the entertainment items chosen will also have changed dramatically. Also availability of new medical techniques and treatments has led to lifestyle choices, due in part perhaps to advertising, that are arguably no healthier than prior home remedies and treatments. Finally whether *items* change due to technology or tastes, price relatives will have a less clear meaning as a measure of inflation than if the items in question were unchanged. Isolating the effects of such quality and taste changes then becomes a major task of the statisticians who compose the indices. This task is aside from the problem of what to do when a wholly new item is introduced or an old one disappears.

Choice of Weights. Even if items were to remain constant in quality once introduced, one has the problem of choosing the appropriate weight for each item in the basket of items. Again, if consumers are involved, the appropriate *market* basket of items presumably should reflect consumer choices in their budgets—or at least that portion of their budgets which they are willing and able to spend on market-priced goods and services. This latter caveat means that we exclude such normal budgetary items as taxes, charitable contributions, and all forms of savings. However, such a basket clearly does not correspond to any *total cost of living.* Here, the main issue is changes in the appropriate budget weights from one period (called the reference period) to any other time period. What period should be that reference? After all, as relative item prices change at different rates, consumers will choose more of some items and less of others; this is the substitution effect (for example, choosing more chicken and less beef as chicken prices fall compared to beef prices). Also as overall budgets change, the proportions of some items will increase or decrease depending upon tastes and preferences (this is the income effect—for example, choosing steak versus hamburger simply because income rises). Both of these effects will cause the budget mix to change in a later period compared with the reference period. Should the weights then be chosen referring to the past, the present, or something in-between? The answers to questions such as these have occupied a vast economic and statistical literature for many years.

The overall answer is that the choice of appropriate weights depends upon the question that is to be answered. For many purposes, the most common question is forward-looking: given the choices of budget items of some *past reference period,* how much more must one pay for the same basket of items today? This means using initial period weights and generates what is called a Laspeyres index. Of the indices shown in Table 10-2, the CPI and the PPI answer that question at least one year from their reference period ahead. The CPI and the PPI try to keep the market basket fixed for all years of the time series shown, whereas the other indices change the weights year by year using a *chain-index* formulation. These latter indices normalize the index to a base reference period, however.

A similar question, which is retrospective, is How much less would someone have paid for the same basket of today, one year earlier? Again, taking the reference period as the base, look one period earlier to obtain this answer from the table for the CPI and the PPI. This means using terminal period weights and generates what is called a Paasche index.

A third type of question would be, How much more or less must one spend this year versus an earlier or later year in order to keep oneself as well off as in the base period (that is, what would it take to keep one's standard of living constant)? It is the answer to this last question that is the goal of a true or *ideal* cost-of-living index (sometimes called a COLI). One choice of weights which might approximate this goal would require a geometric average of the two types of indices (the Laspeyres and the Paasche) noted above for any two periods. This calculation would generate what is called a Fisher *ideal index* and is the system currently used to generate the PDGDP index, the export price index, PDX, and the PDCE index shown in the table.

What Is the Nature of the Change?

Bias in the CPI as a measure of a true cost-of-living index has been a contentious issue for many years—certainly back to 1959. It is a vitally important issue to many retirees because the CPI is used on an annual basis to adjust much of federal entitlement spending including social security. It is also used on a regular basis to adjust income tax brackets, certain union wage contracts, as well as many public and private pension plans. The major recent controversy about bias in the CPI as a measure of the COLI stems from the Boskin Commission report to the Senate Finance Committee in December 1996 (titled *Toward a More Accurate Measure of the Cost of Living*). As might be expected from the discussion above, the main arguments deal with measurement (choices of items, choices of weights), and application (choices of which index for which purpose).

Measurement. Calculation of the CPI by the BLS presents an awesome task if we consider that their responsibility requires monthly samples of 71,000 item prices from 22,000 outlets for 44 geographic areas. Separately, they gather monthly information from 5,000 renters and 10,000 homeowners for the housing components of the CPI which is the largest component of the overall index (see table 10-3 for the 1982–1984 based weights currently used). The commission found that there were four sources of bias—all on balance in the direction of upward bias (see table 10-4). Upper-level substitution bias refers to the weighting issue discussed earlier as between, for example, chicken and beef or between starches and vegetables. Switching from the Laspeyres-type fixed weights toward a more *ideal* set of composite weights is estimated to account for an upward bias of .15 percentage points. The lower-level substitution bias, for example, between beef steak and beef hamburger is said to cause a bias of .25 percentage points, even though the degree of switching between such items is not well understood. New outlet bias is another form of substitution bias which refers to the fact that suburban shopping mall superstores (such as Wal-Mart Stores) have replaced downtown outlets (such as Macy's stores). The main criticism is that this type of switch is only caught with a long-time delay. New outlet bias is estimated to be worth .10 percentage points. All these separate substitution biases have been studied by the BLS itself over many years, and these estimates fall within the range of

TABLE 10-3
Relative Importance of Items in the CPI-U, U.S. City Average, December 1995 (Based on 1982–1984 Expenditure Weights)

Major Components		Relative Importance in Percent
1. Food and beverages		17.33
2. Housing		41.35
a. Shelter	28.29	
b. Fuels	3.79	
c. All other	9.27	
3. Apparel and upkeep		5.52
4. Transportation		16.95
a. New vehicles	5.03	
b. Used cars	1.34	
c. Motor fuel	2.91	
d. All other	7.61	
5. Medical care		7.36
6. Entertainment		4.37
7. Other goods and services		7.12
a. Personal and educational expenses	4.34	
b. All others	2.78	
TOTAL		100.00

Source: Bureau of Labor Statistics, *Monthly Labor Review*

BLS estimates although they are not strictly additive. (For example, buying at a suburban discount supermarket may lead to a choice of more beef, less chicken, even though overall our society is choosing more chicken, less beef).

TABLE 10-4
Estimates of Biases in the CPI-Based Measure of the Cost of Living (Percentage Points Per Annum)[1]

Sources of Bias	Estimate
Upper level substitution	0.15
Lower level substitution	0.25
New products/quality change	0.60
New outlets	0.10
Total	**1.10**
Plausible range	(0.80–1.60)

The largest recommended adjustment for upward bias targets the issues of new product introduction (such as VCRs) into the CPI and quality change (improvement) in the itemized goods and services already in the item list of the CPI (longevity for automobiles). This purported failure to adequately measure new products and quality change is said to cause an upward bias of .60 percentage points—the largest single source of bias. Adding all of these sources together, as if they are independent, leads to the overall estimate of bias as being of the order of 1.10 percentage points per annum with a plausible range of 0.80 to 1.60. This is a large estimate of bias considering that the CPI itself has averaged 3.6 percent over the last 10 years.

The Commission's critique of the CPI as a strongly upward-biased estimator of the COLI has itself been criticized on the following grounds:[2]

- Quality and new-goods bias—The Commission's estimates continue to lack comprehensiveness and may not apply with equal force to the average consumer; most examples have an anecdotal quality and are not the outcome of rigorous economic analysis.
- Substitution bias—The Commission disagrees with the Bureau of Labor Statistics (BLS) as to the size of some of the components of this bias and how to correct for each of them; the Commission treats these component biases as additive, a view that BLS and other researchers dispute.

---

1. Michael J. Boskin et. al. *Toward a More Accurate Measure of the Cost of Living: Final Report to the Senate Finance Committee from the Advisory Commission to Study the Consumer Price Index,* December 4, 1996, Washington, DC.
2. Joel Popkin and Company. *CPI Commission's Findings Are Not Convincing: Final Report to the Senate Finance Committee from the Advisory Commission to Study the Consumer Price Index.* Prepared for American Association for Retired Persons, January 6, 1997, Washington, DC, pp. 2, 13, 15.

- With respect to other issues of quality of life such as crime, the deteriorating environment, and longer commuting time that must be considered for a cost-of-living index, the Commission provides evidence that is scantier than that on quality change and new goods.
- The Commission fails to consider the need for a CPI/COLI for older people due to differences in expenditure weights and patterns and items chosen.
- Research recommendations of the Commission are narrowly devoted to correcting for upward bias rather than being comprehensive toward improvement.

How and When Does This Change Affect Clients?

If the CPI bias problem is to be solved, the solution must arise from the BLS itself. Several corrective measures are already in place for the next major revision in 1998 when the CPI's new reference base years will be 1993–1995. Although it is unlikely that all of the recommendations of the Boskin report will be incorporated, the anticipated effect of certain corrections will likely be to slow CPI/COLI growth compared to historical inflation rates. Immediately, this means that annual social security payments and tax brackets will be adjusted less than prior projections. In addition, the inflation component used for annuity and pension planning will be less, thus requiring less wealth and income to be set aside for a given real standard-of-living projection. Interest rate and yield assumptions may also have to be adjusted downward because the financial markets might require and expect less nominal return in order to achieve a certain real return after inflation.

Does CPI Correction Have Other Effects Upon Other Indices? The issue of bias in measurement is more far-reaching than the CPI. The other indices shown in Table 10-2 will be affected if new product and quality change adjustments are made by the BLS, since many of the bias-adjusted components of the CPI would affect components of those indices as well. In particular, the PDCE deflator, the PDX deflator and, hence, the overall PDGDP deflator (which uses the former as components) would all be affected. This is good news in the sense that integrated systems of price measurement imply that improvements anywhere become generalized. The PPI will also be improved in part, insofar as the components for consumer goods in the finished goods index are improved. Furthermore, improvements in the techniques of adjustment for quality change would improve all indices to some extent.

Are There Any Other Issues or Opportunities regarding Other Indices aside from the CPI? During the Nixon Administration the federal government chose the CPI as the most appropriate (popular and available) indicator of the cost of living, in a period when inflationary pressures were rising and fairness in treatment of social security (CSI) retirees was a big issue. From 1935 to the early 1970s, intermittent inflation-related adjustments to SSI payouts had been made as Congress and the President saw fit. The 1972 legislation codified the process of indexation, removed discretion, and improved the process of management of entitlements. (Unfortunately, poorly written legislation was enacted, and age 65 retirees from 1972 to 1976 got a double dose of inflation protection. This was corrected using a *notch* adjustment for retirees after 1976.)

At the time, the dispute about bias in the CPI as a measure of the cost of living was moot because it was so widely used as a *cost-of-living adjustment* (COLA) mechanism in labor contracts and (some) defined-benefit pension plan adjustments in private and public pension plan management. In truth, the alleged bias was recognized as a possibility much earlier in congressional hearings of the early 60s. The BLS was adamant then (as it is now), that the CPI was not and was never intended to be a measure of the cost of living. Rather, it was intended to be an indicator of inflationary pressures on urban clerical and blue-collar workers (now named CPI-W and covering about 32 percent of the population as of today). Those hearings led to some new procedures and, most important, to broadening the sample size of household expenditures to include all urban consumers (called CPI-U and covering about 80 percent of the population). The essential methods for the two indices remain the same and any biases in one will be reflected in the other.

Recently, as we have noted, the CPI is widely criticized as an inadequate indicator of the cost of living, even though it or its subcomponents are ever more widely used for unintended purposes such as adjustment of tax brackets and rental-contract indexation, as well as the uses mentioned earlier. Significantly, medicare Supplement B inflation adjustments use a subset of the CPI dealing with medical services inflation. The Boskin Commission claims that this particular subset has been upward biased by approximately 3 percent per annum prior to 1995. Are there other indices that might be used for some of these purposes?

Turning back to Table 10-2, we have already noted that the consumer expenditures deflator (PDCE) is a chain-weighted ideal index, composed of almost identically the same components and items as the CPI. It clearly could be used in preference to the CPI as a proxy for the cost of living, since it has more current expenditure patterns built into its very construction. For this reason, it might have been chosen initially as the index for SSI and income tax bracket adjustments if it were more widely known. The Congress and the President could make this change today through a simple legislative adjustment—it would remove much of the *product substitution* and *new product bias* in the CPI. Bias due to *quality change* and outlet substitution would still remain, however.

The components of the PPI are frequently used in long-term purchase contracts by the federal government (defense and procurement items), and by private firms (for example, energy items purchased by utilities, aluminum companies, and pipelines; chemical item feedstocks purchased by chemical companies; pulp purchased by paper companies; and such). The problems of quality change are much easier to handle in commodity-type price indices. Construction contracts are also often written with clauses identifying price adjustments using PPI item prices (steel reinforcing bars, cement, asphalt, and such).

What Should Be Done?

Financial services professionals should be aware of what indices are available when they are called upon to consider inflation adjustments in estate planning cases involving business valuation. Forecasts of these indices are widely available from specialist forecasting firms and are much preferred to casual use of the CPI as the only choice of inflation indicator for such purposes. Similarly for pension planning, the consumption expenditures deflator is probably to be preferred to the CPI for most households due to its more current weighting.

Finally in the field of portfolio management, the CPI is frequently misused as the sole indicator of inflation when calculating inflation-adjusted returns to assets over various time periods. Generally, financial markets will discount inflation expectations into the required rates of return of different financial instruments. For example, when inflation expectations fall, interest rates (discount rates) fall raising the present values of stocks and bonds. But which indicator(s) of inflation is (are) appropriate? In the case of returns to individual investors, who are all considered ultimately to be households or consumers, a consumption-based cost-of-living index may be appropriate. But are all investors in the market ultimately *households*? That is, are all financial intermediaries such as banks, mutual funds, pension plans, and insurance companies ultimately acting for (agents of) consumers? Or are they acting as well for some other economic entities whose requirements for inflation protection are entirely different, such as state governments, charitable trusts, college endowment funds, property-casualty insurance funds, nonfinancial corporations, and all the other myriad "ultimate" asset holders in the economy?

To question does raise the point that a more broad-based index of inflation, such as the GDP deflator (PDGDP in table 10-2), may in fact be more appropriate as the gauge of financial markets' inflation expectations than even a bias-corrected CPI. For financial planning purposes for individual clients, cost-of-living inflation protection is probably most appropriate. Financial markets as a whole may be using a different gauge, however, and this difference means that discounts for inflation are likely to be less than what they would be using even a bias-corrected CPI. Therefore required rates of return built into asset values in the market may be less than the typical client's requirements.

Hedging, using PDCE projections, therefore, would be a preferred alternative for client purposes. This would accomplish most of the COLI result without overstating the differences between client inflation risk protection versus the markets' built-in inflation risk protection.

Where Can I Find Out More?

- Bureau of Labor Statistics, *Monthly Labor Review*, U.S. Government Printing Office, Washington, DC, monthly.
- Also see footnotes.

Public and Private Economic Security Mechanisms

Proposals for social security privatization in whole or part, both in the U.S. and abroad, have been in the news for some time. The larger question is demographic as well as financial: Will the *total* savings-spending balance between workers and retirees in the mid-21st century be capable of maintaining appropriate living standards for both groups, given that the growth of the U.S. economy and other developed economies is modest, and that the ratio of people over 60 years of age to people in the normal working ages of 16 to 59 is growing rapidly in all countries? This discussion outlines the main issues in the debate and shows that considerable further research must be done *soon*.

What Is the Current Situation?

Government-sponsored social security schemes in the United States go back to 1935 when the federal government passed the Social Security Act. We know it today as the Old Age, Survivors and Disability Insurance Program (OASDI). The disability portion will not be discussed here, even though the OASI and DI funds are actually held in trust together. We will use the term SSI to refer to all the federal government's social insurance programs.

The meaning of the trust funds themselves requires explanation. Since 1983 and the Greenspan Commission's recommended adjustments (discussed later), the trust funds hold surplus accumulations (contributions from employers and employees less benefits paid), plus nominal interest earned on the accumulations, plus some portion of federal income taxes paid on social security benefits by high-income recipients. The basic system is still designed as pay-as-you-go (PAYG) with the current surpluses designed originally in 1983 to cover the expected *bubble* of baby-boomer retirements beginning about 2010, growing through 2030 (when the last of the baby-boomers retires), and ending in 2050 (assuming an average mortality at age 85). There has never been a reserve fund to cover all obligated and contingent liabilities as is found in all private pension schemes. Thus, by its nature, SSI has always had unfunded liabilities. The issues now arise because some of the underlying assumptions of the Greenspan Commission have not been borne out, and it is now 14 years later. Thus for a 75-year fix, as before, the *bubble* must be addressed again. Under current (intermediate) projections, social security benefits exceed all sources of revenue by 2019 (13 years earlier than originally projected). Then the trust funds begin to decline, and by 2029 the trust funds disappear (about 30 years earlier than expected) and annual obligations exceed annual receipts. Social security taxes then finance only about 77 percent of obligated benefits, so SSI becomes technically bankrupt.

The Greenspan Commission thought they had made a 75-year fix to the system by delaying cost-of-living adjustments, raising the overall SSI tax rate by 2.4 percent, pushing up payroll taxes on the self-employed, raising the retirement age, and taxing up to 50 percent of high-income recipients' benefits. The trust funds' accumulations were the result and they did buy some time, but other aspects of the projections were incorrect. From 1983 to 1996 economic growth was slower, unemployment was higher, money wages barely kept up with inflation, and male participation in the workforce slowed more than expected, raising the retiree-to-worker ratios even faster. These changes to economic assumptions were approximately offset by changes to demographic assumptions, however. The main sources of net forecast error were much larger disability payments (as the government liberalized the definition of disability) and "one shot changes in the methodology used in the projections."[3] It is estimated now, on a basis of present discounted values, that the difference between SSI revenues and expenditures averages 2.2 percent of payroll over 75 years. Therefore, one fix to the system would require an increase in the payroll tax by about 18 percent (2.2 percent on top of 12.4 percent currently paid in equal portions by employees and employers). An alternative fix would require a similar percentage decrease in benefits for all current and future beneficiaries for 75 years.

What Is the Nature of the Change?

The usual downside risks to this intermediate scenario are legion. Aside from possible forecast-type errors about growth, unemployment, inflation, and worker-retiree ratios as occurred before, new issues with regard to medicare-funding requirements and the overall savings-consumption balance in the economy have become more important. In addition, employees have started to take defensive actions which may also inhibit some of the easy solutions of the past.

The medicare trust funds are in more of a crisis than social security and are projected to be depleted much earlier, perhaps by 2001. A partial solution to that situation is likely to require another payroll tax increase. Moreover, the medicare deficits will also be compounded even more than the social security funds by the baby boomers' arrival after 2010. Therefore, avoiding even a small payroll tax increase for social security is more critical than usual.

Another solution would be merited because of decreasing payback to workers who continue to be in the system—and hence decreasing political support for the system. After the year 2010, it is estimated that no single (unmarried) workers will earn as much as a 2 percent real rate of return on their contributions (including employer contributions) to the system. A 2 percent real return is considered a reasonable gauge of the break-even real

---

3. *Economic Report of the President*, p. 103.

return for an alternative low-risk investment. Whereas, social security paybacks have shown fantastic real returns (well above a 5 percent, virtually riskless real return) for nearly all cohorts and all income groups, married and single, since inception to about 1980, that has changed dramatically. After the year 2000, more and more two-earner couples will be effectively getting paybacks of less than 2 percent real. Only the declining number of single-earner couples will be continuing to earn returns in the 5 to 10 percent range (due primarily to the survivorship provisions of SSI). What has happened to cause this? The baby-boomer demographics and the slowing economy have finally removed the *chain-letter* effect of the system. As a result, political support for the current system is waning among younger cohorts, and that is a devastating blow to one of the most well-supported and successful social insurance schemes ever devised in the United States.

Privatization of at least a portion of the SSI program becomes more and more attractive to future recipients and current politicians. President Clinton's quadrennial Social Security Advisory Council has agreed on the basic facts outlined above. They differ significantly on the nature of the *fix,* however.

Plan A—the Maintenance of Benefits Plan—supported by 6 out of 13, would basically keep the present system, tunes, tightens and taxes again along the lines of the Greenspan Commission (adding 1.6 percent increase in payroll tax after 2145), and permits the steady increasing allocation of up to 40 percent of the trust funds into common equity investments by 2014.

Plan B—the Individual Accounts Plan—supported by two members, would keep payroll tax as is, tunes along the same lines as in Plan A, but most importantly requires a mandatory individual account, like an IRA to be created using a payroll contribution of an additional 1.6 percent (equally drawn from employers and employees). Such contributions while mandatory are not considered a tax, since they would not be included in federal budget calculations. The assets in the accounts would be administered by the SSI system with portfolio allocation decisions made by individuals from among a small number of stock and bond index funds. Payouts would only be available as an annuity after retirement.

Plan C—the Personal Security Accounts Plan—proposed by five members, is the clearest break with the current program. Five percent of the 12.4 percent payroll tax would be extracted and put into mandatory IRAs for all workers. The funds thus set aside would be controlled by individuals outside of SSI. At retirement, the funds could be taken out as a lump sum or as an annuity. Another 2.4 percent would be used to fund existing SDI requirements, with the remaining 5 percent devoted to a minimum level defined benefit, independent of earnings (equivalent to $410 per month in 1996 dollars, which is about 57 percent of the average current retiree benefit). In spite of the reduction of the defined benefit, coverage of the remaining unfunded liability for current retirees is still required. For this, Plan C envisions new federal borrowing with a payback using the proceeds of an additional 1.5 percent payroll tax over the next 72 years.

How Does This Change Affect Clients?

The main motivation behind some form of SSI privatization is the hope that average returns can be raised above the expected low real returns under the current SSI program. Some of these hopes are based on a false premise, however. It is not possible to raise *total* returns to capital (savings) in the economy as a whole in the future, unless the economy-wide growth rate is raised—and this can only happen if capital investment today or other growth-enhancing initiatives (for example, more education, research and development, etc.) are taking place. Nothing in the plans outlined above is targeted to increase growth rates, however, The proponents of Plans B and C hope that net savings rates will rise due to a more efficient private allocation and use of at least a portion of the payroll tax receipts. But this begs the question about private versus public uses of receipts being more or less efficient. The broader point is that higher returns earned by a portion of SSI receipts may be at the expense of exactly offsetting lower returns elsewhere for other forms of investment, *unless* the overall economy-wide growth rate is increased. Therefore the *total* return to savers as they retire may not be raised at all—just the sources will be redistributed. The SSI program will gain but other pension sources will lose.

Another point is raised by the whole notion that the SSI program should have a favored place in the totality of American economic security mechanisms. Why not let the payout fall to 77 percent of current obligations after 2019? After all, this level of benefit would still be considerably higher in real terms than current benefits—it simply wouldn't be as high in relative terms compared to payrolls at that time. Why not simply change employees' *expectations* now rather than change the *program* itself over the next 75 years. It has more than done its work of raising many of our senior citizens out of the poverty trap of the 1950s and 60s. Why should preservation of SSI payouts be sacred? Why not encourage other sources of income for seniors?

For example, Table 10-5 shows the distribution of income receipts by all seniors over 65 in 1994.[4] It is clear that there are other major sources of income for seniors that could be enhanced through wise public policy. In particular, with increasing longevity, employment income could be encouraged rather than discouraged as it is now for the over-65 cohorts. Such earnings constituted 26 percent of total income of older persons in 1962 as compared with the 18 percent in 1994. These figures are in spite of the depression era and labor-union inspired penalties for working beyond age 65, in terms of loss of SSI benefits if certain wage income limits are exceeded before age 70. Imagine how much larger this income might be if such

---

4. Yung-Ping Chen, "The Role of the Fourth Pillar in the Redesign of Social Security," *Studies on the Four Pillars, The Geneva Papers on Risk and Insurance*, October 1996, number 81, Geneva, pp. 469–477.

penalties were removed. It would help seniors who want to work and help correct the demographic load by raising the proportion of workers to (full-time) retirees. Partial pensions for partial retirement have been proposed in several European countries in order to help mitigate the problem of a shrinking workforce. Prolongation of working life should be more of an option for more people. Aside from the perversity of the penalty noted above, the delayed retirement credit (DRE), which is 4.5 percent for retirees born in 1929 and 1930 and is designed to compensate workers for not receiving benefits when they defer retirement, should be made actuarially fair now. This could be done at an 8 percent rate rather than waiting until 2009 for those born in 1943 and later to receive an actuarially fair return. Encouraging work after first retirement should be a primary goal of public policy.

TABLE 10-5
1994 Percentage of Income Received

Social security	42%
Asset income	18%
Occupational pensions	19%
(private pensions)	(10%)
Employment income	18%

Source: Y.P. Chen—see footnotes.

In fact, note that the *grey* labor market in the U.S. is growing anyway, with many seniors not reporting their labor income in order to avoid the penalties noted above. Other defensive actions that seniors are taking include annuitizing much of their estate (through such gimmicks as taking reverse mortgages), thereby *consuming* the estate, rather than leaving it as a family asset (bequeathing it). The overall result of this annuitization of resources is that savings rates among seniors are lower now than ever before in our history.[5] This helps explain a large part of the decline in household savings rates in U.S. society compared to other countries. This trend, in turn, has had deleterious effects upon our national saving and investment rate and our long-term growth prospects.

Some of the arguments for resolving SSI's unfunded obligations are based on intergenerational equity consideration. The first baby boomers have recently turned 50. In about 15 years they will reach normal retirement age with the effects noted earlier. They should now be bearing as much of the burden on society as is feasible for their own retirement costs. To the extent that they save more(and invest wisely) now, they make it easier on themselves and the rest of society when they retire. Herein lies the dispute between those who think the federal government is part of the problem, not part of the solution. To the extent that the SSI program and its trust funds are federalized

---

5. Jagadeesh Gokhale, Lawrence J. Kotlikoff, and John Sabelhaus, "Understanding the Postwar Decline in U.S. Saving: A Cohort Analysis," *Brookings Papers on Economic Activity,* no. 1 (1996), Washington, DC: Brookings Institution, pp. 315–407.

and are counted in the federal budget, it is claimed that any potential capital accumulation will forever be held hostage to the wasteful whims of politicians. True savings (and investment) of the current surpluses wrung out of the baby boomers will never bear fruit for their retirement years. Hence privatization is necessary even if the baby-boomer problem is exaggerated! That is the argument anyway.

What Should Be Done?

The decline in bequeathable resources and the rise of annuitized resources as a percent of all resources of the elderly was dramatic from 1960–61 to 1987–90 as shown in table 10-6.[6] A large part of the shift was due to the relative growth of SSI benefits, which are treated as an annuity in this calculus. Now, SSI is at risk. Whether it is saved another time or not, the best advice to clients is to harbor more resources in other forms, because society as a whole will be ever more stretched to meet the needs of its nonworking, aging (but healthy) seniors with the toil of its younger generations. Therefore the calculus of expected and required retirement income should now be planned to include larger proportions of asset income, occupational pensions, and employment income in order to reach the required replacement ratios of normal working age income. SSI should henceforth be viewed as a risky *asset*. A calculus assuming SSI benefits to be about 75 percent of today's benefits in real terms would be a constructive and conservative assumption for retirement and estate planning purposes.

TABLE 10-6
Elderly Persons Resources: Shares of Annuitized and Bequeathable Resources in Total Resources

Measure and Period	Males	Females
Annuitized resources		
1960–61	0.16	0.18
1972–73	0.28	0.36
1984–86	0.39	0.49
1987–90	0.41	0.50
Bequeathable resources		
1960–61	0.84	0.82
1972–73	0.72	0.64
1984–86	0.61	0.51
1987–90	0.59	0.50

Source: J. Gokhale, L.J. Kotlikoff, J. Sabelhaus—see footnotes.

---

6. Table adapted from J. Gokhale et al., op. cit., pp. 361, 362, Tables 11 and 12.

Where Can I Find Out More?

Aside from the sources in the footnotes:

- *Report of the 1994–1996 Advisory Council on Social Security* Volume I: Findings and Recommendations, Washington, DC, January 1997.
- *Economic Report of the President*, chapter 3, Washington, DC, February 1997.
- Joseph Quinn. *Entitlements and the Federal Budget: Securing the Future,* Washington, DC: National Academy on Aging, May 1996.

11

HUMAN BEHAVIOR PERSPECTIVES

Michael J. Roszkowski

Introduction

The family-owned business has become a major focus for the financial services industry, for justifiable reasons. It is estimated that family-owned businesses account for 90 percent of all businesses, employing 50 percent of all American workers and contributing over 50 percent to the U.S. Gross Domestic Product. Certain sectors of the economy are dominated by family-owned businesses, namely real estate, construction, and distribution. Although most of these family-owned firms are small, some of the world's largest companies are also family-owned or -controlled concerns (for example, DuPont). Approximately 20 percent of Fortune 500 firms can be considered family businesses. Family-run firms differ from other businesses. There is evidence to show that such firms tend to treat workers more fairly and provide better customer service. Compared to other businesses, family-owned firms tend to be younger and have fewer formalized operating procedures and less bureaucracy. Decision making tends to be centralized, frequently in the hands of an autocratic, patriarchal founder. Family firms tend to resist change more than non-family-owned businesses and have greater aversion to debt. Transitions in leadership are usually difficult in family-owned businesses. An often-quoted statistic is that only about 30 percent of family businesses successfully pass to the second generation and only 15 percent into the third generation. Because family members who work in the family business have multiple roles (employees, owners, relatives), many of the family difficulties spill over into the business.

The family-owned business market can be lucrative to the financial services provider; but to be successful, the professional must understand its unique characteristics. Many professionals, including attorneys, accountants, insurance agents, financial planners, and psychologists, are involved in advising or servicing the family-owned business. The training and expertise of each professional differs, and no one can be an expert in all aspects of the family business. While the serious psychological problems confronting the family business should be referred to therapists specializing in this area, all professionals involved with the family business should have at least some exposure to the psychological issues confronting the typical family business. This chapter deals with some of the psychological issues involved in working with the family firm.

Psychological Characteristics of the Entrepreneur

What Was the Situation Before?

Founders of family-owned businesses are generally entrepreneurs. Until recently, studies considering the psychological characteristics of entrepreneurs tried to isolate personality factors that distinguish between entrepreneurs and other occupations. A large variety of personality characteristics have been examined, with most studies not able to differentiate very well between entrepreneurs and nonentrepreneurs on most such characteristics, leading to the conclusion that there is no one "typical" entrepreneurial profile. Usually the differences that have been found between entrepreneurs and nonentrepreneurs, while statistically significant, are fairly small.

A list of personality characteristics that at one time or another have been used to describe the entrepreneur is shown below. As one can see, some of these traits are even contradictory (for example, dominant and easygoing).

Table 11-1
Character Traits of Entrepreneurs

Adaptable	Disciplined	Involved	Realistic
Agreeable	Dominant	Logical	Reliable
Analytical	Easygoing	Loyal	Reserved
Bold	Effective	Mainstream	Responsible
Calm	Efficient	Mature	Scientific
Cheerful	Energetic	Modest	Sensitive
Clear-thinking	Enthusiastic	Objective	Serious
Committed	Factual	Observant	Sincere
Confident	Forward-looking	Open-minded	Soft-spoken
Conscientious	Frank	Organized	Stable
Conservative	Friendly	Outgoing	Stimulating
Considerate	Goal-oriented	Painstaking	Sympathetic
Controlled	Gracious	Patient	Systematic
Cooperative	Idealistic	Perceptive	Tactful
Creative	Imaginative	Persevering	Thoughtful
Curious	Independent	Persistent	Tolerant
Decisive	Ingenious	Persuasive	Trouble-shooter
Dependable	Innovative	Practical	Understanding
Determined	Intellectual	Quick	Warm
Diplomatic	Intelligent	Quiet	

Source: Joseph F. Singer, "Differentiating the Entrepreneur: A Functional-Personality Theory." University of Arkansas Web Site.

Note that the above list contains the word "innovative." While it is true that entrepreneurs are somewhat more innovative than managers, this is not always so. Most entrepreneurs are not "inventors" in the strict sense of the word. Rather, most get their ideas for starting their businesses by working in that particular field and merely replicating or simply modifying an existing concept. Furthermore, the longer the entrepreneur has been in a particular business, the less innovative he or she tends to be. The more innovative entrepreneurs tend to have started a larger number of businesses but not to have endured in them for long. The reasons for this are not understood fully, but it is believed that the innovative entrepreneur gets bored with the existing venture and desires to move on to another one. As evidence, note for example that in one study the innovative entrepreneurs spent only 18 percent of their time on administration, compared to 45 percent for the less innovative. Innovativeness does not necessarily equate with survival.

The personality characteristics that have been linked with entrepreneurship most consistently are (1) need for achievement, (2) risk tolerance, (3) internal locus of control, (4) need for autonomy, and (5) optimism. These are the personality dimensions most likely to separate the entrepreneur from the nonentrepreneur.

- *Need for Achievement.* Most studies find that entrepreneurs have a very strong drive to achieve.
- *Risk Tolerance.* While ability to deal with risk is part of the definition of entrepreneur, most studies find that entrepreneurs are moderate risk takers rather than either very high or very low risk takers. Moderate risks are preferred because they allow the entrepreneur to use skill to control his or her exposure to risk. With too much risk, success is strictly a matter of chance. With too little, anyone can do it.
- *Locus of Control.* When asked to account for success or failure in their life, most entrepreneurs ascribe their fate to their own personal efforts rather than to luck or chance factors. This type of attribution is called *internal locus of control*, whereas attribution of success or failure to chance or luck is termed *external locus of control.* People with an internal locus of control can handle stress better, and being an entrepreneur has been shown to be quite stressful.
- *Need for Autonomy.* Entrepreneurs do not like being under the control of another person.
- *Optimism.* Entrepreneurs are willing to start another venture even after repeated failures. They believe that they have learned from past mistakes and that the current venture will be successful.

While other traits such as leadership and creativity are frequently found among entrepreneurs, they are also characteristics of individuals who are successful managers and hence cannot be considered unique to entrepreneurs. The other reported characteristics have not been replicated sufficiently and may be descriptive of only certain types of entrepreneurs. For example, some studies note that entrepreneurs are lonely people who did not participate in group activities while in school (for example, team sports and clubs) and later in life were misfits in conventional organizations.

Environmental factors fostering entrepreneurship have also been studied. There are extensive data to show that entrepreneurs had parents who owned their own businesses and that such parents encouraged independence, responsibility, and achievement in their offspring.

Entrepreneurs generally grow up in middle- to upper-class families, although many were born to immigrant parents or are themselves immigrants. Only limited support can be gathered for the contention that entrepreneurs are first-born or only children, who presumably received more parental attention, which in turn leads to greater self-confidence and the willingness to engage in new ventures.

Data about the educational level of entrepreneurs are similarly equivocal, although a fair number of studies suggest that entrepreneurs have limited education, except for those engaged in high-tech ventures. Perhaps it is fairest to conclude that entrepreneurs are better educated than the general public, but less educated than managers, and that in school they were not the top students. Table 11-2 compares traits of managers and entrepreneurs.

Table 11-2
Traits of Managers and Entrepreneurs

Trait	Traditional Managers	Entrepreneurs
Primary motives	Promotion and other traditional corporate rewards, (office, staff, and power)	Independence, opportunity to create, and money
Time orientation	Short run—meeting quotas and budgets; weekly, monthly, quarterly, and annual planning horizons	Survival and achieving 5- to 10-year growth of business
Activity	Delegates and supervises	Direct involvement
Risk	Careful	Moderate risk taker
Status	Concerned about status symbols	No concern about status symbols
Failure and mistakes	Tries to avoid mistakes and surprises	Deals with mistakes and failures
Decisions	Usually agrees with those in upper management positions	Follows dream
Serves whom?	Others	Self and customers
Family history	Family members worked for large organizations	Entrepreneurial small-business, professional, or farm background
Relationship with others	Hierarchy as basic relationship	Transactions and deal making as basic relationship

Source: Modified from table appearing in *American Psychologist,* 1990, vol. 45, no. 2, p. 209.

What Is the Nature of the Change?

Until recently, research on entrepreneurs and the family-owned business did not consider women entrepreneurs. With the increase in the number of women in the workforce, the situation is changing. These days women are starting businesses at a faster rate than men. Presently about a third of businesses in the United States are owned by women. Research comparing male and female entrepreneurs is increasing. Although they are more similar than different, female and male entrepreneurs differ in the following ways:

- Women are somewhat older when they start their first entrepreneurial venture (35–45 years of age for women versus 25–35 for men).
- Women are more likely to start a service business.
- Male entrepreneurs generally have educational backgrounds in business or technical fields; female entrepreneurs are more likely to have a liberal arts education.
- Women are more likely to have an entrepreneurial mother.
- Women are more likely to use outside sources for support and information (for example, trade associations).
- Woman-owned businesses are smaller.
- Female small-business owners devote more time to family than do male small-business owners.
- Several studies document that women starting a business have a harder time securing new venture financing, perhaps because failure rates for woman-owned businesses are higher.

Women are still discouraged from joining the family business, especially as partners or in a leadership capacity. (How many times have you seen "Smith & Daughter" or "Jones Sisters" on a storefront?) Seldom are they the founders' primary choice for a successor. If they are allowed to join, they are relegated to staff positions such as customer service or human resources and so are unable to make major decisions.

The 1995 MassMutual annual survey of family business owners showed that in 34 percent of the businesses, a son is involved in the business in some way, but only 16 percent of these businesses report the involvement of a daughter. Likewise, whereas 26 percent of the family business owners report that they have a brother involved in the business, only 11 percent report a sister's involvement. While 72 percent of the brothers and 56 percent of the sons were key decision makers in the family business, only 37 percent of the sisters and 30 percent of the daughters were reported to be thus involved.

It should be noted, however, that although the representation of women in top management positions in family-owned businesses is low, it is still higher than in non-family businesses.

The reasons for this gender gap in the family businesses is probably attributable to the same factors as have been identified for women in the workplace in all types of settings. It has been shown that sexual role stereotypes are more prevalent among men and that men prefer promoting other men. Some research findings show that women have lower career aspirations than men, perhaps because women's aspirations are limited by gender stereotypes. Older adults have been found to gender-stereotype more than younger adults. It is encouraging that if a man has been exposed to, read about, or even heard about a woman who was successful in a typically male occupation, the degree of gender bias decreases. Less encouraging is research showing that even though the percentage of dual-earner couples has risen dramatically, sharing of domestic responsibilities by husbands has not risen proportionately; working women are still handling the lion's share of housework and child rearing.

Recent research on the characteristics of entrepreneurs is conducted under the assumption that there are different types of entrepreneurs and that each type probably has different personality characteristics. A number of different typologies have been proposed. For example, a recent study of Australian female business founders suggests three psychological types of female entrepreneurs:

1. need achiever

2. pragmatic

3. managerial

The *need achiever* entrepreneur has a high need for achievement; the *managerial* entrepreneur, for power; and the *pragmatic* entrepreneur, a moderate need for both achievement and power.

A typology of family business owners, encompassing founders as well as heirs, has been recently developed by Russ Alan Prince and Karen Maru File. Eight family business personality types have been identified, based on research on 985 family business owners. The system is detailed in *Marketing to Family Business Owners*. The eight personalities are shown in table 11-3.

Table 11-3
Eight Family Business Owner Personalities

Personality	Frequency	Core Motivation
Loving Parents	34%	Family involvement in business
Autocrats	19%	Control all aspects of the business
Empire Builders	13%	Create a business empire
Fortune Hunters	9%	Become wealthy
Recruits	8%	Drafted into the business by family
Rebels	6%	Prove that they can be successful
Status Seekers	6%	Recognition for success
Social Benefactors	5%	Make the world a better place

What Should Be Done?

Financial services professionals need to be aware that these eight personalities are interested in various financial products to different degrees. Furthermore, the products must be positioned differently to appeal to each personality type. For example, Fortune Hunters are most likely to use life insurance to pay estate taxes, whereas Recruits are least likely to do so. (See table 11-4.)

Table 11-4
Percent of Each Personality That Believes in Using Life Insurance to Pay Estate Taxes

Fortune Hunters	96%
Status Seekers	91%
Autocrats	90%
Social Benefactors	88%
Empire Builders	86%
Rebels	86%
Loving Parents	77%
Recruits	54%

Consider the differences in the importance of various executive benefits, as judged by the eight personalities, shown in table 11-5.

Table 11-5
Percent of Each Personality Type That Considers the Benefit Important

Personality Type	Life Insurance	Disability Insurance	Corporate Car	Restricted Stock/Stock Option
Social Benefactors	96%	93%	0%	10%%
Status Seekers	90%	11%	96%	23%
Recruits	84%	46%	12%	29%
Rebels	81%	60%	18%	21%
Loving Parents	40%	81%	19%	57%
Empire Builders	35%	52%	3%	35%
Fortune Hunters	16%	30%	59%	0%
Autocrats	15%	20%	43%	3%

Positioning statements for six classes of products are presented: Executive Benefits, Retirement Planning, Business Succession and Estate Planning, Asset Protection Planning, Investment Management, and Charitable Estate Planning. Position statements advocated by Prince and File for the first two classes, by personality type, are shown below. The statement is meant to appeal to the core motivation driving the family business owner.

Positioning Statements on Executive Benefits:

- *Loving Parents:* An executive benefits plan enables you to take care of your family.
- *Empire Builders:* An executive benefits plan helps you keep people focused and committed to building the business.
- *Autocrats:* An executive benefits plan helps you keep employees motivated in the right direction.
- *Rebels:* A well-thought-through executive benefits plan allows you to be seen as a high-quality manager.
- *Recruits:* There are certain kinds of benefits family members expect.
- *Fortune Hunters:* Executive benefits allow you to maximize your wealth through the business.
- *Status Seekers:* Executive benefits allow you to reward yourself and to be recognized.
- *Social Benefactors:* Executive benefits reflect the social responsibility of every company.

Positioning Statements on Retirement Planning:

- *Loving Parents:* A retirement plan can be used to take care of future financial needs of the family.
- *Empire Builders:* A retirement plan is designed to maximize growth in the business faster.
- *Autocrats:* A retirement plan is an effective way of increasing and controlling managerial retention and commitment.
- *Rebels:* A retirement plan can be better than any large company's retirement plan.
- *Recruits:* A retirement plan can be designed to meet your family's expectations.
- *Fortune Hunters:* A retirement plan can provide a substantial payout to the owners.
- *Status Seekers:* A retirement plan enables you to live in the future with the same status you enjoy now.
- *Social Benefactors:* A retirement plan reflects your ethical responsibility to your people.

Where Can I Find Out More?

- HS 331 Planning for Business Owners and Professionals. The American College.
- GS 836 Business Succession Planning I. The American College.
- M. W. Begley and D. P. Boyd. "Psychological Characteristics Associated with Performance in Entrepreneurial Firms and Small Businesses," *Journal of Business Venturing*, 1987, vol. 2, pp. 79–93.
- R. H. Brockhaus, Sr. and P. S. Horowitz. "The Psychology of the Entrepreneur," *The Art and Science of Entrepreneurship*, D. L. Sexton and R. W. Smilor, eds., Cambridge: Ballinger, 1986, pp. 25–48.
- J. Langan-Fox and S. Roth. "Achievement Motivation and Female Entrepreneurs," *Journal of Occupational and Organizational Psychology*, 1995, vol. 68, pp. 209–218.
- M. E. Mangelsdorf. "The Entrepreneurial Personality," *Inc. Magazine*, August 1988, p. 18.
- S. Parasuraman, Y. S. Purohit, and V. M. Godshalk. "Work and Family Variables, Entrepreneurial Career Success and Psychological Well-being," *Journal of Vocational Behavior*, 1996, vol. 48, pp. 275–300.
- R. A. Prince and K. M. File. *Marketing to Family Business Owners*. Cincinnati: National Underwriter, 1995, 307 pages. (Along with data on purchasing behavior and positioning statements, the book contains exercises designed to help the financial services professional become proficient in classifying clients into the eight personality types.)
- E. H. Scheis. "The Role of the Founder in Creating Organizational Culture," *Family Business Review*, 1995, vol. 8, no. 3, pp. 221–238.

- H. P. Welsch and L. K. Gundry. "Differences in Familial Influence among Women-owned Businesses," *Family Business Review,* 1994, vol. 7, pp. 273–286.

Successful Family-Owned Business Succession

What Was the Situation Before?

Research results show that family business owners with children encourage their offspring to become involved in the family business, based on the belief that it is a good opportunity for the children and a worthwhile continuance of a family tradition. According to the 1995 MassMutual survey of family business owners, only 19 percent of parents either "somewhat" or "strongly" discourage their offsprings' participation in the business.

Until recently, advisers of family businesses also believed that liquidating or selling a family-owned business to a nonfamily member should be avoided at all costs. The family-owned business was considered a legacy that was to be passed on to one's children or some other close relative. The family-owned business was to remain in the family at all costs because it was intrinsically good to have a family business.

What Is the Nature of the Change?

It is now recognized that "success" should not always be equated with "succession." Some family businesses should be liquidated rather than passed on to the next generation because of the misery they can create for individuals who are pressured to take over and who are ill-suited to fulfill this role (the so-called "trapped child syndrome"). Furthermore, in some dysfunctional families the founder uses the family business to keep children and grandchildren close by, preventing the offspring from finding their own identity. The offspring are forced to subordinate their needs to those of the family. In a recent study 14 percent of college juniors and seniors felt that they would let someone down if they did not enter the family business. The pressure seems to come more from the father than the mother. Approximately 38 percent of the sample indicated that their father would like them to enter the business, compared to 24 percent who stated that this sentiment came from their mother. Frequently the founder's children are reluctant to reveal their true feelings about the family business to their parents because they fear the disclosure would hurt their parents' feelings.

The following reasons have been identified for children's reluctance or refusal to get involved in the family business:

1. lack confidence in ability to live up to parents' expectations

2. fear sibling rivalry

3. see limited career growth opportunities

4. want to establish own identity

5. lack interest in the particular business

6. see family-owned business as too all-consuming

One study suggests that father-son working relationships in the family business are fairly harmonious when the father is 50 to 59 years of age and the son is 23 to 32 years old. The relationship is problematic when (a) the son is 17 to 22 and the father is 41 to 45 years old and (b) son is 34 to 40 and dad is 60 to 69.

Other research shows that the more mutual respect there is between father and son, the more successful the succession. Unfortunately, according to a recent study, the level of mutual respect between father and son in the family-owned business leaves a lot of room for improvement. The percentage of the sons indicating that their degree of mutual respect/understanding was very high was 10 percent; high, 10 percent; moderate, 50 percent; and low, 30 percent.

In this same study, sibling relationships among the offspring of family business owners were also less than ideal. Asked about their degree of accommodation, over 15 percent of the siblings said it was very high, 60 percent said it was moderate, and the remaining 25 percent indicated that it was low (characterized by infighting).

What Should Clients Do?

If a child does not want to be the heir apparent to the family business, in most instances the person's wish should be honored. As parental pressures increase, children experience identity difficulties and begin to doubt their ability to succeed outside the family business. Coercion will result in the offspring resenting and regretting his or her capitulation to the parents' wish. The offspring will probably always have a feeling of having been deprived of a more fulfilling career. At best the offspring will be unmotivated, and at worst he or she will become rebellious.

If an offspring's personality does not match the abilities and interests required by the job, then job dissatisfaction will result, and job performance may suffer. Psychologists have found that vocational interests can be reduced to about four to seven basic types. The most widely accepted typology, based on extensive empirical research, was developed by psychologist John L. Holland, who identified six basic occupational personality types: Realistic, Investigative, Artistic, Social, Enterprising, and Conventional. Adjacent personality types are more similar to each other, as shown in the diagram that follows.

```
              Realistic
Conventional           Investigative


Enterprising            Artistic

              Social
```

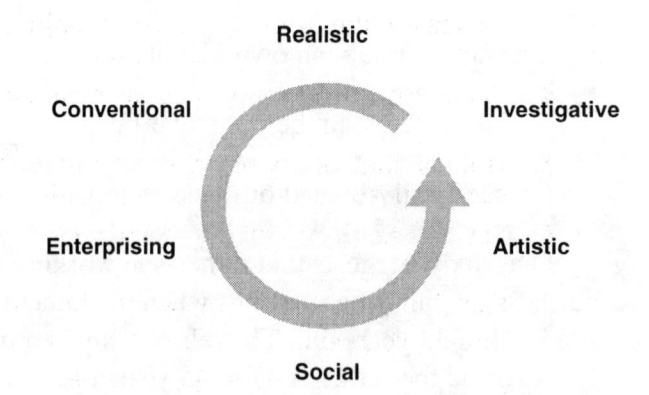

The *Realistic* personality prefers to work alone in outdoor and manual activities. Most of these jobs are blue-collar in nature, except for a few technical positions, such as engineer. The *Investigative* personality type, which occurs among scientists, is marked by interest in working with ideas rather than people or things. *Artistic* personalities are most interested in working with ideas and things but like to create new ideas or things, rather than working within a conventional framework. *Social* personalities prefer to work with other people, especially those in distress, wishing to assist them (for example, social workers and teachers). The *Enterprising* personality type also likes working with people but wants to control and dominate rather than assist them. The Enterprising personality is very goal oriented and likes to manage the work being done by others. The *Conventional* personality type likes to work with things rather than people or ideas, especially if the work is detail oriented. This type of individual prefers unambiguous routine tasks, characteristic of jobs such as a clerk.

Career interest tests are available to determine which type of pursuits an offspring prefers. Family business advisers should avail themselves of such career counseling services.

If an offspring expresses interest in joining the family business, steps can be taken to prevent problems with the father and siblings. The following measures have been found to be effective:

1. Prior to entering the family business, children should work elsewhere for a couple of years. Furthermore, they should be eased into the business by assigning them progressively greater responsibilities.

2. It is better to place independent-minded offspring in a branch office than the headquarters, where friction between father and offspring is likely to occur. Similar autonomy can be provided by placing the offspring in a new division or in charge of a new product line.

3. To avoid sibling rivalries, assign them different jobs and responsibilities. Do not have one sibling report to another.

4. Spend time together outside the business.

5. Hold annual family retreats to bring problems out in the open.

6. Set up a family council to make recommendations on policy.

7. Develop formal codes of conduct, written for family members by family members.

Elaboration of some of these points is in order. The family council and the board of directors should not be one and the same. Even though they may appear to have similar functions, one major difference between these two bodies of overseers lies in their primary objective. The family council has the best interest of the family at heart, whereas the board of directors is more concerned about what's best for the business. Given the differences in mission, tensions between the family council and the board of directors are likely to exist. One way of minimizing conflicts is to have some overlapping membership between these two boards.

An example of a family code of conduct developed by a successful family business appears in Arthur Andersen's *Family Business Advisor* (June 1995). It includes the following principles to guide family meetings:

1. Allow others to complete their thoughts without interruption.

2. Assume that others are acting in good faith.

3. Allow for the personal growth and development of others.

4. Involve as many family members as possible in a decision.

5. Respond to requests in a timely manner.

6. Seek consensus.

While this is just common sense, it frequently needs to be repeated, lest we forget.

Where Can I Find Out More?

- HS 331 Planning for Business Owners and Professionals. The American College.
- GS 836 Business Succession Planning I. The American College.
- GS 838 Business Succession Planning II. The American College.
- J. A. Barach and J. B. Ganitsky. "Successful Succession in Family Business," *Family Business Review*, 1995, vol. 8, no. 2, pp. 131–155.

- C. J. Eckrich and T. A. Loughead. "Effects of Family Business Membership and Psychological Separation on the Career Development of Late Adolescents," *Family Business Review*, 1995, vol. 9, no. 4, pp. 369–386.
- W. C. Handler. "Key Interpersonal Relationships of Next-Generation Family Members in Family Firms," *Journal of Small Business Management*, July 1991, pp. 21–32.
- K. Kaye. "When the Family Business is a Sickness," *Family Business Review*, 1995, vol. 9, no. 4, pp. 347–368.

Decision-Making Styles and Succession

What Was the Situation Before?

Most founders are very reluctant to give up control of the business. Succession and estate planning were once considered to be relevant issues only when the founder's career was drawing to an end.

What Is the Nature of the Change?

A recent national survey of the heirs of failed family businesses indicates that the major trigger for the transition in leadership and ultimate collapse of the business was not the founder's retirement, but the founder's death (78 percent of the cases). In over a third of these instances, the death was "unexpected."

It is generally recommended that (a) succession planning start 5 to 20 years in advance of the anticipated date of retirement, (b) the succession plan be in writing, and (c) an advisory board be set up to help with the process. While advisers to the family business now realize that these issues need to be addressed continuously, because they are processes rather than events, the evidence suggests that this point of view is not yet accepted by the founders themselves.

A recent study shows that 63 percent of founders believe that the successor should be selected no more than 5 years prior to retirement. Only 35 percent feel it necessary for the plan to be in writing, and an even lower proportion (27 percent) feel that a board of advisors is necessary to assist in the process.

Recent research on the decision-making strategies of entrepreneurs sheds light on why this state of affairs exists. Most successful entrepreneurs are not long-term strategic planners. They tend to be *intuitive* thinkers who abhor what they perceive to be unnecessary bureaucracy.

On the Myers-Briggs personality scale, 60 percent of founders are *intuitive* decision makers, whereas 86 percent of managers are *sensing* types. Sensing decision makers need external information to make decisions, whereas intuitive types rely on their own internal judgments, such as imagination. It's been observed that sensing types like to have specific detailed facts, whereas intuitives prefer to have just a general overview. It's been reported that certain words are more likely to appeal to the intuitive type, whereas other words are more appealing to the sensing type. Their respective vocabularies are as follows:

Intuitive	Sensing
hunch	experience
future	past
speculative	realistic
inspiration	perspiration
possible	actual
head-in-clouds	down-to-earth
fantasy	utility
fiction	fact
ingenuity	practicality
imaginative	sensible

New findings also indicate that many successful founders do not spend much time researching and analyzing. Entrepreneurs seize the moment. If something is analyzed too long, the opportunity could disappear. The analyses conducted by entrepreneurs are characterized by (a) a quick screening of opportunities, (b) focusing on just a small number of important issues, (c) acting without having all the answers (partial information). Most entrepreneurs feel that some unknowns cannot be answered through more research. They prefer informal methods of learning about their customers' needs and indicate a mistrust of formal market research.

A typology of family business owners, based primarily on who makes the important decisions, is presented in the 1995 MassMutual Annual Survey of 1,029 Family Business Owners. Seven types of family businesses are identified, based on a statistical technique called cluster analysis:

1. *Mom and Pop* (17 percent of family businesses). A husband and wife run the business jointly, with two-thirds intending to pass the business to their children. The average age of the owners is 52. The businesses are smaller than average.

2. *Sibling Team* (6 percent). Two or more siblings run the business, which is typically a first-generation (78 percent) venture. Family disagreements regarding the business occur frequently.

3. *Dominant Owner* (12 percent). In this family business, "the owner is king," and this individual makes all the decisions. Family disagreements are infrequent because there is only one decision maker. These businesses are mainly first generation and smaller than average. The average age of the owner is 52. While 90 percent of these owners

have offspring, less than half plan to transfer the business to the next generation.

4. *Looking Ahead* (16 percent). The average age of the owner is 62, and this individual is starting to recognize that the business will not remain in his hands forever. The children are becoming involved in decision making, but the final decision still rests with the owner.

5. *Parental Oversight* (13 percent). These are family businesses in transition from one generation to the next. Primary responsibility for decision making has been passed from parent to offspring (average age, 37), but the parent continues to be involved in the business, leading to frequent disagreements about how the business should be run.

6. *Outside Assistance* (33 percent). This type of family business has the smallest number of decision makers (average is 3), and it is also unusual because the primary decision makers are *not* family members. The average age of the owner is 49.

7. *The Mega Firm* (4 percent). The mega firm is at the opposite end of the spectrum from the "outside assistance" firm in terms of the number of decision makers (average is 10) and contains both family members and non-family employees as key decision makers. This firm is generally large (average number of employees is 347). A greater-than-average level of discord characterizes these family businesses.

What Should Clients Do?

Advisers working with the family business founder need to be sensitive to who makes the decisions, as well as the person's decision-making style, when presenting information. When dealing with a founder, do not overload the person with too many details, because founders are usually good at extrapolating patterns and trends from limited data. Too much detail will bore them. Don't expect them to have an orderly, disciplined approach to information collection.

Many decisions about the purchase of financial services for the firm often involve parties not directly working in the firm, the so-called "shadow influencers." Partly due to this situation, decisions about purchasing a financial service or product take longer for a family business than for another type of concern.

Efforts by advisers to alert family business owners about the dangers of not having a written succession plan may be having an effect, based on results of MassMutual's third annual survey of family business owners. In 1993 only 21 percent of respondents had a written succession plan. By 1994 the comparable percentage was 28 percent. In the 1995 survey almost half (48 percent) of family business owners reported having a written succession plan in place.

Interestingly, the survey found that large family businesses (i.e., more than 100 employees) were no more likely than small businesses (i.e., fewer than 25 employees) to have a formal succession plan. Likewise, only a small difference was found based on the generation of the business (33 percent of first generation business owners had a succession plan, compared to 29 percent of third generation owners). However, women business owners were less likely to have a written succession plan (33 percent of women versus 46 percent of the men).

As might be expected, the older the owner, the more likely that a written succession plan exists.

Age	Percent Who Have a Succession Plan
under 50	38%
50-64	43%
65 or older	63%

While these statistics are encouraging, especially when compared to the earlier studies, it is still quite shocking that 37 percent of family business owners past the normal retirement age have not created a formal succession plan.

Founders are generally reluctant to transfer the enterprise to a successor because their own identity is tied to the business. Frequently the business becomes their sole interest, dominating all other aspects of their lives. A founder is especially unlikely to "let go" if he or she is involved in every detail of the business and has not regularly delegated the more routine and mundane tasks to subordinates. According to Prince and File, the "Autocrat" is the family business owner type least likely to consider the inevitability of having to get out of the business at some point. Consequently, this personality type is not very interested in retirement planning.

The possible reasons why founders are reluctant to plan succession are eloquently stated by Ernest A. Doud, who uses David Letterman's "top ten" format to identify the reasons and then indicate why the rationale underlying this pattern of thought is wrong. With Ernie Doud's kind permission, we have reproduced the list, which was presented on the World Wide Web by Doud Hausner and Associates of Glendale, California. Since there is some evidence that compared to other people, entrepreneurs like to employ metaphors in their speech, they will probably respond well to the arguments presented by Doud.

Top Ten Reasons Founders Won't Let Go
Doud Hausner and Associates

10. "Too many people I've known have died soon after they retired (or acted like they were dead)." There's no correlation between mortality and retirement. However, it helps to develop interests outside the business to which you can turn your attention.

9. "Without me, the business is nothing." Get your ego down to a more realistic size. In fact, under your successors, the business may evolve in ways you've never imagined.

8. "Without the business, I'm nothing." It doesn't have to be an "all or nothing" proposition. There are many constructive ways you can maintain your identity and connection with the business, spend time with your successors and trusted advisors investigating all the possibilities.

7. "I hate gardening, find cruises boring, and get sunburned if I play too much golf." So find other leisure activities that excite you. Do those things you've always wanted to do, but for which you never had the time. (We know one founder who rekindled his interest in music. His combo now appears in jazz festivals all over the world).

6. "I need someplace to go." My wife keeps reminding me she married me for better or for worse—but not for lunch! There is no denying the fact that major changes can add new stresses to any relationship. If you don't develop a new focus in your life, then you're liable to have time on your hands while your spouse maintains her/his normally busy schedule. To help avoid unnecessary post-retirement stress in your marriage, re-read numbers 8 and 7.

5. "The 'kids' want to change the way the business is run. If I'm not there, they will change what I've built!" If the business doesn't change to keep up with new demands, it will suffer. If you took over from a previous generation, you made changes. And if you are the founder, the business has changed from the first day it started. Businesses can thrive on infusions of fresh ideas and energy.

4. "I don't want to choose between my 'kids' to name a successor." Well, you could let them "duke it out" after you're gone. Better yet, involve them in the decision. If you have a strategic vision and plan for the business it will be easier to determine who has the skills and talents needed to lead it.

3. "The business is my major source of income. I have to stay active to protect it." There are a vast array of strategies for turning your illiquid business investment into an asset that can provide a stream of retirement income. Check them out!

2. "Nobody can run the business as well as I can." You may not realize it, but you're probably not the only one running your business now. You may make major decisions, but chances are, you're not involved in all the details. Step back! Look around. You may find untapped potential.

1. "They may run it better than I did!" And what's wrong with that? Don't let your ego get in the way. Comprehensive succession planning that is done well will help your business thrive under the next generation. This is one of the most important legacies you can create.

Where Can I Find Out More?

- HS 331 Planning for Business Owners and Professionals. The American College.
- GS 836 Business Succession Planning I. The American College.
- GS 838 Business Succession Planning II. The American College.
- J. A. Barach and J. B. Ganitsky. "Successful Succession in Family Business," *Family Business Review,* 1995, vol. 8, no. 2, pp. 131–155.
- A. Bhinde. "How Entrepreneurs Craft Strategies That Work," *Harvard Business Review*, March-April 1994, pp. 150–161.
- E. H. Buttner and N. Gryskiewicz. "Entrepreneurs' Problem-solving Styles: An Empirical Study Using the Kirton Adaptation/Innovation Theory," *Journal of Small Business Management*, January 1993, pp. 22–31.
- T. J. Callahan and M. D. Cassar. "Small Business Owners' Assessments of Their Abilities to Perform and Interpret Formal Market Studies," *Journal of Small Business Management*, October 1995, pp. 1–9.
- D. A. Kirby and T. J. Lee. "Succession Management in Family Firms in the Northeast of England," *Family Business Review*, 1996, vol. 9, no. 1, pp. 75–81.
- M. E. Mangelsdorf. "The Entrepreneurial Personality," *Inc. Magazine*, August 1988, p. 18.
- Mathew Greenwald & Associates. *MassMutual 1995 Annual Survey of Family Business Owners*, September 1995, Massachusetts Mutual Life Insurance Company, Springfield, MA, 59 pages.
- R. A. Prince and K. M. File. *Marketing to Family Business Owners.* Cincinnati: National Underwriter, 1995.

12

USING THE INTERNET FOR INSURANCE AND FINANCIAL SERVICES

Alan C. Bugbee, Jr.

What if you could access all of the financial markets in the world any time and all the time? What if you could review the states' regulations for insurance instantaneously? What if you could have worldwide discussions with other people in insurance and financial services any time, day or night? What if you could search for the best price for _____ (fill in the blank) on a worldwide basis? What if you could have your entire company or companies available at your fingertips any time, anywhere? What if you could do all of this and more?

You can, on the Internet! "Only the imagination limits the types of information products or services that insurers can deliver via the Web," (Krohm, 1996, p. 533).

Why Should You Learn About and Use the Internet?

The Internet is a fact. This was established a long time ago (at least in terms of computers). If the appeal of what you can do on the Internet doesn't convince you to use it, consider this: You need to know about the Internet because your clients will have access to it. You do not want to be upstaged by them. Nothing is worse than being or appearing to be ignorant about a tool that is vital to your business. The Internet is no longer merely an interesting thing to know about; it is a necessity. This chapter will help you learn about the Internet and start you on your way to becoming proficient in its use.

What Is the Internet?

Internet is an acronym for International Network. Simply put, the Internet is a network of networks; it is a connection between a wide number of computers and computer networks throughout the world. It provides access to millions of other computers, billions of words, and trillions of bytes of information. Each day over 100 million words are added to the Internet. It can be thought of as a gigantic library, but it is much, much more. In addition to the vast array of text, it contains audio, pictures, graphics, video, live action, animation, and direct audio (telephony). It can be used to sell merchandise, keep track of stocks, bonds and mutual funds, have a live conference with others half a world away, telephone friends, send messages around the world, observe what's happening in Tokyo, San Diego, or Antarctica, buy merchandise in Brussels, Tierra del Fuego, Seoul or Chicago, and take courses. There is little you cannot do on the Internet. It is the "backbone" of the body that brings together diverse parts to form a whole working system.[1]

The benefits of the Internet are especially evident in the fields of financial services and insurance. Information about these fields is open to everyone with Internet access. The Internet also can provide information about who is accessing them to the sponsor(s) or owner(s) of the home page. It is an excellent source of information about federal and state regulations governing financial services, and it provides detailed information (including prospectuses) about stocks, bonds, mutual funds, IPOs, futures, and so on. "(The Internet is) currently limited in what it can do by bandwidth constraints." (Batman, 1997, p. 5-11)

The Internet is composed of six general parts or operations. The most widely used part is *Electronic Mail*, or *e-mail* for short (Hafner, 1997). This enables messages to be sent around the world at high speed and minimal cost. The best known part is the *World Wide Web (www)*. The World Wide Web is a collection of multimedia documents connected by hyperlinks. It is the most recent addition to the Internet, having become commercially available in February 1994. Since its introduction, it has grown by leaps and bounds and is now considered synonymous with the Internet. However, the other parts should not be overlooked because they provide a wealth of useful information.

Gopher[2] is the precursor to the World Wide Web. It is a menu of text-based Internet resources. Gopher can be accessed by any Web browser, but it contains no pictures, tables, or graphics. By current standards, it seems primitive. It has existed for quite a while and contains a very large amount of information. It is especially good for examining the history and background of companies and institutions.

Related to Gopher is *ftp*, or *file transfer protocol*. This function of the Internet is used to browse files and, as its name implies, to transfer files from their site to a personal computer. While this part of the Internet cannot display pictures (it shows "<IMAGE>" instead), it can retrieve World Wide Web documents in their entirety. This can be helpful because it can operate independently of the browser through MS-DOS commands.

Telnet and *Usenet* are commands that allow the user to remotely connect to another Internet host; this host could be another computer, network, or system. Unlike the use of a browser, through Telnet you are actually logged onto that computer. It is very similar to having a terminal connected to a minicomputer or mainframe computer. As a rule, if a site will allow you to use

---

1. Actually, as analogies go, it is closer to *Star Trek*'s the Borg, a linked collection of different species for a common purpose, than it is to the human body.
2. It got its name because it was developed at the University of Minnesota, the home of the Golden Gophers.

Telnet, you would enter your e-mail address as your name and "anonymous" as your password. As with the other non-www or e-mail parts of the Internet, it can provide some very interesting and useful resources.

Newsgroups and discussion groups are, as their names imply, essentially bulletin boards where you can post and read messages about a topic. These groups are probably the third most popular feature of the Internet. (Nelson, 1995, p. 98) They can involve almost anything. They may be "moderated" or "unmoderated," which means that either all messages go through a site, which is responsible for determining whether the material is appropriate for the newsgroup, or messages are posted directly from users to the newsgroup without being reviewed. Both approaches have their merits. Understand, however, that "anything goes" applies to an unmoderated site. This concept will be discussed more later.

Two other functions of the Internet that are not generally among its main uses but are helpful are *finger* and *Whois*. Both are used with *shell accounts*, which connect your computer to a host computer. In effect, a shell account transforms your computer into a monitor and keyboard on another computer. Finger allows you to find out who someone is on the Internet. This is useful, especially in finding out the true names of persons in discussion groups, newsgroups, or who sent you e-mail. To do this, you only need the person's e-mail address—that is, name@hostname. If the host you've fingered responds to your request (not all of them will), finger will tell you who he or she is. It may also provide detailed information about him or her.

Another way to get information is through the command *Whois*. This operates in the same way as finger and will provide similar information. Like the other commands, if it is supported by the browser you are using, it can be entered in the command line and will return the results on the screen.

What Does "Surfing the Web" Mean?

Contrary to popular belief (or at least usage in the popular press), *surfing the Web* does not mean selecting one site, going to it, viewing it, then selecting another site, going to it, and so forth. Rather, it means following links within Web pages and seeing where they take you. Truly surfing the Internet can take you far afield. You'll probably end up in a site with very flimsy connections to where you began. However, doing your daily routine of logging on, then reading today's *Dilbert* cartoon (*http://www.unitedmedia.com/ comics/ dilbert/*), then checking on the stock market (see Appendix), then reading your e-mail is not surfing the Web. This is mentioned to protect you from having ridicule heaped upon you by more sophisticated Internet users for misusing this term.

Who Owns the Internet and the Information on It?

As mentioned previously, the Internet is a network of computer networks around the globe.[3] Because whatever is on the Internet can, at least in theory, be seen by anyone in the world, the posting of information is considered to be exportation and falls under the jurisdiction of the U.S. Department of Commerce's export restrictions! This is based on two main legal points. First, exporting anything requires a license. Second, exporting a service is roughly equivalent to exporting the pieces necessary to provide that service. Therefore, if you ship, carry, transfer a file, or electronically mail anything out of the United States (as you would by posting something on an Internet discussion group), it needs to be covered by an export license. This would seem to defeat the use of the Internet for free and open exchange of information. Fortunately, there is a loophole. It is called a *general license* and it allows you to export anything that is not specifically restricted from export. Therefore, have no fear of sending messages or posting information on the Internet unless what you are sending is owned by somebody else or is restricted from export.

The other legal restriction stipulates that, if a physical part or thing is restricted from export, then remote access to it is also excluded. This restriction is to keep the plans for something that cannot be exported from being copied and reproduced elsewhere.

Who Is Responsible for What's Put on a Computer Network? Suppose someone posts restricted information on the Internet. Is the operator of the network responsible for what has been put on it? According to the Corporation for Research and Educational Networking's (CREN) interpretation of the law, a network operator is responsible for illegal export only if the operator was aware of the violation and failed to inform proper authorities. The operator is not responsible for monitoring usage and determining whether or not it is legal. This view has been upheld by the courts.

What Are Your Property Rights If You Put Something on the Internet? While someone on the Internet cannot change your message or home page without your authorization (or by cracking your network sign-ons), almost anything on the Internet can be copied and posted elsewhere. Don't put anything on the Internet that you don't want to appear anywhere else.

A related point is, "How much credence should be given to information and/or advice that is on the Internet?" Suppose a hot stock tip is posted on a discussion group to which you belong. What should you do about it? In general, treat advice on the Internet—especially in a chat room[4]—the same

---

3. In the case of some NASA sites, it goes beyond the earth, too. See *http://www.jpl.nasa.gov* to view images from the Hubble telescope.
4. A *chat room* is an interactive discussion (via keyboard) about a specific topic that is hosted on a *bulletin board system (BBS)* on an on-line service such as America On Line or CompuServe.

way that you would treat advice received at a cocktail party, in a bar, or via a phone call. How much credence you give it should depend on how well you know the person providing it.

How Do I Get on the Internet?

A number of different things are required to get on the Internet. They are briefly covered below. If you are already connected to the Internet and understand how it works, you can bypass this section.

Access. You must have an account with an *Internet Service Provider (ISP)*. The provider could be with your company, organization, or school, or with a commercial service like America On Line (AOL), Erol's, and so on. You can also get direct satellite connection (direct PC satellite dish), but it is expensive and has a fairly high monthly cost. Regardless of how you do it, you *must* have a connection. There is no other way to access the Internet.

Hardware. While you don't need a full-flown personal computer to use the Internet, you do need a good-quality screen (17" is the current standard), a keyboard, sufficient computer memory (Intel 386 is absolute minimum), and a modem (at least 14.4 kilobits per second [Kbps], preferably at least 28.8). You do not need disk memory space to use the Internet, although without it you can't save anything. Computer manufacturers are introducing inexpensive computers called *network computers*, which can operate on the Internet (you can use your TV as a monitor with the Philips/Magnavox Web TV) but can do nothing else. They are very much like the terminals that were connected to mainframe computers before the rise of personal computers. It remains to be seen whether or not this type of Internet access will be successful.

Software. While there are a number of different types of software for the Internet, at present there are two primary Internet software packages—Netscape Navigator and Microsoft Explorer. (Oracle has one called Power Browser, but it does not seem to be used by many.) Both packages have benefits. At the time this chapter was written, Netscape is dominant, but Explorer is coming up fast. Either is a good choice.

Many commercial services come with Internet software. If you are purchasing access through a commercial service, be sure that the software is included. If it isn't, see what software the service recommends.

Time. Unless you have an express purpose and only one delineated site that you want to visit, expect to spend a lot of time on the Internet, especially at the beginning. One of the most fascinating things about the Internet, particularly the World Wide Web, is that your journey on it can take you anywhere in the world (or, in cases like the NASA sites, beyond). To do this, of course, takes a lot of time. This is not to say that you will become an Internet addict if you use it. Rather, because it is so large and growing so fast, exploring it takes time. Once you become familiar with it, however, exploration time is significantly reduced. Think of this as analogous to searching for a topic in a library. Once you know where to look, it is much easier to find what you're looking for.

Money. The cost of the Internet is a conglomeration of the costs of access, hardware, software, and time. Hardware and software obviously cost money, and time is money, at least in the sense that, if you're using the Internet, you're not doing something else. Potentially the most prohibitive cost of the Internet is the only real variable cost: access and connection-time costs. If you are gaining Internet access through a commercial service, you must pay for it. Until you know what you'll be doing with the Internet, get a service with unlimited access time. This is more expensive than the options with limited hours, but will be well worth it if you are new to the Internet. Also, make sure that you can change your service if you find you need less time.

I Now Know What the Internet Is and How to Get On It. Now What?

There are over 30 million Web sites on the Internet. According to one estimate (Baranoff, 1996, p. 23), the number of insurance companies with Web sites is doubling every 53 days. A 1995 LIMRA study found 2,200 insurance and insurance-related companies with their own Web sites. It would take considerably more space than is available in this chapter (or this book) to list and summarize all Internet sites that are related to insurance and financial services. On the other hand, it would not be too helpful merely to show you how to search the Internet (as the next section will do) without giving you some knowledge of what's there. As a compromise, some Web sites that are related to insurance and financial services will be briefly discussed. What identifies these sites for inclusion is that they are all on The American College's home page under Internet Resources. To reach this listing directly, go to *http://www.amercoll.edu/pages/level2/fspgs.htm* or click Internet Resources, then Insurance and Financial Services Web Sites. In addition to this Web site summary, a listing of Web sites, their Internet addresses (called *uniform resource locations* or *URLs),* and brief comments about what they do is included as an appendix to this chapter.

The American College (http://www.amercoll.edu) The College's Web site provides detailed information about its educational programs, certifications (CLU, ChFC, RHU, REBC) and graduate degrees (MSFS, MSM). It also contains information about the College's Gregg Center and the surrounding Delaware Valley. In addition, the College's Web site includes two forms of Internet resources: general search engines and insurance and financial services Web sites. It is an excellent resource for finding things on the Internet.

American Risk and Insurance Association or ARIA (http://www.aria.org/aria.html) This Web site provides access to relevant sources of information about risk and insurance. These include the *Journal of Risk and Insurance* in full-text form on-line, risk and insurance working papers, and other resources. ARIA also has links to especially pertinent schools (Georgia State University, the University of Georgia, the University of Texas at Austin, and the University of Pennsylvania) with programs in risk management and insurance. Of particular relevance and usefulness is this Web site's listings and linkages to news and announcements in risk management and insurance.

American Society of CLU & ChFC (http://www.agents-online.com/asclu/ index.htm) The Society's home page includes information about its mission, products, services, membership activities, news releases, and calendar of events. It also lists the American Business Ethics awards. In addition and very importantly, this Web site features questions and answers about the Society's Life Insurance Illustration Questionnaire (IQ) and Replacement Questionnaire (RQ). Agents can learn more about both questionnaires and hence can better explain their use and value to clients.

American Institute of CPCU and Insurance Institute of America (http://www.insweb.com/educator/aicpcu-iia.org) This Web site provides detailed information about the American Institute for Chartered Property Casualty Underwriters (AICPCU) and the Insurance Institute of America's educational programs and professional certification. It also contains sections on *frequently asked questions* (*FAQs* in Internet-speak) and insurance-related Web sites.

Certified Financial Planner Board of Standards (http://www.cfp-board.org/ This is the Web site of the professional regulatory agency that oversees the requirements for financial planning. This site instructs users about how to become a CFP and what is needed to retain this certification, including education, tests, experience requirements, and ethics. It also has—as many general sites do—links to related Web sites.

EINET Galaxy for Insurance (http://galaxy.einet.net/galaxy/business-and-commerce/general-products-and-services/insurance.htm) This Web site is actually a sub-site of the Galaxy search engine (*http://galaxy.einet.net*). This particular section deals exclusively with insurance. It covers related topics (providing links to other insurance-related areas such as health and medicine and finance), new topics (less than 7 days old), product and service descriptions, commercial organizations, and nonprofit organizations. Because of the nature of this site (a *category-based search engine,* to be discussed below), detailed descriptions are provided about the sites listed under these topics.

Infomanage-Investment (http://www.infomanage.com/investment/ default. htm). This site is a veritable cornucopia of investment resources. It has 14 general topics that each contain specific site links under them. These topics (and their number of links[5]) are: Exchanges on the www (55), International Stock Information (11), Financial News (7), Investment Banks, etc., (22), Venture Capital (5), Currency Rates (31), Edgar (7), Bonds (18), Futures and

---

5. As of February 26, 1997.

Options (19), Stocks and Reports/Analysis (33), Stock Quotes-Real Time/20 minutes delayed (15), Finance/Taxes (12), Computers/Technology (10), and Brokerages (4). You really can't go wrong with this site as a source on financial services, at least as a starting point.

The Insurance Agent's Online Network (http://www.agents-online.com/) This is, as its name implies, a multiple-member site that provides Web access to six organizations: AALU, ASHIA, ASCLU, GAMA, MDRT, and NALU. All six have home pages at this Web site. As is apparent from its membership, this is a very thorough source of information about life and health insurance. The Web sites of these organizations can also be reached directly by entering the following http addresses:

AALU—Association for Advanced Life Underwriting *(http://www.agents-online.com/AALU/index.htm)*

AHIA—Association of Health Insurance Agents *(http://www.agents-online.com/AHIA/ahia.htm)*

ASCLU—American Society of CLU & ChFC *(http://www.agents-online.com/ASCLU/index.htm)*

GAMA—General Agents and Managers Association *(http://gamaweb.com)*

MDRT—Million Dollar Round Table *(http://www.agents-online.com/MDRT/index.html)*

NALU—National Association of Life Underwriters *(http://www.agents-online.com/NALU/NALUhome.html)*

Insurance Companies & Resources on the Net (http://lattanze.loyola.edu/users/cwebb/insure.htm) This site lists the Web sites on the Internet that are related to insurance. These are primarily insurance company sites, but are not exclusively so. A helpful feature of this site is that it is alphabetically indexed so you don't have to go through many screens to find a particular site listing. Its only real limitation (but it is a very significant one) is that it hasn't been updated since February 4, 1996. Because, as noted above, the number of insurance and insurance-related companies with Web sites doubles every 53 days, there are about 256 times as many sites now (March 13, 1997) as there were when this site was last updated. However, it is still well worth checking. Hopefully, its developer, Chris Webb (*cwebb@lattanze.loyola.edu*), will update it soon, as the beginning paragraph of this site promises.

Insurance News Network (http://www.insure.com) This Web site updates developments in automobile, life, and home insurance. It also includes information on annuities, state regulations, and company ratings, and has an insurance glossary. Like other general sites, this one also permits access to search engines. What is most important about this site is its recent news about events that affect insurance; in addition to summarizing the news, it also provides links to the selected story as well as retaining previous news stories and news releases. It is an excellent source for background material.

InsWeb (http://www.insweb.com) InsWeb is "the Internet gateway to the insurance industry." This Web site has information for both consumers and insurance/financial services professionals. It consists of three general sections. *Consumer Information & Purchasing Center* is, as its name implies, geared toward consumers. This section contains relevant news and events, general search utilities, research information, and survey information. In addition, it allows users to get instant quotes on the cost of insurance. It also has an agent locator, which helps consumers find insurance agents in their area who can meet their particular needs. *Insurance Industry Center* is aimed at meeting the needs of professionals. It has subsections in Life and Health Insurance, Property and Casualty Insurance, What's New on InsWeb, information about and links to insurance companies, and a Weekly Tax Update. The third section is *Career Center*. This lists job opportunities in insurance and financial services. It is a good source for both the neophyte who is seeking to enter the field and the seasoned professional who is thinking about changing companies and/or locations.

LIFE: Life and Health Insurance Foundation for Education (http://www.life-line.org/site1/cgi) LIFE is a Web site aimed primarily at providing information to consumers. It contains four general sections. *Insurance 101* is an introduction to insurance concepts and terminology; it also covers the history of insurance. *Life Calculators* estimates how much insurance a person needs by asking a number of interactive questions. *Health for Life* provides a monthly digest of Internet sources that can help users maintain or improve their health and fitness. Users may subscribe to this digest, which is then sent to their e-mail address. *Facts of Life* includes information about LIFE—what it is and what it is attempting to do. One interesting feature of this site is its *Life-Line Facts*. A box on the first page shows the year-to-date payments made to policyholders by life insurance companies in the United States and Canada.

LIMRA (http://tccn.com/limra-international/home.htm) This Web site, which is available to anyone on the Internet[6] provides news and information about LIMRA and the financial services field. Its first page includes a weekly update of events at LIMRA, in the industry, and on the Internet. It also contains sections on financial services careers and a sampler of its extensive database. One very interesting section, *Hot Topic*, lists resources in LIMRA's database for conducting literature searches on special themes of interest in insurance and financial services. The "hot topic" changes weekly.

---

6. LIMRA also has a paid subscription line, LIMRA Online, which allows access to its extensive marketing research data.

LOMA (http://www.loma.org) LOMA's Web site provides extensive information about the management and operations of life and health insurance and financial services companies. Its home page contains 15 sections, concentrating on its programs and designations, education, management, and operations. Of particular interest is the *CyberTalk* section. This part of LOMA's Web site discusses developments by insurance and financial services companies on the Internet. In addition to its current topic of discussion, it has an archive of prior topics. This is a good place to look for information about how the Internet is being used in life and health insurance and financial services.

Money Personal Finance Center (http://www.moneypages.com/syndicate) This Web site, developed by the *New York Times* syndicate, deals with stocks, bonds, and mutual funds. It also has a current price index for stocks (although you must know a stock's ticker name to get a quote). This Web site also has an extensive collection of financial links on the Internet. One very useful section is *Broker's Corner*. It is specifically for stockbrokers and includes such diverse topics as CFP and CFA requirements, NASD licenses, trade magazines, information on government regulations and regulators, and marketing on the Internet.

National Association of Insurance Commissioners (http://www.naic.org/) This Web site is the place to find out about insurance regulations. It will inform you what NAIC is doing, including its committee activities, and provides an interactive map of the United States for a detailed description of the insurance commissioners (including pictures, phone numbers, and addresses). It also contains NAIC's newsletters and news releases. Inquiries about state insurance regulations should begin here.

RISKWeb (http://www.riskweb.com/). This Web site, developed and maintained by Jim Garven, focuses on helping professionals and academics in the field of risk management and insurance. It contains a search engine on its front page drawing from eight general search engines (discussed below), 17 news sources, or 19 reference materials sources. In addition, RISKWeb presents an extensive listing of links to relevant resources in risk management. You can also subscribe to RISKNet by filling in an on-line bibliographic survey. This subscription will put you on RISKNet's mailing list and, if you desire, it will enable you to receive an entire day's messages in a single digest. The mailing list feature enables the user to join in a discussion group on risk management and insurance. Give this helpful and informative resource a try. If you find that it isn't what you want, you can easily unsubscribe to it.

Society for Insurance Research (http://connectyou.com/sir/) This Web site provides rapid access to insurance research abstracts by author and by subject. It must be noted, however, that the articles are only available by purchasing them either through LEXIS/NEXIS or through SIR. For this reason, this site is probably best used to supplement other information or as a source when the information sought cannot be found anywhere else. This Web site also has an insurance career center that allows job seekers to post and edit their resume on-line and search for jobs. Employers can post jobs and search through candidates' on-line resumes. In addition, this site has a good listing of links of insurance-related home pages, broken down by topic.

Up to this point, 18 different Web sites of special interest to professionals in insurance and financial services have been examined. Perhaps you think that this covers the entire gamut of relevant Internet sites in these areas. Think again: These sites are only about 7/100 of one percent of Internet Web sites on insurance and financial services. How do you find the Web sites you want? The next section addresses this.

General Search Procedures

Because the Internet is so vast and contains such a wide array of information, it can be quite intimidating. The previous section gave brief sketches of some sites which may or may not provide users with exactly what they're looking for. There are at least 30 million pages on the World Wide Web; Usenet and Gopher probably double that number. How is one to dig through all of this information to find some that is useful and relevant?

Fortunately, the answer lies in *search engines*. These special World Wide Web sites enable the user to find documents on the Internet (and sometimes elsewhere) that address specified topics, phrases, or subjects. The Internet includes a large number of different search engines, but only a select few have gained dominance. Two of these, *Alta Vista* and *Excite*, will be covered in detail below. However, some general information about search engines and how to conduct specific searches will be discussed first.

There are two types of search engines: *category-based* and *indexed*. A category-based search engine has general areas of information, such as business, humor, computers, and so on. You select one of these categories and are presented with another set of subcategories for the one selected. For example, if you picked business, the subcategories might be stock market, transportation, health care, insurance, financial services, and so forth. The subcategory selected would lead to more sub-fields, each related to the one selected. The selection of fields continues until you find the Web sites you are looking for. In other words, the user follows a tree-like hierarchy that becomes more and more defined until he or she arrives at the Web sites that fulfill the criteria of interest.

Category-based search engines utilize reviews of Web sites that define how those sites should be categorized. Because they require defining reviews, these search engines have a smaller number of usable links. They may also be somewhat dated, depending on how many reviewers they have. They do, however, include more detailed analyses of the documents and Web sites contained within their tree structures. They are good sources for detailed and in-depth information about well-established sites and can be efficient starting points for a search. However, remember that they may be dated in their reviews and may not include new or recently revised sites.

An *indexed* search engine, on the other hand, is not bounded by the need to have sites defined and cross-referenced. This type of searcher takes a word or words you enter in the search box and seeks out Web sites that contain those search words. Alta Vista and Excite are indexed search engines. In effect, this type of search engine can find anything on the Internet. Some engines search only World Wide Web sites. Some let you choose what to search—for example, World Wide Web, Newsgroups, or Usenet classified ads. Some will search non-Internet sites. As a rule, however, the latter sites do not allow free access to their information. You must pay to access it—perhaps $1 to download a particular paper from a non-Internet site. Generally, the information from these sources is not available anywhere else.

Indexed search engines are best used either for searches that require access to the entire Internet (or its components) or to find answers to questions that cannot be categorized easily. As is to be expected with something that searches through millions of documents and billions of words, it takes some skill to tell the indexed search engines how to find precisely what you are looking for. Before considering specific search engines, some general rules of indexed searching will be discussed.

Be sure of your spelling; the Internet is quite literal and unforgiving. A simple misspelling can take you on a lengthy detour to places you're not looking for. Before launching a search, check to see that what you've put in the search box is what you want it to be.

Search engines can be case sensitive. As a rule, unless you know that what you are looking for is capitalized, use lowercase letters. This will return both uppercase and lowercase letters. Be prepared, however, to get more (sometimes a lot more) results this way. For example, an Alta Vista search for "The American College" (quotation marks will be discussed below) finds 700 documents. Exactly the same search in lowercase and without quotation marks finds over one million documents. The first search done with Excite finds 3,807 documents; the second search finds 3,285,720 documents. Despite these massive returns, use lowercase rather than uppercase. In a preliminary search, it is better to start big and whittle down to specifics.

One very worthwhile feature of both Netscape Navigator and Microsoft Explorer which is related to searches is *Bookmarks*. This feature allows you to "tag" a Web site and create a link from your computer to the site just by clicking a headline. For example, if you were using Netscape Navigator and wanted to get to The American College home page any time, you would enter *http://www.amercoll.edu* in the link box of Netscape. When the College's home page was displayed, you could click Bookmarks, then Add to Bookmarks. From that point on, when you press Bookmarks, a list of sites you want to access quickly is displayed. To get to one of these sites, highlight that site and double click the mouse button. You'll be automatically transported to that Web site.

Finally, use the KISS (Keep It Simple, Stupid) principle whenever possible. Simplicity will help you find what you want more quickly. Do not use complex (not to be confused with advanced) searches when simple ones will do.

Search Engines: Alta Vista and Excite

Two search engines will be explored here: Alta Vista and Excite. There are many others. (The *All-In-One* Web site lists all known search engines.) Alta Vista and Excite have been selected because they provide the largest amount of information and are the fastest searchers available. When you become comfortable with the Internet, experiment with different search engines and select the one(s) that best suit your needs. See the Appendix of this chapter for a listing of other search engines.

Alta Vista, Latin for "high view" or "to see high or far," is debatably the fastest of the search engines. Depending upon how busy the Internet is, Alta Vista can conduct a search through millions of Web sites in a short period (usually no more than one minute).

Alta Vista has two types of searches, simple and advanced. The simple search utilizes a word or words and finds out where they appear on Web sites throughout the Internet. Once its search is completed, it reports the results—with titles, link, and description—to your screen. Alta Vista reports how many sites it found in the search and then presents them in sets of ten. (It tends to use round numbers, rather than an exact count, when it gets a lot of "hits" in a search.)

Simple searches can contain a single word, several words, and/or phrases. When Alta Vista sees a group of words separated by white spaces, it understands that one or more of these words is the focus of the search. In other words, in a simple search, the use of the words *insurance financial services* would return any Web sites with the word "insurance" and/or "financial" and/or "services" within it. This is called the *default* **OR** *operator*. The Web sites the search finds are sorted by the frequency of occurrences of the search words, so sites containing all three words would come first, sites with two of the search words would come next, and sites with only one search word would come last. Alta Vista reads the terms from left to right, so sites containing the word "insurance" would come before "financial" and "services," "financial" would be next, then "services."

Needless to say, Alta Vista's assumption of **OR** between search words can lead to excessively large results. Fortunately, there are ways to define how you would like search terms to be treated. This is known as *gluing* words together. The easiest way is to put a specific phrase in quotes. For example, if you wanted to perform a search for financial services, list "financial services" as the search term. This tells Alta Vista that the results must contain the entire term "financial services," not just "financial" and/or "services," as in the previous example.

Another useful device is the *plus sign (+)*. This indicates that a word must be in the document found in the search. For example, the search terms +insurance "financial services" would tell Alta Vista that the word "insurance" must be in the document found and that the term "financial services" is desired, but not necessary (the **OR** assumption). If "+" was put ahead of "financial services" in this search, it would mean both the terms "insurance" and "financial services" must appear in the document.

The opposite of this is the *minus sign (–)*. Its inclusion before a word in a search tells Alta Vista that this word or term must *not* appear in the document. For example, suppose you wanted to conduct a search on all kinds of life insurance except term insurance. You would specify "life insurance" –term. This would return all documents containing the term "life insurance" but would exclude any that include the word "term."

Another useful feature of Alta Vista simple searches is the *wild card (*)*. This lets the user specify only parts of a search word. It is useful when there are spelling variations of a word (for example, "colo*r" would yield "color" and "colour"; "cantalo*" would yield "cantaloup," "cantaloupe," and "cantalope"). The wild card is also useful when you want a search to include plurals of a word without writing them out (for example, "qualit*" would yield "quality" and "qualities") or when you aren't sure of the spelling of a word (for example, "alumin*" would produce documents with the American *aluminum* and the British *aluminium*).

The wild card has some limitations. It cannot be used at the beginning of a word and must have at least three letters ahead of it. It will match from zero to five letters, in lowercase only. In other words, a search for the word "cas*" would find documents containing the words "case," "casing," "casket," and "cashier." It would not, however, find documents containing "cassette" or "castanets." Along this same line, the use of "*" can create too many matches. This will cause Alta Vista to ignore the search and return the result: **No documents match this query**.

An advanced search in Alta Vista is quite different from a simple search. It employs full *Boolean* search features. A Boolean search allows the user to give exact specifications of what is to be found. In addition, it allows the user to stipulate how the results of the search will be ranked. A Boolean search is a much easier way to generate links that are much closer to the search term.

Unlike simple searches, advanced searches require binary operators **AND**, **OR**, and **NOT** to glue words and phrases together. The +, –, and white spacing of the simple search do not apply here. Quotation marks, however, can be used in the same way.

One feature of these operators which is not available in a simple search is *NEAR*. This option is like **AND**, which specifies that the two words connected by it must both appear in a document. **NEAR** specifies that the words must appear within ten words of each other. This helps avoid the search turning up documents that coincidentally contain the cited words.

Another helpful feature of advanced search is the use of parentheses. In Boolean operations like computer programming, parentheses enable the user to give exacting specifications of what is being looked for in the search. For example, if you wanted to find growth or balanced mutual funds related to life insurance or health insurance, you could specify "mutual funds" **AND** (growth **OR** balanced) **NEAR** (life **OR** health) **AND** (insurance). This would ensure that you'd find the results you were looking for in your search.

Both simple and advanced searches in Alta Vista have extensive Help sections. To view the Help section in a simple search, click the right mouse button at the top of the Alta Vista screen. To get help for an advanced search, first click the Advanced button (second from the left on the Alta Vista screen).then click the Help button. Alta Vista, especially the advanced search, takes some getting used to, particularly if the user has no experience in programming. However, it is well worth the time spent learning it.

Another very useful search engine is Excite. This engine accesses over 50 million pages on the Internet. It is said that if you can't find it on Excite, it isn't on the Internet. Excite can be used for category-based searches or indexed searches; the indexed searches can be done with or without Boolean operators. In addition, the user may select which database to search. Excite allows the choice of World Wide Web, Web Site Reviews (category-based), Usenet Newsgroups, and Usenet Classified advertisements.[7] Excite searches utilize the same operations as previously discussed under Alta Vista, except the **NEAR** operator, which is not available.

One very useful feature of Excite is the **More Like This** option. This phrase appears to the right of each title listed in the search results. If you find that a particular document is especially what you are looking for, click on **More Like This.** Excite will conduct another search using the document as an example. This will help you find documents and Internet links that more exactly match with what you are looking for.

---

7. Alta Vista also allows the search of Newsgroups (Usenet). You must select this option before entering the words to search in the box. Alta Vista automatically defaults to searching the Internet World Wide Web.

Excite also has a **Sort By Site** feature. This will list results by the Web site in which they are contained. **Sort By Site** defines results more tightly and limits the number of times the same site will appear as the result of a search.

Excite also has an advanced search feature, although it is not nearly as sophisticated as the one in Alta Vista. Actually, the Excite advanced search enables the use of the "+" sign for words a document must contain and a "–" sign for words it must not contain. It also allows the use of Boolean operators.

Both Excite and Alta Vista will open the door for you when you decide to journey beyond a few known and specified Web sites, like those mentioned in the previous section of this chapter. In effect, Alta Vista and Excite make the entire Internet available to you. Where you go, what you see, and how you use it is up to you.

Go Forth and Ride

Don't think of the Internet as a train that already left the station and you need to catch up with it. Think of it as an conveyor belt that's always moving and can get you from one place to another more quickly.

In this chapter, you have been shown where this conveyor belt is, how it operates, where to get on it, what some of its stops are, and how to find more. Enjoy your trip!

Where Can I Find Out More?

- Robert M. Baranoff. "The Net Benefit." *LIMRA's Marketfacts* (July/August 1996), pp. 23–27.
- S.A. Batman. *Financial Planning in Cyberspace: The New Frontiers for Practice Management and Client Service.* 1996.
- Katie Hafner. "Look Who's Talking." *Newsweek* (February 17, 1997), pp. 70–72.
- Gregory Krohm. "A Survey of Insurance Industry and Regulatory Applications on the Internet." *Journal of Insurance Regulation*, Vol.14, No.4 (Summer 1996), pp. 518–548.
- S.L. Nelson. *Field Guide to the Internet.* Redmond, WA: Microsoft Press, 1995.

CHAPTER 12 APPENDIX
SELECTED WEB SITES

Search Engines

All-In-One
Address (URL): www.albany.net/allinone
Comments: Every known search engine on the Internet linked together at one site.

Alta Vista
Address (URL): www.altavista.digital.com
Comments: Possibly the fastest of the indexed search engines. Has both simple and advanced searches. Advanced searches allow for sophisticated and comprehensive searches.

EINET Galaxy
Address (URL): galaxy.einet.net
Comments: This is a good general search engine with both indexed and category-based capabilities.

Excite
Address (URL): www.excite.com
Comments: Possibly the most comprehensive search engine. Has both category-based and indexed searches. If you can't find it on Excite, it probably isn't on the Internet.

InfoSeek
Address (URL): www.infoseek.com
Comments: A good overall search engine. Has both indexed and category-based capabilities. Allows access to non-www Internet sites, including Yellow Pages search.

Lycos
Address (URL): lycos.cs.cmu.edu
Comments: A good search engine for conducting complex searches.

NLightN
Address (URL): www.nlightn.com
Comments: A good source for searching Internet Web sites and non-Web sites. Provides a great deal of information in its search results.

WebCrawler
>*Address (URL):* www.webcrawler.com
>*Comments:* A well-liked search engine from America On Line (AOL).

Yahoo
>*Address (URL):* www.yahoo.com
>*Comments:* Probably the best-known of the search engines. Primarily a category-based searcher, but also has indexed capabilities.

Insurance

American Risk and Insurance Association
>*Address (URL):* www.aria.org/aria.html
>*Comments:* One Web site for professionals and academics in insurance and risk management. RISKWeb is the other main site on this topic.

EINET Galaxy for Insurance
>*Address (URL):* galaxy.einet.net/galaxy/business-and-commerce/general-products-and-services/insurance.htm
>*Comments:* A good comprehensive content-based search engine specializing in insurance.

Insurance Agent's Online Network
>*Address (URL):* www.agents-online.com
>*Comments:* The mega-site holding the home pages of AALU, ASHIA, ASCLU, GAMA, MDRT, and NALU.

Insurance Companies and Resources on the Internet
>*Address (URL):* lattanze.loyola.edu/users/cwebb/insure.htm
>*Comments:* A comprehensive, although dated (last updated 2/4/96), guide to insurance companies and resources on the Internet.

Insurance News Network
>*Address (URL):* www.insure.com
>*Comments:* A detailed and well laid out Web site to provide information about auto, home, and life insurance, annuities, company ratings, and state laws and regulations.

Insure Market
>*Address (URL):* www.insuremarket.com
>*Comments:* A Web site run by Intuit's Quicken for personal insurance. Three general sections: quotes, insurance basics, and risk evaluation for automobiles. Lists many insurance companies and their sites.

InsWeb
- *Address (URL):* www.insweb.com
- *Comments:* Calls itself "The Internet Gateway to the Insurance Industry," and it is.

LIFE: Life and Health Insurance Foundation for Education
- *Address (URL):* www.life-line.org/site1/cgi
- *Comments:* A Web site aimed at producing an informed consumer in matters of insurance.

National Association of Insurance Commissioners
- *Address (URL):* www.naic.org
- *Comments:* There is no better place than this to find out about insurance regulations and regulators.

RISKWeb
- *Address (URL):* www.riskweb.com
- *Comments:* One main Web site (ARIA is the other one) for professionals and academics in the field of risk management and insurance.

Society for Insurance Research
- *Address (URL):* connectyou.com/sir
- *Comments:* A good source for research on insurance, but it costs money to get it. Use as a last resort if you cannot find the information you want elsewhere.

Investment/Financial Services

Bank.Net
- *Address (URL):* bank.net/home.rich.html
- *Comments:* A detailed listing and linkage Internet resource for banking and finance investment resources.

CNN Financial News
- *Address (URL):* www.cnnfn.com
- *Comments:* The Financial News Network on the Internet from Cable News Network (CNN).

EDGAR
- *Address (URL):* www.sec.gov
- *Comments:* The searchable database of the Securities and Exchange Commission. EDGAR is the Electronic Data Gathering, Analysis, and Retrieval tool of the SEC. It shows itself very well on the Internet.

Financial Times
Address (URL): www.usa.ft.com (U.S. edition)
www.ft.com/ (U.K./world edition)
Comments: A worldwide financial resource. Has both a U.S. edition and a United Kingdom and Worldwide edition.

FINdex
Address (URL): www.findex.com
Comments: A very helpful Web site for obtaining information about financial services. Includes sections on accounting and taxes, banking, insurance, investments, legal and regulatory issues, and mortgages.

FinWEB
Address (URL): www.finweb.com
Comments: This Web site provides a comprehensive listing and linkage of other Web sites dealing with economics and financial services.

InfoManage-Investment
Address (URL): www.infomanage.com/investment/default.htm
Comments: A very good index of Web sites on investment and financial services. Includes listings and linkages to most exchanges around the world and includes a section on the use of computers and technology in finance.

Money Personal Finance Center
Address (URL): www.moneypages.com/syndicate
Comments: A nice overview of monetary matters from the *New York Times* syndicate.

Trader's Financial Resource Guide
Address (URL): www.libertynet.org/~beausaug
Comments: A highly detailed Web site source for financial services information. A listing and linkage to financial service newspapers on the Internet is especially useful.

USA Today Money
Address (URL): www.USAtoday.com/money/mfront.htm
Comments: "McPaper" with fries and a Coke.

The Wall Street Journal
Addresses: www.wsj.com *or* update.wsj.com
Comments: The interactive edition of the *Wall Street Journal*. Allows users to get extensive information about finance and investments.

News and Information

Cable News Network
    Address (URL):   www.cnn.com
    Comments: The Internet version of CNN.

The Detroit News
    Address (URL):   www.detnews.com
    Comments: A well done and highly detailed newspaper from the Motor City.

New York Times Syndicate
    Address (URL):   nytsyn.com:80/website.html
    Comments: Includes ten newspapers (such as the *New York Times* and the *Boston Globe*), six information services, six magazines, and two television stations.

PathFinder
    Address (URL):   www.pathfinder.com
    Comments: Provides on-line guides to multiple journals, magazines (including *Time, Life,* and *Money)* and news services.

The Press Association News Centre
    Address (URL):   www.pa.press.net
    Comments: The British news wire service.

San Francisco Newspaper
    Address (URL):   www.sfgate.com
    Comments: Both of San Francisco's major newspapers, the *Chronicle* and *Examiner,* on-line.

USA Today
    Address (URL):   www.usatoday.com
    Comments: "McPaper" on the Internet.

The Washington Post
    Address (URL):   www.washington.post.com
    Comments: The entire *Washington Post*, including sports, classified ads, and even the comics.

Associations and Educational Sites

The American College
    Address (URL):   www.amercoll.edu
    Comments: A premiere Web site for information about the College and its programs. A very good source for information about and

access to insurance and financial services Web sites and general search engines.

American Institute of Certified Public Accountants
Address (URL): www.aicpa.org/index.htm
Comments: A very good Web site for matters related to accounting and taxation. Leads with "Hot Topics" and has both brief and detailed directories of its contents.

American Institute for CPCU and Insurance Institute of America
Address (URL): www.insweb.com/educator/aicpcu-iia.org
Comments: *The* Web site for property and casualty insurance.

The American Society of CLU & ChFC
Address (URL): www.agents-online.com/asclu/index.htm
Comments: The Web site of the Society provides information about its activities and programs. Especially helpful in explaining its IQ and RQ forms.

CFP Board of Standards
Address (URL): www.cfp-board.org
Comments: The home page of the professional regulatory organization for financial planners.

International Association of Financial Planners
Address (URL): www.iafp.org/
Comments: The Web site of financial planners (primarily for members). Has three general sections: consumer services, professional information, and member services.

LIMRA
Address (URL): tccn.com/limra-international/home.htm
Comments: The home page of the Life Insurance Marketing Research Association. Generally, an advertisement for its database Web site, which costs money to access.

LOMA
Address (URL): www.loma.org
Comments: The home page of the Life Office Management Association.

Miscellaneous

CIA World Fact Book
Address (URL): www.yahoo.com/regional/CIA_World_Factbook/
Comments: An excellent resource for information about regions and countries throughout the world. You'd be hard-pressed to

find a better place to learn about locations, their populace, and their economy.

Dilbert
Address (URL): www.unitedmedia.com/comics/dilbert/
Comments: Seen daily by millions (and worth it).

FedWorld
Address (URL): www.fedworld.gov
Comments: Everything (and more) you ever wanted to know about the federal government. This is the directory of federal Internet sites.

SwitchBoard
Address (URL): www.switchboard.com
Comments: The white pages of the Internet. If a name is in the United States phone books, it's here. Includes Internet addresses and more.

World Wide Yellow Pages
Address (URL): www.cba.uh.edu/ylowpges/ylowpges.html
Comments: The business services phone directory of the Internet.

13

ETHICS

Ronald F. Duska

What Was the Situation Before?

In one sense ethics doesn't change. Lying has always been lying, cheating has always been cheating, and scamming customers has always been scamming. New technologies and products may create new opportunities for cheating and increase the asymmetry of knowledge, thus making it easier for an agent to manipulate the behavior of a client, but such behavior violates the Golden Rule, "Do unto others as you would have them do unto you," which still reigns in ethics, along with the requirements for avoiding harm, doing good, and being fair and honest. However, with the media blitz criticizing financial services, cultures, and practices, and the immense amount of litigation directed against those in the financial services industry, a new consciousness of the necessity to do the right thing (or at least the legal thing) has been forced on the members of the financial services professions.

In the last several years a number of companies in the financial and insurance sectors have been accused of unethical practices. In some cases, companies driven by profit, with a single-minded focus on increased productivity, set up instruments and incentive and reward systems that contributed to their agents' forgetting that the primary focus of a financial services professional should be the needs of the client. In other cases, greedy agents convinced unsuspecting customers to replace policies that weren't in need of replacing, in effect skimming their clients' cash value to pay the commission on the new policies. The scandals and lawsuits that have arisen as a result of such questionable market behavior made the industry and the individuals in the industry reexamine the ethics of their practices and institute compliance programs to help avoid such missteps in the future. Hence a sense of complacency about ethics and compliance has turned into a sense of urgency with respect to determining what is right and encouraging right behavior. In this regard we should take note of four trends.

What Is the Nature of the Change?

1. Going Beyond Compliance. In the past there was a tendency to reduce ethics to mere legality. If what I was doing was legal it was acceptable, and all that was required was to follow the law. What has been recognized though is that it is important to do more than just obey the letter of the law. It is important to follow the spirit of the law. This is clear when one reflects on what the law is. The law generally is an ordinance of reason promulgated by one in authority for the common good. The law and regulations generally are not needed if the society is functioning well. But if individuals begin to harm others with their behavior or take advantage of them, violating their moral rights, the law will step in to protect those rights. The law adds public promulgation and sanctions to morality. So the law is the servant of morality, and behind any good law is a moral spirit. Ethics demands following the spirit of the law and not mere compliance with the letter of the law. For example, certain marketing practices may meet legal requirements, but if they take advantage of the customers by not fully disclosing what is necessary to make an informed decision, they are unethical.

There are, according to Lynn Sharpe Paine, two distinct approaches to ethical situations, or two solutions to correcting unethical practices—a compliance-based approach and an ethical-based approach. Since compliance means obeying the rules, in a compliance-based approach the control of the behavior comes from the rules, which are externally imposed. Conversely, in an ethics-based approach the rules are internalized and control is from within. In this case, the person is self-governed. The purposes of the two approaches are also different. While the purpose of compliance is to avoid legal violations and sanctions, the purpose of ethics is to generate responsible action. Since compliance is informed by the law it is most efficiently directed by attorneys, while ethical approaches are initiated and directed by managers. Compliance is established and enforced by education, threats, and reduced discretion, while ethical behavior is established by education, self-control, and accountability. The desired organizational result from a compliance perspective is to remain legal, while the desired result from an ethical point of view is productivity spurred on in accordance with lived ethical values.

In the long run a compliance approach "encourages indifference to the moral legitimacy of choices," and appears to be "stability insurance" for top managers. Such an approach is "unlikely to release much moral imagination, rarely addresses the root cause of misconduct, and usually doesn't seek to inspire moral commitment."

In a compliance-oriented culture we are treating the symptoms but haven't gotten to the cause of the disease. As Paine says, "Managers who define ethics as legal compliance are implicitly endorsing a code of moral mediocrity." So one of the newer lessons in ethics is to emphasize that we need to go beyond a mere compliance mentality.

2. Virtue Ethics. A second significant change is in the shift from looking at ethics as merely a set of rules, a set of do's and don'ts, to looking at ethics as a guide to how to be. In this latter view the goal is living well, or excellence in activity, which involves character development. The popular name for this approach to ethics is called virtue ethics. Instead of trying to create an ultimate set of do's and don'ts, ethicists have come to recognize that it may be more important to concentrate on the development of character traits that are dispositions to do the right thing, called virtues, as opposed to character traits that are dispositions to do the wrong thing, called vices. In this way the rules can become internalized so that rather than simply having the rule to be honest, there will be a development of the character trait of honesty. Rather than simply having the rule to look out for the best interest of one's client, there will be the character traits of fidelity, loyalty, and dedication.

But with all this emphasis on virtues and character traits, one needs to inquire, what roots of character traits are necessary? There are a variety of lists. One such list is found in the International Association of Financial Planners Code of conduct, which stresses *integrity, objectivity, fairness,* and *confidentiality.*

We will look at this list briefly. While one important aspect of integrity is honesty, and honesty is an essential character trait for being an ethical person, there is a meaning of integrity that goes beyond honesty and signifies *wholeness.* In colloquial speech we recognize such a character trait when we say people "have their act together." The earliest of philosophers and religious ethicists would have taken integrity to mean a combination of the essential virtues or character traits of *prudence, justice, temperance,* and *courage,* which were the foundational virtues, often called the "cardinal" virtues. Prudence is the first and involves knowing what is right and good as well as desiring it. Temperance is the virtue necessary for pursuing the good and right we recognize by controlling the desires and passions that tend to lead us away from that good or right. Courage is the trait that gives us the willpower to overcome the fears that keep us from pursuing the good and right. Justice gives us a necessary concern for the good of others, the virtue of being able to temper our self-interest for the sake of another. Such a virtue or character excellence feeds into the second IAFP virtue of *objectivity.*

Objectivity demands the ability to get out of oneself and put oneself in the place of another with compassion. (The Golden Rule requires objectivity.) Without the capacity to empathize with others, to see the world as others see it, ethics would be virtually impossible. Such objectivity leads to the next IAFP virtue, the virtue of *fairness.*

Fairness demands that we treat all people the same way unless there is some relevant reason for not doing so. It is obvious, of course, that fairness is almost the same as justice, the virtue that insists on treating others as they ought to be treated.

Confidentiality is not so much a character trait as a state that requires one to respect another's right to privacy, and fidelity to the good of one's client. Confidentiality means one must not only honor the client's right to privacy, but also must safeguard it, and never use information about a client in any way that would harm that client.

3. Professionalism. Beyond the virtues described in the IAFP code, we add a third concern to the ethics of financial planning: professionalism. The general argument for professionalism is that professionals have a special obligation to their clients. What are the characteristics of a professional? According to most accounts, a professional is a person working in a field that requires specialized knowledge, and that has entry and behavior requirements that are policed by the profession. Because of the professional's specialized knowledge his or her client is in a dependent position, having to trust the advice of the professional. Hence the professional has the welfare of the client in his or her hands, and an altruistic dedication to the best interest of the client is required to avoid using the client as a means to the professional's ends. In the words of Solomon Huebner, the founder of The American College:

> "In the application of that knowledge, the professional should abandon the strictly selfish commercial view and ever keep in mind the advantage of the client."

This looking out for the best interest of the client is the ultimate ethical concern.

4. Corporate Culture. There is one more important trend in the state of the art, and that is the attempt to wrestle with the question, "Why do good people do bad things?" The latest studies try to answer this question by citing the influence of the corporate culture. Here organizational behavior studies blend with ethical concerns to try to determine ways of altering behavior. It should be noted that all living things, from plants to humans, are affected by their environment, and that just as a tomato depends on good soil and enough, but not too much, sun and water if it is to flourish, so human beings depend on a good environment if they are to flourish in the aspect of their character. One of the environmental factors that has significant influence in the financial services industry is the matter of incentives. If a corporate culture rewards only productivity and takes no account of ethical behavior, it will inadvertently encourage behavior that is solely bottom-line oriented. In the financial services industry, then, this leads to the reexamination of the commission structures, the evaluation of leadership, and the emphasis on ethical training of the new agent.

What Should Be Done?

To overcome the selfish commercial view, we must cease using others merely as a means to our own ends. "Do unto others as you would have them do unto you" is still the basis of ethics. But additionally we need certain other things:

1. A well articulated sense of what is important. If companies keep pushing profit over the emphasis on the Golden Rule or a concern for the client, then the level of ethical behavior will not rise.
2. An emphasis on professionalism.
3. Leadership that "walks the talk."
4. A watchful eye on potential trouble spots.

5. Ethics-based policies, culture, and rewards and sanctions, rather than compliance-based policies and culture.
6. Commission structures need to be examined. We need to recognize that incentive programs lead people to behave in certain ways.
7. Adequate recruiting and training programs. We need to help trainees understand why certain things are unacceptable. We need role models and mentoring. Those who have succeeded by dint of hard work and honesty must show the way.

Where Can I Find Out More?

- GS 831 Ethics and Human Values. The American College.
- *Readings and Applications in Ethics for Field Managers.* The American College, 1995.
- Burke A. Christensen and Ken Cooper, eds. *The Best of Strictly Speaking.* The American College, 1995.
- Dennis M. Groner and Mary B. Petersen. *Compliance: The Life Practitioner's Practical Survival Guide,* 1995.
- Norman E. Bowie and Ronald F. Duska. *Business Ethics,* 2d ed., 1990.
- Cynthia Davidson. *The Market Conduct Handbook for Agents.* Merritt Professional Publishing, 1997.
- *Ethical Practices.* Indianapolis: Pictorial, 1994.
- *Ethics for the Insurance Professional.* Dearborn, R&R Newkirk, 1992.

14

CHARITABLE GIVING

Jennifer J. Alby

Fair-Market-Value Deduction for Gifts of Publicly Traded Stock to Private Foundations

What Was the Situation Before?

Gifts of highly appreciated securities to a private foundation have enjoyed favorable treatment in the past. For pre-1995 gifts of publicly traded long-term appreciated securities to private foundations the donor could deduct the securities' full fair market value. The special treatment for pre-1995 gifts was available to the extent the contribution, along with all prior contributions of stock in the same corporation by the donor and the donor's family, did not exceed 10 percent of the value of the corporation's outstanding stock.[1] In 1995 Congress removed the fair-market-value deduction for appreciated stock gifts to private foundations, limiting the charitable deduction to the donor's basis in the stock.

What Is the Nature of the Change?

Congress has temporarily restored the fair-market-value deduction for gifts of publicly traded stock to private foundations—but only for gifts made during the period of July 1, 1996, to May 31, 1997.[2] By print, this news will be old. However, a bill currently in Congress, HR 519, would permanently restore this provision.

What Should Be Done?

Financial service professionals must pay close attention to legislative developments regarding deductions for gifts of publicly traded stocks to private foundations so that they can inform clients of the tax consequences.

Where Can I Find Out More?

- PL 104-108. Small Business and Job Protection Act of 1996.

---

1. IRC Sec. 170(e)(5).
2. IRC Sec. 1206, Small Business and Job Protection Act of 1996.

Charitable Gift Annuity Rates Raised

What Are Charitable Gift Annuities?

Charitable gift annuities (CGAs) are often promoted by charities as a useful way for a donor to make a charitable gift while retaining an income stream that will give the donor additional retirement protection. Nonprofit organizations are able to provide an annuity income to a donor in exchange for a gift under Internal Revenue Code Sec. 501(m)(5). How this technique works is that the donor and the charity form an agreement, whereby the donor makes a donation to the charity in exchange for a life annuity backed by the assets of the charitable organization. It is not a *quid pro quo* transaction because the fair market value of the gift exceeds the present value of the life annuity. Since the life annuity is not equivalent to the lump-sum gift, the charity will receive a benefit (that is, any funds remaining from the lump-sum gift above the cost of the life annuity) at the annuitant's death. The donor is entitled to an income tax deduction at the time of the gift but must recognize income tax upon receipt of annuity payments pursuant to the annuity taxation rules.

According to the gift annuity agreement between the donor and the charity, the charity agrees to an annuity payment rate for the donor's life. The American Council on Gift Annuities (ACGA) has prescribed a set of rates to which most charities adhere. These charitable gift annuity rates are actuarially determined based on the donor's life expectancy and the applicable federal midterm rate for the current or previous 2 months (the donor can select the most favorable rate). This predetermined rate is not equal to what a commercial annuity would provide because the ACGA rates assume that the property that passes to the charity at the annuitant's death is at least 50 percent of the amount of the donated property.

How Do They Work?

After the gift annuity agreement is signed and executed pursuant to state law, the donor contributes cash or property to the charity. The donor's income tax deduction is the difference between the fair market value of the property given and the present value of the life annuity. The present value is determined by finding the annuity factor in IRS Publication 1457, Actuarial Values Alpha Volume. This amount is fully deductible within the percentage limitations of IRC Sec. 170.

Although the donor receives an income tax deduction upon transfer of the property to the charity, the donor must recognize income upon receipt of annuity payments. A portion of the payment will reflect a return of principal, which is determined by dividing the investment in the contract by the expected return. This results in an exclusion ratio, which shelters a portion of each annuity payment from tax. The investment in the contract is the lesser of the present value of the annuity or the fair market value of the property transferred. The expected return is the annual annuity amount multiplied by the donor's life expectancy.

The annuity taxation rules provide for a portion of every payment to be excluded from income tax and the remaining portion generally to be included as taxable income. However, the character of the taxable portion of the annuity could result in both ordinary income and capital gains treatment if an appreciated capital asset is contributed to the charity.[3] Although tax is avoided on any appreciation of capital gain upon transfer to the charity, a percentage of unrealized capital gain will be allocated to each annuity payment. The result is that each annuity payment may have parts that are nontaxable, parts that are taxable as ordinary income, and parts that are taxable as capital gain. If the annuitant lives beyond his or her life expectancy, each payment he or she receives will be entirely subject to ordinary income tax.

The following example illustrates the advantages of making a gift of appreciated property to a charity in the form of a charitable gift annuity:

> *Example:* Sue has $500,000 worth of publicly held AT&T stock with a tax basis of $100,000. She wants to make a gift to The American College, but she needs a guaranteed income stream. Sue is 65 years old, and the American Council on Gift Annuities provides for a 6.5 percent annuity payout rate for her life expectancy. She decides to give the stock to the College in exchange for a charitable gift annuity for her life. Sue will receive an income tax deduction of $231,830, which will be limited to 30 percent of her adjusted gross income because appreciated property is being donated (under the percentage limitations in IRC Sec. 170); carryover rules are applicable. Sue will be paid an annual annuity of $32,500 for the rest of her life, of which $2,749.50 will be tax free and the balance taxable as ordinary income and capital gain.

Charitable gift annuities appeal to individuals like Sue who have charitable aspirations, wish to avoid tax, and need a guaranteed income stream without any worries.

What Is the Nature of the Change?

The American Council on Gift Annuities has recently raised the charitable gift annuity rates. The goal of these rates is to have at least 50 percent of the gift distributed to the charity and the other half paid to noncharitable beneficiaries in the form of annuity payments. The new ACGA rates are based on an interest rate of 6.25 percent (7 percent total minus administrative costs

---

3. This is different from the tax rules for commercial annuities, which do not include a capital gain element.

of .75 percent). The old rates were based on an interest rate of 5.5 percent. The new rates are also based on new mortality assumptions.

The following example illustrates the use of the new rates:

> *Example:* Assume the same facts as in the example above. Sue, who is 65 years old, has $500,000 worth of publicly held AT&T stock with a tax basis of $100,000. She wants to make a gift to The American College but needs a guaranteed income stream, so she decides to give the stock to the College in exchange for a charitable gift annuity for her life. Now the American Council on Gift Annuities provides for a 7.2 percent annuity payout rate for Sue's life expectancy. In this scenario, Sue will receive an income tax deduction of $202,950, which is $28,880 less than it was using the old ACGA rates. This represents about $11,436 in tax savings. This deduction will again be limited to 30 percent of Sue's adjusted gross income, and the carryover rules are still applicable. Sue will receive an annual annuity payment of $36,000 for the rest of her life; $3,045 will be tax free, and the balance will be taxable as ordinary income and capital gain. This annual payment is $3,500 greater than payments under the old ACGA rates.

As you can see, the tax deduction in this example is less than in the previous example. However, the income Sue receives each year is several thousand dollars greater, which will more than make up for the tax savings lost.

Charitable gift annuities are devices that require relatively little planning from the donor's perspective, while providing a lifetime retirement benefit and ultimately making a gift to charity. The advantage of creating a CGA now is that the new rates enable CGAs to better compete with other fixed investment vehicles.

What Should Be Done?

Congress responded to challenges to charitable gift annuities with the Charitable Gift Annuity Antitrust Relief Act of 1995 (P.L. 104-63) and the Philanthropy Protection Act of 1995. These acts removed charitable gift annuities from antitrust scrutiny and limited the applicability of securities laws to charitable organizations.

Some states continue to have stringent rules for charities offering charitable gift annuities. These states regulate reserve limits, have investment requirements, and may require a permit to issue CGAs.[4] These regulations

---

4. See California Insurance Code Sec. 11420 *et seq.* and New York Consolidated Laws Sec. 1110 *et seq.*

make it difficult for the charity to provide even a moderate payout when chances are fairly good that investment performance will not yield much of a remainder interest. Since the charity backs the annuity payments with corporate assets, if the charity cannot earn enough to pay the annuity and principal is depleted, the charity may receive nothing at the donor's death. Thus the risks to the charity are lower than expected investment returns and annuitants outliving their life expectancy.

Financial service professionals should familiarize themselves with both federal and state regulations on charitable gift annuities and monitor any changes in these regulations or in the ACGA rates.

Where Can I Find Out More?

- "New Rates for Gift Annuities," *Planned Giving Today,* January 1997, vol. 8, no. 1.
- *Taxwise Giving,* January 1997.
- NumberCruncher Software. (610) 527-5216.
- PG Calc Software. (617) 497-4970.

Charitable Planning with S Corporation Stock

What Was the Situation Before?

Many small corporations have opted to make the subchapter S election to take advantage of pass-through taxation while enjoying limited liability. Generally, in order to qualify as an S corporation, an entity must, among other requirements, have only individual shareholders (with some exceptions, not including a charity or charitable trust). If a charity is a shareholder, the corporation loses its S corporation status and becomes a C corporation. This presents a problem for owners of S corporation stock who wish to make a contribution to charity and avoid capital gain.

What is the Nature of the Change?

The Small Business Job Protection Act of 1996[5] provides among other things that beginning in the year 1998, charities will be eligible owners of S corporation stock pursuant to IRC Sec. 1361 (c)(7). The good news is that this gives small business owners who own stock in such corporations the opportunity to make charitable contributions of S corporation stock. This stock is often the largest assets these shareholders own. The downside is that an S corporation's income and losses will flow through to the charity shareholder, resulting in unrelated business taxable income. For a more detailed description of this change see chapter 3, "Business Planning."

---

5. Public Law 104-188 (August 20, 1996).

What Is Unrelated Business Taxable Income?

Generally, an exempt organization receives tax-exempt treatment only if its primary purpose is to engage in the type of activity that qualified it for the exemption. Exempt organizations may operate trades or businesses that further their exempt purpose. If the trade or business is outside the scope of its exempt purpose, however, the exempt organization may be subject to income tax for any income earned from the unrelated business.[6]

The irony is that when a charity owns nondebt-financed real estate, any income earned on the real estate is not deemed to be unrelated business taxable income. However, if an S corporation owns real estate and the charity owns shares of the S corporation's stock, the same income generated by the real estate will be unrelated business taxable income to the charity.

What Should Be Done?

Financial planners should be alert to the potential benefits of charitable deductions of S corporation stock, particularly in situations where the disadvantages to the charity, as described above, can be minimized.

Where Can I Find Out More?

- For more information contact The American College Development Division. (610) 526-1000.
- PL 104-188. Small Business Job Protection Act of 1996.

Charitable Planning with Qualified Plan Assets

What Was the Situation Before?

Prior to January 1, 1997, individuals who took distributions from qualified plans or individual retirement accounts were subject to a 15 percent excise tax on the amount in excess of the threshold distribution indexed for inflation. This 15 percent tax proved to be a *dis*incentive for the people who wanted to take large distributions during life.

A qualified plan or IRA is also subject to a 15 percent excise tax on excess accumulations at death. The result is a double-edged sword. If an individual does not take distributions and recognize excise tax on excess distributions during life, he or she dies with the excise tax on the accumulation at death. The 15 percent excise tax applies even when the amount is given to a charity.

---

6. For an example of the devastating effect, see *Newhall Unitrust v. Comm'r.*, Docket #95-7051 (9th Cir. 1/23/97).

What Is the Nature of the Change?

The 3-year moratorium on the excise tax (effective for taxable years 1997 through 1999) for excess distributions from qualified plans or IRAs may entice some people to do some charitable planning. (See "The 15 Percent Excise Tax Moratorium—Should You Bite?" in chapter 5.)

What Should Be Done?

Financial services professionals should examine the options carefully. Also see "Estate Planning for Retirement Benefits, chapter 2, in which we examined the multilayer tax impact on qualified plans and IRAs includible in a decedent's estate.

Suppose, in our example in chapter 2, Mrs. Adams named her children as beneficiaries of her $2 million IRA. The tax consequences on her $6 million estate result in the following taxes:

Federal estate tax	$2,173,203
State death tax	492,940
Excise tax on excess accumulations	148,831
Income tax (income in respect of a decedent)	472,038
Total taxes	$3,287,012
Balance to heirs	$2,712,988
Percentage to heirs	45%

In the above scenario, Mrs. Adams left the IRA to her children. The problem is that the children must recognize income tax because the property has income in respect of a decedent (IRD). Therefore, an alternative plan may be to leave a charity an asset with IRD and to transfer non-IRD assets to heirs. The charity will not recognize income tax because it is a tax-exempt entity. Likewise, the children will not recognize any income tax because they will receive assets that do not carry income in respect of a decedent.

Option 1. Assume that Mrs. Adams leaves her $2 million IRA to The American College and the balance of her gross estate of $6 million to her two children. The children will not recognize income tax and Mrs. Adams's estate will receive a charitable deduction for the full value of the IRA passing to the College pursuant to IRC Sec. 2055. Unfortunately, the 15 percent excise tax on excess accumulations will still apply to the $2 million IRA left to the College (the 3-year moratorium applies only to excess distributions; excess accumulations continue to be subject to the 15 percent tax).

The taxes for her estate and her IRA are as follows:

Estate Tax Calculation

Gross estate	$6,000,000
Excise tax deduction	148,831
Charitable deduction	2,000,000
Taxable estate	$3,851,169
Tentative federal estate tax	1,758,943
Unified credit	(192,800)
State death tax credit	(264,922)
Net federal estate tax	$1,301,221

Total Taxes

Federal estate tax	$1,301,221
Assumed state death tax	264,922
Excess accumulations tax	148,831
Income tax	0
Total taxes	$1,714,974
Estate remaining after taxes	$2,285,026
Percentage of estate passing to heirs	38%

Although less money will pass to Mrs. Adams's heirs, less will also pass to the government. Thus, a philanthropically minded individual who plans on giving assets to a charitable organization at death may opt for this plan.

Option 2. Because the 3-year moratorium on the 15 percent excise tax applies only to excess distributions and not to excess accumulations, there may be a greater incentive to set up a charitable remainder trust (CRT) to begin removing the accumulation and thereby avoid both excise taxes. This planning opportunity involves taking a lifetime distribution from the qualified plan or IRA and making a net after-tax contribution to the CRT.

A charitable remainder trust is an irrevocable trust that will be income tax exempt if drafted properly pursuant to IRC Sec. 664. The donor will receive an immediate income tax charitable deduction for the present value of the remainder interest that will eventually pass to charity. This will help offset the income tax on the distribution from the plan. With the 3-year moratorium on the excise tax on excess distributions, an individual can take distributions without being subject to the excise tax. This option may be a good one for a person who is at or near age 70 1/2 and will not be able to take advantage of additional deferrals.

A charitable remainder trust can be an annuity trust or a unitrust. The main difference between the two is that annual payments in an annuity trust must be at least 5 percent of the *initial* value of the trust, while in a unitrust payments must be at least 5 percent of the value *determined annually*. The unitrust percentage is based on the increase in corpus due to investment growth.

The donor of the charitable remainder trust may retain the right to receive income for life or for a term of years not to exceed 20, and he or she may also designate others as income beneficiaries. The trustee of the CRT will make distributions of the payout amount to income beneficiaries, who will have to recognize income tax on those distributions. Distributions made to beneficiaries are taxed under a tier system pursuant to IRC Sec. 664. Essentially, a distribution to a beneficiary is taxed as ordinary income to the extent that the trust has ordinary income in the current year and undistributed ordinary income from prior years. Thereafter, the distribution is taxed as capital gain to the extent the trust has realized capital gains form prior years. Any excess amount of the distribution is tax free to the beneficiary.

Suppose that instead of naming The American College as the beneficiary of the qualified plan, Mrs. Adams decides to fund a charitable remainder unitrust (CRUT) by taking a $2 million lump-sum distribution from her IRA. She recognizes income tax of $688,000 on the distribution, but she does not recognize excise tax because of the 3-year moratorium. She makes a contribution to the charitable remainder trust of the net after-tax amount of $1,312,000. This contribution to the trust generates an income tax deduction for the present value of the remainder interest of $769,134, which passes to the College at her death. Mrs. Adams will receive an income payout of 6 percent from the trust.

Assume for purposes of the following calculation that Mrs. Adams dies in the year of the distribution and does not have the advantage of receiving *any* income from the CRT. The taxes for her estate and her IRA are as follows:

Tax on Distribution from IRA

Income tax on the IRA (assume 34.4% income tax rate on lump-sum distribution of $2 million due to 5-year averaging)	$688,000
Excise tax on excess distribution	0

Tax Deduction for Transfer to CRUT

Net after-tax amount contributed to a CRUT	$1,312,000
Income tax charitable deduction (assume the entire amount is deductible in current year)	$769,134

Estate Tax

Gross estate (includes $304,577—the income tax saved by the charitable deduction)	$4,304,577
Tentative federal estate tax	2,308,317
Unified credit	(192,800)
Credit for state death tax	(313,713)
Federal estate tax	$1,801,804

Total Taxes

Federal estate tax	$1,801,804
Assumed state death tax	313,713
Excess accumulations tax	0
Income tax	688,000
Total taxes	$2,803,517
Estate remaining after taxes	$3,196,483
Percentage of estate passing to heirs	53%

(Note: This calculation assumes death occurs in the year of distribution. If Mrs. Adams survives additional years, the estate will appreciate. Likewise, Mrs. Adams will receive annual income payments from the CRUT that will be subject to income tax in accordance with the four-tier system.)

Option 3. Now suppose that Mrs. Adams wants to give her children additional income at her death but also wants to benefit The American College. She decides to name a testamentary CRT as beneficiary of her IRA at death. Her children will be the income beneficiaries for their lives, and The American College will receive the remainder interest. The trust will pay out 6 percent of the income it earns to the two children for the rest of their lives. Assume that one child is 51 years old, and the other is 46. The College will receive the remaining principal at the death of the surviving child.

The tax consequences are as follows:

Estate Tax Calculation

Gross estate	$6,000,000
Excise tax deduction	148,831
Estate tax charitable deduction	291,140
Taxable estate	$5,560,029
Tentative federal estate tax	2,698,816
Unified credit	192,800
State death tax credit	458,003
Federal estate tax	$2,048,013

Total Taxes

Federal estate tax	$2,048,013
Assumed state death tax	458,003
Excess accumulations tax	148,831
Income tax	0
Total taxes	$2,654,847
Total reduction of estate ($6,000,000 minus $291,140 minus all taxes)	$3,054,013
Percentage of estate passing to heirs	51%

Option 3 saves the estate $160,127 in federal estate and state death taxes over the initial plan. What's more, there will be no income taxes on the IRA until Mrs. Adams's children receive their annual payments from the CRT. The present value of the payments they will receive during their lifetimes is $1,708,860.

Where Can I Find Out More?

- *Charitable Giving and Solicitation,* October 16, 1996.
- Leimberg's Pension and Excise Tax Calculator. (610) 527-5216.
- PG Calc Software. (617) 497-4970.
- NumberCruncher Software. (610) 527-5216.

15

GAAP VERSUS SAP:
CRITICAL INFORMATION FOUND IN FINANCIAL STATEMENTS

Charles S. Di Lullo

Differences in Principles, Objectives, and Audiences

The financial statements for life insurance companies differ substantially from those of other businesses. The reason for such differences is due to the application of statutory accounting principles (SAP) in the preparation of life insurance financial statements versus generally accepted accounting principles (GAAP) that are applied to the financial statements of other types of businesses.

Differences also exist within life insurance companies themselves. These differences are found in whether a particular life insurance company is a stock company or a mutual company. A stock company has stockholders to whom the board of directors and management must account, whereas a mutual company must account to its policyholders who are in fact the owners of the company. (See figure 15-1.) Different presentation approaches exist in support of these two different types of accountabilities.

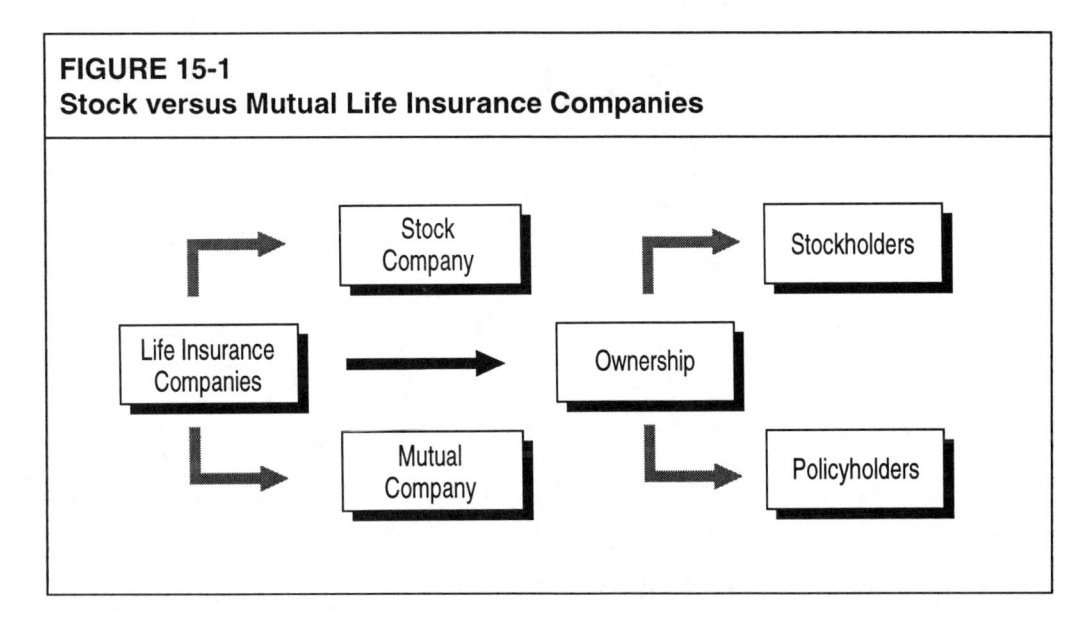

FIGURE 15-1
Stock versus Mutual Life Insurance Companies

Life Insurance Companies → Stock Company / Mutual Company → Ownership → Stockholders / Policyholders

The objectives, audiences, and structure associated with the formation and dissemination of GAAP versus SAP are also substantially different. (See figure 15-2.)

GAAP is concerned with the measurement of economic activities, the time when such measurements are made and recorded, the proper disclosures surrounding these economic activities, and the preparation and presentation of summarized economic activities in financial statements. The resulting financial statements are prepared and presented in published or unpublished reports issued by a company along with other pertinent information, and/or they are reflected in financial reports audited and issued with a related opinion by an external CPA—either an individual or a firm. The audiences that GAAP-prepared financial statements generally serve are investors, creditors, prospective investors, security and exchange commission, company management and board, company employees, and various financial and security analysts.

SAP is concerned with the methods and measurements of reflecting the degree of solvency or the amount of asset coverage that a life insurance company must have to meet the present and future claims on such assets. In addition to the reports issued by a company and/or the related audited CPA report as issued under GAAP, a life insurance company under SAP must submit to the state a statutory financial report. The audiences that SAP-prepared financial statements serve, in addition to those served by GAAP, are state insurance regulators, rating agencies, prospective policyowners, and company agents. SAP has the additional requirement over GAAP of satisfying within its financial statements the state regulatory authorities.

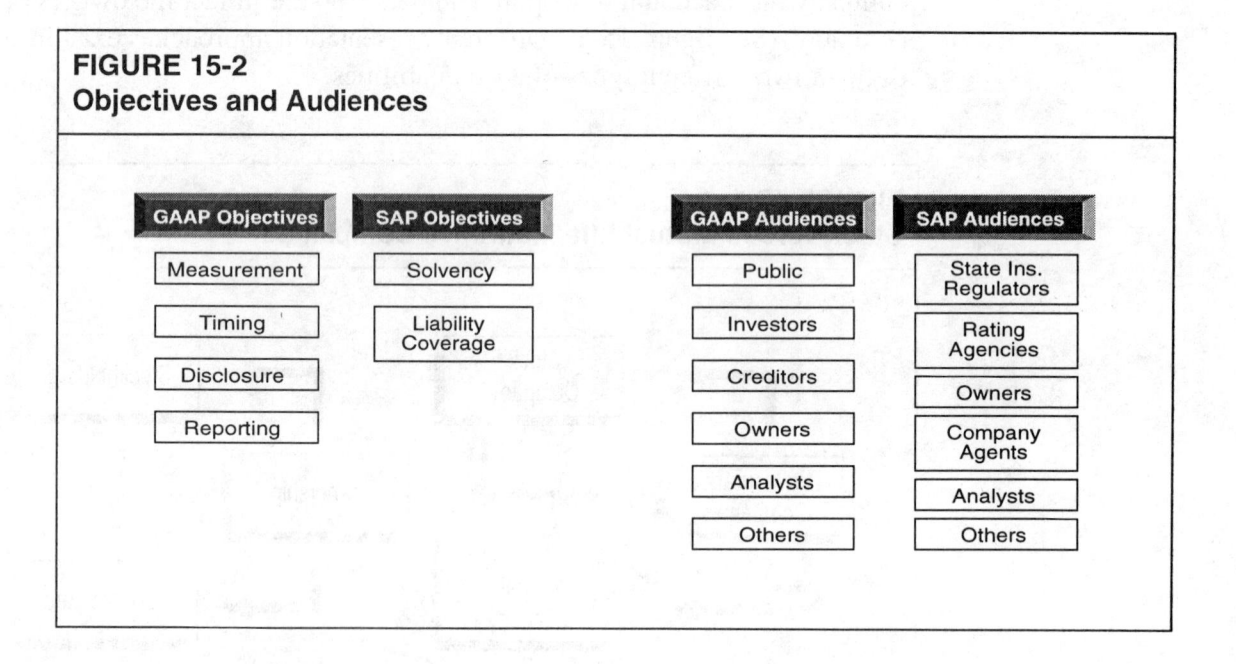

FIGURE 15-2
Objectives and Audiences

GAAP Objectives	SAP Objectives	GAAP Audiences	SAP Audiences
Measurement	Solvency	Public	State Ins. Regulators
Timing	Liability Coverage	Investors	Rating Agencies
Disclosure		Creditors	Owners
Reporting		Owners	Company Agents
		Analysts	Analysts
		Others	Others

The Beginnings and its Evolution

The evolution of GAAP over the years has been from a number of different sources, such as industry practices, professional opinions and pronouncements, and professional publications. Currently, the primary body that oversees existing principles and issues new or revised principles is the Financial Accounting Standards Board (FASB). It is the successor of the old Accounting Principles Board (APB) that came into existence in 1959 and issued its first opinion in 1962. The APB consisted exclusively of CPAs who provided their time and efforts on a voluntary basis. The FASB has a wider and more diversified financial disciplines representation of its members, and they are compensated for their responsibilities.

SAP had its origin in 1875 when the first annual statement was adopted by the National Association of Insurance Commissioners (NAIC). This statement, commonly referred to—even today—as the blank or blue blank statutory report, must be filed in each state where an insurance company is licensed to do business. The reporting requirements for SAP, unlike GAAP, are established by each state's legislature. The state's insurance department interprets and enforces the state's statutory requirements. The NAIC, which consists of membership from various state insurance departments, has as one of its objectives the fostering of uniformity in the recording requirements among the various states.

In the early 1970s, both the Security and Exchange Commission (SEC) and the American Institute of Certified Public Accountants (AICPA) had concerns relative to the different recording requirements being established by the various states. This resulted in the AICPA developing GAAP requirements for insurance companies. These requirements were restricted to those insurance companies who were stock companies, since they were similar to other types of corporations. They did not address mutual life insurance companies. Supposedly, the formulation of GAAP requirements for mutual life insurance companies is currently being deliberated. Stock companies issue two reports, a SAP report for the state and a GAAP report for all other purposes; mutual companies issue only a SAP report.

Underlying Concepts

The principles supporting GAAP versus SAP requirements are totally different. GAAP's objective is the reporting of a company's financial status and results of operations for a specified period. SAP's objective is to reflect the degree of solvency and asset coverage needed to meet a company's current and future liabilities. (See figure 15-3.)

The underlying concepts supporting GAAP fall into nine basic principles. Each represents a component of the building blocks applicable to accomplishing the overall objective of GAAP. (See figure 15-4.) Those concepts are

- *Relevancy*: reflection of the useful data on financial statements that affects or is directly associated with the process of making pertinent financial decisions

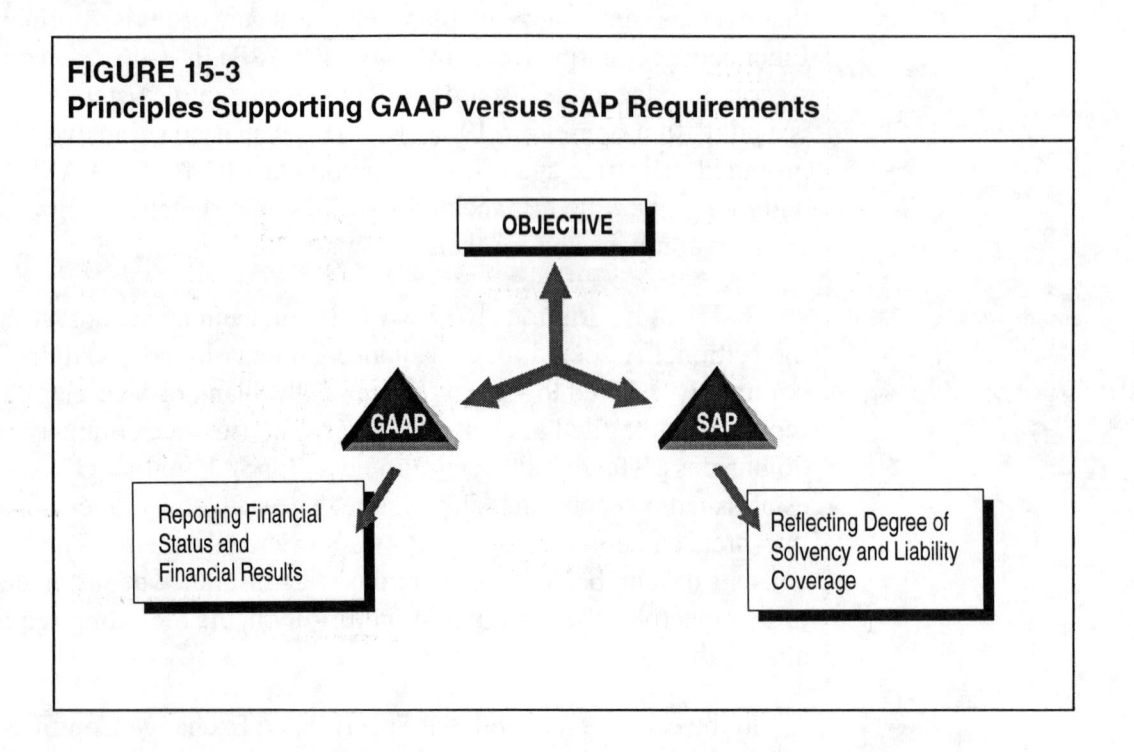

FIGURE 15-3
Principles Supporting GAAP versus SAP Requirements

[Diagram: OBJECTIVE at top, with GAAP triangle leading to "Reporting Financial Status and Financial Results" and SAP triangle leading to "Reflecting Degree of Solvency and Liability Coverage"]

- *Uniformity*: consistency in the accounting practices within and across different businesses for enhanced understanding and for viable comparative analysis
- *Consistency*: application within a business of similar accounting practices over time for appropriate comparative analysis of performance in one year as compared with another
- *Accrual*: recognition of revenues and expenses in the accounting period when earned or incurred versus the period received or paid
- *Cost*: conservation of the initial exchange price for an asset, liability, or capital, and maintaining such price as the historic cost basis
- *Conservatism*: if necessary, understating rather than overstating net income or net assets; in other words, never anticipate profits and always provide for losses
- *Materiality*: disclosure of events that are of relative importance to a business's performance and for understanding its financial statements
- *Monetary Unit*: reflection of only those transactions of economic activities or occurrences that can be measured in monetary terms
- *Going Concern*: assumption that a business will remain in existence indefinitely

Under SAP the underlying principle is liquidity. All financial data is recorded on a cash basis. All transactions are reflected on a liquidation value basis (current market value).

FIGURE 15-4
GAAP Principles

- Relevancy
- Going Concern
- Uniformity
- Monetary Unit
- GAAP Principles
- Consistency
- Accrual
- Materiality
- Cost
- Conservatism

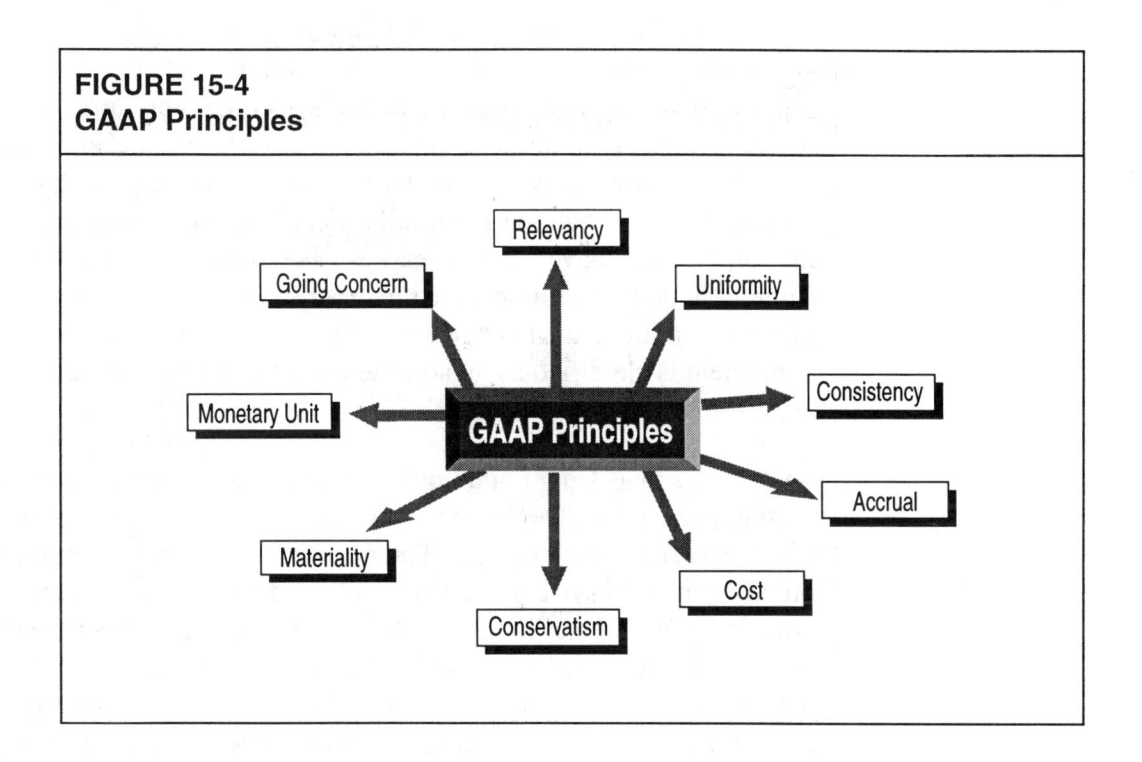

Critical Differences

The critical differences between GAAP and SAP are found in their underlying principles. GAAP concentrates on matching revenues and expenses (accrual concept); SAP utilizes cash-base accounting. GAAP focuses primarily on the income and cash-flow statements; SAP focuses on the balance sheet and emphasizes solvency. (See figure 15-5.)

Under SAP accounting, both admitted and nonadmitted asset accounts and ledger and nonledger accounts exist. (See figure 15-6.) Conversely, under GAAP accounting no such difference exists.

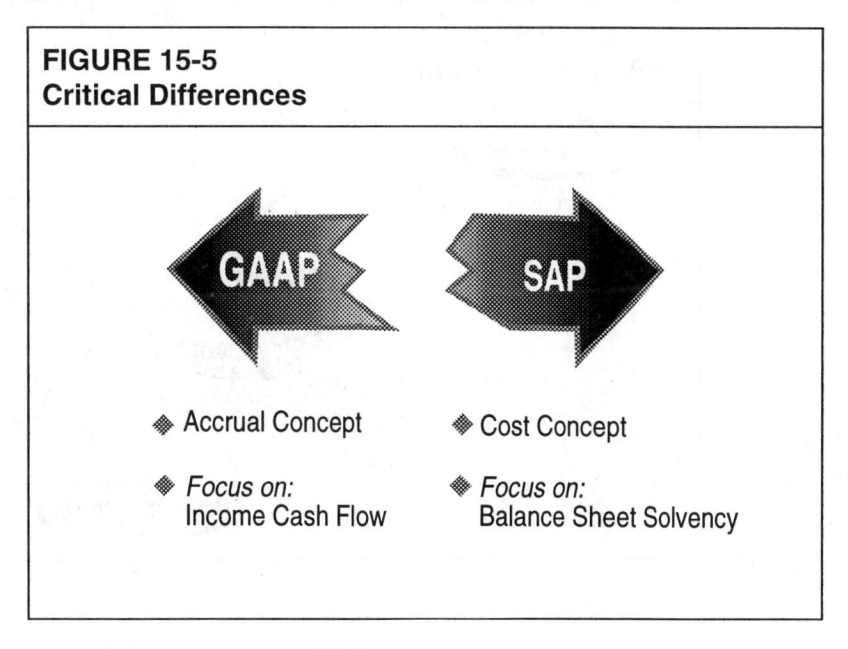

FIGURE 15-5
Critical Differences

GAAP ← → SAP

- Accrual Concept
- Focus on: Income Cash Flow

- Cost Concept
- Focus on: Balance Sheet Solvency

Admitted assets are reflected on an insurance company's annual statement. These assets concern themselves with both revenue and expense accounts that are directly associated with a company's product premiums, investments, and related product benefit cost. Nonadmitted assets are not reflected on the annual statement. They fall into two categories: those partially admitted and those entirely nonadmitted. Partially admitted assets, as an example, include investments that have a lower market value than their current book value. Entirely nonadmitted assets are those acquired in carrying out the normal process of doing business, such as furniture, most equipment (computer equipment is classified as an admitted asset), and amounts advanced to agents against future commissions.

SAP also has ledger and nonledger accounts, a difference that does not exist under GAAP. The ledger accounts are those that are maintained on a cash-basis accounting system. The nonledger accounts are those that are not on the cash-basis system but are maintained on a separate worksheet and are not part of the general ledger. Unlike the nonadmitted assets, the nonledger accounts are reflected on the annual statement. To keep the ledger and nonledger accounts in balance on the general ledger, a balancing account is maintained as a ledger account, which could be considered a composite total of all of a company's nonledger accounts.

The application of the underlying principles supporting both GAAP and SAP to their related financial statements affects the "what, how, and why" of those statements. To find and properly interpret the critical information in those statements, it is important to understand what they reflect, how they can be used to help a business attain its objectives (financial and other), how the underlying principles impact various methods of data presentation, and what tools and techniques are available to extract information needed to understand the why of what occurred, which will help any decision process and related action plan.

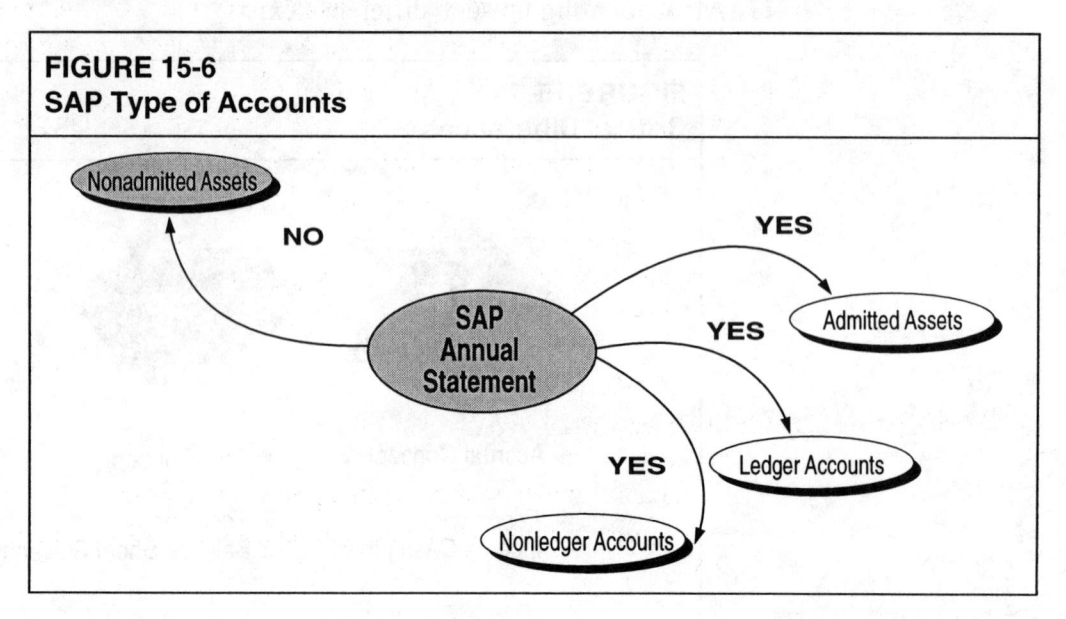

FIGURE 15-6
SAP Type of Accounts

The preparation of financial statements is an art. Many different methods of presenting financial data are both available and legitimate. The art must be understood so that proper interpretation of such data can be made.

The objectives supporting the preparation of financial statements can have a dramatic impact on the "what, how, and why" of the information presented. Statements can be prepared for different audiences, under different bases, utilizing different methods, or with different goals. (See figure 15-7.)

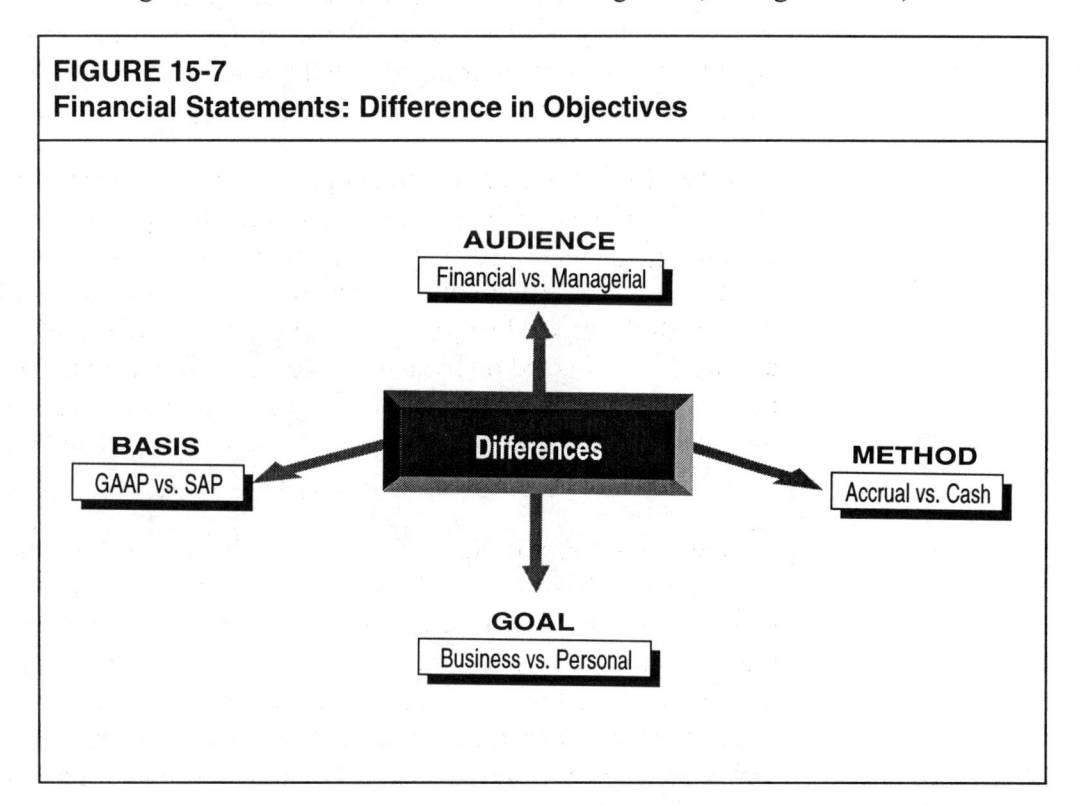

FIGURE 15-7
Financial Statements: Difference in Objectives

- Different audiences (such as external audited statements for investors and creditors versus internal detailed statements for management to utilize in evaluating a business plan)
- Different bases (such as GAAP versus SAP statements)
- Different methods (such as the accrual method for business purposes versus the cash method for tax purposes)
- Different goals (such as the presentation of a company's financial status and results of operations under a going concern concept versus personal financial statements that are based on current market value)

Basic Financial Statements

The basic financial statements applicable to both GAAP and SAP are the balance sheet, the income statement, and the cash-flow statement. (See figure 15-8.)

FIGURE 15-8
Types of Financial Statements

BALANCE SHEET:
Liab. + Equity = *Assets*

INCOME STATEMENT:
Revenues − Expense = *Profit/Loss*

CASH FLOW STATEMENT:
Cash from Operations + Investments + Financing

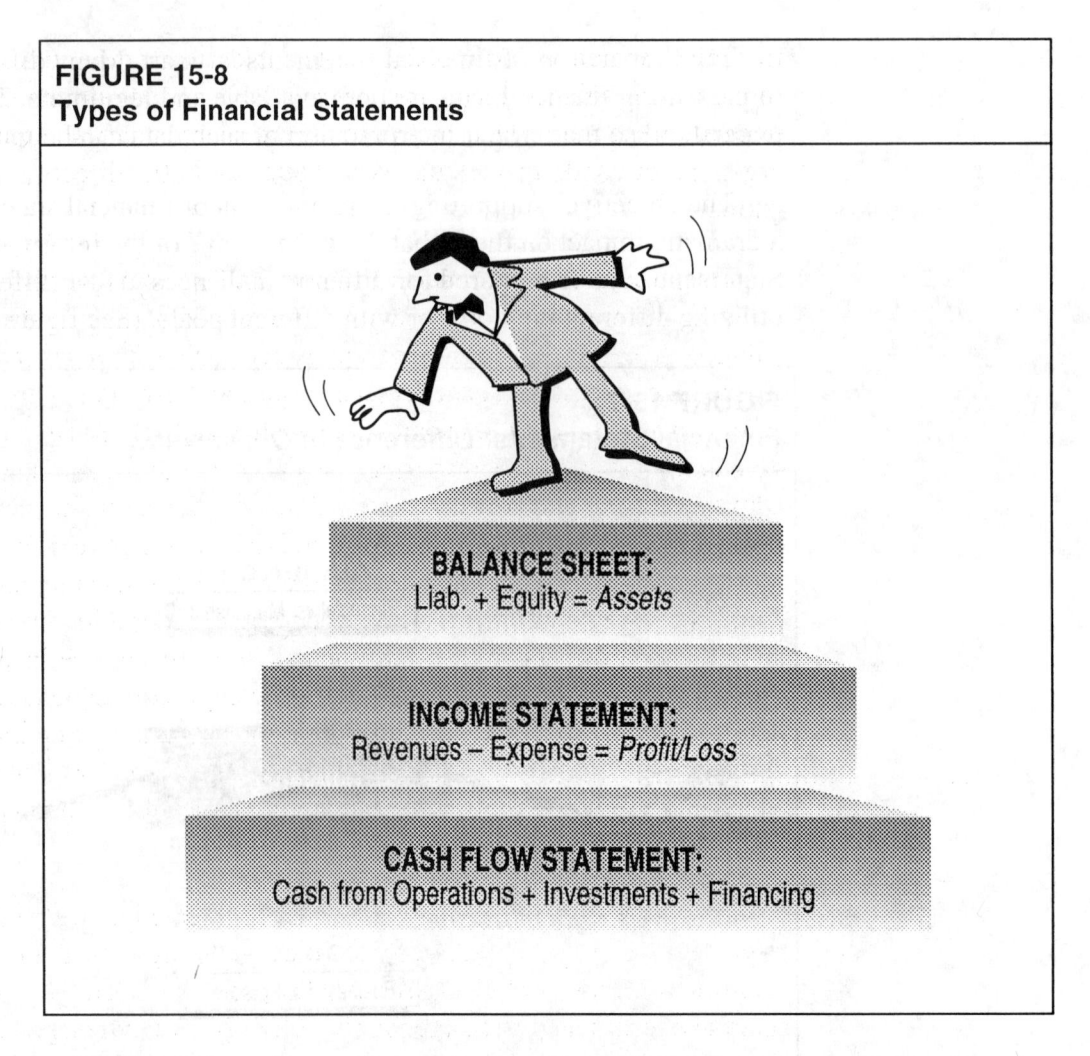

The balance sheet reflects a business's financial status at a point in time, that is, on a particular date such as December 31. Included within the statement are all business assets, liabilities, and equity. The strength of the financial status will depend on the type and related funding of the business's assets. Such funding is either by debt or by equity.

The income statement reflects the results of operations for a period of time, such as January 1 through December 31. The statement accounts for all revenues earned and expenses incurred during the period being measured. The results of operations (a business's profit or loss) will depend on whether revenues exceed expenses, which is a profit, or expenses exceed revenues, which is a loss.

The cash-flow statement reflects, by using both the balance sheet and income statement, a business's overall increase or decrease in cash over a specified period of time. The statement accounts for the sources and uses of cash from three different perspectives. The first perspective is from operations, which is extracted from the income statement and the working capital (current assets minus current liabilities) found on the balance sheet. The next perspective is from investments, the acquisition and/or disposal of long-term assets found on the balance sheet. The final perspective is from financing, which includes both long-term debt and equity transactions also found on the balance sheet. The statement is an excellent management evaluation tool. It reflects a cash basis, the sources of cash available to an organization, and, through the uses of such cash, the direction management is taking.

The structure of the financial statements for GAAP versus SAP differs according to the type of accounts that are reflected on each statement. The balance sheet under GAAP generally is divided between current assets (cash, marketable securities, accounts receivables, and inventory) and long-term assets (property, plant, and equipment) whereas SAP assets, in addition to cash and marketable securities, are reflected mainly as invested assets, other admitted assets, deferred due, accrued income, and separate account assets. Invested assets are those assets that produce income in the form of interest, rent, dividends, and capital gains. Other admitted assets include electronic data-processing equipment, reinsurance ceded, federal income tax recoverable, and other items that can be established as necessary by the insured. Deferred, due, and accrued income consist of investment income due and accrued, and deferred and uncollected premiums on policies in force. Separate account assets are those assets that are maintained apart from a company's general accounts. They are usually invested in nonguaranteed insurance products and/or employee benefit plans.

Liabilities under GAAP are generally segregated by current accounts payable, taxes payable, accrued liabilities, and long-term debt payable. SAP liabilities include nonledger accounts for policies currently in force or policies that have terminated with a remaining liability, policy reserves, amounts on deposit, claims incurred but not yet paid, dividend liabilities, accrued expense other than claims, unearned income, and amounts temporarily held for disposition.

Equity under GAAP usually consists of capital stock, retained earnings, and any capital surplus or paid-in capital accounts. Under SAP there is capital stock for stock companies and surplus for both stock and mutual companies. Surplus usually consists of contributed surplus for the excess over par value on issued capital stock, special surplus for reserves applicable to general contingencies, and unassigned surplus, which represents accumulated operating and other earnings.

The income statement under GAAP reflects the revenues and related costs associated with a company's operating and other activities. Similarly SAP reflects the revenues or income from insurance contracts and/or net income from investments, and expenses for policy benefits, policy reserves costs, commissions, general expenses, taxes, and policy dividends.

The Why and What of Evaluation

Financial statements can be evaluated for a number of reasons that include but are not limited to evaluation of performance, evaluation of stability, evaluation for identifying funding sources, evaluation for identifying debt collateral, evaluation for investment, and evaluation for determination of a business's worth. (See figure 15-9.)

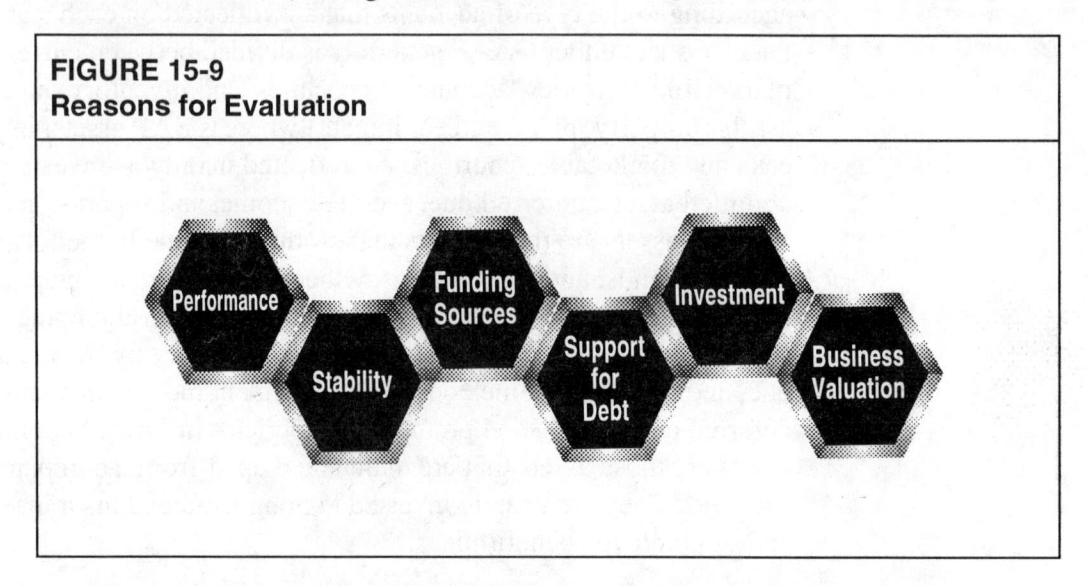

FIGURE 15-9
Reasons for Evaluation

Performance • Stability • Funding Sources • Support for Debt • Investment • Business Valuation

A number of different evaluation tools are available to analyze and understand GAAP-prepared financial statements. Such tools as common-size analysis, trend analysis, ratio analysis, break-even analysis, and even a number of external publications are available. (See figure 15-10.)

Common-size analysis is a tool that converts dollars to percentages and relates the components of total assets to the individual asset accounts, total liabilities and equity to the individual liabilities and equity accounts, and net sales to the individual revenue and expense accounts. Its advantages are that percentages are easier to work with than absolute dollars, and that it eliminates any differences in overall dollar size of two companies that are being compared.

Trend analysis is also a percentage statement. It identifies a base year as 100 percent and relates each successive year's percentages as a relationship of each account to the base year. Its advantage is that it reflects the impact of inflation and other external factors on profitability and growth. Ratio analysis provides a series of specific ratios that measures different components of a business for comparison with prior performance, other businesses, or industry averages. Such ratios can measure liquidity, capital structure, returns on investment, asset utilization, and market performance. Break-even analysis is another tool that can assist in determining the break-even point for proposed products or projected courses of action.

**FIGURE 15-10
Evaluation Tools**

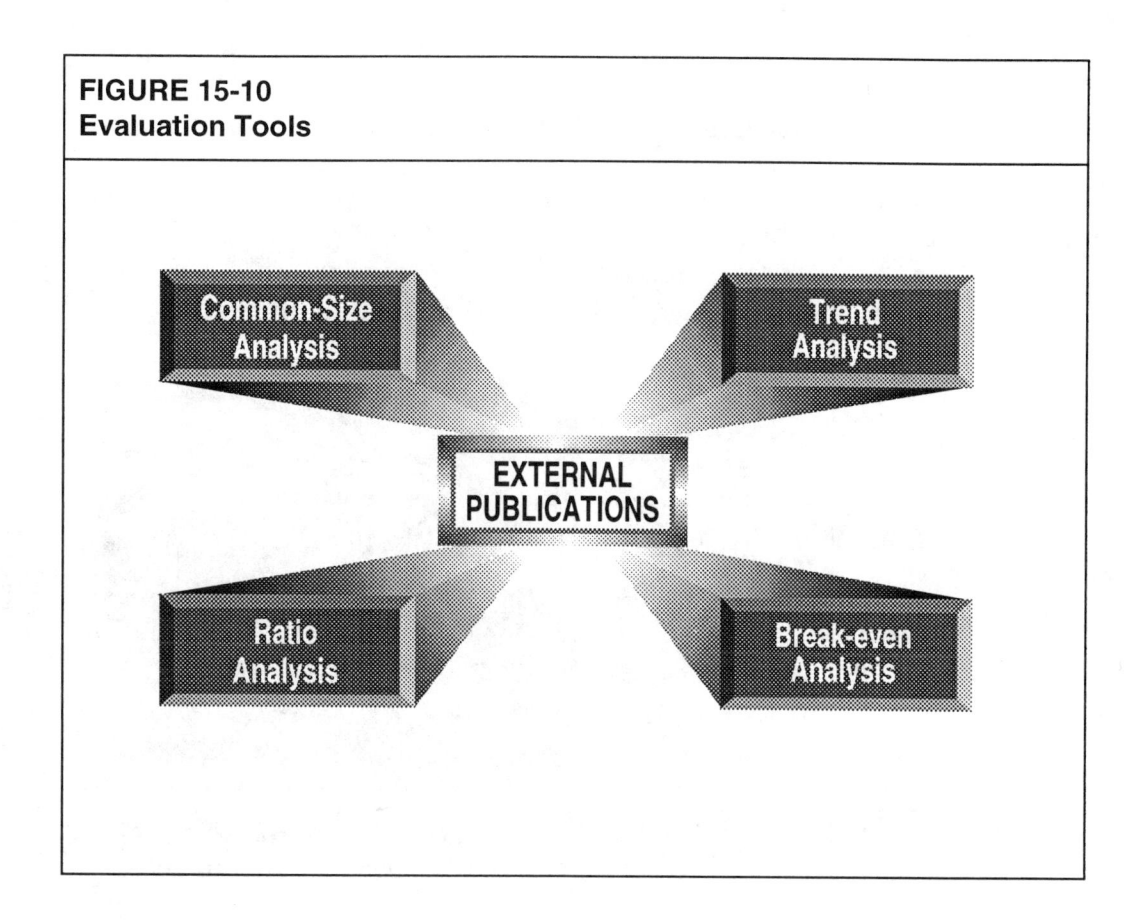

- Common-Size Analysis
- Trend Analysis
- EXTERNAL PUBLICATIONS
- Ratio Analysis
- Break-even Analysis

Risk Based Capital

The evaluation methods available for financial statements prepared under GAAP are also available for those prepared under SAP. In addition, under SAP the concept of risk based capital can be applied. The risk based capital concept and related formula and performance levels provide a vehicle to assist the management of companies, the state regulators, and the general public in maintaining good business practices. It provides the necessary early warning signals to allow sufficient time for corrective action, and it will help, along with other good management, product and investment objectives and related performances to enhance consumer confidence in the industry.

The National Association of Insurance Commissioners (NAIC) adopted the Risk Based Capital for Life and Health Insurance Model Act on December 6, 1992. The act established higher minimum capital requirements in support of continued financial stability. It has as its overall objective the strengthening of companies that are undercapitalized. It identifies early warning signals of companies with unstable capital, which can be rectified through improving their capital structure. Finally, it strengthens the authority of state regulators over life companies experiencing capital structure problems. (See figure 15-11.)

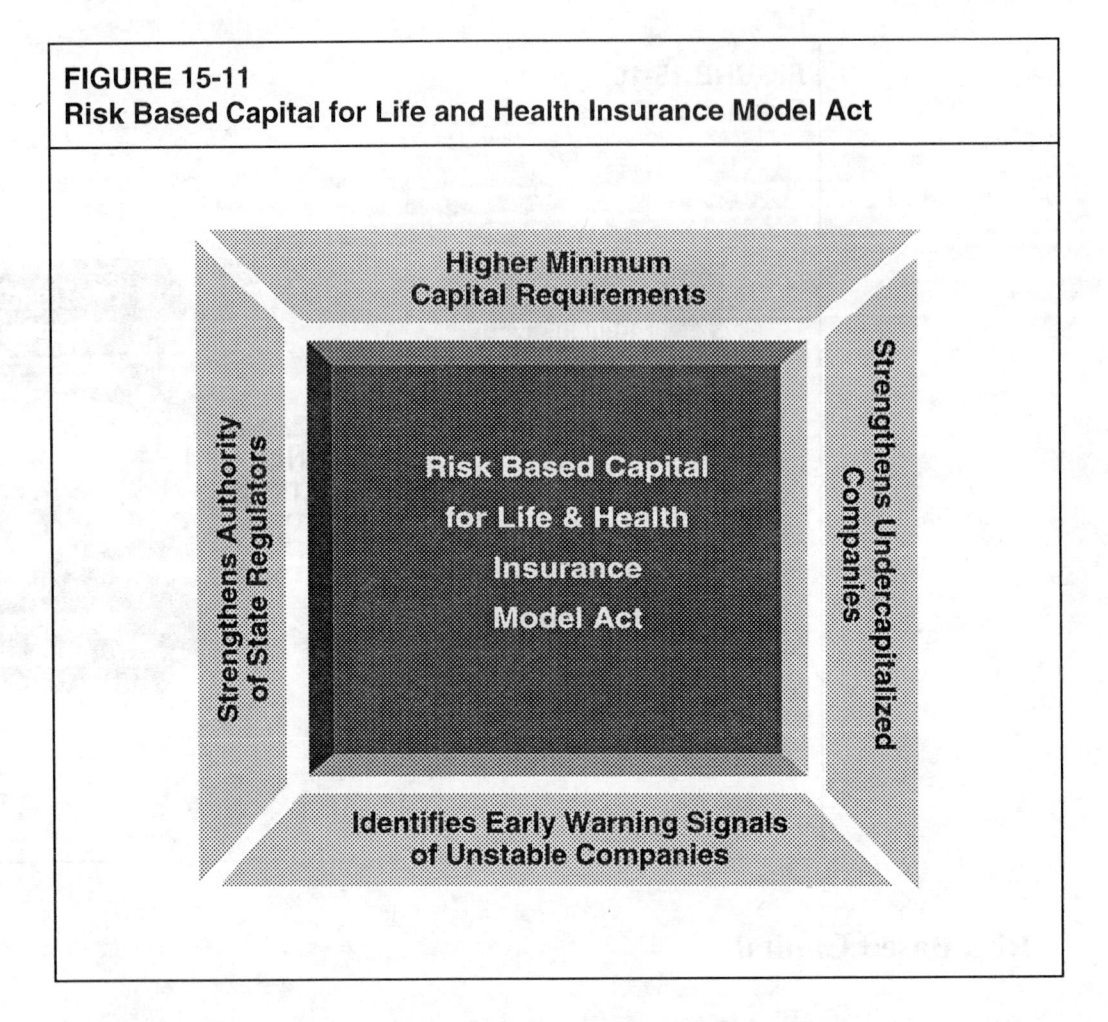

FIGURE 15-11
Risk Based Capital for Life and Health Insurance Model Act

- Higher Minimum Capital Requirements
- Strengthens Authority of State Regulators
- Strengthens Undercapitalized Companies
- Identifies Early Warning Signals of Unstable Companies

Risk Based Capital for Life & Health Insurance Model Act

Under the act every company must submit to the NAIC—and to the state in which it does business upon written request from the state—on or before the filing date a risk based capital report reflecting its risk based capital levels as of the end of the previous calendar year. The risk based capital levels fall into one of four event categories: company action level, regulatory action level, authorized control level, or mandatory control level.

A strong capital structure within a company assists in providing the necessary protection from investment and insurance risk. Such risks are associated with unforeseen events that can have a substantial negative impact and/or drain on a company's assets and reserves.

The amount of capital that is set aside to minimize risk exposure should be reflective of the type of risk that exists. The higher the risk, the higher the required capital support. The lower the risk, the lower the required capital support. With the use of a risk based capital formula, assistance is provided in quantifying the funds that a company should set aside for the various risks taken in its business operations.

The concept of utilizing various formulas to measure appropriate capital is not new. Over the years, both rating agencies and companies have been using internally developed formulas to accomplish this objective. The rating agencies still use their formula to establish levels of capital that they want to maintain, which are referred to by various surplus names such as required, target, or benchmark surplus. In comparing actual capital to a target, a company can plan courses of action to follow either with excess capital or with capital to enhance product line, or formulate steps with capital deficiencies to reduce capital needs or increase the capital base.

Internally developed formulas are sometimes utilized for other financial and operating purposes, such as allocating capital by profit centers and evaluating performance by the return on capital invested in each center, which assists management in determining the most productive use of capital.

The risk based capital concept provides a means of establishing regulatory capital standards for overall business operations relative to the size and risk profile of various companies.

The four major risks associated with the risk profile that are involved in the calculation of a risk based capital formula are

- asset risk: the risk of asset default
- insurance risk: the risk of adverse mortality and morbidity experience
- interest rate risk: the disintermediation risk of policyholders withdrawing funds
- general business risk: the normal business and management risk (See figure 15-12.)

The risk based capital for a particular company is determined or calculated by applying established factors to various asset, premium, and reserve balances. Such factors are higher for those account items with greater underlying risk, and lower for those accounts items that are less risky. The following are examples of the accounts and other items to which factors are applied:

- asset risk accounts: bonds, mortgages, preferred and common stocks, separated accounts, real estate and other long-term assets, miscellaneous and reinsurance accounts, and off-balance sheet items
- insurance risk accounts: medical insurance premiums, disability income premiums, claim reserves, various life insurance premiums, and premium stabilization reserves
- interest rate risk accounts: low risk category accounts and medium and high risk category accounts
- general business risk accounts: life and annuity premiums and health premiums

FIGURE 15-12
Major Risk in Risk Profile

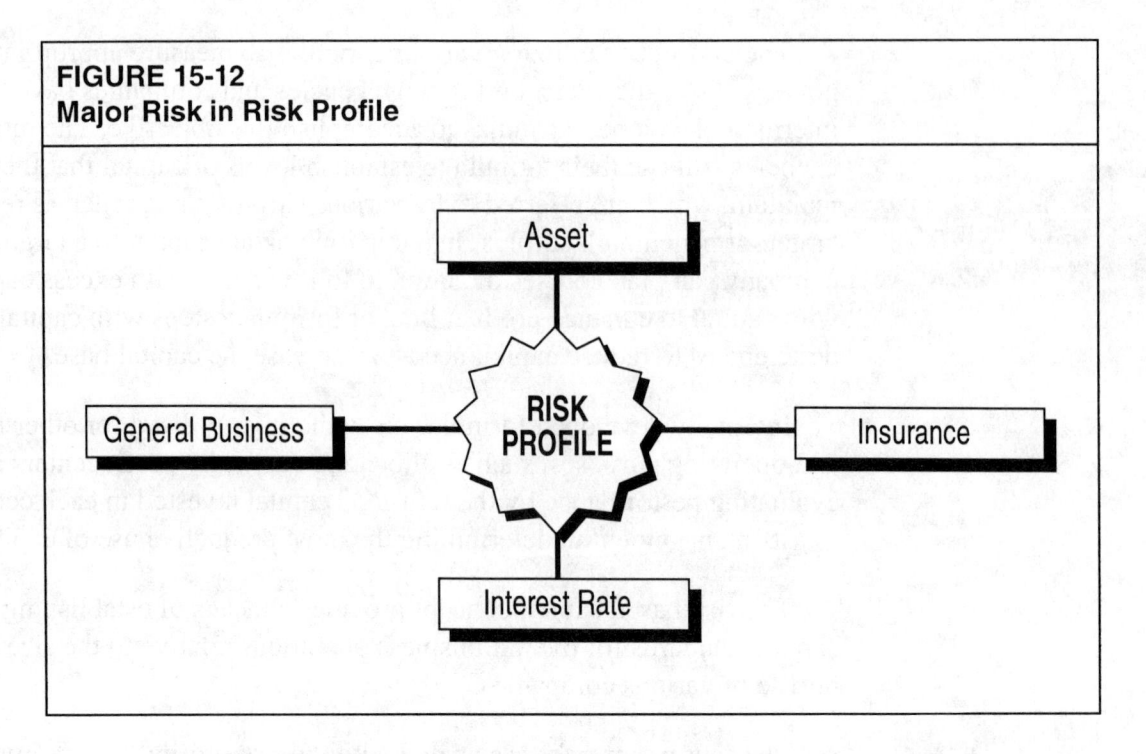

```
                    ┌─────────┐
                    │  Asset  │
                    └────┬────┘
                         │
    ┌──────────────┐   ╔═╧═══════╗   ┌───────────┐
    │General Business├──╢  RISK   ╟──┤ Insurance │
    └──────────────┘   ║ PROFILE ║   └───────────┘
                       ╚═╤═══════╝
                         │
                    ┌────┴─────────┐
                    │Interest Rate │
                    └──────────────┘
```

The risk based capital standards are used by regulators to assist in determining appropriate actions relating to companies who, as a result of applying a formula, reflect signs of deteriorating financial conditions. The risk based capital standards also provide an additional standard for measuring minimum capital requirements; companies that fall below this standard would be placed under regulatory control.

Established risk based capital factors exist for each category as well as the levels of risk within each category of a company's accounts. These factors are applied to the values reflected in a company's annual statement. Within the asset risk accounts, factors exist for

- different categories and sizes of government bonds
- mortgages in good standing versus mortgages that are 90 days overdue or are overdue with unpaid taxes or are in foreclosure
- different risk categories of preferred stock
- affiliated and unaffiliated common stock
- separate accounts
- occupied real estate, real estate investments, or foreclosed real estate
- other long-term assets
- miscellaneous assets such as policy loans and short-term investments
- various categories of reinsurance
- off-balance sheet accounts such as noncontrolled accounts and contingent liabilities

Within the insurance risk accounts, factors exist for different categories and amounts for individuals and group major medical, disability, and other coverages with limited benefits and with claim reserves; for different categories and amounts applied to net amount at risk for ordinary and group life in force; and for premium stabilization reserves.

Within the interest rate risk accounts, factors exist for various types of low-, medium-, and high-risk annuities, GICs, and life insurance reserves.

The product of the application of the factors to the various accounts provides the basis for determining the various individual risk exposures, that is, asset, insurance, interest, and general business risks.

The total risk based capital of a company estimates the capital required to deal with losses caused by catastrophic financial events. The chances that all of the various individual risks will occur simultaneously is remote. In fact, some of the risks are mutually exclusive. Therefore adding all of the individual risks together to determine a company's total risk based capital would overstate the total risk and not be appropriate. To deal with this problem, the individual risks are modified within a formula to compute the total risk based capital. The formula takes into consideration what is referred to as the covariance adjustment and is as follows:

Total Risk Based Capital
Equals
$\sqrt{[(\text{Asset Risk} + \text{Interest Rate Risk})^2 + (\text{Insurance Risk})^2]} + \text{Business Risk}$

The total risk based capital results represent the foundation for computing the various risk based capital levels that are compared with a company's total adjusted capital. This comparison determines the extent, if any, to which state regulators become involved in a company and its operations.

Total adjusted capital is determined by modifying a company's capital and surplus to include asset valuation and voluntary investment reserves and to also include 50 percent of the company's dividend liability.

The risk based capital is compared with the total adjusted capital for determining the risk based capital level. As indicated earlier, the risk based capital level falls into one of four event categories. They consist of a company action level event, a regulatory action level event, an authorized control level event, and a mandatory control level event. Each requires a different action by a company. (See figure 15-13.)

A company action level event exists when the filing of a risk based capital report indicates that the total adjusted capital is greater than or equal to the regulatory action level but less than its company action level; or that the total adjusted capital is greater than or equal to the company action level but less than the product of the authorized control level and 2.5.

If such an event occurs, a company must submit a comprehensive financial plan that identifies the condition for the existence of the event, a proposal of corrective actions, projected financial results for the current year and at least the next 4 years—giving consideration to what would occur with or without the corrective actions, and an explanation of the major assumptions affecting the projections and the sensitivity of the projections to the assumptions.

The comprehensive financial plan must be submitted within 45 days after the year-end in which the company action level event occurred. Then, within 60 days after its submission the company will receive feedback relative to the acceptance, modification, or rejection of the plan. Hearing procedures exist for situations in which the feedback decision is challenged.

A regulatory action level event exists when the filing of a risk based capital report indicates that the total adjusted capital is greater than or equal to its authorized control level but less than its regulatory action level. If such an event occurs, the state regulators may require an examination and analysis (either internally and/or by a third-party consultant for which all costs and fees would be borne by the company) of the risk based capital plan and of the company's assets, liabilities, and operations. Such an examination and analysis results in an order, referred to as the Corrective Order, specifying whatever corrective actions the state regulator requires. Within 45 days after the year-end in which the regulatory action level event occurred, the company must submit a comprehensive financial plan. Hearing procedures exist for situations in which any corrective order is challenged.

An authorized control level event exists when the filing of a risk based capital report indicates that the total adjusted capital is greater than or equal to the mandatory control level but less than the authorized control level.

As under the regulatory action level event, if such an event occurs the state regulators may require an examination and analysis (either internally and/or by a third-party consultant for which all costs and fees would be borne by the company) of the risk based capital plan and of the company's assets, liabilities, and operations.

If deemed to be in the best interest of policyholders, creditors, and the general public, the state regulators will take such action to cause a company to be placed under regulatory control. The event is deemed sufficient grounds for the regulatory control action to take place. Hearing procedures exist for situations in which any corrective order and/or regulatory control is challenged.

A mandatory control level event exists when the filing of a risk based capital report indicates that the total adjusted capital is less than the mandatory control level.

As under the authorized control level event, if it is deemed to be in the best interest of policyholders, creditors, and the general public, such action can be taken to cause a company to be placed under regulatory control. The event is deemed sufficient grounds for the regulatory control action to take place. Hearing procedures exist for situations in which the regulatory control is challenged.

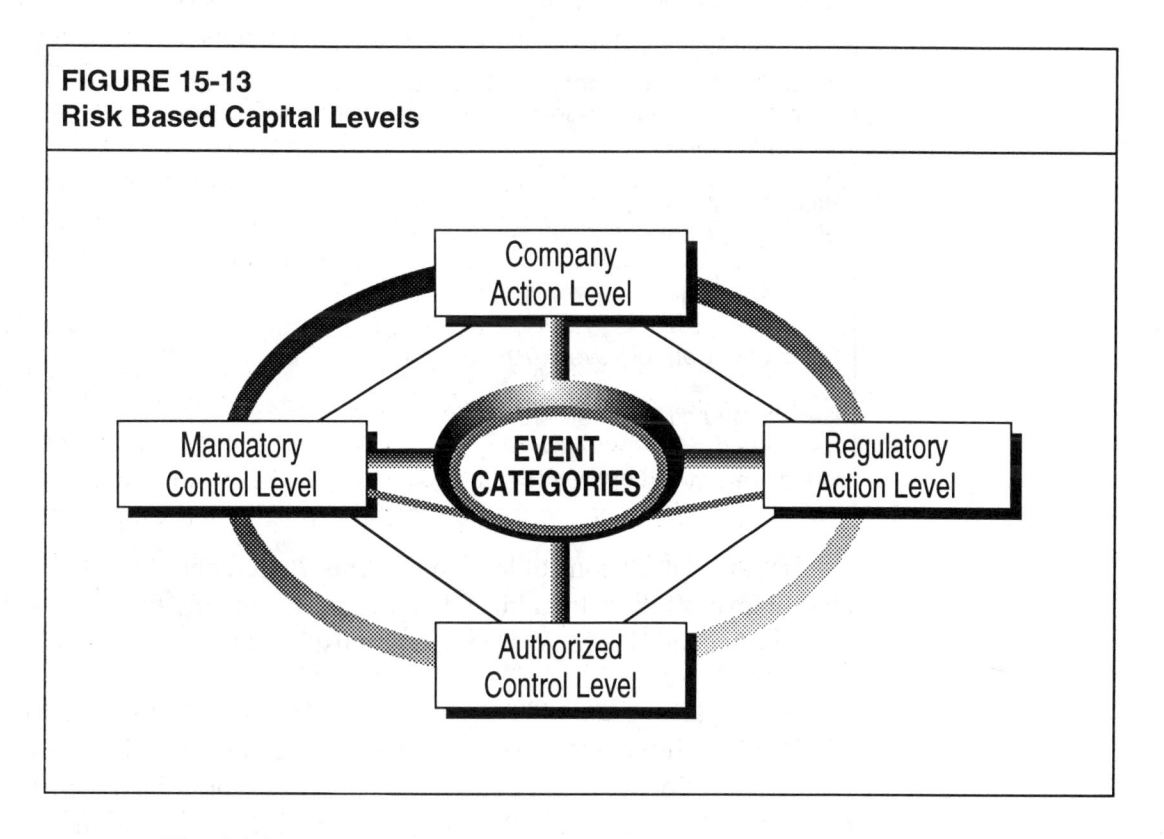

FIGURE 15-13
Risk Based Capital Levels

- Company Action Level
- Regulatory Action Level
- Authorized Control Level
- Mandatory Control Level
- EVENT CATEGORIES

The Risk Based Capital for Life and Health Insurance Model Act increased the state regulator's ability to evaluate a company and also increased the regulator's authority over a company whose financial condition has deteriorated. The act requires that each year every life insurance company calculate its minimum capital requirement using the risk based capital formula. The results of the formula are compared with the company's actual total adjusted capital balance, and, if the company's capital balance falls below the formula, the state regulator will take some form of action depending on the severity of the deficiency. The act requires the determination of the four event levels that are used to determine if regulatory action is necessary. (See table 15-1.)

The initial base level, which represents 50 percent of the risk based capital formula calculation, is referred to as the 100 percent authorized control level. If the total adjusted capital of a company falls below the authorized capital control level but equals or exceeds the mandatory control level, the company must file a corrective plan and submit to an examination, and the company may, as a result of the examination, be placed under regulatory control.

TABLE 15-1
Company Control Levels

Total Risk Based Capital (Based on application of the risk based capital formula)	$73,400
Total Adjusted Capital (Based on modified capital and surplus to include asset valuation and voluntary investment reserves plus 50% of dividend liability)	$80,000
Base Adjusted Capital (Represents 50% of risk based capital)	$36,700
Authorized Control Level—100% of BAC	$36,700
Mandatory Control Level—70% of ACL	$25,690
Regulatory Action Level—150% of ACL	$55,050
Company Action Level—200% of ACL	$73,400

The mandatory control level represents 70 percent of the authorized control level. If the total adjusted capital of a company falls below the mandatory control level, the company must be put under regulatory control.

The regulatory action level represents 150 percent of the authorized control level. If the total adjusted capital of a company falls below the regulatory action level but equals or exceeds the authorized control level, the company must file a corrective plan, submit to an examination, and follow any orders for corrective action.

The company action level represents 200 percent of the authorized control level. If the total adjusted capital of a company is between 200 percent and 250 percent of the authorized control level, the company is required to prepare a trend test. If the total adjusted capital is below the company action level but above the regulatory action level, the company must submit within 45 days a financial plan that identifies the cause of the capital problem and the proposed course of action to correct it.

A trend test calculates the greater of the decrease in the margin between the current year's authorized control level and the prior year, and the average of the past 3 years. It also assumes that the decrease in the authorized control level could occur again in the coming year. Any company that trends below 1.9 times its authorized control level would trigger regulatory action. (See table 15-2.)

Under a sensitivity test, a company, depending on certain considerations, recalculates its risk based capital or total adjusted capital using a specific alternative for a particular factor in the formula and reports to the state regulator the recalculated amount.

TABLE 15-2
Required Action Determination

Event Level	Amount	Total Adjusted Capital	Action Plan
ACL	$36,700	$80,000	None
MCL	$25,690	$80,000	None
RAL	$55,050	$80,000	None
CAL	$73,400	$80,000	None
Trend Test	$73,400–$91,750	$80,000	Test Required

Every company has the opportunity to prepare and submit to the state regulator a written report and analysis of its risk based capital results that could also include any other appropriate comments.

As indicated at the outside, the financial statements for life insurance companies differ substantially from those of other businesses. With a better understanding of the underlying concepts of GAAP and SAP and their differences in principles, objectives, and audiences, a clearer base for interpreting and analyzing such statements should occur.

APPENDIX

SMALL BUSINESS JOB PROTECTION ACT OF 1996: ANALYSIS OF QUALIFIED PLAN PROVISIONS (SECTIONS 1316, 1401-1461)

Qualified plan design through and after the year 2000 will be significantly affected if not dominated by the provisions summarized here, which were adopted as part of the 1996 tax legislation. Note that effective dates vary over this period, with some provisions becoming effective in later years and some phased in over the period through 2000. In addition to this summary, many of the most significant provisions are discussed in the main text.

Subject	Act Section(s)	Code Section(s)	Effective Date(s)
Qualified plan trust can hold S corp stock	1316(a)(2)	1361(c)(7)	Taxable years beginning after December 31, 1997

Prior Law: A trust established under a qualified plan (Code Sec. 401(a) trust) was not a permitted shareholder in an S corporation. For qualified plan purposes, the primary consequence of this was that a qualified plan sponsored by an S corporation could not invest in company stock. This precluded the use of such stock in the company's profit-sharing plan and prohibited the adoption of stock bonus plans or ESOPs by the S corporation.

New Law: A Sec. 401(c) trust will be a permitted shareholder in an S corporation. This will open the door to qualified plan techniques not formerly available to S corporations.

Subject	Act Section(s)	Code Section(s)	Effective Date(s)
Repeal of 5-year averaging	1401	402	Taxable years beginning after 1999

Prior Law: Certain lump-sum distributions from qualified plans were eligible for special 5-year averaging, which reduced the tax on the amount by allowing it to be taxed in lower tax brackets as if received over a 5-year period. Ten-year averaging, permitted under pre-1986 law, continued to be available to taxpayers who attained age 50 before January 1, 1986.

New Law: Five-year averaging is repealed effective after 1999. Taxpayers eligible to elect 10-year averaging under prior law will continue to be able to do so.

Commentary: This provision will primarily affect small-to-moderate qualified plan accumulations. Taxpayers in this category should consider taking lump-sum distributions now, while this provision is still available. For larger distributions, deferral generally has been and will be more advantageous than current withdrawal and taxation. However, see the discussion of Act Section 1452, below.

Subject	Act Section(s)	Code Section(s)	Effective Date
Repeal of $5,000 employee death benefit	1402	101(b)	Deaths after August 20, 1996

Prior Law: Death benefits (insured or noninsured) payable by an employer to an employee's beneficiary were free of income tax up to $5,000.

New Law: This provision is repealed.

Commentary: This provision dates from many decades ago, and because the amount was never increased to reflect inflation, it had already become largely irrelevant in planning employee death benefits.

Subject	Act Section(s)	Code Section(s)	Effective Date
Rules for recovery of basis from qualified annuity payments	1403	72(d)	Annuity starting dates after 90th day following August 20, 1996

Prior Law: If a participant in a qualified plan had a basis in the plan accumulation, as would be the case, for example, if he had made after-tax contributions to the plan, this basis was recovered under one of two ways: an "exact" method and a safe-harbor method.

New Law: Under the new law the safe harbor method is the primary way to recover basis. The law provides that the total basis is to be divided by a number from a prescribed table, and the resultant amount is the amount of each payment that is nontaxable. The table is as follows:

Age on annuity starting date	Number of anticipated payments
Not more than 55	360
More than 55—60	310
More than 60—65	260
More than 65—70	210
More than 70	160

Subject	*Act Section(s)*	*Code Section(s)*	*Effective Date*
Minimum distribution beginning date	1404	401(a)(9)	Years beginning after December 31, 1996

Prior Law: Qualified plan, IRA, and 403(b) plan distributions had to begin by April 1 of the year following the year in which the participant attained age 70 ½ even if the participant continued working (and thus in some cases the employer had to continue contributions to the plan).

New Law: The new law reverts to a pre-1986 rule under which distributions do not have to begin at age 70 ½ if the participant continues working; distributions are required in that case by April 1 of the year following the year of actual retirement. The "actual retirement" provision, however, is not available to 5 percent owners as defined in the top-heavy rules (an owner of more than 5 percent of the business).

Commentary: While this provision eliminates an awkward feature of prior law, for plan participants who continue to work after age 70 ½, delaying distributions until retirement will mean that the annual distribution then required under the minimum distribution rules will be considerably larger. For large account balances this delay could therefore push the required minimum distribution above the $155,000 (indexed) threshold amount for the 15 percent excess-distribution penalty. In such situations, the participant should consider the advisability of taking distributions even before retirement.

Existing plans will have to be amended to permit deferral of distributions to actual retirement. However, the IRS has indicated that during the transition employees other than 5 percent owners who attain age 70 ½ after 1995 can defer distributions to actual retirement even though the plan has not been formally amended. Ann. 97-24, 1997-11 IRB.

Subject	*Act Section(s)*	*Code Section(s)*	*Effective Date*
SIMPLE Plans	1421, 1422	408(p), 401(k)	Taxable years beginning after December 31, 1996

Prior Law: No provision for such plans. However, the Code included provisions whereby SEPs (Simplified Employee Pensions) could be funded through employee salary reductions (SARSEPs).

New Law: The provision for SARSEPs is repealed, but existing SARSEPs may continue, as in effect on December 31, 1996. The provisions for regular SEPs (employer-funded only) remain unchanged.

The new law provides for plans referred to as "savings incentive match plans for employees" (SIMPLE), with the following major features:

- available to employers with 100 or fewer employees (only employees with at least $5000 in compensation for the prior year are counted) on any day in the year
- available only to employers who do not sponsor another qualified plan, 403(b) plan, or SEP
- contributions can be made to each employee's IRA or to the employee's 401(k) account
- employees who earned at least $5000 from the employer in the preceding 2 years, and who are reasonably expected to earn at least $5000 in the current year, can contribute (through salary reductions) up to $6,000 (indexed) annually
- required employer contribution equal to either
  - (a) a dollar-for-dollar matching contribution up to 3 percent of the employee's compensation (the employer can elect a lower percentage, not less than 1 percent, in not more than 2 out of the past 5 years), or
  - (b) 2 percent of compensation for all eligible employees earning at least $5,000 (whether or not they elect salary reductions)

Further detailed rules are included in the instructions with new IRS forms for adopting these plans, forms 5304-SIMPLE and 5305-SIMPLE.

Commentary: The new SIMPLE plans are somewhat simpler to administer and explain than the SARSEPs available under prior law, and SIMPLEs are available to a broader range of employers (up to 100 employees instead of 25). However, the benefits to employees are potentially somewhat lower than from SARSEPs because of the $6,000 limitation (the 1996 SARSEP limitation was $9,500). Also, from the employer viewpoint, contributions to a SIMPLE are less flexible than for SARSEPs.

In general most practitioners believe that the 401(k)/SIMPLE option will be little used since it offers few if any advantages over a regular 401(k) plan. SIMPLE/IRAs will be advantageous primarily for very small businesses that want to adopt the simplest possible pension arrangement funded through employee salary reductions. Note that regular SEPs (without the salary reduction feature) are still available and continue to be attractive as an alternative for small businesses seeking a simple plan.

See detailed discussion in chapter 5.

Subject	*Act Section(s)*	*Code Section(s)*	*Effective Date*
401(k) plans for tax exempts	1426	401(k)(4)	Plan years beginning after December 31, 1996

Prior Law: Governments and tax-exempt organizations could not maintain 401(k) plans, except for certain plans grandfathered under prior law.

New Law: Tax-exempt organizations and Indian tribal governments (but not other state or local governments or governmental organizations) may adopt 401(k) plans.

Commentary: This provision expands the choices available to tax-exempt organizations for their retirement plans. Some tax exempts, primarily those exempt under Section 501(c)(3) (educational, charitable, and health organizations) continue to be eligible to adopt 403(b) plans as well as now having the opportunity to adopt 401(k) plans. Total salary reductions, however, are limited to $9,500 (indexed) per employee. See detailed discussion in Chapter 5.

Subject	*Act Section(s)*	*Code Section(s)*	*Effective Date*
Spousal IRA limitation increased	1427	219(c)	Taxable years beginning after December 31, 1996

Prior Law: An individual filing a joint return, whose spouse had no compensation for the taxable year, was allowed to make a contribution to an IRA for the spouse; the total individual and spousal contribution could not exceed $2,250.

New Law: The limit on the total individual and spousal contribution has been increased to $4,000, so long as the combined compensation of both spouses exceeds that amount. The contribution for each spouse, as under prior law, cannot exceed $2,000 for the year.

Under the new law, a spousal IRA is available for the (joint return) spouse whose compensation is the lesser (including a spouse with no income), rather than, as under prior law, only for the spouse with no compensation income at all.

Subject	*Act Section(s)*	*Code Section(s)*	*Effective Date*
Definition of highly compensated; family aggregation rules	1431	414(q)	Years beginning after December 31, 1996

Prior Law: <u>Highly compensated.</u> For purposes of various nondiscrimination rules relating to qualified plans, "highly compensated employee" was defined as an employee who, during the year or any preceding year

- owned more than 5 percent of the business
- received compensation from the employer of more than $100,000 (1996)
- received compensation from the employer of more than $66,000 (1996) and was in the most highly paid 20 percent of employees of the employer
- was an officer and received compensation from the employer of more than $60,000 (1996)

<u>Family aggregation.</u> For purposes of the $150,000 limit on compensation used in determining qualified plan limitations, all members of a family were considered a single employee. For example, if a husband and wife operated a business and each earned $100,000 from the business, total qualified plan benefits for both would have to be based on a total salary of $150,000 rather than the actual total of $200,000.

New Law: Highly compensated. A highly compensated employee is defined as an employee who

- owned more than 5 percent of the business at any time during the year or the preceding year
- for the preceding year had compensation from the employer in excess of $80,000 (to be indexed for inflation) and, if the employer elects, was in the most highly paid 20 percent of employees of the employer for the preceding year

Family aggregation. The family aggregation rule is repealed.

Commentary: The new definition of highly compensated simplifies plan administration and in many cases will reduce the number of employees deemed highly compensated, making it easier to comply with nondiscrimination rules. The employer election to add the top-paid 20 percent limitation to the $80,000 limit will generally be made if it reduces the number of highly compensated employees. This may be the case if the employer's workforce is highly paid.

The repeal of family aggregation removes a rule that, though it rarely applied, produced very harsh and unjust results when it did. (See discussion in chapter 5.)

Subject	*Act Section(s)*	*Code Section(s)*	*Effective Date*
50/40% participation rule	1432	401(a)(26)	Years beginning after December 31, 1996

Prior Law: In addition to all the other applicable participation rules of the Code, every qualified plan had to cover a minimum of the lesser of 50 employees or 40 percent of the employer's employees. The purpose was to eliminate a former practice under which an employer adopted a separate plan with generous benefits that covered only a few highly compensated employees.

New Law: The 50/40% rule has been modified so that it covers only defined-benefit plans. Apparently Congress has determined that the abuse described above is significant only in the case of defined-benefit plans covering a few employees.

Commentary: This provision expands the options available in designing qualified plan arrangements that provide significant benefits for key employees and executives.

Subject	Act Section(s)	Code Section(s)	Effective Date
Alternative methods of satisfying 401(k) nondiscrimination tests	1433	401(k); 401(m)	Years beginning after December 31, 1998, except provisions relating to use of prior year for ADP computation effective for years beginning after December 31, 1996

Prior Law: A special nondiscrimination test, the ADP test, applies to 401(k) plans. This test limits the salary reduction contributions available to highly compensated employees under a formula based on actual deferrals made by nonhighly compensated employees. Matching contributions by employers are subject to a similar test, the ACP test.

New Law: The new law simplifies these tests in several ways:

- The test is based on deferral percentages for nonhighly compensated employees for the preceding rather than the current year, which allows predictability and reduces the need to distribute excess contributions after the year-end.
- An additional "safe harbor" ADP test is provided. Under this test, the nondiscrimination requirements are satisfied if the employer (a) satisfies a matching contribution requirement (100 percent of the employee contribution up to 3 percent of compensation, plus 50 percent from 3 to 5 percent) or (b) the employer makes a nonelective (nonmatching) contribution for all eligible nonhighly compensated employees equal to at least 3 percent of compensation.
- A safe harbor for the ACP test is also provided. Under this safe harbor, no match can be made for employee deferrals in excess of 6 percent of compensation, and the rate of match must not increase as the employee deferral rate increases. Also, matching contribution rates for highly compensated employees must not be greater than those for nonhighly compensated employees.

Commentary: These improvements are an attempt to improve compliance by 401(k) plans, especially by smaller plans which have had difficulty in dealing with the complexity and administrative costs of the prior rules. See detailed discussion in chapter 5.

Subject	Act Section(s)	Code Section(s)	Effective Date
Definition of compensation	1434	415(c)(3)	Years beginning after December 31, 1997

Prior Law: For purposes of the Section 415 limit on annual additions to a participant's account (limited to the lesser of 25% of compensation or $30,000, as indexed), compensation did not include elective deferrals such as salary reductions in a 401(k) plan.

New Law: Compensation for purposes of the annual additions limit is "grossed up" to include elective deferrals in 401(k) plans, 403(b) plans, 457 plans, and Section 125 (flexible-benefit) plans.

Commentary: The effect of this provision is to increase the base for the Section 415 limitation, which could allow some employees to contribute more to qualified defined-contribution and 403(b) plans than under prior law.

For example, suppose an employee's gross salary is $40,000 and he contributes $4,000 of this by salary reduction (elective deferral) to a Section 125 plan. The maximum annual addition that could be made to his account in the employer's defined-contribution plan under prior law was $9,000 (25 percent of $36,000). Under the new law (after 1997) the maximum is $10,000 (25 percent of $40,000).

Subject	Act Section(s)	Code Section(s)	Effective Date
Aggregation rules for unincorporated businesses	1441	401(d)	Years beginning after December 31, 1996

Prior Law: There are (and remain) general rules requiring aggregation of commonly controlled businesses for purposes of applying the nondiscrimination tests. In addition, prior law included a special additional rule that applied to plans covering owners of unincorporated businesses such as proprietorships and partnerships.

New Law: The special aggregation rules for unincorporated businesses are repealed. These entities continue to be subject to the general aggregation rules applicable to all businesses.

Commentary: This provision eliminates an obsolete and complex provision that was a trap for the unwary.

Subject	Act Section(s)	Code Section(s)	Effective Date
Elimination of special vesting rule for multiemployer plans	1442	411(a)	Years beginning on or after January 1, 1997, with transition provisions

This provision eliminates the ability to use 10-year cliff vesting in multiemployer plans.

Subject	Act Section(s)	Code Section(s)	Effective Date
Distributions under rural cooperative plans	1443	401(k)(7)	Distributions after August 20, 1996; public utility provisions effective for plan years beginning after December 31, 1996

This provision permits hardship distributions and distributions after age 59 ½ by rural cooperative plans.

Subject	Act Section(s)	Code Section(s)	Effective Date
Treatment of governmental plans under Section 415	1444	415(b)(10)	Generally, years beginning after December 31, 1994

Under this provision, defined-benefit plans of governmental employers will be subject only to the dollar limit of Sec. 415 ($125,000 annually, as indexed) and not to the 100 percent of compensation limit.

Subject	Act Section(s)	Code Section(s)	Effective Date
Social Security retirement age as uniform retirement age	1445	401(a)(5)	Years beginning after December 31, 1996

This provision conforms certain provisions in the qualified plan law (those requiring a "uniform retirement age") to the recent changes in social security that provide a range of retirement ages.

Subject	Act Section(s)	Code Section(s)	Effective Date
Contributions on behalf of disabled participants	1446	415(c)(3)(C)	Years beginning after December 31, 1996

Prior Law: Contributions to a qualified plan on behalf of disabled highly compensated employees were not permitted. An employer election was required for contributions on behalf of other disabled employees.

New Law: These restrictions are eliminated if a defined-contribution plan provides for contributions on behalf of all disabled participants.

Subject	Act Section(s)	Code Section(s)	Effective Date
Changes in rules for 457 plans	1447, 1448	457	Taxable years beginning after December 31, 1996, except trust requirement effective to assets and income held by a plan on and after August 20, 1996 (existing plans, January 1, 1999)

Prior Law: Section 457 governs nonqualified deferred-compensation plans of governmental organizations and tax-exempt employers. In an eligible Section 457 plan, the annual amount deferred by an employee was limited to the lesser of $7,500 (unindexed) or one-third of compensation. Plans were required to be unfunded, with no assets set aside in trust for employees.

New Law: These provisions make the following reforms:

- Plans can permit involuntary cashouts of up to $3,500 if no amount has been deferred by the participant for 2 years, and there has been no prior distribution.
- The $7,500 limit will be indexed for inflation.
- In the case of governmental plans, assets must be held in trusts or custodial accounts.

Commentary: These provisions of the act do not resolve the current conflict between the funding requirements of ERISA applicable to certain plans of tax-exempt organizations and the requirement of Section 457 that such plans must be unfunded. Thus 457 plans continue to be of very restricted usefulness to nongovernmental tax-exempt organizations.

Subject	Act Section(s)	Code Section(s)	Effective Date
GATT interest and mortality rate assumptions	1449	415(b)(2)(E)	As if included in GATT, with transitional rule

This provision makes it possible to delay, until plan years beginning after 1999, the effectiveness of the 1994 GATT provisions that prescribed interest and mortality assumptions for calculating lump-sum payments from defined-benefit plans. This may make it possible for participants to receive larger lump-sum distributions from defined-benefit plans during the transition period than GATT would have allowed. Formal amendment of the defined-benefit plan may be required in order to take advantage of this transitional rule.

Subject	Act Section(s)	Code Section(s)	Effective Date
Section 403(b) changes	1450	403(b)	Years after December 31, 1995

The act makes the following changes applicable to 403(b) tax-deferred annuity plans:

- The rules for making elections are conformed to those applicable to 401(k) plans. This eliminates an awkward rule under which only one 403(b) election could be made each calendar year.
- Indian tribal governments are deemed eligible to sponsor 403(b) programs for contracts purchased in a plan year beginning before January 1, 1995, and such contracts may be rolled over to a 401(k) plan sponsored by the tribal government. This provision in effect rescues these contracts from being disqualified.
- 403(b) contracts must explicitly incorporate the $9,500 (indexed) salary reduction limit. There is a 90-day period after the date of enactment to make changes to existing contracts.

Subject	Act Section(s)	Code Section(s)	Effective Date
Joint and survivor notice period	1451	417(a)	Plan years beginning after December 31, 1996

The Code and ERISA require that a written explanation of the joint and survivor annuity option must be given no less than 30 nor more than 90 days before the beginning date. Treasury regulations allow the participant and spouse to waive this requirement. This provision codifies the provision in the regulations.

Subject	*Act Section(s)*	*Code Section(s)*	*Effective Date*
Repeal of combined fraction and suspension of 15% excess-distribution tax	1452	415(e) (repealed)	Limitation years beginning after December 31, 1999; excise tax suspended 1997 through 1999

Prior Law: Code Section 415 (enacted as part of ERISA in 1974) provides limits on annual additions to a defined-contribution plan (the lesser of 25 percent of compensation or $30,000, as indexed) and limits on benefit under a defined-benefit plan (the lesser of 100 percent of average compensation or $120,000, as indexed). Under Section 415(e), if a participant was covered under both a defined-benefit plan and a defined-contribution plan of the same employer, a complex computation involving a "combination fraction" had to be made each year to limit total benefits so that it was not possible to maximize both the defined-benefit and defined-contribution amounts.

The Tax Reform Act of 1986 added another provision aimed at preventing excessive qualified plan accumulations by highly compensated employees, the 15 percent excess-distribution tax. Under this provision, an excise tax of 15 percent is enacted on annual plan distributions exceeding $155,000 (indexed), in addition to the regular income tax. There are provisions exempting accrued benefits in excess of $562,500 as of August 1, 1986 (the grandfathered amount). There is also an additional 15 percent estate tax on excess accumulations at death.

New Law: Congress has apparently determined that the existence of both the provisions described above constitutes overkill and has repealed one of these, the combination fraction computation of Section 415(e), effective after 1999. To provide relief during the interim, the 15 percent excess-distribution tax (but not the excess-accumulation tax) is suspended for years beginning after December 31, 1996, and before January 1, 2000. Distributions during this period are deemed to be made first from non-grandfathered amounts.

Commentary: The repeal of Section 415(e) is welcome and will simplify administration of plans covering owners and executives, as well as open new opportunities for creative plan design.

The suspension of the 15 percent excise tax is something of a Trojan horse, since it may encourage some participants to take distributions (and pay income taxes) earlier than they otherwise would have. In many cases, deferral of distributions and taxes would save participants more money than the 15 percent excise tax saving involved in taking a distribution during the suspension period. Advisors will have to evaluate this decision based on the age and health status of the participant and spouse. If their joint life expectancy is relatively limited, current withdrawals may be beneficial. Note that 5-year averaging continues to be available through 1999 to further reduce the impact of any total distribution taken during this period.

The need for money may be another factor. If money has to be withdrawn over a relatively short-term period, making long-term deferral impossible, then distributions should probably be made during this interim period if the 15 percent excise tax is a factor.

Fundamentally, however, for the vast majority of plan participants who are aged 70 or less and whose qualified accounts total less than $1 million, the amount of 15 percent excise tax imposed on regular minimum distributions will be small or zero and the 3-year moratorium provides no significant benefit.

Subject	Act Section(s)	Code Section(s)	Effective Date
Prohibited transaction penalty	1453	4975	Prohibited transactions occurring after August 20, 1996

The initial prohibited transaction penalty has been raised from 5 percent to 10 percent.

Subject	Act Section(s)	Code Section(s)	Effective Date
Leased employee definition	1454	414(n)	Years beginning after December 31, 1996

Prior Law: A leased employee is treated as the service recipient's employee for pension purposes if the leased employee does work "historically performed by employees."

New Law: The "historically performed" provision has been replaced by a provision covering services that "are performed under primary direction or control by the recipient."

Commentary: This change reduces uncertainty in application of the leased employee rules. It will facilitate contracting out of various jobs such as maintenance, by reducing concern that the leased employees will have to be taken into account for purposes of the service recipient's pension plans.

Subject	Act Section(s)	Code Section(s)	Effective Date
Uniform penalty provisions	1455	6724, 6047	Returns, etc., with due date after December 31, 1996

This provision makes certain pension-related penalties more uniform.

Subject	Act Section(s)	Code Section(s)	Effective Date
Retirement benefits of ministers not subject to self-employment tax	1456	1402	Years beginning before, on, or after December 31, 1994

This provision exempts the rental value of parsonages or any other retirement benefit from a church plan after the clergyman retires.

Subject	Act Section(s)	Code Section(s)	Effective Date
Sample language for spousal consent and QDRO forms	1457	417(a), 414(p)	Not later than January 1, 1997

The Treasury is directed to develop the sample language referred to. This will affect an increasingly important legal practice issue, the procuring of informed consents from spouses who relinquish spousal rights in qualified plans.

Subject	Act Section(s)	Code Section(s)	Effective Date
Awards to volunteer firefighters, etc.	1458	457	Accruals and amounts paid after December 31, 1996

Length-of-service awards paid to volunteer firefighters or emergency medical or ambulance volunteers will not be considered deferred compensation subject to the limitations of Section 457.

Subject	Act Section(s)	Code Section(s)	Effective Date
Special ADP testing for pre-21 401(k) participants	1459	401(k)(3)	Plan years beginning after December 31, 1998

Prior Law: Many employers would have liked to extend 401(k) eligibility to younger workers (those aged under 21). However, this was rarely done because these younger workers were less likely to participate and this low participation would make it harder to meet the ADP or ACP tests for the overall plan, thus reducing the salary reduction amounts available to highly compensated employees.

New Law: In performing the ADP tests of Section 401(k) or the ACP tests of Section 401(m), the employer may elect to exclude eligible employees who have not attained age 21 or one year of service. The plan must meet Section 410(b) tests with respect to these under-21/one-year participants.

Subject	*Act Section(s)*	*Code Section(s)*	*Effective Date*
Application of ERISA to insurance company general accounts	1460	ERISA Section 401	Not later than June 30, 1997

The Department of Labor is directed to issue regulations providing guidance in determining when assets held by an insurance company on behalf of insurance policies issued to a pension plan constitute plan assets. These regulations are intended to clarify the issues raised by the Supreme Court in <u>John Hancock v. Harris Trust</u>, 510 U.S. 86 (1993), which held that certain such assets held in an insurance company's general account should be considered plan assets. The outcome of this regulatory project could have significant impact on the marketing of insurance contracts to pension plans.

Subject	*Act Section(s)*	*Code Section(s)*	*Effective Date*
Church plan changes	1461	401 et seq.	Years beginning after December 31, 1996

This provision allows self-employed ministers, or ministers employed by non-501(c)(3) organizations, the benefit of the favorable church plan rules for their retirement plans and adds various other provisions favoring the clergy.

ABOUT THE AUTHORS

JENNIFER J. ALBY, JD, is director of planned giving at The American College. Ms. Alby received her BA from the University of Minnesota and her JD from William Mitchell College of Law.

GEORGE ALDEN, MBA, MSFS, is a registered representative of NYLIFE Securities, Inc. He has been with New York Life since March 1979. Mr. Alden received his BA from Texas A&M in 1974 and his MBA from the University of Wyoming in 1977. In 1996 he earned his MSFS degree from The American College.

BURTON T. BEAM, Jr., MBA, MA, CLU, ChFC, CPCU, is director of continuing education at The American College. He is also responsible for the course material on health insurance and group insurance in the programs leading to the Chartered Life Underwriter (CLU), Registered Health Underwriter (RHU), and Registered Employee Benefits Consultant (REBC) professional designations. Mr. Beam received his BA and his MBA from the University of Oregon and his MA from the University of Pennsylvania.

ROGER C. BIRD, PhD, holds the Frank M. Engle Distinguished Chair in Economic Security Research at The American College and is also professor of economics. He is responsible for course material on financial institutions, portfolio management, and mutual funds in the Graduate School program. Dr. Bird received his BA degree from Lafayette College and his MA and PhD from the University of Pennsylvania.

ALAN C. BUGBEE, JR., PhD, is the director of psychometric services at the American Registry of Radiologic Technologists in St. Paul, Minnesota. He is the former director of educational systems and former associate professor of psychology at The American College. Dr. Bugbee received his BA from the University of Vermont, his MA Ed and MPA from George Washington University, and his PhD from the University of Pittsburgh.

DAVID M. CORDELL, PhD, CFA, CFP, CLU, is associate professor of finance at The American College. His course responsibilities are in the areas of financial and retirement planning. Dr. Cordell earned his BA at The

University of Texas at Austin, where he also received his MBA and PhD in financial management and investments.

CHARLES S. DI LULLO, MBA, CPA, CLU, ChFC, PFS, is the vice president of finance and treasurer of The American College. He is also an associate professor of accounting, responsible for the Graduate School program's Financial Statement Analysis and Business Valuation courses. Mr. Di Lullo received his BA from St. Joseph's University and his MBA from Drexel University.

RONALD F. DUSKA, PhD, holds the Charles Lamont Post Chair of Ethics and the Professions and is professor of ethics at The American College. He is responsible for course material on ethics in the Graduate School programs. Dr. Duska received his BA from St. Mary's Seminary, his MA from St. John's University, and his PhD from Northwestern University.

THOMAS A. DZIADOSZ, MA, CLU, ChFC, is associate professor of economics at The American College. He is responsible for HS 322 The Financial System in the Economy and examination development for various Huebner School and Graduate School courses. Mr. Dziadosz received his BA from LaSalle University and his MA from the University of Connecticut.

CONSTANCE J. FONTAINE, JD, LLM, CLU, ChFC, is associate professor of taxation at The American College and develops examination material for courses in estate planning and taxation. She is also responsible for HS 330 Fundamentals of Estate Planning I. Ms. Fontaine received her BS from Beaver College, her JD from Widener University School of Law, and her LLM from Villanova University.

EDWARD E. GRAVES, MA, CLU, ChFC, is associate professor of insurance at The American College. He is responsible for the courses in the CLU and ChFC designation programs dealing with individual insurance products and insurance law. Mr. Graves earned his BS from California State University at Los Angeles and his MA at the University of Pennsylvania.

JAMES F. IVERS III, JD, LLM, ChFC, is professor of taxation at The American College. His responsibilities at the College include revising and developing HS 321 Income Taxation. He is an author or editor of several books in the College's Huebner School series. Mr. Ivers received his BA from the Villanova University Honors Program and his JD and LLM from Boston University School of Law.

TED KURLOWICZ, JD, LLM, CLU, ChFC, is professor of taxation at The American College. His College responsibilities include preparation of courses in estate planning and planning for business owners and professionals. He received his BS from the University of Connecticut, his MA from the University of Pennsylvania, his JD from the Delaware Law School, and his LLM from the Villanova University School of Law.

THOMAS P. LANGDON, JD, LLM, MBA, MSFS, CLU, ChFC, CFA, is assistant professor of taxation for The American College. He is responsible for material on estate planning and business succession planning for various Heubner School and Graduate School courses. Mr. Langdon earned his BS and MBA degrees from the University of Connecticut, his MSFS degree from The American College, and his JD from Western New England College School of Law.

STEPHAN R. LEIMBERG, JD, CLU, is professor of taxation and estate planning at The American College. He is also adjunct professor of estate planning in the Tax Master's program of Temple University's School of Law. Mr. Leimberg holds a BA from Temple University and a JD from Temple University School of Law.

DAVID A. LITTELL, JD, is associate professor of taxation at The American College. He is responsible for course and textbook development for HS 326 Planning for Retirement Needs, HS 336 Financial Decision Making at Retirement, and HS 341 Selected Retirement Planning Topics. Mr. Littell received a BA in psychology from Northwestern University and earned his JD at the Boston University School of Law.

JOHN J. McFADDEN, MA, JD, is professor of taxation at The American College. Mr. McFadden is responsible for the College's graduate courses in advanced pension and retirement planning and executive compensation. His BA is from Lehigh University, with an MA from the University of Rochester and a JD from Harvard Law School.

MICHAEL J. ROSZKOWSKI, PhD, is associate professor of psychology and director of marketing research at The American College. Dr. Roszkowski earned his BS at St. Joseph's University and his MEd and PhD at Temple University. He is a licensed psychologist.

WILLIAM J. RUCKSTUHL, MBA, CLU, ChFC, is associate professor of finance at The American College. He is responsible for course material on investment and financial planning in the programs leading to both the CLU and ChFC designations. Mr. Ruckstuhl received his BS from Grove City College and his MBA from the University of Pennsylvania.

Index

Above the line deduction, 1.3
Accounting Principles Board (APB), 15.3
Accounts, ledger and nonledger, 15.5, 15.6
Accrual, 15.4
Accrued liabilities, 15.9
Advance health care directive, 2.36
Advance medical directives, 2.38
Advanced search, 12.14
Agent for a natural person, 1.15
American Institute of Certified Public Accountants (AICPA), 15.3
Annual exclusion, 2.1
Annuity, 14.3
Antifraud provisions, 9.2
Asset allocation, 8.1–33
Asset, admitted and nonadmitted, 15.5, 15.6
Assets under management, 9.5
Association of Advanced Life Underwriters (AALU), 4.30
Association taxable as a corporation, 3.16
Associations and educational web sites, 12.21
ATM cards, 8.39–41

Bagley v. United States, 4.5
Balance sheet, 15.5, 15.7–8
Beneficiaries, 2.1
Beyond Leverage: Split-dollar Funding of the GST-Exempt Trust, 4.48
Bookmarks, 12.12
Boolean search, 12.14
Break-even analysis, 15.10
Brody, 4.16
Built-in gains tax, 3.26
Business succession, 11.10

C corporation, 3.14
Cash-base accounting, 15.5
Cash-flow statement, 15.5, 15.7–8
Category-based search engines, 12.11
Centralized management, 3.16
Changing order, 3.21
Charitable remainder trust (CRT), 2.17, 3.4, 3.23, 14.8
Charitable remainder unitrust (CRUT), 14.9
Charitable gift annuities (CGAs), 14.2
Chasman, 4.15
Check-the-box regulations, 3.17
Childs v. Comm'r., 4.15
Chronically ill individual, 1.6
Circuit breakers, 8.25
COBRA, 7.9–10
Code Sec. 2035, 4.35
Code Sec. 2042, 4.35
Code Sec. 61, 4.11
Code Sec. 72, 4.17
Code Sec. 7702(f)(7), 4.29
Cohen v. Comm'r, 4.21
COLI, 10.13
Common-size analysis, 15.10
Company-owned life insurance (COLI), 3.28
Competition in financial services, 10.1
    bank holding companies, 10.4
    banking industry, 10.1
    Barnett Bank, 10.3
    credit unions, 10.1
    insurance industry, 10.1
    market share of assets, 10.1
    mutual funds, 10.1
    S&Ls, 10.1
Compliance, 13.1
Compliance-oriented culture, 13.2
Conduit, 8.34

Confidentiality, 13.3
Conservatism, 15.4
Consistency, 15.4
Constrained allocation, 8.12, 8.17, 8.22–23, 8.24
Continuity of life, 3.16
Controlling and sole shareholder, 4.35
Controlling shareholder, 4.2
Corporate culture, 13.4
Cost, 15.4
Credit cards, 8.39–47
    terms, 8.41–47
Cristofani v. Comm'r., 2.1
Crummey, 2.1
Current accounts payable, 15.9
Current assets, 15.9
Custom Asset Management Program (CAMP), 8.5

Debit cards, 8.39–41
Delayed retirement credit (DRE), 10.23
Dividend reinvestment plans (DRIPs), 8.28
Domestic corporation, 3.6
Domestic international sales corporation (DISC) 3.6
Durable medical power of attorney, 2.37

Efficient frontier line, 8.4
Electing small business trust (ESBT), 3.4, 3.11, 3.23
Emergency fund, 8.36–39
Employee stock ownership plans (ESOPs), 3.22
Entrepreneurs, 11.2, 11.14,
Equity, 15.9
Equity indexed annuities, 6.1–7
    annuitization, 6.4
    asset match, 6.5
    criminalization of donors, 6.7
    giving away assets, 6.7
Equity split-dollar, 4.10
ERISA, 4.4
    HIPAA changes, 7.11

Ethics, 13.1
Evolving Edge of the Split-dollar Envelope, 4.49
Excess-accumulations tax, 2.11
Excise tax, 14.6
Excise tax moratorium, 5.16
    combination fraction, 5.16
    15 percent excess, 5.16
Exclusion ratio, 14.2
Executive benefits, 11.8

Fairness, 13.3
Family-owned businesses, 11.1
Favorable PLR on Private Split-dollar Arrangement, 4.42
Financial Accounting Standards Board (FASB), 15.3
Financial adviser, role, 8.6
501(c)(3) organizations, 5.19
Foreign property limitation, 2.30
Form ADV-S, 9.4
Form ADV-T, 9.5
401(k) plans, 5.11–15
    ACP testing, 5.12, 5.14
    ADP testing, 5.12, 5.14
    compensation with Code Sec. 415, 5.15
    early participations, 5.14
    eligibility expanded, 5.12
    family aggregation, 5.14
    highly compensated employees, 5.12
401(k) SIMPLE, 5.6, 5.10
    advantages, 5.10
    disadvantages, 5.1
Free transferability of interest, 3.16

General Counsel Memorandum 32941, 4.12
General partners, 3.14
Generally accepted accounting principles (GAAP), 15.1
Gift splitting, 2.2
Gift Tax Consequences of Private Split Dollar, 4.42
Global diversification, 8.5

Going concern, 15.4
Golden Rule, 13.1
Goos v. Comm'r., 4.1
Greensberg, Norman, 4.8
Greenspan Commissions, 10.19
Grantor trusts, 1.16, 3.7, 3.23

Hardship, 2.27
Health care proxy, 2.44
Health Insurance Portability and
        Accountability Act, 7.1–17
    COBRA changes, 7.9–10
    ERISA changes, 7.10–11
    increased availability of coverage, 7.1–5
    medical savings accounts, 7.11–17
    portability, 7.5–9
Healy v. United States, 4.7
Howard Johnson v. Comm'r., 4.43

Illustrations, life insurance, 6.9
Income in respect of a decedent (IRD), 2.10, 3.14
Income statement, 15.7-8
Indexed search engine, 12.12
Insurance web sites, 12.18
Integrity, 13.3
International Association of Financial
        Planners Code of conduct, 13.3
Internet, 12.1
    Corporation for Research and
        Educational Networking, 12.4
    discussion groups, 12.3
    Electronic Mail, 12.2
    e-mail, 12.2
    file transfer protocol, 12.2
    Gopher, 12.2
    home page, 12.2
        American Society of CLU & ChFC, 12.7
        American Institute of CPCU and
            Insurance Institute of America, 12.7
        Certified Financial Planner Board of
            Standards, 12.7

        CyberTalk, 12.10
        EINET Galaxy for Insurance, 12.7
        Infomanage-investment, 12.7
        Insurance Companies & Resources on
            the Net, 12.8
        Insurance News Network, 12.8
        InsWeb, 12.9
        LEXIS, NEXIS, 12.10
        LIFE: Life and Health Insurance
            Foundation for Education, 12.9
        LIMRA, 12.9
        LOMA, 12.10
        Money Personal Finance Center, 12.10
        National Association of Insurance
            Commissioners, 12.10
        RISKWeb, 12.10
        Society for Insurance Research, 12.10
        The American College, 12.6
        The Insurance Agent's Online
            Network, 12.8
    Internet Service Provider (ISP), 12.5
    network computers, 12.5
    newsgroups, 12.3
    shell accounts, 12.3
    surfing the web, 12.3
    Telnet, 12.2
    World Wide Web, 12.2
Invested assets, 15.9
Investment adviser, 9.1
Investment Advisers Act of 1940, 9.1
Investment Advisers Supervision
        Coordination Act (IASCA), 9.1
Investments, 8.1–47
Investment/financial services web sites, 12.19
IRC 7872 below-market interest rate loan
        issues, 4.42
Irrevocable annuity trust, 1.17
Irrevocable life insurance trust (ILIT), 2.1

Janitor insurance, 3.28
Jensen, J., 4.22
Joint life policies, 1.11
Joint-life payout, 2.14

Key person coverage, 3.28
KISS (Keep It Simple, Stupid), 12.13
Kraus, 4.19

Large QDOTs, 2.29
Life insurance company as a stock company or a mutual company, 15.1
Life insurance policy illustrations, 6.9
Life insurance: taxation and products, 4.37
Limited liability, 3.16
Limited liability companies (LLCs), 3.1, 3.14, 4.45
Limited partners, 3.14
LIMRA, 12.9
Living trust, 2.17
Long-term assets, 15.9
Long-term debt payable, 15.9
Ltr. Rul. 8003094, 4.7
Lumpkin v. Comm'r., 4.36
Lwry, Mark, 4.47

Majority Shareholder Estate Taxation and Split-Dollar Plans, 4.39
Marital trust, 2.15
Market timing, 8.1–8.3
Matching revenues and expenses, 15.5
Materiality, 15.4
Mean-variance optimization (MVO), 8.1
Medical savings accounts, 7.11–17
Mental Health Parity Act, 7.19–20
Minimum distribution, 2.14
Minor v. U.S., 4.15
Monetary unit, 15.4
Moody's Average, 3.31
Mortality tables, 2.25
Mutual funds, 8.6

NAIC model regulation, illustrations, 6.10–15
National Association of Insurance Commissioners (NAIC), 15.3

National Association of Securities Dealers (NASD) 9.3
Nesbitt v. Comm'r., 4.21
Newborns' and Mothers' Health Protection Act, 7.17–18
News and information web sites, 12.21
Nonprofit organizations, 5.18
Nonresident alien, 3.4

Objectivity, 13.3
Old Age, Survivors and Disability Insurance Program (OASDI), 10.19
Optimization software, 8.5
Organ and tissue donations, 2.43
Organ donor card, 2.46

Paine, Lynn Sharpe, 13.2
Pass-through entity, 3.1
Pass-through taxation, 14.5
Pass-through treatment 3.22
Pay-as-you-go (PAYG), 10.19
Permissible shareholders, 3.2, 3.3
PLR 7916029, 4.15, 4.25
PLR 8310027, 4.15, 4.25
PLR 8547006, 4.7
PLR 9037012, 4.37
PLR 9235020, 4.44
PLR 9309046, 4.43
PLR 9318007, 4.43, 4.44
PLR 9331009, 4.43, 4.44
PLR 9452004, 4.7
PLR 9511046, 4.37
PLR 961017, 4.38
PLR 9623024, 4.46
PLR 9636033, 4.41
PLR 9639053, 4.45
PLR 9651017, 4.43
PLR 9651030, 4.39
PLR 9709027, 4.39, 4.43
Policy illustrations, 6.9
Portability, medical expense coverage, 7.11–17
Possessions corporation, 3.6

Premarital agreements, 3.4
Price indices, 10.10
    cost-of-living index (COLI), 10.13
    Fisher *ideal index,* 10.13
Private foundation, 14.1
Professionalism, 13.3
Property, 4.13
PS 38 rates, 4.8
PS 38 Table, 4.8

QTIP trust, 2.15
Qualified adoption expenses, 1.8–9
Qualified domestic trust (QDOT), 2.19
Qualified interest, 3.32
Qualified joint and survivor annuity (QJSA), 2.12
Qualified retirement plans, 2.9
Qualified Subchapter S Subsidiary (QSSS), 3.6
Qualified Subchapter S trusts (QSSTs), 3.2, 3.7
Qualified terminable interest property trust (QTIP trust), 3.9

Raby, 4.18
Rated insureds, 4.9
Ratio analysis, 15.10
Reallocation, 8.14–15
Relevancy, 15.3
Replacement questionnaire, 6.15–17
Retirement Equity Act (REA), 2.13
Retirement planning, 11.9, 11.17
Rev. Rul. 64-328, 4.5, 4.6, 4.12
Rev. Rul. 66-110, 4.5, 4.6, 4.12
Rev. Rul. 76-274, 4.36
Rev. Rul. 78-420, 4.7, 4.8
Rev. Rul. 79-50, 4.7
Rev. Rul. 79-129, 4.36
Rev. Rul. 81-198, 4.48
Rev. Rul. 82-145, 4.37
Reverse split-dollar (RSD), 4.30–31
Risk, 8.4–5, 8.8, 8.18, 8.19
Risk based capital, 15.11
    asset risk, 15.13
    authorized control level event, 15.15, 15.16
    company action level, 15.18
    company action level event, 15.15
    comprehensive financial, 15.16
    four major risks, 15.13
    general business risk, 15.13
    general business risk accounts, 15.13
    insurance risk, 15.13
    interest rate risk, 15.13
    interest rate risk accounts, 15.13
    initial base level, 15.17
    mandatory control level, 15.18
    mandatory control level event, 15.15, 15.16
    regulatory action level, 15.18
    regulatory action level event, 15.15
    Risk Based Capital for Life and Health Insurance Model Act, 15.11
    total adjusted capital, 15.15
    total risk based capital, 15.15
    sensitivity test, 15.18
    trend test, 15.18
Risk tolerance, 11.3
Rollover, 2.12

S corporations, 3.1, 3.2, 3.14, 14.5
Saks, 4.18
Salary reduction SEPs, 5.18
Same insured requirement, 1.12
SARSEPs, 5.1
Separate account, 15.9
Search engines, 12.11
SECs Release No. 1A-770, 9.2
SEC Release No. 1A-1601, 9.4
SEC Release No. 1A-1602, 9.4
Sec. 83, 4.10
Sec. 401(a), 3.4
Sec. 401(k) plans, 5.18
Sec. 403(b) annuity plans, 5.18
Sec. 501(c)(3), 3.4
Sec. 2042—From Soup to Nuts, 4.35, 4.40
Sec. 7520, 2.25

Securities and Exchange Commission (SEC), 9.1, 15.3
Security requirements for QDOTs, 2.29
Security, 9.2
Self-employed, 1.4
Sercl v. United States, 4.5
Shareholder, 4.2
Simmons, S., 4.7
SIMPLE, 5.1–11, 5.19
    adopting a plan, 5.4
    advantages, 5.8
    contributions, 5.2
    disadvantages, 5.8
    eligibility requirements, 5.3
    eligible employers, 5.2
    funding vehicles, 5.4
    plan operations, 5.5
    withdrawals, 5.6
SIMPLE IRA, 5.1
Simple searches, 12.13
Single beneficiary trust, 1.15
Small QDOTs, 2.29
Social Security Advisory Council, 10.21
Some Advanced Uses of Life Insurance in Financial and Estate Planning, 4.40
Special allocations, 3.24
Split Dollar, the Bifurcated Peso: Split, Rip, or Tear?, 4.30
SSI, 10.19
Statute of limitations, 2.6
Statutory accounting principles (SAP), 15.1
Straight debt, 3.12
Street name, 8.29
Substantial economic effect, 3.24
Succession planning, 11.14, 11.17
Super annual exclusion, 2.20
Survivorship (second-to-die), 4.8

TAM 7832012, 4.8
TAM 9604001, 4.13
Tax Planning with Life Insurance, 4.30
Taxable economic benefit, 4.5
Taxes payable, 15.9
Terminally ill individual, 1.6
Testamentary trusts, 3.8

The Federal Income Tax Law, 4.17
Tools & Techniques of Life Insurance Planning, 4.30
Tools and Techniques of Employee Benefit and Retirement Planning, 4.31
Trading collar, 8.25
Trend analysis, 15.10
Triple tax, 2.11
20 Years of Sunshine, Stone Crabs, and Estate Planning Strategies, 4.39

Unconstrained allocation, 8.11–12, 8.17, 8.18, 8.20–21, 8.24
Unified credit shelter trust (UCST), 2.16
U.S. Life Table 38, 4.8
Unitrust, 14.8
Uniformity, 15.4
Unrelated business taxable income (UBTI), 3.5
Unrelated business taxable income, 3.23

Viatical settlement provider, 1.6
Virtue ethics, 13.2
Voting trusts, 3.7–8

West, 4.18

Young et ux. et al. v. Comm'r., 4.20
YRT, 4.5